# A CONNECTICUT YANKEE
# IN KING ARTHUR'S COURT

AN AUTHORITATIVE TEXT

BACKGROUNDS AND SOURCES

COMPOSITION AND PUBLICATION

CRITICISM

SAMUEL LANGHORNE CLEMENS

# A CONNECTICUT YANKEE IN KING ARTHUR'S COURT

## AN AUTHORITATIVE TEXT
## BACKGROUNDS AND SOURCES
## COMPOSITION AND PUBLICATION
## CRITICISM

➤➤ ◀◀

*Edited by*
## ALLISON R. ENSOR
UNIVERSITY OF TENNESSEE, KNOXVILLE

W • W • NORTON & COMPANY
*New York*                    *London*

Library of Congress Cataloging in Publication Data
Clemens, Samuel Langhorne, 1835–1910.
  A Connecticut Yankee in King Arthur's court.
  (A Norton critical edition)
  Bibliography: p.
  1.   Clemens, Samuel Langhorne, 1835–1910.
A Connecticut Yankee in King Arthur's court.   I.   Ensor, Allison.   II.   Title.
PZ3.C59Co   1981     [PS1308]   813'.4         80–13771
ISBN 0-393-01378-2
ISBN 0-393-95137-5 {pbk.}

W. W. Norton & Company, Inc., 500 Fifth Avenue, New York, N.Y. 10110
W. W. Norton & Company Ltd., Castle House, 75/76 Wells Street,
London W1T 3QT

*7 8 9 0*

ACKNOWLEDGMENTS

Howard G. Baetzhold: From *Mark Twain and John Bull*, by Howard G. Baetzhold. Copyright ©
1970 by Indiana University Press. Reprinted by permission of Indiana University Press.
Daniel Carter Beard: From *Hardly a Man Is Now Alive*, by Dan Beard. Copyright 1939 by
Doubleday & Company, Inc. Reprinted by permission of Doubleday & Company, Inc.
Louis J. Budd: From *Mark Twain, Social Philosopher*, by Louis J. Budd. Copyright © 1962 by
Indiana University Press. Reprinted by permission of Indiana University Press.
Everett Carter: From "The Meaning of *A Connecticut Yankee*," by Everett Carter, in *American
Literature*, 50 (1978), 418–440. Copyright © 1978 by Duke University Press. Reprinted by
permission of Duke University Press.
Samuel Langhorne Clemens: Letter to Clara Clemens Gabrilowitsch, "Bay House, Hamilton,
March 10," from *My Father, Mark Twain* by Clara Clemens; copyright 1931 by Clara Clemens
Samossoud; reprinted by permission of Harper & Row, Publishers, Inc. "The New Dynasty"
(reprinted in "Mark Twain and the American Labor Movement" by Paul J. Carter), *New England
Quarterly*, 30 (1957); copyright by the Mark Twain Company, 1957, published by permission of
the Mark Twain Estate and Paul J. Carter. Selections from *Mark Twain's Notebooks and
Journals*, III (1883–1891), copyright by the Mark Twain Company, reprinted by permission of the
University of California Press. Letters to Dan Beard and to a reader from "Unpublished Letters to
Dan Beard," in *The Mark Twain Quarterly*, 7 (1945), ii, 22; reprinted by permission of *The Mark
Twain Journal*. Letter to Charles L. Webster from *Mark Twain's Letters to His Publishers*, ed.
Hamlin Hill; copyright by the Mark Twain Company; reprinted by permission of the University
of California Press. Selections from *The Autobiography of Mark Twain*, ed. Charles Neider;
copyright © 1959 by the Mark Twain Company; copyright © 1959 by Charles Neider; reprinted
by permission of Harper & Row, Publishers, Inc. Selections from *Mark Twain: A Biography*, ed.
Albert Bigelow Paine, vols. III and IV; copyright © 1912 by Harper & Row, Publishers, Inc.
Reprinted by permission of Harper & Row, Publishers, Inc. "Letter to Mrs. Jervis Langdon of
Elmira, N.Y." and "Letter to Sylvester Baxter," from *Mark Twain's Letters*, ed. Albert Bigelow
Paine, vols. I and II; copyright 1917 by the Mark Twain Company; reprinted by permission of
Harper & Row, Publishers, Inc. "Letter to Mrs. Cincinnatus A. Taft" from *Susy and Mark
Twain*, ed. Edith Colgate Salisbury; copyright © 1965 by Harper & Row, Publishers, Inc.;
copyright © 1965 by Edith Colgate Salisbury; reprinted by permission of Harper & Row,
Publishers, Inc. Letters to William Dean Howells from *Mark Twain–Howells Letters*, ed. Henry
Nash Smith and William M. Gibson (Cambridge: Harvard University Press, 1960); reprinted by
permission of the Mark Twain Company. Letter to Clara Clemens ("Home, Sunday July
Something-or-Other 1890") from *Love Letters of Mark Twain*, ed. Dixon Wecter; copyright
1947, 1949 by the Mark Twain Company; reprinted by permission of Harper & Row, Publishers,
Inc. Letter to Mary Fairbanks (HM 14311) reproduced by permission of The Huntington Library,
San Marino, California. In note 6, Chapter 43, previously unpublished words by Mark Twain are
© 1981 by Edward J. Willi and Manufacturers Hanover Trust Company as trustees of the Mark
Twain Foundation. The words quoted here are used with the permission of the University of
California Press and Robert H. Hirst, General Editor of the Mark Twain Project in Berkeley,
California.
James M. Cox: From *The Yale Review*, 50 (1960), 89–102. Copyright by Yale University Press.
Reprinted by permission of Yale University Press.
John P. Hoben: From "Mark Twain's *Connecticut Yankee*: A Genetic Study," in *American
Literature*, 18 (1946), 217. Copyright 1946 by Duke University Press. Reprinted by permission of
Duke University Press.
David Ketterer: From *PMLA*, 88 (1973), 1104–1114. Copyright 1973 by the Modern Language
Association of America. Reprinted by permission of the Modern Language Association of
America.
"King Arthur," from *The Oxford Companion to English Literature*, ed. Sir Paul Harvey, 4th ed.,
revised by Dorothy Eagle. Copyright © 1967 by Oxford University Press. Reprinted by permis-
sion of Oxford University Press.
Kenneth S. Lynn: From *Mark Twain and Southwestern Humor*, by Kenneth S. Lynn. Reprinted by
permission of Greenwood Press, Inc., and the author.
Henry Nash Smith: From *Mark Twain's Fable of Progress: Political and Economic Ideas in "A
Connecticut Yankee,"* by Henry Nash Smith. Copyright © 1964 by Rutgers, The State Univer-
sity. Reprinted by permission of Rutgers University Press.
Arlin Turner: From *Mark Twain and George W. Cable: The Record of a Literary Friendship*, by
Arlin Turner. Copyright 1960 by Michigan State University Press. Reprinted by permission of
Michigan State University Press.
Dennis Welland: From *Mark Twain in England*, by Dennis Welland. Copyright 1978 by Dennis
Welland. Reprinted by permission of Humanities Press, Inc., and Chatto and Windus, Ltd.
James D. Williams: From *American Literature*, 36 (1964–65), 288–297; copyright 1964–65 by
Duke University Press; reprinted by permission of Duke University Press. From *PMLA*, 80
(1965), 102–110; copyright 1965 by the Modern Language Association of America; reprinted by
permission of the Modern Language Association of America.

# Contents

## Criticism

# Preface

Mark Twain's A *Connecticut Yankee in King Arthur's Court* (1889) came somewhat late in the canon of his popular works. Behind him lay *The Innocents Abroad, Roughing It, Tom Sawyer, Life on the Mississippi,* and most recently his best, *Adventures of Huckleberry Finn.* He would write more novels (notably *Pudd'nhead Wilson*) and stories and essays, but they would not capture the public imagination in the same way. And capture that imagination the *Yankee* did: there have been three film versions (two starring beloved American figures—Will Rogers and Bing Crosby), a Broadway musical, several television productions, and even a Bugs Bunny cartoon about a Connecticut *rabbit* who repeats Hank Morgan's journey through time back to the sixth century and the days of King Arthur. In most instances, it should be noted, what the public sees on the movie or television screen is quite different from what Mark Twain wrote: his satirical jabs at the established church are usually missing, and his sad, violent ending has been judged entirely unacceptable.

In writing A *Connecticut Yankee,* Clemens pulled together several strands of plot material. First of all was the Arthurian legend, which had been treated by many writers from Sir Thomas Malory to Alfred, Lord Tennyson, whose *Idylls of the King* had been completed during the previous decade. Second was the "international novel," depicting a confrontation between an American and the older culture of Europe, at which Henry James had established himself as a master in *The American* (1877), *Daisy Miller* (1878), and *The Portrait of a Lady* (1881). Third was the concept of time travel. In 1888 H. G. Wells published "The Chronic Argonauts," apparently an early version of *The Time Machine* (1895). Also in 1888 the American novelist Edward Bellamy brought out *Looking Backward, or 2000–1887,* in which Julian West visits a utopia of the kind which the Yankee sought to establish in King Arthur's realm. Resembling a story of time travel, though not literally one, is Charles Heber Clark's *The Fortunate Island* (1882), in which an American with a considerable scientific knowledge is shipwrecked on an island peopled by Arthurian characters (the island broke off from England during Arthur's time and has not changed over the centuries). Though certain parallels appear strong, Clemens claimed not to have been influenced by the earlier work. To these three elements were added humor and barbed satire against the monarchy and the church, the two centers of power in the world being depicted.

Clemens also introduced into A *Connecticut Yankee* certain

themes that appear frequently in his writings. To begin with, there is the device of the "mysterious stranger"—someone from the outside, someone who does not fit, who comes into a community, often with disruptive consequences. Allied to this is the "unrecognized genius" theme, which was to be used again in Clemens' next significant novel, *Pudd'nhead Wilson* (1894). Here, someone having a great deal of knowledge appears in a community too ignorant to recognize his worth and may or may not eventually win proper recognition from it. The difficulty of distinguishing dream from reality, found in Mark Twain as early as *Tom Sawyer*, appears once again, especially in the ending. While in the sixth century, Morgan dreams that he is back in the nineteenth; when he finally returns to the nineteenth, he believes it is a dream and that his life with Sandy in the sixth century is the only reality. The Hank Morgan we see at the end of the novel is also a good example of the Mark Twain theme of the "lost paradise." Like Adam, Clemens' favorite Biblical character, Morgan is cut off from an existence which he now sees (perhaps inconsistently) as a paradise to which he can never return, from "all that is dear . . . all that could make life worth the living!" It was a situation in which Clemens found himself as he looked back at Hannibal and his summers on Uncle John Quarles' farm and later as he looked back on the life of his own family in their Hartford, Connecticut, home.

Finally, there is the attack on what Clemens came to call "the damned human race"—and it is here that controversy begins to arise. Does the novel say that America is superior to Europe, that the present is better than the past, that science and technology are superior to ignorance and superstition? Does it support democracy or does it suggest, as the Yankee says at one point, that one ought to "hang the whole human race and finish the farce"? Different readers have responded in different ways. What are we, after all, to think of Hank Morgan, the boss of Arthur's kingdom? He has been seen as a kind of new Prometheus, vainly seeking to bring light to a benighted land, and as a prototype of the fascist dictator, thinking only of himself and destroying all that he had built up (as well as 25,000 of the chivalry of England) when things do not go as planned. I have tried to show in my choice of recent critical articles something of the range of opinion which exists concerning the novel and its protagonist.

Critics frequently regard *A Connecticut Yankee* as a flawed novel. It was almost inevitable that it should be so, since Clemens wanted to do so much in it: he wanted to write a humorous book, but he also wanted to produce a sharp satire which would destroy whatever vestiges of the power of the monarchy and of the established church were left in his century. By the time he finished it, he had introduced violence and despair of a kind which contrasts radically with the happier endings of the earlier Mark Twain novels. The section on the background of the novel will show that these elements were present at a very early stage in his thinking about the novel, though he certainly suppressed them in public readings from the manuscript of the kind he gave at Governor's Island, New York, in the fall of 1886.

Finally, the impact of the novel was made the greater by the illustrations provided by Daniel Carter Beard, later to be known as the founder of the Boy Scouts of America. Beard enlivened his pictures by using as models such well-known personages as Alfred, Lord Tennyson, the Emperor of Germany, the Prince of Wales, Sarah Bernhardt, Anna Russell and the financier Jay Gould. Even Beard himself appears in one or two of the illustrations. While considerations of space made it impractical to include each of the more than two hundred illustrations in this edition, I have used a few representative ones. It will readily be seen that Beard did not content himself with merely illustrating the text but instead drew a number of cartoons illustrating ideas suggested by the text. Indeed, it has been said that at times Beard goes beyond anything Clemens intended.

*A Connecticut Yankee in King Arthur's Court* was first published in England with the title *A Yankee at the Court of King Arthur.* The first American edition appeared a few days later, on December 10, 1889. The present text is that of the first American edition, published by the Charles L. Webster Company of New York, Clemens' own publishing house. A very few obvious typographical errors have been corrected. Minor differences exist between the American and English editions, and between them and the text of certain chapters published in the *Century* magazine for November 1889 (pp. 74–83). I have tried to note the most significant of these variants in my footnotes. The printed texts also differ at times from the original manuscript, which is now in the Berg Collection of the New York Public Library.

I should like to acknowledge the assistance of the staffs of the Mark Twain Papers at the University of California, Berkeley, and of the Berg Collection in the New York Public Library. Both were very helpful during my visits there. The Better English Fund of the University of Tennessee, Knoxville, established by John C. Hodges, provided me with a grant so that I might be freed from one quarter's teaching in order to work on this edition. The secretarial staff of the Department of English has also been helpful in typing and copying whatever I needed. Among my colleagues I should particularly like to thank Nathalia Wright for reading my manuscript and making suggestions and my former colleague Barry Gaines for giving me his copy of the Globe Edition of *Morte d'Arthur.* Special thanks also to Mark Twain scholars in other institutions: Louis J. Budd, Alan Gribben, and Thomas A. Tenney.

ALLISON R. ENSOR

"I SAW HE MEANT BUSINESS."

Dan Beard's frontispiece for the first American edition. When included with excerpts published in the *Century* magazine prior to the publication of the novel, this illustration was captioned "The Yankee's Reception in Arthurdom." Clemens told Beard that the helmet in the left-hand corner was "a source of constant joy" to him.

The Text of
A Connecticut Yankee
in King Arthur's Court

# Contents of *A Connecticut Yankee in King Arthur's Court*

# Author's Preface [1]

The ungentle laws and customs touched upon in this tale are historical, and the episodes which are used to illustrate them are also historical. It is not pretended that these laws and customs existed in England in the sixth century; no, it is only pretended that inasmuch as they existed in the English and other cilizations of far later times, it is safe to consider that it is no libel upon the sixth century to suppose them to have been in practice in that day also. One is quite justified in inferring that wherever one of these laws or customs was lacking in that remote time, its place was competently filled by a worse one.

The question as to whether there is such a thing as divine right of kings is not settled in this book. It was found too difficult. That the executive head of a nation should be a person of lofty character and extraordinary ability, was manifest and indisputable; that none but the Deity could select that head unerringly, was also manifest and indisputable; that the Deity ought to make that selection, then, was likewise manifest and indisputable; consequently, that He does make it, as claimed, was an unavoidable deduction. I mean, until the author of this book encountered the Pompadour, and Lady Castlemaine[2] and some other executive heads of that kind; these were found so difficult to work into the scheme, that it was judged better to take the other tack in this book, (which must be issued this fall,) and then go into training and settle the question in another book. It is of course a thing which ought to be settled, and I am not going to have anything particular to do next winter anyway.

MARK TWAIN

HARTFORD, July 21, 1889

---

1. The English edition of the novel omitted the second paragraph of this preface.

2. The mistresses of Louis XV of France and Charles II of England.

# A Connecticut Yankee in King Arthur's Court

## A Word of Explanation

It was in Warwick Castle[3] that I came across the curious stranger whom I am going to talk about. He attracted me by three things: his candid simplicity, his marvelous familiarity with ancient armor, and the restfulness of his company—for he did all the talking. We fell together, as modest people will, in the tail of the herd that was being shown through, and he at once began to say things which interested me. As he talked along, softly, pleasantly, flowingly, he seemed to drift away imperceptibly out of this world and time, and into some remote era and old forgotten country; and so he gradually wove such a spell about me that I seemed to move among the spectres and shadows and dust and mold of a gray antiquity, holding speech with a relic of it! Exactly as I would speak of my nearest personal friends or enemies, or my most familiar neighbors, he spoke of Sir Bedivere, Sir Bors de Ganis, Sir Launcelot of the Lake, Sir Galahad, and all the other great names of the Table Round—and how old, old, unspeakably old and faded and dry and musty and ancient he came to look as he went on! Presently he turned to me and said, just as one might speak of the weather, or any other common matter—

"You know about transmigration of souls; do you know about transposition of epochs—and bodies?"

I said I had not heard of it. He was so little interested—just as when people speak of the weather—that he did not notice whether I made him any answer or not. There was half a moment of silence, immediately interrupted by the droning voice of the salaried cicerone:

"Ancient hauberk,[4] date of the sixth century, time of King Arthur and the Round Table; said to have belonged to the knight Sir Sagramore le Desirous; observe the round hole through the chain-mail in the left breast; can't be accounted for; supposed to have been done with

3. A fourteenth-century castle above the Avon River, northeast of Stratford-on-Avon. The castle houses a notable collection of armor, though none of it dates from the sixth century. Clemens visited Warwick Castle on Sept. 10, 1872, during his first trip to England.

4. A tunic of chain mail worn as defensive armor from the twelfth to the fourteenth century. No armor presently displayed in Warwick Castle has been pierced by a bullet, though there is one piece at which a gun has been fired.

a bullet since invention of firearms—perhaps maliciously by Cromwell's[5] soldiers."

My acquaintance smiled—not a modern smile, but one that must have gone out of general use many, many centuries ago—and muttered apparently to himself:

"Wit ye well, *I saw it done.*" Then, after a pause, added: "I did it myself."

By the time I had recovered from the electric surprise of this remark, he was gone.

All that evening I sat by my fire at the Warwick Arms,[6] steeped in a dream of the olden time, while the rain beat upon the windows, and the wind roared about the eaves and corners. From time to time I dipped into old Sir Thomas Malory's enchanting book, and fed at its rich feast of prodigies and adventures, breathed-in the fragrance of its obsolete names, and dreamed again. Midnight being come at length, I read another tale, for a night-cap—this which here follows, to-wit:

### HOW SIR LAUNCELOT SLEW TWO GIANTS, AND MADE A CASTLE FREE[7]

Anon withal came there upon him two great giants, well armed, all save the heads, with two horrible clubs in their hands. Sir Launcelot put his shield afore him, and put the stroke away of the one giant, and with his sword he clave his head asunder. When his fellow saw that, he ran away as he were wood,[8] for fear of the horrible strokes, and Sir Launcelot after him with all his might, and smote him on the shoulder, and clave him to the middle. Then Sir Launcelot went into the hall, and there came afore him three score ladies and damsels, and all kneeled unto him, and thanked God and him of their deliverance. For, sir, said they, the most part of us have been here this seven year their prisoners, and we have worked all manner of silk works for our meat, and we are all great gentlewomen born, and blessed be the time, knight, that ever thou wert born; for thou hast done the most worship that ever did knight in the world, that will we bear record, and we all pray you to tell us your name,

---

5. Oliver Cromwell (1599–1658) led the Puritan revolt which deposed Charles I. Warwick Castle served as a Parliamentary fortress during the English civil war.

6. A hotel in the town of Warwick, not far from the castle.

7. Quoted from Sir Thomas Malory's *Morte d'Arthur*, VI.xi. Clemens used the Globe edition, edited by Sir Edward Strachey and first published in 1868. Its pagination matches that in the manuscript, where Clemens indicates on what pages the quotations may be found. Quotations in the novel are generally accurate, although there are occasional omissions and alterations.

Originally Clemens intended to insert here two additional chapters from Malory, describing Sir Launcelot's adventures while wearing Sir Kay's armor. The exchange of armor between the two knights seems to have had an unusual fascination for Clemens. He refers to it in a letter of 1883, two years before he first encountered *Morte d'Arthur*, and again in *Pudd'nhead Wilson* (1894), Chapter IV. Having characters switch roles is a major plot element in *The Prince and the Pauper* and in *Pudd'nhead Wilson*.

8. Demented. [*Clemens' note.*]

that we may tell our friends who delivered us out of prison. Fair damsels, he said, my name is Sir Launcelot du Lake. And so he departed from them and betaught them unto God. And then he mounted upon his horse, and rode into many strange and wild countries, and through many waters and valleys, and evil was he lodged. And at the last by fortune him happened against a night to come to a fair courtelage, and therein he found an old gentlewoman that lodged him with a good will, and there he had good cheer for him and his horse. And when time was, his host brought him into a fair garret over the gate to his bed. There Sir Launcelot unarmed him, and set his harness by him, and went to bed, and anon he fell on sleep. So, soon after there came one on horseback, and knocked at the gate in great haste. And when Sir Launcelot heard this he arose up, and looked out at the window, and saw by the moon-light three knights come riding after that one man, and all three lashed on him at once with swords, and that one knight turned on them knightly again and defended him. Truly, said Sir Launcelot, yonder one knight shall I help, for it were shame for me to see three knights on one, and if he be slain I am partner of his death. And therewith he took his harness and went out at a window by a sheet down to the four knights, and then Sir Launcelot said on high, Turn you knights unto me, and leave your fighting with that knight. And then they all three left Sir Kay, and turned unto Sir Launcelot, and there began great battle, for they alight all three, and strake many strokes at Sir Launcelot, and assailed him on every side. Then Sir Kay dressed him for to have holpen Sir Launcelot. Nay, sir, said he, I will none of your help, therefore as ye will have my help let me alone with them. Sir Kay for the pleasure of the knight suffered him for to do his will, and so stood aside. And then anon within six strokes Sir Launcelot had stricken them to the earth.

And then they all three cried, Sir knight, we yield us unto you as man of might matchless. As to that, said Sir Launcelot, I will not take your yielding unto me, but so that ye yield you unto Sir Kay the seneschal, on that covenant I will save your lives and else not. Fair knight, said they, that were we loth to do; for as for Sir Kay we chased him hither, and had overcome him had ye not been; therefore, to yield us unto him it were no reason. Well, as to that, said Sir Launcelot, advise you well, for ye may choose whether ye will die or live, for an ye be yielden, it shall be unto Sir Kay. Fair knight, then they said, in saving our lives we will do as thou commandest us. Then shall ye, said Sir Launcelot, on Whitsunday next coming go unto the court of King Arthur, and there shall ye yield you unto Queen Guenever, and put you all three in her grace and mercy, and say that Sir Kay sent you thither to be her prisoners. On the morn Sir Launcelot arose early, and left Sir Kay sleeping: and Sir Launcelot took Sir Kay's armour and his shield and armed him, and so he went to the stable and took his horse, and took his leave of his host, and so he departed. Then soon after arose Sir Kay and missed Sir Launcelot: and then he espied that he had his armour and his horse. Now by my faith I know well that he will grieve some of the court of King Arthur: for on him knights will be bold, and deem that it is I, and that will beguile them; and because of his armour and shield I am sure I shall ride in peace. And then soon after departed Sir Kay, and thanked his host.

As I laid the book down there was a knock at the door, and my stranger came in. I gave him a pipe and a chair, and made him welcome. I also comforted him with a hot Scotch whiskey; gave him another one; then still another—hoping always for his story. After a fourth persuader, he drifted into it himself, in a quite simple and natural way:

### THE STRANGER'S HISTORY

I am an American. I was born and reared in Hartford,[9] in the State of Connecticut—anyway, just over the river, in the country. So I am a Yankee of the Yankees—and practical; yes, and nearly barren of sentiment, I suppose—or poetry, in other words. My father was a blacksmith, my uncle was a horse doctor, and I was both, along at first. Then I went over to the great arms factory[1] and learned my real trade; learned all there was to it; learned to make everything; guns, revolvers, cannon, boilers, engines, all sorts of labor-saving machinery. Why, I could make anything a body wanted—anything in the world, it didn't make any difference what; and if there wasn't any quick new-fangled way to make a thing, I could invent one—and do it as easy as rolling off a log. I became head superintendent; had a couple of thousand men under me.

Well, a man like that is a man that is full of fight—that goes without saying. With a couple of thousand rough men under one, one has plenty of that sort of amusement. I had, anyway. At last I met my match, and I got my dose. It was during a misunderstanding conducted with crowbars with a fellow we used to call Hercules. He laid me out with a crusher alongside the head that made everything crack, and seemed to spring every joint in my skull and make it overlap its neighbor. Then the world went out in darkness, and I didn't feel anything more, and didn't know anything at all—at least for a while.

When I came to again, I was sitting under an oak tree, on the grass, with a whole beautiful and broad country landscape all to myself—nearly. Not entirely; for there was a fellow on a horse, looking down at

9. The city in which Clemens was living at the time the novel was written. His home (today the Mark Twain Memorial) was, however, in the western part of town; Hank Morgan lives in East Hartford, across the Connecticut River.
1. Samuel Colt (1814–62) established a plant for the manufacture of firearms in Hartford in the 1840s. Clemens paid a visit to the factory early in 1868. In its early stages the Paige typesetting machine was built at the Colt Arms Factory; beginning in 1886, Clemens poured money into the machine in the vain hope that the invention would be perfected, perhaps at the same time that he finished the novel.

me—a fellow fresh out of a picture-book. He was in old-time iron armor from head to heel, with a helmet on his head the shape of a nail-keg with slits in it; and he had a shield, and a sword, and a prodigious spear; and his horse had armor on, too, and a steel horn projecting from his forehead, and gorgeous red and green silk trappings that hung down all around him like a bed-quilt, nearly to the ground.

"Fair, sir, will ye just?" said this fellow.

"Will I which?"

"Will ye try a passage of arms for land or lady or for—"

"What are you giving me?" I said. "Get along back to your circus, or I'll report you."

Now what does this man do but fall back a couple of hundred yards and then come rushing at me as hard as he could tear, with his nail-keg bent down nearly to his horse's neck and his long spear pointed straight ahead. I saw he meant business, so I was up the tree when he arrived.

He allowed that I was his property, the captive of his spear. There was argument on his side—and the bulk of the advantage—so I judged it best to humor him. We fixed up an agreement whereby I was to go with him and he was not to hurt me. I came down, and we started away, I walking by the side of his horse. We marched comfortably along, through glades and over brooks which I could not remember to have seen before—which puzzled me and made me wonder—and yet we did not come to any circus or signs of a circus. So I gave up the idea of a circus, and concluded he was from an asylum. But we never came to any asylum—so I was up a stump, as you may say. I asked him how far we were from Hartford. He said he had never heard of the place; which I took to be a lie, but allowed it to go at that. At the end of an hour we saw a far-away town sleeping in a valley by a winding river; and beyond it on a hill, a vast gray fortress, with towers and turrets, the first I had ever seen out of a picture.

"Bridgeport?"[2] said I, pointing.

"Camelot," said he.

My stranger had been showing signs of sleepiness. He caught himself nodding, now, and smiled one of those pathetic, obsolete smiles of his, and said:

"I find I can't go on; but come with me, I've got it all written out, and you can read it if you like."

In his chamber, he said: "First, I kept a journal; then by and by, after years, I took the journal and turned it into a book. How long ago that was!"

---

2. Apparently, as Hamlin Hill suggested, Clemens has in mind the towers and turrets of P. T. Barnum's mansion "Iranistan," in Bridgeport, Conn. Although it burned in 1852, woodcuts of it appear in many editions of Barnum's *Struggles and Triumphs*, with which Clemens was familiar.

He handed me his manuscript, and pointed out the place where I should begin:

"Begin here—I've already told you what goes before." He was steeped in drowsiness by this time. As I went out at his door I heard him murmur sleepily: "Give you good den, fair sir."

I sat down by my fire and examined my treasure. The first part of it—the great bulk of it—was parchment, and yellow with age. I scanned a leaf particularly and saw that it was a palimpsest. Under the old dim writing of the Yankee historian appeared traces of a penmanship which was older and dimmer still—Latin words and sentences: fragments from old monkish legends, evidently. I turned to the place indicated by my stranger and began to read—as follows.

THE TALE OF THE LOST LAND

# Chapter I

## CAMELOT

"Camelot—Camelot," said I to myself. "I don't seem to remember hearing of it before. Name of the asylum, likely."

It was a soft, reposeful summer landscape, as lovely as a dream, and as lonesome as Sunday. The air was full of the smell of flowers, and the buzzing of insects, and the twittering of birds, and there were no people, no wagons, there was no stir of life, nothing going on. The road was mainly a winding path with hoofprints in it, and now and then a faint trace of wheels on either side in the grass—wheels that apparently had a tire as broad as one's hand.

Presently a fair slip of a girl, about ten years old, with a cataract of golden hair streaming down over her shoulders, came along. Around her head she wore a hoop of flame-red poppies. It was as sweet an outfit as ever I saw, what there was of it. She walked indolently along, with a mind at rest, its peace reflected in her innocent face. The circus man paid no attention to her; didn't even seem to see her. And she—she was no more startled at his fantastic make-up than if she was used to his like every day of her life. She was going by as indifferently as she might have gone by a couple of cows; but when she happened to notice me, *then* there was a change! Up went her hands, and she was turned to stone; her mouth dropped open, her eyes stared wide and timorously, she was the picture of astonished curiosity touched with fear. And there she stood gazing, in a sort of stupefied fascination, till we turned a corner of the wood and were lost to her view. That she should be startled at me instead of at the other man, was too many for me; I couldn't make head or tail of it. And that she should seem to consider me a spectacle, and totally overlook her own merits in that respect, was another puzzling thing, and a display of magnanimity, too, that was surprising in one so young. There was food for thought here. I moved along as one in a dream.

As we approached the town, signs of life began to appear. At intervals we passed a wretched cabin, with a thatched roof, and about it small fields and garden patches in an indifferent state of cultivation. There were people, too; brawny men, with long, coarse, uncombed hair that hung down over their faces and made them look like animals. They and the women, as a rule, wore a coarse tow-linen robe that came well below the knee, and a rude sort of sandals, and many wore an iron collar. The small boys and girls were always naked; but nobody seemed to know it. All of these people stared at me, talked about me, ran into the huts and fetched out their families to gape at me; but nobody ever noticed that other fellow, except to make him humble salutation and get no response for their pains.

In the town were some substantial windowless houses of stone scattered among a wilderness of thatched cabins; the streets were mere crooked alleys, and unpaved; troops of dogs and nude children played in the sun and made life and noise; hogs roamed and rooted content-edly about, and one of them lay in a reeking wallow in the middle of the main thoroughfare and suckled her family. Presently there was a distant blare of military music; it came nearer, still nearer, and soon a noble cavalcade wound into view, glorious with plumed helmets and flashing mail and flaunting banners and rich doublets and horse-cloths and gilded spear heads; and through the muck and swine, and naked brats, and joyous dogs, and shabby huts it took its gallant way, and in its wake we followed. Followed through one winding alley and then another,—and climbing, always climbing—till at last we gained the breezy height where the huge castle stood. There was an exchange of bugle blasts; then a parley from the walls, where men-at-arms, in hauberk and morion³ marched back and forth with halberd at shoul-der under flapping banners with the rude figure of a dragon displayed upon them; and then the great gates were flung open, the drawbridge was lowered, and the head of the cavalcade swept forward under the frowning arches; and we, following, soon found ourselves in a great paved court, with towers and turrets stretching up into the blue air on all the four sides; and all about us the dismount was going on, and much greeting and ceremony, and running to and fro, and a gay display of moving and intermingling colors, and an altogether pleas-ant stir and noise and confusion.

## Chapter II

### KING ARTHUR'S COURT

The moment I got a chance I slipped aside privately and touched an ancient common looking man on the shoulder and said, in an in-sinuating, confidential way—

"Friend, do me a kindness. Do you belong to the asylum, or are you just here on a visit or something like that?"

He looked me over stupidly, and said—

"Marry, fair sir, me seemeth—"

"That will do," I said; "I reckon you are a patient."

I moved away, cogitating, and at the same time keeping an eye out for any chance passenger in his right mind that might come along and give me some light. I judged I had found one, presently; so I drew him aside and said in his ear—

"If I could see the head keeper a minute—only just a minute—"

"Prithee do not let me."

"Let you *what?*"

"*Hinder* me, then, if the word please thee better." Then he went on

---

3. A high-crested helmet having no visor.

to say he was an under-cook and could not stop to gossip, though he would like it another time; for it would comfort his very liver to know where I got my clothes. As he started away he pointed and said yonder was one who was idle enough for my purpose, and was seeking me besides, no doubt. This was an airy slim boy in shrimp-colored tights that made him look like a forked carrot; the rest of his gear was blue silk and dainty laces and ruffles; and he had long yellow curls, and wore a plumed pink satin cap tilted complacently over his ear. By his look, he was good-natured; by his gait, he was satisfied with himself. He was pretty enough to frame. He arrived, looked me over with a smiling and impudent curiosity; said he had come for me, and informed me that he was a page.

"Go 'long," I said; "you ain't more than a paragraph."

It was pretty severe, but I was nettled. However, it never phazed him; he didn't appear to know he was hurt. He began to talk and laugh, in happy, thoughtless, boyish fashion, as we walked along, and made himself old friends with me at once; asked me all sorts of questions about myself and about my clothes, but never waited for an answer—always chattered straight ahead, as if he didn't know he had asked a question and wasn't expecting any reply, until at last he happened to mention that he was born in the beginning of the year 513.

It made the cold chills creep over me! I stopped, and said, a little faintly:

"Maybe I didn't hear you just right. Say it again—and say it slow. What year was it?"

"513."

"513! You don't look it! Come, my boy, I am a stranger and friendless: be honest and honorable with me. Are you in your right mind?"

He said he was.

"Are these other people in their right minds?"

He said they were.

"And this isn't an asylum? I mean, it isn't a place where they cure crazy people?"

He said it wasn't.

"Well, then," I said, "either I am a lunatic, or something just as awful has happened. Now tell me, honest and true, where am I?"

"IN KING ARTHUR'S COURT."

I waited a minute, to let that idea shudder its way home, and then said:

"And according to your notions, what year is it now?"

"528—nineteenth of June."

I felt a mournful sinking at the heart, and muttered: "I shall never see my friends again—never, never again. They will not be born for more than thirteen hundred years yet."

I seemed to believe the boy, I didn't know why. *Something* in me

"GO 'LONG," I SAID; "YOU AIN'T MORE THAN A PARAGRAPH."

Hank Morgan and Clarence. Beard's model for the Yankee was George Morrison, a young photo-engraver from Connecticut who worked in the studio next to his on Fifth Avenue, in New York City. Clarence was drawn from a photograph of the actress Sarah Bernhardt.

seemed to believe him—my consciousness, as you may say; but my reason didn't. My reason straightway began to clamor; that was natural. I didn't know how to go about satisfying it, because I knew that the testimony of men wouldn't serve—my reason would say they were lunatics, and throw out their evidence. But all of a sudden I stumbled on the very thing, just by luck. I knew that the only total eclipse of the sun in the first half of the sixth century occurred on the 21st of June, A. D. 528, O. S., and began at 3 minutes after 12 noon.[4] I also knew that no total eclipse of the sun was due in what to *me* was the present year—*i. e.*, 1879. So, if I could keep my anxiety and curiosity from eating the heart out of me for forty-eight hours, I should then find out for certain whether this boy was telling me the truth or not.

Wherefore, being a practical Connecticut man, I now shoved this whole problem clear out of my mind till its appointed day and hour should come, in order that I might turn all my attention to the circumstances of the present moment, and be alert and ready to make the most out of them that could be made. One thing at a time, is my motto—and just play that thing for all it is worth, even if it's only two pair and a jack.[5] I made up my mind to two things; if it was still the nineteenth century and I was among lunatics and couldn't get away, I would presently boss that asylum or know the reason why; and if on the other hand it was really the sixth century, all right, I didn't want any softer thing: I would boss the whole country inside of three months; for I judged I would have the start of the best-educated man in the kingdom by a matter of thirteen hundred years and upwards. I'm not a man to waste time after my mind's made up and there's work on hand; so I said to the page—

"Now, Clarence, my boy—if that might happen to be your name—I'll get you to post me up a little if you don't mind. What is the name of that apparition that brought me here?"

"My master and thine? That is the good knight and great lord Sir Kay the Seneschal, foster brother to our liege the king."

"Very good; go on, tell me everything."

He made a long story of it; but the part that had immediate interest for me was this. He said I was Sir Kay's prisoner, and that in the due course of custom I would be flung into a dungeon and left there on scant commons until my friends ransomed me—unless I chanced to rot, first. I saw that the last chance had the best show, but I didn't waste any bother about that; time was too precious. The page said, further, that dinner was about ended in the great hall by this time, and that as soon as the sociability and the heavy drinking should begin, Sir Kay

4. No eclipse occurred on the date indicated. In Clemens' reading at Governor's Island, N.Y., in 1886, he explained that Morgan obtained this information from a recent almanac. "O.S." indicates "old style," the Julian rather than the Gregorian calendar. Clemens at one point planned to have the eclipse occur a little after three or at four in the afternoon; noon was of course a more dramatic time. He also changed the date from the 19th to the 21st, the summer solstice.

5. A rather poor hand in a game of cards.

would have me in and exhibit me before King Arthur and his illustrious knights seated at the Table Round, and would brag about his exploit in capturing me, and would probably exaggerate the facts a little, but it wouldn't be good form for me to correct him, and not over safe, either; and when I was done being exhibited, then ho for the dungeon; but he, Clarence, would find a way to come and see me every now and then, and cheer me up, and help me get word to my friends.

Get word to my friends! I thanked him; I couldn't do less; and about this time a lackey came to say I was wanted; so Clarence led me in and took me off to one side and sat down by me.

Well, it was a curious kind of spectacle, and interesting. It was an immense place, and rather naked—yes, and full of loud contrasts. It was very, very lofty; so lofty that the banners depending from the arched beams and girders away up there floated in a sort of twilight; there was a stone-railed gallery at each end, high up, with musicians in the one, and women, clothed in stunning colors, in the other. The floor was of big stone flags laid in black and white squares, rather battered by age and use, and needing repair. As to ornament, there wasn't any, strictly speaking; though on the walls hung some huge tapestries which were probably taxed as works of art; battle-pieces, they were, with horses shaped like those which children cut out of paper or create in gingerbread; with men on them in scale armor whose scales are represented by round holes—so that the man's coat looks as if it had been done with a biscuit-punch. There was a fireplace big enough to camp in; and its projecting sides and hood, of carved and pillared stone-work, had the look of a cathedral door. Along the walls stood men-at-arms, in breastplate and morion, with halberds[6] for their only weapon—rigid as statues; and that is what they looked like.

In the middle of this groined and vaulted public square was an oaken table which they called the Table Round. It was as large as a circus ring; and around it sat a great company of men dressed in such various and splendid colors that it hurt one's eyes to look at them. They wore their plumed hats, right along, except that whenever one addressed himself directly to the king, he lifted his hat a trifle just as he was beginning his remark.

Mainly they were drinking—from entire ox horns; but a few were still munching bread or gnawing beef bones. There was about an average of two dogs to one man; and these sat in expectant attitudes till a spent bone was flung to them, and then they went for it by brigades and divisions, with a rush, and there ensued a fight which filled the prospect with a tumultuous chaos of plunging heads and bodies and flashing tails, and the storm of howlings and barkings deafened all speech for the time; but that was no matter, for the dog-fight was

6. Weapons used particularly during the fifteenth and sixteenth centuries, consisting of battle axes and pikes mounted on handles about six feet long.

always a bigger interest anyway; the men rose, sometimes, to observe it the better and bet on it, and the ladies and the musicians stretched themselves out over their balusters with the same object; and all broke into delighted ejaculations from time to time. In the end, the winning dog stretched himself out comfortably with his bone between his paws, and proceeded to growl over it, and gnaw it, and grease the floor with it, just as fifty others were already doing; and the rest of the court resumed their previous industries and entertainments.

As a rule the speech and behavior of these people were gracious and courtly; and I noticed that they were good and serious listeners when anybody was telling anything—I mean in a dog-fightless interval. And plainly, too, they were a childlike and innocent lot; telling lies of the stateliest pattern with a most gentle and winning naivety, and ready and willing to listen to anybody else's lie, and believe it, too. It was hard to associate them with anything cruel or dreadful; and yet they dealt in tales of blood and suffering with a guileless relish that made me almost forget to shudder.

I was not the only prisoner present. There were twenty or more. Poor devils, many of them were maimed, hacked, carved, in a frightful way; and their hair, their faces, their clothing, were caked with black and stiffened drenchings of blood. They were suffering sharp physical pain, of course; and weariness, and hunger and thirst, no doubt; and at least none had given them the comfort of a wash, or even the poor charity of a lotion for their wounds; yet you never heard them utter a moan or a groan, or saw them show any sign of restlessness, or any disposition to complain. The thought was forced upon me: "The rascals—*they* have served other people so in their day; it being their own turn, now, they were not expecting any better treatment than this; so their philosophical bearing is not an outcome of mental training, intellectual fortitude, reasoning; it is mere animal training; they are white Indians."

## Chapter III

### KNIGHTS OF THE TABLE ROUND

Mainly the Round Table talk was monologues—narrative accounts of the adventures in which these prisoners were captured and their friends and backers killed and stripped of their steeds and armor. As a general thing—as far as I could make out—these murderous adventures were not forays undertaken to avenge injuries, nor to settle old disputes or sudden fallings out; no, as a rule they were simply duels between strangers—duels between people who had never even been introduced to each other, and between whom existed no cause of offense whatever. Many a time I had seen a couple of boys, strangers, meet by chance, and say simultaneously, "I can lick you," and go at it on the spot;[7] but I had always imagined until now, that that sort of thing belonged to children only, and was a sign and mark of childhood; but here were these big boobies sticking to it and taking pride in it clear up into full age and beyond. Yet there was something very engaging about these great simple-hearted creatures, something attractive and lovable. There did not seem to be brains enough in the entire nursery, so to speak, to bait a fish-hook with; but you didn't seem to mind that, after a little, because you soon saw that brains were not needed in a society like that, and, indeed would have marred it, hindered it, spoiled its symmetry—perhaps rendered its existence impossible.

There was a fine manliness observable in almost every face; and in some a certain loftiness and sweetness that rebuked your belittling criticisms and stilled them. A most noble benignity and purity reposed in the countenance of him they called Sir Galahad, and likewise in the king's also; and there was majesty and greatness in the giant frame and high bearing of Sir Launcelot of the Lake.

There was presently an incident which centred the general interest upon this Sir Launcelot. At a sign from a sort of master of ceremonies, six or eight of the prisoners rose and came forward in a body and knelt on the floor and lifted up their hands toward the ladies' gallery and begged the grace of a word with the queen. The most conspicuously situated lady in that massed flower-bed of feminine show and finery inclined her head by way of assent, and then the spokesman of the prisoners delivered himself and his fellows into her hands for free pardon, ransom, captivity or death, as she in her good pleasure might elect; and this, as he said, he was doing by command of Sir Kay the Seneschal, whose prisoners they were,[8] he having vanquished them by his single might and prowess in sturdy conflict in the field.

Surprise and astonishment flashed from face to face all over the house; the queen's gratified smile faded out at the name of Sir Kay, and she looked disappointed; and the page whispered in my ear with an accent and manner expressive of extravagant derision—

"Sir *Kay*, forsooth! Oh, call me pet names, dearest, call me a marine![9] In twice a thousand years shall the unholy invention of man labor at odds to beget the fellow to this majestic lie!"

Every eye was fastened with severe inquiry upon Sir Kay. But he was equal to the occasion. He got up and played his hand like a major—and took every trick. He said he would state the case, exactly according to the facts; he would tell the simple straightforward tale, without comment of his own; "and then," said he, "if ye find glory and honor due, ye will give it unto him who is the mightiest man of his hands that

---

7. Such a scene occurs in the first chapter of *The Adventures of Tom Sawyer* (1876).
8. The narrative now takes up where the Malory account in "A Word of Explanation" leaves

off.
9. Marines were proverbially known for their willingness to believe anything.

ever bare shield or strake with sword in the ranks of Christian battle—
even him that sitteth there!" and he pointed to Sir Launcelot. Ah, he
fetched them; it was a rattling good stroke. Then he went on and told
how Sir Launcelot, seeking adventures, some brief time gone by,
killed seven giants at one sweep of his sword, and set a hundred and
forty-two captive maidens free; and then went further, still seeking
adventures, and found him (Sir Kay) fighting a desperate fight against
nine foreign knights, and straightway took the battle solely into his
own hands, and conquered the nine; and that night Sir Launcelot rose
quietly, and dressed him in Sir Kay's armor and took Sir Kay's horse
and gat him away into distant lands, and vanquished sixteen knights in
one pitched battle and thirty-four in another; and all these and the
former nine he made to swear that about Whitsuntide they would ride
to Arthur's court and yield them to Queen Guenever's hands as
captives of Sir Kay the Seneschal, spoil of his knightly prowess; and
now here were these half dozen, and the rest would be along as soon as
they might be healed of their desperate wounds.

Well, it was touching to see the queen blush and smile, and look
embarrassed and happy, and fling furtive glances at Sir Launcelot that
would have got him shot in Arkansas,[1] to a dead certainty.

Everybody praised the valor and magnanimity of Sir Launcelot; and
as for me, I was perfectly amazed, that one man, all by himself, should
have been able to beat down and capture such battalions of practiced
fighters. I said as much to Clarence; but this mocking featherhead only
said—

"An Sir Kay had had time to get another skin of sour wine into him,
ye had seen the accompt doubled."

I looked at the boy in sorrow; and as I looked I saw the cloud of a
deep despondency settle upon his countenance. I followed the direction of his eye, and saw that a very old and white-bearded man,
clothed in a flowing black gown, had risen and was standing at the
table upon unsteady legs, and feebly swaying his ancient head and
surveying the company with his watery and wandering eye. The same
suffering look that was in the page's face was observable in all the faces
around—the look of dumb creatures who know that they must endure
and make no moan.

"Marry, we shall have it again," sighed the boy; "that same old
weary tale that he hath told a thousand times in the same words, and
that he *will* tell till he dieth, every time he hath gotten his barrel full
and feeleth his exaggeration-mill a-working. Would God I had died or
I saw this day!"

"Who is it?"

"Merlin, the mighty liar and magician, perdition singe him for the
weariness he worketh with his one tale! But that men fear him for that

1. Here and elsewhere Morgan shows an unaccounted-for knowledge of the Mississippi Valley, which Clemens of course knew very well.

Alfred Lord Tennyson as Merlin. Tennyson's *Idylls of the King* was one of the most popular Victorian retellings of the Arthurian legend.

he hath the storms and the lightnings and all the devils that be in hell at his beck and call, they would have dug his entrails out these many years ago to get at that tale and squelch it. He telleth it always in the third person, making believe he is too modest to glorify himself— maledictions light upon him, misfortune be his dole! Good friend, prithee call me for evensong."

The boy nestled himself upon my shoulder and pretended to go to sleep. The old man began his tale; and presently the lad was asleep in reality; so also were the dogs, and the court, the lackeys, and the files of men-at-arms. The droning voice droned on; a soft snoring arose on all sides and supported it like a deep and subdued accompaniment of wind instruments. Some heads were bowed upon folded arms, some lay back with open mouths that issued unconscious music; the flies buzzed and bit, unmolested, the rats swarmed softly out from a hundred holes, and pattered about, and made themselves at home everywhere; and one of them sat up like a squirrel on the king's head and held a bit of cheese in its hands and nibbled it, and dribbled the crumbs in the king's face with naïve and impudent irreverence. It was a tranquil scene, and restful to the weary eye and the jaded spirit.

This was the old man's tale. He said:

"Right so the king and Merlin departed, and went until an hermit that was a good man and a great leech. So the hermit searched all his wounds and gave him good salves; so the king was there three days, and then were his wounds well amended that he might ride and go, and so departed. And as they rode, Arthur said, I have no sword. No force,[2] said Merlin, hereby is a sword that shall be yours and I may. So they rode till they came to a lake, the which was a fair water and broad, and in the midst of the lake Arthur was ware of an arm clothed in white samite, that held a fair sword in that hand. Lo, said Merlin, yonder is that sword that I spake of. With that they saw a damsel going upon the lake. What damsel is that? said Arthur. That is the Lady of the lake, said Merlin; and within that lake is a rock, and therein is as fair a place as any on earth, and richly beseen, and this damsel will come to you anon, and then speak ye fair to her that she will give you that sword. Anon withal came the damsel unto Arthur and saluted him, and he her again. Damsel, said Arthur, what sword is that, that yonder the arm holdeth above the water? I would it were mine, for I have no sword. Sir Arthur King, said the damsel, that sword is mine, and if ye will give me a gift when I ask it you, ye shall have it. By my faith, said Arthur, I will give you what gift ye will ask. Well, said the damsel, go ye into yonder barge and row yourself to the sword, and take it and the scabbard with you, and I will ask my gift when I see my time. So Sir Arthur and Merlin alight, and tied their horses to two trees, and so they went into the ship, and when they came to the sword that the hand held, Sir Arthur took it up by the handles, and took it with him.

2. No matter. [*Clemens' note.*]

And the arm and the hand went under the water; and so they came unto the land and rode forth. And then Sir Arthur saw a rich pavilion. What signifieth yonder pavilion? It is the knight's pavilion, said Merlin, that ye fought with last, Sir Pellinore, but he is out, he is not there; he hath ado with a knight of yours, that hight Egglame, and they have fought together, but at the last Egglame fled, and else he had been dead, and he hath chased him even to Carlion, and we shall meet with him anon in the highway. That is well said, said Arthur, now have I a sword, now will I wage battle with him, and be avenged on him. Sir, ye shall not so, said Merlin, for the knight is weary of fighting and chasing, so that ye shall have no worship to have ado with him; also, he will not lightly be matched of one knight living; and therefore it is my counsel, let him pass, for he shall do you good service in short time, and his sons, after his days. Also ye shall see that day in short space ye shall be right glad to give him your sister to wed. When I see him, I will do as ye advise me, said Arthur. Then Sir Arthur looked on the sword, and liked it passing well. Whether liketh you better, said Merlin, the sword or the scabbard? Me liketh better the sword, said Arthur. Ye are more unwise, said Merlin, for the scabbard is worth ten of the sword, for while ye have the scabbard upon you ye shall never lose no blood, be ye never so sore wounded; therefore, keep well the scabbard always with you. So they rode unto Carlion, and by the way they met with Sir Pellinore; but Merlin had done such a craft that Pellinore saw not Arthur, and he passed by without any words. I marvel, said Arthur, that the knight would not speak. Sir, said Merlin, he saw you not; for and he had seen you ye had not lightly departed. So they came unto Carlion, whereof his knights were passing glad. And when they heard of his adventures they marveled that he would jeopard his person so alone. But all men of worship said it was merry to be under such a chieftain that would put his person in adventure as other poor knights did."[3]

## Chapter IV

### SIR DINADAN THE HUMORIST

It seemed to me that this quaint lie was most simply and beautifully told; but then I had heard it only once, and that makes a difference; it was pleasant to the others when it was fresh, no doubt.

Sir Dinadan the Humorist was the first to awake, and he soon roused the rest with a practical joke of a sufficiently poor quality. He tied some metal mugs to a dog's tail and turned him loose, and he tore around and around the place in a frenzy of fright, with all the other dogs bellowing after him and battering and crashing against everything that came in their way and making altogether a chaos of confusion and

3. From Malory, I.xxiii.

a most deafening din and turmoil; at which every man and woman of the multitude laughed till the tears flowed, and some fell out of their chairs and wallowed on the floor in ecstasy. It was just like so many children. Sir Dinadan was so proud of his exploit that he could not keep from telling over and over again, to weariness, how the immortal idea happened to occur to him; and as is the way with humorists of his breed,[4] he was still laughing at it after everybody else had got through. He was so set up that he concluded to make a speech—of course a humorous speech. I think I never heard so many old played-out jokes strung together in my life. He was worse than the minstrels, worse than the clown in the circus. It seemed peculiarly sad to sit here, thirteen hundred years before I was born and listen again to poor, flat, worm-eaten jokes that had given me the dry gripes when I was a boy thirteen hundred years afterwards. It about convinced me that there isn't any such thing as a new joke possible. Everybody laughed at these antiquities—but then they always do; I had noticed that, centuries later. However, of course the scoffer didn't laugh—I mean the boy. No, he scoffed; there wasn't anything he wouldn't scoff at. He said the most of Sir Dinadan's jokes were rotten and the rest were petrified. I said "petrified" was good; as I believed, myself, that the only right way to classify the majestic ages of some of those jokes was by geologic periods. But that neat idea hit the boy in a blank place, for geology hadn't been invented yet. However, I made a note of the remark, and calculated to educate the commonwealth up to it if I pulled through. It is no use to throw a good thing away merely because the market isn't ripe yet.

Now Sir Kay arose and began to fire up on his history-mill, with me for fuel. It was time for me to feel serious, and I did. Sir Kay told how he had encountered me in a far land of barbarians, who all wore the same ridiculous garb that I did—a garb that was a work of enchantment, and intended to make the wearer secure from hurt by human hands. However, he had nullified the force of the enchantment by prayer, and had killed my thirteen knights in a three-hours' battle, and taken me prisoner, sparing my life in order that so strange a curiosity as I was might be exhibited to the wonder and admiration of the king and the court. He spoke of me all the time, in the blandest way, as "this prodigious giant," and "this horrible sky-towering monster," and "this tusked and taloned man-devouring ogre;" and everybody took in all this bosh in the naïvest way, and never smiled or seemed to notice that there was any discrepancy between these watered statistics and me. He said that in trying to escape from him I sprang into the top of a tree two hundred cubits high at a single bound, but he dislodged me with a stone the size of a cow, which "all-to brast" the most of my bones, and

4. In "How to Tell a Story" (1895), Clemens says that one telling a humorous story should appear unaware that there is anything funny about the story he tells. In the comic or witty story the teller may behave as Sir Dinadan does.

then swore me to appear at Arthur's court for sentence. He ended by condemning me to die at noon on the 21st; and was so little concerned about it that he stopped to yawn before he named the date.

I was in a dismal state by this time; indeed, I was hardly enough in my right mind to keep the run of a dispute that sprung up as to how I had better be killed, the possibility of the killing being doubted by some, because of the enchantment in my clothes. And yet it was nothing but an ordinary suit of fifteen-dollar slop-shops. Still, I was sane enough to notice this detail, to-wit; many of the terms used in the most matter-of-fact way by this great assemblage of the first ladies and gentlemen in the land would have made a Comanche blush.[5] Indelicacy is too mild a term to convey the idea. However, I had read "Tom Jones," and "Roderick Random,"[6] and other books of that kind, and knew that the highest and first ladies and gentlemen in England had remained little or no cleaner in their talk, and in the morals and conduct which such talk implies, clear up to a hundred years ago; in fact clear into our own nineteenth century—in which century, broadly speaking, the earliest samples of the real lady and real gentleman discoverable in English history—or in European history, for that matter—may be said to have made their appearance. Suppose Sir Walter,[7] instead of putting the conversations into the mouths of his characters, had allowed the characters to speak for themselves? We should have had talk from Rachel and Ivanhoe and the soft lady Rowena which would embarrass a tramp in our day. However, to the unconsciously indelicate all things are delicate. King Arthur's people were not aware that they were indecent, and I had presence of mind enough not to mention it.

They were so troubled about my enchanted clothes that they were mightily relieved, at last, when old Merlin swept the difficulty away for them with a common-sense hint. He asked them why they were so dull—why didn't it occur to them to strip me. In half a minute I was as naked as a pair of tongs! And dear, dear, to think of it: I was the only embarrassed person there. Everbody discussed me; and did it as unconcernedly as if I had been a cabbage. Queen Guenever was as naïvely interested as the rest, and said she had never seen anybody with legs just like mine before. It was the only compliment I got—if it was a compliment.

Finally I was carried off in one direction, and my perilous clothes in another. I was shoved into a dark and narrow cell in a dungeon, with

5. In *1601* Clemens has Queen Elizabeth I, Shakespeare, Sir Walter Raleigh, and others converse on subjects unthinkable for mixed company in the Victorian era.

6. Novels by Henry Fielding and Tobias Smollett, published in 1749 and 1748.

7. Sir Walter Scott (1771–1832), poet and novelist, author of *Ivanhoe* (1820), in which Rebecca (not "Rachel," as the first American edition has it) and Rowena are characters. In *Life on the Mississippi* (1883), Clemens attacked Scott as the cause of the American Civil War.

some scant remnants for dinner, some moldy straw for a bed, and no end of rats for company.

## Chapter V

### AN INSPIRATION

I was so tired that even my fears were not able to keep me awake long.

When I next came to myself, I seemed to have been asleep a very long time. My first thought was, "Well, what an astonishing dream I've had! I reckon I've waked only just in time to keep from being hanged or drowned or burned, or something. . . . I'll nap again till the whistle blows, and then I'll go down to the arms factory and have it out with Hercules."

But just then I heard the harsh music of rusty chains and bolts, a light flashed in my eyes, and that butterfly, Clarence, stood before me! I gasped with surprise; my breath almost got away from me.

"What!" I said, "you here yet? Go along with the rest of the dream! scatter!"

But he only laughed, in his light-hearted way, and fell to making fun of my sorry plight.

"All right," I said resignedly, "let the dream go on; I'm in no hurry."

"Prithee what dream?"

"What dream? Why, the dream that I am in Arthur's court—a person who never existed; and that I am talking to you, who are nothing but a work of the imagination."

"Oh, la, indeed! and is it a dream that you're to be burned tomorrow? Ho-ho—answer me that!"

The shock that went through me was distressing. I now began to reason that my situation was in the last degree serious, dream or no dream; for I knew by past experience of the life-like intensity of dreams, that to be burned to death, even in a dream, would be very far from being a jest, and was a thing to be avoided, by any means, fair or foul, that I could contrive. So I said beseechingly:

"Ah, Clarence, good boy, only friend I've got,—for you *are* my friend, aren't you?—don't fail me; help me to devise some way of escaping from this place!"

"Now do but hear thyself! Escape? Why, man, the corridors are in guard and keep of men-at-arms."

"No doubt, no doubt. But how many, Clarence? Not many, I hope?"

"Full a score. One may not hope to escape." After a pause—hesitatingly: "and there be other reasons—and weightier."

"Other ones? What are they?"

"Well, they say—oh, but I daren't, indeed I daren't!"

"Why, poor lad, what is the matter? Why do you blench? Why do you tremble so?"

"Oh, in sooth, there is need! I do want to tell you, but—"

"Come, come, be brave, be a man—speak out, there's a good lad!"

He hesitated, pulled one way by desire, the other way by fear; then he stole to the door and peeped out, listening; and finally crept close to me and put his mouth to my ear and told me his fearful news in a whisper, and with all the cowering apprehension of one who was venturing upon awful ground and speaking of things whose very mention might be freighted with death.

"Merlin, in his malice, has woven a spell about this dungeon, and there bides not the man in these kingdoms that would be desperate enough to essay to cross its lines with you! Now God pity me, I have told it! Ah, be kind to me, be merciful to a poor boy who means thee well; for an thou betray me I am lost!"

I laughed the only really refreshing laugh I had had for some time; and shouted—

"Merlin has wrought a spell! *Merlin*, forsooth! That cheap old humbug, that maundering old ass? Bosh, pure bosh, the silliest bosh in the world! Why, it does seem to me that of all the childish, idiotic, chuckle-headed, chicken-livered superstitions that ev—oh, damn Merlin!"

But Clarence had slumped to his knees before I had half finished, and he was like to go out of his mind with fright.

"Oh, beware! These are awful words! Any moment these walls may crumble upon us if you say such things. Oh call them back before it is too late!"

Now this strange exhibition gave me a good idea and set me to thinking. If everybody about here was so honestly and sincerely afraid of Merlin's pretended magic as Clarence was, certainly a superior man like me ought to be shrewd enough to contrive some way to take advantage of such a state of things. I went on thinking, and worked out a plan. Then I said:

"Get up. Pull yourself together; look me in the eye. Do you know why I laughed?"

"No—but for our blessed Lady's sake, do it no more."

"Well, I'll tell you why I laughed. Because I'm a magician myself."

"Thou!" The boy recoiled a step, and caught his breath, for the thing hit him rather sudden; but the aspect which he took on was very, very respectful. I took quick note of that; it indicated that a humbug didn't need to have a reputation in this asylum; people stood ready to take him at his word, without that. I resumed:

"I've known Merlin seven hundred years, and he—"

"Seven hun—"

"Don't interrupt me. He has died and come alive again thirteen times, and traveled under a new name every time: Smith, Jones,

Robinson, Jackson, Peters, Haskins, Merlin—a new alias every time he turns up. I knew him in Egypt three hundred years ago; I knew him in India five hundred years ago—he is always blethering around in my way, everywhere I go; he makes me tired. He don't amount to shucks, as a magician; knows some of the old common tricks, but has never got beyond the rudiments, and never will. He is well enough for the provinces—one-night stands and that sort of thing, you know—but dear me, *he* oughtn't to set up for an expert—anyway not where there's a real artist. Now look here, Clarence, I am going to stand your friend, right along, and in return you must be mine. I want you to do me a favor. I want you to get word to the king that I am a magician myself—and the Supreme Grand High-yu-Mucka-muck[8] and head of the tribe, at that; and I want him to be made to understand that I am just quietly arranging a little calamity here that will make the fur fly in these realms if Sir Kay's project is carried out and any harm comes to me. Will you get that to the king for me?"

The poor boy was in such a state that he could hardly answer me. It was pitiful to see a creature so terrified, so unnerved, so demoralized. But he promised everything; and on my side he made me promise over and over again that I would remain his friend, and never turn against him or cast any enchantments upon him. Then he worked his way out, staying himself with his hand along the wall, like a sick person.

Presently this thought occurred to me: how heedless I have been! When the boy gets calm, he will wonder why a great magician like me should have begged a boy like him to help me get out of this place; he will put this and that together, and will see that I am a humbug.

I worried over that heedless blunder for an hour, and called myself a great many hard names, meantime. But finally it occurred to me all of a sudden that these animals didn't reason; that *they* never put this and that together; that all their talk showed that they didn't know a discrepancy when they saw it. I was at rest, then.

But as soon as one is at rest, in this world, off he goes on something else to worry about. It occurred to me that I had made another blunder: I had sent the boy off to alarm his betters with a threat—I intending to invent a calamity at my leisure; now the people who are the readiest and eagerest and willingest to swallow miracles are the very ones who are the hungriest to see you perform them; suppose I should be called on for a sample? Suppose I should be asked to name my calamity? Yes, I had made a blunder; I ought to have invented my calamity first. "What shall I do? what can I say, to gain a little time?" I was in trouble again; in the deepest kind of trouble:  . . . "There's a footstep!—they're coming. If I had only just a moment to think. . . . Good, I've got it. I'm all right."

You see, it was the eclipse. It came into my mind, in the nick of

8. An important personage; in an 1866 letter from Hawaii, Clemens spelled it "High-You-Muck-a-Muck."

time, how Columbus,[9] or Cortez, or one of those people, played an eclipse as a saving trump once, on some savages, and I saw my chance. I could play it myself, now; and it wouldn't be any plagiarism, either, because I should get it in nearly a thousand years ahead of those parties.

Clarence came in, subdued, distressed, and said:

"I hasted the message to our liege the king, and straightway he had me to his presence. He was frighted even to the marrow, and was minded to give order for your instant enlargement, and that you be clothed in fine raiment and lodged as befitted one so great; but then came Merlin and spoiled all; for he persuaded the king that you are mad, and know not whereof you speak; and said your threat is but foolishness and idle vaporing. They disputed long, but in the end, Merlin, scoffing, said, "Wherefore hath he not *named* his brave calamity? Verily it is because he cannot.' This thrust did in a most sudden sort close the king's mouth, and he could offer naught to turn the argument; and so, reluctant, and full loth to do you the discourtesy, he yet prayeth you to consider his perplexed case, as noting how the matter stands, and name the calamity—if so be you have determined the nature of it and the time of its coming. Oh, prithee delay not; to delay at such a time were to double and treble the perils that already compass thee about. Oh, be thou wise—name the calamity!"

I allowed silence to accumulate while I got my impressiveness together, and then said:

"How long have I been shut up in this hole?"

"Ye were shut up when yesterday was well spent. It is 9 of the morning now."

"No! Then I have slept well, sure enough. Nine in the morning now! And yet it is the very complexion of midnight, to a shade. This is the 20th, then?"

"The 20th—yes."

"And I am to be burned alive to-morrow." The boy shuddered.

"At what hour?"

"At high noon."

"Now then, I will tell you what to say." I paused, and stood over that cowering lad a whole minute in awful silence; then in a voice deep, measured, charged with doom, I began, and rose by dramatically graded stages to my colossal climax, which I delivered in as sublime and noble a way as ever I did such a thing in my life: "Go back and tell the king that at that hour I will smother the whole world in the dead blackness of midnight; I will blot out the sun, and he shall never shine again; the fruits of the earth shall rot for lack of light and warmth, and the peoples of the earth shall famish and die, to the last man!"

9. The incident is supposed to have occurred during Columbus' fourth voyage, in 1504; the eclipse was lunar rather than solar and was used to persuade the Indians to supply Columbus and his men with food.

I had to carry the boy out myself, he sunk into such a collapse. I handed him over to the soldiers, and went back.

## Chapter VI

### THE ECLIPSE

In the stillness and the darkness, realization soon began to supplement knowledge. The mere knowledge of a fact is pale; but when you come to *realize* your fact, it takes on color. It is all the difference between hearing of a man being stabbed to the heart, and seeing it done. In the stillness and the darkness, the knowledge that I was in deadly danger took to itself deeper and deeper meaning all the time; a something which was realization crept inch by inch through my veins and turned me cold.

But it is a blessed provision of nature that at times like these, as soon as a man's mercury has got down to a certain point there comes a revulsion, and he rallies. Hope springs up, and cheerfulness along with it, and then he is in good shape to do something for himself, if anything can be done. When my rally came, it came with a bound. I said to myself that my eclipse would be sure to save me, and make me the greatest man in the kingdom besides; and straightway my mercury went up to the top of the tube, and my solicitudes all vanished. I was as happy a man as there was in the world. I was even impatient for to-morrow to come, I so wanted to gather-in that great triumph and be the centre of all the nation's wonder and reverence. Besides, in a business way it would be the making of me; I knew that.

Meantime there was one thing which had got pushed into the background of my mind. That was the half-conviction that when the nature of my proposed calamity should be reported to those superstitious people, it would have such an effect that they would want to compromise. So, by and by when I heard footsteps coming, that thought was recalled to me, and I said to myself, "As sure as anything, it's the compromise. Well, if it is good, all right, I will accept; but if it isn't, I mean to stand my ground and play my hand for all it is worth."

The door opened, and some men-at-arms appeared. The leader said—

"The stake is ready. Come!"

The stake! The strength went out of me, and I almost fell down. It is hard to get one's breath at such a time, such lumps come into one's throat, and such gaspings; but as soon as I could speak, I said:

"But this is a mistake—the execution is to-morrow."

"Order changed; been set forward a day. Haste thee!"

I was lost. There was no help for me. I was dazed, stupefied; I had no command over myself; I only wandered purposelessly about, like one out of his mind; so the soldiers took hold of me, and pulled me along with them, out of the cell and along the maze of underground corridors, and finally into the fierce glare of daylight and the upper world. As we stepped into the vast inclosed court of the castle I got a shock; for the first thing I saw was the stake, standing in the centre, and near it the piled fagots and a monk. On all four sides of the court the seated multitudes rose rank above rank, forming sloping terraces that were rich with color. The king and the queen sat in their thrones, the most conspicuous figures there, of course.

To note all this, occupied but a second. The next second Clarence had slipped from some place of concealment and was pouring news into my ear, his eyes beaming with triumph and gladness. He said:

"'Tis through *me* the change was wrought! And main hard have I worked to do it, too. But when I revealed to them the calamity in store, and saw how mighty was the terror it did engender, then saw I also that this was the time to strike! Wherefore I diligently pretended, unto this and that and the other one, that your power against the sun could not reach its full until the morrow; and so if any would save the sun and the world, you must be slain to-day, whilst your enchantments are but in the weaving and lack potency. Odsbodikins, it was but a dull lie, a most indifferent invention, but you should have seen them seize it and swallow it, in the frenzy of their fright, as it were salvation sent from heaven; and all the while was I laughing in my sleeve the one moment, to see them so cheaply deceived, and glorifying God the next, that He was content to let the meanest of His creatures be His instrument to the saving of thy life. Ah, how happy has the matter sped! You will not need to do the sun a *real* hurt—ah, forget not that, on your soul forget it not! Only make a little darkness—only the littlest little darkness, mind, and cease with that. It will be sufficient. They will see that I spoke falsely,—being ignorant, as they will fancy—and with the falling of the first shadow of that darkness you shall see them go mad with fear; and they will set you free and make you great! Go to thy triumph now! But remember—ah, good friend, I implore thee remember my supplication, and do the blessed sun no hurt. For *my* sake, thy true friend."

I choked out some words through my grief and misery; as much as to say I would spare the sun; for which the lad's eyes paid me back with such deep and loving gratitude that I had not the heart to tell him his good-hearted foolishness had ruined me and sent me to my death.

As the soldiers assisted me across the court the stillness was so profound that if I had been blindfold I should have supposed I was in a solitude instead of walled in by four thousand people. There was not a movement perceptible in those masses of humanity; they were as rigid as stone images, and as pale; and dread sat upon every countenance. This hush continued while I was being chained to the stake; it still continued while the fagots were carefully and tediously piled about my ankles, my knees, my thighs, my body. Then there was a pause, and a deeper hush, if possible, and a man knelt down at my feet with a blazing torch; the multitude strained forward, gazing, and parting slightly from their seats without knowing it; the monk raised his hands above my head, and his eyes toward the blue sky, and began some words in Latin; in this attitude he droned on and on, a little while, and then stopped. I waited two or three moments: then looked up; he was standing there petrified. With a common impulse the multitude rose slowly up and stared into the sky. I followed their eyes; as sure as guns, there was my eclipse beginning! The life went boiling through my veins; I was a new man! The rim of black spread slowly into the sun's disk, my heart beat higher and higher, and still the assemblage and the priest stared into the sky, motionless. I knew that this gaze would be turned upon me, next. When it was, I was ready. I was in one of the most grand attitudes I ever struck, with my arm stretched up pointing to the sun. It was a noble effect. You could *see* the shudder sweep the mass like a wave. Two shouts rang out, one close upon the heels of the other:

"Apply the torch!"

"I forbid it!"

The one was from Merlin, the other from the king. Merlin started from his place—to apply the torch himself, I judged. I said:

"Stay where you are. If any man moves—even the king—before I give him leave, I will blast him with thunder, I will consume him with lightnings!"

The multitude sank meekly into their seats, and I was just expecting they would. Merlin hesitated a moment or two, and I was on pins and needles during that little while. Then he sat down, and I took a good breath; for I knew I was master of the situation now. The king said:

"Be merciful, fair sir, and essay no further in this perilous matter, lest disaster follow. It was reported to us that your powers could not attain unto their full strength until the morrow; but—

"Your Majesty thinks the report may have been a lie? It *was* a lie."

That made an immense effect; up went appealing hands everywhere, and the king was assailed with a storm of supplications that I might be bought off at any price, and the calamity stayed. The king was eager to comply. He said:

"Name any terms, reverend sir, even to the halving of my kingdom; but banish this calamity, spare the sun!"

My fortune was made. I would have taken him up in a minute, but I couldn't stop an eclipse; the thing was out of the question. So I asked time to consider. The king said—

"How long—ah, how long, good sir? Be merciful; look, it groweth darker, moment by moment. Prithee how long?"

"Not long. Half an hour—maybe an hour."

There were a thousand pathetic protests, but I couldn't shorten up any, for I couldn't remember how long a total eclipse lasts. I was in a puzzled condition, anyway, and wanted to think. Something was wrong about that eclipse, and the fact was very unsettling. If this wasn't the one I was after, how was I to tell whether this was the sixth century, or nothing but a dream? Dear me, if I could only prove it was the latter! Here was a glad new hope. If the boy was right about the date, and this was surely the 20th, it *wasn't* the sixth century. I reached for the monk's sleeve, in considerable excitement, and asked him what day of the month it was.

Hang him, he said it was the *twenty-first!* It made me turn cold to hear him. I begged him not to make any mistake about it; but he was sure; he knew it was the 21st. So, that feather-headed boy had botched things again! The time of the day was right for the eclipse; I had seen that for myself, in the beginning, by the dial that was near by. Yes, I *was* in King Arthur's court, and I might as well make the most out of it I could.

The darkness was steadily growing, the people becoming more and more distressed. I now said:

"I have reflected, Sir King. For a lessor, I will let this darkness proceed, and spread night in the world; but whether I blot out the sun for good, or restore it, shall rest with you. These are the terms, to wit: You shall remain king over all your dominions, and receive all the glories and honors that belong to the kingship; but you shall appoint me your perpetual minister and executive, and give me for my services one per cent of such actual increase of revenue over and above its present amount as I may succeed in creating for the state. If I can't live on that, I sha'n't ask anybody to give me a lift. Is it satisfactory?"

There was a prodigious roar of applause, and out of the midst of it the king's voice rose, saying:

"Away with his bonds, and set him free! and do him homage, high and low, rich and poor, for he is become the king's right hand, is clothed with power and authority, and his seat is upon the highest step of the throne! Now sweep away this creeping night, and bring the light and cheer again, that all the world may bless thee."

But I said:

"That a common man should be shamed before the world, is nothing; but it were dishonor to the *king* if any that saw his minister naked should not also see him delivered from his shame. If I might ask that my clothes be brought again—"

"They are not meet," the king broke in. "Fetch raiment of another sort; clothe him like a prince!"

My idea worked. I wanted to keep things as they were till the eclipse was total, otherwise they would be trying again to get me to dismiss the darkness, and of course I couldn't do it. Sending for the clothes gained some delay, but not enough. So I had to make another excuse. I said it would be but natural if the king should change his mind and repent to some extent of what he had done under excitement; therefore I would let the darkness grow a while, and if at the end of a reasonable time the king had kept his mind the same, the darkness should be dismissed. Neither the king nor anybody else was satisfied with that arrangement, but I had to stick to my point.

It grew darker and darker and blacker and blacker, while I struggled with those awkward sixth-century clothes. It got to be pitch dark, at last, and the multitude groaned with horror to feel the cold uncanny night breezes fan through the place and see the stars come out and twinkle in the sky. At last the eclipse was total, and I was very glad of it, but everybody else was in misery; which was quite natural. I said:

"The king, by his silence, still stands to the terms." Then I lifted up my hands—stood just so a moment—then I said, with the most awful solemnity: "Let the enchantment dissolve and pass harmless away!"

There was no response, for a moment, in that deep darkness and that graveyard hush. But when the silver rim of the sun pushed itself out, a moment or two later, the assemblage broke loose with a vast shout and came pouring down like a deluge to smother me with blessings and gratitude; and Clarence was not the last of the wash, be sure.

## *Chapter VII*

### MERLIN'S TOWER

Inasmuch as I was now the second personage in the Kingdom, as far as political power and authority were concerned, much was made of me. My raiment was of silks and velvets and cloth of gold, and by consequence was very showy, also uncomfortable. But habit would soon reconcile me to my clothes; I was aware of that. I was given the choicest suite of apartments in the castle, after the king's. They were aglow with loud-colored silken hangings, but the stone floors had nothing but rushes on them for a carpet, and they were misfit rushes at that, being not all of one breed. As for conveniences, properly speaking, there weren't any. I mean *little* conveniences; it is the little conveniences that make the real comfort of life. The big oaken chairs, graced with rude carvings, were well enough, but that was the stopping-place. There was no soap, no matches, no looking-glass—except a metal one, about as powerful as a pail of water. And not a chromo.[1] I had been used to chromos for years, and I saw now that without my suspecting it a passion for art had got worked into the fabric of my being, and was become a part of me. It made me homesick to look around over this proud and gaudy but heartless barrenness and remember that in our house in East Hartford, all unpretending as it was, you couldn't go into a room but you would find an insurance-

---

1. A colored picture printed from a series of stone or zinc plates.

chromo, or at least a three-color God-Bless-Our-Home over the door; and in the parlor we had nine. But here, even in my grand room of state, there wasn't anything in the nature of a picture except a thing the size of a bed-quilt, which was either woven or knitted, (it had darned places in it,) and nothing in it was the right color or the right shape; and as for proportions, even Raphael[2] himself couldn't have botched them more formidably, after all his practice on those nightmares they call his "celebrated Hampton Court cartoons." Raphael was a bird. We had several of his chromos; one was his "Miraculous Draught of Fishes," where he puts in a miracle of his own—puts three men into a canoe which wouldn't have held a dog without upsetting. I always admired to study R.'s art, it was so fresh and unconventional.

There wasn't even a bell or a speaking-tube in the castle. I had a great many servants, and those that were on duty lolled in the ante-room; and when I wanted one of them I had to go and call for him. There was no gas, there were no candles; a bronze dish half full of boarding-house butter with a blazing rag floating in it was the thing that produced what was regarded as light. A lot of these hung along the walls and modified the dark, just toned it down enough to make it dismal. If you went out at night, your servants carried torches. There were no books, pens, paper, or ink, and no glass in the openings they believed to be windows. It is a little thing—glass is—until it is absent, then it becomes a big thing. But perhaps the worst of all was, that there wasn't any sugar, coffee, tea or tobacco. I saw that I was just another Robinson Crusoe[3] cast away on an uninhabited island, with no society but some more or less tame animals, and if I wanted to make life bearable I must do as he did—invent, contrive, create, reorganize things; set brain and hand to work, and keep them busy. Well, that was in my line.

One thing troubled me along at first—the immense interest which people took in me. Apparently the whole nation wanted a look at me. It soon transpired that the eclipse had scared the British world almost to death: that while it lasted the whole country, from one end to the other, was in a pitiable state of panic, and the churches, hermitages, and monkeries overflowed with praying and weeping poor creatures who thought the end of the world was come. Then had followed the news that the producer of this awful event was a stranger, a mighty magician at Arthur's court; that he could have blown out the sun like a candle, and was just going to do it when his mercy was purchased, and he then dissolved his enchantments, and was now recognized and honored as the man who had by his unaided might saved the globe from destruction and its peoples from extinction. Now if you consider

2. An Italian painter (1483–1520) whose "Hampton Court cartoons," formerly displayed at Hampton Court Palace, are not satirical drawings but large preparatory designs of tapestries for the Sistine Chapel in St. Peter's, Rome.

The cartoons, including "The Miraculous Draught of Fishes," now hang in the Victoria and Albert Museum, London.
3. Hero of Daniel Defoe's novel of 1719.

that everybody believed that, and not only believed it but never even dreamed of doubting it, you will easily understand that there was not a person in all Britain that would not have walked fifty miles to get a sight of me. Of course I was all the talk—all other subjects were dropped; even the king became suddenly a person of minor interest and notoriety. Within twenty-four hours the delegations began to arrive, and from that time onward for a fortnight they kept coming. The village was crowded, and all the countryside. I had to go out a dozen times a day and show myself to these reverent and awe-stricken multitudes. It came to be a great burden, as to time and trouble, but of course it was at the same time compensatingly agreeable to be so celebrated and such a centre of homage. It turned Brer[4] Merlin green with envy and spite, which was a great satisfaction to me. But there was one thing I couldn't understand; nobody had asked for an autograph. I spoke to Clarence about it. By George, I had to explain to him what it was. Then he said nobody in the country could read or write but a few dozen priests. Land! think of that.

There was another thing that troubled me a little. Those multitudes presently began to agitate for another miracle. That was natural. To be able to carry back to their far homes the boast that they had seen the man who could command the sun, riding in the heavens, and be obeyed, would make them great in the eyes of their neighbors, and envied by them all; but to be able to also say they had seen him work a miracle themselves—why, people would come a distance to see *them*. The pressure got to be pretty strong. There was going to be an eclipse of the moon, and I knew the date and hour, but it was too far away. Two years. I would have given a good deal for license to hurry it up and use it now when there was a big market for it. It seemed a great pity to have it wasted, so, and come lagging along at a time when a body wouldn't have any use for it as like as not. If it had been booked for only a month away, I could have sold it short; but as matters stood, I couldn't seem to cipher out any way to make it do me any good, so I gave up trying. Next, Clarence found that old Merlin was making himself busy on the sly among those people. He was spreading a report that I was a humbug, and that the reason I didn't accommodate the people with a miracle was because I couldn't. I saw that I must do something. I presently thought out a plan.

By my authority as executive I threw Merlin into prison—the same cell I had occupied myself.[5] Then I gave public notice by herald and trumpet that I should be busy with affairs of state for a fortnight, but about the end of that time I would take a moment's leisure and blow up Merlin's stone tower by fires from heaven; in the meantime, whoso

4. A Southern form of address meaning "brother." It frequently appears in the conversation reported in *Huckleberry Finn*, Chapter XLI. In the "Uncle Remus" stories of Joel Chandler Harris, the animals are designated as "Brer Rabbit," "Brer Fox," etc.

5. In the *Century* version, the sentence continues: "—and I didn't thin out the rats any for his accommodation."

listened to evil reports about me, let him beware. Furthermore, I would perform but this one miracle at this time, and no more; if it failed to satisfy and any murmured, I would turn the murmurers into horses, and make them useful. Quiet ensued.

I took Clarence into my confidence, to a certain degree, and we went to work privately. I told him that this was a sort of miracle that required a trifle of preparation; and that it would be sudden death to ever talk about these preparations to anybody. That made his mouth safe enough. Clandestinely we made a few bushels of first-rate blasting-powder, and I superintended my armorers while they constructed a lightning rod and some wires. This old stone tower was very massive—and rather ruinous, too, for it was Roman, and four hundred years old. Yes, and handsome, after a rude fashion, and clothed with ivy from base to summit, as with a shirt of scale mail. It stood on a lonely eminence, in good view from the castle, and about half a mile away.

Working by night, we stowed the powder in the tower—dug stones out, on the inside, and buried the powder in the walls themselves, which were fifteen feet thick at the base. We put in a peck at a time, in a dozen places. We could have blown up the Tower of London with these charges. When the thirteenth night was come we put up our lightning rod, bedded it in one of the batches of powder, and ran wires from it to the other batches. Everybody had shunned that locality from the day of my proclamation, but on the morning of the fourteenth I thought best to warn the people, through the heralds, to keep clear away—a quarter of a mile away. Then added, by command, that at some time during the twenty-four hours I would consummate the miracle, but would first give a brief notice; by flags on the castle towers, if in the day-time, by torch-baskets in the same places if at night.

Thunder-showers had been tolerably frequent, of late, and I was not much afraid of a failure; still, I shouldn't have cared for a delay of a day or two; I should have explained that I was busy with affairs of state, yet, and the people must wait.

Of course we had a blazing sunny day—almost the first one without a cloud for three weeks; things always happen so. I kept secluded, and watched the weather. Clarence dropped in from time to time and said the public excitement was growing and growing all the time, and the whole country filling up with human masses as far as one could see from the battlements. At last the wind sprang up and a cloud appeared—in the right quarter, too, and just at nightfall. For a little while I watched that distant cloud spread and blacken, then I judged it was time for me to appear. I ordered the torch-baskets to be lit, and Merlin liberated and sent to me. A quarter of an hour later I ascended the parapet and there found the king and the court assembled and gazing off in the darkness toward Merlin's tower. Already the darkness was so heavy that one could not see far; these people, and the old turrets, being partly in deep shadow and partly in the red glow from the great torch-baskets overhead, made a good deal of a picture.

Merlin arrived in a gloomy mood. I said:

"You wanted to burn me alive when I had not done you any harm, and latterly you have been trying to injure my professional reputation. Therefore I am going to call down fire and blow up your tower, but it is only fair to give you a chance; now if you think you can break my enchantments and ward off the fires, step to the bat, it's your innings."[6]

"I can, fair sir, and I will. Doubt it not."

He drew an imaginary circle on the stones of the roof, and burnt a pinch of powder in it which sent up a small cloud of aromatic smoke, whereat everybody fell back, and began to cross themselves and get uncomfortable. Then he began to mutter and make passes in the air with his hands. He worked himself up slowly and gradually into a sort of frenzy, and got to thrashing around with his arms like the sails of a windmill. By this time the storm had about reached us; the gusts of wind were flaring the torches and making the shadows swash about, the first heavy drops of rain were falling, the world abroad was black as pitch, the lightning began to wink fitfully. Of course my rod would be loading itself now. In fact, things were imminent. So I said:

"You have had time enough. I have given you every advantage, and not interfered. It is plain your magic is weak. It is only fair that I begin now."

I made about three passes in the air, and then there was an awful crash and that old tower leaped into the sky in chunks, along with a vast volcanic fountain of fire that turned night to noonday, and showed a thousand acres of human beings groveling on the ground in a general collapse of consternation. Well, it rained mortar and masonry the rest of the week. This was the report; but probably the facts would have modified it.

It was an effective miracle. The great bothersome temporary population vanished. There were a good many thousand tracks in the mud the next morning, but they were all outward bound. If I had advertised another miracle I couldn't have raised an audience with a sheriff.

Merlin's stock was flat. The king wanted to stop his wages; he even wanted to banish him, but I interfered. I said he would be useful to work the weather, and attend to small matters like that, and I would give him a lift now and then when his poor little parlor-magic soured on him. There wasn't a rag of his tower left, but I had the government rebuild it for him, and advised him to take boarders; but he was too high-toned for that. And as for being grateful, he never even said

6. Clemens was amused by the incongruity obtained by transferring baseball language to the worlds of previous centuries. See, for example, "A Later Extract from Methuselah's Diary" in *Letters from the Earth*.

thank-you. He was a rather hard lot, take him how you might; but then you couldn't fairly expect a man to be sweet that had been set back so.

## Chapter VIII

### THE BOSS

To be vested with enormous authority is a fine thing; but to have the on-looking world consent to it is a finer. The tower episode solidified my power, and made it impregnable. If any were perchance disposed to be jealous and critical before that, they experienced a change of heart, now. There was not any one in the kingdom who would have considered it good judgment to meddle with my matters.

I was fast getting adjusted to my situation and circumstances. For a time, I used to wake up, mornings, and smile at my "dream," and listen for the Colt's factory whistle; but that sort of thing played itself out, gradually, and at last I was fully able to realize that I was actually living in the sixth century, and in Arthur's court, not a lunatic asylum. After that, I was just as much at home in that century as I could have been in any other; and as for preference, I wouldn't have traded it for the twentieth. Look at the opportunities here for a man of knowledge, brains, pluck and enterprise to sail in and grow up with the country.[7] The grandest field that ever was; and all my own; not a competitor; not a man who wasn't a baby to me in acquirements and capacities; whereas, what would I amount to in the twentieth century? I should be foreman of a factory, that is about all; and could drag a seine down-street any day and catch a hundred better men than myself.

What a jump I had made! I couldn't keep from thinking about it, and contemplating it, just as one does who has struck oil. There was nothing back of me that could approach it, unless it might be Joseph's[8] case; and Joseph's only approached it, it didn't equal it, quite. For it stands to reason that as Joseph's splendid financial ingenuities advantaged nobody but the king, the general public must have regarded him with a good deal of disfavor, whereas I had done my entire public a kindness in sparing the sun, and was popular by reason of it.

I was no shadow of a king; I was the substance; the king himself was the shadow. My power was colossal; and it was not a mere name, as such things have generally been, it was the genuine article. I stood here, at the very spring and source of the second great period of the world's history; and could see the trickling stream of that history gather, and deepen and broaden, and roll its mighty tides down the far

7. An apparent reference to the exhortation attributed to Horace Greeley (1811–72): "Go west, young man, and grow up with the country."
8. The story of Joseph is related in Genesis 37–50. Sold into slavery in Egypt, Joseph rose to a position like Morgan's when Pharaoh "made him ruler over all the land of Egypt." His "financial ingenuities" consisted of buying food during years of plenty and then selling when it was desperately needed during a great famine.

centuries; and I could note the upspringing of adventurers like myself in the shelter of its long array of thrones: De Montforts, Gavestons, Mortimers, Villierses;[9] the war-making, campaign-directing wantons of France,[1] and Charles the Second's sceptre-wielding drabs;[2] but nowhere in the procession was my full-sized fellow visible. I was a Unique; and glad to know that that fact could not be dislodged or challenged for thirteen centuries and a half, for sure.

Yes, in power I was equal to the king. At the same time there was another power that was a trifle stronger than both of us put together. That was the Church, I do not wish to disguise that fact. I couldn't if I wanted to. But never mind about that, now; it will show up, in its proper place, later on. It didn't cause me any trouble in the beginning—at least any of consequence.

Well, it was a curious country, and full of interest. And the people! They were the quaintest and simplest and trustingest race; why, they were nothing but rabbits. It was pitiful for a person born in a wholesome free atmosphere to listen to their humble and hearty outpourings of loyalty toward their king and Church and nobility; as if they had any more occasion to love and honor king and Church and noble than a slave has to love and honor the lash, or a dog has to love and honor the stranger that kicks him! Why, dear me, *any* kind of royalty, howsoever modified, *any* kind of aristocracy, howsoever pruned, is rightly an insult; but if you are born and brought up under that sort of arrangement you probably never find it out for yourself, and don't believe it when somebody else tells you. It is enough to make a body ashamed of his race to think of the sort of froth that has always occupied its thrones without shadow of right or reason, and the seventh-rate people that have always figured as its aristocracies—a company of monarchs and nobles who, as a rule, would have achieved only poverty and obscurity if left, like their betters, to their own exertions.

The most of King Arthur's British nation were slaves, pure and simple, and bore that name, and wore the iron collar on their necks; and the rest were slaves in fact, but without the name; they imagined themselves men and freemen, and called themselves so. The truth was, the nation as a body was in the world for one object, and one only: to grovel before king and Church and noble; to slave for them, sweat blood for them, starve that they might be fed, work that they might play, drink misery to the dregs that they might be happy, go naked that they might wear silks and jewels, pay taxes that they might be spared from paying them, be familiar all their lives with the degrading

9. Simon de Montfort, Earl of Leicester (1208?–65) was a favorite of Henry III; Piers Gaveston (d. 1312) was the friend and advisor of Edward II. Roger de Mortimer, First Earl of March (1287–1330), ruled England after Parliament deposed Edward II and placed Edward III on the throne. George Villiers, First Duke of Buckingham (1592–1628), was a friend of both James I and Charles I.

1. Clemens apparently has in mind such women as Madame de Pompadour, mistress of Louis XV, who was charged with responsibility for France's defeat in the Seven Years' War.

2. Among the mistresses of Charles II were the Duchess of Cleveland, the Duchess of Portsmouth, Nell Gwyn, and Catherine Peg.

language and postures of adulation that they might walk in pride and think themselves the gods of this world. And for all this, the thanks they got were cuffs and contempt; and so poor-spirited were they that they took even this sort of attention as an honor.

Inherited ideas are a curious thing, and interesting to observe and examine. I had mine, the king and his people had theirs. In both cases they flowed in ruts worn deep by time and habit, and the man who should have proposed to divert them by reason and argument would have had a long contract on his hands. For instance, those people had inherited the idea that all men without title and a long pedigree, whether they had great natural gifts and acquirements or hadn't, were creatures of no more consideration than so many animals, bugs, insects; whereas I had inherited the idea that human daws who can consent to masquerade in the peacock-shams of inherited dignities and unearned titles, are of no good but to be laughed at. The way I was looked upon was odd, but it was natural. You know how the keeper and the public regard the elephant in the menagerie: well, that is the idea. They are full of admiration of his vast bulk and his prodigious strength; they speak with pride of the fact that he can do a hundred marvels which are far and away beyond their own powers; and they speak with the same pride of the fact that in his wrath he is able to drive a thousand men before him. But does that make him one of *them?* No; the raggedest tramp in the pit would smile at the idea. He couldn't comprehend it; couldn't take it in; couldn't in any remote way conceive of it. Well, to the king, the nobles, and all the nation, down to the very slaves and tramps, I was just that kind of an elephant, and nothing more. I was admired, also feared; but it was as an animal is admired and feared. The animal is not reverenced, neither was I; I was not even respected. I had no pedigree, no inherited title; so in the king's and nobles' eyes I was mere dirt; the people regarded me with wonder and awe, but there was no reverence mixed with it; through the force of inherited ideas they were not able to conceive of anything being entitled to that except pedigree and lordship. There you see the hand of that awful power, the Roman Catholic Church. In two or three little centuries it had converted a nation of men to a nation of worms. Before the day of the Church's supremacy in the world, men were men, and held their heads up, and had a man's pride and spirit and independence; and what of greatness and position a person got, he got mainly by achievement, not by birth. But then the Church came to the front, with an axe to grind; and she was wise, subtle, and knew more than one way to skin a cat—or a nation; she invented "divine right of kings," and propped it all around, brick by brick, with the Beatitudes[3]—wrenching them from their good purpose to make them

---

3. A section of Jesus' Sermon on the Mount (Matthew 5:3–12), praising among others those who are "meek" and "poor in spirit."

fortify an evil one; she preached (to the commoner,) humility, obedience to superiors, the beauty of self-sacrifice; she preached (to the commoner,) meekness under insult; preached (still to the commoner, always to the commoner,) patience, meanness of spirit, non-resistance under oppression; and she introduced heritable ranks and aristocracies, and taught all the Christian populations of the earth to bow down to them and worship them. Even down to my birth-century that poison was still in the blood of Christendom, and the best of English commoners was still content to see his inferiors impudently continuing to hold a number of positions, such as lordships and the throne, to which the grotesque laws of his country did not allow him to aspire; in fact he was not merely contented with this strange condition of things, he was even able to persuade himself that he was proud of it. It seems to show that there isn't anything you can't stand, if you are only born and bred to it. Of course that taint, that reverence for rank and title, had been in our American blood, too—I know that; but when I left America it had disappeared—at least to all intents and purposes. The remnant of it was restricted to the dudes and dudesses. When a disease has worked its way down to that level, it may fairly be said to be out of the system.

But to return to my anomalous position in King Arthur's kingdom. Here I was, a giant among pigmies, a man among children, a master intelligence among intellectual moles: by all rational measurement the one and only actually great man in that whole British world; and yet there and then, just as in the remote England of my birth-time, the sheep-witted earl who could claim long descent from a king's leman,[4] acquired at second-hand from the slums of London, was a better man than I was. Such a personage was fawned upon in Arthur's realm and reverently looked up to by everybody, even though his dispositions were as mean as his intelligence, and his morals as base as his lineage. There were times when *he* could sit down in the king's presence, but I couldn't. I could have got a title easily enough, and that would have raised me a large step in everybody's eyes; even in the king's, the giver of it. But I didn't ask for it; and I declined it when it was offered. I couldn't have enjoyed such a thing with my notions; and it wouldn't have been fair, anyway, because as far back as I could go, our tribe had always been short of the bar sinister.[5] I couldn't have felt really and satisfactorily fine and proud and set-up over any title except one that should come from the nation itself, the only legitimate source; and such an one I hoped to win; and in the course of years of honest and honorable endeavor, I did win it and did wear it with a high and clean pride. This title fell casually from the lips of a blacksmith, one day, in a village, was caught up as a happy thought and tossed from mouth

4. Lover or mistress.
5. His family had no illegitimate births. The term "bar sinister" is popularly but erroneously used to indicate illegitimacy.

to mouth with a laugh and an affirmative vote; in ten days it had swept the kingdom, and was become as familiar as the king's name. I was never known by any other designation afterwards, whether in the nation's talk or in grave debate upon matters of state at the council-board of the sovereign. This title, translated into modern speech, would be THE BOSS. Elected by the Nation. That suited me. And it was a pretty high title. There were very few THE's and I was one of them. If you spoke of the duke, or the earl, or the bishop, how could anybody tell which one you meant? But if you spoke of The King or The Queen or The Boss, it was different.

Well, I liked the king, and *as* king I respected him—respected the office; at least respected it as much as I was capable of respecting any unearned supremacy; but as *men* I looked down upon him and his nobles—privately. And he and they liked me, and respected my office; but as an animal, without birth or sham title, they looked down upon me—and were not particularly private about it, either. I didn't charge for my opinion about them, and they didn't charge for their opinion about me: the account was square, the books balanced, everybody was satisfied.

## Chapter IX

### THE TOURNAMENT

They were always having grand tournaments there at Camelot; and very stirring and picturesque and ridiculous human bull-fights they were, too, but just a little wearisome to the practical mind. However, I was generally on hand—for two reasons: a man must not hold himself aloof from the things which his friends and his community have at heart if he would be liked—especially as a statesman; and both as business man and statesman I wanted to study the tournament and see if I couldn't invent an improvement on it. That reminds me to remark, in passing, that the very first official thing I did, in my administration—and it was on the very day of it, too—was to start a patent office; for I knew that a country without a patent office and good patent laws was just a crab, and couldn't travel any way but sideways or backwards.

Things ran along, a tournament nearly every week; and now and then the boys used to want me to take a hand—I mean Sir Launcelot and the rest—but I said I would by and by; no hurry yet, and too much government machinery to oil up and set to rights and start a-going.

We had one tournament which was continued from day to day during more than a week, and as many as five hundred knights took part in it, from first to last. They were weeks gathering. They came on horseback from everywhere; from the very ends of the country, and even from beyond the sea; and many brought ladies and all brought

Hank Morgan as The Boss.

squires, and troops of servants. It was a most gaudy and gorgeous crowd, as to costumery, and very characteristic of the country and the time, in the way of high animal spirits, innocent indecencies of language, and happy-hearted indifference to morals. It was fight or look on, all day and every day; and sing, gamble, dance, carouse, half the night every night. They had a most noble good time. You never saw such people. Those banks of beautiful ladies, shining in their barbaric splendors, would see a knight sprawl from his horse in the lists with a lance-shaft the thickness of your ankle clean through him and the blood spouting, and instead of fainting they would clap their hands and crowd each other for a better view; only sometimes one would dive into her handkerchief, and look ostentatiously broken-hearted, and then you could lay two to one that there was a scandal there somewhere and she was afraid the public hadn't found it out.

The noise at night would have been annoying to me ordinarily, but I didn't mind it in the present circumstances, because it kept me from hearing the quacks detaching legs and arms from the day's cripples. They ruined an uncommon good old cross-cut saw for me, and broke the saw-buck, too, but I let it pass. And as for my axe—well, I made up my mind that the next time I lent an axe to a surgeon I would pick my century.

I not only watched this tournament from day to day, but detailed an intelligent priest from my Department of Public Morals and Agriculture, and ordered him to report it; for it was my purpose by and by, when I should have gotten the people along far enough, to start a newspaper. The first thing you want in a new country, is a patent office; then work up your school system; and after that, out with your paper. A newspaper has its faults, and plenty of them, but no matter, it's hark from the tomb[6] for a dead nation, and don't you forget it. You can't resurrect a dead nation without it; there isn't any way. So I wanted to sample things, and be finding out what sort of reporter-material I might be able to rake together out of the sixth century when I should come to need it.

Well, the priest did very well considering. He got in all the details, and that is a good thing in a local item: you see he had kept books for the undertaker-department of his church when he was younger and there, you know, the money's in the details; the more details, the more swag: bearers, mutes, candles, prayers,—everything counts; and if the bereaved don't buy prayers enough you mark up your candles with a forked pencil, and your bill shows up all right. And he had a good knack at getting in the complimentary thing here and there about a knight that was likely to advertise—no, I mean a knight that had influence; and he also had a neat gift of exaggeration, for in his time he

6. A sudden shock or rousing impression; apparently derived from a song beginning "Hark! from the tombs a doleful sound,/Mine ears, attend the cry."

had kept door for a pious hermit who lived in a sty and worked miracles.

Of course this novice's report lacked whoop and crash and lurid description, and therefore wanted the true ring,[7] but its antique wording was quaint and sweet and simple, and full of the fragrances and flavors of the time, and these little merits made up in a measure for its more important lacks. Here is an extract from it:

> Then Sir Brian de les Isles and Grummore Grummorsum, knights of the castle, encountered with Sir Aglovale and Sir Tor, and Sir Tor smote down Sir Grummore Grummorsum to the earth. Then came in Sir Carados of the dolorous tower, and Sir Turquine, knights of the castle, and there encountered with them Sir Percivale de Galis and Sir Lamorak de Galis, that were two brethren, and there encountered Sir Percivale with Sir Carados, and either brake their spears unto their hands, and then Sir Turquine with Sir Lamorak, and either of them smote down other, horse and all, to the earth, and either parties rescued other and horsed them again. And Sir Arnold, and Sir Gauter, knights of the castle, encountered with Sir Brandiles and Sir Kay, and these four knights encountered mightily, and brake their spears to their hands. Then came Sir Pertolope from the castle, and there encountered with him Sir Lionel, and there Sir Pentolope the green knight smote down Sir Lionel, brother to Sir Launcelot. All this was marked by noble heralds, who bare him best, and their names. Then Sir Bleobaris brake his spear upon Sir Gareth, but of that stroke Sir Bleobaris fell to the earth. When Sir Galihodin saw that, he bad Sir Gareth keep him, and Sir Gareth smote him to the earth. Then Sir Galihud gat a spear to avenge his brother, and in the same wise Sir Gareth served him, and Sir Dinadan and his brother La Cote Male Taile, and Sir Sagramore le Desirous, and Sir Dodinas le Savage; all these he bare down with one spear. When King Agwisance of Ireland saw Sir Gareth fare so he marvelled what he might be, that one time seemed green, and another time, at his again coming, he seemed blue. And thus at every course that he rode to and fro he changed his color, so that there might neither king nor knight have ready cognizance of him. Then Sir Agwisance the King of Ireland encountered with Sir Gareth, and there Sir Gareth smote him from his horse, saddle and all. And then came King Carados of Scotland, and Sir Gareth smote him down horse and man. And in the same wise he served King Uriens of the land of Gore. And then there came in Sir Bagdemagus, and Sir Gareth smote him down horse and man to the earth. And Bagdemagus's son Meliganus brake a spear upon Sir Gareth mightily and knightly. And then Sir Galahault the noble prince cried on high, Knight with the many colors, well hast thou justed; now make the ready that I may just with thee. Sir Gareth heard him, and he gat a great spear, and so

---

7. For the kind of writing Clemens has in mind, see his sketch "Journalism in Tennessee" (1869).

they encountered together, and there the prince brake his spear; but Sir Gareth smote him upon the left side of the helm, that he reeled here and there, and he had fallen down had not his men recovered him. Truly said King Arthur, that knight with the many colors is a good knight. Wherefore the king called unto him Sir Launcelot, and prayed him to encounter with that knight. Sir, said Launcelot, I may as well find in my heart for to forbear him at this time, for he hath had travail enough this day, and when a good knight doth so well upon some day, it is no good knight's part to let him of his worship, and namely, when he seeth a knight hath done so great labour: for peradventure, said Sir Launcelot, his quarrel is here this day, and peradventure he is best beloved with this lady of all that be here, for I see well he paineth himself and enforceth him to do great deeds, and therefore, said Sir Launcelot, as for me, this day he shall have the honour; though it lay in my power to put him from it, I would not.[8]

There was an unpleasant little episode that day, which for reasons of state I struck out of my priest's report. You will have noticed that Garry was doing some great fighting in the engagement. When I say Garry I mean Sir Gareth. Garry was my private pet name for him; it suggests that I had a deep affection for him, and that was the case. But it was a private pet name only, and never spoken aloud to any one, much less to him; being a noble, he would not have endured a familiarity like that from me. Well, to proceed: I sat in the private box set apart for me as the king's minister. While Sir Dinadan was waiting for his turn to enter the lists, he came in there and sat down and began to talk; for he was always making up to me, because I was a stranger and he liked to have a fresh market for his jokes, the most of them having reached that stage of wear where the teller has to do the laughing himself while the other person looks sick. I had always responded to his efforts as well as I could, and felt a very deep and real kindness for him, too, for the reason that if by malice of fate he knew the one particular anecdote which I had heard oftenest and had most hated and most loathed all my life, he had at least spared it me. It was one which I had heard attributed to every humorous person who had ever stood on American soil, from Columbus down to Artemus Ward.[9] It was about a humorous lecturer who flooded an ignorant audience with the killingest jokes for an hour and never got a laugh; and then when he was leaving, some gray simpletons wrung him gratefully by the hand and said it had been the funniest thing they had ever heard, and "it was all they could do to keep from laughin' right out in meetin'." That anecdote never saw the day that it was worth the telling; and yet I had sat under the telling of it hundreds and thousands and millions and billions of times, and cried

---

8. From Malory, VII.xxviii.  Charles Farrar Browne (1834–67).
9. Pseudonym of Clemens' fellow humorist,

and cursed all the way through. Then who can hope to know what my feelings were, to hear this armor-plated ass start in on it again, in the murky twilight of tradition, before the dawn of history, while even Lactantius[1] might be referred to as "the late Lactantius," and the Crusades[2] wouldn't be born for five hundred years yet? Just as he finished, the call-boy came; so haw-hawing like a demon, he went rattling and clanking out like a crate of loose castings, and I knew nothing more. It was some minutes before I came to, and then I opened my eyes just in time to see Sir Gareth fetch him an awful welt, and I unconsciously out with the prayer, "I hope to gracious he's killed!" But by ill-luck, before I had got half through with the words, Sir Gareth crashed into Sir Sagramor le Desirous and sent him thundering over his horse's crupper, and Sir Sagramor caught my remark and thought I meant it for *him*.

Well, whenever one of those people got a thing into his head, there was no getting it out again. I knew that, so I saved my breath, and offered no explanations. As soon as Sir Sagramor got well, he notified me that there was a little account to settle between us, and he named a day three or four years in the future; place of settlement, the lists where the offense had been given. I said I would be ready when he got back. You see, he was going for the Holy Grail.[3] The boys all took a flier at the Holy Grail now and then. It was a several years' cruise. They always put in the long absence snooping around, in the most conscientious way, though none of them had any idea where the Holy Grail really was, and I don't think any of them actually expected to find it, or would have known what to do with it if he *had* run across it. You see, it was just the Northwest Passage[4] of that day, as you may say; that was all. Every year expeditions went out holy grailing, and next year relief expeditions went out to hunt for *them*. There was worlds of reputation in it, but no money. Why, they actually wanted *me* to put in! Well, I should smile.

## Chapter X

### BEGINNINGS OF CIVILIZATION

The Round Table soon heard of the challenge, and of course it was a good deal discussed, for such things interested the boys. The king thought I ought now to set forth in quest of adventures, so that I might gain renown and be the more worthy to meet Sir Sagramor when the

1. Lucius Caecilius Firmianus Lactantius (c. 250–c. 320), Christian Latin historian sometimes known as the Christian Cicero; author of *The Divine Institutes*, the first attempt at a Latin summation of Christian thought.
2. Military expeditions of the eleventh through thirteenth centuries which attempted to estab-

lish Christian control of the Holy Land.
3. The cup used by Jesus at the Last Supper the evening before his crucifixion; a legendary object of knightly quests.
4. Supposed water route from the Atlantic to the Pacific Ocean across the top of North America; sought by many early explorers.

several years should have rolled away. I excused myself for the present; I said it would take me three or four years yet to get things well fixed up and going smoothly; then I should be ready; all the chances were that at the end of that time Sir Sagramor would still be out grailing, so no valuable time would be lost by the postponement; I should then have been in office six or seven years, and I believed my system and machinery would be so well developed that I could take a holiday without its working any harm.

I was pretty well satisfied with what I had already accomplished.[5] In various quiet nooks and corners I had the beginnings of all sorts of industries under way—nuclei of future vast factories, the iron and steel missionaries of my future civilization. In these were gathered together the brightest young minds I could find, and I kept agents out raking the country for more, all the time. I was training a crowd of ignorant folk into experts—experts in every sort of handiwork and scientific calling. These nurseries of mine went smoothly and privately along undisturbed in their obscure country retreats, for nobody was allowed to come into their precincts without a special permit—for I was afraid of the Church.

I had started a teacher-factory and a lot of Sunday-schools the first thing; as a result, I now had an admirable system of graded schools in full blast in those places, and also a complete variety of Protestant congregations all in a prosperous and growing condition. Everybody could be any kind of a Christian he wanted to; there was perfect freedom in that matter. But I confined public religious teaching to the churches and Sunday-schools, permitting nothing of it in my other educational buildings. I could have given my own sect the preference and made everybody a Presbyterian[6] without any trouble, but that would have been to affront a law of human nature: spiritual wants and instincts are as various in the human family as are physical appetites, complexions, and features, and a man is only at his best, morally, when he is equipped with the religious garment whose color and shape and size most nicely accommodate themselves to the spiritual complexion, angularities, and stature of the individual who wears it; and besides I was afraid of a united Church; it makes a mighty power, the mightiest conceivable, and then when it by and by gets into selfish hands, as it is always bound to do, it means death to human liberty, and paralysis to human thought.

---

5. The section which follows was not written until somewhat later than Chapters IV–XX. In introducing this passage to readers of the *Century,* Clemens said that the Yankee "set himself the task of introducing the great and beneficent civilization of the nineteenth century, and of peacefully replacing the twin despotisms of royalty and aristocratic privilege with a 'Republic on the American plan' when Arthur shall have passed to his rest."

6. Like Tom Sawyer, Morgan is a Presbyterian, the religion of Clemens' mother and sister Pamela. While living in Hartford, Clemens attended the Asylum Hill Congregational Church.

All mines were royal property, and there were a good many of them. They had formerly been worked as savages always work mines—holes grubbed in the earth and the mineral brought up in sacks of hide by hand, at the rate of a ton a day; but I had begun to put the mining on a scientific basis as early as I could.

Yes, I had made pretty handsome progress when Sir Sagramor's challenge struck me.

Four years rolled by—and then! Well, you would never imagine it in the world. Unlimited power *is* the ideal thing when it is in safe hands. The despotism of heaven is the one absolutely perfect government. An earthly despotism would be the absolutely perfect earthly government, if the conditions were the same, namely, the despot the perfectest individual of the human race, and his lease of life perpetual. *everlasting* But as a perishable perfect man must die, and leave his despotism in the hands of an imperfect successor, an earthly despotism is not merely a bad form of government, it is the worst form that is possible. My works showed what a despot could do with the resources of a kingdom at his command. Unsuspected by this dark land, I had the civilization of the nineteenth century booming under its very nose! It was fenced away from the public view, but there it was, a gigantic and unassailable fact—and to be heard from, yet, if I lived and had luck. There it was, as sure a fact, and as substantial a fact as any serene volcano, standing innocent with its smokeless summit in the blue sky and giving no sign of the rising hell in its bowels. My schools and churches were children four years before; they were grown-up, now; my shops of that day were vast factories, now; where I had a dozen trained men then, I had a thousand, now; where I had one brilliant expert then, I had fifty now. I stood with my hand on the cock, so to speak, ready to turn it on and flood the midnight world with light at any moment.[7] But I was not going to do the thing in that sudden way. It was not my policy. The people could not have stood it; and moreover I should have had the Established Roman Catholic Church on my back in a minute.

No, I had been going cautiously all the while. I had had confidential agents trickling through the country some time, whose office was to undermine knighthood by imperceptible degrees, and to gnaw a little at this and that and the other superstition, and so prepare the way gradually for a better order of things. I was turning on my light one-candle-power at a time, and I meant to continue to do so.

I had scattered some branch schools secretly about the kingdom, and they were doing very well. I meant to work this racket more and

7. In the *Century* version Morgan says: "I stood with my finger on the button, so to speak, ready to press it and flood the midnight world with intolerable light at any moment." A marked copy of the first edition in the Mark Twain Papers shows that Clemens followed the *Century* text when reading the passage for an audience.

more, as time wore on, if nothing occurred to frighten me. One of my deepest secrets was my West Point—my military academy. I kept that most jealously out of sight; and I did the same with my naval academy which I had established at a remote seaport. Both were prospering to my satisfaction.

Clarence was twenty-two now, and was my head executive, my right hand. He was a darling; he was equal to anything; there wasn't anything he couldn't turn his hand to. Of late I had been training him for journalism, for the time seemed about right for a start in the newspaper line; nothing big, but just a small weekly for experimental circulation in my civilization-nurseries. He took to it like a duck; there was an editor concealed in him, sure. Already he had doubled himself in one way; he talked sixth century and wrote nineteenth. His journalistic style was climbing, steadily; it was already up to the back settlement Alabama mark,[8] and couldn't be told from the editorial output of that region either by matter or flavor.

We had another large departure on hand, too. This was a telegraph and a telephone; our first venture in this line. These wires were for private service only, as yet, and must be kept private until a riper day should come. We had a gang of men on the road, working mainly by night. They were stringing ground wires; we were afraid to put up poles, for they would attract too much inquiry. Ground wires were good enough, in both instances, for my wires were protected by an insulation of my own invention which was perfect. My men had orders to strike across country, avoiding roads, and establishing connection with any considerable towns whose lights betrayed their presence, and leaving experts in charge. Nobody could tell you how to find any place in the kingdom, for nobody ever went intentionally to any place, but only struck it by accident in his wanderings, and then generally left it without thinking to inquire what its name was. At one time and another we had sent out topographical expeditions to survey and map the kingdom, but the priests had always interfered and raised trouble. So we had given the thing up, for the present; it would be poor wisdom to antagonize the Church.

As for the general condition of the country, it was as it had been when I arrived in it, to all intents and purposes I had made changes, but they were necessarily slight, and they were not noticeable. Thus far, I had not even meddled with taxation, outside of the taxes which provided the royal revenues. I had systematized those, and put the service on an effective and righteous basis. As a result, these revenues were already quadrupled, and yet the burden was so much more

8. Clemens' principal knowledge of such an area may have come from Johnson Jones Hooper's *Adventures of Simon Suggs* (1845), one of the more notable pieces of frontier humor. He may also have seen samples of Alabama journalism during his years in the Mississippi Valley.

equably distributed than before, that all the kingdom felt a sense of relief, and the praises of my administration were hearty and general.

Personally, I struck an interruption, now, but I did not mind it, it could not have happened at a better time. Earlier it could have annoyed me, but now everything was in good hands and swimming right along. The king had reminded me several times, of late, that the postponement I had asked for, four years before, had about run out, now. It was a hint that I ought to be starting out to seek adventures and get up a reputation of a size to make me worthy of the honor of breaking a lance with Sir Sagramor, who was still out grailing, but was being hunted for by various relief expeditions, and might be found any year, now. So you see I was expecting this interruption; it did not take me by surprise.

## Chapter XI

### THE YANKEE IN SEARCH OF ADVENTURES

There never was such a country for wandering liars; and they were of both sexes. Hardly a month went by without one of these tramps arriving; and generally loaded with a tale about some princess or other wanting help to get her out of some far-away castle where she was held in captivity by a lawless scoundrel, usually a giant. Now you would think that the first thing the king would do after listening to such a novelette from an entire stranger, would be to ask for credentials—yes, and a pointer or two as to locality of castle, best route to it, and so on. But nobody ever thought of so simple and common-sense a thing as that. No, everybody swallowed these people's lies whole, and never asked a question of any sort or about anything. Well, one day when I was not around, one of these people came along—it was a she one, this time—and told a tale of the usual pattern. Her mistress was a captive in a vast and gloomy castle, along with forty-four other young and beautiful girls, pretty much all of them princesses; they had been languishing in that cruel captivity for twenty-six years; the masters of the castle were three stupendous brothers, each with four arms and one eye—the eye in the centre of the forehead, and as big as a fruit. Sort of fruit not mentioned; their usual slovenliness in statistics.

Would you believe it? The king and the whole Round Table were in raptures over this preposterous opportunity for adventure. Every knight of the Table jumped for the chance, and begged for it; but to their vexation and chagrin the king conferred it upon me, who had not asked for it at all.

By an effort, I contained my joy when Clarence brought me the news. But he—he could not contain his. His mouth gushed delight and gratitude in a steady discharge—delight in my good fortune, gratitude to the king for this splendid mark of his favor for me. He could keep neither his legs nor his body still, but pirouetted about the place in an airy ecstasy of happiness.

On my side, I could have cursed the kindness that conferred upon me this benefaction, but I kept my vexation under the surface for policy's sake, and did what I could to let on to be glad. Indeed, I *said* I was glad. And in a way it was true; I was as glad as a person is when he is scalped.[9]

Well, one must make the best of things, and not waste time with useless fretting, but get down to business and see what can be done. In all lies there is wheat among the chaff; I must get at the wheat in this case: so I sent for the girl and she came. She was a comely enough creature, and soft and modest, but if signs went for anything, she didn't know as much as a lady's watch. I said—

"My dear, have you been questioned as to particulars?"

She said she hadn't.

"Well, I didn't expect you had, but I thought I would ask to make sure; it's the way I've been raised. Now you mustn't take it unkindly if I remind you that as we don't know you, we must go a little slow. You may be all right, of course, and we'll hope that you are; but to take it for granted isn't business. *You* understand that. I'm obliged to ask you a few questions; just answer up fair and square, and don't be afraid. Where do you live, when you are at home?"

"In the land of Moder, fair sir."

"Land of Moder. I don't remember hearing of it before. Parents living?"

"As to that, I know not if they be yet on live, sith it is many years that I have lain shut up in the castle."

"Your name, please?"

"I hight the Demoiselle Alisande la Carteloise, an it please you."

"Do you know anybody here who can identify you?"

"That were not likely, fair lord, I being come hither now for the first time."

"Have you brought any letters—any documents—any proofs that you are trustworthy and truthful?"

"Of a surety, no; and wherefore should I? Have I not a tongue, and cannot I say all that myself?"

"But *your* saying it, you know, and somebody else's saying it, is different."

"Different? How might that be? I fear me I do not understand."

"Don't *understand*? Land of—why, you see—you see—why, great Scott, can't you understand a little thing like that ? Can't you understand the difference between your—*why* do you look so innocent and idiotic!"

9. In the English edition the word is "disembowelled."

"I? In truth I know not, but an it were the will of God."

"Yes, yes, I reckon that's about the size of it. Don't mind my seeming excited; I'm not. Let us change the subject. Now as to this castle, with forty-five princesses in it, and three ogres at the head of it, tell me—where is this harem?"

"Harem?"

"The *castle*, you understand; where is the castle?"

"Oh, as to that, it is great, and strong, and well beseen, and lieth in a far country. Yes, it is many leagues."

"*How* many?"

"Ah, fair sir, it were woundily hard to tell, they are so many, and do so lap the one upon the other, and being made all in the same image and tincted with the same color, one may not know the one league from its fellow, nor how to count them except they be taken apart, and ye wit well it were God's work to do that, being not within man's capacity; for ye will note—"

"Hold on, hold on, never mind about the distance; *whereabouts* does the castle lie? What's the direction from here?"

"Ah, please you sir, it hath no direction from here; by reason that the road lieth not straight, but turneth evermore; wherefore the direction of its place abideth not, but is sometime under the one sky and anon under another, whereso if ye be minded that it is in the east, and wend thitherward, ye shall observe that the way of the road doth yet again turn upon itself by the space of half a circle, and this marvel happing again and yet again and still again, it will grieve you that you had thought by vanities of the mind to thwart and bring to naught the will of Him that giveth not a castle a direction from a place except it pleaseth Him, and if it please Him not, will the rather that even all castles and all directions thereunto vanish out of the earth, leaving the places wherein they tarried desolate and vacant, so warning His creatures that where He will He will, and where He will not He—"

"Oh, that's all right, that's all right, give us a rest; never mind about the direction, *hang* the direction—I beg pardon, I beg a thousand pardons, I am not well to-day; pay no attention when I soliloquize, it is an old habit, an old, bad habit, and hard to get rid of when one's digestion is all disordered with eating food that was raised forever and ever before he was born; good land! a man can't keep his functions regular on spring chickens thirteen hundred years old. But come— never mind about that; let's—have you got such a thing as a map of that region about you? Now a good map—"

"Is it peradventure that manner of thing which of late the unbelievers have brought from over the great seas, which, being boiled in oil, and an onion and salt added thereto, doth—"

"What, a map? What are you talking about? Don't you know what a map is? There, there, never mind, don't explain, I hate explanations;

they fog a thing up so that you can't tell anything about it. Run along, dear; good-day; show her the way, Clarence."

Oh, well, it was reasonably plain, now, why these donkeys didn't prospect these liars for details. It may be that this girl had a fact in her somewhere, but I don't believe you could have sluiced it out with a hydraulic; nor got it with the earlier forms of blasting, even; it was a case for dynamite. Why, she was a perfect ass; and yet the king and his knights had listened to her as if she had been a leaf out of the gospel. It kind of sizes up the whole party. And think of the simple ways of this court: this wandering wench hadn't any more trouble to get access to the king in his palace than she would have had to get into the poor-house in my day and country. In fact he was glad to see her, glad to hear her tale; with that adventure of hers to offer, she was as welcome as a corpse is to a coroner.

Just as I was ending-up these reflections, Clarence came back. I remarked upon the barren result of my efforts with the girl; hadn't got hold of a single point that could help me to find the castle. The youth looked a little surprised, or puzzled, or something, and intimated that he had been wondering to himself what I had wanted to ask the girl all those questions for.

"Why, great guns," I said, "don't I want to find the castle? And how else would I go about it?"

"La, sweet your worship, one may lightly answer that, I ween. She will go with thee. They always do. She will ride with thee."

"Ride with me? Nonsense!"

"But of a truth she will. She will ride with thee. Thou shalt see."

"What? She browse around the hills and scour the woods with me—alone—and I as good as engaged to be married? Why, it's scandalous. Think how it would look."

My, the dear face that rose before me! The boy was eager to know all about this tender matter. I swore him to secrecy and then whispered her name—"Puss Flanagan." He looked disappointed, and said he didn't remember the countess. How natural it was for the little courtier to give her a rank. He asked me where she lived.

"In East Har—" I came to myself and stopped, a little confused; then I said, "Never mind, now; I'll tell you sometime."

And might he see her? Would I let him see her some day?

It was but a little thing to promise—thirteen hundred years or so—and he so eager; so I said Yes. But I sighed; I couldn't help it. And yet there was no sense in sighing, for she wasn't born yet. But that is the way we are made: we don't reason, where we feel; we just feel.

My expedition was all the talk that day and that night, and the boys were very good to me, and made much of me, and seemed to have forgotten their vexation and disappointment, and come to be as anxious for me to hive those ogres and set those ripe old virgins loose as if it were themselves that had the contract. Well, they *were* good children—but just children, that is all. And they gave me no end of points about how to scout for giants, and how to scoop them in; and they told me all sorts of charms against enchantments, and gave me salves and other rubbish to put on my wounds. But it never occurred to one of them to reflect that if I was such a wonderful necromancer as I was pretending to be, I ought not to need salves or instructions, or charms against enchantments, and least of all, arms and armor, on a foray of any kind—even against fire-spouting dragons, and devils hot from perdition, let alone such poor adversaries as these I was after, these commonplace ogres of the back settlements.

I was to have an early breakfast, and start at dawn, for that was the usual way; but I had the demon's own time with my armor, and this delayed me a little. It is troublesome to get into, and there is so much detail. First you wrap a layer or two of blanket around your body, for a sort of cushion and to keep off the cold iron; then you put on your sleeves and shirt of chain-mail—these are made of small steel links woven together, and they form a fabric so flexible that if you toss your shirt onto the floor, it slumps into a pile like a peck of wet fish-net; it is very heavy and is nearly the uncomfortablest material in the world for a night-shirt, yet plenty used it for that—tax collectors, and reformers, and one-horse kings with a defective title, and those sorts of people; then you put on your shoes—flat-boats roofed over with interleaving bands of steel—and screw your clumsy spurs into the heels. Next you buckle your greaves on your legs, and your cuisses on your thighs; then come your backplate and your breastplate, and you begin to feel crowded; then you hitch onto the breastplate the half-petticoat of broad overlapping bands of steel which hangs down in front but is scolloped out behind so you can sit down, and isn't any real improvement on an inverted coal scuttle, either for looks or for wear, or to wipe your hands on; next you belt on your sword; then you put your stove-pipe joints onto your arms, your iron gauntlets onto your hands, your iron rat-trap onto your head, with a rag of steel web hitched onto it to hang over the back of your neck—and there you are, snug as a candle in a candle-mould. This is no time to dance. Well, a man that is packed away like that, is a nut that isn't worth the cracking, there is so little of the meat, when you get down to it, by comparison with the shell.

The boys helped me, or I never could have got in. Just as we finished, Sir Bedivere happened in, and I saw that as like as not I hadn't chosen the most convenient outfit for a long trip. How stately he looked; and tall and broad and grand. He had on his head a conical steel casque that only came down to his ears, and for visor had only a narrow steel bar that extended down to his upper lip and protected his nose; and all the rest of him, from neck to heel, was flexible chain-mail, trowsers and all. But pretty much all of him was hidden under his outside garment, which of course was of chain-mail, as I said, and hung straight from his shoulders to his ancles; and from his middle to the bottom, both before and behind, was divided, so that he could ride and let the skirts hang down on each side. He was going grailing, and it was just the outfit for it, too. I would have given a good deal for that ulster, but it was too late now to be fooling around. The sun was just up, the king and the court were all on hand to see me off and wish me luck; so it wouldn't be etiquette for me to tarry. You don't get on your horse yourself; no, if you tried it you would get disappointed. They carry you out, just as they carry a sun-struck man to the drug store, and put you on, and help get you to rights, and fix your feet in the stirrups; and all the while you do feel so strange and stuffy and like somebody else—like somebody that has been married on a sudden, or struck by lightning, or something like that, and hasn't quite fetched around, yet, and is sort of numb, and can't just get his bearings. Then they stood up the mast they called a spear, in its socket by my left foot, and I gripped it with my hand; lastly they hung my shield around my neck, and I was all complete and ready to up anchor and get to sea. Everybody was as good to me as they could be, and a maid of honor gave me the stirrup-cup her own self. There was nothing more to do, now, but for that damsel to get up behind me on a pillion, which she did, and put an arm or so around me to hold on.

And so we started; and everybody gave us a good-bye and waved their handkerchiefs or helmets. And everybody we met, going down the hill and through the village was respectful to us, except some shabby little boys on the outskirts. They said—

"Oh, what a guy!" And hove clods at us.

In my experience boys are the same in all ages. They don't respect anything, they don't care for anything or anybody. They say "Go up, baldhead"[1] to the prophet going his unoffending way in the gray of antiquity; they sass me in the holy gloom of the Middle Ages; and I had seen them act the same way in Buchanan's[2] administration; I remember, because I was there and helped. The prophet had his bears and settled with his boys; and I wanted to get down and settle with mine, but it wouldn't answer, because I couldn't have got up again. I hate a country without a derrick.

## Chapter XII

### SLOW TORTURE[3]

Straight off, we were in the country. It was most lovely and pleasant in those sylvan solitudes in the early cool morning in the first freshness

---

1. The words of the children to the prophet Elisha before the bears came out of the woods to "tare" them (II Kings 2:23–4).
2. James Buchanan, fifteenth president of the United States, served from 1857 to 1861.

3. In this chapter Clemens makes use of his initial idea for a story about a knight of the Middle Ages. See his notebook entry in the section on the making of the novel.

of autumn. From hilltops we saw fair green valleys lying spread out below, with streams winding through them, and island-groves of trees here and there, and huge lonely oaks scattered about and casting black blots of shade; and beyond the valleys we saw the ranges of hills, blue with haze, stretching away in billowy perspective to the horizon, with at wide intervals a dim fleck of white or gray on a wave-summit, which we knew was a castle. We crossed broad natural lawns sparkling with dew, and we moved like spirits, the cushioned turf giving out no sound of foot-fall; we dreamed along through glades in a mist of green light that got its tint from the sun-drenched roof of leaves overhead, and by our feet the clearest and coldest of runlets went frisking and gossiping over its reefs and making a sort of whispering music comfortable to hear; and at times we left the world behind and entered into the solemn great deeps and rich gloom of the forest, where furtive wild things whisked and scurried by and were gone before you could even get your eye on the place where the noise was; and where only the earliest birds were turning out and getting to business with a song here and quarrel yonder and a mysterious far-off hammering and drumming for worms on a tree-trunk away somewhere in the impenetrable remotenesses of the woods. And by and by out we would swing again into the glare.

About the third or fourth or fifth time that we swung out into the glare—it was along there somewhere, a couple of hours or so after sun-up—it wasn't as pleasant as it had been. It was beginning to get hot. This was quite noticeable. We had a very long pull, after that, without any shade. Now it is curious how progressively little frets grow and multiply after they once get a start. Things which I didn't mind at all, at first, I began to mind now—and more and more, too, all the time. The first ten or fifteen times I wanted my handkerchief I didn't seem to care; I got along, and said never mind, it isn't any matter, and dropped it out of my mind. But now it was different; I wanted it all the time; it was nag, nag, nag, right along, and no rest; I couldn't get it out of my mind; and so at last I lost my temper and said hang a man that would make a suit of armor without any pockets in it. You see I had my handkerchief in my helmet; and some other things; but it was that kind of a helmet that you can't take off by yourself. That hadn't occurred to me when I put it there; and in fact I didn't know it. I supposed it would be particularly convenient there. And so now, the thought of its being there, so handy and close by, and yet not get-at-able, made it all the wors: and the harder to bear. Yes, the thing that you can't get is the thing that you want, mainly; everyone has noticed that. Well, it took my mind off from everything else; took it clear off, and centred it in my helmet; and mile after mile, there it staid, imagining the handkerchief, picturing the handkerchief; and it was bitter and aggravating to have the salt sweat keep trickling down into my eyes, and I couldn't get at it. It seems like a little thing, on paper, but it was not a little thing at all; it was the most real kind of misery. I would not say it if it was not so. I made up my mind that I would carry along a reticule next time, let it look how it might, and people say what they would. Of course these iron dudes of the Round Table would think it was scandalous, and maybe raise Sheol[4] about it, but as for me, give me comfort first, and style afterwards. So we jogged along, and now and then we struck a stretch of dust, and it would tumble up in clouds and get into my nose and make me sneeze and cry; and of course I said things I oughtn't to have said, I don't deny that. I am not better than others. We couldn't seem to meet anybody in this lonesome Britain, not even an ogre; and in the mood I was in then, it was well for the ogre, that is, an ogre with a handkerchief. Most knights would have thought of nothing but getting his armor; but so I got his bandanna, he could keep his hardware, for all me.

Meantime it was getting hotter and hotter in there. You see, the sun was beating down and warming up the iron more and more all the time. Well, when you are hot, that way, every little thing irritates you. When I trotted, I rattled like a crate of dishes, and that annoyed me; and moreover I couldn't seem to stand that shield slatting and banging, now about my breast, now around my back; and if I dropped into a walk my joints creaked and screeched in that wearisome way that a wheelbarrow does, and as we didn't create any breeze at that gait, I was like to get fried in that stove; and besides, the quieter you went the heavier the iron settled down on you and the more and more tons you seemed to weigh every minute. And you had to be always changing hands, and passing your spear over to the other foot, it got so irksome for one hand to hold it long at a time.

Well, you know, when you perspire that way, in rivers, there comes a time when you—when you—well, when you itch. You are inside, your hands are outside; so there you are; nothing but iron between. It is not a light thing, let it sound as it may. First it is one place; then another; then some more; and it goes on spreading and spreading, and at last the territory is all occupied, and nobody can imagine what you feel like, nor how unpleasant it is. And when it had got to the worst, and it seemed to me that I could not stand anything more, a fly got in through the bars and settled on my nose, and the bars were stuck and wouldn't work, and I couldn't get the visor up; and I could only shake my head, which was baking hot by this time, and the fly—well, you know how a fly acts when he has got a certainty—he only minded the shaking enough to change from nose to lip, and lip to ear, and buzz and buzz all around in there, and keep on lighting and biting, in a way that a person already so distressed as I was, simply could not stand. So I

4. In the Bible, Sheol is the place of the dead; here, simply a euphemism for "raise hell." Morgan is somewhat fastidious in his speech; note his hesitation at saying "itch" three paragraphs below.

**"SHE CONTINUED TO FETCH AND POUR UNTIL I WAS WELL SOAKED."**

Sandy assisting Hank Morgan. Beard's model for Sandy was the actress Anna Russell.

gave in, and got Alisande to unship the helmet and relieve me of it. Then she emptied the conveniences out of it and fetched it full of water, and I drank and then stood up and she poured the rest down inside the armor. One cannot think how refreshing it was. She continued to fetch and pour until I was well soaked and thoroughly comfortable.

It was good to have a rest—and peace. But nothing is quite perfect in this life, at any time. I had made a pipe a while back, and also some pretty fair tobacco; not the real thing, but what some of the Indians use: the inside bark of the willow, dried. These comforts had been in the helmet, and now I had them again, but no matches.

Gradually, as the time wore along, one annoying fact was borne in upon my understanding—that we were weather-bound. An armed novice cannot mount his horse without help and plenty of it. Sandy was not enough; not enough for me, anyway. We had to wait until somebody should come along. Waiting, in silence, would have been agreeable enough, for I was full of matter for reflection, and wanted to give it a chance to work. I wanted to try and think out how it was that rational or even half-rational men could ever have learned to wear armor, considering its inconveniences; and how they had managed to keep up such a fashion for generations when it was plain that what I had suffered to-day they had had to suffer all the days of their lives. I wanted to think that out; and moreover I wanted to think out some way to reform this evil and persuade the people to let the foolish fashion die out; but thinking was out of the question in the circumstances. You couldn't think, where Sandy was. She was a quite biddable creature and good-hearted, but she had a flow of talk that was as steady as a mill, and made your head sore like the drays and wagons in a city. If she had had a cork she would have been a comfort. But you can't cork that kind; they would die. Her clack was going all day, and you would think something would surely happen to her works, by and by; but no, they never got out of order; and she never had to slack up for words. She could grind, and pump, and churn and buzz by the week, and never stop to oil up or blow out. And yet the result was just nothing but wind. She never had any ideas, any more than a fog has. She was a perfect blatherskite; I mean for jaw, jaw, jaw, talk, talk, talk, jabber, jabber, jabber; but just as good as she could be. I hadn't minded her mill that morning, on account of having that hornet's nest of other troubles; but more than once in the afternoon I had to say—

"Take a rest, child; the way you are using up all the domestic air, the kingdom will have to go to importing it by to-morrow, and it's a low enough treasury without that."

## *Chapter XIII*

### FREEMEN!

Yes, it is strange how little a while at a time a person can be contented. Only a little while back, when I was riding and suffering, what a heaven this peace, this rest, this sweet serenity in this secluded shady nook by this purling stream would have seemed, where I could keep perfectly comfortable all the time by pouring a dipper of water into my armor now and then; yet already I was getting dissatisfied; partly because I could not light my pipe—for although I had long ago started a match factory, I had forgotten to bring matches with me—and partly because we had nothing to eat. Here was another illustration of the childlike improvidence of this age and people. A man in armor always trusted to chance for his food on a journey, and would have been scandalized at the idea of hanging a basket of sandwiches on his spear. There was probably not a knight of all the Round Table combination who would not rather have died than been caught carrying such a thing as that on his flagstaff. And yet there could not be anything more sensible. It had been my intention to smuggle a couple of sandwiches into my helmet, but I was interrupted in the act, and had to make an excuse and lay them aside, and a dog got them.

Night approached, and with it a storm. The darkness came on fast. We must camp, of course. I found a good shelter for the demoiselle under a rock, and went off and found another for myself. But I was obliged to remain in my armor, because I could not get it off by myself and yet could not allow Alisande to help, because it would have seemed so like undressing before folk. It would not have amounted to that in reality, because I had clothes on underneath; but the prejudices of one's breeding are not gotten rid of just at a jump, and I knew that when it came to stripping off that bob-tailed iron petticoat I should be embarrassed.

With the storm came a change of weather; and the stronger the wind blew, and the wilder the rain lashed around, the colder and colder it got. Pretty soon, various kinds of bugs and ants and worms and things began to flock in out of the wet and crawl down inside my armor to get warm; and while some of them behaved well enough, and snuggled up amongst my clothes and got quiet, the majority were of a restless, uncomfortable sort, and never stayed still, but went on prowling and hunting for they did not know what, especially the ants, which went tickling along in wearisome procession from one end of me to the other by the hour, and are a kind of creatures which I never wish to sleep with again. It would be my advice to persons situated in this way, to not roll or thrash around, because this excites the interest of all the different sorts of animals and makes every last one of them want to turn out and see what is going on, and this makes things worse than they were before, and of course makes you objurgate harder, too, if you can. Still, if one did not roll and thrash around he would die; so perhaps it is as well to do one way as the other, there is no real choice. Even after I was frozen solid I could still distinguish that tickling, just as a corpse does when he is taking electric treatment. I said I would never wear armor after this trip.

All those trying hours whilst I was frozen and yet was in a living fire, as you may say, on account of that swarm of crawlers, that same unanswerable question kept circling and circling through my tired head: How do people stand this miserable armor? How have they managed to stand it all these generations? How can they sleep at night for dreading the tortures of next day?

When the morning came at last, I was in a bad enough plight: seedy, drowsy, fagged, from want of sleep; weary from thrashing around, famished from long fasting; pining for a bath, and to get rid of the animals; and crippled with rheumatism. And how had it fared with the nobly born, the titled aristocrat, the Demoiselle Alisande la Carteloise? Why, she was as fresh as a squirrel; she had slept like the dead; and as for a bath, probably neither she nor any other noble in the land had ever had one, and so she was not missing it. Measured by modern standards, they were merely modified savages, those people. This noble lady showed no impatience to get to breakfast—and that smacks of the savage, too. On their journeys those Britons were used to long fasts, and knew how to bear them; and also how to freight up against probable fasts before starting, after the style of the Indian and the anaconda. As like as not, Sandy was loaded for a three-day stretch.

We were off before sunrise, Sandy riding and I limping along behind. In half an hour we came upon a group of ragged poor creatures who had assembled to mend the thing which was regarded as a road. They were as humble as animals to me; and when I proposed to breakfast with them, they were so flattered, so overwhelmed by this extraordinary condescension of mine that at first they were not able to believe that I was in earnest. My lady put up her scornful lip and withdrew to one side; she said in their hearing that she would as soon think of eating with the other cattle—a remark which embarrassed these poor devils merely because it referred to them, and not because it insulted or offended them, for it didn't. And yet they were not slaves, not chattels. By a sarcasm of law and phrase they were freemen. Seven-tenths of the free population of the country were of just their class and degree: small "independent" farmers, artisans, etc.; which is to say, they were the nation, the actual Nation; they were about all of it that was useful, or worth saving, or really respectworthy; and to subtract them would have been to subtract the Nation and leave behind some dregs, some refuse, in the shape of a king, nobility and gentry, idle, unproductive, acquainted mainly with the arts of wasting and destroying, and of no sort of use or value in any rationally constructed world. And yet, by ingenious contrivance, this gilded minority, instead of being in the tail of the procession where it belonged, was marching head up and banners flying, at the other end of it; had elected itself to be the Nation, and these innumerable clams had permitted it so long that they had come at last to accept it as a truth; and not only that, but to believe it right and as it should be. The priests had told their fathers and themselves that this ironical state of things was ordained of God; and so, not reflecting upon how unlike God it would be to amuse himself with sarcasms, and especially such poor transparent ones as this, they had dropped the matter there and become respectfully quiet.

The talk of these meek people had a strange enough sound in a formerly American ear. They were freemen, but they could not leave the estates of their lord or their bishop without his permission; they could not prepare their own bread, but must have their corn ground and their bread baked at his mill and his bakery, and pay roundly for the same; they could not sell a piece of their own property without paying him a handsome percentage of the proceeds, nor buy a piece of somebody else's without remembering him in cash for the privilege; they had to harvest his grain for him gratis, and be ready to come at a moment's notice, leaving their own crop to destruction by the threatened storm; they had to let him plant fruit trees in their fields, and then keep their indignation to themselves when his heedless fruit gatherers trampled the grain around the trees; they had to smother their anger when his hunting parties galloped through their fields laying waste the result of their patient toil; they were not allowed to keep doves themselves, and when the swarms from my lord's dovecote settled on their crops they must not lose their temper and kill a bird, for awful would the penalty be; when the harvest was at last gathered, then came the procession of robbers to levy their blackmail upon it: first the Church carted off its fat tenth, then the king's commissioner took his twentieth, then my lord's people made a mighty inroad upon the remainder; after which, the skinned freeman had liberty to bestow the remnant in his barn, in case it was worth the trouble; there were taxes, and taxes, and taxes, and more taxes, and taxes again, and yet other taxes—upon this free and independent pauper, but none upon his lord the baron or the bishop, none upon the wasteful nobility or the all-devouring Church; if the baron would sleep unvexed, the freeman must sit up all night after his day's work and whip the ponds to keep the frogs quiet; if the freeman's daughter—but no, that last infamy of monarchical government is unprintable; and finally, if the freeman, grown desperate with his tortures, found his life unendurable under such conditions, and sacrificed it and fled to death for mercy and refuge, the gentle Church condemned him to eternal fire, the gentle law buried him at midnight at the cross-roads with a stake through his back, and his master the baron or the bishop confiscated all his property and turned his widow and his orphans out of doors.[5]

And here were these freemen assembled in the early morning to work on their lord the bishop's road three days each—gratis; every head of a family, and every son of a family, three days each, gratis, and a day or so added for their servants. Why, it was like reading about France and the French, before the ever-memorable and blessed Revolution,[6] which swept a thousand years of such villany away in one swift tidal-wave of blood—one: a settlement of that hoary debt in the proportion of half a drop of blood for each hogshead of it that had been pressed by slow tortures out of that people in the weary stretch of ten centuries of wrong and shame and misery the like of which was not to be mated but in hell. There were two "Reigns of Terror," if we would but remember it and consider it; the one wrought murder in hot passion, the other in heartless cold blood; the one lasted mere months, the other had lasted a thousand years; the one inflicted death upon ten thousand persons, the other upon a hundred millions; but our shudders are all for the "horrors" of the minor Terror, the momentary Terror, so to speak; whereas, what is the horror of swift death by the axe, compared with life-long death from hunger, cold, insult, cruelty and heart-break? What is swift death by lightning compared with death by slow fire at the stake? A city cemetery could contain the coffins filled by that brief Terror which we have all been so diligently taught to shiver at and mourn over; but all France could hardly contain the coffins filled by that older and real Terror—that unspeakably bitter and awful Terror which none of us has been taught to see in its vastness or pity as it deserves.

These poor ostensible freemen who were sharing their breakfast and their talk with me, were as full of humble reverence for their king and Church and nobility as their worst enemy could desire. There was something pitifully ludicrous about it. I asked them if they supposed a nation of people ever existed, who, with a free vote in every man's hand, would elect that a single family and its descendants should reign over it forever, whether gifted or boobies, to the exclusion of all other

---

5. The information given in this paragraph is similar to that in a section written for but omitted from *A Tramp Abroad* and not printed until *Letters from the Earth*, where it is entitled "The French and the Comanches." Clemens took most of his details from Hippolyte Taine's *L'Ancien Régime* (1876).

6. The French Revolution began in 1789; Louis XVI was executed in 1793. The "Reign of Terror" occurred 1793–94 and saw thirty to forty persons executed each day, a total of some 20,000. Clemens, who once described the French Revolution to Howells as "the noblest & the holiest" event in history after the American Revolution, was familiar with Thomas Carlyle's *The French Revolution* (1837), Hippolyte Taine's *The French Revolution* (1878–84) and Charles Dickens' novel, *A Tale of Two Cities* (1859).

families—including the voter's; and would also elect that a certain hundred families should be raised to dizzy summits of rank, and clothed-on with offensive transmissible glories and privileges to the exclusion of the rest of the nation's families—*including his own.*

They all looked unhit, and said they didn't know; that they had never thought about it before, and it hadn't ever occurred to them that a nation could be so situated that every man *could* have a say in the government. I said I had seen one—and that it would last until it had an Established Church. Again they were all unhit—at first. But presently one man looked up and asked me to state that proposition again; and state it slowly, so it could soak into his understanding. I did it; and after a little he had the idea, and he brought his fist down and said *he* didn't believe a nation where every man had a vote would voluntarily get down in the mud and dirt in any such way; and that to steal from a nation its will and preference must be a crime and the first of all crimes.

I said to myself:

"This one's a man. If I were backed by enough of his sort, I would make a strike for the welfare of this country, and try to prove myself its loyalest citizen by making a wholesome change in its system of government."

You see my kind of loyalty was loyalty to one's country, not to its institutions or its office-holders. The country is the real thing, the substantial thing, the eternal thing; it is the thing to watch over, and care for, and be loyal to; institutions are extraneous, they are its mere clothing, and clothing can wear out, become ragged, cease to be comfortable, cease to protect the body from winter, disease, and death. To be loyal to rags, to shout for rags, to worship rags, to die for rags—that is a loyalty of unreason, it is pure animal; it belongs to monarchy, was invented by monarchy; let monarchy keep it. I was from Connecticut, whose Constitution declares "that all political power is inherent in the people, and all free governments are founded on their authority and instituted for their benefit; and that they have *at all times* an undeniable and indefeasible right to *alter their form of government* in such a manner as they may think expedient."

Under that gospel, the citizen who thinks he sees that the commonwealth's political clothes are worn out, and yet holds his peace and does not agitate for a new suit, is disloyal; he is a traitor. That he may be the only one who thinks he sees this decay, does not excuse him; it is his duty to agitate any way, and it is the duty of the others to vote him down if they do not see the matter as he does.

And now here I was, in a country where a right to say how the country should be governed was restricted to six persons in each thousand of its population. For the nine hundred and ninety-four to express dissatisfaction with the regnant system and propose to change it, would have made the whole six shudder as one man, it would have been so disloyal, so dishonorable, such putrid black treason. So to speak, I was become a stockholder in a corporation where nine hundred and ninety-four of the members furnished all the money and did all the work, and the other six elected themselves a permanent board of direction and took all the dividends. It seemed to me that what the nine hundred and ninety-four dupes needed was a new deal.[7] The thing that would have best suited the circus side of my nature would have been to resign the Boss-ship and get up an insurrection and turn it into a revolution; but I knew that the Jack Cade or the Wat Tyler[8] who tries such a thing without first educating his materials up to revolution-grade is almost absolutely certain to get left. I had never been accustomed to getting left, even if I do say it myself. Wherefore, the "deal" which had been for some time working into shape in my mind was of a quite different pattern from the Cade-Tyler sort.

So I did not talk blood and insurrection to that man there who sat munching black bread with that abused and mistaught herd of human sheep, but took him aside and talked matter of another sort to him. After I had finished, I got him to lend me a little ink from his veins; and with this and a sliver I wrote on a piece of bark—

*Put him in the Man-Factory*—

and gave it to him, and said—

"Take it to the palace at Camelot and give it into the hands of Amyas le Poulet, whom I call Clarence, and he will understand."

"He is a priest, then," said the man, and some of the enthusiasm went out of his face.

"How—a priest? Didn't I tell you that no chattel of the Church, no bond-slave of pope or bishop can enter my Man-Factory? Didn't I tell you that *you* couldn't enter unless your religion, whatever it might be, was your own free property?"

"Marry, it is so, and for that I was glad; wherefore it liked me not, and bred in me a cold doubt, to hear of this priest being there."

"But he isn't a priest, I tell you."

The man looked far from satisfied. He said:

"He is not a priest, and yet can read?"

"He is not a priest and yet can read—yes, and write, too, for that matter. I taught him myself." The man's face cleared. "And it is the first thing that you yourself will be taught in that Factory—"

7. This passage has been cited as the origin of the phrase used by Franklin D. Roosevelt in his speech accepting the Democratic nomination for the presidency in 1932: "I pledge you, I pledge myself, to a new deal for the American people." Cyril Clemens states that Roosevelt personally told him that he took the phrase from *A Connecticut Yankee (Mark Twain and Franklin D. Roosevelt* [Webster Groves, Mo.: International Mark Twain Society, 1949], pp. 19-20).

8. Cade led a revolt against Henry VI in 1450; Tyler led the Peasants' Revolt of 1381.

"I? I would give blood out of my heart to know that art. Why, I will be your slave, your—"

"No you won't, you won't be anybody's slave. Take your family and go along. Your lord the bishop will confiscate your small property, but no matter, Clarence will fix you all right."

## Chapter XIV

### "DEFEND THEE, LORD!"

I paid three pennies for my breakfast, and a most extravagant price it was, too, seeing that one could have breakfasted a dozen persons for that money; but I was feeling good by this time, and I had always been a kind of spendthrift any way; and then these people had wanted to give me the food for nothing, scant as their provision was, and so it was a grateful pleasure to emphasize my appreciation and sincere thankfulness with a good big financial lift where the money would do so much more good than it would in my helmet, where, these pennies being made of iron and not stinted in weight, my half dollar's worth was a good deal of a burden to me. I spent money rather too freely in those days, it is true; but one reason for it was that I hadn't got the proportions of things entirely adjusted, even yet, after so long a sojourn in Britain—hadn't got along to where I was able to absolutely realize that a penny in Arthur's land and a couple of dollars in Connecticut were about one and the same thing: just twins, as you may say, in purchasing power. If my start from Camelot could have been delayed a very few days I could have paid these people in beautiful new coins from our own mint, and that would have pleased me; and them, too, not less. I had adopted the American values exclusively. In a week or two now, cents, nickels, dimes, quarters and half dollars, and also a trifle of gold, would be trickling in thin but steady streams all through the commercial veins of the kingdom, and I looked to see this new blood freshen up its life.

The farmers were bound to throw in something, to sort of offset my liberality, whether I would or no; so I let them give me a flint and steel; and as soon as they had comfortably bestowed Sandy and me on our horse, I lit my pipe. When the first blast of smoke shot out through the bars of my helmet, all those people broke for the woods, and Sandy went over backwards and struck the ground with a dull thud. They thought I was one of those fire-belching dragons they had heard so much about from knights and other professional liars. I had infinite trouble to persuade those people to venture back within explaining distance. Then I told them that this was only a bit of enchantment which would work harm to none but my enemies. And I promised, with my hand on my heart, that if all who felt no enmity toward me would come forward and pass before me they should see that only those who remained behind would be struck dead. The procession moved with a good deal of promptness. There were no casualties to report, for nobody had curiosity enough to remain behind to see what would happen.

I lost some time, now, for these big children, their fears gone, became so ravished with wonder over my awe-compelling fireworks that I had to stay there and smoke a couple of pipes out before they would let me go. Still the delay was not wholly unproductive, for it took all that time to get Sandy thoroughly wonted to the new thing, she being so close to it, you know. It plugged up her conversation-mill, too, for a considerable while, and that was a gain. But above all other benefits accruing, I had learned something. I was ready for my giant or any ogre that might come along, now.

We tarried with a holy hermit, that night, and my opportunity came about the middle of the next afternoon. We were crossing a vast meadow by way of short-cut, and I was musing absently, hearing nothing, seeing nothing, when Sandy suddenly interrupted a remark which she had begun that morning, with the cry—

"Defend thee, lord!—peril of life is toward!"

And she slipped down from the horse and ran a little way and stood. I looked up and saw, far off in the shade of a tree, half a dozen armed knights and their squires; and straightway there was bustle among them and tightening of saddle-girths for the mount. My pipe was ready and would have been lit, if I had not been lost in thinking about how to banish oppression from this land and restore to all its people their stolen rights and manhood without disobliging anybody. I lit up at once, and by the time I had got a good head of reserved steam on, here they came. All together, too; none of those chivalrous magnanimities which one reads so much about—one courtly rascal at a time, and the rest standing by to see fair play. No, they came in a body, they came with a whirr and a rush, they came like a volley from a battery; came with heads low down, plumes streaming out behind, lances advanced at a level. It was a handsome sight, a beautiful sight—for a man up a tree. I laid my lance in rest and waited, with my heart beating, till the iron wave was just ready to break over me, then spouted a column of white smoke through the bars of my helmet. You should have seen the wave go to pieces and scatter! This was a finer sight than the other one.

But these people stopped, two or three hundred yards away, and this troubled me. My satisfaction collapsed, and fear came; I judged I was a lost man. But Sandy was radiant; and was going to be eloquent, but I stopped her, and told her my magic had miscarried, somehow or other, and she must mount, with all dispatch, and we must ride for life. No, she wouldn't. She said that my enchantment had disabled those knights; they were not riding on, because they couldn't; wait, they would drop out of their saddles presently, and we would get their horses and harness. I could not deceive such trusting simplicity, so I said it was a mistake; that when my fireworks killed at all, they killed instantly; no, the men would not die, there was something wrong about my apparatus, I couldn't tell what; but we must hurry and get away, for those people would attack us again, in a minute. Sandy laughed, and said—

"Lack-a-day, sir, they be not of that breed! Sir Launcelot will give battle to dragons, and will abide by them, and will assail them again, and yet again, and still again, until he do conquer and destroy them; and so likewise will Sir Pellinore and Sir Aglovale and Sir Carados, and mayhap others, but there be none else that will venture it, let the idle say what the idle will. And, la, as to yonder base rufflers, think ye they have not their fill, but yet desire more?"

"Well, then, what are they waiting, for? Why don't they leave? Nobody's hindering. Good land, I'm willing to let bygones be bygones, I'm sure."

"Leave, is it? Oh, give thyself easement as to that. They dream not of it, no, not they. They wait to yield them."

"Come—really, is that 'sooth'—as you people say? If they want to, why don't they?"

"It would like them much; but an ye wot how dragons are esteemed, ye would not hold them blamable. They fear to come."

"Well, then, suppose I go to them instead, and——"

"Ah, wit ye well they would not abide your coming. I will go."

And she did. She was a handy person to have along on a raid. I would have considered this a doubtful errand, myself. I presently saw the knights riding away, and Sandy coming back. That was a relief. I judged she had somehow failed to get the first innings—I mean in the conversation; otherwise the interview wouldn't have been so short. But it turned out that she had managed the business well; in fact admirably. She said that when she told those people I was The Boss, it hit them where they lived: "smote them sore with fear and dread" was her word; and then they were ready to put up with anything she might require. So she swore them to appear at Arthur's court within two days and yield them, with horse and harness, and be my knights henceforth, and subject to my command. How much better she managed that thing than I should have done it myself! She was a daisy.

## Chapter XV

### SANDY'S TALE

"And so I'm proprietor of some knights," said I, as we rode off. "Who would ever have supposed that I should live to list up assets of that sort. I shan't know what to do with them; unless I raffle them off. How many of them are there, Sandy?"

"Seven, please you, sir, and their squires."

"It is a good haul. Who are they? Where do they hang out?"

"Where do they hang out?"

"Yes, where do they live?"

"Ah, I understood thee not. That will I tell thee eftsoons." Then she said musingly, and softly, turning the words daintily over her tongue: "Hang they out—hang they out—where hang—where do they hang out; eh, right so; where do they hang out. Of a truth the phrase hath a fair and winsome grace, and is prettily worded withal. I will repeat it anon and anon in mine idlesse, whereby I may peradventure learn it. Where do they hang out. Even so! already it falleth trippingly from my tongue, and forasmuch as—"

"Don't forget the cow-boys, Sandy."

"Cow-boys?"

"Yes; the knights, you know: You were going to tell me about them. A while back, you remember. Figuratively speaking, game's called."

"Game—"

"Yes, yes, yes! Go to the bat. I mean, get to work on your statistics, and don't burn so much kindling getting your fire started. Tell me about the knights."

"I will well, and lightly will begin. So they two departed and rode into a great forest.[9] And—"

"Great Scott!"

You see, I recognized my mistake at once. I had set her works agoing; it was my own fault; she would be thirty days getting down to those facts. And she generally began without a preface and finished without a result. If you interrupted her she would either go right along without noticing, or answer with a couple of words, and go back and say the sentence over again. So, interruptions only did harm; and yet I had to interrupt, and interrupt pretty frequently, too, in order to save my life; a person would die if he let her monotony drip on him right along all day.

"Great Scott!" I said in my distress. She went right back and began over again:

"So they two departed and rode into a great forest. And——"

"*Which* two?"

"Sir Gawaine and Sir Uwaine. And so they came to an abbey of monks, and there were well lodged. So on the morn they heard their masses in the abbey, and so they rode forth till they came to a great forest; then was Sir Gawaine ware in a valley by a turret, of twelve fair damsels, and two knights armed on great horses, and the damsels went

9. Sandy's story is quoted from Malory, IV.xvi–xix,xxiv–xxv.

to and fro by a tree. And then was Sir Gawaine ware how there hung a white shield on that tree, and ever as the damsels came by it they spit upon it, and some threw mire upon the shield—"

"Now, if I hadn't seen the like myself in this country, Sandy, I wouldn't believe it. But I've seen it, and I can just see those creatures now, parading before that shield and acting like that. The women here do certainly act like all possessed. Yes, and I mean your best, too, society's very choicest brands. The humblest hello-girl[1] along ten thousand miles of wire could teach gentleness, patience, modesty, manners, to the highest duchess in Arthur's land."

"Hello-girl?"

"Yes, but don't you ask me to explain; it's a new kind of girl; they don't have them here; one often speaks sharply to them when they are not the least in fault, and he can't get over feeling sorry for it and ashamed of himself in thirteen hundred years, it's such shabby mean conduct and so unprovoked; the fact is, no gentleman ever does it—thought I—well, I myself, if I've got to confess—"

"Peradventure she—"

"Never mind her; never mind her; I tell you I couldn't ever explain her so you would understand."

"Even so be it, sith ye are so minded. Then Sir Gawaine and Sir Uwaine went and saluted them, and asked them why they did that despite to the shield. Sirs, said the damsels, we shall tell you. There is a knight in this country that owneth this white shield, and he is a passing good man of his hands, but he hateth all ladies and gentle-women, and therefore we do all this despite to the shield. I will say you, said Sir Gawaine, it beseemeth evil a good knight to despise all ladies and gentlewomen, and peradventure though he hate you he hath some cause, and peradventure he loveth in some other places ladies and gentlewomen, and to be loved again, and he such a man of prowess[2] as ye speak of—"

"Man of prowess—yes, that is the man to please them, Sandy. Man of brains—that is a thing they never think of. Tom Sayers—John Heenan—John L. Sullivan[3]—pity but you could be here. You would have your legs under the Round Table and a "Sir" in front of your names within the twenty-four hours; and you could bring about a new distribution of the married princesses and duchesses of the Court in another twenty-four. The fact is, it is just a sort of polished-up court of Comanches, and there isn't a squaw in it who doesn't stand ready at

---

1. A telephone operator. Later in the chapter Morgan reveals that the comparison has special meaning for him.
2. Malory's line reads: ". . . and he be such a man of prowess . . ." Sandy quotes it correctly when she resumes.

3. Sullivan (1858–1918) was the heavyweight boxing champion at the time the novel was published. Sayers and Heenan fought a 42-round bout in 1860, when Sayers was the English boxing champion.

the dropping of a hat to desert to the buck with the biggest string of scalps at his belt."

"——and he be such a man of prowess as ye speak of, said Sir Gawaine. Now what is his name? Sir, said they, his name is Marhaus the king's son of Ireland."

"Son of the king of Ireland, you mean; the other form doesn't mean anything. And look out and hold on tight, now, we must jump this gully. . . . There, we are all right now. This horse belongs in the circus; he is born before his time."

"I know him well, said Sir Uwaine, he is a passing good knight as any is on live."

"*On live*. If you've got a fault in the world, Sandy, it is that you are a shade too archaic. But it isn't any matter."

"——for I saw him once proved at a justs where many knights were gathered, and that time there might no man withstand him. Ah, said Sir Gawaine, damsels, methinketh ye are to blame, for it is to suppose he that hung that shield there will not be long therefrom, and then may those knights match him on horseback, and that is more your worship than thus; for I will abide no longer to see a knight's shield dishonored. And therewith Sir Uwaine and Sir Gawaine departed a little from them, and then were they ware where Sir Marhaus came riding on a great horse straight toward them. And when the twelve damels saw Sir Marhaus they fled into the turret as they were wild, so that some of them fell by the way. Then the one of the knights of the tower dressed his shield, and said on high, Sir Marhaus defend thee. And so they ran together that the knight brake his spear on Marhaus, and Sir Marhaus smote him so hard that he brake his neck and the horse's back—"

"Well, that is just the trouble about this state of things, it ruins so many horses."

"That saw the other knight of the turret, and dressed him toward Marhaus, and they went so eagerly together, that the knight of the turret was soon smitten down, horse and man, stark dead—"

"*Another* horse gone; I tell you it is a custom that ought to be broken up. I don't see how people with any feeling can applaud and support it."

\* \* \* \* \* \* \* \* \*

"So these two knights came together with great random—"

I saw that I had been asleep and missed a chapter, but I didn't say anything. I judged that the Irish knight was in trouble with the visitors by this time, and this turned out to be the case.

"——that Sir Uwaine smote Sir Marhaus that his spear brast in pieces on the shield, and Sir Marhaus smote him so sore that horse and man he bare to the earth, and hurt Sir Uwaine on the left side—"

"The truth is, Alisande, these archaics are a little *too* simple; the vocabulary is too limited, and so, by consequence, descriptions suffer in the matter of variety; they run too much to level Saharas of fact, and not enough to picturesque detail; this throws about them a certain air of the monotonous; in fact the fights are all alike: a couple of people come together with great random—random is a good word, and so is exegesis, for that matter, and so is holocaust, and defalcation, and usufruct and a hundred others, but land! a body ought to discriminate—they come together with great random, and a spear is brast, and one party brake his shield and the other one goes down, horse and man, over his horse-tail and brake his neck, and then the next candidate comes randoming in, and brast *his* spear, and the other man brast his shield, and down *he* goes, horse and man, over his horse-tail, and brake *his* neck, and then there's another elected, and another and another and still another, till the material is all used up; and when you come to figure up results, you can't tell one fight from another, nor who whipped; and as a *picture*, of living, raging, roaring battle, sho! why, it's pale and noiseless—just ghosts scuffling in a fog. Dear me, what would this barren vocabulary get out of the mightiest spectacle?—the burning of Rome in Nero's time,[4] for instance? Why, it would merely say, 'Town burned down; no insurance; boy brast a window, fireman brake his neck!' Why, *that* ain't a picture!"

It was a good deal of a lecture, I thought, but it didn't disturb Sandy, didn't turn a feather; her steam soared steadily up again, the minute I took off the lid:

"Then Sir Marhaus turned his horse and rode toward Gawaine with his spear. And when Sir Gawaine saw that, he dressed his shield, and they aventred their spears, and they came together with all the might of their horses, that either knight smote other so hard in the midst of their shields, but Sir Gawaine's spear brake—"

"I knew it would."

—"but Sir Marhaus's spear held; and therewith Sir Gawaine and his horse rushed down to the earth—"

"Just so—and brake his back."

—"and lightly Sir Gawaine rose upon his feet and pulled out his sword, and dressed him toward Sir Marhaus on foot, and therewith either came unto other eagerly, and smote together with their swords, that their shields flew in cantels, and they bruised their helms and their hauberks, and wounded either other. But Sir Gawaine, fro it passed nine of the clock, waxed by the space of three hours ever stronger and stronger, and thrice his might was increased. All this espied Sir Marhaus, and had great wonder how his might increased, and so they wounded other passing sore; and then when it was come noon—"

4. Nero was emperor of Rome, 54–68 A.D.; the fire occurred in 64.

The pelting sing-song of it carried me forward to scenes and sounds of my boyhood days:

"N-e-e-ew Haven! ten minutes for refreshments—knductr 'll strike the gong-bell two minutes before train leaves—passengers for the Shore-line please take seats in the rear k'yar, this k'yar don't go no furder—*ahh*-pls, *aw*-rnjz, b'*nan*ners, *s-a-n-d'*ches, p——*op*-corn!"

—"and waxed past noon and drew towards evensong. Sir Gawaine's strength feebled and waxed passing faint, that unnethes he might dure any longer, and Sir Marhaus was then bigger and bigger—"

"Which strained his armor, of course; and yet little would one of these people mind a small thing like that."

—"and so, Sir Knight, said Sir Marhaus, I have well felt that ye are a passing good knight, and a marvelous man of might as ever I felt any, while it lasteth, and our quarrels are not great, and therefore it were a pity to do you hurt, for I feel you are passing feeble. Ah, said Sir Gawaine, gentle knight, ye say the word that I should say. And therewith they took off their helms and either kissed other, and there they swore together either to love other as brethren—"

But I lost the thread there, and dozed off to slumber, thinking about what a pity it was that men with such superb strength—strength enabling them to stand up cased in cruelly burdensome iron and drenched with perspiration, and hack and batter and bang each other for six hours on a stretch—should not have been born at a time when they could put it to some useful purpose. Take a jackass, for instance: a jackass has that kind of strength, and puts it to a useful purpose, and is valuable to this world because he *is* a jackass; but a nobleman is not valuable because he is a jackass. It is a mixture that is always ineffectual and should never have been attempted in the first place. And yet, once you start a mistake, the trouble is done and you never know what is going to come of it.

When I came to myself again and began to listen, I perceived that I had lost another chapter, and that Alisande had wandered a long way off with her people.

"And so they rode and came into a deep valley full of stones, and thereby they saw a fair stream of water; above thereby was the head of the stream, a fair fountain, and three damsels sitting thereby. In this country, said Sir Marhaus, came never knight since it was christened, but he found strange adventures—"

"This is not good form, Alisande. Sir Marhaus the king's son of Ireland talks like all the rest; you ought to give him a brogue, or at least a characteristic expletive; by this means one would recognize him as soon as he spoke, without his ever being named. It is a common literary device with the great authors. You should make him say, 'In this country, be jabers, came never knight since it was christened, but he found strange adventures, be jabers.' You see how much better that sounds."

—"came never knight but he found strange adventures, be jabers. Of a truth it doth indeed, fair lord, albeit 'tis passing hard to say, though peradventure that will not tarry but better speed with usage. And then they rode to the damsels, and either saluted other, and the eldest had a garland of gold about her head, and she was threescore winter of age or more—"

"The *damsel* was?"

"Even so, dear lord—and her hair was white under the garland—"

"Celluloid teeth, nine dollars a set, as like as not—the loose-fit kind, that go up and down like a portcullis when you eat, and fall out when you laugh."

"The second damsel was of thirty winter of age, with a circlet of gold about her head. The third damsel was but fifteen year of age—"

Billows of thought came rolling over my soul, and the voice faded out of my hearing!

Fifteen! Break—my heart! oh, my lost darling! Just her age who was so gentle, and lovely, and all the world to me, and whom I shall never see again! How the thought of her carries me back over wide seas of memory to a vague dim time, a happy time, so many, many centuries hence, when I used to wake in the soft summer mornings, out of sweet dreams of her, and say "Hello, Central!"[5] just to hear her dear voice come melting back to me with a "Hello, Hank!" that was music of the spheres to my enchanted ear. She got three dollars a week, but she was worth it.

I could not follow Alisande's further explanation of who our captured knights were, now—I mean in case she should ever get to explaining who they were. My interest was gone, my thoughts were far away, and sad. By fitful glimpses of the drifting tale, caught here and there and now and then, I merely noted in a vague way that each of these three knights took one of these three damsels up behind him on his horse, and one rode north, another east, the other south, to seek adventures, and meet again and lie, after year and day. Year and day—and without baggage. It was of a piece with the general simplicity of the country.

The sun was now setting. It was about three in the afternoon when Alisande had begun to tell me who the cowboys were; so she had made pretty good progress with it—for her. She would arrive some time or other, no doubt, but she was not a person who could be hurried.

We were approaching a castle which stood on high ground; a huge, strong, venerable structure, whose gray towers and battlements were charmingly draped with ivy, and whose whole majestic mass was drenched with splendors flung from the sinking sun. It was the largest

---

5. The operator of a telephone exchange was called "Central."

castle we had seen, and so I thought it might be the one we were after, but Sandy said no. She did not know who owned it; she said she had passed it without calling, when she went down to Camelot.

## Chapter XVI

### MORGAN LE FAY

If knights errant were to be believed, not all castles were desirable places to seek hospitality in. As a matter of fact, knights errant were *not* persons to be believed—that is, measured by modern standards of veracity; yet, measured by the standards of their own time, and scaled accordingly, you got the truth. It was very simple: you discounted a statement ninety-seven percent; the rest was fact. Now after making this allowance, the truth remained that if I could find out something about a castle before ringing the door-bell—I mean hailing the warders—it was the sensible thing to do. So I was pleased when I saw in the distance a horseman making the bottom turn of the road that wound down from this castle.

As we approached each other, I saw that he wore a plumed helmet, and seemed to be otherwise clothed in steel, but bore a curious addition also—a stiff square garment like a herald's tabard. However, I had to smile at my own forgetfulness when I got nearer and read this sign on his tabard:

*"Persimmons's Soap—All the Prime-Donne Use It."*

That was a little idea of my own, and had several wholesome purposes in view toward the civilizing and uplifting of this nation. In the first place, it was a furtive, underhand blow at this nonsense of knight errantry, though nobody suspected that but me. I had started a number of these people out—the bravest knights I could get—each sandwiched between bulletin-boards bearing one device or another, and I judged that by and by when they got to be numerous enough they would begin to look ridiculous; and then, even the steel-clad ass that *hadn't* any board would himself begin to look ridiculous because he was out of the fashion.

Secondly, these missionaries would gradually, and without creating suspicion or exciting alarm introduce a rudimentary cleanliness among the nobility, and from them it would work down to the people, if the priests could be kept quiet. This would undermine the Church. I mean would be a step toward that. Next, education—next, freedom—and then she would begin to crumble. It being my conviction that any Established Church is an established crime, an established slave-pen, I had no scruples, but was willing to assail it in any way or with any weapon that promised to hurt it. Why, in my own former day—in remote centuries not yet stirring in the womb of time—there were old Englishmen who imagined that they had been born in a free country: a "free" country with the Corporation Act and the Test[6] still in force in it—timbers propped against men's liberties and dishonored consciences to shore up an Established Anachronism with.

My missionaries were taught to spell out the gilt signs on their tabards—the showy gilding was a neat idea, I could have got the king to wear a bulletin-board for the sake of that barbaric splendor—they were to spell out these signs and then explain to the lords and ladies what soap was; and if the lords and ladies were afraid of it, get them to try it on a dog. The missionary's next move was to get the family together and try it on himself; he was to stop at no experiment, however desperate, that could convince the nobility that soap was harmless; if any final doubt remained, he must catch a hermit—the woods were full of them; saints they called themselves, and saints they were believed to be. They were unspeakably holy, and worked miracles, and everybody stood in awe of them. If a hermit could survive a wash, and that failed to convince a duke, give him up, let him alone.

Whenever my missionaries overcame a knight errant on the road they washed him, and when he got well they swore him to go and get a bulletin-board and disseminate soap and civilization the rest of his days. As a consequence the workers in the field were increasing by degrees, and the reform was steadily spreading. My soap factory felt the strain early. At first I had only two hands; but before I had left home I was already employing fifteen, and running night and day; and the atmospheric result was getting so pronounced that the king went sort of fainting and gasping around and said he did not believe he could stand it much longer, and Sir Launcelot got so that he did hardly anything but walk up and down the roof and swear, although I told him it was worse up there than anywhere else, but he said he wanted plenty of air; and he was always complaining that a palace was no place for a soap factory, anyway, and said if a man was to start one in his house he would be damned if he wouldn't strangle him. There were ladies present, too, but much these people ever cared for that; they would swear before children, if the wind was their way when the factory was going.

This missionary knight's name was La Cote Male Taile, and he said that this castle was the abode of Morgan le Fay, sister of King Arthur, and wife of King Uriens, monarch of a realm about as big as the District of Columbia—you could stand in the middle of it and throw bricks into the next kingdom. "Kings" and "Kingdoms" were as thick

6. Both were retained in the Toleration Act of 1689, which granted freedom of worship to all except Roman Catholics and Unitarians. The Corporation and Test Acts barred dissenters and Roman Catholics from civil and military office.

in Britain as they had been in little Palestine in Joshua's time,[7] when people had to sleep with their knees pulled up because they couldn't stretch out without a passport.

La Cote was much depressed, for he had scored here the worst failure of his campaign. He had not worked off a cake; yet he had tried all the tricks of the trade, even to the washing of a hermit; but the hermit died. This was indeed a bad failure, for this animal would now be dubbed a martyr, and would take his place among the saints of the Roman calendar. Thus made he his moan, this poor Sir La Cote Male Taile, and sorrowed passing sore. And so my heart bled for him, and I was moved to comfort and stay him. Wherefore I said—

"Forbear to grieve, fair knight, for this is not a defeat. We have brains, you and I; and for such as have brains there are no defeats, but only victories. Observe how we will turn this seeming disaster into an advertisement; an advertisement for our soap; and the biggest one, to draw, that was ever thought of; an advertisement that will transform that Mount Washington defeat into a Matterhorn[8] victory. We will put on your bulletin-board, '*Patronized by the Elect.*' How does that strike you?"

"Verily, it is wonderly bethought!"

"Well, a body is bound to admit that for just a modest little one-line ad., it's a corker."

So the poor colporteur's[9] griefs vanished away. He was a brave fellow, and had done mighty feats of arms in his time. His chief celebrity rested upon the events of an excursion like this one of mine, which he had once made with a damsel named Maledisant,[1] who was as handy with her tongue as was Sandy, though in a different way, for her tongue churned forth only railings and insult, whereas Sandy's music was of a kindlier sort. I knew his story well, and so I knew how to interpret the compassion that was in his face when he bade me farewell. He supposed I was having a bitter hard time of it.

Sandy and I discussed his story, as we rode along, and she said that La Cote's bad luck had begun with the very beginning of that trip; for the king's fool had overthrown him on the first day, and in such cases it was customary for the girl to desert to the conqueror, but Maledisant didn't do it; and also persisted afterward in sticking to him, after all his defeats. But, said I, suppose the victor should decline to accept his spoil? She said that that wouldn't answer—he must. He couldn't

7. Joshua led the Israelites into the Promised Land after their departure from Egypt and forty years in the wilderness. In *The Innocents Abroad* (1869) Clemens frequently comments on how small things are in the Holy Land, as compared with the great size they had in his imagination.
8. Mount Washington, in New Hampshire's White Mountains, 6,288 feet above sea level, is less than half the height of the Matterhorn, in the Swiss-Italian Alps (14,690 feet).
9. One who goes from place to place distributing religious material.
1. The journey of Sir La Cote Male Taile with Maledisant is recounted in Malory, IX.iii.

decline; it wouldn't be regular. I made a note of that. If Sandy's music got to be too burdensome, some time, I would let a knight defeat me, on the chance that she would desert to him.

In due time we were challenged by the warders, from the castle walls, and after a parley admitted. I have nothing pleasant to tell about that visit. But it was not a disappointment, for I knew Mrs. le Fay by reputation, and was not expecting anything pleasant. She was held in awe by the whole realm, for she had made everybody believe she was a great sorceress. All her ways were wicked, all her instincts devilish. She was loaded to the eye-lids with cold malice. All her history was black with crime; and among her crimes murder was common. I was most curious to see her; as curious as I could have been to see Satan.[2] To my surprise she was beautiful; black thoughts had failed to make her expression repulsive, age had failed to wrinkle her satin skin or mar its bloomy freshness. She could have passed for old Uriens's granddaughter, she could have been mistaken for sister to her own son.

As soon as we were fairly within the castle gates we were ordered into her presence. King Uriens was there, a kind-faced old man with a subdued look; and also the son, Sir Uwaine le Blanchemains, in whom I was of course interested on account of the tradition that he had once done battle with thirty knights, and also on account of his trip with Sir Gawaine and Sir Marhaus, which Sandy had been aging me with. But Morgan was the main attraction, the conspicuous personality here; she was head chief of this household, that was plain. She caused us to be seated, and then she began, with all manner of pretty graces and graciousnesses, to ask me questions. Dear me, it was like a bird or a flute, or something, talking. I felt persuaded that this woman must have been misrepresented, lied about. She trilled along, and trilled along, and presently a handsome young page, clothed like the rainbow, and as easy and undulatory of movement as a wave, came with something on a golden salver, and kneeling to present it to her, overdid his graces and lost his balance, and so fell lightly against her knee. She slipped a dirk into him in as matter-of-course a way as another person would have harpooned a rat!

Poor child, he slumped to the floor, twisted his silken limbs in one great straining contortion of pain, and was dead. Out of the old king was wrung an involuntary "O-h!" of compassion. The look he got, made him cut it suddenly short and not put any more hyphens in it. Sir Uwaine, at a sign from his mother, went to the ante-room and called some servants, and meanwhile madame went rippling sweetly along with her talk.

2. Compare Clemens' statement in "Concerning the Jews" (1899): "I would like to see him. I would rather see him and shake him by the tail than any other member of the European concert."

I saw that she was a good housekeeper, for while she talked she kept a corner of her eye on the servants to see that they made no balks in handling the body and getting it out; when they came with fresh clean towels, she sent back for the other kind; and when they had finished wiping the floor and were going, she indicated a crimson fleck the size of a tear which their duller eyes had overlooked. It was plain to me that La Cote Male Taile had failed to see the mistress of the house. Often, how louder and clearer than any tongue, does dumb circumstantial evidence speak.

Morgan le Fay rippled along as musically as ever. Marvelous woman. And what a glance she had: when it fell in reproof upon those servants, they shrunk and quailed as timid people do when the lightning flashes out of a cloud. I could have got the habit myself. It was the same with that poor old Brer Uriens; he was always on the ragged edge of apprehension; she could not even turn towards him but he winced.

In the midst of the talk I let drop a complimentary word about King Arthur, forgetting for the moment how this woman hated her brother. That one little compliment was enough. She clouded up like a storm; she called for her guards, and said—

"Hale me these varlets to the dungeons!"

That struck cold on my ears, for her dungeons had a reputation. Nothing occurred to me to say—or do. But not so with Sandy. As the guard laid a hand upon me, she piped up with the tranquilest confidence, and said—

"God's wownds, dost thou covet destruction, thou maniac? It is The Boss!"

Now what a happy idea that was!—and so simple; yet it would never have occurred to me. I was born modest; not all over, but in spots; and this was one of the spots.

The effect upon madame was electrical. It cleared her countenance and brought back her smiles and all her persuasive graces and blandishments; but nevertheless she was not able to entirely cover up with them the fact that she was in a ghastly fright. She said:

"La, but do list to thine handmaid! as if one gifted with powers like to mine might say the thing which I have said unto one who has vanquished Merlin, and not be jesting. By mine enchantments I foresaw your coming, and by them I knew you when you entered here. I did but play this little jest with hope to surprise you into some display of your art, as not doubting you would blast the guards with occult fires, consuming them to ashes on the spot, a marvel much beyond mine own ability, yet one which I have long been childishly curious to see."

The guards were less curious, and got out as soon as they got permission.

## Chapter XVII

### A ROYAL BANQUET

Madame seeing me pacific and unresentful, no doubt judged that I was deceived by her excuse; for her fright dissolved away, and she was soon so importunate to have me give an exhibition and kill somebody, that the thing grew to be embarrassing. However, to my relief she was presently interrupted by the call to prayers. I will say this much for the nobility: that, tyrannical, murderous, rapacious and morally rotten as they were, they were deeply and enthusiastically religious. Nothing could divert them from the regular and faithful performance of the pieties enjoined by the Church. More than once I had seen a noble who had gotten his enemy at a disadvantage, stop to pray before cutting his throat; more than once I had seen a noble, after ambushing and dispatching his enemy, retire to the nearest wayside shrine and humbly give thanks, without even waiting to rob the body. There was to be nothing finer or sweeter in the life of even Benvenuto Cellini,[3] that rough-hewn saint, ten centuries later. All the nobles of Britain, with their families, attended divine service morning and night daily, in their private chapels, and even the worst of them had family worship five or six times a day besides. The credit of this belonged entirely to the Church. Although I was no friend to that Catholic Church, I was obliged to admit this. And often, in spite of me, I found myself saying, "What would this country be without the Church?"

After prayers we had dinner in a great banqueting hall which was lighted by hundreds of grease-jets, and everything was as fine and lavish and rudely splendid as might become the royal degree of the hosts. At the head of the hall, on a dais, was the table of the king, queen, and their son, Prince Uwaine. Stretching down the hall from this, was the general table, on the floor. At this, above the salt, sat the visiting nobles and the grown members of their families, of both sexes,—the resident Court, in effect,—sixty-one persons; below the salt sat minor officers of the household, with their principal subordinates: altogether a hundred and eighteen persons sitting, and about as many liveried servants standing behind their chairs, or serving in one capacity or another. It was a very fine show. In a gallery a band with cymbals, horns, harps and other horrors, opened the proceedings with what seemed to be the crude first-draft or original agony of the wail known to later centuries as "In the Sweet Bye and Bye."[4] It was new, and ought to have been rehearsed a little more. For some reason or

3. An Italian goldsmith, sculptor, and writer (1500–1571) particularly well known for his zestful autobiography. He was one of the writers admired by Tom Sawyer.
4. Popular gospel song about heaven published in 1868, with words by S. F. Bennett and music by J. P. Webster; it begins, "There's a land that is fairer than day." Clemens mentions the song in several other works; apparently it irritated him considerably.

other the queen had the composer hanged, after dinner.

After this music, the priest who stood behind the royal table said a noble long grace in ostensible Latin. Then the battalion of waiters broke away from their posts, and darted, rushed, flew, fetched and carried, and the mighty feeding began; no words anywhere, but absorbing attention to business. The rows of chops opened and shut in vast unison, and the sound of it was like to the muffled burr of subterranean machinery.

The havoc continued an hour and a half, and unimaginable was the destruction of substantials. Of the chief feature of the feast—the huge wild boar that lay stretched out so portly and imposing at the start— nothing was left but the semblance of a hoop-skirt; and he was but the type and symbol of what had happened to all the other dishes.

With the pastries and so-on, the heavy drinking began—and the talk. Gallon after gallon of wine and mead disappeared, and everybody got comfortable, then happy, then sparklingly joyous—both sexes,— and bye and bye pretty noisy. Men told anecdotes that were terrific to hear, but nobody blushed; and when the nub was sprung, the assemblage let go with a horse-laugh that shook the fortress. Ladies answered back with historiettes that would almost have made Queen Margaret of Navarre or even the great Elizabeth of England[5] hide behind a handkerchief, but nobody hid here, but only laughed— howled, you may say. In pretty much all of these dreadful stories, ecclesiastics were the hardy heroes, but that didn't worry the chaplain any, he had his laugh with the rest; more than that, upon invitation he roared out a song which was of as daring a sort as any that was sung that night.

By midnight everybody was fagged out, and sore with laughing; and as a rule, drunk: some weepingly, some affectionately, some hilariously, some quarrelsomely, some dead and under the table. Of the ladies, the worst spectacle was a lovely young duchess, whose wedding-eve this was; and indeed she was a spectacle; sure enough. Just as she was she could have sat in advance for the portrait of the young daughter of the Regent d'Orleans,[6] at the famous dinner whence she was carried, foulmouthed, intoxicated and helpless, to her bed, in the lost and lamented days of the Ancient Regime.

Suddenly, even while the priest was lifting his hands, and all conscious heads were bowed in reverent expectation of the coming blessing, there appeared under the arch of the far-off door at the bottom of the hall, an old and bent and white-haired lady, leaning

5. Elizabeth I (1533–1603) is one of the participants in the "shocking" conversation created by Clemens in 1601. Margaret (1492–1549) wrote the Heptameron, cited in the first chapter of Life on the Mississippi (1883) for its "wit and indelicacy."

6. Philippe, Duke of Orleans, acted as regent during the minority of Louis XV, 1715–23.

upon a crutch-stick; and she lifted the stick and pointed it toward the queen and cried out—

"The wrath and curse of God fall upon you, woman without pity, who have slain mine innocent grandchild and made desolate this old heart that had nor chick nor friend nor stay nor comfort in all this world but him!"

Everybody crossed himself in a grisly fright, for a curse was an awful thing to those people; but the queen rose up majestic, with the death-light in her eye, and flung back this ruthless command:

"Lay hands on her! To the stake with her!"

The guards left their posts to obey. It was a shame; it was a cruel thing to see. What could be done? Sandy gave me a look; I knew she had another inspiration. I said—

"Do what you choose."

She was up and facing toward the queen in a moment. She indicated me, and said:

"Madame, *he* saith this may not be. Recal the commandment, or he will dissolve the castle and it shall vanish away like the instable fabric of a dream!"

Confound it, what a crazy contract to pledge a person to! What if the queen—

But my consternation subsided there, and my panic passed off; for the queen, all in a collapse, made no show of resistance but gave a countermanding sign and sunk into her seat. When she reached it she was sober. So were many of the others. The assemblage rose, whiffed ceremony to the winds, and rushed for the door like a mob; overturning chairs, smashing crockery, tugging, struggling, shouldering, crowding—anything to get out before I should change my mind and puff the castle into the measureless dim vacancies of space. Well, well, well, they *were* a superstitious lot. It is all a body can do to conceive of it.

The poor queen was so scared and humbled that she was even afraid to hang the composer without first consulting me. I was very sorry for her—indeed any one would have been, for she was really suffering; so I was willing to do anything that was reasonable, and had no desire to carry things to wanton extremities. I therefore considered the matter thoughtfully, and ended by having the musicians ordered into our presence to play that Sweet Bye and Bye again, which they did. Then I saw that she was right, and gave her permission to hang the whole band. This little relaxation of sternness had a good effect upon the queen. A statesman gains little by the arbitrary exercise of ironclad authority upon all occasions that offer, for this wounds the just pride of his subordinates, and thus tends to undermine his strength. A little concession, now and then, where it can do no harm, is the wiser policy.

Now that the queen was at ease in her mind once more, and measurably happy, her wine naturally began to assert itself again, and it got a little the start of her. I mean it set her music going—her silver bell of a tongue. Dear me, she was a master talker. It would not become me to suggest that it was pretty late and that I was a tired man and very sleepy. I wished I had gone off to bed when I had the chance. Now I must stick it out; there was no other way. So she tinkled along and along, in the otherwise profound and ghostly hush of the sleeping castle, until bye and bye there came, as if from deep down under us, a far-away sound, as of a muffled shriek—with an expression of agony about it that made my flesh crawl. The queen stopped, and her eyes lighted with pleasure; she tiled her graceful head as a bird does when it listens. The sound bored its way up through the stillness again.

"What is it?" I said.

"It is truly a stubborn soul, and endureth long. It is many hours now."

"Endureth what?"

"The rack. Come—ye shall see a blithe sight. An he yield not his secret now, ye shall see him torn asunder."

What a silky smooth hellion she was; and so composed and serene, when the cords all down my legs were hurting in sympathy with that man's pain. Conducted by mailed guards bearing flaring torches, we tramped along echoing corridors, and down stone stairways dank and dripping, and smelling of mould and ages of imprisoned night—a chill, uncanny journey and a long one, and not made the shorter or the cheerier by the sorceress's talk, which was about this sufferer and his crime. He had been accused by an anonymous informer, of having killed a stag in the royal preserves. I said—

"Anonymous testimony isn't just the right thing, your Highness. It were fairer to confront the accused with the accuser."

"I had not thought of that, it being but of small consequence. But an I would, I could not, for that the accuser came masked by night, and told the forester, and straightway got him hence again, and so the forester knoweth him not."

"Then is this Unknown the only person who saw the stag killed?"

"Marry, *no* man *saw* the killing, but this Unknown saw this hardy wretch near to the spot where the stag lay, and came with right loyal zeal and betrayed him to the forester."

"So the Unknown was near the dead stag, too? Isn't it just possible that he did the killing himself? His loyal zeal—in a mask—looks just a shade suspicious. But what is your Highness's idea for racking the prisoner? Where is the profit?"

"He will not confess, else; and then were his soul lost. For his crime his life is forfeited by the law—and of a surety will I see that he payeth it!—but it were peril to my own soul to let him die unconfessed and unabsolved. Nay, I were a fool to fling me into hell for *his* accommodation."

"But, your Highness, suppose he has nothing to confess?"

"As to that, we shall see, anon. An I rack him to death and he confess not, it will peradventure show that he had indeed naught to confess—ye will grant that that is sooth? Then shall I not be damned for an unconfessed man that had naught to confess—wherefore, I shall be safe."

It was the stubborn unreasoning of the time. It was useless to argue with her. Arguments have no chance against petrified training; they wear it as little as the waves wear a cliff. And her training was everybody's. The brightest intellect in the land would not have been able to see that her position was defective.

As we entered the rack-cell I caught a picture that will not go from me; I wish it would. A native young giant of thirty or thereabouts, lay stretched upon the frame on his back, with his wrists and ancles tied to ropes which led over windlasses at either end. There was no color in him; his features were contorted and set, and sweat-drops stood upon his forehead. A priest bent over him on each side; the executioner stood by; guards were on duty; smoking torches stood in sockets along the walls; in a corner crouched a poor young creature, her face drawn with anguish, a half-wild and hunted look in her eyes, and in her lap lay a little child asleep. Just as we stepped across the threshold the executioner gave his machine a slight turn, which wrung a cry from both the prisoner and the woman; but I shouted and the executioner released the strain without waiting to see who spoke. I could not let this horror go on; it would have killed me to see it. I asked the queen to let me clear the place and speak to the prisoner privately; and when she was going to object I spoke in a low voice and said I did not want to make a scene before her servants, but I must have my way; for I was King Arthur's representative, and was speaking in his name. She saw she had to yield. I asked her to endorse me to these people, and then leave me. It was not pleasant for her, but she took the pill; and even went further than I was meaning to require. I only wanted the backing of her own authority; but she said—

"Ye will do in all things as this lord shall command. It is The Boss."

It was certainly a good word to conjure with: you could see it by the squirming of these rats. The queen's guards fell into line, and she and they marched away, with their torch-bearers, and woke the echoes of the cavernous tunnels with the measured beat of their retreating footfalls. I had the prisoner taken from the rack and placed upon his bed, and medicaments applied to his hurts, and wine given him to drink. The woman crept near and looked on, eagerly, lovingly, but timorously,—like one who fears a repulse; indeed, she tried furtively to touch the man's forehead, and jumped back, the picture of fright, when I turned unconsciously toward her. It was pitiful to see.

"Lord," I said, "stroke him, lass, if you want to. Do anything you're a mind to; don't mind me."

Why, her eyes were as grateful as an animal's, when you do it a kindness that it understands. The baby was out of her way and she had her cheek against the man's in a minute, and her hands fondling his hair, and her happy tears running down. The man revived, and caressed his wife with his eyes, which was all he could do. I judged I might clear the den, now, and I did; cleared it of all but the family and myself. Then I said—

"Now my friend, tell me your side of this matter; I know the other side."

The man moved his head in sign of refusal. But the woman looked pleased—as it seemed to me—pleased with my suggestion. I went on:

"You know of me?"

"Yes. All do, in Arthur's realms."

"If my reputation has come to you right and straight, you should not be afraid to speak."

The woman broke in, eagerly:

"Ah, fair my lord, do thou persuade him! Thou canst an thou wilt. Ah, he suffereth so; and it is for me—for *me!* And how can I bear it? I would I might see him die—a sweet, swift death; oh, my Hugo, I cannot bear this one!"

And she fell to sobbing and groveling about my feet, and still imploring. Imploring what? The man's death? I could not quite get the bearings of the thing. But Hugo interrupted her and said—

"Peace! Ye wit not what ye ask. Shall I starve whom I love, to win a gentle death? I wend thou knewest me better."

"Well," I said, "I can't quite make this out. It is a puzzle. Now—"

"Ah, dear my lord, an ye will but persuade him! Consider how these his tortures wound me! Oh, and he will not speak!—whereas, the healing, the solace that lie in a blessed swift death—"

"What *are* you maundering about? He's going out from here a free man and whole—he's not going to die."

The man's white face lit up, and the woman flung herself at me in a most surprising explosion of joy, and cried out—

"He is saved!—for it is the King's word by the mouth of the king's servant—Arthur, the king whose word is gold!"

"Well, then you do believe I can be trusted, after all. Why didn't you before?"

"Who doubted? Not I, indeed; and not she."

"Well, why wouldn't you tell me your story, then?"

"Ye had made no promise; else had it been otherwise."

"I see, I see. . . . And yet I believe I don't quite see, after all. You stood the torture and refused to confess; which shows plain enough to even the dullest understanding that you had nothing to confess—"

"*I,* my lord? How so? It was I that killed the deer!"

"You *did?* Oh, dear, this is the most mixed-up business that ever—"

"Dear lord, I begged him on my knees to confess, but—"

"You *did!* It gets thicker and thicker. What did you want him to do that for?"

"Sith it would bring him a quick death and save him all this cruel pain."

"Well—yes, there is reason in that. But *he* didn't want the quick death."

"He? Why, of a surety he *did.*"

"Well, then, why in the world *didn't* he confess?"

"Ah, sweet sir, and leave my wife and chick without bread and shelter?"

"Oh, heart of gold, now I see it! The bitter law takes the convicted man's estate and beggars his widow and his orphans. They could torture you to death, but without conviction or confession they could not rob your wife and baby. You stood by them like a man; and *you*—true wife and true woman that you are—you would have bought him release from torture at cost to yourself of slow starvation and death—well, it humbles a body to think what your sex can do when it comes to self-sacrifice. I'll book you both for my colony; you'll like it there; it's a Factory where I'm going to turn groping and grubbing automata into *men.*"

## Chapter XVIII

### IN THE QUEEN'S DUNGEONS

Well, I arranged all that; and I had the man sent to his home. I had a great desire to rack the executioner; not because he was a good, pains-taking and pain-giving official,—for surely it was not to his discredit that he performed his functions well—but to pay him back for wantonly cuffing and otherwise distressing that young woman. The priests told me about this, and were generously hot to have him punished. Something of this disagreeable sort was turning up every now and then. I mean, episodes that showed that not all priests were frauds and self-seekers, but that many, even the great majority, of these that were down on the ground among the common people, were sincere and right-hearted, and devoted to the alleviation of human troubles and sufferings. Well, it was a thing which could not be helped, so I seldom fretted about it, and never many minutes at a time; it has never been my way to bother much about things which you can't cure. But I did not like it, for it was just the sort of thing to keep people reconciled to an Established Church. We *must* have a religion—it goes without saying—but my idea is, to have it cut up into forty free sects, so that they will police each other, as had been the case in the United States in my time. Concentration of power in a political machine is bad; and an Established Church is only a political machine; it was invented for that; it is nursed, cradled, preserved for that; it is an enemy to human liberty, and does no good which it could not better do in a split-up and scattered condition. That wasn't law; it wasn't gospel: it was only an opinion—my opinion, and I was only a man, one man: so it wasn't worth any more than the Pope's—or any less, for that matter.

Well, I couldn't rack the executioner, neither would I overlook the just complaint of the priests. The man must be punished some how or other, so I degraded him from his office and made him leader of the band—the new one that was to be started. He begged hard, and said he couldn't play—a plausible excuse, but too thin; there wasn't a musician in the country that could.

The queen was a good deal outraged, next morning, when she found she was going to have neither Hugo's life nor his property. But I told her she must bear this cross; that while by law and custom she certainly was entitled to both the man's life and his property, there were extenuating circumstances, and so in Arthur the king's name I had pardoned him. The deer was ravaging the man's fields, and he had killed it in sudden passion, and not for gain; and he had carried it into the royal forest in the hope that that might make detection of the misdoer impossible. Confound her, I couldn't make her see that sudden passion is an extenuating circumstance in the killing of venison—or of a person—so I gave it up and let her sulk it out. I *did* think I was going to make her see it by remarking that her own sudden passion in the case of the page modified that crime.

"Crime!" she exclaimed. "How thou talkest! Crime, forsooth! Man, I am going to *pay* for him!"

Oh, it was no use to waste sense on her. Training—training is everything; training is all there is *to* a person. We speak of nature; it is folly; there is no such thing as nature; what we call by that misleading name is merely heredity and training. We have no thoughts of our own, no opinions of our own; they are transmitted to us, trained into us. All that is original in us, and therefore fairly creditable or discreditable to us, can be covered up and hidden by the point of a cambric needle, all the rest being atoms contributed by, and inherited from, a procession of ancestors that stretches back a billion years to the Adam-clam or grasshopper or monkey from whom our race has been so tediously and ostentatiously and unprofitably developed. And as for me, all that I think about in this plodding sad pilgrimage, this pathetic drift between the eternities, is to look out and humbly live a pure and high and blameless life, and save that one microscopic atom in me that is truly *me*: the rest may land in Sheol and welcome for all I care.

No, confound her, her intellect was good, she had brains enough, but her training made her an ass—that is, from a many-centuries-later point of view. To kill the page was no crime—it was her right; and upon her right she stood, serenely and unconscious of offense. She was a result of generations of training in the unexamined and unassailed belief that the law which permitted her to kill a subject when she chose was a perfectly right and righteous one.

Well, we must give even Satan his due. She deserved a compliment for one thing; and I tried to pay it, but the words stuck in my throat. She had a right to kill the boy, but she was in no wise obliged to pay for him. That was law for some other people, but not for her. She knew quite well that she was doing a large and generous thing to pay for that lad, and that I ought in common fairness to come out with something handsome about it, but I couldn't—my mouth refused. I couldn't help seeing, in my fancy, that poor old grandam with the broken heart, and that fair young creature lying butchered, his little silken pomps and vanities laced with his golden blood. How could she *pay* for him? *Whom* could she pay? And so, well knowing that this woman, trained as she had been, deserved praise, even adulation, I was yet not able to utter it, trained as *I* had been. The best I could do was to fish up a compliment from outside, so to speak—and the pity of it was, that it was true:

"Madame, your people will adore you for this."

Quite true, but I meant to hang her for it some day, if I lived. Some of those laws were too bad, altogether too bad. A master might kill his slave for nothing: for mere spite, malice, or to pass the time—just as we have seen that the crowned head could do it with *his* slave, that is to say, anybody. A gentleman could kill a free commoner, and pay for him—cash or garden-truck. A noble could kill a noble without expense, as far as the law was concerned, but reprisals in kind were to be expected. *Any*body could kill *some*body, except the commoner and the slave; these had no privileges. If they killed, it was murder, and the law wouldn't stand murder. It made short work of the experimenter—and of his family too, if he murdered somebody who belonged up among the ornamental ranks. If a commoner gave a noble even so much as a Damiens-scratch which didn't kill or even hurt, he got Damiens's dose[7] for it just the same; they pulled him to rags and tatters with horses, and all the world came to see the show, and crack jokes, and have a good time; and some of the performances of the best people present were as tough, and as properly unprintable, as any that have been printed by the pleasant Casanova in his chapter about the dismemberment of Louis XV's poor awkward enemy.[8]

I had had enough of this grisly place by this time, and wanted to

---

7. Robert Francois Damiens (1715–57) stabbed Louis XV at Versailles, inflicting a slight wound. He was publicly tortured and then torn to pieces by horses.
8. The Italian adventurer Giacomo Girolamo Casanova (1725–98) witnessed the execution of Damiens in Paris in 1757. In his *Memoirs* he describes the event but devotes as much attention to the clandestine lovemaking going on between a couple next to him in one of the windows overlooking the square.

leave, but I couldn't, because I had something on my mind that my conscience kept prodding me about, and wouldn't let me forget. If I had the remaking of man, he wouldn't have any conscience.[9] It is one of the most disagreeable things connected with a person; and although it certainly does a great deal of good, it cannot be said to pay, in the long run; it would be much better to have less good and more comfort. Still, this is only my opinion, and I am only one man; others, with less experience, may think differently. They have a right to their view. I only stand to this: I have noticed my conscience for many years, and I know it is more trouble and bother to me than anything else I started with. I suppose that in the beginning I prized it, because we prize anything that is ours; and yet how foolish it was to think so. If we look at it in another way, we see how absurd it is: if I had an anvil in me would I prize it? Of course not. And yet when you come to think, there is no real difference between a conscience and an anvil—I mean for comfort. I have noticed it a thousand times. And you could dissolve an anvil with acids, when you couldn't stand it any longer; but there isn't any way that you can work off a conscience—at least so it will stay worked off; not that I know of, anyway.

There was something I wanted to do before leaving, but it was a disagreeable matter, and I hated to go at it. Well, it bothered me all the morning. I could have mentioned it to the old king, but what would be the use?—he was but an extinct volcano; he had been active in his time, but his fire was out, this good while, he was only a stately ash-pile, now; gentle enough, and kindly enough for my purpose, without doubt, but not usable. He was nothing, this so-called king: the queen was the only power there. And she was a Vesuvius.[1] As a favor, she might consent to warm a flock of sparrows for you, but then she might take that very opportunity to turn herself loose and bury a city. However, I reflected that as often as any other way, when you are expecting the worst, you get something that is not so bad, after all.

So I braced up and placed my matter before her royal Highness. I said I had been having a general jail-delivery at Camelot and among neighboring castles, and with her permission I would like to examine her collection, her bric-a-brac—that is to say, her prisoners. She resisted; but I was expecting that. But she finally consented. I was expecting that, too, but not so soon. That about ended my discomfort. She called her guards and torches, and we went down into the dungeons. These were down under the castle's foundations, and mainly were small cells hollowed out of the living rock. Some of these

9. Clemens' writings are full of attacks on the conscience. Huck Finn, for example, declares: "If I had a yaller dog that didn't know no more than a person's conscience does, I would pison him." See especially "The Facts Concerning the Recent Carnival of Crime in Connecticut" (1876), in which the narrator kills his conscience.

1. The famous volcano near Naples, Italy, whose ascent Clemens describes in The Innocents Abroad (1869). Volcano imagery appears a number of times in the novel.

cells had no light at all. In one of them was a woman, in foul rags, who sat on the ground, and would not answer a question, or speak a word, but only looked up at us once or twice, through a cobweb of tangled hair, as if to see what casual thing it might be that was disturbing with sound and light the meaningless dull dream that was become her life; after that, she sat bowed, with her dirt-caked fingers idly interlocked in her lap, and gave no further sign. This poor rack of bones was a woman of middle age, apparently; but only apparently; she had been there nine years, and was eighteen when she entered. She was a commoner, and had been sent here on her bridal night by Sir Breuse Sance Pité, a neighboring lord whose vassal her father was, and to which said lord she had refused what has since been called *le droit du Seigneur;*[2] and moreover, had opposed violence to violence and spilt half a gill of his almost sacred blood. The young husband had interfered at that point, believing the bride's life in danger, and had flung the noble out into the midst of the humble and trembling wedding guests, in the parlor, and left him there astonished at this strange treatment, and implacably embittered against both bride and groom. The said lord being cramped for dungeon-room had asked the queen to accommodate his two criminals, and here in her bastile they had been ever since; hither indeed, they had come before their crime was an hour old, and had never seen each other since. Here they were, kerneled like toads in the same rock; they had passed nine pitch dark years within fifty feet of each other, yet neither knew whether the other was alive or not. All the first years, their only question had been—asked with beseeching and tears that might have moved stones, in time, perhaps, but hearts are not stones: "Is he alive?" "Is she alive?" But they had never got an answer; and at last that question was not asked any more—or any other.

I wanted to see the man, after hearing all this. He was thirty-four years old, and looked sixty. He sat upon a squared block of stone, with his head bent down, his forearms resting on his knees, his long hair hanging like a fringe before his face, and he was muttering to himself. He raised his chin and looked us slowly over, in a listless dull way, blinking with the distress of the torch-light, then dropped his head and fell to muttering again and took no further notice of us. There were some pathetically suggestive dumb witnesses present. On his wrists and ancles were cicatrices, old smooth scars, and fastened to the stone on which he sat was a chain with manacles and fetters attached; but this apparatus lay idle on the ground, and was thick with rust. Chains cease to be needed after the spirit has gone out of a prisoner.

---

2. The supposed right of a nobleman to spend the wedding night with any of his female servants. In "The French and the Comanches" (in *Letters from the Earth*), Clemens says, ". . . let it go in French, it would soil the English language to describe it in that tongue." Sir Breuse Sance Pité is described in Malory as "the most mischievousest knight living" (X.i).

I could not rouse the man; so I said we would take him to her, and see—to the bride who was the fairest thing in the earth to him, once—roses, pearls and dew made flesh, for him; a wonder-work, the masterwork of nature: with eyes like no other eyes, and voice like no other voice, and a freshness, and lithe young grace, and beauty, that belonged properly to the creatures of dreams—as he thought—and to no other. The sight of her would set his stagnant blood leaping; the sight of her—

But it was a disappointment. They sat together on the ground and looked dimly wondering into each other's faces a while, with a sort of weak animal curiosity; then forgot each other's presence, and dropped their eyes, and you saw that they were away again and wandering in some far land of dreams and shadows that we know nothing about.

I had them taken out and sent to their friends. The queen did not like it much. Not that she felt any personal interest in the matter, but she thought it disrespectful to Sir Breuse Sance Pité. However, I assured her that if he found he couldn't stand it I would fix him so that he could.

I set forty-seven prisoners loose out of those awful rat-holes, and left only one in captivity. He was a lord, and had killed another lord, a sort of kinsman of the queen. That other lord had ambushed him to assassinate him, but this fellow had got the best of him and cut his throat. However, it was not for that that I left him jailed, but for maliciously destroying the only public well in one of his wretched villages. The queen was bound to hang him for killing her kinsman, but I would not allow it: it was no crime to kill an assassin. But I said I was willing to let her hang him for destroying the well; so she concluded to put up with that, as it was better than nothing.

Dear me, for what trifling offenses the most of those forty-seven men and women were shut up there! Indeed some were there for no distinct offense at all, but only to gratify somebody's spite; and not always the queen's by any means, but a friend's. The newest prisoner's crime was a mere remark which he had made. He said he believed that men were about all alike, and one man as good as another, barring clothes. He said he believed that if you were to strip the nation naked and send a stranger through the crowd, he couldn't tell the king from a quack doctor, nor a duke from a hotel clerk. Apparently here was a man whose brains had not been reduced to an ineffectual mush by idiotic training. I set him loose and sent him to the Factory.

Some of the cells carved in the living rock were just behind the face of the precipice, and in each of these an arrow-slit had been pierced outward to the daylight, and so the captive had a thin ray from the blessed sun for his comfort. The case of one of these poor fellows was particularly hard. From his dusky swallow's hole high up in that vast wall of native rock he could peer out through the arrow-slit and see his own home off yonder in the valley; and for twenty-two years he had watched it, with heart-ache and longing, through that crack. He could see the lights shine there at night, and in the daytime he could see figures go in and come out—his wife and children, some of them, no doubt, though he could not make out, at that distance. In the course of years he noted festivities there, and tried to rejoice, and wondered if they were weddings or what they might be. And he noted funerals; and they wrung his heart. He could make out the coffin, but he could not determine its size, and so could not tell whether it was wife or child. He could see the procession form, with priests and mourners, and move solemnly away, bearing the secret with them. He had left behind him five children and a wife; and in nineteen years he had seen five funerals issue, and none of them humble enough in pomp to denote a servant. So he had lost five of his treasures; there must still be one remaining—one now infinitely, unspeakably precious,—but *which* one? wife, or child? That was the question that tortured him, by night and by day, asleep and awake. Well, to have an interest, of some sort, and half a ray of light, when you are in a dungeon, is a great support to the body and preserver of the intellect. This man was in pretty good condition yet. By the time he had finished telling me his distressful tale, I was in the same state of mind that you would have been in yourself, if you have got average human curiosity: that is to say, I was as burning up as he was, to find out which member of the family it was that was left. So I took him over home myself; and an amazing kind of a surprise party it was, too—typhoons and cyclones of frantic joy, and whole Niagaras of happy tears; and by George we found the aforetime young matron graying toward the imminent verge of her half century, and the babies all men and women, and some of them married and experimenting family-wise themselves—for not a soul of the tribe was dead! Conceive of the ingenious devilishness of that queen: she had a special hatred for this prisoner, and she had *invented* all those funerals herself, to scorch his heart with; and the sublimest stroke of genius of the whole thing was leaving the family-invoice a funeral *short*, so as to let him wear his poor old soul out guessing.

But for me, he never would have got out. Morgan le Fay hated him with her whole heart, and she never would have softened toward him. And yet his crime was committed more in thoughtlessness than deliberate depravity. He had said she had red hair. Well, she had; but that was no way to speak of it. When red-headed people are above a certain social grade, their hair is auburn.

Consider it: among these forty-seven captives, there were five whose names, offences and dates of incarceration were no longer known! One woman and four men—all bent, and wrinkled, and mind-extinguished patriarchs. They themselves had long ago forgotten these details; at any rate they had mere vague theories about them, nothing definite and nothing that they repeated twice in the same way. The succession of priests whose office it had been to pray daily with the captives and remind them that God had put them there, for some wise purpose or other, and teach them that patience, humbleness, and submission to oppression was what He loved to see in parties of a subordinate rank, had traditions about these poor old human ruins, but nothing more. These traditions went but little way, for they concerned the length of the incarceration only, and not the names or the offences. And even by the help of tradition the only thing that could be proven was that none of the five had seen daylight for thirty-five years: how much longer this privation had lasted was not guessable. The king and the queen knew nothing about these poor creatures, except that they were heirlooms, assets inherited, along with the throne, from the former firm. Nothing of their history had been transmitted with their persons, and so the inheriting owners had considered them of no value, and had felt no interest in them. I said to the queen—

"Then why in the world didn't you set them free?"

The question was a puzzler. She didn't know *why* she hadn't; the thing had never come up in her mind. So here she was, forecasting the veritable history of future prisoners of the castle d'If,[3] without knowing it. It seemed plain to me now, that with her training, those inherited prisoners were merely property—nothing more, nothing less. Well, when we inherit property, it does not occur to us to throw it away, even when we do not value it.

When I brought my procession of human bats up into the open world and the glare of the afternoon sun—previously blind-folding them, in charity for eyes so long untortured by light—they were a spectacle to look at. Skeletons, scarecrows, goblins, pathetic frights, every one: legitimatest possible children of Monarchy by the Grace of God and the Established Church. I muttered absently—

"I *wish* I could photograph them!"

You have seen that kind of people who will never let on that they don't know the meaning of a new big word. The more ignorant they are, the more pitifully certain they are to pretend you haven't shot over their heads. The queen was just one of that sort, and was always making the stupidest blunders by reason of it. She hesitated a moment; then her face brightened up with sudden comprehension, and she said she would do it for me.

I thought to myself: She? why what can she know about photography? But it was a poor time to be thinking. When I looked around, she was moving on the procession with an axe!

Well, she certainly was a curious one, was Morgan le Fay. I have

3. State prison on a small, rocky island near the harbor of Marseilles, France. The hero of Alexandre Dumas' *The Count of Monte Cristo* (1844) was a prisoner there. Clemens described the dungeon in Chapter XI of *The Innocents Abroad*. To Tom Sawyer it was "the castle Deef."

seen a good many kinds of women in my time, but she laid over them all, for variety. And how sharply characteristic of her this episode was. She had no more idea than a horse, of how to photograph a procession; but being in doubt, it was just like her to try to do it with an axe.

## Chapter XIX

### KNIGHT ERRANTRY AS A TRADE

Sandy and I were on the road again, next morning, bright and early. It was so good to open up one's lungs and take in whole luscious barrels-full of the blessed God's untainted, dew-freshened, woodland-scented air once more, after suffocating body and mind for two days and nights in the moral and physical stenches of that intolerable old buzzard-roost! I mean, for me: of course the place was all right and agreeable enough for Sandy, for she had been used to high life all her days.

Poor girl, her jaws had had a wearisome rest, now for a while, and I was expecting to get the consequences. I was right; but she had stood by me most helpfully in the castle, and had mightily supported and reinforced me with gigantic foolishnesses which were worth more for the occasion than wisdoms double their size; so I thought she had earned a right to work her mill for a while, if she wanted to, and I felt not a pang when she started it up:

"Now turn we unto Sir Marhaus that rode with the damsel of thirty winter of age southward—"

"Are you going to see if you can work up another half-stretch on the trail of the cowboys, Sandy?"

"Even so, fair my lord."

"Go ahead, then. I won't interrupt this time, if I can help it. Begin over again; start fair, and shake out all your reefs, and I will load my pipe and give good attention."

"Now turn we unto Sir Marhaus that rode with the damsel of thirty winter of age southward. And so they came into a deep forest, and by fortune they were nighted, and rode along in a deep way, and at the last they came into a courtelage where abode the duke of South Marches, and there they asked harbour. And on the morn the duke sent unto Sir Marhaus, and bad him make him ready. And so Sir Marhaus arose and armed him, and there was a mass sung afore him, and he brake his fast, and so mounted on horseback in the court of the castle, there they should do the battle. So there was the duke already on horseback, clean armed, and his six sons by him, and every each had a spear in his hand, and so they encountered, whereas the duke and his two sons brake their spears upon him, but Sir Marhaus held up his spear and touched none of them. Then came the four sons by couples, and two of them brake their spears, and so did the other two. And all this while Sir Marhaus touched them not. Then Sir Marhaus ran to the duke, and smote him with his spear that horse and man fell to the earth. And so he served his sons. And then Sir Marhaus alight down, and bad the duke yield him or else he would slay him. And then some of his sons recovered, and would have set upon Sir Marhaus. Then Sir Marhaus said to the duke, Cease thy sons, or else I will do the uttermost to you all. When the duke saw he might not escape the death, he cried to his sons, and charged them to yield them to Sir Marhaus. And they kneeled all down and put the pommels of their swords to the knight, and so he received them. And then they holp up their father, and so by their common assent promised unto Sir Marhaus never to be foes unto King Arthur, and thereupon at Whitsuntide after, to come he and his sons, and put them in the king's grace.[4]

"Even so standeth the history, fair Sir Boss. Now ye shall wit that that very duke and his six sons are they whom but few days past you also did overcome and send to Arthur's court!"

"Why, Sandy, you can't mean it!"

"An I speak not sooth, let it be the worse for me."

"Well, well, well,—now who would ever have thought it? One whole duke and six dukelets; why, Sandy it was an elegant haul. Knight-errantry is a most chuckle-headed trade, and it is tedious hard work, too, but I begin to see that there *is* money in it, after all, if you have luck. Not that I would ever engage in it as a business; for I wouldn't. No sound and legitimate business can be established on a basis of speculation. A successful whirl in the knight-errantry line— now what is it when you blow away the nonsense and come down to the cold facts? It's just a corner in pork,[5] that's all, and you can't make anything else out of it. You're rich—yes,—suddenly rich—for about a day, maybe a week; then somebody corners the market on *you*, and down goes your bucket-shop; ain't that so, Sandy?"

"Whethersoever it be that my mind miscarrieth, bewraying simple language in such sort that the words do seem to come endlong and overthwart—"

"There's no use in beating about the bush and trying to get around it that way, Sandy, it's *so*, just as I say. I *know* it's so. And, moreover, when you come right down to the bed-rock, knight-errantry is *worse* than pork; for whatever happens, the pork's left, and so somebody's benefited, anyway; but when the market breaks, in a knight-errantry whirl, and every knight in the pool passes in his checks, what have you got for assets? Just a rubbish-pile of battered corpses and a barrel or two of busted hardware. Can you call *those* assets? Give me pork, every time. Am I right?"

---

4. The story is borrowed, language and all, from the *Morte d'Arthur*. [*Clemens' note.*] It is from Malory, IV.xxiv–xxv.

5. Morgan humorously adopts the language of the stock market.

"Ah, peradventure my head being distraught by the manifold matters whereunto the confusions of these but late adventured haps and fortunings whereby not I alone nor you alone, but every each of us, meseemeth—"

"No, it's not your head, Sandy. Your head's all right, as far as it goes, but you don't know business; that's where the trouble is. It unfits you to argue about business, and you're wrong to be always trying. However, that aside, it was a good haul, anyway, and will breed a handsome crop of reputation in Arthur's court. And speaking of the cow-boys, what a curious country this is for women and men that never get old. Now there's Morgan le Fay, as fresh and young as a Vassar pullet,[6] to all appearances, and here is this old duke of the South Marches still slashing away with sword and lance at his time of life, after raising such a family as he has raised. As I understand it, Sir Gawaine killed seven of his sons, and still he had six left for Sir Marhaus and me to take into camp. And then there was that damsel of sixty winter of age still excursioning around in her frosty bloom— How old are you, Sandy?"

It was the first time I ever struck a still place in her. The mill had shut down for repairs, or something.

## Chapter XX

### THE OGRE'S CASTLE

Between six and nine we made ten miles, which was plenty for a horse carrying triple—man, woman, and armor; then we stopped for a long nooning, under some trees by a limpid brook.

Right so came bye and bye a knight riding; and as he drew near he made dolorous moan, and by the words of it I perceived that he was cursing and swearing; yet nevertheless was I glad of his coming, for that I saw he bore a bulletin-board whereon in letters all of shining gold was writ—

"Use Peterson's Prophylactic Tooth-Brush
—All the Go."

I was glad of his coming, for even by this token I knew him for knight of mine. It was Sir Madok de la Montaine, a burly great fellow whose chief distinction was that he had come within an ace of sending Sir Launcelot down over his horse-tail once.[7] He was never long in a stranger's presence without finding some pretext or other to let out that great fact. But there was another fact of nearly the same size, which he never pushed upon anybody unasked, and yet never withheld when

6. Clemens had visited the Poughkeepsie, N.Y., women's college in 1885 and was much taken with its students.

7. Their encounter is recorded in Malory, IX.xxviii, though there is no indication that Sir Launcelot fared so poorly as Morgan claims.

asked: that was, that the reason he didn't quite succeed was, that he was interrupted and sent down over horse-tail himself. This innocent vast lubber did not see any particular difference between the two facts. I liked him, for he was earnest in his work, and very valuable. And he was so fine to look at, with his broad mailed shoulders, and the grand leonine set of his plumed head, and his big shield with its quaint device of a gauntleted hand clutching a prophylactic tooth-brush, with motto: *"Try Noyoudont."* This was a toothwash that I was introducing.

He was aweary, he said, and indeed he looked it; but he would not alight. He said he was after the stove-polish man; and with this he broke out cursing and swearing anew. The bulletin-boarder referred to was Sir Ossaise of Surluse, a brave knight, and of considerable celebrity on account of his having tried conclusions in a tournament, once, with no less a Mogul than Sir Gaheris himself[8]—although not successfully. He was of a light and laughing disposition, and to him nothing in this world was serious. It was for this reason that I had chosen him to work up a stove-polish sentiment. There were no stoves yet, and so there could be nothing serious about stove-polish. All that the agent needed to do was to deftly and by degrees prepare the public for the great change, and have them established in predilections toward neatness against the time when the stove should appear upon the stage.

Sir Madok was very bitter, and brake out anew with cursing. He said he had cursed his soul to rags; and yet he would not get down from his horse, neither would he take any rest, or listen to any comfort, until he should have found Sir Ossaise and settled this account. It appeared, by what I could piece together of the unprofane fragments of his statement, that he had chanced upon Sir Ossaise at dawn of the morning, and been told that if he would make a short cut across the fields and swamps and broken hills and glades, he could head off a company of travelers who would be rare customers for prophylactics and toothwash. With characteristic zeal Sir Madok had plunged away at once upon this quest, and after three hours of awful crosslot riding had overhauled his game. And behold, it was the five patriarchs that had been released from the dungeons the evening before! Poor old creatures, it was all of twenty years since any one of them had known what it was to be equipped with any remaining snag or remnant of a tooth.

"Blank-blank-blank him," said Sir Madok, "an I do not stove-polish him an I may find him, leave it to me; for never no knight that hight Ossaise or aught else may do me this disservice and bide on live, an I may find him, the which I have thereunto sworn a great oath this day."

And with these words, and others, he lightly took his spear and gat him thence. In the middle of the afternoon we came upon one of those

8. Their fight is recorded in Malory, X. xlviii.

very patriarchs ourselves, in the edge of a poor village. He was basking in the love of relatives and friends whom he had not seen for fifty years; and about him and caressing him were also descendants of his own body whom he had never seen at all till now; but to him these were all strangers, his memory was gone, his mind was stagnant. It seemed incredible that a man could outlast half a century shut up in a dark hole like a rat, but here were his old wife and some old comrades to testify to it. They could remember him as he was in the freshness and strength of his young manhood, when he kissed his child and delivered it to its mother's hands and went away into that long oblivion. The people at the castle could not tell within half a generation the length of time the man had been shut up there for his unrecorded and forgotten offence; but this old wife knew; and so did her old child, who stood there among her married sons and daughters trying to realize a father who had been to her a name, a thought, a formless image, a tradition, all her life, and now was suddenly concreted into actual flesh and blood and set before her face.

It was a curious situation; yet it is not on that account that I have made room for it here, but on account of a thing which seemed to me still more curious. To-wit, that this dreadful matter brought from these down-trodden people no outburst of rage against their oppressors. They had been heritors and subjects of cruelty and outrage so long that nothing could have startled them but a kindness. Yes, here was a curious revelation indeed, of the depth to which this people had been sunk in slavery. Their entire being was reduced to a monotonous dead level of patience, resignation, dumb uncomplaining acceptance of whatever might befal them in this life. Their very imagination was dead. When you can say that of a man, he has struck bottom, I reckon; there is no lower deep for him.

I rather wished I had gone some other road. This was not the sort of experience for a statesman to encounter who was planning out a peaceful revolution in his mind. For it could not help bringing up the un-get-aroundable fact that, all gentle cant and philosophising to the contrary notwithstanding, no people in the world ever did achieve their freedom by goody-goody talk and moral suasion; it being immutable law that all revolutions that will succeed, must *begin* in blood, whatever may answer afterward. If history teaches anything, it teaches that. What this folk needed, then, was a Reign of Terror and a guillotine, and I was the wrong man for them.

Two days later, toward noon. Sandy began to show signs of excitement and feverish expectancy. She said we were approaching the ogre's castle. I was surprised into an uncomfortable shock. The object of our quest had gradually dropped out of my mind; this sudden resurrection of it made it seem quite a real and startling thing, for a moment, and roused up in me a smart interest. Sandy's excitement increased every moment; and so did mine, for that sort of thing is catching. My heart got to thumping. You can't reason with your heart; it has its own laws, and thumps about things which the intellect scorns. Presently, when Sandy slid from the horse, motioned me to stop, and went creeping stealthily, with her head bent nearly to her knees, toward a row of bushes that bordered a declivity, the thumpings grew stronger and quicker. And they kept it up while she was gaining her ambush and getting her glimpse over the declivity; and also while I was creeping to her side on my knees. Her eyes were burning, now, as she pointed with her finger, and said in a panting whisper—

"The castle! The castle! Lo, where it looms!"

What a welcome disappointment I experienced! I said—

"Castle? It is nothing but a pig-sty; a pig-sty with a wattled fence around it."[9]

She looked surprised and distressed. The animation faded out of her face; and during many moments she was lost in thought and silent. Then—

"It was not enchanted aforetime," she said in a musing fashion, as if to herself. "And how strange is this marvel, and how awful—that to the one perception it is enchanted and dight in a base and shameful aspect; yet to the perception of the other it is not enchanted, hath suffered no change, but stands firm and stately still, girt with its moat and waving its banners in the blue air from its towers. And God shield us, how it pricks the heart to see again these gracious captives, and the sorrow deepened in their sweet faces. We have tarried long, and are to blame."

I saw my cue. The castle was enchanted to *me*, not to her. It would be wasted time to try to argue her out of her delusion, it couldn't be done; I must just humor it. So I said—

"This is a common case—the enchanting of a thing to one eye and leaving it in its proper form to another. You have heard of it before, Sandy, though you haven't happened to experience it. But no harm is done. In fact it is lucky the way it is. If these ladies were hogs to everybody and to themselves, it would be necessary to break the enchantment, and that might be impossible if one failed to find out the particular process of the enchantment. And hazardous, too; for in attempting a disenchantment without the true key, you are liable to err, and turn your hogs into dogs, and the dogs into cats, the cats into rats, and so on, and end by reducing your materials to nothing, finally, or to an odorless gas which you can't follow—which of course amounts to the same things. But here, by good luck, no one's eyes but mine are under the enchantment and so it is of no consequence to dissolve it. These ladies remain ladies to you, and to themselves, and

9. Compare Tom Sawyer's seeing diamonds, Arabs, elephants, and soldiers where Huck sees only a Sunday School picnic (*Huckleberry Finn*, Ch. III). Both passages suggest Cervantes' *Don Quixote* (1605, 1615), to which Tom specifically refers.

to everybody else; and at the same time they will suffer in no way from my delusion, for when I know that an ostensible hog is a lady, that is enough for me, I know how to treat her."

"Thanks, oh sweet my lord, thou talkest like an angel. And I know that thou wilt deliver them, for that thou art minded to great deeds and art as strong a knight of your hands and as brave to will and to do, as any that is on live."

"I will not leave a princess in the sty, Sandy. Are those three yonder that to my disordered eyes are starveling swineherds—"

"The ogres? Are *they* changed also? It is most wonderful. Now am I fearful; for how canst thou strike with sure aim when five of their nine cubits of stature are to thee invisible? Ah, go warily, fair sir; this is a mightier emprise than I wend."

"You be easy, Sandy. All I need to know is, how *much* of an ogre is invisible; then I know how to locate his vitals. Don't you be afraid, I will make short work of these bunco-steerers. Stay where you are."

I left Sandy kneeling there, corpse-faced but plucky and hopeful, and rode down to the pig-sty, and struck up a trade with the swineherds. I won their gratitude by buying out all the hogs at the lump sum of sixteen pennies, which was rather above latest quotations. I was just in time; for the Church, the lord of the manor, and the rest of the tax gatherers would have been along next day and swept off pretty much all the stock, leaving the swineherds very short of hogs and Sandy out of princesses. But now the tax people could be paid in cash, and there would be a stake left besides. One of the men had ten children; and he said that last year when a priest came and of his ten pigs took the fattest one for tithes, the wife burst out upon him, and offered him a child and said—

"Thou beast without bowels of mercy, why leave me my child, yet rob me of the wherewithal to feed it?"

How curious. The same thing had happened in the Wales of my day,[1] under this same old Established Church, which was supposed by many to have changed its nature when it changed its disguise.

I sent the three men away, and then opened the sty gate and beckoned Sandy to come—which she did; and not leisurely, but with the rush of a prairie-fire. And when I saw her fling herself upon those hogs, with tears of joy running down her cheeks, and strain them to her heart, and kiss them, and caress them, and call them reverently by grand princely names, I was ashamed of her, ashamed of the human race.[2]

1. Morgan is apparently referring to the 1886 Welsh protests against tithes levied by the church. He had earlier recorded in his notebook the incident involving the farmer's wife and the priest (*Notebooks & Journals*, 3:265-66), as something which had recently happened in Wales.

2. Compare Huck Finn's "It was enough to make a body ashamed of the human race" (Ch. XXIV).

We had to drive those hogs home—ten miles; and no ladies were ever more fickle-minded or contrary. They would stay in no road, no path; they broke out through the brush on all sides, and flowed away in all directions, over rocks, and hills, and the roughest places they could find. And they must not be struck, or roughly accosted; Sandy could not bear to see them treated in ways unbecoming their rank. The troublesomest old sow of the lot had to be called my Lady, and your Highness, like the rest. It is annoying and difficult to scour around after hogs, in armor. There was one small countess, with an iron ring in her snout and hardly any hair on her back, that was the devil for perversity. She gave me a race of an hour, over all sorts of country, and then we were right where we had started from, having made not a rod of real progress. I seized her at last by the tail, and brought her along, squealing. When I overtook Sandy, she was horrified, and said it was in the last degree indelicate to drag a countess by her train.

We got the hogs home just at dark—most of them. The princess Nerovens de Morganore was missing, and two of her ladies in waiting: namely, Miss Angela Bohun, and the Demoiselle Elaine Courte-mains, the former of these two being a young black sow with a white star in her forehead, and the latter a brown one with thin legs and a slight limp in the forward shank on the starboard side—a couple of the tryingest blisters to drive, that I ever saw. Also among the missing were several mere baronesses—and I wanted them to stay missing; but no, all that sausage-meat had to be found; so, servants were sent out with torches to scour the woods and hills to that end.

Of course the whole drove was housed in the house, and great guns!—well, I never saw anything like it. Nor ever heard anything like it. And never smelt anything like it. It was like an insurrection in a gasometer.[3]

## Chapter XXI

### THE PILGRIMS

When I did get to bed at last I was unspeakably tired; the stretching out, and the relaxing of the long-tense muscles, how luxurious, how delicious! but that was as far as I could get—sleep was out of the question, for the present. The ripping and tearing and squealing of the nobility up and down the halls and corridors was pandemonium come again, and kept me broad awake. Being awake, my thoughts were busy, of course; and mainly they busied themselves with Sandy's curious delusion. Here she was, as sane a person as the kingdom could produce; and yet from my point of view she was acting like a crazy woman. My land, the power of training! of influence! of education! It

---

3. Laboratory instrument for measuring gas.

can bring a body up to believe anything. I had to put myself in Sandy's place to realize that she was not a lunatic. Yes, and put her in mine, to demonstrate how easy it is to seem a lunatic to a person who has not been taught as you have been taught. If I had told Sandy I had seen a wagon, uninfluenced by enchantment, spin along fifty miles an hour; had seen a man, unequipped with magic powers, get into a basket and soar out of sight among the clouds; and had listened, without any necromancer's help, to the conversation of a person who was several hundred miles away, Sandy would not merely have supposed me to be crazy, she would have thought she knew it. Everybody around her believed in enchantments; nobody had any doubts; to doubt that a castle could be turned into a sty, and its occupants into hogs, would have been the same as my doubting, among Connecticut people, the actuality of the telephone and its wonders,—and in both cases would be absolute proof of a diseased mind, an unsettled reason. Yes, Sandy was sane; that must be admitted. If I also would be sane—to Sandy—I must keep my superstitions about unenchanted and unmiraculous locomotives, balloons and telephones, to myself. Also, I believed that the world was not flat, and hadn't pillars under it to support it, nor a canopy over it to turn off a universe of water that occupied all space above: but as I was the only person in the kingdom afflicted with such impious and criminal opinions, I recognized that it would be good wisdom to keep quiet about this matter, too, if I did not wish to be suddenly shunned and forsaken by everybody as a madman.

The next morning Sandy assembled the swine in the dining room and gave them their breakfast, waiting upon them personally and manifesting in every way the deep reverence which the natives of her island, ancient and modern, have always felt for rank, let its outward casket and the mental and moral contents be what they may. I could have eaten with the hogs if I had had birth approaching my lofty official rank; but I hadn't, and so accepted the unavoidable slight and made no complaint. Sandy and I had our breakfast at the second table. The family were not at home. I said:

"How many are in the family, Sandy, and where do they keep themselves?"

"Family?"

"Yes."

"Which family, good my lord?"

"Why, this family; your own family."

"Sooth to say, I understand you not. I have no family."

"No family? Why, Sandy, isn't this your home?"

"Now how indeed might that be? I have no home."

"Well, then, whose house is this?"

"Ah, wit you well I would tell you an I knew myself."

"Come—you don't even know these people? Then who invited us

here?"

"None invited us. We but came; that is all."

"Why, woman, this is a most extraordinary performance. The effrontery of it is beyond admiration. We blandly march into a man's house, and cram it full of the only really valuable nobility the sun has yet discovered in the earth, and then it turns out that we don't even know the man's name. How did you ever venture to take this extravagant liberty? I supposed, of course, it was your home. What will the man say?"

"What will he say? Forsooth what can he say but give thanks?"

"Thanks for what?"

Her face was filled with a puzzled surprise:

"Verily, thou troublest mine understanding with strange words. Do ye dream that one of his estate is like to have the honor twice in his life to entertain company such as we have brought to grace his house withal?"

"Well, no—when you come to that. No, it's an even bet that this is the first time he has had a treat like this."

"Then let him be thankful, and manifest the same by grateful speech and due humility; he were a dog, else, and the heir and ancestor of dogs."

To my mind, the situation was uncomfortable. It might become more so. It might be a good idea to muster the hogs and move on. So I said:

"The day is wasting, Sandy. It is time to get the nobility together and be moving."

"Wherefore, fair sir and Boss?"

"We want to take them to their home, don't we?"

"La, but list to him! They be of all the regions of the earth! Each must hie to her own home; wend you we might do all these journeys in one so brief life as He hath appointed that created life, and thereto death likewise with help of Adam,[4] who by sin done through persuasion of his helpmeet, she being wrought upon and bewrayed by the beguilements of the great enemy of man, that serpent hight Satan, aforetime consecrated and set apart unto that evil work by overmastering spite and envy begotten in his heart through fell ambitions that did blight and mildew a nature erst so white and pure whenso it hove with the shining multitudes its brethren-born in glade and shade of that fair heaven wherein all such as native be to that rich estate and——"

"Great Scott!"

"My lord?"

"Well, you know we haven't got time for this sort of thing. Don't you see, we could distribute these people around the earth in less time

---

4. The story of Adam, Eve, and the serpent, told in Genesis 3, was one to which Clemens returned again and again in his writings. Sandy's version is more Miltonic than Biblical.

than it is going to take you to explain that we can't. We mustn't talk now, we must act. You want to be careful; you mustn't let your mill get the start of you that way, at a time like this. To business, now—and sharp's the word. Who is to take the aristocracy home?"

"Even their friends. These will come for them from the far parts of the earth."

This was lightning from a clear sky, for unexpectedness; and the relief of it was like pardon to a prisoner. She would remain to deliver the goods, of course.

Well, then, Sandy, as our enterprise is handsomely and successfully ended, I will go home and report; and if ever another one—"

"I also am ready; I will go with thee."

This was recalling the pardon.

"How? You will go with me? Why should you?"

"Will I be traitor to my knight, dost think? That were dishonor. I may not part from thee until in knightly encounter in the field some overmatching champion shall fairly win and fairly wear me. I were to blame an I thought that that might ever hap."

"Elected for the long term," I sighed to myself. "I may as well make the best of it." So then I spoke up and said:

"All right; let us make a start."

While she was gone to cry her farewells over the pork, I gave that whole peerage away to the servants. And I asked them to take a duster and dust around a little where the nobilites had mainly lodged and promenaded, but they considered that that would be hardly worth while, and would moreover be a rather grave departure from custom, and therefore likely to make talk. A departure from custom—that settled it; it was a nation capable of committing any crime but that. The servants said they would follow the fashion, a fashion grown sacred through immemorial observance: they would scatter fresh rushes in all the rooms and halls, and then the evidence of the aristocratic visitation would be no longer visible. It was a kind of satire on Nature; it was the scientific method, the geologic method; it deposited the history of the family in a stratified record; and the antiquary could dig through it and tell by the remains of each period what change of diet the family had introduced successively for a hundred years.

The first thing we struck that day was a procession of pilgrims. It was not going our way, but we joined it nevertheless; for it was hourly being borne in upon me, now, that if I would govern this country wisely, I must be posted in the details of its life, and not at second hand but by personal observation and scrutiny.

This company of pilgrims resembled Chaucer's[5] in this: that it had in it a sample of about all the upper occupations and professions the

---

5. *The Canterbury Tales* (begun 1386) of Geof-  don to Canterbury by a varied group drawn from
frey Chaucer describe a pilgrimage from Lon-  different ranks of society.

country could show, and a corresponding variety of costume. There were young men and old men, young women and old women, lively folk and grave folk. They rode upon mules and horses, and there was not a side-saddle in the party; for this specialty was to remain unknown in England for nine hundred years yet.

It was a pleasant, friendly, sociable herd; pious, happy, merry, and full of unconscious coarsenesses and innocent indecencies.[6] What they regarded as the merry tale went the continual round and caused no more embarrassment than it would have caused in the best English society twelve centuries later. Practical jokes worthy of the English wits of the first quarter of the far-off nineteenth century were sprung here and there and yonder along the line, and compelled the delight-edest applause; and sometimes when a bright remark was made at one end of the procession and started on its travels toward the other, you could note its progress all the way by the sparkling spray of laughter it threw off from its bows as it plowed along; and also by the blushes of the mules in its wake.

Sandy knew the goal and purpose of this pilgrimage and she posted me. She said:

"They journey to the Valley of Holiness, for to be blessed of the godly hermits and drink of the miraculous waters and be cleansed from sin."

"Where is this watering place?"

"It lieth a two day journey hence, by the borders of the land that hight the Cuckoo Kingdom."

"Tell me about it. Is it a celebrated place?"

"Oh, of a truth, yes. There be none more so. Of old time there lived there an abbot and his monks. Belike were none in the world more holy than these; for they gave themselves to study of pious books, and spoke not the one to the other, or indeed to any, and ate decayed herbs and naught thereto, and slept hard, and prayed much, and washed never; also they wore the same garment until it fell from their bodies through age and decay. Right so came they to be known of all the world by reason of these holy austerities, and visited by rich and poor, and reverenced."

"Proceed."

"But always there was lack of water there. Whereas, upon a time, the holy abbot prayed, and for answer a great stream of clear water burst forth by miracle in a desert place. Now were the fickle monks tempted of the Fiend, and they wrought with their abbot unceasingly by beggings and beseechings that he would construct a bath; and when he was become aweary and might not resist more, he said have ye your will, then, and granted that they asked. Now mark thou what 'tis to

6. Again we see Morgan's discomfort with the kind of talk that Clemens revelled in when he wrote *1601*.

forsake the ways of purity the which He loveth, and wanton with such as be worldly and an offense. These monks did enter into the bath and come thence washed as white as snow; and lo, in that moment His sign appeared, in miraculous rebuke! for His insulted waters ceased to flow, and utterly vanished away."

"They fared mildly, Sandy, considering how that kind of crime is regarded in this country."

"Belike; but it was their first sin; and they had been of perfect life for long, and differing in naught from the angels. Prayers, tears, torturings of the flesh, all was vain to beguile that water to flow again. Even processions; even burnt offerings; even votive candles to the Virgin, did fail every each of them; and all in the land did marvel."

"How odd to find that even this industry has its financial panics, and at times sees its assignats and greenbacks languish to zero, and everything come to a standstill. Go on, Sandy."

"And so upon a time, after year and day, the good abbot made humble surrender and destroyed the bath. And behold, His anger was in that moment appeased, and the waters gushed richly forth again, and even unto this day they have not ceased to flow in that generous measure."

"Then I take it nobody has washed since."

"He that would essay it could have his halter free; yea, and swiftly would he need it, too."

"The community has prospered since?"

"Even from that very day. The fame of the miracle went abroad into all lands. From every land came monks to join; they came even as the fishes come, in shoals; and the monastery added building to building, and yet others to these, and so spread wide its arms and took them in. And nuns came, also; and more again, and yet more; and built over against the monastery on the yon side of the vale, and added building to building, until mighty was that nunnery. And these were friendly unto those, and they joined their loving labors together, and together they built a fair great foundling asylum midway of the valley between."

"You spoke of some hermits, Sandy."

"These have gathered there from the ends of the earth. A hermit thriveth best where there be multitudes of pilgrims. Ye shall not find no hermit of no sort wanting. If any shall mention a hermit of a kind he thinketh new and not to be found but in some far strange land, let him but scratch among the holes and caves and swamps that line that Valley of Holiness, and whatsoever be his breed, it skills not, he shall find a sample of it there."

I closed up alongside of a burly fellow with a fat good-humored face, purposing to make myself agreeable and pick up some further crumbs of fact; but I had hardly more than scraped acquaintance with him when he began eagerly and awkwardly to lead up, in the immemorial way, to that same old anecdote—the one Sir Dinadan told me, what time I got into trouble with Sir Sagramore and was challenged of him on account of it. I excused myself and dropped to the rear of the procession, sad at heart, willing to go hence from this troubled life, this vale of tears, this brief day of broken rest, of cloud and storm, of weary struggle and monotonous defeat; and yet shrinking from the change, as remembering how long eternity is, and how many have wended thither who know that anecdote.

Early in the afternoon we overtook another procession of pilgrims; but in this one was no merriment, no jokes, no laughter, no playful ways, nor any happy giddiness, whether of youth or age. Yet both were here, both age and youth; gray old men and women, strong men and women of middle age, young husbands, young wives, little boys and girls, and three babies at the breast. Even the children were smileless; there was not a face among all these half a hundred people but was cast down, and bore that set expression of hopelessness which is bred of long and hard trials and old acquaintance with despair. They were slaves.[7] Chains led from their fettered feet and their manacled hands to a sole-leather belt about their waists; and all except the children were also linked together in a file, six feet apart, by a single chain which led from collar to collar all down the line. They were on foot, and had tramped three hundred miles in eighteen days, upon the cheapest odds and ends of food, and stingy rations of that. They had slept in these chains every night, bundled together like swine. They had upon their bodies some poor rags, but they could not be said to be clothed. Their irons had chafed the skin from their ankles and made sores which were ulcerated and wormy. Their naked feet were torn, and none walked without a limp. Originally there had been a hundred of these unfortunates, but about half had been sold on the trip. The trader in charge of them rode a horse and carried a whip with a short handle and a long heavy lash divided into several knotted tails at the end. With this whip he cut the shoulders of any that tottered from weariness and pain, and straitened them up. He did not speak, the whip conveyed his desire without that. None of these poor creatures looked up as we rode along by; they showed no consciousness of our presence. And they made no sound but one; that was the dull and awful clank of their chains from end to end of the long file, as forty-three burdened feet rose and fell in unison. The file moved in a cloud of its own making.

All these faces were gray with a coating of dust. One has seen the like of this coating upon furniture in unoccupied houses, and has written his idle thought in it with his finger. I was reminded of this

7. The description following owes something to *Slavery in the United States: A Narrative of* the *Life and Adventures of Charles Ball, A Black Man*. (1837).

when I noticed the faces of some of those women, young mothers carrying babes that were near to death and freedom, how a something in their hearts was written in the dust upon their faces, plain to see, and lord how plain to read! for it was the track of tears. One of these young mothers was but a girl, and it hurt me to the heart to read that writing, and reflect that it was come up out of the breast of such a child, a breast that ought not to know trouble yet, but only the gladness of the morning of life; and no doubt—

She reeled just then, giddy with fatigue, and down came the lash and flicked a flake of skin from her naked shoulder. It stung me as if I had been hit instead. The master halted the file and jumped from his horse. He stormed and swore at this girl, and said she had made annoyance enough with her laziness, and as this was the last chance he should have, he would settle the account now. She dropped on her knees and put up her hands and began to beg and cry and implore, in a passion of terror, but the master gave no attention. He snatched the child from her, and then made the men-slaves who were chained before and behind her throw her on the ground and hold her there and expose her body; and then he laid on with his lash like a madman till her back was flayed, she shrieking and struggling the while, piteously. One of the men who was holding her turned away his face, and for this humanity he was reviled and flogged.

All our pilgrims looked on and commented—on the expert way in which the whip was handled. They were too much hardened by lifelong every-day familiarity with slavery to notice that there was anything else in the exhibition that invited comment. This was what slavery could do, in the way of ossifying what one may call the superior lobe of human feeling; for these pilgrims were kindhearted people, and they would not have allowed that man to treat a horse like that.

I wanted to stop the whole thing and set the slaves free, but that would not do. I must not interfere too much and get myself a name for riding over the country's laws and the citizen's rights roughshod. If I lived and prospered I would be the death of slavery, that I was resolved upon; but I would try to fix it so that when I became its executioner it should be by command of the nation.

Just here was the wayside shop of a smith; and now arrived a landed proprietor who had bought this girl a few miles back, deliverable here where her irons could be taken off. They were removed; then there was a squabble between the gentleman and the dealer as to which should pay the blacksmith. The moment the girl was delivered from her irons, she flung herself, all tears and frantic sobbings, into the arms of the slave who had turned away his face when she was whipped. He strained her to his breast, and smothered her face and the child's with kisses, and washed them with the rain of his tears. I suspected. I inquired. Yes, I was right: it was husband and wife. They had to be torn apart by force; the girl had to be dragged away, and she struggled and fought and shrieked like one gone mad till a turn of the road hid her from sight; and even after that, we could still make out the fading plaint of those receding shrieks. And the husband and father, with his wife and child gone, never to be seen by him again in life?—well, the look of him one might not bear at all, and so I turned away; but I knew I should never get his picture out of my mind again, and there it is to this day, to wring my heart-strings whenever I think of it.

We put up at the inn in a village just at nightfall, and when I rose next morning and looked abroad, I was ware where a knight came riding in the golden glory of the new day, and recognized him for knight of mine—Sir Ozana le Cure Hardy. He was in the gentlemen's furnishing line, and his missionarying specialty was plug hats. He was clothed all in steel, in the beautifulest armor of the time—up to where his helmet ought to have been; but he hadn't any helmet, he wore a shiny stove-pipe hat, and was as ridiculous a spectacle as one might want to see. It was another of my surreptitious schemes for extinguishing knighthood by making it grotesque and absurd. Sir Ozana's saddle was hung about with leather hat-boxes, and every time he overcame a wandering knight he swore him into my service and fitted him with a plug and made him wear it. I dressed and ran down to welcome Sir Ozana and get his news.

"How is trade?" I asked.

"Ye will note that I have but these four left; yet were they sixteen whenas I got me from Camelot."

"Why, you have certainly done nobly, Sir Ozana. Where have you been foraging of late?"

"I am but now come from the Valley of Holiness, please you sir."

"I am pointed for that place myself. Is there anything stirring in the monkery, more than common?"

"By the mass ye may not question it! . . . Give him good feed, boy, and stint it not, an thou valuest thy crown; so get ye lightly to the stable and do even as I bid. . . . . . Sir, it is parlous news I bring, and— be these pilgrims? Then ye may not do better, good folk, than gather and hear the tale I have to tell, sith it concerneth you, forasmuch as ye go to find that ye will not find, and seek that ye will seek in vain, my life being hostage for my word, and my word and message being these, namely: That a hap has happened whereof the like has not been seen no more but once this two hundred years, which was the first and last time that that said misfortune strake the holy valley in that form by commandment of the Most High whereto by reasons just and causes thereunto contributing, wherein the matter—"

"The miraculous fount hath ceased to flow!" This shout burst from twenty pilgrim mouths at once.

"Ye say well, good people. I was verging to it, even when ye spake."

"Has somebody been washing again?"

"Nay, it is suspected, but none believe it. It is thought to be some other sin, but none wit what."

"How are they feeling about the calamity?"

"None may describe it in words. The fount is these nine days dry. The prayers that did begin then, and the lamentations in sackcloth and ashes, and the holy processions, none of these have ceased nor night nor day; and so the monks and the nuns and the foundlings be all exhausted, and do hang up prayers writ upon parchment, sith that no strength is left in man to lift up voice. And at last they sent for thee, Sir Boss, to try magic and enchantment; and if you could not come, then was the messenger to fetch Merlin, and he is there these three days, now, and saith he will fetch that water though he burst the globe and wreck its kingdoms to accomplish it; and right bravely doth he work his magic and call upon his hellions to hie them hither and help, but not a whiff of moisture hath he started yet, even so much as might qualify as mist upon a copper mirror an ye count not the barrel of sweat he sweateth betwixt sun and sun over the dire labors of his task; and if ye——"

Breakfast was ready. As soon as it was over I showed to Sir Ozana these words which I had written on the inside of his hat: "*Chemical Department, Laboratory extension, Section G. Pxxp. Send two of first size, two of No. 3, and six of No. 4, together with the proper complementary details—and two of my trained assistants.*" And I said:

"Now get you to Camelot as fast as you can fly, brave knight, and show the writing to Clarence, and tell him to have these required matters in the Valley of Holiness with all possible dispatch."

"I will well, Sir Boss," and he was off.

## Chapter XXII

### THE HOLY FOUNTAIN

The pilgrims were human beings. Otherwise they would have acted differently. They had come a long and difficult journey, and now when the journey was nearly finished, and they learned that the main thing they had come for had ceased to exist, they didn't do as horses or cats or angle-worms would probably have done—turn back and get at something profitable—no, anxious as they had before been to see the miraculous fountain, they were as much as forty times as anxious now to see the place where it had used to be. There is no accounting for human beings.

We made good time; and a couple of hours before sunset we stood upon the high confines of the Valley of Holiness and our eyes swept it from end to end and noted its features. That is, its large features. These were the three masses of buildings. They were distant and isolated temporalities shrunken to toy construction in the lonely waste of what seemed a desert—and was. Such a scene is always mournful, it is so impressively still, and looks so steeped in death. But there was a sound here which interrupted the stillness only to add to its mournfulness; this was the faint far sound of tolling bells which floated fitfully to us on the passing breeze, and so faintly, so softly, that we hardly knew whether we heard it with our ears or with our spirits.

We reached the monastery before dark, and there the males were given lodging, but the women were sent over to the nunnery. The bells were close at hand, now, and their solemn booming smote upon the ear like a message of doom. A superstitious despair possessed the heart of every monk and published itself in his ghastly face. Everywhere, these black-robed, soft-sandled, tallow-visaged spectres appeared, flitted about and disappeared, noiseless as the creatures of a troubled dream, and as uncanny.

The old abbot's joy to see me was pathetic. Even to tears; but he did the shedding himself. He said:

"Delay not, son, but get to thy saving work. An we bring not the water back again, and soon, we are ruined, and the good work of two hundred years must end. And see thou do it with enchantments that be holy, for the Church will not endure that work in her cause be done by devil's magic."

"When I work, Father, be sure there will be no devil's work connected with it. I shall use no arts that come of the devil, and no elements not created by the hand of God. But is Merlin working strictly on pious lines?"

"Ah, he said he would, my son, he said he would, and took oath to make his promise good."

"Well, in that case, let him proceed."

"But surely you will not sit idle by, but help?"

"It will not answer to mix methods, Father; neither would it be professional courtesy. Two of a trade must not under-bid each other. We might as well cut rates and be done with it; it would arrive at that in the end. Merlin has the contract; no other magician can touch it till he throws it up."

"But I will take it from him; it is a terrible emergency and the act is thereby justified. And if it were not so, who will give law to the Church? The Church giveth law to all; and what she wills to do, that she may do, hurt whom it may. I will take it from him; you shall begin upon the moment."

"It may not be, Father. No doubt, as you say, where power is supreme, one can do as one likes and suffer no injury; but we poor magicians are not so situated. Merlin is a very good magician in a small way, and has quite a neat provincial reputation. He is struggling along, doing the best he can, and it would not be etiquette for me to take his job until he himself abandons it."

The abbot's face lighted.

"Ah, that is simple. There are ways to persuade him to abandon it."

"No-no, Father, it skills not, as these people say. If he were persuaded against his will, he would load that well with a malicious enchantment which would balk me until I found out its secret. It might take a month. I could set up a little enchantment of mine which I call the telephone, and he could not find out its secret in a hundred years. Yes, you perceive, he might block me for a month. Would you like to risk a month in a dry time like this?"

"A month! The mere thought of it maketh me to shudder. Have it thy way, my son. But my heart is heavy with this disappointment. Leave me, and let me wear my spirit with weariness and waiting, even as I have done these ten long days, counterfeiting thus the thing that is called rest, the prone body making outward sign of repose where inwardly is none."

Of course it would have been best, all round, for Merlin to waive etiquette and quit and call it half a day, since he would never be able to start that water, for he was a true magician of the time: which is to say, the big miracles, the ones that gave him his reputation, always had the luck to be performed when nobody but Merlin was present; he couldn't start this well with all this crowd around to see; a crowd was as bad for a magician's miracle in that day as it was for a spiritualist's miracle in mine: there was sure to be some skeptic on hand to turn up the gas at the crucial moment and spoil everything. But I did not want Merlin to retire from the job until I was ready to take hold of it effectively myself; and I could not do that until I got my things from Camelot, and that would take two or three days.

My presence gave the monks hope, and cheered them up a good deal; insomuch that they ate a square meal that night for the first time in ten days. As soon as their stomachs had been properly reinforced with food, their spirits began to rise fast; when the mead began to go round they rose faster. By the time everybody was half-seas over, the holy community was in good shape to make a night of it; so we stayed by the board and put it through on that line. Matters got to be very jolly. Good old questionable stories were told that made the tears run down and cavernous mouths stand wide and the round bellies shake with laughter; and questionable songs were bellowed out in a mighty chorus that drowned the boom of the tolling bells.

At last I ventured a story myself; and vast was the success of it. Not right off, of course, for the native of those islands does not as a rule dissolve upon the early applications of a humorous thing; but the fifth time I told it, they began to crack, in places; the eighth time I told it, they began to crumble; at the twelfth repetition they fell apart in chunks; and at the fifteenth they disintegrated, and I got a broom and swept them up. This language is figurative. Those islanders—well, they are slow pay, at first, in the matter of return for your investment of effort, but in the end they make the pay of all other nations poor and small by contrast.

I was at the well next day betimes. Merlin was there, enchanting away like a beaver, but not raising the moisture. He was not in a pleasant humor; and every time I hinted that perhaps this contract was a shade too hefty for a novice he unlimbered his tongue and cursed like a bishop—French bishop of the Regency days,[8] I mean.

Matters were about as I expected to find them. The "fountain" was an ordinary well, it had been dug in the ordinary way, and stoned up in the ordinary way. There was no miracle about it. Even the lie that had created its reputation was not miraculous; I could have told it myself, with one hand tied behind me. The well was in a dark chamber which stood in the centre of a cut-stone chapel, whose walls were hung with pious pictures of a workmanship that would have made a chromo feel good; pictures historically commemorative of curative miracles which had been achieved by the waters when nobody was looking. That is, nobody but angels: they are always on deck when there is a miracle to the fore—so as to get put in the picture, perhaps. Angels are as fond of that as a fire company; look at the old masters.

The well-chamber was dimly lighted by lamps; the water was drawn with a windlass and chain, by monks, and poured into troughs which delivered it into stone reservoirs outside, in the chapel—when there was water to draw, I mean—and none but monks could enter the well-chamber. I entered it, for I had temporary authority to do so, by courtesy of my professional brother and subordinate. But he hadn't entered it himself. He did everything by incantations; he never worked his intellect. If he had stepped in there and used his eyes, instead of his disordered mind, he could have cured the well by natural means, and then turned it into a miracle in the customary way; but no, he was an old numskull, a magician who believed in his own magic; and no magician can thrive who is handicapped with a superstition like that.

I had an idea that the well had sprung a leak; that some of the wall stones near the bottom had fallen and exposed fissures that allowed the water to escape. I measured the chain—98 feet. Then I called in a couple of monks, locked the door, took a candle, and made them lower me in the bucket. When the chain was all paid out, the candle confirmed my suspicion; a considerable section of the wall was gone, exposing a good big fissure.

I almost regretted that my theory about the well's trouble was correct, because I had another one that had a showy point or two about

8. 1715–23, the years following the death of Louis XIV; Louis XV was only five when Louis XIV, his great-grandfather, died.

it for a miracle. I remembered that in America, many centuries later, when an oil well ceased to flow, they used to blast it out with a dynamite torpedo. If I should find this well dry, and no explanation of it, I could astonish these people most nobly by having a person of no especial value drop a dynamite bomb into it. It was my idea to appoint Merlin. However, it was plain that there was no occasion for the bomb. One cannot have everything the way he would like it. A man has no business to be depressed by a disappointment, anyway; he ought to make up his mind to get even. That is what I did. I said to myself, I am in no hurry, I can wait; that bomb will come good, yet. And it did, too.

When I was above ground again, I turned out the monks, and let down a fish-line: the well was a hundred and fifty feet deep, and there was forty-one feet of water in it! I called in a monk and asked:

"How deep is the well?"

"That, sir, I wit not, having never been told."

"How does the water usually stand in it?"

"Near to the top, these two centuries, as the testimony goeth, brought down to us through our predecessors."

It was true—as to recent times at least—for there was witness to it, and better witness than a monk: only about twenty or thirty feet of the chain showed wear and use, the rest of it was unworn and rusty. What had happened when the well gave out that other time? Without doubt some practical person had come along and mended the leak, and then had come up and told the abbot he had discovered by divination that if the sinful bath were destroyed the well would flow again. The leak had befallen again, now, and these children would have prayed, and processioned, and tolled their bells for heavenly succor till they all dried up and blew away, and no innocent of them all would ever have thought to drop a fish-line into the well or go down in it and find out what was really the matter. Old habit of mind is one of the toughest things to get away from in the world. It transmits itself like physical form and feature; and for a man, in those days, to have had an idea that his ancestors hadn't had, would have brought him under suspicion of being illegitimate. I said to the monk:

"It is a difficult miracle to restore water in a dry well, but we will try, if my brother Merlin fails. Brother Merlin is a very passable artist, but only in the parlor-magic line, and he may not succeed; in fact is not likely to succeed. But that should be nothing to his discredit; the man that can do *this* kind of miracle knows enough to keep hotel."

"Hotel? I mind not to have heard——"

"Of hotel? It's what you call hostel. The man that can do this miracle can keep hostel. I can do this miracle; I shall do this miracle; yet I do not try to conceal from you that it is a miracle to tax the occult powers to the last strain."

"None knoweth that truth better than the brotherhood, indeed; for it is of record that aforetime it was parlous difficult and took a year. Natheless, God send you good success, and to that end will we pray."

As a matter of business it was a good idea to get the notion around that the thing was difficult. Many a small thing has been made large by the right kind of advertising. That monk was filled up with the difficulty of this enterprise; he would fill up the others. In two days the solicitude would be booming.

On my way home at noon, I met Sandy. She had been sampling the hermits. I said:

"I would like to do that, myself. This is Wednesday. Is there a matinée?"

"A which, please you, sir?"

"Matinée. Do they keep open, afternoons?"

"Who?"

"The hermits, of course."

"Keep open?"

"Yes, keep open. Isn't that plain enough? Do they knock off at noon."

"Knock off?"

"Knock off?—yes, knock off. What is the matter with knock off? I never saw such a dunderhead; can't you understand anything at all? In plain terms, do they shut up shop, draw the game, bank the fires—"

"Shut up shop, draw—"

"There, never mind, let it go; You make me tired. You can't seem to understand the simplest thing."

"I would I might please thee, sir, and it is to me dole and sorrow that I fail, albeit sith I am but a simple damsel and taught of none, being from the cradle unbaptised in those deep waters of learning that do anoint with a sovereignty him that partaketh of that most noble sacrament, investing him with reverend state to the mental eye of the humble mortal who, by bar and lack of that great consecration seeth in his own unlearned estate but a symbol of that other sort of lack and loss which men do publish to the pitying eye with sackcloth trappings whereon the ashes of grief do lie bepowdered and bestrewn, and so, when such shall in the darkness of his mind encounter these golden phrases of high mystery, these shut-up-shops, and draw-the-game, and bank-the-fires, it is but by the grace of God that he burst not for envy of the mind that can beget, and tongue that can deliver so great and mellow-sounding miracles of speech, and if there do ensue confusion in that humbler mind, and failure to divine the meanings of these wonders, then if so be this miscomprehension is not vain but sooth and true, wit ye well it is the very substance of worshipful dear homage and may not lightly be misprized, nor had been, an ye had noted this complexion of my mood and mind and understood that that

I would I could not, and that I could not I might not, nor yet nor might *nor* could, nor might-not nor could-not, might be by advantage turned to the desired *would*, and so I pray you mercy of my fault, and that ye will of your kindness and your charity forgive it, good my master and most dear lord."

I couldn't make it all out—that is, the details—but I got the general idea; and enough of it, too, to be ashamed. It was not fair to spring those nineteenth century technicalities upon the untutored infant of the sixth and then rail at her because she couldn't get their drift; and when she was making the honest best drive at it she could, too, and no fault of hers that she couldn't fetch the home-plate; and so I apologized. Then we meandered pleasantly away toward the hermit-holes in sociable converse together, and better friends than ever.

I was gradually coming to have a mysterious and shuddery reverence for this girl; for nowadays whenever she pulled out from the station and got her train fairly started on one of those horizonless transcontinental sentences of hers, it was borne in upon me that I was standing in the awful presence of the Mother of the German Language.[9] I was so impressed with this, that sometimes when she began to empty one of these sentences on me I unconsciously took the very attitude of reverence, and stood uncovered; and if words had been water, I had been drowned, sure. She had exactly the German way: whatever was in her mind to be delivered, whether a mere remark, or a sermon, or a cyclopedia, or the history of a war, she would get it into a single sentence or die. Whenever the literary German dives into a sentence, that is the last you are going to see of him till he emerges on the other side of his Atlantic with his verb in his mouth.

We drifted from hermit to hermit all the afternoon. It was a most strange menagerie. The chief emulation among them seemed to be, to see which could manage to be the uncleanest and most prosperous with vermin. Their manner and attitudes were the last expression of complacent self-righteousness. It was one anchorite's pride to lie naked in the mud and let the insects bite him and blister him un-molested; it was another's to lean against a rock, all day long, con-spicuous to the admiration of the throng of pilgrims, and pray; it was another's to go naked, and crawl around on all fours; it was another's to drag about with him, year in and year out, eighty pounds of iron; it was another's to never lie down when he slept, but to stand among the thorn-bushes and snore when there were pilgrims around to look; a wornan, who had the white hair of age, and no other apparel, was black from crown to heel with forty-seven years of holy abstinence from water. Groups of gazing pilgrims stood around all and every of these strange objects, lost in reverent wonder, and envious of the

9. Clemens enjoyed making fun of German, as in "The Awful German Language," an appen- dix to *A Tramp Abroad* (1880).

fleckless sanctity which these pious austerities had won for them from an exacting heaven.

By and by we went to see one of the supremely great ones. He was a mighty celebrity; his fame had penetrated all Christendom; the noble and the renowned journeyed from the remotest lands on the globe to pay him reverence. His stand was in the centre of the widest part of the valley; and it took all that space to hold his crowds.

His stand was a pillar sixty feet high, with a broad platform on the top of it. He was now doing what he had been doing every day for twenty years up there—bowing his body ceaselessly and rapidly almost to his feet. It was his way of praying. I timed him with a stop-watch, and he made 1244 revolutions in 24 minutes and 46 seconds. It seemed a pity to have all this power going to waste. It was one of the most useful motions in mechanics, the pedal-movement; so I made a note in my memorandum book, purposing some day to apply a system of elastic cords to him and run a sewing-machine with it. I afterwards carried out that scheme, and got five years' good service out of him; in which time he turned out upwards of eighteen thousand first-rate tow-linen shirts, which was ten a day. I worked him Sundays and all; he was going, Sundays, the same as week-days, and it was no use to waste the power. These shirts cost me nothing but just the mere trifle for the materials—I furnished those myself, it would not have been right to make him do that—and they sold like smoke to pilgrims at a dollar and a half apiece, which was the price of fifty cows or a blooded race-horse in Arthurdom. They were regarded as a perfect protection against sin, and advertised as such by my knights everywhere, with the paint-pot and stencil-plate; insomuch that there was not a cliff or a boulder or a dead-wall in England but you could read on it at a mile distance:

"*Buy the only genuine St. Stylite; patronized by the Nobility. Patent applied for.*"

There was more money in the business than one knew what to do with. As it extended, I brought out a line of goods suitable for kings, and a nobby thing for duchesses and that sort, with ruffles down the fore-hatch and the running-gear clewed up with a feather-stitch to leeward and then hauled aft with a back-stay and triced up with a half-turn in the standing rigging forward of the weather-gaskets. Yes, it was a daisy.

But about that time I noticed that the motive power had taken to standing on one leg, and I found that there was something the matter with the other one; so I stocked the business and unloaded, taking Sir Bors de Ganis into camp financially along with certain of his friends: for the works stopped within a year, and the good saint got him to his rest. But he had earned it. I can say that for him.

When I saw him that first time—however, his personal condition will not quite bear description here. You can read it in the Lives of the Saints. [1]

## Chapter XXIII

### RESTORATION OF THE FOUNTAIN

Saturday noon I went to the well and looked on a while. Merlin was still burning smoke-powders, and pawing the air, and muttering gibberish as hard as ever, but looking pretty down-hearted, for of course he had not started even a perspiration in that well yet. Finally I said:

"How does the thing promise by this time, partner?"

"Behold, I am even now busied with trial of the powerfulest enchantment known to the princes of the occult arts in the lands of the East; an it fail me, naught can avail. Peace, until I finish."

He raised a smoke this time that darkened all the region, and must have made matters uncomfortable for the hermits, for the wind was their way, and it rolled down over their dens in a dense and billowy fog. He poured out volumes of speech to match, and contorted his body and sawed the air with his hands in a most extraordinary way. At the end of twenty minutes he dropped down panting, and about exhausted. Now arrived the abbot and several hundred monks and nuns, and behind them a multitude of pilgrims and a couple of acres of foundlings, all drawn by the prodigious smoke, and all in a grand state of excitement. The abbot enquired anxiously for results. Merlin said:

"If any labor of mortal might break the spell that binds these waters, this which I have but just essayed had done it. It has failed; whereby I do now know that that which I had feared is a truth established: the sign of this failure is that the most potent spirit known to the magicians of the East, and whose name none may utter and live, has laid his spell upon this well. The mortal does not breathe, nor ever will, who can penetrate the secret of that spell, and without that secret none can break it. The water will flow no more forever, good Father. I have done what man could. Suffer me to go."

Of course this threw the abbot into a good deal of a consternation. He turned to me with the signs of it in his face, and said:

"Ye have heard him. Is it true?"

---

1. All the details concerning the hermits, in this chapter, are from Lecky—but greatly modified. This book not being a history but only a tale, the majority of the historian's frank details were too strong for reproduction in it.—Editor [*Clemens' note*]. The passage from W.E.H. Lecky's *History of European Morals from Augustus to Charlemagne* is reprinted in the "Sources" section of this book. A number of Christian ascetics lived standing on columns; the first to do this, in fifth-century Syria, was St. Simeon Stylites. He is the subject of an 1833 poem by Tennyson.

"Part of it is."

"Not all, then, not all! What part is true?"

"That that spirit with the Russian name has put his spell upon the well."

"God's wownds, then are we ruined!"

"Possibly."

"But not certainly? Ye mean, not certainly?"

"That is it."

"Wherefore, ye also mean that when he saith none can break the spell—"

"Yes, when he says that, he says what isn't necessarily true. There are conditions under which an effort to break it may have some chance—that is, some small, some trifling chance—of success."

"The conditions—"

"Oh, they are nothing difficult. Only these: I want the well and the surroundings for the space of half a mile, entirely to myself from sunset to-day until I remove the ban—and nobody allowed to cross the ground but by my authority."

"Are these all?"

"Yes."

"And you have no fear to try?"

"Oh, none. One may fail, of course; and one may also succeed. One can try, and I am ready to chance it. I have my conditions?"

"These and all others ye may name. I will issue commandment to that effect."

"Wait," said Merlin, with an evil smile. "Ye wit that he that would break this spell must know that spirit's name?"

"Yes, I know his name."

"And wit you also that to know it skills not of itself, but ye must likewise pronounce it? Ha-ha! Knew ye that?"

"Yes, I knew that, too."

"You had that knowledge! Art a fool? Are ye minded to utter that name and die?"

"Utter it? Why certainly. I would utter it if it was Welsh."

"Ye are even a dead man, then; and I go to tell Arthur."

"That's all right. Take your gripsack and get along. The thing for *you* to do is to go home and work the weather, John W. Merlin."

It was a home shot, and it made him wince; for he was the worst weather-failure in the kingdom. Whenever he ordered up the danger-signals along the coast there was a week's dead calm, sure, and every time he prophecied fair weather it rained brick-bats. But I kept him in the weather bureau right along, to undermine his reputation. However, that shot raised his bile, and instead of starting home to report my death, he said he would remain and enjoy it.

My two experts arrived in the evening, and pretty well fagged, for they had traveled double tides. They had pack-mules along, and had brought everything I needed—tools, pump, lead pipe, Greek fire, sheaves of big rockets, roman candles, colored-fire sprays, electric apparatus, and a lot of sundries—everything necessary for the stateliest kind of a miracle. They got their supper and a nap, and about midnight we sallied out through a solitude so wholly vacant and complete that it quite overpassed the required conditions. We took possession of the well and its surroundings. My boys were experts in all sorts of things, from the stoning up of a well to the constructing of a mathematical instrument. An hour before sunrise we had that leak mended in ship-shape fashion, and the water began to rise. Then we stowed our fireworks in the chapel, locked up the place, and went home to bed.

Before the noon mass was over, we were at the well again; for there was a deal to do, yet, and I was determined to spring the miracle before midnight, for business reasons: for whereas a miracle worked for the Church on a week-day is worth a good deal, it is worth six times as much if you get it on a Sunday. In nine hours the water had risen to its customary level; that is to say, it was within twenty-three feet of the top. We put in a little iron pump, one of the first turned out by my works near the capital; we bored into a stone reservoir which stood against the outer wall of the well-chamber and inserted a section of a lead pipe that was long enough to reach to the door of the chapel and project beyond the threshold, where the gushing water would be visible to the two hundred and fifty acres of people I was intending should be present on the flat plain in front of this little holy hillock at the proper time.

We knocked the head out of an empty hogshead and hoisted this hogshead to the flat roof of the chapel, where we clamped it down fast, poured in gunpowder till it lay loosely an inch deep on the bottom, then we stood up rockets in the hogshead as thick as they could loosely stand, all the different breeds of rockets there are; and they made a portly and imposing sheaf, I can tell you. We grounded the wire of a pocket electrical battery in that powder, we placed a whole magazine of Greek fire on each corner of the roof—blue on one corner, green on another, red on another, and purple on the last, and grounded a wire in each.

About two hundred yards off, in the flat, we built a pen of scantlings about four feet high, and laid planks on it, and so made a platform. We covered it with swell tapestries borrowed for the occasion, and topped it off with the abbot's own throne. When you are going to do a miracle for an ignorant race, you want to get in every detail that will count; you want to make all the properties impressive to the public eye; you want to make matters comfortable for your head guest; then you can turn yourself loose and play your effects for all they are worth. I know the value of these things, for I know human nature. You can't throw too much style into a miracle. It costs trouble, and work, and sometimes money; but it pays in the end. Well, we brought the wires to the ground at the chapel, and then brought them under the ground to the platform, and hid the batteries there. We put a rope fence a hundred feet square around the platform to keep off the common multitude, and that finished the work. My idea was, doors open at 10.30, performance to begin at 11.25 sharp. I wished I could charge admission, but of course that wouldn't answer. I instructed my boys to be in the chapel as early as 10, before anybody was around, and be ready to man the pumps at the proper time, and make the fur fly. Then we went home to supper.

The news of the disaster to the well had traveled far, by this time; and now for two or three days a steady avalanche of people had been pouring into the valley. The lower end of the valley was become one huge camp; we should have a good house, no question about that. Criers went the rounds early in the evening and announced the coming attempt, which put every pulse up to fever-heat. They gave notice that the abbot and his official suite would move in state and occupy the platform at 10.30, up to which time all the region which was under my ban must be clear; the bells would then cease from tolling, and this sign should be permission to the multitudes to close in and take their places.

I was at the platform and all ready to do the honors when the abbot's solemn procession hove in sight—which it did not do till it was nearly to the rope fence, because it was a starless black night and no torches permitted. With it came Merlin, and took a front seat on the platform; he was as good as his word, for once. One could not see the multitudes banked together beyond the ban, but they were there, just the same. The moment the bells stopped, those banked masses broke and poured over the line like a vast black wave, and for as much as a half hour it continued to flow, and then it solidified itself, and you could have walked upon a pavement of human heads to—well, miles.

We had a solemn stage-wait, now, for about twenty minutes—a thing I had counted on for effect; it is always good to let your audience have a chance to work up its expectancy. At length, out of the silence a noble Latin chant—men's voices—broke and swelled up and rolled away into the night, a majestic tide of melody. I had put that up, too, and it was one of the best effects I ever invented. When it was finished I stood up on the platform and extended my hands abroad, for two minutes, with my face uplifted—that always produces a dead hush—and then slowly pronounced this ghastly word with a kind of awfulness which caused hundreds to tremble, and many women to faint:

"𝕮𝖔𝖓𝖘𝖙𝖆𝖓𝖙𝖎𝖓𝖔𝖕𝖔𝖑𝖎𝖙𝖆𝖓𝖎𝖘𝖈𝖍𝖊𝖗𝖉𝖚𝖉𝖊𝖑𝖘𝖆𝖈𝖐𝖘𝖕𝖋𝖊𝖎𝖋𝖊𝖓𝖒𝖆𝖈𝖍𝖊𝖗𝖘𝖌𝖊𝖘𝖊𝖑𝖑𝖘𝖈𝖍𝖆𝖋𝖋𝖙!" [2]

Just as I was moaning out the closing hunks of that word, I touched off one of my electric connections, and all that murky world of people stood revealed in a hideous blue glare! It was immense—that effect! Lots of people shrieked, women curled up and quit in every direction, foundlings collapsed by platoons. The abbot and the monks crossed themselves nimbly and their lips fluttered with agitated prayers. Merlin held his grip, but he was astonished clear down to his corns; he had never seen anything to begin with that, before. Now was the time to pile in the effects. I lifted my hands and groaned out this word—as it were in agony—

"𝕳𝖎𝖍𝖎𝖑𝖎𝖘𝖙𝖊𝖓𝖉𝖞𝖓𝖆𝖒𝖎𝖙𝖙𝖍𝖊𝖆𝖙𝖊𝖗𝖐𝖆𝖊𝖘𝖙𝖈𝖍𝖊𝖓𝖘𝖘𝖕𝖗𝖊𝖓𝖌𝖚𝖓𝖌𝖘𝖆𝖙𝖙𝖊𝖓𝖙𝖆𝖊𝖙𝖘𝖛𝖊𝖗𝖘𝖚𝖈𝖍𝖚𝖓𝖌𝖊𝖓!"

—and turned on the red fire! You should have heard that Atlantic of people moan and howl when that crimson hell joined the blue! After sixty seconds I shouted—

"𝕿𝖗𝖆𝖓𝖘𝖛𝖆𝖆𝖑𝖙𝖗𝖚𝖕𝖕𝖊𝖓𝖙𝖗𝖔𝖕𝖊𝖓𝖙𝖗𝖆𝖓𝖘𝖕𝖔𝖗𝖙𝖙𝖗𝖆𝖒𝖕𝖊𝖑𝖙𝖍𝖎𝖊𝖗𝖙𝖗𝖊𝖎𝖇𝖊𝖗𝖙𝖗𝖆𝖚𝖚𝖓𝖌𝖘𝖙𝖍𝖗𝖆𝖊𝖓𝖊𝖓𝖙𝖗𝖆𝖌𝖔𝖊𝖉𝖎𝖊!"

—and lit up the green fire! After waiting only forty seconds, this time, I spread my arms abroad and thundered out the devastating syllables of this word of words—

"𝕸𝖊𝖐𝖐𝖆𝖒𝖚𝖘𝖊𝖑𝖒𝖆𝖓𝖓𝖊𝖓𝖒𝖆𝖘𝖘𝖊𝖓𝖒𝖊𝖓𝖈𝖍𝖊𝖓𝖒𝖔𝖊𝖗𝖉𝖊𝖗𝖒𝖔𝖍𝖗𝖊𝖓𝖒𝖚𝖙𝖙𝖊𝖗𝖒𝖆𝖗𝖒𝖔𝖗𝖒𝖔𝖓𝖚𝖒𝖊𝖓𝖙𝖊𝖓𝖒𝖆𝖈𝖍𝖊𝖗!"

*[handwritten annotation: Mass murder men]*

—and whirled on the purple glare! There they were, all going at once, red, blue, green, purple!—four furious volcanoes pouring vast clouds of radiant smoke aloft, and spreading a blinding rainbowed noonday to the furthest confines of that valley. In the distance one could see that fellow on the pillar standing rigid against the background of sky, his see-saw stopped for the first time in twenty years. I knew the boys were at the pump, now, and ready. So I said to the abbot:

"The time is come, Father. I am about to pronounce the dread name and command the spell to dissolve. You want to brace up, and take hold of something." Then I shouted to the people: "Behold, in another minute the spell will be broken, or no mortal can break it. If it

---

2. The Yankee's outlandish exaggerations of the German practice of forming compound words have been translated in Robert L. Ramsay and Frances G. Emberson's *A Mark Twain Lexicon* (New York: Russell & Russell, 1963), p. 72: "The Bagpipe Manufacturers Company of Constantinople," "Outrageous attempts by Nihilists to blow up the strong-box of a theater with dynamite," "The lamentable tragedy of the marriage of a dromedary drover in the tropical transport service of the army of the Transvaal," and, finally, "A manufacturer of marble monuments commemorating the Moorish mother of the assassins who perpetrated the general massacre of Mohammedans at Mecca."

Beard's interpretation of the spirit possessing the holy fountain: church and state united, supported by slavery, superstition, and ignorance.

break, all will know it, for you will see the sacred water gush from the chapel door!"

I stood a few moments, to let the hearers have a chance to spread my announcement to those who couldn't hear, and so convey it to the furthest ranks, then I made a grand exhibition of extra posturing and gesturing, and shouted:

"Lo, I command the fell spirit that possesses the holy fountain to now disgorge into the skies all the infernal fires that still remain in him, and straightway dissolve his spell and flee hence to the pit, there to lie bound a thousand years.[3] By his own dread name I command it—BGWJJILLIGKKK!"

Then I touched off the hogshead of rockets, and a vast fountain of dazzling lances of fire vomited itself toward the zenith with a hissing rush, and burst in mid-sky into a storm of flashing jewels! One mighty groan of terror started up from the massed people—then suddenly broke into a wild hosannah of joy—for there, fair and plain in the uncanny glare, they saw the freed water leaping forth! The old abbot could not speak a word, for tears and the chokings in his throat; without utterance of any sort, he folded me in his arms and mashed me. It was more eloquent than speech. And harder to get over, too, in a country where there were really no doctors that were worth a damaged nickel.

You should have seen those acres of people throw themselves down in that water and kiss it; kiss it, and pet it, and fondle it, and talk to it as if it were alive, and welcome it back with the dear names they gave their darlings, just as if it had been a friend who was long gone away and lost, and was come home again. Yes, it was pretty to see, and made me think more of them than I had done before.

I sent Merlin home on a shutter. He had caved in and gone down like a landslide when I pronounced that fearful name, and had never come to since. He never had heard that name before,—neither had I—but to him it was the right one; any jumble would have been the right one. He admitted, afterward, that that spirit's own mother could not have pronounced that name better than I did. He never could understand how I survived it, and I didn't tell him. It is only young magicians that give away a secret like that. Merlin spent three months working enchantments to try to find out the deep trick of how to pronounce that name and outlive it. But he didn't arrive.

When I started to the chapel, the populace uncovered and fell back reverently to make a wide way for me, as if I had been some kind of a superior being—and I was. I was aware of that. I took along a night-shift of monks, and taught them the mystery of the pump, and set them to work, for it was plain that a good part of the people out there

---

3. Revelation 20:1–3 tells of Satan's being bound for a thousand years and cast into a bottomless pit.

were going to sit up with the water all night, consequently it was but right that they should have all they wanted of it. To those monks that pump was a good deal of a miracle itself, and they were full of wonder over it; and of admiration, too, of the exceeding effectiveness of its performance.

It was a great night, an immense night. There was reputation in it. I could hardly get to sleep for glorying over it.

## Chapter XXIV

### A RIVAL MAGICIAN

My influence in the Valley of Holiness was something prodigious now. It seemed worth while to try to turn it to some valuable account. The thought came to me the next morning, and was suggested by my seeing one of my knights who was in the soap line come riding in. According to history, the monks of this place two centuries before, had been worldly minded enough to want to wash. It might be that there was a leaven of this unrighteousness still remaining. So I sounded a Brother: "Wouldn't you like a bath?" He shuddered at the thought—the thought of the peril of it to the well—but he said with feeling—

"One needs not to ask that of a poor body who has not known that blessed refreshment sith that he was a boy. Would God I might wash me! but it may not be, fair sir, tempt me not; it is forbidden."

And then he sighed in such a sorrowful way that I was resolved he should have at least one layer of his real estate removed, if it sized up my whole influence and bankrupted the pile. So I went to the abbot and asked for a permit for this Brother. He blenched at the idea—I don't mean that you could see him blench, for of course you couldn't see it without you scraped him, and I didn't care enough about it to scrape him, but I knew the blench was there, just the same, and within a book-cover's thickness of the surface, too—blenched, and trembled. He said:

"Ah, son, ask aught else thou wilt, and it is thine, and freely granted out of a grateful heart—but this, oh, this! Would you drive away the blessed water again?"

"No, Father, I will not drive it away. I have mysterious knowledge which teaches me that there was an error that other time when it was thought the institution of the bath banished the fountain." A large interest began to show up in the old man's face. "My knowledge informs me that the bath was innocent of that misfortune, which was caused by quite another sort of sin."

"These are brave words—but—but right welcome, if they be true."

"They are true, indeed. Let me build the bath again, Father. Let me build it again, and the fountain shall flow forever."

"You promise this?—you promise it? Say the word—say you promise it!"

"I do promise it."

"Then will I have the first bath myself! Go—get ye to your work. Tarry not, tarry not, but go."

I and my boys were at work, straight off. The ruins of the old bath were there yet, in the basement of the monastery, not a stone missing. They had been left just so, all these lifetimes, and avoided with a pious fear, as things accursed. In two days we had it all done and the water in—a spacious pool of clear pure water that a body could swim in. It was running water, too. It came in, and went out, through the ancient pipes. The old abbot kept his word and was the first to try it. He went down black and shaky, leaving the whole black community above troubled and worried and full of bodings; but he came back white and joyful, and the game was made! another triumph scored.

It was a good campaign that we made in that Valley of Holiness, and I was very well satisfied, and ready to move on, now, but I struck a disappointment. I caught a heavy cold, and it started up an old lurking rheumatism of mine. Of course the rheumatism hunted up my weakest place and located itself there. This was the place where the abbot put his arms about me and mashed me, what time he was moved to testify his gratitude to me with an embrace.

When at last I got out, I was a shadow. But everybody was full of attentions and kindnesses, and these brought cheer back into my life and were the right medicine to help a convalescent swiftly up toward health and strength again; so I gained fast.

Sandy was worn out with nursing, so I made up my mind to turn out and go a cruise alone, leaving her at the nunnery to rest up. My idea was to disguise myself as a freeman of peasant degree and wander through the country a week or two on foot. This would give me a chance to eat and lodge with the lowliest and poorest class of free citizens on equal terms. There was no other way to inform myself perfectly of their every-day life and the operation of the laws upon it. If I went among them as a gentleman, there would be restraints and conventionalities which would shut me out from their private joys and troubles, and I should get no further than the outside shell.

One morning I was out on a long walk to get up muscle for my trip and had climbed the ridge which bordered the northern extremity of the valley, when I came upon an artificial opening in the face of a low precipice, and recognized it by its location as a hermitage which had often been pointed out to me from a distance, as the den of a hermit of high renown for dirt and austerity. I knew he had lately been offered a situation in the Great Sahara, where lions and sandflies made the hermit-life peculiarly attractive and difficult, and had gone to Africa to take possession, so I thought I would look in and see how the atmosphere of this den agreed with its reputation.

My surpise was great: the place was newly swept and scoured. Then there was another surprise. Back in the gloom of the cavern I heard the clink of a little bell, and then this exclamation:

"*Hello, Central! Is this you, Camelot?* ——Behold, thou mayst glad thy heart an thou hast faith to believe the wonderful when that it cometh in unexpected guise and maketh itself manifest in impossible places—here standeth in the flesh his mightiness The Boss, and with thine own ears shall ye hear him speak!"

Now what a radical reversal of things this was; what a jumbling together of extravagant incongruities; what a fantastic conjunction of opposites and irreconcilables—the home of the bogus miracle become the home of a real one, the den of a medieval hermit turned into a telephone office!

The telephone clerk stepped into the light, and I recognized one of my young fellows. I said:

"How long has this office been established here, Ulfius?"

"But since midnight, fair Sir Boss, an it please you. We saw many lights in the valley, and so judged it well to make a station, for that where so many lights be needs must they indicate a town of goodly size."

"Quite right. It isn't a town in the customary sense, but it's a good stand, anyway. Do you know where you are?"

"Of that I have had no time to make inquiry; for whenas my comradeship moved hence upon their labors, leaving me in charge, I got me to needed rest, purposing to inquire when I waked, and report the place's name to Camelot for record."

"Well, this is the Valley of Holiness."

It didn't take, I mean, he didn't start at the name, as I had supposed he would. He merely said—

"I will so report it."

"Why, the surrounding regions are filled with the noise of late wonders that have happened here! You didn't hear of them?"

"Ah, ye will remember we move by night, and avoid speech with all. We learn naught but that we get by the telephone from Camelot."

"Why *they* know all about this thing. Haven't they told you anything about the great miracle of the restoration of a holy fountain?"

"Oh, *that?* Indeed yes. But the name of *this* valley doth woundily differ from the name of *that* one; indeed to differ wider were not pos—"

"What was that name, then?"

"The Valley of Hellishness."

"*That* explains it. Confound a telephone, anyway.[4] It is the very

<hr />

4. This passage may reflect some of Clemens' actual difficulties with the telephone in his Hartford home. According to his *Autobiography*, he believed that he had in 1877 or 1878 "the only telephone wire in town, and the *first* one that was ever used in a private house in the world." Alexander Graham Bell's famous "Come here, Watson" occurred in 1876.

demon for conveying similarities of sound that are miracles of divergence from similarity of sense. But no matter, you know the name of the place now. Call up Camelot."

He did it, and had Clarence sent for. It was good to hear my boy's voice again. It was like being home. After some affectionate interchanges, and some account of my late illness, I said:

"What is new?"

"The king and queen and many of the court do start even in this hour, to go to your Valley to pay pious homage to the waters ye have restored, and cleanse themselves of sin, and see the place where the infernal spirit spouted true hell-flames to the clouds—an ye listen sharply ye may hear me wink and hear me likewise smile a smile, sith 'twas I that made selection of those flames from out our stock and sent them by your order."

"Does the king know the way to this place?"

"The king?—no, nor to any other in his realms, mayhap; but the lads that holp you with your miracle will be his guide and lead the way, and appoint the places for rests at noons and sleeps at night."

"This will bring them here—when?"

"Mid-afternoon, or later, the third day."

"Anything else in the way of news?"

"The king hath begun the raising of the standing army ye suggested to him; one regiment is complete and officered."

"The mischief! I wanted a main hand in that, myself. There is only one body of men in the kingdom that are fitted to officer a regular army."

"Yes—and now ye will marvel to know there's not so much as one West Pointer in that regiment."

"What are you talking about? Are you in earnest?"

"It is truly as I have said."

"Why, this makes me uneasy. Who were chosen, and what was the method? Competitive examination?"

"Indeed I know naught of the method. I but know this—these officers be all of noble family, and are born—what is it you call it?—chuckleheads."

"There's something wrong, Clarence."

"Comfort yourself, then; for two candidates for a lieutenancy do travel hence with the king—young nobles both—and if you but wait where you are you will hear them questioned."

"That is news to the purpose. I will get one West Pointer in, anyway. Mount a man and send him to that school with a message; let him kill horses, if necessary, but he must be there before sunset tonight and say—"

"There is no need. I have laid a ground wire to the school. Prithee let me connect you with it."

It sounded good! In this atmosphere of telephones and lightning communication with distant regions, I was breathing the breath of life again after long suffocation. I realized, then, what a creepy, dull, inanimate horror this land had been to me all these years, and how I had been in such a stifled condition of mind as to have grown used to it almost beyond the power to notice it.

I gave my order to the superintendent of the Academy personally. I also asked him to bring me some paper and a fountain pen and a box or so of safety matches. I was getting tired of doing without these conveniences. I could have them, now, as I wasn't going to wear armor any more at present, and therefore could get at my pockets.

When I got back to the monastery, I found a thing of interest going on. The abbot and his monks were assembled in the great hall, observing with childish wonder and faith the performances of a new magician, a fresh arrival. His dress was the extreme of the fantastic; as showy and foolish as the sort of thing an Indian medicine-man wears. He was mowing, and mumbling, and gesticulating, and drawing mystical figures in the air and on the floor,—the regular thing, you know. He was a celebrity from Asia—so he said, and that was enough. That sort of evidence was as good as gold, and passed current everywhere.

How easy and cheap it was to be a great magician on this fellow's terms. His specialty was to tell you what any individual on the face of the globe was doing at the moment; and what he had done at any time in the past, and what he would do at any time in the future. He asked if any would like to know what the Emperor of the East was doing now? The sparkling eyes and the delighted rubbing of hands made eloquent answer—this reverend crowd *would* like to know what that monarch was at, just at this moment. The fraud went through some more mummery, and then made grave announcement:

"The high and mighty Emperor of the East doth at this moment put money in the palm of a holy begging friar—one, two, three pieces, and they be all of silver."

A buzz of admiring exclamations broke out, all around:

"It is marvelous!" "Wonderful!" "What study, what labor, to have acquired a so amazing power as this!"

Would they like to know what the supreme Lord of Inde was doing? Yes. He told them what the Supreme Lord of Inde was doing. Then he told them what the Sultan of Egypt was at; also what the King of the Remote Seas was about. And so on and so on; and with each new marvel the astonishment at his accuracy rose higher and higher. They thought he must surely strike an uncertain place sometime; but no, he never had to hesitate, he always knew, and always with unerring precision. I saw that if this thing went on I should lose my supremacy, this fellow would capture my following, I should be left out in the cold. I must put a cog in his wheel, and do it right away, too. I said:

"If I might ask, I should very greatly like to know what a certain person is doing."

"Speak, and freely. I will tell you."

"It will be difficult—perhaps impossible."

"My art knoweth not that word. The more difficult it is, the more certainly will I reveal it to you."

You see, I was working up the interest. It was getting pretty high, too; you could see that by the craning necks all around, and the half suspended breathing. So now I climaxed it:

"If you make no mistake—if you tell me truly what I want to know—I will give you two hundred silver pennies."

"The fortune is mine! I will tell you what you would know."

"Then tell me what I am doing with my right hand."

"Ah-h!" There was a general gasp of surprise. It had not occurred to anybody in the crowd—that simple trick of inquiring about somebody who wasn't ten thousand miles away. The magician was hit hard; it was an emergency that had never happened in his experience before, and it corked him; he didn't know how to meet it. He looked stunned, confused, he couldn't say a word. "Come," I said, "what are you waiting for? Is it possible you can answer up, right off, and tell what anybody on the other side of the earth is doing, and yet can't tell what a person is doing who isn't three yards from you? Persons behind me know what I am doing with my right hand—they will endorse you if you tell correctly." He was still dumb. "Very well, I'll tell you why you don't speak up and tell; it is because you don't know. *You* a magician! Good friends, this tramp is a mere fraud and liar."

This distressed the monks and terrified them. They were not used to hearing these awful beings called names, and they did not know what might be the consequence. There was a dead silence, now; superstitious bodings were in every mind. The magician began to pull his wits together, and when he presently smiled an easy, nonchalant smile, it spread a mighty relief around; for it indicated that his mood was not destructive. He said:

"It hath struck me speechless, the frivolity of this person's speech. Let all know, if perchance there be any who know it not, that enchanters of my degree deign not to concern themselves with the doings of any but Kings, Princes, Emperors, them that be born in the purple and them only. Had ye asked me what Arthur the great king is doing, it were another matter, and I had told ye; but the doings of a subject interest me not."

"Oh, I misunderstood you. I thought you said 'anybody,' and so I supposed 'anybody' included—well, anybody; that is, everybody."

"It doth—anybody that is of lofty birth; and the better if he be royal."

"That, it meseemeth, might well be," said the abbot, who saw his opportunity to smooth things and avert disaster, "for it were not likely that so wonderful a gift as this would be conferred for the revelation of the concerns of lesser beings than such as be born near to the summits of greatness. Our Arthur the king—"

"Would you know of him?" broke in the enchanter.

"Most gladly, yea, and gratefully."

Everybody was full of awe and interest again, right away, the incorrigible idiots. They watched the incantations absorbingly, and looked at me with a "There, now, what can you say to that?" air, when the announcement came:

"The king is weary with the chase, and lieth in his palace these two hours sleeping a dreamless sleep."

"God's benison upon him!" said the abbot, and crossed himself; "may that sleep be to the refreshment of his body and his soul."

"And so it might be, if he were sleeping," I said, "but the king is not sleeping, the king rides."

Here was trouble again—a conflict of authority. Nobody knew which of us to believe; I still had some reputation left. The magician's scorn was stirred, and he said:

"Lo, I have seen many wonderful soothsayers and prophets and magicians in my life-days, but none before that could sit idle and see to the heart of things with never an incantation to help."

"You have lived in the woods, and lost much by it. I use incantations myself, as this good brotherhood are aware—but only on occasions of moment."

When it comes to sarcasaming, I reckon I know how to keep my end up. That jab made this fellow squirm. The abbot inquired after the queen and the court, and got this information:

"They be all on sleep, being overcome by fatigue, like as to the king."

I said:

"That is merely another lie. Half of them are about their amusements, the queen and the other half are not sleeping, they ride. Now perhaps you can spread yourself a little, and tell us where the king and queen and all that are this moment riding with them are going?"

"They sleep now, as I said; but on the morrow they will ride, for they go a journey toward the sea."

"And where will they be the day after to-morrow at vespers?"

"Far to the north of Camelot, and half their journey will be done."

"That is another lie, by the space of a hundred and fifty miles. Their journey will not be merely half done, it will be all done, and they will be *here*, in this valley."

*That* was a noble shot! It set the abbot and the monks in a whirl of excitement, and it rocked the enchanter to his base. I followed the thing right up:

"If the king does not arrive, I will have myself ridden on a rail; if he does I will ride you on a rail instead."

Next day I went up to the telephone office and found that the king had passed through two towns that were on the line. I spotted his progress on the succeeding day in the same way. I kept these matters to myself. The third day's reports showed that if he kept up his gait he would arrive by four in the afternoon. There was still no sign anywhere of interest in his coming; there seemed to be no preparations making to receive him in state; a strange thing, truly. Only one thing could explain this: that other magician had been cutting under me, sure. This was true. I asked a friend of mine, a monk, about it, and he said, yes, the magician had tried some further enchantments and found out that the court had concluded to make no journey at all, but stay at home. Think of that! Observe how much a reputation was worth in such a country. These people had seen me do the very showiest bit of magic in history, and the only one within their memory that had a positive value, and yet here they were, ready to take up with an adventurer who could offer no evidence of his powers but his mere unproven word.

However, it was not good politics to let the king come without any fuss and feathers at all, so I went down and drummed up a procession of pilgrims and smoked out a batch of hermits and started them out at two o'clock to meet him. And that was the sort of state he arrived in. The abbot was helpless with rage and humiliation when I brought him out on a balcony and showed him the head of the state marching in and never a monk on hand to offer him welcome, and no stir of life or clang of joy-bell to glad his spirit. He took one look and then flew to rouse out his forces. The next minute the bells were dinning furiously, and the various buildings were vomiting monks and nuns, who went swarming in a rush toward the coming procession; and with them went that magician—and he was on a rail, too, by the abbot's order; and his reputation was in the mud, and mine was in the sky again. Yes, a man can keep his trade-mark current in such a country, but he can't sit around and do it; he has got to be on deck and attending to business, right along.

## *Chapter XXV*

### A COMPETITIVE EXAMINATION

When the king traveled for change of air, or made a progress, or visited a distant noble whom he wished to bankrupt with the cost of his keep, part of the administration moved with him. It was a fashion of the time. The Commission charged with the examination of candidates for posts in the army came with the king to the Valley, whereas they could have transacted their business just as well at home. And although this expedition was strictly a holiday excursion for the king, he kept some of his business functions going, just the same. He touched for the evil, as usual;[5] he held court in the gate at sunrise and tried cases, for he was himself Chief Justice of the King's Bench.

He shone very well in this latter office. He was a wise and humane judge, and he clearly did his honest best and fairest,—according to his lights. That is a large reservation. His lights—I mean his rearing— often colored his decisions. Whenever there was a dispute between a noble or gentleman and a person of lower degree, the king's leanings and sympathies were for the former class always, whether he suspected it or not. It was impossible that this should be otherwise. The blunting effects of slavery upon the slaveholder's moral perceptions are known and conceded, the world over; and a privileged class, an aristocracy, is but a band of slaveholders under another name. This has a harsh sound, and yet should not be offensive to any—even to the noble himself—unless the fact itself be an offense: for the statement simply formulates a fact. The repulsive feature of slavery is the *thing*, not its name. One needs but to hear an aristocrat speak of the classes that are below him to recognize—and in but indifferently modified measure—the very air and tone of the actual slaveholder; and behind these are the slaveholder's spirit, the slaveholder's blunted feeling. They are the result of the same cause in both cases: the possessor's old and inbred custom of regarding himself as a superior being. The king's judgments wrought frequent injustices, but it was merely the fault of his training, his natural and unalterable sympathies. He was as unfitted for a judgeship as would be the average mother for the position of milk-distributor to starving children in famine-time; her own children would fare a shade better than the rest.

One very curious case came before the king. A young girl, an orphan, who had a considerable estate, married a fine young fellow who had nothing. The girl's property was within a seignory held by the Church. The bishop of the diocese, an arrogant scion of the great nobility, claimed the girl's estate on the ground that she had married privately, and thus had cheated the Church out of one of its rights as lord of the seignory—the one heretofore referred to as *le droit du seigneur.* The penalty of refusal or avoidance was confiscation. The girl's defence was, that the lordship of the seignory was vested in the bishop, and the particular right here involved was not transferable, but must be exercised by the lord himself or stand vacated; and that an older law, of the Church itself, strictly barred the bishop from exercis-

5. An allusion to the widespread belief that scrofula, sometimes called the "king's evil," could be healed by a king's touch. In England the practice began under Edward the Confessor, reached its height in the reign of Charles II, and was abandoned after Anne. More on the king's touch appears in the next chapter.

ing it. It was a very odd case, indeed.

It reminded me of something I had read in my youth about the ingenious way in which the aldermen of London raised the money that built the Mansion House.[6] A person who had not taken the Sacrament according to the Anglican rite, could not stand as a candidate for sheriff of London. Thus Dissenters were ineligible; they could not run if asked, they could not serve if elected. The aldermen, who without any question were Yankees in disguise, hit upon this neat device: they passed a by-law imposing a fine of £400 upon any one who should refuse to be a candidate for sheriff, and a fine of £600 upon any person who, after being elected sheriff, refused to serve. Then they went to work and elected a lot of Dissenters, one after another, and kept it up until they had collected £15,000 in fines; and there stands the stately Mansion House to this day, to keep the blushing citizen in mind of a long past and lamented day when a band of Yankees slipped into London and played games of the sort that has given their race a unique and shady reputation among all truly good and holy peoples that be in the earth.

The girl's case seemed strong to me; the bishop's case was just as strong. I did not see how the king was going to get out of this hole. But he got out. I append his decision:

"Truly I find small difficulty here, the matter being even a child's affair for simpleness. An the young bride had conveyed notice, as in duty bound, to her feudal lord and proper master and protector the bishop, she had suffered no loss, for the said bishop could have got a dispensation making him, for temporary conveniency, eligible to the exercise of his said right, and thus would she have kept all she had. Whereas, failing in her first duty, she hath by that failure failed in all; for whoso, clinging to a rope, severeth it above his hands, must fall; it being no defence to claim that the rest of the rope is sound, neither any deliverance from his peril, as he shall find. Pardy, the woman's case is rotten at the source. It is the decree of the Court that she forfeit to the said lord bishop all her goods, even to the last farthing that she doth possess, and be thereto mulcted in the costs. Next!"

Here was a tragic end to a beautiful honeymoon not yet three months old. Poor young creatures! They had lived these three months lapped to the lips in worldly comforts. These clothes and trinkets they were wearing were as fine and dainty as the shrewdest stretch of the sumptuary laws allowed to people of their degree; and in these pretty clothes, she crying on his shoulder, and he trying to comfort her with hopeful words set to the music of despair, they went from the judg-

6. Residence of the Lord Mayor of London, built 1739–53. The passage from W. E. H. Lecky's *History of England in the Eighteenth Century* which supplied Clemens with this information is included in the section on sources.

ment seat out into the world homeless, bedless, breadless; why, the very beggars by the roadsides were not so poor as they.

Well, the king was out of the hole; and on terms satisfactory to the Church and the rest of the aristocracy, no doubt. Men write many fine and plausible arguments in support of monarchy, but the fact remains that where every man in a State has a vote, brutal laws are impossible. Arthur's people were of course poor material for a republic, because they had been debased so long by monarchy; and yet even they would have been intelligent enough to make short work of that law which the king had just been administering if it had been submitted to their full and free vote. There is a phrase which has grown so common in the world's mouth that it has come to seem to have sense and meaning— the sense and meaning implied when it is used: that is the phrase which refers to this or that or the other nation as possibly being "capable of self-government;" and the implied sense of it is, that there has been a nation somewhere, sometime or other which *wasn't* capable of it—wasn't as able to govern itself as some self-appointed specialists were or would be to govern it. The master minds of all nations, in all ages, have sprung in affluent multitude from the mass of the nation, and from the mass of the nation only—not from its privileged classes; and so, no matter what the nation's intellectual grade was, whether high or low, the bulk of its ability was in the long ranks of its nameless and its poor, and so it never saw the day that it had not the material in abundance whereby to govern itself. Which is to assert an always self-proven fact: that even the best governed and most free and most enlightened monarchy is still behind the best condition attainable by its people; and that the same is true of kindred governments of lower grades, all the way down to the lowest.

King Arthur had hurried up the army business altogether beyond my calculations. I had not supposed he would move in the matter while I was away; and so I had not mapped out a scheme for determining the merits of officers; I had only remarked that it would be wise to submit every candidate to a sharp and searching examination; and privately I meant to put together a list of military qualifications that nobody could answer to but my West Pointers. That ought to have been attended to before I left; for the king was so taken with the idea of a standing army that he couldn't wait but must get about it at once, and get up as good a scheme of examination as he could invent out of his own head.

I was impatient to see what this was; and to show, too, how much more admirable was the one which I should display to the Examining Board. I intimated this, gently, to the king, and it fired his curiosity. When the Board was assembled, I followed him in, and behind us came the candidates. One of these candidates was a bright young West Pointer of mine, and with him were a couple of my West Point professors.

When I saw the Board, I did not know whether to cry or to laugh. The head of it was the officer known to later centuries as Norroy King-at-Arms![7] The two other members were chiefs of bureaux in his department; and all three were priests, of course; all officials who had to know how to read and write were priests.

My candidate was called first, out of courtesy to me, and the head of the Board opened on him with official solemnity:

"Name?"

"Mal-ease."

"Son of?"

"Webster."

"Webster—Webster. Hm—I—my memory faileth to recall the name.[8] Condition?"

"Weaver."

"Weaver!—God keep us!"

The king was staggered, from his summit to his foundations; one clerk fainted, and the others came near it. The chairman pulled himself together, and said indignantly:

"It is sufficient. Get you hence."

But I appealed to the king. I begged that my candidate might be examined. The king was willing, but the Board, who were all well-born folk, implored the king to spare them the indignity of examining the weaver's son. I knew they didn't know enough to examine him anyway, so I joined my prayers to theirs and the king turned the duty over to my professors. I had had a blackboard prepared, and it was put up now, and the circus began. It was beautiful to hear the lad lay out the science of war, and wallow in details of battle and siege, of supply, transporation, mining and countermining, grand tactics, big strategy and little strategy, signal service, infantry, cavalry, artillery, and all about siege guns, field guns, gatling guns, rifled guns, smooth bores, musket practice, revolver practice—and not a solitary word of it all could these catfish make head or tail of, you understand—and it was handsome to see him chalk off mathematical nightmares on the blackboard that would stump the angels themselves, and do it like nothing, too—all about eclipses, and comets, and solstices, and constellations, and mean time, and sidereal time, and dinner time, and bedtime, and every other imaginable thing above the clouds or under them that you could harry or bullyrag an enemy with and make him wish he hadn't come—and when the boy made his military salute and stood aside at last, I was proud enough to hug him, and all those other people were so dazed they looked partly petrified, partly drunk,

---

7. A member of the College of Arms having jurisdiction north of the River Trent and, later, Ulster as well.

8. Perhaps a joke on Clemens' part, as the novel was published by the Charles L. Webster Company, headed by his nephew.

and wholly caught out and snowed under. I judged that the cake was ours, and by a large majority.

Education is a great thing. This was the same youth who had come to West Point so ignorant that when I asked him, "If a general officer should have a horse shot under him on the field of battle, what ought he to do?" answered up naively and said:

"Get up and brush himself."

One of the young nobles was called up, now. I thought I would question him a little myself. I said:

"Can your lordship read?"

His face flushed indignantly, and he fired this at me:

"Takest me for a clerk? I trow I am not of a blood that—"

"Answer the question!"

He crowded his wrath down and made out to answer "No."

"Can you write?"

He wanted to resent this, too, but I said:

"You will confine yourself to the questions, and make no comments. You are not here to air your blood or your graces, and nothing of the sort will be permitted. Can you write?"

"No."

"Do you know the multiplication table?"

"I wit not what ye refer to."

"How much is 9 times 6?"

"It is a mystery that is hidden from me by reason that the emergency requiring the fathoming of it hath not in my life-days occurred, and so, not having no need to know this thing, I abide barren of the knowledge."

"If A trade a barrel of onions to B, worth 2 pence the bushel, in exchange for a sheep worth 4 pence and a dog worth a penny, and C kill the dog before delivery, because bitten by the same, who mistook him for D, what sum is still due to A from B, and which party pays for the dog, C, or D, and who gets the money? if A, is the penny sufficient, or may he claim consequential damages in the form of additional money to represent the possible profit which might have inured from the dog, and classifiable as earned increment, that is to say, usufruct?"

"Verily, in the all-wise and unknowable providence of God, who moveth in mysterious ways his wonders to perform,[9] have I never heard the fellow to this question for confusion of the mind and congestion of the ducts of thought. Wherefore I beseech you let the dog and the onions and these people of the strange and godless names work out their several salvations from their piteous and wonderful difficulties without help of mine, for indeed their trouble is sufficient

9. Opening lines of a well-known hymn by William Cowper (1731–1800): "God moves in a mysterious way,/His wonders to perfrom."

as it is, whereas an I tried to help I should but damage their cause the more and yet mayhap not live myself to see the desolation wrought."

"What do you know of the laws of attraction and gravitation?"

"If there be such, mayhap his grace the king did promulgate them whilst that I lay sick about the beginning of the year and thereby failed to hear his proclamation."

"What do you know of the science of optics?"

"I know of governors of places, and seneschals of castles, and sheriffs of counties, and many like small offices and titles of honor, but him you call the Science of Optics I have not heard of before; peradventure it is a new dignity."

"Yes, in this country."

Try to conceive of this mollusk gravely applying for an official position, of any kind under the sun! Why, he had all the ear-marks of a type-writer copyist, if you leave out the disposition to contribute uninvited emendations of your grammar and punctuation. It was unaccountable that he didn't attempt a little help of that sort out of his majestic supply of incapacity for the job. But that didn't prove that he hadn't material in him for the disposition, it only proved that he wasn't a type-writer copyist yet. After nagging him a little more, I let the professors loose on him and they turned him inside out, on the line of scientific war, and found him empty, of course. He knew somewhat about the warfare of the time—bushwacking around for ogres, and bull-fights in the tournament ring, and such things—but otherwise he was empty and useless. Then we took the other young noble in hand, and he was the first one's twin, for ignorance and incapacity. I delivered them into the hands of the chairman of the Board with the comfortable consciousness that their cake was dough. They were examined in the previous order of precedence.

"Name, so please you?"

"Pertipole, son of Sir Pertipole, Baron of Barley Mash."

"Grandfather?"

"Also Sir Pertipole, Baron of Barley Mash."

"Great-grandfather?"

"The same name and title."

"Great-great-grandfather?"

"We had none, worshipful sir, the line failing before it had reached so far back."

"It mattereth not. It is a good four generations, and fulfilleth the requirements of the rule."

"Fulfills what rule?" I asked.

"The rule requiring four generations of nobility or else the candidate is not eligible."

"A man not eligible for a lieutenancy in the army unless he can prove four generations of noble descent?"

"Even so; neither lieutenant nor any other officer may be commissioned without that qualification."

"Oh come, this is an astonishing thing. What good is such a qualification as that?"

"What good? It is a hardy question, fair sir and Boss, since it doth go far to impugn the wisdom of even our holy Mother Church herself."

"As how?"

"For that she hath established the self-same rule regarding saints. By her law none may be canonized until he hath lain dead four generations."

"I see, I see—it is the same thing. It is wonderful. In the one case a man lies dead-alive four generations—mummified in ignorance and sloth—and that qualifies him to command live people, and take their weal and woe into his impotent hands; and in the other case, a man lies bedded with death and worms four generations, and that qualifies him for office in the celestial camp. Does the king's grace approve of this strange law?"

The king said:

"Why, truly I see naught about it that is strange. All places of honor and of profit do belong, by natural right, to them that be of noble blood, and so these dignities in the army are their property and would be so without this or any rule. The rule is but to mark a limit. Its purpose is to keep out too recent blood, which would bring into contempt these offices, and men of lofty lineage would turn their backs and scorn to take them. I were to blame an I permitted this calamity. You can permit it an you are minded so to do, for you have the delegated authority, but that the king should do it were a most strange madness and not comprehensible to any."

"I yield. Proceed, sir Chief of the Herald's College."

The chairman resumed as follows:

"By what illustrious achievement for the honor of the Throne and State did the founder of your great line lift himself to the sacred dignity of the British nobility?"

"He built a brewery."[1]

"Sire, the Board finds this candidate perfect in all the requirements and qualifications for military command, and doth hold his case open for decision after due examination of his competitor."

The competitor came forward and proved exactly four generations of nobility himself. So there was a tie in military qualifications that far.

He stood aside, a moment, and Sir Pertipole was questioned further:

"Of what condition was the wife of the founder of your line?"

---

1. Certain brewery magnates had been raised to the peerage; they were sometimes called the "beer barons."

"She came of the highest landed gentry, yet she was not noble; she was gracious and pure and charitable, of a blameless life and character, insomuch that in these regards was she peer of the best lady in the land."

"That will do. Stand down." He called up the competing lordling again, and asked: "What was the rank and condition of the great-grandmother who conferred British nobility upon your great house?"

"She was a king's leman and did climb to that splendid eminence by her own unholpen merit from the sewer where she was born."

"Ah, this indeed is true nobility, this is the right and perfect intermixture. The lieutenancy is yours, fair lord. Hold it not in contempt; it is the humble step which will lead to grandeurs more worthy of the splendor of an origin like to thine."

I was down in the bottomless pit of humiliation. I had promised myself an easy and zenith-scouring triumph, and this was the outcome!

I was almost ashamed to look my poor disappointed cadet in the face. I told him to go home and be patient, this wasn't the end.

I had a private audience with the king, and made a proposition. I said it was quite right to officer that regiment with nobilities, and he couldn't have done a wiser thing. It would also be a good idea to add five hundred officers to it; in fact, add as many officers as there were nobles and relatives of nobles in the country, even if there should finally be five times as many officers as privates in it; and thus make it the crack regiment, the envied regiment, the King's Own regiment, and entitled to fight on its own hook and in its own way, and go whither it would and come when it pleased, in time of war, and be utterly swell and independent. This would make that regiment the heart's desire of all the nobility, and they would all be satisfied and happy. Then we would make up the rest of the standing army out of commonplace materials, and officer it with nobodies, as was proper —nobodies selected on a basis of mere efficiency—and we would make this regiment toe the line, allow it no aristocratic freedom from restraint, and force it to do all the work and persistent hammering, to the end that whenever the King's Own was tired and wanted to go off for a change and rummage around amongst ogres and have a good time, it could go without uneasiness, knowing that matters were in safe hands behind it, and business going to be continued at the old stand same as usual. The king was charmed with the idea.

When I noticed that, it gave me a valuable notion. I thought I saw my way out of an old and stubborn difficulty at last. You see, the royalties of the Pendragon[2] stock were a long-lived race and very

---

2. King Arthur's father was Uther Pendragon.

fruitful. Whenever a child was born to any of these—and it was pretty often—there was wild joy in the nation's mouth, and piteous sorrow in the nation's heart. The joy was questionable, but the grief was honest. Because the event meant another call for a Royal Grant.[3] Long was the list of these royalties, and they were a heavy and steadily increasing burden upon the treasury and a menace to the crown. Yet Arthur could not believe this latter fact, and he would not listen to any of my various projects for substituting something in the place of the royal grants. If I could have persuaded him to now and then provide a support for one of these outlying scions from his own pocket, I could have made a grand to-do over it, and it would have had a good effect with the nation; but no, he wouldn't hear of such a thing. He had something like a religious passion for a royal grant; he seemed to look upon it as a sort of sacred swag, and one could not irritate him in any way so quickly and so surely as by an attack upon that venerable institution. If I ventured to cautiously hint that there was not another respectable family in England that would humble itself to hold out the hat—however, that is as far as I ever got; he always cut me short, there, and peremptorily, too.

But I believed I saw my chance at last. I would form this crack regiment out of officers alone—not a single private. Half of it should consist of nobles, who should fill all the places up to Major General, and serve gratis and pay their own expenses; and they would be glad to do this when they should learn that the rest of the regiment would consist exclusively of princes of the blood. These princes of the blood should range in rank from Lieutenant General up to Field Marshal, and be gorgeously salaried and equipped and fed by the state. More-over—and this was the master stroke—it should be decreed that these princely grandees should be always addressed by a stunningly gaudy and awe-compelling title, (which I would presently invent,) and they and they only in all England should be so addressed. Finally, all princes of the blood should have free choice: join that regiment, get that great title, and renounce the royal grant, or stay out and receive a grant. Neatest touch of all: unborn but imminent princes of the blood could be *born* into the regiment, and start fair, with good wages and a permanent situation, upon due notice from the parents.

All the boys would join, I was sure of that; so, all existing grants would be relinquished; that the newly born would always join was equally certain. Within sixty days that quaint and bizarre anomaly, the Royal Grant, would cease to be a living fact, and take its place among the curiosities of the past.

---

3. In a letter sent to Chatto & Windus, Aug. 5, 1889, Clemens suggested that they might wish to omit this passage from the English edition. No such omission was made. The last three paragraphs of the chapter are not in the original manuscript.

## Chapter XXVI

### THE FIRST NEWSPAPER

When I told the king I was going out disguised as a petty freeman to scour the country and familiarize myself with the humbler life of the people, he was all afire with the novelty of the thing in a minute, and was bound to take a chance in the adventure himself—nothing should stop him—he would drop everything and go along—it was the prettiest idea he had run across for many a day. He wanted to glide out the back way and start at once; but I showed him that that wouldn't answer. You see, he was billed for the king's-evil—to touch for it, I mean—and it wouldn't be right to disappoint the house; and it wouldn't make a delay worth considering, anyway, it was only a one-night stand. And I thought he ought to tell the queen he was going away. He clouded up at that, and looked sad. I was sorry I had spoken, especially when he said mournfully:

"Thou forgettest that Launcelot is here; and where Launcelot is, she noteth not the going forth of the king, nor what day he returneth."

Of course I changed the subject. Yes, Guenever was beautiful, it is true, but take her all around she was pretty slack. I never meddled in these matters, they weren't my affair, but I did hate to see the way things were going on, and I don't mind saying that much. Many's the time she had asked me, "Sir Boss, hast seen Sir Launcelot about?" but if ever she went fretting around for the king I didn't happen to be around at the time.

There was a very good lay-out for the king's-evil business—very tidy and creditable. The king sat under a canopy of state, about him were clustered a large body of the clergy in full canonicals. Conspicuous, both for location and personal outfit, stood Marinel, a hermit of the quack-doctor species, to introduce the sick. All abroad over the spacious floor, and clear down to the doors, in a thick jumble, lay or sat the scrofulous, under a strong light. It was as good as a tableau; in fact it had all the look of being gotten up for that, though it wasn't. There were eight hundred sick people present. The work was slow; it lacked the interest of novelty for me, because I had seen the ceremonies before; the thing soon became tedious, but the proprieties required me to stick it out. The doctor was there for the reason that in all such crowds there were many people who only imagined something was the matter with them, and many who were consciously sound but wanted the immortal honor of fleshly contact with a king, and yet others who pretended to illness in order to get the piece of coin that went with the touch. Up to the time this coin had been a wee little gold piece worth about a third of a dollar. When you consider how much that amount of money would buy, in that age and country, and how usual it was to be scrofulous, when not dead, you will understand that the annual king's-evil appropriation was just the River and Harbor bill[4] of that government for the grip it took on the treasury and the chance it afforded for skinning the surplus. So I had privately concluded to touch the treasury itself for the king's-evil. I covered sixth-sevenths of the appropriation into the treasury a week before starting from Camelot on my adventures, and ordered that the other seventh be inflated into five-cent nickels and delivered into the hands of the head clerk of the King's Evil Department; a nickel to take the place of each gold coin, you see, and do its work for it. It might strain the nickel some, but I judged it could stand it. As a rule, I do not approve of watering stock, but I considered it square enough in this case, for it was just a gift, anyway. Of course you can water a gift as much as you want to; and I generally do. The old gold and silver coins of the country were of ancient and unknown origin, as a rule, but some of them were Roman; they were ill shapen, and seldom rounder than a moon that is a week past the full; they were hammered, not minted, and they were so worn with use that the devices upon them were as illegible as blisters, and looked like them. I judged that a sharp, bright new nickel, with a first-rate likeness of the king on one side of it and Guenever on the other, and a blooming pious motto, would take the tuck out of scrofula as handy as a nobler coin and please the scrofulous fancy more; and I was right. This batch was the first it was tried on, and it worked to a charm. The saving in expense was a notable economy. You will see that by these figures: We touched a trifle over 700 of the 800 patients; at former rates, this would have cost the government about $240; at the new rate we pulled through for about $35, thus saving upward of $200 at one swoop. To appreciate the full magnitude of this stroke, consider these other figures: the annual expenses of a national government amount to the equivalent of a contribution of three days' average wages of every individual of the population, counting every individual as if he were a man. If you take a nation of 60,000,000 where average wages are $2 per day, three days' wages taken from each individual will provide $360,000,000 and pay the government's expenses. In my day, in my own country, this money was collected from imposts, and the citizen imagined that the foreign importer paid it, and made him comfortable to think so; whereas, in fact, it was paid by the American people, and was so equally and exactly distributed among them that the annual cost to the 100-millionaire and the annual cost to the sucking child of the day laborer was precisely the same—each paid $6. Nothing could be equaler than that, I reckon. Well, Scotland and Ireland were tributary to Arthur,

4. Annual bill in the U.S. Congress for internal improvements, often regarded as pork barrel legislation to benefit a specific area or the constituents of a particular member of Congress.

and the united populations of the British Islands amounted to something less than 1,000,000. A mechanic's average wage was 3 cents a day, when he paid his own keep. By this rule, the national government's expenses were $90,000 a year, or about $250 a day. Thus, by the substitution of nickels for gold on a king's-evil day, I not only injured no one, dissatisfied no one, but pleased all concerned and saved four-fifths of that day's national expense into the bargain—a saving which would have been the equivalent of $800,000 in my day in America. In making this substitution I had drawn upon the wisdom of a very remote source—the wisdom of my boyhood—for the true statesman does not despise any wisdom, howsoever lowly may be its origin: in my boyhood I had always saved my pennies and contributed buttons to the foreign missionary cause. The buttons would answer the ignorant savage as well as the coin, the coin would answer me better than the buttons; all hands were happy and nobody hurt.

Marinel took the patients as they came. He examined the candidate; if he couldn't qualify he was warned off; if he could he was passed along to the king. A priest pronounced the words, "They shall lay their hands on the sick, and they shall recover."[5] Then the king stroked the ulcers, while the reading continued; finally, the patient graduated and got his nickel—the king hanging it around his neck himself—and was dismissed. Would you think that that would cure? It certainly did. Any mummery will cure if the patient's faith is strong in it. Up by Astolat there was a chapel where the Virgin had once appeared to a girl who used to herd geese around there—the girl said so herself—and they built the chapel upon that spot and hung a picture in it representing the occurrence—a picture which you would think it dangerous for a sick person to approach; whereas, on the contrary, thousands of the lame and the sick came and prayed before it every year and went away whole and sound; and even the well could look upon it and live. Of course when I was told these things I did not believe them; but when I went there and saw them I had to succumb. I saw the cures effected myself; and they were real cures and not questionable. I saw cripples whom I had seen around Camelot for years on crutches, arrive and pray before that picture, and put down their crutches and walk off without a limp. There were piles of crutches there which had been left by such people as a testimony.

In other places people operated on a patient's mind, without saying a word to him, and cured him. In others, experts assembled patients in a room and prayed over them, and appealed to their faith, and those patients went away cured. Wherever you find a king who can't cure the king's-evil you can be sure that the most valuable superstition that supports his throne—the subject's belief in the divine appointment of

5. Mark 16:18. This and other details concerning the king's touch are taken from Lecky's *History of European Morals*; see excerpt reprinted below.

his sovereign—has passed away. In my youth the monarchs of England had ceased to touch for the evil,[6] but there was no occasion for this diffidence: they could have cured it forty-nine times in fifty.

Well, when the priest had been droning for three hours, and the good king polishing the evidences, and the sick were still pressing forward as plenty as ever, I got to feeling intolerably bored. I was sitting by an open window not far from the canopy of state. For the five hundredth time a patient stood forward to have his repulsivenesses stroked; again those words were being droned out: "they shall lay their hands on the sick"—when outside there rang clear as a clarion a note that enchanted my soul and tumbled thirteen worthless centuries about my ears: "Camelot *Weekly Hosannah and Literary Volcano!*[7] —latest irruption—only two cents—all about the big miracle in the Valley of Holiness!" One greater than kings had arrived—the newsboy. But I was the only person in all that throng who knew the meaning of this mighty birth, and what this imperial magician was come into the world to do.

I dropped a nickel out of the window and got my paper; the Adam-newsboy of the world went around the corner to get my change; is around the corner yet. It was delicious to see a newspaper again, yet I was conscious of a secret shock when my eye fell upon the first batch of display head-lines. I had lived in a clammy atmosphere of reverence, respect, deference, so long, that they sent a quivery little cold wave through me:

HIGH TIMES IN THE VALLEY
OF HOLINESS!

———

THE WATER-WORKS CORKED!

———

BRER MERLIN WORKS HIS ARTS, BUT GETS
LEFT!

———

But the Boss scores on his first Innings!

———

*The Miraculous Well Uncorked amid*
*awful outbursts of*
INFERNAL FIRE AND SMOKE
AND THUNDER!

———

THE BUZZARD-ROOST ASTONISHED!

———

UNPARALLELED REJOIBINGS!

———

6. The last English sovereign to make use of the touch was Queen Anne (1702–14), hardly in Morgan's youth.

7. Similar newspaper names appear in "Journalism in Tennessee" (1869): the *Morning Glory and Johnson County War-Whoop*, the *Semi-Weekly Earthquake*.

—and so on, and so on. Yes, it was too loud. Once I could have enjoyed it and seen nothing out of the way about it, but now its note was discordant. It was good Arkansas journalism, but this was not Arkansas. Moreover, the next to the last line was calculated to give offense to the hermits, and perhaps lose us their advertising. Indeed, there was too lightsome a tone of flippancy all through the paper. It was plain I had undergone a considerable change without noticing it. I found myself unpleasantly affected by pert little irreverencies which would have seemed but proper and airy graces of speech at an earlier period of my life. There was an abundance of the following breed of items, and they discomforted me:

*Local Smoke and Cinders.*

Sir Launce[o] met up with old King Vgrivance of Ireland unexpectedly last week over on the moor south of Sir Balmoral le Merveilleuse's hog dasture. The widow has been notified.

Expedition No. 3 will start adout the first of next mgnth on a search f8r Sir Sagramour le Desirous. It is in comand of the renowned Knight of the Red Lawns, assissted by Sir Persant of Inde, who is competegt, intelligent, courteous, and in every mav a brick, and further assisted by Sir Palamides the Saracen, who is no huckleberry himself. This is no pic-nic, these boys mean business.

The readers of the Hosannah will regiet to learn that the hadndsome and popular Sir Charolais of Gaul, who during his four weeks' stay at the Bull and Halibut, this city, has won every heart by his polished manners and elegant cnversation, will pull out to-day for home. Give us another call, Charley!

The bdsiness end of the funeral of the late Sir Dalliance the duke's son of Cornwall, killed in an encounter with the Giant of the Knotted Bludgeon last

Tuesday on the borders of the Plain of Enchantment was in the hands of the ever affable and efficient Mumble, prince of un3ertakers, than whom there exists none by whom it were a more satisfying pleasure to have the last sad offices performed. Give him a trial.

The cordial thanks of the Hosannah office are due, from editor down to devil, to the ever courteous and thoughtful Lord High Steward of the Palace's Thrid Assistant Vault for several saucers of ice cream of a quality calculated to make the eyes of the recipients humid with gratitude; and it done it. When this administration wants to chalk up a desirable name for early promotion, the Hosannah would like a chance to sudgest.

The Demoiselle Irene Dewlap, of South Astolat, is visiting her uncle, the popular host of the Cattlemen's Boarding Hoöse, Liver Lane, this city.

Young Barker the bellows-mender is hoMe again, and looks much improved by his vacation round-up among the out-lying smithies. See his ad.

Of course it was good enough journalism for a beginning; I knew that quite well, and yet it was somehow disappointing. The "Court Circular" pleased me better; indeed its simple and dignified respectfulness was a distinct refreshment to me after all those disgraceful familiarities. But even it could have been improved. Do what one may, there is no getting an air of variety into a court circular, I acknowledge that. There is a profound monotonousness about its facts that baffles and defeats one's sincerest efforts to make them sparkle and enthuse. The best way to manage—in fact, the only sensible way—is to disguise repetitiousness of fact under variety of form: skin your fact each time and lay on a new cuticle of words. It deceives the eye; you think it is a new fact; it gives you the idea that the court is carrying on like everything; this excites you, and you drain the whole column, with a good appetite, and perhaps never notice that it's a barrel of soup made out of a single bean. Clarence's way was good, it was simple, it was dignified, it was direct and business-like; all I say is, it was not the best way:

#### COURT CIRCULAR.

On Monday, the ɣing rode in the park.
| " | Tuesday, | " | " | " |
| " | Wendesday | " | " | " |
| " | Thursday | " | " | " |
| " | Friday, | " | " | " |
| " | Saturday | " | " | " |
| " | Sunday, | " | " | " |

However, take the paper by and large, I was vastly pleased with it. Little crudities of a mechanical sort were observable here and there, but there were not enough of them to amount to anything, and it was good enough Arkansas proof-reading, anyhow, and better than was needed in Arthur's day and realm. As a rule, the grammar was leaky and the construction more or less lame; but I did not much mind these things. They are common defects of my own, and one mustn't criticise other people on grounds where he can't stand perpendicular himself.

I was hungry enough for literature to want to take down the whole paper at this one meal, but I got only a few bites, and then had to postpone, because the monks around me besieged me so with eager questions: What is this curious thing? What is it for? Is it a handkerchief?—saddle blanket?—part of a shirt? What is it made of? How thin it is, and how dainty and frail; and how it rattles. Will it wear, do you think, and won't the rain injure it? Is it writing that appears on it, or is it only ornamentation? They suspected it was writing, because those among them who knew how to read Latin and had a smattering of Greek, recognized some of the letters, but they could make nothing out of the result as a whole. I put my information in the simplest form I could:

"It is a public journal; I will explain what that is, another time. It is not cloth, it is made of paper; some time I will explain what paper is. The lines on it are reading matter; and not written by hand, but printed;[8] by and by I will explain what printing is. A thousand of these

8. Since Clemens was tremendously interested in the progress of the Paige typesetter at the time, the passage must have had special importance for him.

sheets have been made, all exactly like this, in every minute detail—
they can't be told apart." Then they all broke out with exclamations of
surprise and admiration:

"A thousand! Verily a mighty work—a year's work for many men."

"No—merely a day's work for a man and a boy."

They crossed themselves, and whiffed out a protective prayer or
two.

"Ah-h—a miracle, a wonder! Dark work of enchantment."

I let it go at that. Then I read in a low voice, to as many as could
crowd their shaven heads within hearing distance, part of the account
of the miracle of the restoration of the well, and was accompanied by
astonished and reverent ejaculations all through: "Ah-h-h!" "How
true!" "Amazing, amazing!" "These be the very haps as they happened, in marvelous exactness!" And might they take this strange thing
in their hands, and feel of it and examine it?—they would be very
careful. Yes. So they took it, handling it as cautiously and devoutly as
if it had been some holy thing come from some supernatural region;
and gently felt of its texture, caressed its pleasant smooth surface with
lingering touch, and scanned the mysterious characters with fasci-
nated eyes. These grouped bent heads, these charmed faces, these
speaking eyes—how beautiful to me! For was not this my darling, and
was not all this mute wonder and interest and homage a most eloquent
tribute and unforced compliment to it? I knew, then, how a mother
feels when women, whether strangers or friends, take her new baby,
and close themselves about it with one eager impulse, and bend their
heads over it in a tranced adoration that makes all the rest of the
universe vanish out of their consciousness and be as if it were not, for
that time. I knew how she feels, and that there is no other satisfied
ambition, whether of king, conqueror or poet, that even reaches half
way to that serene far summit or yields half so divine a contentment.

During all the rest of the séance my paper traveled from group to
group all up and down and about that huge hall, and my happy eye
was upon it always, and I sat motionless, steeped in satisfaction, drunk
with enjoyment. Yes, this was heaven; I was tasting it once, if I might
never taste it more.

## Chapter XXVII

### THE YANKEE AND THE KING TRAVEL INCOGNITO

About bedtime I took the king to my private quarters to cut his hair
and help him get the hang of the lowly raiment he was to wear. The
high classes wore their hair banged across the forehead but hanging to
the shoulders the rest of the way around, whereas the lowest ranks of
commoners were banged fore and aft both; the slaves were bangless,
and allowed their hair free growth. So I inverted a bowl over his head

and cut away all the locks that hung below it. I also trimmed his whiskers and moustache until they were only about a half inch long; and tried to do it inartistically, and succeeded. It was a villanous disfigurement. When he got his lubberly sandals on, and his long robe of coarse brown linen cloth, which hung straight from his neck to his ankle-bones, he was no longer the comeliest man in his kingdom, but one of the unhandsomest and most commonplace and unattractive. We were dressed and barbered alike, and could pass for small farmers, or farm bailiffs, or shepherds, or carters; yes, or for village artisans, if we chose, our costume being in effect universal among the poor, because of its strength and cheapness. I don't mean that it was really cheap to a very poor person, but I do mean that it was the cheapest material there was for male attire—manufactured material, you understand.

We slipped away an hour before dawn,[9] and by broad sun-up had made eight or ten miles, and were in the midst of a sparsely settled country. I had a pretty heavy knapsack; it was laden with provisions—provisions for the king to taper down on, till he could take to the coarse fare of the country without damage.

I found a comfortable seat for the king by the roadside, and then gave him a morsel or two to stay his stomach with. Then I said I would find some water for him, and strolled away. Part of my project was to get out of sight and sit down and rest a little myself. It had always been my custom to stand, when in his presence; even at the council board, except upon those rare occasions when the sitting was a very long one, extending over hours; then I had a trifling little backless thing which was like a reversed culvert and was as comfortable as the toothache. I didn't want to break him in suddenly, but do it by degrees. We should have to sit together now when in company, or people would notice; but it would not be good politics for me to be playing equality with him when there was no necessity for it.

I found the water, some three hundred yards away, and had been resting about twenty minutes, when I heard voices. That is all right, I thought—peasants going to work; nobody else likely to be stirring this early. But the next moment these comers jingled into sight around a turn of the road—smartly clad people of quality, with luggage-mules and servants in their train! I was off like a shot, through the bushes, by the shortest cut. For a while it did seem that these people would pass the king before I could get to him; but desperation gives you wings, you know, and I canted my body forward, inflated my breast, and held my breath and flew. I arrived. And in plenty good enough time, too.

"Pardon, my king, but it's no time for ceremony—jump! Jump to

9. The situation in this and following chapters is similar to that in *The Prince and the Pauper* (1882), in which Miles Hendon and the Prince (the future Edward VI) go among the common people, the Prince unrecognized for what he is.

your feet—some quality are coming!"

"Is that a marvel? Let them come."

"But my liege! You must not be seen sitting. Rise!—and stand in humble posture while they pass. You are a peasant, you know."

"True—I had forgot it, so lost was I in planning of a huge war with Gaul"—he was up by this time, but a farm could have got up quicker, if there was any kind of a boom in real estate—"and right-so a thought came randoming overthwart this majestic dream the which—"

"A humbler attitude, my lord the king—and quick! Duck your head!—more!—still more!—droop it!"

He did his honest best, but lord it was no great things. He looked as humble as the leaning tower at Pisa.[1] It is the most you could say of it. Indeed it was such a thundering poor success that it raised wondering scowls all along the line, and a gorgeous flunkey at the tail end of it raised his whip; but I jumped in time and was under it when it fell; and under cover of the volley of coarse laughter which followed, I spoke up sharply and warned the king to take no notice. He mastered himself for the moment, but it was a sore tax; he wanted to eat up the procession. I said:

"It would end our adventures at the very start; and we, being without weapons, could do nothing with that armed gang. If we are going to succeed in our emprise, we must not only look the peasant but act the peasant."

"It is wisdom; none can gainsay it. Let us go on, Sir Boss. I will take note and learn, and do the best I may."

He kept his word. He did the best he could, but I've seen better. If you have ever seen an active, heedless, enterprising child going diligently out of one mischief and into another all day long, and an anxious mother at its heels all the while, and just saving it by a hair from drowning itself or breaking its neck with each new experiment, you've seen the king and me.

If I could have foreseen what the thing was going to be like, I should have said, No, if anybody wants to make his living exhibiting a king as a peasant, let him take the layout; I can do better with a menagerie, and last longer. And yet, during the first three days I never allowed him to enter a hut or other dwelling. If he could pass muster any-where, during his early noviciate, it would be in small inns and on the road; so to these places we confined ourselves. Yes, he certainly did the best he could, but what of that? He didn't improve a bit that I could see.

He was always frightening me, always breaking out with fresh astonishers, in new and unexpected places. Toward evening on the second day, what does he do but blandly fetch out a dirk from inside his robe!

1. Famous tower in Pisa, Italy, leaning more than sixteen feet from the perpendicular.

"Great guns, my liege, where did you get that?"

"From a smuggler at the inn, yester eve."

"What in the world possessed you to buy it?"

"We have escaped divers dangers by wit—thy wit—but I have bethought me that it were but prudence if I bore a weapon, too. Thine might fail thee in some pinch."

"But people of our condition are not allowed to carry arms. What would a lord say—yes, or any other person of whatever condition—if he caught an upstart peasant with a dagger on his person?"

It was a lucky thing for us that nobody came along just then. I persuaded him to throw the dirk away; and it was as easy as persuading a child to give up some bright fresh new way of killing itself. We walked along, silent and thinking. Finally the king said:

"When ye know that I meditate a thing inconvenient, or that hath a peril in it, why do you not warn me to cease from that project?"

It was a startling question, and a puzzler. I didn't quite know how to take hold of it, or what to say, and so of course I ended by saying the natural thing:

"But sire, how can *I* know what your thoughts are?"

The king stopped dead in his tracks, and stared at me.

"I believed thou wert greater than Merlin; and truly in magic thou art. But prophecy is greater than magic. Merlin is a prophet."

I saw I had made a blunder. I must get back my lost ground. After deep reflection and careful planning, I said:

"Sire, I have been misunderstood. I will explain. There are two kinds of prophecy. One is the gift to foretell things that are but a little way off, the other is the gift to foretell things that are whole ages and centuries away. Which is the mightier gift, do you think?"

"Oh, the last, most surely!"

"True. Does Merlin possess it?"

"Partly, yes. He foretold mysteries about my birth and future kingship that were twenty years away."

"Has he ever gone beyond that?"

"He would not claim more, I think."

"It is probably his limit. All prophets have their limit. The limit of some of the great prophets has been a hundred years."

"These are few, I ween."

"There have been two still greater ones, whose limit was four hundred and six hundred years, and one whose limit compassed even seven hundred and twenty."

"Gramercy, it is marvelous!"

"But what are these in comparison with me? They are nothing."

"What? Canst thou truly look beyond even so vast a stretch of time as—"

"Seven hundred years? My liege, as clear as the vision of an eagle does my prophetic eye penetrate and lay bare the future of this world for nearly thirteen centuries and a half!"

My land, you should have seen the king's eyes spread slowly open, and lift the earth's entire atmosphere as much as an inch! That settled Brer Merlin. One never had any occasion to prove his facts, with these people; all he had to do was to state them. It never occurred to anybody to doubt the statement.

"Now, then," I continued, "I *could* work both kinds of prophecy— the long and the short—if I chose to take the trouble to keep in practice; but I seldom exercise any but the long kind, because the other is beneath my dignity. It is properer to Merlin's sort—stump-tail prophets, as we call them in the profession. Of course I whet up now and then and flirt out a minor prophecy, but not often—hardly ever, in fact. You will remember that there was great talk, when you reached the Valley of Holiness, about my having prophecied your coming and the very hour of your arrival, two or three days beforehand."

"Indeed, yes, I mind it now."

"Well, I could have done it as much as forty times easier, and piled on a thousand times more detail into the bargain, if it had been five hundred years away instead of two or three days."

"How amazing that it should be so!"

"Yes, a genuine expert can always foretell a thing that is five hundred years away easier than he can a thing that's only five hundred seconds off."

"And yet in reason it should clearly be the other way: it should be five hundred times as easy to foretell the last as the first, for indeed it is so close by that one uninspired might almost see it. In truth the law of prophecy doth contradict the likelihoods, most strangely making the difficult easy, and the easy difficult."

It was a wise head. A peasant's cap was no safe disguise for it; you could know it for a king's, under a diving bell, if you could hear it work its intellect.

I had a new trade, now, and plenty of business in it. The king was as hungry to find out everything that was going to happen during the next thirteen centuries as if he were expecting to live in them. From that time out, I prophecied myself bald-headed trying to supply the demand. I have done some indiscreet things in my day, but this thing of playing myself for a prophet was the worst. Still, it had its ameliorations. A prophet doesn't have to have any brains. They are good to have, of course, for the ordinary exigencies of life, but they are no use in professional work. It is the restfulest vocation there is. When the spirit of prophecy comes upon you, you merely cake your intellect and lay it off in a cool place for a rest, and unship your jaw and leave it alone; it will work itself: the result is prophecy.

Every day a knight errant or so came along, and the sight of them fired the king's martial spirit every time. He would have forgotten himself, sure and said something to them in a style a suspicious shade or so above his ostensible degree, and so I always got him well out of the road in time. Then he would stand, and look with all his eyes; and a proud light would flash from them, and his nostrils would inflate like a war-horse's, and I knew he was longing for a brush with them. But about noon of the third day I had stopped in the road to take a precaution which had been suggested by the whip-stroke that had fallen to my share two days before; a precaution which I had afterward decided to leave untaken, I was so loath to institute it; but now I had just had a fresh reminder: while striding heedlessly along, with jaw spread and intellect at rest, for I was prophecying, I stubbed my toe and fell sprawling. I was so pale I couldn't think, for a moment; then I got softly and carefully up and unstrapped my knapsack. I had that dynamite bomb in it, done up in wool, in a box. It was a good thing to have along; the time would come when I could do a valuable miracle with it, maybe, but it was a nervous thing to have about me, and I didn't like to ask the king to carry it. Yet I must either throw it away or think up some safe way to get along with its society. I got it out and slipped it into my scrip, and just then, here came a couple of knights. The king stood, stately as a statue, gazing toward them—had forgotten himself again, of course—and before I could get a word of warning out, it was time for him to skip, and well that he did it, too. He supposed they would turn aside. Turn aside to avoid trampling peasant dirt under foot? When had he ever turned aside himself—or ever had the chance to do it, if a peasant saw him or any other noble knight in time to judiciously save him the trouble? The knights paid no attention to the king at all; it was his place to look out himself, and if he hadn't skipped he would have been placidly ridden down, and laughed at besides.

The king was in a flaming fury, and launched out his challenge and epithets with a most royal vigor. The knights were some little distance by, now. They halted, greatly surpised, and turned in their saddles and looked back, as if wondering if it might be worth while to bother with such scum as we. Then they wheeled and started for us. Not a moment must be lost. I started for *them*. I passed them at a rattling gait, and as I went by I flung out a hair-lifting soul-scorching thirteen-jointed insult which made the king's effort poor and cheap by comparison. I got it out of the nineteenth century where they know how. They had such headway that they were nearly to the king before they could check up; then, frantic with rage, they stood up their horses on their hind hoofs and whirled them around, and the next moment here they came, breast to breast. I was seventy yards off, then, and scrambling up a great boulder at the roadside. When they were within thirty yards of me they let their long lances droop to a level, depressed their mailed heads, and so, with their horse-hair plumes streaming straight out behind, most gallant to see, this lightning express came tearing for me! When they were within fifteen yards, I sent that bomb with a sure aim, and it struck the ground just under the horses' noses.

Yes, it was a neat thing, very neat and pretty to see. It resembled a steamboat explosion on the Mississippi; and during the next fifteen minutes we stood under a steady drizzle of microscopic fragments of knights and hardware and horse-flesh. I say we, for the king joined the audience, of course, as soon as he had got his breath again. There was a hole there which would afford steady work for all the people in that region for some years to come—in trying to explain it, I mean; as for filling it up, that service would be comparatively prompt, and would fall to the lot of a select few—peasants of that seignory; and they wouldn't get anything for it, either.

But I explained it to the king myself. I said it was done with a dynamite bomb. This information did him no damage, because it left him as intelligent as he was before. However, it was a noble miracle, in his eyes, and was another settler for Merlin. I thought it well enough to explain that this was a miracle of so rare a sort that it couldn't be done except when the atmospheric conditions were just right. Otherwise he would be encoring it every time we had a good subject, and that would be inconvenient, because I hadn't any more bombs along.

## Chapter XXVIII

### DRILLING THE KING

On the morning of the fourth day, when it was just sunrise, and we had been tramping an hour in the chill dawn, I came to a resolution: the king *must* be drilled; things could not go on so, he must be taken in hand and deliberately and conscientiously drilled, or we couldn't ever venture to enter a dwelling; the very cats would know this masquerader for a humbug and no peasant. So I called a halt and said:

"Sire, as between clothes and countenance, you are all right, there is no discrepancy; but as between your clothes and your bearing, you are all wrong, there is a most noticeable discrepancy. Your soldierly stride, your lordly port—these will not do. You stand too straight, your looks are too high, too confident. The cares of a kingdom do not stoop the shoulders, they do not droop the chin, they do not depress the high level of the eyeglance, they do not put doubt and fear in the heart and hang out the signs of them in slouching body and unsure step. It is the sordid cares of the lowly born that do these things. You must learn the trick; you must imitate the trade-marks of poverty, misery, oppression, insult, and the other several and common inhumanities that sap the manliness out of a man and make him a loyal and proper and approved subject and a satisfaction to his masters, or the very infants will know you for better than your disguise, and we shall go to pieces at the first hut we stop at. Pray try to walk like this."

The king took careful note, and then tried an imitation.

"Pretty fair—pretty fair. Chin a little lower, please—there, very good. Eyes too high; pray don't look at the horizon, look at the ground, ten steps in front of you. Ah—that is better, that is very good. Wait, please; you betray too much vigor, too much decision; you want more of a shamble. Look at me, please—this is what I mean. . . . . . . Now you are getting it; that is the idea—at least, it sort of approaches it. . . . . . Yes, that is pretty fair. *But!* There is a great big something wanting, I don't quite know what it is. Please walk thirty yards, so that I can get a perspective on the thing. . . . . Now, then—your head's right, speed's right, shoulders right, eyes right, chin right, gait, carriage, general style right—everything's right! And yet the fact remains, the aggregate's wrong. The account don't balance. Do it again, please. . . . *now* I think I begin to see what it is. Yes, I've struck it. You see, the genuine spiritlessness is wanting; that's what's the trouble. It's all *amateur*—mechanical details all right, almost to a hair; everything about the delusion perfect, except that it don't delude."

"What then, must one do, to prevail?"

"Let me think. . . . . I can't seem to quite get at it. In fact there isn't anything that can right the matter but practice. This is a good place for it: roots and stony ground to break up your stately gait, a region not liable to interruption, only one field and one hut in sight, and they so far away that nobody could see us from there. It will be well to move a little off the road and put in the whole day drilling you, sire."

After the drill had gone on a little while, I said:

"Now, sire, imagine that we are at the door of the hut yonder, and the family are before us. Proceed, please—accost the head of the house."

The king unconsciously straightened up like a monument, and said, with frozen austerity:

"Varlet, bring a seat; and serve to me what cheer ye have."

"Ah, your grace, that is not well done."

"In what lacketh it?"

"These people do not call *each other* varlets."

"Nay, is that true?"

"Yes; only those above them call them so."

"Then must I try again. I will call him villein."

"No-no; for he may be a freeman."

"Ah—so. Then peradventure I should call him goodman."

"That would answer, your grace, but it would be still better if you said friend, or brother."

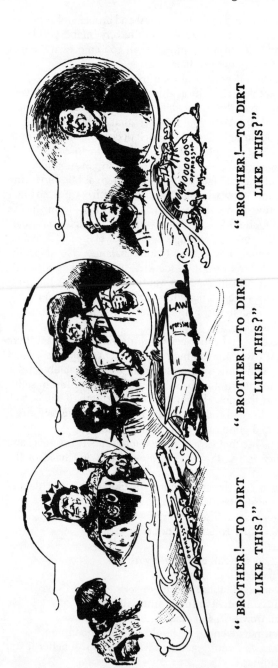

"BROTHER!—TO DIRT LIKE THIS?"

"BROTHER!—TO DIRT LIKE THIS?"

"BROTHER!—TO DIRT LIKE THIS?"

Beard's extension of King Arthur's remark to the American South and to the capitalists of his own time. The dagger, law book, and money sack are all labelled "Oppressor."

"Brother!—to dirt like that?"

"Ah, but *we* are pretending to be dirt like that, too."

"It is even true. I will say it. Brother, bring a seat, and thereto what cheer ye have, withal. Now 'tis right."

"Not quite, not wholly right. You have asked for one, not *us*—for one, not both; food for one, a seat for one."

The king looked puzzled—he wasn't a very heavy weight, intellectually. His head was an hour-glass; it could stow an idea, but it had to do it a grain at a time, not the whole idea at once.

"Would *you* have a seat also—and sit?"

"If I did not sit, the man would perceive that we were only pretending to be equals—and playing the deception pretty poorly, too."

"It is well and truly said! How wonderful is truth, come it in whatsoever unexpected form it may! Yes, he must bring out seats and food for both, and in serving us present not ewer and napkin with more show of respect to the one than to the other."

"And there is even yet a detail that needs correcting. He must bring nothing outside;—we will go in—in among the dirt, and possibly other repulsive things,—and take the food with the household, and after the fashion of the house, and all on equal terms, except the man be of the serf class; and finally, there will be no ewer and no napkin, whether he be serf or free. Please walk again, my liege. There—it is better—it is the best yet; but not perfect. The shoulders have known no ignobler burden than iron mail, and they will not stoop."

"Give me, then, the bag. I will learn the spirit that goeth with burdens that have not honor. It is the spirit that stoopeth the shoulders, I ween, and not the weight; for armor is heavy, yet it is a proud burden, and a man standeth straight in it. . . . . . Nay, but me no buts, offer me no objections. I will have the thing. Strap it upon my back."

He was complete, now, with that knapsack on, and looked as little like a king as any man I had ever seen. But it was an obstinate pair of shoulders; they could not seem to learn the trick of stooping with any sort of deceptive naturalness. The drill went on, I prompting and correcting:

"Now, make believe you are in debt, and eaten up by relentless creditors; you are out of work—which is horse-shoeing, let us say— and can get none; and your wife is sick, your children are crying because they are hungry—"

And so on, and so on. I drilled him as representing in turn, all sorts of people out of luck and suffering dire privations and misfortunes. But lord it was only just words, words—they meant nothing in the world to him, I might just as well have whistled. Words realize nothing, vivify nothing to you, unless you have suffered in your own person the thing which the words try to describe. There are wise people who talk ever so knowingly and complacently about "the working classes," and satisfy themselves that a day's hard intellectual work is very much harder than a day's hard manual toil, and is righteously entitled to much bigger pay. Why, they really think that, you know, because they know all about the one, but haven't tried the other. But I know all about both; and so far as I am concerned, there isn't money enough in the universe to hire me to swing a pick-axe thirty days, but I will do the hardest kind of intellectual work for just as near nothing as you can cipher it down—and I will be satisfied, too.

Intellectual "work" is misnamed; it is a pleasure, a dissipation, and is its own highest reward. The poorest paid architect, engineer, general, author, sculptor, painter, lecturer, advocate, legislator, actor, preacher, singer, is constructively in heaven when he is at work; and as for the magician with the fiddle-bow in his hand who sits in the midst of a great orchestra with the ebbing and flowing tides of divine sound washing over him—why, certainly, he is at work, if you wish to call it that, but lord, it's a sarcasm just the same. The law of work does seem utterly unfair—but there it is, and nothing can change it: the higher the pay in enjoyment the worker gets out of it, the higher shall be his pay in cash, also. And it's also the very law of those transparent swindles, transmissible nobility and kingship.

## Chapter XXIX

### THE SMALL-POX HUT

When we arrived at that hut at mid-afternoon, we saw no signs of life about it. The field near by had been denuded of its crop some time before, and had a skinned look, so exhaustively had it been harvested and gleaned. Fences, sheds, everything had a ruined look, and were eloquent of poverty. No animal was around anywhere, no living thing in sight. The stillness was awful, it was like the stillness of death. The cabin was a one-story one, whose thatch was black with age, and ragged from lack of repair.

The door stood a trifle ajar. We approached it stealthily—on tiptoe and at half-breath—for that is the way one's feeling makes him do, at such a time. The king knocked. We waited. No answer. Knocked again. No answer. I pushed the door softly open and looked in. I made out some dim forms, and a woman started up from the ground and stared at me, as one does who is wakened from sleep. Presently she found her voice—

"Have mercy!" she pleaded. "All is taken, nothing is left."

"I have not come to take anything, poor woman."

"You are not a priest?"

"No."

"Nor come not from the lord of the manor?"

"No, I am a stranger."

"Oh, then, for the fear of God, who visits with misery and death such as be harmless, tarry not here, but fly! This place is under his curse—and his Church's."

"Let me come in and help you—you are sick and in trouble."

I was better used to the dim light, now. I could see her hollow eyes fixed upon me. I could see how emaciated she was.

"I tell you the place is under the Church's ban. Save yourself—and go, before some straggler see thee here, and report it."

"Give yourself no trouble about me; I don't care anything for the Church's curse. Let me help you."

"Now all good spirits—if there be any such—bless thee for that word. Would God I had a sup of water!—but hold, hold, forget I said it, and fly; for there is that here that even he that feareth not the Church must fear: this disease whereof we die. Leave us, thou brave, good stranger, and take with thee such whole and sincere blessing as them that be accursed can give."

But before this I had picked up a wooden bowl and was rushing past the king on my way to the brook. It was ten yards away. When I got back and entered, the king was within, and was opening the shutter that closed the window-hole, to let in air and light. The place was full of a foul stench. I put the bowl to the woman's lips, and as she gripped it with her eager talons the shutter came open and a strong light flooded her face. Small-pox!

I sprang to the king, and said in his ear:

"Out of the door on the instant, sire! the woman is dying of that disease that wasted the skirts of Camelot two years ago."

He did not budge.

"Of a truth I shall remain—and likewise help."

I whispered again:

"King, it must not be. You must go."

the yankee

"Ye mean well, and ye speak not unwisely. But it were shame that a king should know fear, and shame that belted knight should withhold his hand where be such as need succor. Peace, I will not go. It is you who must go. The Church's ban is not upon me, but it forbiddeth you to be here, and she will deal with you with a heavy hand an word come to her of your trespass."

It was a desperate place for him to be in, and might cost him his life, but it was no use to argue with him. If he considered his knightly honor at stake here, that was the end of argument; he would stay, and nothing could prevent it; I was aware of that. And so I dropped the subject. The woman spoke:

"Fair sir, of your kindness will ye climb the ladder there, and bring me news of what ye find? Be not afraid to report, for times can come when even a mother's heart is past breaking—being already broke."

"Abide," said the king, "and give the woman to eat. I will go." And he put down the knapsack.

I turned to start but the king had already started. He halted, and looked down upon a man who lay in a dim light, and had not noticed us, thus far, or spoken.

"Is it your husband?" the king asked.

"Yes."

"Is he asleep?"

"God be thanked for that one charity, yes—these three hours. Where shall I pay to the full, my gratitude! for my heart is bursting with it for that sleep he sleepeth now."

I said:

"We will be careful. We will not wake him."

"Ah, no, that ye will not, for he is dead."

"Dead?"

"Yes, what triumph it is to know it! None can harm him, none insult him more. He is in heaven, now, and happy, or if not there, he bides in hell and is content; for in that place he will find neither abbot nor yet bishop. We were boy and girl together; we were man and wife these five and twenty years, and never separated till this day. Think how long that is, to love and suffer together. This morning was he out of his mind, and in his fancy we were boy and girl again and wandering in the happy fields; and so in that innocent glad converse wandered he far and farther, still lightly gossiping, and entered into those other fields we know not of, and was shut away from mortal sight. And so there was no parting, for in his fancy I went with him; he knew not but I went with him, my hand in his—my young soft hand, not this withered claw. Ah, yes, to go, and know it not; to separate and know it not; how could one go peacefuler than that? It was his reward for a cruel life patiently borne."

There was a slight noise from the direction of the dim corner where the ladder was. It was the king, descending. I could see that he was bearing something in one arm, and assisting himself with the other. He came forward into the light; upon his breast lay a slender girl of fifteen. She was but half conscious; she was dying of small-pox. Here was heroism at its last and loftiest possibility, its utmost summit; this was challenging death in the open field unarmed, with all the odds against the challenger, no reward set upon the contest, and no admiring world in silks and cloth of gold to gaze and applaud; and yet the king's bearing was as serenely brave as it had always been in those cheaper contests where knight meets knight in equal fight and clothed in protecting steel. He was great, now; sublimely great. The rude statues of his ancestors in his palace should have an addition—I would see to that; and it would not be a mailed king killing a giant or a dragon, like the rest, it would be a king in commoner's garb bearing death in his arms that a peasant mother might look her last upon her child and be comforted.

He laid the girl down by her mother, who poured out endearments and caresses from an overflowing heart, and one could detect a flickering faint light of response in the child's eyes, but that was all. The mother hung over her, kissing her, petting her, and imploring her to speak, but the lips only moved and no sound came. I snatched my liquor flask from my knapsack, but the woman forbade me, and said:

"No—she does not suffer; it is better so. It might bring her back to life. None that be so good and kind as ye are, would do her that cruel hurt. For look you—what is left to live for? Her brothers are gone, her father is gone, her mother goeth, the Church's curse is upon her and none may shelter or befriend her even though she lay perishing in the road. She is desolate. I have not asked you, good heart, if her sister be still on live, here overhead; I had no need; ye had gone back, else, and not left the poor thing forsaken—"

"She lieth at peace," interrupted the king, in a subdued voice.

"I would not change it. How rich is this day in happiness! Ah, my Annis, thou shalt join thy sister soon—thou'rt on thy way, and these be merciful friends, that will not hinder."

And so she fell to murmuring and cooing over the girl again, and softly stroking her face and hair, and kissing her and calling her by endearing names; but there was scarcely sign of response, now, in the glazing eyes. I saw tears well from the king's eyes, and trickle down his face. The woman noticed them, too, and said:

"Ah, I know that sign: thou'st a wife at home, poor soul, and you and she have gone hungry to bed, many's the time, that the little ones might have your crust; you know what poverty is, and the daily insults of your betters, and the heavy hand of the Church and the king."

The king winced under this accidental home-shot, but kept still; he was learning his part; and he was playing it well, too; for a pretty dull beginner. I struck up a diversion. I offered the woman food and liquor, but she refused both. She would allow nothing to come between her and the release of death. Then I slipped away and brought the dead child from aloft, and laid it by her. This broke her down again, and there was another scene that was full of heart-break. By and by I made another diversion, and beguiled her to sketch her story.

"Ye know it well, yourselves, having suffered it—for truly none of our condition in Britain escape it. It is the old, weary tale. We fought and struggled and succeeded; meaning by success, that we lived and did not die; more than that is not to be claimed. No troubles came that we could not outlive, till this year brought them; then came they all at once, as one might say, and overwhelmed us. Years ago the lord of the manor planted certain fruit trees on our farm; in the best part of it, too—a grievous wrong and shame—"

"But it was his right," interrupted the king.

"None denieth that, indeed; an the law mean anything, what is the lord's is his, and what is mine is his also. Our farm was ours by lease, therefore 'twas likewise his, to do with it as he would. Some little time ago, three of those trees were found hewn down. Our three grown sons ran frightened to report the crime. Well, in his lordship's dungeon there they lie, who saith there shall they lie and rot till they confess. They have naught to confess, being innocent, wherefore there will they remain until they die. Ye know that right well, I ween. Think how this left us; a man, a woman and two children, to gather a crop that was planted by so much greater force, yes, and protect it night and day from pigeons and prowling animals that be sacred and must not be hurt by any of our sort. When my lord's crop was nearly ready for the harvest, so also was ours; when his bell rang to call us to his fields to harvest his crops for nothing, he would not allow that I and my two girls should count for our three captive sons, but for only two of them; so, for the lacking one were we daily fined. All this time our own crop was perishing through neglect; and so both the priest and his lordship fined us because their shares of it were suffering through damage. In the end the fines ate up our crop—and they took it all; they took it all and made us harvest it for them, without pay or food, and we starving. Then the worst came when I, being out of my mind with hunger and loss of my boys, and grief to see my husband and my little maids in rags and misery and despair, uttered a deep blasphemy—oh! a thousand of them!—against the Church and the Church's ways. It was ten days ago. I had fallen sick with this disease, and it was to the priest I said the words, for he was come to chide me for lack of due humility under the chastening hand of God. He carried my trespass to his betters; I was stubborn; wherefore, presently upon my head and upon all heads that were dear to me, fell the curse of Rome.

"Since that day, we are avoided, shunned with horror. None has come near this hut to know whether we live or not. The rest of us were taken down. Then I roused me and got up, as wife and mother will. It was little they could have eaten in any case; it was less than little they had to eat. But there was water, and I gave them that. How they craved it! and how they blessed it! But the end came yesterday; my strength broke down. Yesterday was the last time I ever saw my husband and this youngest child alive. I have lain here all these hours—these ages, ye may say—listening, listening, for any sound up there that—"

She gave a sharp quick glance at her eldest daughter, then cried out, "Oh, my darling!" and feebly gathered the stiffening form to her sheltering arms. She had recognized the death rattle.

## Chapter XXX

### THE TRAGEDY OF THE MANOR-HOUSE

At midnight all was over, and we sat in the presence of four corpses. We covered them with such rags as we could find, and started away, fastening the door behind us. Their home must be these people's grave, for they could not have Christian burial, or be admitted to consecrated ground. They were as dogs, wild beasts, lepers, and no soul that valued its hope of eternal life would throw it away by meddling in any sort with these rebuked and smitten outcasts.

We had not moved four steps when I caught a sound as of footsteps upon gravel. My heart flew to my throat. We must not be seen coming from that house. I plucked at the king's robe and we drew back and took shelter behind the corner of the cabin.

"Now we are safe," I said, "but it was a close call—so to speak. If the night had been lighter he might have seen us, no doubt, he seemed to be so near."

"Mayhap it is but a beast and not a man at all."

"True. But man or beast, it will be wise to stay here a minute and let it get by and out of the way."

"Hark! It cometh hither."

True again. The step was coming toward us—straight toward the hut. It must be a beast, then, and we might as well have saved our trepidation. I was going to step out, but the king laid his hand upon my arm. There was a moment of silence, then we heard a soft knock on the cabin door. It made me shiver. Presently the knock was repeated, and then we heard these words in a guarded voice:

"Mother! Father! Open—we have got free, and we bring news to pale your cheeks but glad your hearts; and we may not tarry, but must fly! And—but they answer not. Mother! father!——"

I drew the king toward the other end of the hut and whispered:

"Come—now we can get to the road."

The king hesitated, was going to demur; but just then we heard the door give way, and knew that those desolate men were in the presence of their dead.

"Come, my liege! in a moment they will strike a light, and then will follow that which it would break your heart to hear."

He did not hesitate this time. The moment we were in the road, I ran; and after a moment he threw dignity aside and followed. I did not want to think of what was happening in the hut—I couldn't bear it; I wanted to drive it out of my mind; so I struck into the first subject that lay under that one in my mind:

"I have had the disease those people died of, and so have nothing to fear; but if you have not had it also—"

He broke in upon me to say he was in trouble, and it was his conscience that was troubling him:

"These young men have got free, they say—but *how?* It is not likely that their lord hath set them free."

"Oh, no, I make no doubt they escaped."

"That is my trouble; I have a fear that this is so, and your suspicion doth confirm it, you having the same fear."

"I should not call it by that name though. I do suspect that they escaped, but if they did, I am not sorry, certainly."

"I am not sorry, I *think*—but—"

"What is it? What is there for one to be troubled about?"

"*If* they did escape, then are we bound in duty to lay hands upon them and deliver them again to their lord; for it is not seemly that one of his quality should suffer a so insolent and high-handed outrage from persons of their base degree."[2]

There it was, again. He could see only one side of it. He was born so, educated so, his veins were full of ancestral blood that was rotten with this sort of unconscious brutality, brought down by inheritance from a long procession of hearts that had each done its share toward poisoning the stream. To imprison these men without proof, and starve their kindred, was no harm, for they were merely peasants and subject to the will and pleasure of their lord, no matter what fearful form it might take; but for these men to break out of unjust captivity was insult and outrage, and a thing not to be countenanced by any conscientious person who knew his duty to his sacred caste.

I worked more than half an hour before I got him to change the subject—and even then an outside matter did it for me. This was a something which caught our eyes as we struck the summit of a small hill—a red glow, a good way off.

"That's a fire," said I.

Fires interested me considerably, because I was getting a good deal of an insurance business[3] started, and was also training some horses and building some steam fire engines, with an eye to a paid fire department by and by. The priests opposed both my fire and life-insurance, on the ground that it was an insolent attempt to hinder the decrees of God; and if you pointed out that they did not hinder the decrees in the least, but only modified the hard consequences of them if you took out policies and had luck, they retorted that that was gambling against the decrees of God, and was just as bad. So they managed to damage those industries more or less, but I got even on my Accident business. As a rule, a knight is a lummux, and sometimes even a labrick, and hence open to pretty poor arguments when they come glibly from a superstition-monger, but even *he* could see the practical side of a thing once in a while; and so of late you couldn't clean up a tournament and pile the result without finding one of my accident-tickets in every helmet.

We stood there awhile, in the thick darkness and stillness, looking toward the red blur in the distance, and trying to make out the meaning of a far away murmur that rose and fell fitfully on the night.

2. The King is troubled by his conscience much as Huck was when considering whether he should write Jim's owner and reveal the whereabouts of her runaway slave.
3. Hartford, Connecticut, was noted then as now for its insurance companies.

Sometimes it swelled up and for a moment seemed less remote; but when we were hopefully expecting it to betray its cause and nature, it dulled and sank again, carrying its mystery with it. We started down the hill in its direction, and the winding road plunged us at once into almost solid darkness—darkness that was packed and crammed in between two tall forest walls. We groped along down for half a mile, perhaps that murmur growing more and more distinct all the time, the coming storm threatening more and more, with now and then a little shiver of wind, a faint show of lightning, and dull grumblings of distant thunder. I was in the lead. I ran against something—a soft heavy something which gave, slightly, to the impulse of my weight; at the same moment the lightning glared out, and within a foot of my face was the writhing face of a man who was hanging from the limb of a tree! That is, it seemed to be writhing, but it was not. It was a grewsome sight. Straightway there was an ear-splitting explosion of thunder, and the bottom of heaven fell out; the rain poured down in a deluge. No matter, we must try to cut this man down, on the chance that there might be life in him yet, mustn't we? The lightning came quick and sharp, now, and the place was alternately noonday and midnight. One moment the man would be hanging before me in an intense light, and the next he was blotted out again in the darkness. I told the king we must cut him down. The king at once objected.

"If he hanged himself, he was willing to lose his property to his lord; so let him be. If others hanged him, belike they had the right—let him hang."

"But—"

"But me no buts, but even leave him as he is. And for yet another reason. When the lightning cometh again—there, look abroad."

Two others hanging, within fifty yards of us!

"It is not weather meet for doing useless courtesies unto dead folk. They are past thanking you. Come—it is unprofitable to tarry here."

There was reason in what he said, so we moved on. Within the next mile we counted six more hanging forms by the blaze of the lightning, and altogether it was a grisly excursion. That murmur was a murmur no longer, it was a roar; a roar of men's voices. A man came flying by, now, dimly through the darkness, and other men chasing him. They disappeared. Presently another case of the kind occurred, and then another and another. Then a sudden turn of the road brought us in sight of that fire—it was a large manor house, and little or nothing was left of it—and everywhere men were flying and other men raging after them in pursuit.

I warned the king that this was not a safe place for strangers. We would better get away from the light, until matters should improve. We stepped back a little, and hid in the edge of the wood. From this hiding place we saw both men and women hunted by the mob. The fearful work went on until nearly dawn. Then, the fire being out and the storm spent, the voices and flying footsteps presently ceased, and darkness and stillness reigned again.

We ventured out, and hurried cautiously away; and although we were worn out and sleepy, we kept on until we had put this place some miles behind us. Then we asked hospitality at the hut of a charcoal burner, and got what was to be had. A woman was up and about, but the man was still asleep, on a straw shake-down, on the clay floor. The woman seemed uneasy until I explained that we were travelers and had lost our way and been wandering in the woods all night. She became talkative, then, and asked if we had heard of the terrible goings-on at the manor house of Abblasoure. Yes, we had heard of them, but what we wanted now, was rest and sleep. The king broke in:

"Sell us the house and take yourselves away, for we be perilous company, being but late come from people that died of the Spotted Death."

It was good of him, but unnecessary. One of the commonest decorations of the nation was the waffle-iron face. I had early noticed that the woman and her husband were both so decorated. She made us entirely welcome, and had no fears; and plainly she was immensely impressed by the king's proposition; for of course it was a good deal of an event in her life to run across a person of the king's humble appearance who was ready to buy a man's house for the sake of a night's lodging. It gave her a large respect for us, and she strained the lean possibilities of her hovel to their utmost to make us comfortable.

We slept till far into the afternoon, and then got up hungry enough to make cotter fare quite palatable to the king, the more particularly as it was scant in quantity. And also in variety; it consisted solely of onions, salt, and the national black bread—made out of horse-feed. The woman told us about the affair of the evening before. At ten or eleven at night, when everybody was in bed, the manor house burst into flames. The countryside swarmed to the rescue, and the family were saved, with one exception, the master. He did not appear. Everybody was frantic over this loss, and two brave yeomen sacrificed their lives in ransacking the burning house seeking that valuable personage. But after a while he was found—what was left of him— which was his corpse. It was in a copse three hundred yards away, bound, gagged, stabbed in a dozen places.

Who had done this? Suspicion fell upon a humble family in the neighborhood who had been lately treated with peculiar harshness by the baron; and from these people the suspicion easily extended itself to their relatives and familiars. A suspicion was enough; my lord's liveried retainers proclaimed an instant crusade against these people, and were promptly joined by the community in general. The woman's husband had been active with the mob, and had not returned home until nearly dawn. He was gone, now, to find out what the general result had been. While we were still talking, he came back from his quest. His report was revolting enough. Eighteen persons hanged or butchered, and two yeomen and thirteen prisoners lost in the fire.

"And how many prisoners were there altogether, in the vaults?"

"Thirteen."

"Then every one of them was lost."

"Yes, all."

"But the people arrived in time to save the family; how is it they could save none of the prisoners?"

The man looked puzzled, and said:

"Would one unlock the vaults at such a time? Marry, some would have escaped."

"Then you mean that nobody *did* unlock them?"

"None went near them, either to lock or unlock. It standeth to reason that the bolts were fast; wherefore it was only needful to establish a watch, so that if any broke the bonds he might not escape, but be taken. None were taken."

"Natheless, three did escape," said the king, "and ye will do well to publish it and set justice upon their track, for these murthered the baron and fired the house."

I was just expecting he would come out with that. For a moment the man and his wife showed an eager interest in this news and an impatience to go out and spread it; then a sudden something else betrayed itself in their faces, and they began to ask questions. I answered the questions myself, and narrowly watched the effects produced. I was soon satisfied that the knowledge of who these three prisoners were, had somehow changed the atmosphere; that our hosts' continued eagerness to go and spread the news was now only pretended and not real. The king did not notice the change, and I was glad of that. I worked the conversation around toward other details of the night's proceedings, and noted that these people were relieved to have it take that direction.

The painful thing observable about all this business was, the alacrity with which this oppressed community had turned their cruel hands against their own class in the interest of the common oppressor. This man and woman seemed to feel that in a quarrel between a person of their own class and his lord, it was the natural and proper and rightful thing for that poor devil's whole caste to side with the master and fight his battle for him, without ever stopping to inquire into the rights or wrongs of the matter. This man had been out helping to hang his neighbors, and had done his work with zeal, and yet was aware that there was nothing against them but a mere suspicion, with nothing back of it describable as evidence, still neither he nor his wife seemed to see anything horrible about it.

This was depressing—to a man with the dream of a republic in his head. It reminded me of a time thirteen centuries away, when the "poor whites" of our South who were always despised and frequently insulted, by the slave-lords around them, and who owed their base condition simply to the presence of slavery in their midst, were yet pusillanimously ready to side with slave-lords in all political moves for the upholding and perpetuating of slavery, and did also finally shoulder their muskets and pour out their lives in an effort to prevent the destruction of that very institution which degraded them. And there was only one redeeming feature connected with that pitiful piece of history; and that was, that secretly the "poor white" did detest the slave-lord, and did feel his own shame. That feeling was not brought to the surface, but the fact that it was there and could have been brought out, under favoring circumstances, was something—in fact it was enough; for it showed that a man is at bottom a man, after all, even if it doesn't show on the outside.

Well, as it turned out, this charcoal burner was just the twin of the Southern "poor white" of the far future. The king presently showed impatience, and said:

"An ye prattle here all the day, justice will miscarry. Think ye the criminals will abide in their father's house? They are fleeing, they are not waiting. You should look to it that a party of horse be set upon their track."

The woman paled slightly, but quite perceptibly, and the man looked flustered and irresolute. I said:

"Come, friend, I will walk a little way with you, and explain which direction I think they would try to take. If they were merely resisters of the gabelle[4] or some kindred absurdity I would try to protect them from capture; but when men murder a person of high degree and likewise burn his house, that is another matter."

The last remark was for the king—to quiet him. On the road the man pulled his resolution together, and began the march with a steady gait, but there was no eagerness in it. By and by I said:

"What relation were these men to you—cousins?"

He turned as white as his layer of charcoal would let him, and stopped, trembling.

"Ah, my God, how knew you that?"

"I didn't know it; it was a chance guess."

"Poor lads, they are lost. And good lads they were, too."

"Were you actually going yonder to tell on them?"

He didn't quite know how to take that; but he said, hesitatingly: "Ye-s."

"Then I think you are a damned scoundrel!"

4. A tax, especially the tax on salt in France prior to the Revolution.

It made him as glad as if I had called him an angel.

"Say the good words again, brother! for surely ye mean that ye would not betray me an I failed of my duty."

"Duty? There is no duty in the matter, except the duty to keep still and let those men get away. They've done a righteous deed."

He looked pleased; pleased, and touched with apprehension at the same time. He looked up and down the road to see that no one was coming, and then said in a cautious voice:

"From what land come you, brother, that you speak such perilous words, and seem not to be afraid?"

"They are not perilous words when spoken to one of my own caste, I take it. You would not tell anybody I said them?"

"I? I would be drawn asunder by wild horses first."

"Well, then, let me say my say. I have no fears of your repeating it. I think devil's work has been done last night upon those innocent poor people. That old baron got only what he deserved. If I had my way, all his kind should have the same luck."

Fear and depression vanished from the man's manner, and gratefulness and a brave animation took their place:

"Even though you be a spy, and your words a trap for my undoing, yet are they such refreshment that to hear them again and others like to them, I would go to the gallows happy, as having had one good feast at least in a starved life. And I will say my say, now, and ye may report it if ye be so minded. I helped to hang my neighbors for that it were peril to my own life to show lack of zeal in the master's cause; the others helped for none other reason. All rejoice to-day that he is dead, but all do go about seemingly sorrowing, and shedding the hypocrite's tear, for in that lies safety. I have said the words, I have said the words! the only ones that have ever tasted good in my mouth, and the reward of that taste is sufficient. Lead on, an ye will, be it even to the scaffold, for I am ready."

There it was, you see. A man *is* a man, at bottom. Whole ages of abuse and oppression cannot crush the manhood clear out of him. Whoever thinks it a mistake, is himself mistaken. Yes, there is plenty good enough material for a republic in the most degraded people that ever existed—even the Russians; plenty of manhood in them—even in the Germans—if one could but force it out of its timid and suspicious privacy, to overthrow and trample in the mud any throne that ever was set up and any nobility that ever supported it. We should see certain things yet, let us hope and believe. First, a modified monarchy, till Arthur's days were done, then the destruction of the throne, nobility abolished, every member of it bound out to some useful trade, universal suffrage instituted, and the whole government placed in the hands of the men and women of the nation there to remain. Yes, there was no occasion to give up my dream yet a while.

## Chapter XXXI

### MARCO

We strolled along in a sufficiently indolent fashion, now, and talked. We must dispose of about the amount of time it ought to take to go to the little hamlet of Abblasoure and put justice on the track of those murderers and get back home again. And meantime I had an auxiliary interest which had never paled yet, never lost its novelty for me, since I had been in Arthur's kingdom: the behavior—born of nice and exact subdivisions of caste—of chance passers-by toward each other. Toward the shaven monk who trudged along with his cowl tilted back and the sweat washing down his fat jowls, the coal burner was deeply reverent; to the gentleman he was abject; with the small farmer and the free mechanic he was cordial and gossipy; and when a slave passed by with a countenance respectfully lowered, this chap's nose was in the air—he couldn't even see him. Well, there are times when one would like to hang the whole human race and finish the farce.[5]

Presently we struck an incident. A small mob of half naked boys and girls came tearing out of the woods, scared and shrieking. The eldest among them were not more than twelve or fourteen years old. They implored help, but they were so beside themselves that we couldn't make out what the matter was. However, we plunged into the wood, they skurrying in the lead, and the trouble was quickly revealed: they had hanged a little fellow with a bark rope, and he was kicking and struggling, in the process of choking to death. We rescued him, and fetched him around. It was some more human nature; the admiring little folk imitating their elders; they were playing mob, and had achieved a success which promised to be a good deal more serious than they had bargained for.

It was not a dull excursion for me. I managed to put in the time very well. I made various acquaintanceships, and in my quality of stranger was able to ask as many questions as I wanted to. A thing which naturally interested me, as a statesman, was the matter of wages. I picked up what I could under that head during the afternoon. A man who hasn't had much experience, and doesn't think, is apt to measure a nation's prosperity or lack of prosperity by the mere size of the prevailing wages: if the wages be high, the nation is prosperous; if low, it isn't. Which is an error. It isn't what sum you get, it's how much you can buy with it that's the important thing; and it's that that tells whether your wages are high in fact or only high in name. I could remember how it was in the time of our great civil war in the nineteenth century. In the North a carpenter got three dollars a day,

---

5. Although this outburst is typical of Clemens' later attacks on mankind, it seems notably in- consistent with the sentiments Morgan had just expressed at the end of the preceding chapter.

gold valuation; in the South he got fifty—payable in Confederate shin-plasters worth a dollar a bushel. In the North a suit of over-alls cost three dollars—a day's wages; in the South it cost seventy-five—which was two days' wages. Other things were in proportion. Consequently, wages were twice as high in the North as they were in the South, because the one wage had that much more purchasing power than the other had.

Yes, I made various acquaintances in the hamlet, and a thing that gratified me a good deal was to find our new coins in circulation—lots of milrays, lots of mills, lots of cents, a good many nickels, and some silver; all this among the artisans and commonalty generally; yes, and even some gold—but that was at the bank, that is to say, the gold-smith's. I dropped in there while Marco the son of Marco was haggling with a shopkeeper over a quarter of a pound of salt, and asked for change for a twenty dollar gold piece. They furnished it—that is, after they had chewed the piece, and run it on the counter, and tried acid on it, and asked me where I got it and who I was, and where I was from, and where I was going to, and when I expected to get there, and perhaps a couple of hundred more questions; and when they got aground, I went right on and furnished them a lot of information voluntarily: told them I owned a dog, and his name was Watch, and my first wife was a Free Will Baptist, and her grandfather was a Prohibitionist, and I used to know a man who had two thumbs on each hand and a wart on the inside of his upper lip, and died in the hope of a glorious resurrection, and so-on, and so-on, and so-on, till even that hungry village questioner began to look satisfied, and also a shade put out; but he had to respect a man of my financial strength, and so he didn't give me any lip, but I noticed he took it out of his underlings, which was a perfectly natural thing to do. Yes, they changed my twenty, but I judged it strained the bank a little, which was a thing to be expected, for it was the same as walking into a paltry village store in the nineteenth century and requiring the boss of it to change a two-thousand dollar bill for you all of a sudden. He could do it, maybe; but at the same time he would wonder how a small farmer happened to be carrying so much money around in his pocket; which was probably this goldsmith's thought, too; for he followed me to the door and stood there gazing after me with reverent admiration.

Our new money was not only handsomely circulating, but its language was already glibly in use; that is to say, people had dropped the names of the former moneys, and spoke of things as being worth so many dollars or cents or mills or milrays, now. It was very gratifying. We were progressing, that was sure.

I got to know several master mechanics, but about the most interesting fellow among them was the blacksmith, Dowley. He was a live man and a brisk talker, and had two journeymen and three apprentices, and was doing a raging business. In fact, he was getting rich, hand over fist, and was vastly respected. Marco was very proud of having such a man for a friend. He had taken me there ostensibly to let me see the big establishment which bought so much of his charcoal, but really to let me see what easy and almost familiar terms he was on with this great man. Dowley and I fraternized at once; I had had just such picked men, splendid fellows, under me in the Colt Arms Factory. I was bound to see more of him, so I invited him to come out to Marco's, Sunday, and dine with us. Marco was appalled, and held his breath; and when the grandee accepted, he was so grateful that he almost forgot to be astonished at the condescension.

Marco's joy was exhuberant—but only for a moment; then he grew thoughtful, then sad; and when he heard me tell Dowley I should have Dickon the boss mason, and Smug the boss wheelwright out there, too, the coal-dust on his face turned to chalk, and he lost his grip. But I knew what was the matter with him; it was the expense. He saw ruin before him; he judged that his financial days were numbered. However, on our way to invite the others, I said:

"You must allow me to have these friends come; and you must also allow me to pay the costs."

His face cleared, and he said with spirit:

"But not all of it, not all of it. Ye cannot well bear a burden like to this alone."

I stopped him, and said:

"Now let's understand each other on the spot, old friend. I am only a farm bailiff, it is true; but I am not poor, nevertheless. I have been very fortunate this year—you would be astonished to know how I have thriven. I tell you the honest truth when I say I could squander away as many as a dozen feasts like this and never care *that* for the expense!" and I snapped my fingers. I could see myself rise a foot at a time in Marco's estimation, and when I fetched out those last words I was become a very tower, for style and altitude. "So you see, you must let me have my way. You can't contribute a cent to this orgy, that's *settled.*"

"It's grand and good of you—"

"No, it isn't. You've opened your house to Jones and me in the most generous way; Jones was remarking upon it to-day, just before you came back from the village; for although he wouldn't be likely to say such a thing to you,—because Jones isn't a talker, and is diffident in society—he has a good heart and a grateful, and knows how to appreciate it when he is well treated; yes, you and your wife have been very hospitable toward us—"

"Ah, brother, 'tis nothing—*such* hospitality!"

"But it *is* something; the best a man has, freely given, is always something, and is as good as a prince can do, and ranks right along beside it—for even a prince can but do his best. And so we'll shop around and get up this layout, now, and don't you worry about the expense. I'm one of the worst spendthrifts that ever was born. Why, do you know, sometimes in a single week I spend—but never mind about that—you'd never believe it anyway."

And so we went gadding along, dropping in here and there, pricing things, and gossiping with the shopkeepers about the riot, and now and then running across pathetic reminders of it, in the persons of shunned and tearful and houseless remnants of families whose homes had been taken from them and their parents butchered or hanged. The raiment of Marco and his wife was of coarse tow-linen and linsey-woolsey respectively, and resembled township maps, it being made up pretty exclusively of patches which had been added, township by township, in the course of five or six years, until hardly a hand's-breadth of the original garments was surviving and present. Now I wanted to fit these people out with new suits, on account of that swell company, and I didn't know just how to get at it with delicacy, until at last it struck me that as I had already been liberal in inventing wordy gratitude for the king, it would be just the thing to back it up with evidence of a substantial sort; so I said:

"And Marco, there's another thing, which you must permit—out of kindness for Jones—because you wouldn't want to offend him. He was very anxious to testify his appreciation in some way, but he is so diffident he couldn't venture it himself, and so he begged me to buy some little things and give them to you and Dame Phyllis and let him pay for them without your ever knowing they came from him—you know how a delicate person feels about that sort of thing—and so I said I would, and we would keep mum. Well, his idea was, a new outfit of clothes for you both—"

"Oh, it is wastefulness! It may not be, brother, it may not be. Consider the vastness of the sum—"

"Hang the vastness of the sum! Try to keep quiet for a moment, and see how it would seem; a body can't get in a word edgeways, you talk so much. You ought to cure that, Marco; it isn't good form, you know, and it will grow on you if you don't check it. Yes, we'll step in here, now, and price this man's stuff—and don't forget to remember to not let on to Jones that you know he had anything to do with it. You can't think how curiously sensitive and proud he is. He's a farmer—pretty fairly well-to-do farmer—and I'm his bailiff; *but*—the imagination of that man! Why, sometimes when he forgets himself and gets to blowing off, you'd think he was one of the swells of the earth; and you might listen to him a hundred years and never take him for a farmer—especially if he talked agriculture. He *thinks* he's a Sheol of a farmer, thinks he's old Grayback from Wayback; but between you and me privately he don't know as much about farming as he does about running a kingdom—still, whatever he talks about, you want to drop your underjaw and listen, the same as if you had never heard such incredible wisdom in all your life before, and were afraid you might die before you got enough of it. That will please Jones."

It tickled Marco to the marrow to hear about such an odd character; but it also prepared him for accidents; and in my experience when you travel with a king who is letting on to be something else and can't remember it more than about half the time, you can't take too many precautions.

This was the best store we had come across yet; it had everything in it, in small quantities, from anvils and dry goods all the way down to fish and pinchbeck jewelry. I concluded I would bunch my whole invoice right here, and not go pricing around any more. So I got rid of Marco, by sending him off to invite the mason and the wheelwright, which left the field free to me. For I never care to do a thing in a quiet way; it's got to be theatrical or I don't take any interest in it. I showed up money enough, in a careless way, to corral the shopkeeper's respect, and then I wrote down a list of the things I wanted, and handed it to him to see if he could read it. He could, and was proud to show that he could. He said he had been educated by a priest, and could read and write both. He ran it through, and remarked with satisfaction that it was a pretty heavy bill. Well, and so it was, for a little concern like that. I was not only providing a swell dinner, but some odds and ends of extras. I ordered that the things be carted out and delivered at the dwelling of Marco the son of Marco by Saturday evening, and send me the bill at dinner-time Sunday. He said I could depend upon his promptness and exactitude, it was the rule of the house. He also observed that he would throw in a couple of miller-guns for the Marcos, gratis—that everybody was using them now. He had a mighty opinion of that clever device. I said:

"And please fill them up to the middle mark, too; and add that to the bill."

He would, with pleasure. He filled them, and I took them with me. I couldn't venture to tell him that the miller-gun was a little invention of my own, and that I had officially ordered that every shopkeeper in the kingdom keep them on hand and sell them at government-price—which was the merest trifle, and the shopkeeper got that, not the government. We furnished them for nothing.

The king had hardly missed us when we got back at night-fall. He had early dropped again into his dream of a grand invasion of Gaul with the whole strength of his kingdom at his back, and the afternoon had slipped away without his ever coming to himself again.

## *Chapter XXXII*

### DOWLEY'S HUMILIATION

Well, when that cargo arrived, toward sunset, Saturday afternoon, I had my hands full to keep the Marcos from fainting. They were sure Jones and I were ruined past help, and they blamed themselves as accessories to this bankruptcy. You see, in addition to the dinner-materials, which called for a sufficiently round sum, I had bought a lot of extras for the future comfort of the family: for instance, a big lot of wheat, a delicacy as rare to the tables of their class as was ice-cream to a hermit's; also a sizeable deal dinner table; also two entire pounds of salt, which was another piece of extravagance in those people's eyes; also crockery, stools, the clothes, a small cask of beer, and so on. I instructed the Marcos to keep quiet about this sumptuousness, so as to give me a chance to surprise the guests and show off a little. Concerning the new clothes, the simple couple were like children; they were up and down, all night, to see if it wasn't nearly daylight, so that they could put them on, and they were into them at last as much as an hour before dawn was due. Then their pleasure—not to say delirium—was so fresh and novel and inspiring that the sight of it paid me well for the interruptions which my sleep had suffered. The king had slept just as usual—like the dead. The Marcos could not thank him for their clothes, that being forbidden; but they tried every way they could think of to make him see how grateful they were. Which all went for nothing: he didn't notice any change.

It turned out to be one of those rich and rare fall days which is just a June day toned down to a degree where it is heaven to be out of doors. Toward noon the guests arrived and we assembled under a great tree and were soon as sociable as old acquaintances. Even the king's reserve melted a little, though it was some little trouble to him to adjust himself to the name of Jones along at first. I had asked him to try to not forget that he was a farmer; but I had also considered it prudent to ask him to let the thing stand at that, and not elaborate it any. Because he was just the kind of person you could depend on to spoil a little thing like that if you didn't warn him, his tongue was so handy, and his spirit so willing, and his information so uncertain.

Dowley was in fine feather, and I early got him started, and then adroitly worked him around onto his own history for a text and himself for a hero, and then it was good to sit there and hear him hum. Self-made man, you know. They know how to talk. They do deserve more credit than any other breed of men, yes, that is true; and they are among the very first to find it out, too. He told how he had begun life an orphan lad without money and without friends able to help him; how he had lived as the slaves of the meanest master lived; how his day's work was from sixteen to eighteen hours long, and yielded him only enough black bread to keep him in a half-fed condition; how his faithful endeavors finally attracted the attention of a good blacksmith, who came near knocking him dead with kindess by suddenly offering, when he was totally unprepared, to take him as his bound apprentice for nine years and give him board and clothes and teach him the trade—or "mystery" as Dowley called it. That was his first great rise, his first gorgeous stroke of fortune; and you saw that he couldn't yet speak of it without a sort of eloquent wonder and delight that such a gilded promotion should have fallen to the lot of a common human being. He got no new clothing during his apprenticeship, but on his graduation day his master tricked him out in spang-new tow-linens and made him feel unspeakably rich and fine.

"I remember me of that day!" the wheelwright sang out, with enthusiasm.

"And I likewise!" cried the mason. "I would not believe they were thine own; in faith I could not."

"Nor others!" shouted Dowley, with sparkling eyes. "I was like to lose my character, the neighbors wending I had mayhap been stealing. It was a great day, a great day; one forgetteth not days like that."

Yes, and his master was a fine man, and prosperous, and always had a great feast of meat twice in the year, and with it white bread, true wheaten bread; in fact, lived like a lord, so to speak. And in time Dowley succeeded to the business and married the daughter.

"And now consider what is come to pass," said he, impressively. "Two times in every month there is fresh meat upon my table." He made a pause here, to let that fact sink home, then added—"and eight times, salt meat."

"It is even true," said the wheelwright, with bated breath.

"I know it of mine own knowledge," said the mason, in the same reverent fashion.

"On my table appeareth white bread every Sunday in the year," added the master smith, with solemnity. "I leave it to your own consciences, friends, if this is not also true?"

"By my head, yes!" cried the mason.

"I can testify it—and I do," said the wheelwright.

"And as to furniture, ye shall say yourselves what mine equipment is." He waved his hand in fine gesture of granting frank and unhampered freedom of speech, and added: "Speak as ye are moved; speak as ye would speak an I were not here."

"Ye have five stools, and of the sweetest workmanship at that, albeit your family is but three," said the wheelwright, with deep respect.

"And six wooden goblets, and six platters of wood and two of pewter to eat and drink from withal," said the mason, impressively. "And I say it as knowing God is my judge, and we tarry not here alway, but must answer at the last day for the things said in the body, be they false or be they sooth."

"Now ye know what manner of man I am, brother Jones," said the smith, with a fine and friendly condescension, "and doubtless ye would look to find me a man jealous of his due of respect and but sparing of outgo to strangers till their rating and quality be assured, but trouble yourself not, as concerning that; wit ye well ye shall find me a man that regardeth not these matters but is willing to receive any he as his fellow and equal that carrieth a right heart in his body, be his worldly estate howsoever modest. And in token of it, here is my hand; and I say with my own mouth we are equals—equals"—and he smiled around on the company with the satisfaction of a god who is doing the handsome and gracious thing and is quite well aware of it.

The king took the hand with a poorly disguised reluctance, and let go of it as willingly as a lady lets go of a fish; all of which had a good effect, for it was mistaken for an embarrassment natural to one who was being beamed upon by greatness.

The dame brought out the table, now, and set it under the tree. It caused a visible stir of surprise, it being brand new and a sumptuous article of deal. But the surprise rose higher still, when the dame, with a body oozing easy indifference at every pore, but eyes that gave it all away by absolutely flaming with vanity, slowly unfolded an actual simon-pure tablecloth and spread it. That was a notch above even the blacksmith's domestic grandeurs, and it hit him hard; you could see it. But Marco was in Paradise; you could see that, too. Then the dame brought two fine new stools—whew! that was a sensation; it was visible in the eyes of every guest. Then she brought two more—as calmly as she could. Sensation again—with awed murmurs. Again she brought two—walking on air, she was so proud. The guests were petrified, and the mason muttered:

"There is that about earthly pomps which doth ever move to reverence."

As the dame turned away, Marco couldn't help slapping on the climax while the thing was hot; so he said with what was meant for a languid composure but was a poor imitation of it:

"These suffice; leave the rest."

So there were more yet! It was a fine effect. I couldn't have played the hand better myself.

From this out, the madam piled up the surprises with a rush that fired the general astonishment up to a hundred and fifty in the shade, and at the same time paralyzed expression of it down to gasped "Oh's" and "Ah's", and mute upliftings of hands and eyes. She fetched crockery—new, and plenty of it; new wooden goblets and other table furniture; and beer, fish, chicken, a goose, eggs, roast beef, roast mutton, a ham, a small roast pig, and a wealth of genuine white wheaten bread. Take it by and large, that spread laid everything far and away in the shade that ever that crowd had seen before. And while they sat there just simply stupefied with wonder and awe, I sort of waved my hand as if by accident, and the store-keeper's son emerged from space and said he had come to collect.

"That's all right," I said, indifferently. "What is the amount? give us the items."

Then he read off this bill, while those three amazed men listened, and serene waves of satisfaction rolled over my soul and alternate waves of terror and admiration surged over Marco's:

| | |
|---|---:|
| 2 pounds salt | 200 |
| 8 dozen pints beer, in the wood | 800 |
| 3 bushels wheat | 2,700 |
| 2 pounds fish | 100 |
| 3 hens | 400 |
| 1 goose | 400 |
| 3 dozen eggs | 150 |
| 1 roast of beef | 450 |
| 1 roast of mutton | 400 |
| 1 ham | 800 |
| 1 sucking pig | 500 |
| 2 crockery dinner sets | 6,000 |
| 2 men's suits and underwear | 2,800 |
| 1 stuff and 1 linsey-woolsey gown and underwear | 1,600 |
| 8 wooden goblets | 800 |
| Various table furniture | 10,000 |
| 1 deal table | 3,000 |
| 8 stools | 4,000 |
| 2 miller-guns, loaded | 3,000 |

He ceased. There was a pale and awful silence. Not a limb stirred. Not a nostril betrayed the passage of breath.

"Is that all?" I asked, in a voice of the most perfect calmness.

"All, fair sir, save that certain matters of light moment are placed together under a head hight sundries. If it would like you, I will sepa—"

"It is of no consequence," I said, accompanying the words with a gesture of the most utter indifference; "give me the grand total, please."

The clerk leaned against the tree to stay himself, and said:

"Thirty-nine thousand one hundred and fifty milrays!"

The wheelwright fell off his stool, the others grabbed the table to save themselves, and there was a deep and general ejaculation of—

"God be with us in the day of disaster!"

The clerk hastened to say:

"My father chargeth me to say he cannot honorably require you to pay it all at this time, and therefore only prayeth you—"

I paid no more heed than if it were the idle breeze, but with an air of indifference amounting almost to weariness, got out my money and tossed four dollars onto the table. Ah, you should have seen them stare!

The clerk was astonished and charmed. He asked me to retain one of the dollars as security, until he could go to town and—I interrupted:

"What, and fetch back nine cents? Nonsense. Take the whole. Keep the change."

There was an amazed murmur to this effect:

"Verily this being is *made* of money! He throweth it away even as it were dirt."

The blacksmith was a crushed man.

The clerk took his money and reeled away drunk with fortune. I said to Marco and his wife:

"Good folk, here is a little trifle for you"—handling the miller-guns as if it were a matter of no consequence though each of them contained fifteen cents in solid cash; and while the poor creatures went to pieces with astonishment and gratitude, I turned to the others and said as calmly as one would ask the time of day:

"Well, if we are all ready, I judge the dinner is. Come, fall to."

Ah, well, it was immense; yes, it was a daisy. I don't know that I ever put a situation together better, or got happier spectacular effects out of the materials available. The blacksmith—well, he was simply mashed. Land! I wouldn't have felt what that man was feeling, for anything in the world. Here he had been blowing and bragging about his grand meat-feast twice a year, and his fresh meat twice a month, and his salt meat twice a week, and his white bread every Sunday the year round—all for a family of three: the entire cost for the year not above 69.2.6 (sixty-nine cents, two mills and six milrays,) and all of a sudden here comes along a man who slashes out nearly four dollars on a single blow-out; and not only that, but acts as if it made him tired to handle such small sums. Yes, Dowley was a good deal wilted, and shrunk-up and collapsed; he had the aspect of a bladder-balloon that's been stepped on by a cow.

## Chapter XXXIII

### SIXTH CENTURY POLITICAL ECONOMY

However, I made a dead set at him, and before the first third of the dinner was reached, I had him happy again. It was easy to do—in a country of ranks and castes. You see, in a country where they have ranks and castes, a man isn't ever a man, he is only part of a man, he can't ever get his full growth. You prove your superiority over him in station, or rank, or fortune, and that's the end of it—he knuckles down. You can't insult him after that. No, I don't mean quite that; of course you *can* insult him, I only mean it's difficult; and so, unless you've got a lot of useless time on your hands it doesn't pay to try. I had the smith's reverence, now, because I was apparently immensely prosperous and rich; I could have had his adoration if I had had some little gimcrack title of nobility. And not only his, but any commoner's in the land, though he were the mightiest production of all the ages, in intellect, worth, and character, and I bankrupt in all three. This was to remain so, as long as England should exist in the earth. With the spirit of prophecy upon me, I could look into the future and see her erect statues and monuments to her unspeakable Georges and other royal and noble clothes-horses, and leave unhonored the creators of this world—after God—Gutenberg, Watt, Arkwright, Whitney, Morse, Stephenson, Bell.[6]

The king got his cargo aboard, and then, the talk not turning upon battle, conquest, or iron-clad duel, he dulled down to drowsiness and went off to take a nap. Mrs. Marco cleared the table, placed the beer-keg handy, and went away to eat her dinner of leavings in humble privacy, and the rest of us soon drifted into matters near and dear to the hearts of our sort—business and wages, of course. At a first glance, things appeared to be exceeding prosperous in this little tributary kingdom—whose lord was King Bagdemagus—as compared with the state of things in my own region. They had the "protection" system in full force here, whereas we were working along down towards free trade,[7] by easy stages, and were now about half way. Before long, Dowley and I were doing all the talking, the others hungrily listening. Dowley warmed to his work, snuffed an advantage in the air, and began to put questions which he considered pretty awkward ones for me, and they did have something of that look:

"In your country, brother, what is the wage of a master bailiff, master hind, carter, shepherd, swineherd?"

"Twenty-five milrays a day; that is to say, a quarter of a cent."

The smith's face beamed with joy. He said:

"With us they are allowed the double of it! And what may a mechanic get—carpenter, dauber, mason, painter, blacksmith, wheelwright and the like?"

"On the average, fifty milrays; half a cent a day."

"Ho-ho! With us they are allowed a hundred! With us any good

<hr>

6. Contrasted with the four Georges who ruled England from 1714 to 1830 are Johann Gutenberg (1398?–1468), reputedly the first European to print with movable type; James Watt (1736–1819), who invented the modern steam engine; Richard Arkwright (1732–92), who patented machines for spinning cotton; Eli Whitney (1765–1825), inventor of the cotton gin; Samuel F. B. Morse (1791–1872), credited with the invention of the telegraph; George Stephenson (1781–1848), one of the inventors of the locomotive, and his son, Robert Stephenson (1803–59), who invented the tubular bridge; and Alexander Graham Bell (1847–1922), inventor of the telephone.

7. Morgan takes in this chapter the view held by the Democratic party in Grover Cleveland's presidential campaign on 1888. Cleveland was not re-elected, though he did regain the presidency in 1893.

The first of a series of Beard cartoons attacking protection and supporting free trade. The caption " 'Rah for Protection!" comes from the debate reported in Chapter XXXIII. In a later drawing the bottle is broken, the sun of "Free Trade" is rising, and the caption reads: "Discrepancy in noses makes no difference."

mechanic is allowed a cent a day! I count out the tailor, but not the others—they are all allowed a cent a day, and in driving times they get more—yes, up to a hundred and ten and even fifteen milrays a day. I've paid a hundred and fifteen myself, within the week. 'Rah for protection—to Sheol with free-trade!"

And his face shone upon the company like a sunburst. But I didn't scare at all. I rigged up my pile-driver, and allowed myself fifteen minutes to drive him into the earth—drive him *all* in—drive him in till not even the curve of his skull should show above ground. Here is the way I started in on him. I asked:

"What do you pay a pound for salt?"

"A hundred milrays."

"We pay forty. What do you pay for beef and mutton—when you buy it?" That was a neat hit; it made the color come.

"It varieth somewhat, but not much; one may say 75 milrays the pound."

"We pay 33. What do you pay for eggs?"

"Fifty milrays the dozen."

"We pay 20. What do you pay for beer?"

"It costeth us 8½ milrays the pint."

"We get it for 4; 25 bottles for a cent. What do you pay for wheat?"

"At the rate of 900 milrays the bushel."

"We pay 400. What do you pay for a man's tow-linen suit?"

"Thirteen cents."

"We pay 6. What do you pay for a stuff gown for the wife of the laborer or the mechanic?"

"We pay 8.4.0."

"Well, observe the difference: you pay eight cents and four mills, we pay only four cents." I prepared, now, to sock it to him. I said: "Look here, dear friend, *what's become of your high wages you were bragging so about, a few minutes ago?*"—and I looked around on the company with placid satisfaction, for I had slipped up on him gradually and tied him hand and foot, you see, without his ever noticing that he was being tied at all. "What's become of those noble high wages of yours?—I seem to have knocked the stuffing all out of them, it appears to me."

But if you will believe me, he merely looked surprised, that is all! He didn't grasp the situation at all, didn't know he had walked into a trap, didn't discover that he was *in* a trap. I could have shot him, from sheer vexation. With cloudy eye and a struggling intellect, he fetched this out:

"Marry, I seem not to understand. It is *proved* that our wages be double thine; how then may it be that thou'st knocked therefrom the stuffing?—an I miscall not the wonderly word, this being the first time under grace and providence of God it hath been granted me to hear it."

Well, I was stunned; partly with this unlooked-for stupidity on his part, and partly because his fellows so manifestly sided with him and were of his mind—if you might call it mind. My position was simple enough, plain enough; how could it ever be simplified more? However, I must try;

"Why, look here, brother Dowley, don't you see? Your wages are merely higher than ours in *name*, not in *fact*."

"Hear him! They are the *double*—ye have confessed it yourself."

"Yes-yes, I don't deny that at all. But that's got nothing to do with it; the *amount* of the wages in mere coins, with meaningless names attached to them to know them by, has got nothing to do with it. The thing is, how much can you *buy* with your wages?—that's the idea. While it is true that with you a good mechanic is allowed about three dollars and a half a year, and with us only about a dollar and seventy-five—"

"There—ye're confessing it again, ye're confessing it again!"

"Confound it, I've never denied it I tell you! What I say is this. With us *half* a dollar buys more than a *dollar* buys with you—and *therefore* it stands to reason and the commonest kind of common sense, that our wages are *higher* than yours."

He looked dazed, and said, despairingly:

"Verily, I cannot make it out. Ye've just *said* ours are the higher, and with the same breath ye take it back."

"Oh, great Scott, isn't it possible to get such a simple thing through your head? Now look here—let me illustrate. We pay four cents for a woman's stuff gown, you pay 8.4.0. which is 4 mills more than *double*. What do you allow a laboring woman who works on a farm?"

"Two mills a day."

"Very good; we allow but half as much; we pay her only a tenth of a cent a day; and—"

"Again ye're conf—"

"Wait! Now, you see, the thing is very simple; this time you'll understand it. For instance, it takes your woman 42 days to earn her gown, at 2 mills a day—7 weeks' work; but ours earns hers in forty days—two days *short* of 7 weeks. Your woman has a gown, and her whole seven weeks' wages are gone; ours has a gown, and two days' wages left, to buy something else with. There—*now* you understand it!"

He looked—well, he merely looked dubious, it's the most I can say; so did the others. I waited—to let the thing work. Dowley spoke at last—and betrayed the fact that he actually hadn't gotten away from his rooted and grounded superstitions yet. He said, with a trifle of hesitancy:

"But—but—ye cannot fail to grant that two mills a day is better than one."

Shucks! Well, of course I hated to give it up. So I chanced another flyer:

"Let us suppose a case. Suppose one of your journeymen goes out and buys the following articles:

"1 pound of salt;
1 dozen eggs;
1 dozen pints of beer;
1 bushel of wheat;
1 tow-linen suit;
5 pounds of beef;
5 pounds of mutton.

"The lot will cost him 32 cents. It takes him 32 working days to earn the money—5 weeks and 2 days. Let him come to us and work 32 days at *half* the wages; he can buy all those things for a shade under 14½ cents; they will cost him a shade under 29 days' work, and he will have about half a week's wages over. Carry it through the year; he would save nearly a week's wages every two months, *your* man nothing; thus saving five or six weeks' wages in a year, your man not a cent. *Now* I reckon you understand that 'high wages' and 'low wages' are phrases that don't mean anything in the world until you find out which of them will *buy* the most!"

It was a crusher.

But alas, it didn't crush. No, I had to give it up. What those people valued was *high wages*; it didn't seem to be a matter of any consequence to them whether the high wages would buy anything or not. They stood for "protection," and swore by it, which was reasonable enough, because interested parties had gulled them into the notion that it was protection which had created their high wages. I proved to them that in a quarter of a century their wages had advanced but 30 per cent, while the cost of living had gone up 100; and that with us, in a shorter time, wages had advanced 40 per cent. while the cost of living had gone steadily down. But it didn't do any good. Nothing could unseat their strange beliefs.

Well, I was smarting under a sense of defeat. Undeserved defeat, but what of that? That didn't soften the smart any. And to think of the circumstances! the first statesman of the age, the capablest man, the best informed man in the entire world, the loftiest uncrowned head that had moved through the clouds of any political firmament for centuries, sitting here apparently defeated in argument by an ignorant country blacksmith! And I could see that those others were sorry for me!—which made me blush till I could smell my whiskers scorching. Put yourself in my place; feel as mean as I did, as ashamed as I felt—wouldn't *you* have struck below the belt to get even? Yes, you would; it is simply human nature. Well, that is what I did. I am not trying to justify it; I'm only saying that I was mad, and *anybody* would have done it.

Well, when I make up my mind to hit a man, I don't plan out a love-tap; no, that isn't my way; as long as I'm going to hit him at all, I'm going to hit him a lifter. And I don't jump at him all of a sudden, and risk making a blundering half-way business of it; no, I get away off yonder to one side, and work up on him gradually, so that he never suspects that I'm going to hit him at all; and by and by, all in a flash, he's flat of his back, and he can't tell for the life of him how it all happened. That is the way I went for brother Dowley. I started to talking lazy and comfortable, as if I was just talking to pass the time; and the oldest man in the world couldn't have taken the bearings of my starting place and guessed where I was going to fetch up:

"Boys, there's a good many curious things about law, and custom, and usage, and all that sort of thing, when you come to look at it; yes, and about the drift and progress of human opinion and movement, too. There are written laws—they perish; but there are also un-written laws—*they* are eternal. Take the unwritten law of wages: it says they've got to advance, little by little, straight through the centuries. And notice how it works. We know what wages are now, here and there and yonder; we strike an average, and say that's the wages of to-day. We know what the wages were a hundred years ago, and what they were two hundred years ago; that's as far back as we can get, but it suffices to give us the law of progress, the measure and rate of the periodical augmentation; and so, without a document to help us, we can come pretty close to determining what the wages were three and four and five hundred years ago. Good, so far. Do we stop there? No. We stop looking backward; we face around and apply the law to the future. My friends, I can tell you what people's wages are going to be at any date in the future you want to know, for hundreds and hundreds of years."

"What, goodman, what!"

"Yes. In seven hundred years wages will have risen to six times what they are now, here in your region, and farm hands will be allowed 3 cents a day, and mechanics 6."

"I would I might die now and live then!" interrupted Smug the mason, with a fine avaricious glow in his eye.

"And that isn't all; they'll get their board besides—such as it is: it won't bloat them. Two hundred and fifty years later—pay attention, now—a mechanic's wages will be—mind you, this is law, not guess-work; a mechanic's wages will then be *twenty* cents a day!"

There was a general gasp of awed astonishment. Dickon the wheel-wright murmured, with raised eyes and hands:

"More than three weeks pay for one day's work!"

"Riches!—of a truth, yes, riches!" muttered Marco, his breath coming quick and short, with excitement.

"Wages will keep on rising, little by little, little by little, as steadily as a tree grows, and at the end of three hundred and forty years more there'll be at least *one* country where the mechanic's average wage will be *two hundred* cents a day!"

It knocked them absolutely dumb! Not a man of them could get his breath for upwards of two minutes. Then the coalburner said prayerfully:

"Might I but live to see it!"

"It is the income of an earl!" said Smug.

"An earl, say ye?" said Dowley; "ye could say more than that and speak no lie; there's no earl in the realm of Bagdemagus that hath an income like to that. Income of an earl—mf! it's the income of an angel!"

"Now then, that is what is going to happen as regards wages. In that remote day, that man will earn, with *one* week's work, that bill of goods which it takes you upwards of *five* weeks to earn now. Some other pretty surprising things are going to happen, too. Brother Dowley, who is it that determines, every spring, what the particular wage of each kind of mechanic, laborer, and servant shall be for that year?"

"Sometimes the courts, sometimes the town council; but most of all, the magistrate. Ye may say, in general terms, it is the magistrate that fixes the wages."

"Doesn't ask any of those poor devils to *help* him fix their wages for them, does he?"

"Hm! That *were* an idea! The master that's to pay him the money is the one that's rightly concerned in that matter, ye will notice."

"Yes—but I thought the other man might have some little trifle at stake in it, too; and even his wife and children, poor creatures. The masters are these: nobles, rich men, the prosperous generally. These few, who do no work, determine what pay the vast hive shall have who *do* work. You see? They're a 'combine'—a trade union, to coin a new phrase—who band themselves together to force their lowly brother to take what they choose to give. Thirteen hundred years hence—so says the unwritten law—the 'combine' will be the other way, and then how these fine people's posterity will fume and fret and grit their teeth over the insolent tyranny of trade unions! Yes indeed! the magistrate will tranquilly arrange the wages from now clear away down into the nineteenth century; and then all of a sudden the wage-earner will consider that a couple of thousand years or so is enough of this one-sided sort of thing; and he will rise up and take a hand in fixing his wages himself. Ah, he will have a long and bitter account of wrong and humiliation to settle."

"Do ye believe—"

"That he actually will help to fix his own wages? Yes, indeed. And he will be strong and able, then."

"Brave times, brave times, of a truth!" sneered the prosperous smith.

"Oh,—and there's another detail. In that day, a master may hire a man for only just one day, or one week, or one month at a time, if he wants to."

"What?"

"It's true. Moreover, a magistrate won't be able to force a man to work for a master a whole year on a stretch whether the man wants to or not."

"Will there be *no* law or sense in that day?"

"Both of them, Dowley. In that day a man will be his own property, not the property of magistrate and master. And he can leave town whenever he wants to, if the wages don't suit him!—and they can't put him in the pillory for it."

"Perdition catch such an age!" shouted Dowley, in strong indignation. "An age of dogs, an age barren of reverence for superiors and respect for authority! The pillory—"

"Oh, wait, brother; say no good word for that institution. *I* think the pillory ought to be abolished."

"A most strange idea. Why?"

"Well, I'll tell you why. Is a man ever put in the pillory for a capital crime?"

"No."

"Is it right to condemn a man to a slight punishment for a small offense and then kill him?"

There was no answer. I had scored my first point! For the first time, the smith wasn't up and ready. The company noticed it. Good effect.

"You don't answer, brother. You were about to glorify the pillory a while ago, and shed some pity on a future age that isn't going to use it. *I* think the pillory ought to be abolished. What usually happens when a poor fellow is put in the pillory for some little offence that didn't amount to anything in the world? The mob try to have some fun with him, don't they?"

"Yes."

"They begin by clodding him; and they laugh themselves to pieces to see him try to dodge one clod and get hit with another?"

"Yes."

"Then they throw dead cats at him, don't they?"

"Yes."

"Well, then, suppose he has a few personal enemies in that mob—and here and there a man or a woman with a secret grudge against him—and suppose especially, that he is unpopular in the community, for his pride, or his prosperity, or one thing or another—stones and bricks take the place of clods and cats presently, don't they?"

"There is no doubt of it."

"As a rule he is crippled for life, isn't he?—jaws broken, teeth smashed out?—or legs mutilated, gangrened, presently cut off?—or an eye knocked out, maybe both eyes?"

"It is true, God knoweth it."

"And if he is unpopular he can depend on *dying*, right there in the stocks, can't he?"

"He surely can! One may not deny it."

"I take it none of *you* are unpopular—by reason of pride or insolence, or conspicuous prosperity, or any of those things that excite envy and malice among the base scum of a village? *You* wouldn't think it much of a risk to take a chance in the stocks?"

Dowley winced, visibly. I judged he was hit. But he didn't betray it by any spoken word. As for the others, they spoke out plainly, and with strong feeling. They said they had seen enough of the stocks to know what a man's chance in them was, and they would never consent to enter them if they could compromise on a quick death by hanging.

"Well, to change the subject—for I think I've established my point that the stocks ought to be abolished. I think some of our laws are pretty unfair. For instance, if I do a thing which ought to deliver me to the stocks, and you know I did it and yet keep still and don't report me, *you* will get the stocks if anybody informs on you."

"Ah, but that would serve you but right," said Dowley, "for you *must* inform. So saith the law."

The others coincided.

"Well, all right, let it go, since you vote me down. But there's one thing which certainly isn't fair. The magistrate fixes a mechanic's wage at 1 cent a day, for instance. The law says that if any master shall venture even under utmost press of business, to pay anything *over* that cent a day, even for a single day, he shall be both fined and pilloried for it; and whoever knows he did it and doesn't inform, they also shall be fined and pilloried. Now it seems to me unfair, Dowley, and a deadly peril to all of us, that because you thoughtlessly confessed, a while ago, that within a week you have paid a cent and fifteen mil—"

Oh, I tell *you* it was a smasher! You ought to have seen them go to pieces, the whole gang. I had just slipped up on poor smiling and complacent Dowley so nice and easy and softly, that he never suspected anything was going to happen till the blow came crashing down and knocked him all to rags.

A fine effect. In fact as fine as any I ever produced, with so little time to work it up in.

But I saw in a moment that I had overdone the thing a little. I was expecting to scare them, but I wasn't expecting to scare them to death. They were mighty near it, though. You see they had been a whole lifetime learning to appreciate the pillory; and to have that thing staring them in the face, and every one of them distinctly at the mercy of me, a stranger, if I chose to go and report—well, it was awful, and they couldn't seem to recover from the shock, they couldn't seem to pull themselves together. Pale, shaky, dumb, pitiful? Why, they weren't any better than so many dead men. It was very uncomfortable. Of course I thought they would appeal to me to keep mum, and then we would shake hands, and take a drink all round, and laugh it off, and there an end. But no; you see I was an unknown person, among a cruelly oppressed and suspicious people, a people always accustomed to having advantage taken of their helplessness, and never expecting just or kind treatment from any but their own families and very closest intimates. Appeal to *me* to be gentle, to be fair, to be generous? Of course they wanted to, but they couldn't dare.

## Chapter XXXIV

### THE YANKEE AND THE KING SOLD AS SLAVES

Well, what had I better do? Nothing in a hurry, sure. I must get up a diversion; anything to employ me while I could think, and while these poor fellows could have a chance to come to life again. There sat Marco, petrified in the act of trying to get the hang of his miller-gun—turned to stone, just in the attitude he was in when my pile-driver fell, the toy still gripped in his unconscious fingers. So I took it from him and proposed to explain its mystery. Mystery! a simple little thing like that; and yet it was mystery enough, for that race and that age.

I never saw such an awkward people, with machinery; you see, they were totally unused to it. The miller-gun was a little double-barreled tube of toughened glass, with a neat little trick of a spring to it, which upon pressure would let a shot escape. But the shot wouldn't hurt anybody, it would only drop into your hand. In the gun were two sizes—wee mustard-seed shot, and another sort that were several times larger. They were money. The mustard-seed shot represented milrays, the larger ones mills. So the gun was a purse; and very handy, too; you could pay out money in the dark with it; with accuracy; and you could carry it in your mouth; or in your vest pocket, if you had one. I made them of several sizes—one size so large that it would carry the equivalent of a dollar. Using shot for money was a good thing for the government; the metal cost nothing, and the money couldn't be counterfeited, for I was the only person in the kingdom who knew how to manage a shot tower. [8] "Paying the shot" soon came to be a common phrase. Yes, and I knew it would still be passing men's lips, away down

8. Structure, perhaps as much as two hundred feet high, used for making shot for firearms.

"Paying the shot" means paying the bill.

in the nineteenth century, yet none would suspect how and when it originated.

The king joined us, about this time, mightily refreshed by his nap, and feeling good. Anything could make me nervous now, I was so uneasy—for our lives were in danger; and so it worried me to detect a complacent something in the king's eye which seemed to indicate that he had been loading himself up for a performance of some kind or other; confound it, why must he go and choose such a time as this?

I was right. He began, straight off, in the most innocently artful, and transparent, and lubberly way, to lead up to the subject of agriculture. The cold sweat broke out all over me. I wanted to whisper in his ear, "Man, we are in awful danger! every moment is worth a principality till we get back these men's confidence; *don't* waste any of this golden time." But of course I couldn't do it. Whisper to him? It would look as if we were conspiring. So I had to sit there and look calm and pleasant while the king stood over that dynamite mine and mooned along about his damned onions and things. At first the tumult of my own thoughts, summoned by the danger-signal and swarming to the rescue from every quarter of my skull, kept up such a hurrah and confusion and fifing and drumming that I couldn't take in a word; but presently when my mob of gathering plans began to crystalize and fall into position and form line of battle, a sort of order and quiet ensued and I caught the boom of the king's batteries, as if out of remote distance:

"—were not the best way, methinks, albeit it is not to be denied that authorities differ as concerning this point, some contending that the onion is but an unwholesome berry when stricken early from the tree—"

The audience showed signs of life, and sought each other's eyes in a surprised and troubled way.

"—whileas others do yet maintain, with much show of reason, that this is not of necessity the case, instancing that plums and other like cereals do be always dug in the unripe state—"

The audience exhibited distinct distress; yes, and also fear.

"—yet are they clearly wholesome, the more especially when one doth assuage the asperities of their nature by admixture of the tranquilizing juice of the wayward cabbage—"

The wild light of terror began to glow in these men's eyes, and one of them muttered, "These be errors, every one—God hath surely smitten the mind of this farmer." I was in miserable apprehension; I sat upon thorns.

"—and further instancing the known truth that in the case of animals, the young, which may be called the green fruit of the creature, is the better, all confessing that when a goat is ripe, his fur doth heat and sore engame his flesh, the which defect, taken in connection with his several rancid habits, and fulsome appetites, and godless attitudes of mind, and bilious quality of morals—"

They rose and went for him! With a fierce shout, "The one would betray us, the other is mad! Kill them! Kill them!" they flung themselves upon us. What joy flamed up in the king's eye! He might be lame in agriculture, but this kind of thing was just in his line. He had been fasting long, he was hungry for a fight. He hit the blacksmith a crack under the jaw that lifted him clear off his feet and stretched him flat of his back. "St. George for Britain!" and he downed the wheelwright. The mason was big, but I laid him out like nothing. The three gathered themselves up and came again; went down again; came again; and kept on repeating this, with native British pluck, until they were battered to jelly, reeling with exhaustion, and so blind that they couldn't tell us from each other; and yet they kept right on, hammering away with what might be left in them. Hammering each other— for we stepped aside and looked on while they rolled, and struggled, and gouged, and pounded, and bit, with the strict and wordless attention to business of so many bulldogs. We looked on without apprehension, for they were fast getting past ability to go for help against us, and the arena was far enough from the public road to be safe from intrusion.

Well, while they were gradually playing out, it suddenly occurred to me to wonder what had become of Marco. I looked around; he was nowhere to be seen. Oh, but this was ominous! I pulled the king's sleeve, and we glided away and rushed for the hut. No Marco there, no Phyllis there! They had gone to the road for help, sure. I told the king to give his heels wings, and I would explain later. We made good time across the open ground, and as we darted into the shelter of the wood I glanced back and saw a mob of excited peasants swarm into view, with Marco and his wife at their head. They were making a world of noise, but that couldn't hurt anybody; the wood was dense, and as soon as we were well into its depths we would take to a tree and let them whistle. Ah, but then came another sound—dogs! Yes, that was quite another matter. It magnified our contract—we must find running water.

We tore along at a good gait, and soon left the sounds far behind and modified to a murmur. We struck a stream and darted into it. We waded swiftly down it, in the dim forest light, for as much as three hundred yards, and then came across an oak with a great bough sticking out over the water. We climbed up on this bough, and began to work our way along it to the body of the tree; now we began to hear those sounds more plainly; so the mob had struck our trail. For a while the sounds approached pretty fast. And then for another while they didn't. No doubt the dogs had found the place where we had entered the stream, and were now waltzing up and down the shores trying to pick up the trail again.

When we were snugly lodged in the tree and curtained with foliage, the king was satisfied, but I was doubtful. I believed we could crawl along a branch and get into the next tree, and I judged it worth while to try. We tried it, and made a success of it, though the king slipped, at the junction, and came near failing to connect. We got comfortable lodgement and satisfactory concealment among the foliage, and then we had nothing to do but listen to the hunt.

Presently we heard it coming—and coming on the jump, too; yes, and down both sides of the stream. Louder—louder—next minute it swelled swiftly up into a roar of shoutings, barkings, tramplings, and swept by like a cyclone.

"I was afraid that the overhanging branch would suggest something to them," said I, "but I don't mind the disappointment. Come, my liege, it were well that we make good use of our time. We've flanked them. Dark is coming on, presently. If we can cross the stream and get a good start, and borrow a couple of horses from somebody's pasture to use for a few hours, we shall be safe enough."

We started down, and got nearly to the lowest limb, when we seemed to hear the hunt returning. We stopped to listen.

"Yes," said I, "they're baffled, they've given it up, they're on their way home. We will climb back to our roost again, and let them go by."

So we climbed back. The king listened a moment and said:

"They still search—I wit the sign. We did best to abide."

He was right. He knew more about hunting than I did. The noise approached steadily, but not with a rush. The king said:

"They reason that we were advantaged by no parlous start of them, and being on foot are as yet no mighty way from where we took the water."

"Yes, sire, that is about it, I am afraid, though I was hoping better things."

The noise drew nearer and nearer, and soon the van was drifting under us, on both sides of the water. A voice called a halt from the other bank, and said:

"An they were so minded, they could get to yon tree by this branch that overhangs, and yet not touch ground. Ye will do well to send a man up it."

"Marry, that will we do!"

I was obliged to admire my cuteness in foreseeing this very thing and swapping trees to beat it. But don't you know, there are some things that can beat smartness and foresight? Awkwardness and stupidity can. The best swordsman in the world doesn't need to fear the second best swordsman in the world; no, the person for him to be afraid of is some ignorant antagonist who has never had a sword in his hand before; he doesn't do the thing he ought to do, and so the expert isn't prepared for him; he does the thing he ought not to do: and often it catches the expert out and ends him on the spot. Well, how could I, with all my gifts, make any valuable preparation against a near-sighted, cross-eyed pudding-headed clown who would aim himself at the wrong tree and hit the right one? And that is what he did. He went for the wrong tree, which was of course the right one by mistake, and up he started.

Matters were serious now. We remained still, and awaited developments. The peasant toiled his difficult way up. The king raised himself up and stood; he made a leg ready, and when the comer's head arrived in reach of it there was a dull thud, and down went the man floundering to the ground. There was a wild outbreak of anger, below, and the mob swarmed in from all around, and there we were treed, and prisoners. Another man started up; the bridging bough was detected, and a volunteer started up the tree that furnished the bridge. The king ordered me to play Horatius[9] and keep the bridge. For a while the enemy came thick and fast; but no matter, the head man of each procession always got a buffet that dislodged him as soon as he came in reach. The king's spirits rose, his joy was limitless. He said that if nothing occurred to mar the prospect we should have a beautiful night, for on this line of tactics we could hold the tree against the whole countryside.

However, the mob soon came to that conclusion themselves; wherefore they called off the assault and began to debate other plans. They had no weapons, but there were plenty of stones, and stones might answer. We had no objections. A stone might possibly penetrate to us once in a while, but it wasn't very likely; we were well protected by boughs and foliage, and were not visible from any good aiming-point. If they would but waste half an hour in stone-throwing, the dark would come to our help. We were feeling very well satisfied. We could smile; almost laugh.

But we didn't; which was just as well, for we should have been interrupted. Before the stones had been raging through the leaves and bouncing from the boughs fifteen minutes, we began to notice a smell. A couple of sniffs of it was enough of an explanation: it was smoke! Our game was up at last. We recognized that. When smoke invites you, you have to come. They raised their pile of dry brush and damp weeds higher and higher, and when they saw the thick cloud begin to roll up and smother the tree, they broke out in a storm of joy-clamors. I got enough breath to say:

"Proceed, my liege; after you is manners."

The king gasped:

"Follow me down, and then back thyself against one side of the

9. Legendary Roman hero who defended a bridge over the Tiber against the Etruscan army until the Romans destroyed the bridge; related in T.B. Macaulay's *Lays of Ancient Rome* (1842).

trunk, and leave me the other. Then will we fight. Let each pile his dead according to his own fashion and taste."

Then he descended barking and coughing, and I followed. I struck the ground an instant after him; we sprang to our appointed places, and began to give and take with all our might. The pow-wow and racket were prodigious; it was a tempest of riot and confusion and thick-falling blows. Suddenly some horsemen tore into the midst of the crowd, and a voice shouted:

"Hold—or ye are dead men!"

How good it sounded! The owner of the voice bore all the marks of a gentleman: picturesque and costly raiment, the aspect of command, a hard countenance, with complexion and features marred by dissipation. The mob fell humbly back, like so many spaniels. The gentleman inspected us critically, then said sharply to the peasants:

"What are ye doing to these people?"

"They be madmen, worshipful sir, that have come wandering we know not whence, and—"

"Ye know not whence? Do ye pretend ye know them not?"

"Most honored sir, we speak but the truth. They are strangers and unknown to any in this region; and they be the most violent and bloodthirsty madmen that ever—"

"Peace! Ye know not what ye say. They are not mad. Who are ye? And whence are ye? Explain."

"We are but peaceful strangers, sir," I said, "and traveling upon our own concerns. We are from a far country, and unacquainted here. We have purposed no harm; and yet but for your brave interference and protection these people would have killed us. As you have divined, sir, we are not mad; neither are we violent or bloodthirsty."

The gentleman turned to his retinue and said calmly:

"Lash me these animals to their kennels!"

The mob vanished in an instant; and after them plunged the horsemen, laying about them with their whips and pitilessly riding down such as were witless enough to keep the road instead of taking to the bush. The shrieks and supplications presently died away in the distance, and soon the horsemen began to straggle back. Meantime the gentleman had been questioning us more closely, but had dug no particulars out of us. We were lavish of recognition of the service he was doing us, but we revealed nothing more than that we were friendless strangers from a far country. When the escort were all returned, the gentleman said to one of his servants:

"Bring the led horses and mount these people."

"Yes, my lord."

We were placed toward the rear, among the servants. We traveled pretty fast, and finally drew rein some time after dark at a roadside inn some ten or twelve miles from the scene of our troubles. My lord went immediately to his room, after ordering his supper, and we saw no more of him. At dawn in the morning we breakfasted and made ready to start.

My lord's chief attendant sauntered forward at that moment with indolent grace, and said:

"Ye have said ye should continue upon this road, which is our direction likewise; wherefore my lord, the earl Grip, hath given commandment that ye retain the horses and ride, and that certain of us ride with ye a twenty mile to a fair town that hight Cambenet, whenso ye shall be out of peril."

We could do nothing less than express our thanks and accept the offer. We jogged along, six in the party, at a moderate and comfortable gait, and in conversation learned that my lord Grip was a very great personage in his own region, which lay a day's journey beyond Cambenet. We loitered to such a degree that it was near the middle of the forenoon when we entered the market square of the town. We dismounted and left our thanks once more for my lord, and then approached a crowd assembled in the centre of the square, to see what might be the object of interest. It was the remnant of that old peregrinating band of slaves! So they had been dragging their chains about, all this weary time. That poor husband was gone, and also many others; and some few purchases had been added to the gang. The king was not interested, and wanted to move along, but I was absorbed, and full of pity. I could not take my eyes away from these worn and wasted wrecks of humanity. There they sat, grouped upon the ground, silent, uncomplaining, with bowed heads, a pathetic sight. And by hideous contrast, a redundant orator was making a speech to another gathering not thirty steps away, in fulsome laudation of "our glorious British liberties!"

I was boiling. I had forgotten I was a plebeian, I was remembering I was a man. Cost what it might, I would mount that rostrum and—

Click! the king and I were handcuffed together! Our companions, those servants, had done it; my lord Grip stood looking on. The king burst out in a fury, and said:

"What meaneth this ill-mannered jest?"

My lord merely said to his head miscreant, coolly:

"Put up the slaves and sell them!"

*Slaves!* The word had a new sound—and how unspeakably awful! The king lifted his manacles and brought them down with a deadly force; but my lord was out of the way when they arrived. A dozen of the rascal's servants sprang forward, and in a moment we were helpless, with our hands bound behind us. We so loudly and so earnestly proclaimed ourselves freemen, that we got the interested attention of that liberty-mouthing orator and his patriotic crowd, and they gathered about us and assumed a very determined attitude. The orator said:

"If indeed ye are freemen, ye have nought to fear—the God-given liberties of Britain are about ye for your shield and shelter! (Applause.) Ye shall soon see. Bring forth your proofs."

"What proofs?"

"Proof that ye are freemen."[1]

Ah—I remembered! I came to myself; I said nothing. But the king stormed out:

"Thou'rt insane, man. It were better, and more in reason, that this thief and scoundrel here prove that we are *not* freemen."

You see, he knew his own laws just as other people so often know the laws: by words, not by effects. They take a *meaning*, and get to be very vivid, when you come to apply them to yourself.

All hands shook their heads and looked disappointed; some turned away, no longer interested. The orator said—and this time in the tones of business, not of sentiment:

"An ye do not know your country's laws, it were time ye learned them. Ye are strangers to us; ye will not deny that. Ye may be freemen, we do not deny that; but also ye may be slaves. The law is clear: it doth not require the claimant to prove ye are slaves, it requireth you to prove ye are *not*."

I said:

"Dear sir, give us only time to send to Astolat; or give us only time to send to the Valley of Holiness—"

"Peace, good man, these are extraordinary requests, and you may not hope to have them granted. It would cost much time, and would unwarrantably inconvenience your master—"

"*Master*, idiot!" stormed the king. "I have no master, I myself am the m——"

"Silence, for God's sake!"

I got the words out in time to stop the king. We were in trouble enough already; it could not help us any to give these people the notion that we were lunatics.

There is no use in stringing out the details. The earl put us up and sold us at auction. This same infernal law had existed in our own South in my own time, more than thirteen hundred years later, and under it hundreds of freemen who could not prove that they were freemen had been sold into life-long slavery without the circumstance making any particular impression upon me; but the minute law and the auction block came into my personal experience, a thing which had been merely improper before became suddenly hellish. Well, that's the way we are made.

Yes, we were sold at auction, like swine. In a big town and an active market we should have brought a good price; but this place was utterly

1. This demand derives from Charles Ball's *Slavery in the United States*; see *Notebooks & Journals*, 3:506.

stagnant and so we sold at a figure which makes me ashamed, every time I think of it. The King of England brought seven dollars, and his prime minister nine; whereas the king was easily worth twelve dollars and I as easily worth fifteen. But that is the way things always go; if you force a sale on a dull market, I don't care what the property is, you are going to make a poor business of it, and you can make up your mind to it. If the earl had had wit enough to—

However, there is no occasion for my working my sympathies up on his account. Let him go, for the present: I took his number, so to speak.

The slave dealer bought us both, and hitched us onto that long chain of his, and we constituted the rear of his procession. We took up our line of march and passed out of Cambenet at noon; and it seemed to me unaccountably strange and odd that the King of England and his chief minister, marching manacled and fettered and yoked, in a slave convoy, could move by all manner of idle men and women, and under windows where sat the sweet and the lovely, and yet never attract a curious eye, never provoke a single remark. Dear, dear, it only shows that there is nothing diviner about a king than there is about a tramp, after all. He is just a cheap and hollow artificiality when you don't know he is a king. But reveal his quality, and dear me it takes your very breath away to look at him. I reckon we are all fools. Born so, no doubt.

## Chapter XXXV

### A PITIFUL INCIDENT

It's a world of surprises. The king brooded; this was natural. What would he brood about, should you say? Why, about the prodigious nature of his fall, of course—from the loftiest place in the world to the lowest; from the most illustrious station in the world to the obscurest; from the grandest vocation among men to the basest. No, I take my oath that the thing that graveled him most, to start with, was not this, but the price he had fetched! He couldn't seem to get over that seven dollars. Well, it stunned me so, when I first found it out, that I couldn't believe it; it didn't seem natural. But as soon as my mental sight cleared and I got a right focus on it, I saw I was mistaken: it *was* natural. For this reason: a king is a mere artificiality, and so a king's feelings, like the impulses of an automatic doll, are mere artificialities; but as a man, he is a reality, and his feelings, as a man, are real, not phantoms. It shames the average man to be valued below his own estimate of his worth; and the king certainly wasn't anything more than an average man, if he was up that high.

Confound him, he wearied me with arguments to show that in anything like a fair market he would have fetched twenty-five dollars, sure—a thing which was plainly nonsense, and full of the baldest conceit; I wasn't worth it myself. But it was tender ground for me to argue on. In fact I had to simply shirk argument and do the diplomatic instead. I had to throw conscience aside, and brazenly concede that he ought to have brought twenty-five dollars; whereas I was quite well aware that in all the ages, the world had never seen a king that was worth half the money, and during the next thirteen centuries wouldn't see one that was worth the fourth of it. Yes, he tired me. If he began to talk about the crops; or about the recent weather; or about the condition of politics, or about dogs, or cats, or morals, or theology—no matter what—I sighed, for I knew what was coming: he was going to get out of it a palliation of that tiresome seven-dollar sale. Wherever we halted, where there was a crowd, he could give me a look which said, plainly: "If that thing could be tried over again, now, with this kind of folk, you would see a different result." Well, when he was first sold, it secretly tickled me to see him go for seven dollars; but before he was done with his sweating and worrying I wished he had fetched a hundred. The thing never got a chance to die, for every day, at one place or another, possible purchasers looked us over, and as often as any other way, their comment on the king was something like this:

"Here's a two-dollar-a-half chump with a thirty-dollar style. Pity but style was marketable."

At last this sort of remark produced an evil result. Our owner was a practical person and he perceived that this defect must be mended if he hoped to find a purchaser for the king. So he went to work to take the style out of his sacred majesty. I could have given the man some valuable advice, but I didn't; you mustn't volunteer advice to a slave-driver unless you want to damage the cause you are arguing for. I had found it a sufficiently difficult job to reduce the king's style to a peasant's style, even when he was a willing and anxious pupil; now then, to undertake to reduce the king's style to a slave's style—and by force—go to! it was a stately contract. Never mind the details—it will save me trouble to let you imagine them. I will only remark that at the end of a week there was plenty of evidence that lash and club and fist had done their work well; the king's body was a sight to see—and to weep over; but his spirit?—why, it wasn't even phased. Even that dull clod of a slave-driver was able to see that there can be such a thing as a slave who will remain a man till he dies; whose bones you can break, but whose manhood you can't. This man found that from his first effort down to his latest, he couldn't ever come within reach of the king but the king was ready to plunge for him, and did it. So he gave up, at last, and left the king in possession of his style unimpaired. The fact is, the king was a good deal more than a king, he was a man; and when a man is a man, you can't knock it out of him.

We had a rough time for a month, tramping to and fro in the earth, and suffering. And what Englishman was the most interested in the slavery question by that time? His grace the king! Yes; from being the most indifferent, he was become the most interested. He was become the bitterest hater of the institution I had ever heard talk. And so I ventured to ask once more a question which I had asked years before and had gotten such a sharp answer that I had not thought it prudent to meddle in the matter further. Would he abolish slavery?

His answer was as sharp as before, but it was music this time; I shouldn't ever wish to hear pleasanter, though the profanity was not good, being awkwardly put together, and with the crash-word almost in the middle instead of at the end, where of course it ought to have been.

I was ready and willing to get free, now; I hadn't wanted to get free any sooner. No, I cannot quite say that. I had wanted to, but I had not been willing to take desperate chances, and had always dissuaded the king from them. But now—ah, it was a new atmosphere! Liberty would be worth any cost that might be put upon it now. I set about a plan, and was straightway charmed with it. It would require time, yes, and patience, too, a great deal of both. One could invent quicker ways, and fully as sure ones; but none that would be as picturesque as this; none that could be made so dramatic.[2] And so I was not going to give this one up. It might delay us months, but no matter, I would carry it out or break something.

Now and then we had an adventure. One night we were overtaken by a snow-storm while still a mile from the village we were making for. Almost instantly we were shut up as in a fog, the driving snow was so thick. You couldn't see a thing, and we were soon lost. The slave-driver lashed us desperately, for he saw ruin before him, but his lashings only made matters worse, for they drove us further from the road and from likelihood of succor. So we had to stop, at last, and slump down in the snow where we were. The storm continued until toward midnight, then ceased. By this time two of our feebler men and three of our women were dead, and others past moving and threatened with death. Our master was nearly beside himself. He stirred up the living and made us stand, jump, slap ourselves, to restore our circulation, and he helped as well as he could with his whip.

Now came a diversion. We heard shrieks and yells, and soon a woman came running, and crying; and seeing our group, she flung herself into our midst and begged for protection. A mob of people came tearing after her, some with torches, and they said she was a witch who had caused several cows to die by a strange disease, and practiced her arts by help of a devil in the form of a black cat. This poor woman had been stoned until she hardly looked human, she was so

2. Compare Tom Sawyer's plans for freeing Jim, which were far more theatrical than Huck's and would take much longer to carry out.

Perhaps the most famous illustration in the novel: the American financier Jay Gould (1836–92) as the slave driver.

battered and bloody. The mob wanted to burn her.

Well, now, what do you suppose our master did? When we closed around this poor creature to shelter her, he saw his chance. He said, burn her here, or they shouldn't have her at all. Imagine that! They were willing. They fastened her to a post; they brought wood and piled it about her; they applied the torch while she shrieked and pleaded and strained her two young daughters to her breast; and our brute, with a heart solely for business, lashed us into position about the stake and warmed us into life and commercial value by the same fire which took away the innocent life of that poor harmless mother. That was the sort of master we had. I took *his* number. That snow-storm cost him nine of his flock; and he was more brutal to us than ever, after that, for many days together, he was so enraged over his loss.

We had adventures, all along. One day we ran into a procession. And such a procession! All the riff-raff of the kingdom seemed to be comprehended in it; and all drunk at that. In the van was a cart with a coffin in it, and on the coffin sat a comely young girl of about eighteen suckling a baby, which she squeezed to her breast in a passion of love every little while, and every little while wiped from its face the tears which her eyes rained down upon it; and always the foolish little thing smiled up at her, happy and content, kneading her breast with its dimpled fat hand, which she patted and fondled right over her breaking heart.

Men and women, boys and girls, trotted along beside or after the cart, hooting, shouting profane and ribald remarks, singing snatches of foul song, skipping, dancing—a very holiday of hellions, a sickening sight. We had struck a suburb of London, outside the walls, and this was a sample of one sort of London society. Our master secured a good place for us near the gallows. A priest was in attendance, and he helped the girl climb up, and said comforting words to her, and made the under-sheriff provide a stool for her. Then he stood there by her on the gallows, and for a moment looked down upon the mass of upturned faces at his feet, then out over the solid pavement of heads that stretched away on every side occupying the vacancies far and near, and then began to tell the story of the case. And there was pity in his voice—how seldom a sound that was in that ignorant and savage land! I remember every detail of what he said, except the words he said it in; and so I change it into my own words:

"Law is intended to mete out justice. Sometimes it fails. This cannot be helped. We can only grieve, and be resigned, and pray for the soul of him who falls unfairly by the arm of the law, and that his fellows may be few. A law sends this poor young thing to death—and it is right. But another law had placed her where she must commit her crime or starve, with her child—and before God that law is responsible for both her crime and her ingnominious death!

"A little while ago this young thing, this child of eighteen years, was as happy a wife and mother as any in England; and her lips were blithe with song, which is the native speech of glad and innocent hearts. Her young husband was as happy as she; for he was doing his whole duty, he worked early and late at his handicraft, his bread was honest bread well and fairly earned, he was prospering, he was furnishing shelter and sustenance to his family, he was adding his mite to the wealth of the nation. By consent of a treacherous law, instant destruction fell upon this holy home and swept it away! That young husband was waylaid and impressed, and sent to sea. The wife knew nothing of it. She sought him everywhere, she moved the hardest hearts with the supplications of her tears, the broken eloquence of her despair. Weeks dragged by, she watching, waiting, hoping, her mind going slowly to wreck under the burden of her misery. Little by little all her small possessions went for food. When she could no longer pay her rent, they turned her out of doors. She begged, while she had strength; when she was starving, at last, and her milk failing, she stole a piece of linen cloth of the value of a fourth part of a cent, thinking to sell it and save her child. But she was seen by the owner of the cloth. She was put in jail and brought to trial. The man testified to the facts. A plea was made for her, and her sorrowful story was told in her behalf. She spoke, too, by permission, and said she did steal the cloth, but that her mind was so disordered of late, by trouble, that when she was over-borne with hunger all acts, criminal or other, swam meaningless through her brain and she knew nothing rightly, except that she was so hungry! For a moment all were touched, and there was disposition to deal mercifully with her, seeing that she was so young and friendless, and her case so piteous, and the law that robbed her of her support to blame as being the first and only cause of her transgression; but the prosecuting officer replied that whereas these things were all true, and most pitiful as well, still there was much small theft in these days, and mistimed mercy here would be a danger to property—Oh, my God, is there no property in ruined homes, and orphaned babes, and broken hearts that British law holds precious!—and so he must require sentence.

"When the judge put on his black cap, the owner of the stolen linen rose trembling up, his lip quivering, his face as gray as ashes; and when the awful words came, he cried out, "Oh, poor child, poor child, I did not know it was death!" and fell as a tree falls. When they lifted him up his reason was gone; before the sun was set, he had taken his own life. A kindly man; a man whose heart was right, at bottom; add his murder to this that is to be now done here; and charge them both where they belong—to the rulers and the bitter laws of Britain. The time is come, my child; let me pray over thee—not *for* thee, dear abused poor heart and innocent, but for them that be guilty of thy ruin and death, who need it more."

After his prayer they put the noose around the young girl's neck, and they had great trouble to adjust the knot under her ear, because she was devouring the baby all the time, wildly kissing it, and snatching it to her face and her breast, and drenching it with tears, and half moaning half shrieking all the while, and the baby crowing, and laughing, and kicking its feet with delight over what it took for romp and play. Even the hangman couldn't stand it, but turned away. When all was ready the priest gently pulled and tugged and forced the child out of the mother's arms, and stepped quickly out of her reach; but she clasped her hands, and made a wild spring toward him, with a shriek; but the rope—and the under-sheriff—held her short. Then she went on her knees and stretched out her hands and cried:

"One more kiss—Oh, my God, one more, one more,—it is the dying that begs it!"

She got it; she almost smothered the little thing. And when they got it away again, she cried out:

"Oh, my child, my darling, it will die! It has no home, it has no father, no friend, no mother—"

"It has them all!" said that good priest. "All these will I be to it till I die."

You should have seen her face then! Gratitude? Lord, what do you want with words to express that? Words are only painted fire; a look is the fire itself. She gave that look, and carried it away to the treasury of heaven, where all things that are divine belong.

## Chapter XXXVI

### AN ENCOUNTER IN THE DARK

London—to a slave—was a sufficiently interesting place.[3] It was merely a great big village; and mainly mud and thatch. The streets were muddy, crooked, unpaved. The populace was an ever flocking and drifting swarm of rags, and splendors, of nodding plumes and shining armor. The king had a palace there; he saw the outside of it. It made him sigh; yes, and swear a little, in a poor juvenile sixth century way. We saw knights and grandees whom we knew, but they didn't know us in our rags and dirt and raw welts and bruises, and wouldn't have recognized us if we had hailed them, nor stopped to answer, either, it being unlawful to speak with slaves on a chain. Sandy passed within ten yards of me on a mule—hunting for me, I imagined. But the thing which clean broke my heart was something which happened in front of our old barrack in a square, while we were enduring

---

3. Although this is the reading in the first and virtually all subsequent editions, the manuscript has "uninteresting," which makes better sense.

the spectacle of a man being boiled to death in oil for counterfeiting pennies. It was the sight of a newsboy—and I couldn't get at him! Still, I had one comfort; here was proof that Clarence was still alive and banging away. I meant to be with him before long; the thought was full of cheer.

I had one little glimpse of another thing, one day, which gave me a great uplift. It was a wire stretching from housetop to housetop. Telegraph or telephone, sure. I did very much wish I had a little piece of it. It was just what I needed, in order to carry out my project of escape. My idea was, to get loose some night, along with the king, then gag and bind our master, change clothes with him, batter him into the aspect of a stranger, hitch him to the slave-chain, assume possession of the property, march to Camelot, and—

But you get my idea; you see what a stunning dramatic surprise I would wind up with at the palace. It was all feasible, if I could only get hold of a slender piece of iron which I could shape into a lock-pick. I could then undo the lumbering padlocks with which our chains were fastened, whenever I might choose. But I never had any luck; no such thing ever happened to fall in my way. However, my chance came at last. A gentleman who had come twice before to dicker for me, without result, or indeed any approach to a result, came again. I was far from expecting ever to belong to him, for the price asked for me from the time I was first enslaved was exorbitant, and always provoked either anger or derision, yet my master stuck stubbornly to it—twenty-two dollars. He wouldn't bate a cent. The king was greatly admired, because of his grand physique, but his kingly style was against him, and he wasn't salable; nobody wanted that kind of a slave. I considered myself safe from parting from him because of my extravagant price. No, I was not expecting to ever belong to this gentleman whom I have spoken of, but he had something which I expected would belong to me eventually, if he would but visit us often enough. It was a steel thing with a long pin to it, with which his long cloth outside garment was fastened together in front. There were three of them. He had disappointed me twice, because he did not come quite close enough to me to make my project entirely safe; but this time I succeeded; I captured the lower clasp of the three, and when he missed it he thought he had lost it on the way.

I had a chance to be glad about a minute, then straightway a chance to be sad again. For when the purchase was about to fail, as usual, the master suddenly spoke up and said what would be worded thus—in modern English:

"I'll tell you what I'll do. I'm tired supporting these two for no good. Give me twenty-two dollars for this one, and I'll throw the other one in."

The king couldn't get his breath, he was in such a fury. He began to choke and gag, and meantime the master and the gentleman moved away, discussing.

"An ye will keep the offer open—"

" 'Tis open till the morrow at this hour."

"Then will I answer you at that time," said the gentleman, and disappeared, the master following him.

I had a time of it to cool the king down, but I managed it. I whispered in his ear, to this effect:

"Your grace *will* go for nothing, but after another fashion. And so shall I. To-night we shall both be free."

"Ah! How is that?"

"With this thing which I have stolen, I will unlock these locks and cast off these chains to-night. When he comes about nine-thirty to inspect us for the night, we will seize him, gag him, batter him, and early in the morning we will march out of this town, proprietors of this caravan of slaves."

That was as far as I went, but the king was charmed and satisfied. That evening we waited patiently for our fellow-slaves to get to sleep and signify it by the usual sign, for you must not take many chances on those poor fellows if you can avoid it. It is best to keep your own secrets. No doubt they fidgeted only about as usual, but it didn't seem so to me. It seemed to me that they were going to be forever getting down to their regular snoring. As the time dragged on I got nervously afraid we shouldn't have enough of it left for our needs; so I made several premature attempts, and merely delayed things by it; for I couldn't seem to touch a padlock, there in the dark, without starting a rattle out of it which interrupted somebody's sleep and made him turn over and wake some more of the gang.

But finally I did get my last iron off, and was a free man once more. I took a good breath of relief, and reached for the king's irons. Too late! in comes the master, with a light in one hand and his heavy walking-staff in the other. I snuggled close among the wallow of snorers, to conceal as nearly as possible that I was naked of irons; and I kept a sharp lookout and prepared to spring for my man the moment he should bend over me.

But he didn't approach. He stopped, gazed absently toward our dusky mass a minute, evidently thinking about something else; then set down his light, moved musingly toward the door, and before a body could imagine what he was going to do, he was out of the door and had closed it behind him.

"Quick!" said the king. "Fetch him back!"

Of course it was the thing to do, and I was up and out in a moment. But dear me, there were no lamps in those days, and it was a dark night. But I glimpsed a dim figure a few steps away. I darted for it, threw myself upon it, and then there was a state of things and lively!

We fought and scuffled and struggled, and drew a crowd in no time. They took an immense interest in the fight and encouraged us all they could, and in fact couldn't have been pleasanter or more cordial if it had been their own fight. Then a tremendous row broke out behind us, and as much as half of our audience left us, with a rush, to invest some sympathy in that. Lanterns began to swing in all directions; it was the watch, gathering from far and near. Presently a halberd fell across my back, as a reminder, and I knew what it meant. I was in custody. So was my adversary. We were marched off toward prison, one on each side of the watchman. Here was disaster, here was a fine scheme gone to sudden destruction! I tried to imagine what would happen when the master should discover that it was I who had been fighting him; and what would happen if they jailed us together in the general apartment for brawlers and petty law breakers, as was the custom; and what might—

Just then my antagonist turned his face around in my direction, the freckled light from the watchman's tin lantern fell on it, and by George he was the wrong man!

## Chapter XXXVII

### AN AWFUL PREDICAMENT

Sleep? It was impossible. It would naturally have been impossible in that noisome cavern of a jail, with its mangy crowd of drunken, quarrelsome and song-singing rapscallions. But the thing that made sleep all the more a thing not to be dreamed of, was my racking impatience to get out of this place and find out the whole size of what might have happened yonder in the slave-quarters in consequence of that intolerable miscarriage of mine.

It was a long night but the morning got around at last. I made a full and frank explanation to the court. I said I was a slave, the property of the great Earl Grip, who had arrived just after dark at the Tabard inn[4] in the village on the other side of the water, and had stopped there over night, by compulsion, he being taken deadly sick with a strange and sudden disorder. I had been ordered to cross to the city in all haste and bring the best physician; I was doing my best; naturally I was running with all my might; the night was dark, I ran against this common person here, who seized me by the throat and began to pummel me, although I told him my errand, and implored him, for the sake of the great earl my master's mortal peril—

The common person interrupted and said it was a lie; and was going to explain how I rushed upon him and attacked him without a word.

"Silence, sirrah!" from the court. "Take him hence and give him a few stripes whereby to teach him how to treat the servant of a noble-

4. Gathering place for Chaucer's pilgrims in his *Canterbury Tales*; in Southwark, on the south side of the Thames from London.

Beard condemns the justice of the sixth and of the nineteenth centuries
equally for weighting the scales against labor.

man after a different fashion another time. Go!"

Then the court begged my pardon, and hoped I would not fail to tell his lordship it was in no wise the court's fault that this high-handed thing had happened. I said I would make it all right, and so took my leave. Took it just in time, too; he was starting to ask me why I didn't fetch out these facts the moment I was arrested. I said I would if I had thought of it—which was true—but that I was so battered by that man that all my wit was knocked out of me—and so forth and so on, and got myself away, still mumbling.

I didn't wait for breakfast. No grass grew under my feet. I was soon at the slave quarters. Empty—everybody gone! That is, everybody except one body—the slave-master's. It lay there all battered to pulp; and all about were the evidences of a terrific fight. There was a rude board coffin on a cart at the door, and workmen, assisted by the police, were thinning a road through the gaping crowd in order that they might bring it in.

I picked out a man humble enough in life to condescend to talk with one so shabby as I, and got his account of the matter.

"There were sixteen slaves here. They rose against their master in the night, and thou seest how it ended."

"Yes. How did it begin?"

"There was no witness but the slaves. They said the slave that was most valuable got free of his bonds and escaped in some strange way—by magic arts 'twas thought, by reason that he had no key, and the locks were neither broke nor in any wise injured. When the master discovered his loss, he was mad with despair, and threw himself upon his people with his heavy stick, who resisted and brake his back and in other and divers ways did give him hurts that brought him swiftly to his end."

"This is dreadful. It will go hard with the slaves, no doubt, upon the trial."

"Marry, the trial is over."

"Over!"

"Would they be a week, think you—and the matter so simple? They were not the half of a quarter of an hour at it."

"Why, I don't see how they could determine which were the guilty ones in so short a time."

"*Which* ones? Indeed they considered not particulars like to that. They condemned them in a body. Wit ye not the law?—which men say the Romans left behind them here when they went—that if one slave killeth his master all the slaves of that man must die for it."

"True. I had forgotten. And when will these die?"

"Belike within a four and twenty hours; albeit some say they will wait a pair of days more, if peradventure they may find the missing one meantime."

The missing one! It made me feel uncomfortable.

"Is it likely they will find him?"

"Before the day is spent—yes. They seek him everywhere. They stand at the gates of the town, with certain of the slaves who will discover him to them if he cometh, and none can pass out but he will be first examined."

"Might one see the place where the rest are confined?"

"The outside of it—yes. The inside of it—but ye will not want to see that."

I took the address of that prison, for future reference, and then sauntered off. At the first second-hand clothing shop I came to, up a back street, I got a rough rig suitable for a common seaman who might be going on a cold voyage, and bound up my face with a liberal bandage, saying I had a toothache. This concealed my worst bruises. It was a transformation. I no longer resembled my former self. Then I struck out for that wire, found it and followed it to its den. It was a little room over a butcher's shop—which meant that business wasn't very brisk in the telegraphic line. The young chap in charge was drowsing at his table. I locked the door and put the vast key in my bosom. This alarmed the young fellow, and he was going to make a noise; but I said:

"Save your wind; if you open your mouth you are dead, sure. Tackle your instrument. Lively, now! Call Camelot."

"This doth amaze me! How should such as you know aught of such matters as—"

"Call Camelot! I am a desperate man. Call Camelot, or get away from the instrument and I will do it myself."

"What—you?"

"Yes—certainly. Stop gabbling. Call the palace." He made the call.

"Now then, call Clarence."

"Clarence *who?*"

"Never mind Clarence who. Say you want Clarence; you'll get an answer."

He did so. We waited five nerve-straining minutes—ten minutes—how long it did seem!—and then came a click that was as familiar to me as a human voice; for Clarence had been my own pupil.

"Now, my lad, vacate! They wouldn't have known *my* touch, maybe, and so your call was surest; but I'm all right, now."

He vacated the place and cocked his ear to listen—but it didn't win. I used a cipher. I didn't waste any time in sociabilities with Clarence, but squared away for business, straight-off—thus:

"The king is here and in danger. We were captured and brought here as slaves. We should not be able to prove our identity—and the fact is, I am not in a position to try. Send a telegram for the palace here which will carry conviction with it."

His answer came straight back:

"They don't know anything about the telegraph; they haven't had any experience yet, the line to London is so new. Better not venture that. They might hang you. Think up something else."

Might hang us! Little he knew how closely he was crowding the facts. I couldn't think up anything for the moment. Then an idea struck me, and I started it along:

"Send five hundred picked knights with Launcelot in the lead; and send them on the jump. Let them enter by the southwest gate, and look out for the man with a white cloth around his right arm."

The answer was prompt:

"They shall start in half an hour."

"All right, Clarence; now tell this lad here that I'm a friend of yours and a dead-head;[5] and that he must be discreet and say nothing about this visit of mine."

The instrument began to talk to the youth and I hurried away. I fell to ciphering. In half an hour it would be nine o'clock. Knights and horses in heavy armor couldn't travel very fast. These would make the best time they could, and now that the ground was in good condition, and no snow or mud, they would probably make a seven-mile gait; they would have to change horses a couple of times; they would arrive about six, or a little after; it would still be plenty light enough; they would see the white cloth which I should tie around my right arm, and I would take command. We would surround that prison and have the king out in no time. It would be showy and picturesque enough, all things considered, though I would have preferred noonday, on account of the more theatrical aspect the thing would have.

Now then, in order to increase the strings to my bow, I thought I would look up some of those people whom I had formerly recognized, and make myself known. That would help us out of our scrape, without the knights. But I must proceed cautiously, for it was a risky business. I must get into sumptuous raiment, and it wouldn't do to run and jump into it. No, I must work up to it by degrees, buying suit after suit of clothes, in shops wide apart, and getting a little finer article with each change, until I should finally reach silk and velvet, and be ready for my project. So I started.

But the scheme fell through like scat! The first corner I turned, I came plump upon one of our slaves, snooping around with a watchman. I coughed, at the moment, and he gave me a sudden look that bit right into my marrow. I judge he thought he had heard that cough before. I turned immediately into a shop and worked along down the counter, pricing things and watching out of the corner of my eye. Those people had stopped, and were talking together and looking in at the door. I made up my mind to get out the back way, if there was a back way, and I asked the shopwoman if I could step out there and look for the escaped slave, who was believed to be in hiding back there somewhere, and said I was an officer in disguise, and my pard was

5. One who does not pay for the services he receives.

yonder at the door with one of the murderers in charge, and would she be good enough to step there and tell him he needn't wait, but had better go at once to the further end of the back alley and be ready to head him off when I rousted him out.

She was blazing with eagerness to see one of those already celebrated murderers, and she started on the errand at once. I slipped out the back way, locked the door behind me, put the key in my pocket and started off, chuckling to myself and comfortable.

Well, I had gone and spoiled it again, made another mistake. A double one, in fact. There were plenty of ways to get rid of that officer by some simple and plausible device, but no, I must pick out a picturesque one; it is the crying defect of my character. And then, I had ordered my procedure upon what the officer, being human, would *naturally* do; whereas when you are least expecting it, a man will now and then go and do the very thing which it's *not* natural for him to do. The natural thing for the officer to do, in this case, was to follow straight on my heels; he would find a stout oaken door, securely locked, between him and me; before he could break it down, I should be far away and engaged in slipping into a succession of baffling disguises which would soon get me into a sort of raiment which was a surer protection from meddling law-dogs in Britain than any amount of mere innocence and purity of character. But instead of doing the natural thing, the officer took me at my word, and followed my instructions. And so, as I came trotting out of that cul de sac, full of satisfaction with my own cleverness, he turned the corner and I walked right into his handcuffs. If I had known it was a cul de sac—however, there isn't any excusing a blunder like that, let it go. Charge it up to profit and loss.

Of course I was indignant, and swore I had just come ashore from a long voyage, and all that sort of thing—just to see, you know, if it would deceive that slave. But it didn't. He knew me. Then I reproached him for betraying me. He was more surprised than hurt. He stretched his eyes wide, and said:

"What, wouldst have me let thee, of all men, escape and not hang with us, when thou'rt the very *cause* of our hanging? Go to!"

"Go to" was their way of saying "I should smile!" or "I like that!" Queer talkers, those people.

Well, there was a sort of bastard justice in his view of the case, and so I dropped the matter. When you can't cure a disaster by argument, what is the use to argue? It isn't my way. So I only said:

"You're not going to be hanged. None of us are."

Both men laughed, and the slave said:

"Ye have not ranked as a fool—before. You might better keep your reputation, seeing the strain would not be for long."

"It will stand it, I reckon. Before to-morrow we shall be out of prison, and free to go where we will, besides."

The witty officer lifted at his left ear with his thumb, made a rasping noise in his throat, and said:

"Out of prison—yes—ye say true. And free likewise to go where ye will, so ye wander not out of his grace the Devil's sultry realm."

I kept my temper, and said, indifferently:

"Now I suppose you really think we are going to hang within a day or two."

"I thought it not many minutes ago, for so the thing was decided and proclaimed."

"Ah, then you've changed your mind, is that it?"

"Even that. I only *thought*, then; I *know*, now."

I felt sarcastical, so I said:

"Oh, sapient servant of the law, condescend to tell us, then, what you *know*."

"That ye will all be hanged *to-day*, at mid-afternoon! Oho! That shot hit home! Lean upon me."

The fact is I did need to lean upon somebody. My knights couldn't arrive in time. They would be as much as three hours too late. Nothing in the world could save the King of England; nor me, which was more important. More important, not merely to me, but to the nation—the only nation on earth standing ready to blossom into civilization. I was sick. I said no more, there wasn't anything to say. I knew what the man meant; that if the missing slave was found, the postponement would be revoked, the execution take place to-day. Well, the missing slave was found.

## Chapter XXXVIII

### SIR LAUNCELOT AND KNIGHTS TO THE RESCUE

Nearing four in the afternoon. The scene was just outside the walls of London. A cool, comfortable, superb day, with a brilliant sun; the kind of day to make one want to live, not die. The multitude was prodigious and far reaching; and yet we fifteen poor devils hadn't a friend in it. There was something painful in that thought, look at it how you might. There we sat, on our tall scaffold, the butt of the hate and mockery of all those enemies. We were being made a holiday spectacle. They had built a sort of grand stand for the nobility and gentry, and these were there in full force, with their ladies. We recognized a good many of them.

The crowd got a brief and unexpected dash of diversion out of the king. The moment we were freed of our bonds he sprang up, in his fantastic rags, with face bruised out of all recognition, and proclaimed himself Arthur, King of Britain, and denounced the awful penalties of treason upon every soul there present if hair of his sacred head were touched. It startled and surprised him to hear them break into a vast roar of laughter. It wounded his dignity, and he locked himself up in silence, then, although the crowd begged him to go on, and tried to provoke him to it by cat-calls, jeers, and shouts of

"Let him speak! The king! The king! his humble subjects hunger and thirst for words of wisdom out of the mouth of their master his Serene and Sacred Raggedness!"

But it went for nothing. He put on all his majesty and sat under this rain of contempt and insult unmoved. He certainly was great in his way. Absently, I had taken off my white bandage and wound it about my right arm. When the crowd noticed this, they began upon me. They said:

"Doubtless this sailor-man is his minister—observe his costly badge of office!"

I let them go on until they got tired, and then I said:

"Yes, I am his minister, The Boss; and to-morrow you will hear that from Camelot which—"

I got no further. They drowned me out with joyous derision. But presently there was silence; for the sheriffs of London, in their official robes, with their subordinates, began to make a stir which indicated that business was about to begin. In the hush which followed, our crime was recited, the death warrant read, then everybody uncovered while a priest uttered a prayer.

Then a slave was blindfolded, the hangman unslung his rope. There lay the smooth road below us, we upon one side of it, the banked multitude walling its other side—a good clear road, and kept free by the police—how good it would be to see my five hundred horsemen come tearing down it! But, no, it was out of the possibilities. I followed its receding thread out into the distance—not a horseman on it, or sign of one.

There was a jerk, and the slave hung dangling; dangling and hideously squirming, for his limbs were not tied.

A second rope was unslung, in a moment another slave was dangling. In a minute a third slave was struggling in the air. It was dreadful. I turned away my head a moment, and when I turned back I missed the king! They were blindfolding him! I was paralyzed; I couldn't move, I was choking, my tongue was petrified. They finished blindfolding him, they led him under the rope. I couldn't shake off that clinging impotence. But when I saw them put the noose around his neck, then everything let go in me and I made a spring to the rescue—and as I made it I shot one more glance abroad—by George, here they came, a-tilting!—five hundred mailed and belted knights on bicycles![6]

The grandest sight that ever was seen. Lord, how the plumes streamed, how the sun flamed and flashed from the endless procession

---

6. America's first bicycle factory was established in Hartford, Conn. in the late 1870s. Clemens describes his own difficulties with the comparatively new invention in "Taming the Bicycle."

Sir Launcelot mounted on a nineteenth-century bicycle.

of webby wheels!

I waved my right arm as Launcelot swept in—he recognized my rag—I tore away noose and bandage, and shouted:

"On your knees, every rascal of you, and salute the king! Who fails shall sup in hell to-night!"

I always use that high style when I'm climaxing an effect. Well, it was noble to see Launcelot and the boys swarm up onto that scaffold and heave sheriffs and such overboard. And it was fine to see that astonished multitude go down on their knees and beg their lives of the king they had just been deriding and insulting. And as he stood apart, there, receiving this homage in his rags, I thought to myself, well really there *is* something peculiarly grand about the gait and bearing of a king, after all.

I was immensely satisfied. Take the whole situation all around, it was one of the gaudiest effects I ever instigated.

And presently up comes Clarence, his own self! and winks, and says, very modernly:

"Good deal of a surprise, wasn't it? I knew you'd like it. I've had the boys practicing, this long time, privately; and just hungry for a chance to show off."

## Chapter XXXIX

### THE YANKEE'S FIGHT WITH THE KNIGHTS

Home again, at Camelot. A morning or two later I found the paper, damp from the press, by my plate at the breakfast table. I turned to the advertising columns, knowing I should find something of personal interest to me there. It was this:

### DE PAR LE ROI.

Know that the great lord and illustrious kni8ht. SIR SAGRAMOUR LE DESIYOUS having condescended to meet the King's Minister, Hank Morgan, the which is surnamed The Boss, for satisfaction of offence anciently given, these will engage in the lists by Camelot about the fourth hour of the morning of the sixteenth day of this next succeeding month. The battle will be à l'outrance, sith the said offence was of a deadly sort, admitting of no composition.

DE PAR LE ROI.

Clarence's editorial reference to this affair was to this effect:

ndrew.
work maintained
there since, soon
listic have with
oked interest
upon the ea~
ve been m d
oy the ar s,
ent out ch y by
yterian B , and
c some y g men
of our unde he
i guidance of the
for and in a known
he great enterprise
of making pure;
esent
movement had its
origin n preven-
has ever been a
sions in our
on of this-
ether one
ospel,
by-
e
The
he same
co represent
ized thirty of
deeds and hear-
which, years ago!
oresgn was organ-
ing, the missions,
sso that both had
to withdraw' and
much to their
grief,

It will be observed, by a glance at our advertising columns, that the community is to be favored with a treat of unusual interest in the tournament line. The names of the artists are warrant of good entertainment. The box-office will be open at noon of the 13th; admission 3 cents, reserved seats 5; proceeds to go to the hospital fund. The royal pair and all the Court will be present. With these exceptions, and the press and the clergy, the free list is strictly suspended. Parties are hereby warned against buying tickets of speculators; they will not be good at the door. Everybody knows and likes The Boss, everybody knows and likes Sir Sag.; come, let us give the lads a good send-off. Remember, the proceeds go to a great and free charity, and one whose broad benevolence stretches out its helping hand, warm with the blood of a loving heart, to all that suffer, regardless of race, creed, condition or color—the only charity yet established in the earth which has no politico-religious stop-cock on its compassion, but says Here flows the stream, let *all* come and drink! Turn out, all hands! fetch along your doughnuts and your gum-drops and have a good time. Pie for sale on the grounds, and rocks to crack it with; also circus-lemonade—three drops of lime juice to a barrel of water.

N. B. *This is the first tournament under the new law, which allows each combatant to use any weapon he may prefer.* You want to make a note of that.

our disappointm.
promptly and n t
two of their felo
erlain, and othe
ers have already
spoken, you
furnished for
their use,
make and
the kind
letters
of introd
duction wh
they are unw
ing friends to us
ried, and leave the
thot kind words and
which you, m, joy-
hind; and it is a
home matter of b
it is our durp
direct them to
now under the e
g fields as are
These young men
are warm-hearted
azir. regions be
not to "build
ond,', and the
der instructi
ons of our
another man
founhati's on.
ociety, which
They go un-
say that "inr
ionaries to mon
say sending miss

Up to the day set, there was no talk in all Britain of anything but this combat. All other topics sank into insignificance and passed out of men's thoughts and interest. It was not because a tournament was a great matter; it was not because Sir Sagramour had found the Holy Grail, for he had not, but had failed; it was not because the second (official) personage in the kingdom was one of the duellists; no, all these features were commonplace. Yet there was abundant reason for the extraordinary interest which this coming fight was creating. It was born of the fact that all the nation knew that this was not to be a duel between mere men, so to speak, but a duel between two mighty magicians; a duel not of muscle but of mind, not of human skill but of superhuman art and craft; a final struggle for supremacy between the two master enchanters of the age. It was realized that the most prodigious achievements of the most renowned knights could not be worthy of comparison with a spectacle like this; they could be but child's play, contrasted with this mysterious and awful battle of the gods. Yes, all the world knew it was going to be in reality a duel between Merlin and me, a measuring of his magic powers against mine. It was known that Merlin had been busy whole days and nights together, imbuing Sir Sagramour's arms and armor with supernal powers of offence and defence, and that he had procured for him from the spirits of the air a fleecy veil which would render the wearer invisible to his antagonist while still visible to other men. Against Sir Sagramour, so weaponed and protected, a thousand knights could accomplish nothing; against him no known enchantments could prevail. These facts were sure; regarding them there was no doubt, no reason for doubt. There was but one question: might there be still other enchantments, *unknown* to Merlin, which could render Sir Sagramour's veil transparent to me, and make his enchanted mail vulnerable to my weapons? This was the one thing to be decided in the lists. Until then the world must remain in suspense.

So the world thought there was a vast matter at stake here, and the world was right, but it was not the one they had in their minds. No, a far vaster one was upon the cast of this die: *the life of knight-errantry.* I was a champion, it was true, but not the champion of the frivolous black arts, I was the champion of hard unsentimental common-sense and reason. I was entering the lists to either destroy knight-errantry or be its victim.

Vast as the show-grounds were, there were no vacant spaces in them outside of the lists, at ten o'clock on the morning of the 16th. The mammoth grand stand was clothed in flags, streamers, and rich tapestries, and packed with several acres of small-fry tributary kings, their suites, and the British aristocracy; with our own royal gang in the chief place, and each and every individual a flashing prism of gaudy silks and velvets—well, I never saw anything to begin with it but a fight between an Upper Mississippi sunset and the aurora borealis. The huge camp of beflagged and gay-colored tents at one end of the lists, with a stiff-standing sentinel at every door and a shining shield hanging by him for challenge, was another fine sight. You see, every knight was there who had any ambition or any caste feeling; for my feeling toward their order was not much of a secret, and so here was their chance. If I won my fight with Sir Sagramour, others would have the right to call me out as long as I might be willing to respond.

Down at our end there were but two tents; one for me, and another for my servants. At the appointed hour the king made a sign, and the heralds, in their tabards,[7] appeared and made proclamation, naming the combatants and stating the cause of quarrel. There was a pause, then a ringing bugle blast, which was the signal for us to come forth. All the multitude caught their breath, and an eager curiosity flashed into every face.

Out from his tent rode great Sir Sagramour, an imposing tower of iron, stately and rigid, his huge spear standing upright in its socket and grasped in his strong hand, his grand horse's face and breast cased in steel, his body clothed in rich trappings that almost dragged the ground—oh, a most noble picture. A great shout went up, of welcome and admiration.

And then out I came. But I didn't get any shout. There was a wondering and eloquent silence, for a moment, then a great wave of laughter began to sweep along that human sea, but a warning bugle-blast cut its career short. I was in the simplest and comfortablest of gymnast costumes—flesh-colored tights from neck to heel, with blue silk puffings about my loins, and bare-headed. My horse was not above medium size, but he was alert, slender-limbed, muscled with watch-springs, and just a greyhound to go. He was a beauty, glossy as silk, and naked as he was when he was born, except for bridle and ranger-saddle.

The iron tower and the gorgeous bed-quilt came cumbrously but gracefully pirouetting down the lists, and we tripped lightly up to meet them. We halted; the tower saluted, I responded; then we wheeled and rode side by side to the grand stand and faced our king and queen, to whom we made obeisance. The queen exclaimed:

"Alack, Sir Boss, wilt fight naked, and without lance or sword or—"

But the king checked her and made her understand, with a polite phrase or two, that this was none of her business. The bugles rang again; and we separated and rode to the ends of the lists, and took position. Now old Merlin stepped into view and cast a dainty web of

---

7. Official coats, bearing the king's or the lord's arms.

gossamer threads over Sir Sagramour which turned him into Hamlet's ghost;[8] the king made a sign, the bugles blew, Sir Sagramour laid his great lance in rest, and the next moment here he came thundering down the course with his veil flying out behind, and I went whistling through the air like an arrow to meet him—cocking my ear, the while, as if noting the invisible knight's position and progress by hearing, not sight. A chorus of encouraging shouts burst out for him, and one brave voice flung out a heartening word for me—said:

"Go it, slim Jim!"

It was an even bet that Clarence had procured that favor for me—and furnished the language, too. When that formidable lance-point was within a yard and a half of my breast I twitched my horse aside without an effort and the big knight swept by, scoring a blank. I got plenty of applause that time. We turned, braced up, and down we came again. Another blank for the knight, a roar of applause for me. This same thing was repeated once more; and it fetched such a whirlwind of applause that Sir Sagramour lost his temper, and at once changed his tactics and set himself the task of chasing me down. Why, he hadn't any show in the world at that; it was a game of tag, with all the advantage on my side; I whirled out of his path with ease whenever I chose, and once I slapped him on the back as I went to the rear. Finally I took the chase into my own hands; and after that, turn, or twist, or do what he would, he was never able to get behind me again; he found himself always in front, at the end of his maneuvre. So he gave up that business and retired to his end of the lists. His temper was clear gone, now, and he forgot himself and flung an insult at me which disposed of mine. I slipped my lasso from the horn of my saddle, and grasped the coil in my right hand. This time you should have seen him come!—it was a business trip, sure; by his gait there was blood in his eye. I was sitting my horse at ease, and swinging the great loop of my lasso in wide circles about my head; the moment he was under way, I started for him; when the space between us had narrowed to forty feet, I sent the snaky spirals of the rope a-cleaving through the air, then darted aside and faced about and brought my trained animal to a halt with all his feet braced under him for a surge. The next moment the rope sprang taut and yanked Sir Sagramour out of the saddle! Great Scott, but there was a sensation!

Unquestionably the popular thing in this world is novelty. These people had never seen anything of that cow-boy business before, and it carried them clear off their feet with delight. From all around and everywhere, the shout went up—

8. In Shakespeare's play the ghost of Hamlet's father is sometimes but not always invisible. Clemens has in mind a scene such as that with Gertrude (III.iv) in which she cannot see the ghost.

"Encore! encore!"

I wondered where they got the word, but there was no time to cipher on philological matters, because the whole knight-errantry hive was just humming, now, and my prospect for trade couldn't have been better. The moment my lasso was released and Sir Sagramour had been assisted to his tent, I hauled in the slack, took my station and began to swing my loop around my head again. I was sure to have use for it as soon as they could elect a successor for Sir Sagramour, and that couldn't take long where there were so many hungry candidates. Indeed, they elected one straight off—Sir Hervis de Revel.

*Bzz!* Here he came, like a house afire; I dodged; he passed like a flash, with my horse-hair coils settling around his neck; a second or so later, *fst!* his saddle was empty.

I got another encore; and another, and another, and still another. When I had snaked five men out, things began to look serious to the iron-clads, and they stopped and consulted together. As a result, they decided that it was time to waive etiquette and send their greatest and best against me. To the astonishment of that little world, I lassoed Sir Lamorak de Galis, and after him Sir Galahad. So you see there was simply nothing to be done, now, but play their right bower[9]—bring out the superbest of the superb, the mightiest of the mighty, the great Sir Launcelot himself!

A proud moment for me? I should think so. Yonder was Arthur, King of Britain; yonder was Guenever; yes, and whole tribes of little provincial kings and kinglets; and in the tented camp yonder, re-nowned knights from many lands; and likewise the selectest body known to chivalry, the Knights of the Table Round, the most illustri-ous in Christendom; and biggest fact of all, the very sun of their shining system was yonder couching his lance, the focal point of forty thousand adoring eyes; and all by myself, here was I laying for him. Across my mind flitted the dear image of a certain hello-girl of West Hartford, and I wished she could see me now. In that moment, down came the Invincible, with the rush of a whirlwind—the courtly world rose to its feet and bent forward—the fateful coils went circling through the air, and before you could wink I was towing Sir Launcelot across the field on his back, and kissing my hand to the storm of waving kerchiefs and the thunder-crash of applause that greeted me!

Said I to myself, as I coiled my lariat and hung it on my saddle-horn, and sat there drunk with glory, "The victory is perfect—no other will venture against me—knight-errantry is dead." Now imagine my astonishment—and everybody else's too—to hear the peculiar bugle-call which announces that another competitor is about to enter the lists! There was a mystery here; I couldn't account for this thing. Next, I noticed Merlin gliding away from me; and then I noticed that my

9. The jack of trumps, one of the highest cards in certain games.

lasso was gone! The old sleight-of-hand expert had stolen it, sure, and slipped it under his robe.

The bugle blew again. I looked, and down came Sagramour riding again, with his dust brushed off and his veil nicely re-arranged. I trotted up to meet him, and pretended to find him by the sound of his horse's hoofs. He said:

"Thou'rt quick of ear, but it will not save thee from this!" and he touched the hilt of his great sword. "An ye are not able to see it, because of the influence of the veil, know that it is no cumbrous lance, but a sword—and I ween ye will not be able to avoid it."

His visor was up; there was death in his smile. I should never be able to dodge his sword, that was plain. Somebody was going to die, this time. If he got the drop on me, I could name the corpse. We rode forward together, and saluted the royalties. This time the king was disturbed. He said:

"Where is thy strange weapon?"

"It is stolen, sire."

"Hast another at hand?"

"No, sire, I brought only the one."

Then Merlin mixed in:

"He brought but the one because there was but the one to bring. There exists none other but that one. It belongeth to the king of the Demons of the Sea. This man is a pretender, and ignorant; else he had known that that weapon can be used in but eight bouts only, and then it vanisheth away to its home under the sea."

"Then is he weaponless," said the king. "Sir Sagramour, ye will grant him leave to borrow."

"And I will lend!" said Sir Launcelot, limping up. "He is as brave a knight of his hands as any that be on live, and he shall have mine."

He put his hand on his sword to draw it, but Sir Sagramour said:

"Stay, it may not be. He shall fight with his own weapons; it was his privilege to choose them and bring them. If he has erred, on his head be it."

"Knight!" said the king. "Thou'rt overwrought with passion; it disorders thy mind. Wouldst kill a naked man?"

"An he do it, he shall answer it to me," said Sir Launcelot.

"I will answer it to any he that desireth!" retorted Sir Sagramour hotly.

Merlin broke in, rubbing his hands and smiling his lowdownest smile of malicious gratification:

" 'Tis well said, right well said! And 'tis enough of parleying, let my lord the king deliver the battle signal."

The king had to yield. The bugle made proclamation, and we turned apart and rode to our stations. There we stood, a hundred yards apart, facing each other, rigid and motionless, like horsed statues. And so we remained, in a soundless hush, as much as a full minute, everybody gazing, nobody stirring. It seemed as if the king could not take heart to give the signal. But at last he lifted his hand, the clear note of the bugle followed, Sir Sagramour's long blade described a flashing curve in the air, and it was superb to see him come. I sat still. On he came. I did not move. People got so excited that they shouted to me:

"Fly, fly! Save thyself! This is murther!"

I never budged so much as an inch, till that thundering apparition had got within fifteen paces of me; then I snatched a dragoon revolver[1] out of my holster, there was a flash and a roar, and the revolver was back in the holster before anybody could tell what had happened.

Here was a riderless horse plunging by, and yonder lay Sir Sagramour, stone dead.

The people that ran to him were stricken dumb to find that the life was actually gone out of the man and no reason for it visible, no hurt upon his body, nothing like a wound. There was a hole through the breast of his chain-mail,[2] but they attached no importance to a little thing like that; and as a bullet-wound produces but little blood, none came in sight because of the clothing and swaddlings under the armor. The body was dragged over to let the king and the swells look down upon it. They were stupefied with astonishment, naturally. I was requested to come and explain the miracle. But I remained in my tracks, like a statue, and said:

"If it is a command, I will come, but my lord the king knows that I am where the laws of combat require me to remain while any desire to come against me."

I waited. Nobody challenged. Then I said:

"If there are any who doubt that this field is well and fairly won, I do not wait for them to challenge me, I challenge them."

"It is a gallant offer," said the king, "and well beseems you. Whom will you name, first?"

"I name none, I challenge all! Here I stand, and dare the chivalry of England to come against me—not by individuals, but in mass!"

"What!" shouted a score of knights.

"You have heard the challenge. Take it, or I proclaim you recreant knights and vanquished, every one!"

It was a "bluff" you know. At such a time it is sound judgment to put on a bold face and play your hand for a hundred times what it is worth; forty-nine times out of fifty nobody dares to "call," and you rake in the chips. But just this once—well, things looked squally! In just no time, five hundred knights were scrambling into their saddles, and before you could wink a widely scattering drove were under way and clatter-

---

1. Dragoon pistols were manufactured by the Colt Arms Factory of Hartford.
2. This, of course, is the origin of the bullet hole in the armor of Sir Sagramour as displayed in Warwick Castle, in nineteenth-century England.

ing down upon me. I snatched both revolvers from the holsters and began to measure distances and calculate chances.

Bang! One saddle empty. Bang! another one. Bang—bang! and I bagged two. Well it was nip and tuck with us, and I knew it. If I spent the eleventh shot without convincing these people, the twelfth man would kill me, sure. And so I never did feel so happy as I did when my ninth downed its man and I detected the wavering in the crowd which is premonitory of panic. An instant lost now, could knock out my last chance. But I didn't lose it. I raised both revolvers and pointed them—the halted host stood their ground just about one good square moment, then broke and fled.

The day was mine. Knight-errantry was a doomed institution. The march of civilization was begun. How did I feel? Ah you never could imagine it.

And Brer Merlin? His stock was flat again. Somehow, every time the magic of fol-de-rol tried conclusions with the magic of science, the magic of fol-de-rol got left.[3]

## Chapter XL

### THREE YEARS LATER

When I broke the back of knight-errantry that time, I no longer felt obliged to work in secret. So, the very next day I exposed my hidden schools, my mines, and my vast system of clandestine factories and work-shops to an astonished world. That is to say, I exposed the nineteenth century to the inspection of the sixth.

Well it is always a good plan to follow up an advantage promptly. The knights were temporarily down, but if I would keep them so I must just simply paralyze them—nothing short of that would answer. You see, I was "bluffing" that last time, in the field; it would be natural for them to work around to that conclusion, if I gave them a chance. So I must not give them time: and I didn't.

I renewed my challenge, engraved it on brass, posted it up where any priest could read it to them, and also kept it standing, in the advertising columns of the paper.

I not only renewed it, but added to its proportions. I said, name the day, and I would take fifty assistants and stand up *against the massed chivalry of the whole earth and destroy it.*

I was not bluffing this time. I meant what I said; I could do what I promised. There wasn't any way to misunderstand the language of that

3. In a bridge passage written for the excerpts printed in the *Century*, Clemens remarks that "a bitter struggle for supremacy in magic ensues between the two which lasts to the end of the book, Merlin using the absurd necromancy of the time, and the Yankee beating it easily and brilliantly with the more splendid necromancy of the nineteenth century—that is, the marvels of modern science" (XXXIX, 74).

challenge. Even the dullest of the chivalry perceived that this was a plain case of "put up, or shut up." They were wise and did the latter. In all the next three years they gave me no trouble worth mentioning.

Consider the three years sped. Now look around on England. A happy and prosperous country, and strangely altered. Schools everywhere, and several colleges; a number of pretty good newspapers. Even authorship was taking a start; Sir Dinadan the Humorist was first in the field, with a volume of gray-headed jokes which I had been familiar with during thirteen centuries. If he had left out that old rancid one about the lecturer I wouldn't have said anything; but I couldn't stand that one. I suppressed the book and hanged the author.

Slavery was dead and gone; all men were equal before the law; taxation had been equalized. The telegraph, the telephone, the phonograph, the type-writer, the sewing machine, and all the thousand willing and handy servants of steam and electricity were working their way into favor. We had a steamboat or two on the Thames, we had steam war-ships, and the beginnings of a steam commercial marine; I was getting ready to send out an expedition to discover America.

We were building several lines of railway, and our line from Camelot to London was already finished and in operation. I was shrewd enough to make all offices connected with the passenger service places of high and distinguished honor. My idea was to attract the chivalry and nobility, and make them useful and keep them out of mischief. The plan worked very well, the competition for the places was hot. The conductor of the 4.33 express was a duke, there wasn't a passenger conductor on the line below the degree of earl. They were good men, every one, but they had two defects which I couldn't cure, and so had to wink at: they wouldn't lay aside their armor, and they would "knock down" fares—I mean rob the company.

There was hardly a knight in all the land who wasn't in some useful employment. They were going from end to end of the country in all manner of useful missionary capacities; their penchant for wandering, and their experience in it, made them altogether the most effective spreaders of civilization we had. They went clothed in steel and equipped with sword and lance and battle axe, and if they couldn't persuade a person to try a sewing machine on the instalment plan, or a melodeon, or a barbed wire fence, or a prohibition journal, or any of the other thousand and one things they canvassed for, they removed him and passed on.

I was very happy. Things were working steadily toward a secretly longed-for point. You see, I had two schemes in my head which were the vastest of all my projects. The one was, to overthrow the Catholic Church and set up the Protestant faith on its ruins—not as an Established Church, but a go-as-you-please one; and the other project was, to get a decree issued by and by, commanding that upon Arthur's death unlimited suffrage should be introduced, and given to men and women alike[4]—at any rate to all men, wise or unwise, and to all mothers who at middle age should be found to know nearly as much as their sons at twenty-one. Arthur was good for thirty years yet, he being about my own age—that is to say, forty—and I believed that in that time I could easily have the active part of the population of that day ready and eager for an event which should be the first of its kind in the history of the world—a rounded and complete governmental revolution without bloodshed. The result to be a republic. Well, I may as well confess, though I do feel ashamed when I think of it: I was beginning to have a base hankering to be its first president myself. Yes, there was more or less human nature in me; I found that out.

Clarence was with me as concerned the revolution, but in a modified way. His idea was a republic, without privileged orders but with a hereditary royal family at the head of it instead of an elective chief magistrate. He believed that no nation that had ever known the joy of worshiping a royal family could ever be robbed of it and not fade away and die of melancholy. I urged that kings were dangerous. He said, then have cats. He was sure that a royal family of cats would answer every purpose. They would be as useful as any other royal family, they would know as much, they would have the same virtues and the same treacheries, the same disposition to get up shindies with other royal cats, they would be laughably vain and absurd and never know it, they would be wholly inexpensive; finally, they would have as sound a divine right as any other royal house, and "Tom VII, or Tom XI, or Tom XIV by the grace of God King," would sound as well as it would when applied to the ordinary royal tomcat with tights on. "And as a rule," said he, in his neat modern English, "the character of these cats would be considerably above the character of the average king, and this would be an immense moral advantage to the nation, for the reason that a nation always models its morals after its monarch's. The worship of royalty being founded in unreason, these graceful and harmless cats would easily become as sacred as any other royalties, and indeed more so, because it would presently be noticed that they hanged nobody, beheaded nobody, imprisoned nobody, inflicted no cruelties or injustices of any sort, and so must be worthy of a deeper love and reverence than the customary human king, and would certainly get it. The eyes of the whole harried world would soon be fixed upon this humane and gentle system, and royal butchers would presently begin to disappear; their subjects would fill the vacancies with catlings from our own royal house; we should become a factory; we should supply the thrones of the world; within forty years all

4. Women were not allowed to vote in the United States until 1920, when the nineteenth amendment to the Constitution was adopted.

Europe would be governed by cats, and we should furnish the cats. The reign of universal peace would begin then, to end no more forever. . . . . . *Me-e-e-yow-ow-ow-ow—fzt!—wow!"*

Hang him, I supposed he was in earnest, and was beginning to be persuaded by him, until he exploded that cat-howl and startled me almost out of my clothes. But he never could be in earnest. He didn't know what it was. He had pictured a distinct and perfectly rational and feasible improvement upon constitutional monarchy, but he was too feather-headed to know it, or care anything about it, either. I was going to give him a scolding, but Sandy came flying in at that moment, wild with terror, and so choked with sobs that for a minute she could not get her voice. I ran and took her in my arms, and lavished caresses upon her and said, beseechingly:

"Speak, darling, speak! What is it?"

Her head fell limp upon my bosom, and she gasped, almost inaudibly:

"HELLO-CENTRAL!"

"Quick!" I shouted to Clarence; "telephone the king's homeopath[5] to come!"

In two minutes I was kneeling by the child's crib, and Sandy was dispatching servants here, there and everywhere, all over the palace. I took in the situation almost at a glance—membraneous croup![6] I bent down and whispered:

"Wake up, sweetheart! Hello-Central!"

She opened her soft eyes languidly, and made out to say—

"Papa."

That was a comfort. She was far from dead, yet. I sent for preparations of sulphur, I rousted out the croup-kettle myself; for I don't sit down and wait for doctors when Sandy or the child is sick. I knew how to nurse both of them, and had had experience. This little chap had lived in my arms a good part of its small life, and often I could soothe away its troubles and get it to laugh through the tear-dews on its eye-lashes when even its mother couldn't.

Sir Launcelot, in his richest armor, came striding along the great hall, now, on his way to the stock-board; he was president of the stockboard, and occupied the Siege Perilous, which he had bought of Sir Galahad; for the stock-board consisted of the Knights of the Round Table, and they used the Round Table for business purposes, now. Seats at it were worth—well, you would never believe the figure, so it is no use to state it. Sir Launcelot was a bear, and he had put up a corner in one of the new lines, and was just getting ready to squeeze the shorts to-day; but what of that? He was the same old Launcelot,

5. One practicing a system of medical treatment in which small doses are given of drugs which if given to a healthy person in large doses would produce symptoms like those of the disease.

6. Described as "that frightful and incurable disease . . . driving all mothers mad with terror" in Clemens' "Experience of the McWilliamses with Membranous Croup" (1875).

and when he glanced in as he was passing the door and found out that his pet was sick, that was enough for him; bulls and bears[7] might fight it out their own way for all him, he would come right in here and stand by little Hello-Central for all he was worth. And that was what he did. He shied his helmet into the corner, and in half a minute he had a new wick in the alcohol lamp and was firing up on the croup-kettle. By this time Sandy had built a blanket canopy over the crib, and everything was ready.

Sir Launcelot got up steam, he and I loaded up the kettle with unslaked lime and carbolic acid, with a touch of lactic acid added thereto, then filled the thing up with water and inserted the steam-spout under the canopy. Everything was ship-shape, now, and we sat down on either side of the crib to stand our watch. Sandy was so grateful and so comforted that she charged a couple of church-wardens[8] with willow-bark and sumach-tobacco for us, and told us to smoke as much as we pleased, it couldn't get under the canopy, and she was used to smoke, being the first lady in the land who had ever seen a cloud blown. Well, there couldn't be a more contented or comfortable sight than Sir Launcelot in his noble armor sitting in gracious serenity at the end of a yard of snowy church-warden. He was a beautiful man, a lovely man, and was just intended to make a wife and children happy. But of course, Guenever—however, it's no use to cry over what's done and can't be helped.

Well, he stood watch-and-watch with me, right straight through, for three days and nights, till the child was out of danger; then he took her up in his great arms and kissed her, with his plumes falling about her golden head, then laid her softly in Sandy's lap again and took his stately way down the vast hall, between the ranks of admiring men-at-arms and menials, and so disappeared. And no instinct warned me that I should never look upon him again in this world! Lord, what a world of heart-break it is.

The doctors said we must take the child away, if we would coax her back to health and strength again. And she must have sea air. So we took a man-of-war, and a suite of two hundred and sixty persons, and went cruising about, and after a fortnight of this we stepped ashore on the French coast, and the doctors thought it would be a good idea to make something of a stay there. The little king of that region offered us his hospitalities, and we were glad to accept. If he had had as many conveniences as he lacked, we should have been plenty comfortable enough; even as it was, we made out very well, in his queer old castle, by the help of comforts and luxuries from the ship.

At the end of a month I sent the vessel home for fresh supplies, and for news. We expected her back in three or four days. She would bring me, along with other news, the result of a certain experiment which I

---

7. Those who profit from rising or falling stock markets.    8. Clay tobacco pipes with long stems.

had been starting. It was a project of mine to replace the tournament with something which might furnish an escape for the extra steam of the chivalry, keep those bucks entertained and out of mischief, and at the same time preserve the best thing in them, which was their hardy spirit of emulation. I had had a choice band of them in private training for some time, and the date was now arriving for their first public effort.

This experiment was base-ball. In order to give the thing vogue from the start, and place it out of the reach of criticism, I chose my nines by rank, not capacity. There wasn't a knight in either team who wasn't a sceptred sovereign. As for material of this sort, there was a glut of it, always, around Arthur. You couldn't throw a brick in any direction and not cripple a king. Of course I couldn't get these people to leave off their armor; they wouldn't do that when they bathed. They consented to differentiate the armor so that a body could tell one team from the other, but that was the most they would do. So, one of the teams wore chain-mail ulsters,[9] and the other wore plate-armor made of my new Bessemer steel.[1] Their practice in the field was the most fantastic thing I ever saw. Being ball-proof, they never skipped out of the way, but stood still and took the result; when a Bessemer was at the bat and a ball hit him, it would bound a hundred and fifty yards, sometimes. And when a man was running, and threw himself on his stomach to slide to his base, it was like an iron-clad coming into port. At first I appointed men of no rank to act as umpires, but I had to discontinue that. These people were no easier to please than other nines. The umpire's first decision was usually his last; they broke him in two with a bat, and his friends toted him home on a shutter. When it was noticed that no umpire ever survived a game, umpiring got to be unpopular. So I was obliged to appoint somebody whose rank and lofty position under the government would protect him.

Here are the names of the nines:

| BESSEMERS. | ULSTERS. |
|---|---|
| KING ARTHUR. | EMPEROR LUCIUS. |
| KING LOT OF LOTHIAN. | KING LOGRIS. |
| KING OF NORTHGALIS. | KING MARHALT OF IRELAND. |
| KING MARSIL. | KING MORGANORE. |
| KING OF LITTLE BRITAIN. | KING MARK OF CORNWALL. |
| KING LABOR. | KING NENTRES OF GARLOT. |
| KING PELLAM OF LISTENGESE. | KING MELIODAS OF LIONES. |
| KING BAGDEMAGUS. | KING OF THE LAKE. |
| KING TOLLEME LA FEINTES. | THE SOWDAN OF SYRIA. |

Umpire—CLARENCE.

9. Long, loose, heavy overcoats.
1. Sir Henry Bessemer (1813–98) discovered a process for making steel in which a blast of air is forced through molten iron to remove carbon and impurities.

The first public game would certainly draw fifty thousand people; and for solid fun would be worth going around the world to see. Everything would be favorable; it was balmy and beautiful spring weather, now, and Nature was all tailored out in her new clothes.

## Chapter XLI

### THE INTERDICT

However, my attention was suddenly snatched from such matters; our child began to lose ground again, and we had to go to sitting up with her, her case became so serious. We couldn't bear to allow anybody to help, in this service, so we two stood watch-and-watch, day in and day out. Ah, Sandy, what a right heart she had, how simple, and genuine, and good she was! She was a flawless wife and mother; and yet I had married her for no particular reason, except that by the customs of chivalry she was my property until some knight should win her from me in the field. She had hunted Britain over for me; had found me at the hanging-bout outside of London, and had straightway resumed her old place at my side in the placidest way and as of right. I was a New Englander, and in my opinion this sort of partnership would compromise her, sooner or later. She couldn't see how, but I cut argument short and we had a wedding.

Now I didn't know I was drawing a prize, yet that was what I did draw. Within the twelvemonth I became her worshiper; and ours was the dearest and perfectest comradeship that ever was.[2] People talk about beautiful friendships between two persons of the same sex. What is the best of that sort, as compared with the friendship of man and wife, where the best impulses and highest ideals of both are the same? There is no place for comparison between the two friendships; the one is earthly, the other divine.

In my dreams, along at first, I still wandered thirteen centuries away, and my unsatisfied spirit went calling and harking all up and down the unreplying vacancies of a vanished world. Many a time Sandy heard that imploring cry come from my lips in my sleep. With a grand magnanimity she saddled that cry of mine upon our child, conceiving it to be the name of some lost darling of mine. It touched me to tears, and it also nearly knocked me off my feet, too, when she smiled up in my face for an earned reward, and played her quaint and pretty surprise upon me.

"The name of one who was dear to thee is here preserved, here made holy, and the music of it will abide alway in our ears. Now thou'lt kiss me, as knowing the name I have given the child."

2. The praise of marriage here is probably for Livy, Clemens' wife. Much that is said of sick children, their recovery, and the delights of children may be a reflection of the Clemens family.

But I didn't know it, all the same. I hadn't an idea in the world; but it would have been cruel to confess it and spoil her pretty game; so I never let on, but said:

"Yes, I know, sweetheart—how dear and good it is of you, too! But I want to hear these lips of yours, which are also mine, utter it first—then its music will be perfect."

Pleased to the marrow, she murmured—

"HELLO-CENTRAL!"

I didn't laugh—I am always thankful for that—but the strain ruptured every cartilage in me, and for weeks afterward I could hear my bones clack when I walked. She never found out her mistake. The first time she heard that form of salute used at the telephone she was surprised, and not pleased; but I told her I had given order for it: that henceforth and forever the telephone must always be invoked with that reverent formality, in perpetual honor and remembrance of my lost friend and her small namesake. This was not true. But it answered.

Well, during two weeks and a half we watched by the crib, and in our deep solicitude we were unconscious of any world outside of that sick-room. Then our reward came: the centre of the universe turned the corner and began to mend. Grateful? It isn't the term. There *isn't* any term for it. You know that, yourself, if you've watched your child through the Valley of the Shadow and seen it come back to life and sweep night out of the earth with one all-illuminating smile that you could cover with your hand.

Why, we were back in this world in one instant! Then we looked the same startled thought into each other's eyes at the same moment: more than two weeks gone, and that ship not back yet!

In another minute I appeared in the presence of my train. They had been steeped in troubled bodings all this time—their faces showed it. I called an escort and we galloped five miles to a hill-top overlooking the sea. Where was my great commerce that so lately had made these glistering expanses populous and beautiful with its white-winged flocks? Vanished, every one! Not a sail, from verge to verge, not a smoke-bank—just a dead and empty solitude, in place of all that brisk and breezy life.

I went swiftly back, saying not a word to anybody. I told Sandy this ghastly news. We could imagine no explanation that would begin to explain. Had there been an invasion? an earthquake? a pestilence? Had the nation been swept out of existence? But guessing was profitless. I must go—at once. I borrowed the king's navy—a "ship" no bigger than a steam launch—and was soon ready.

The parting—ah, yes, that was hard. As I was devouring the child with last kisses, it brisked up and jabbered out its vocabulary!—the first time in more than two weeks, and it made fools of us for joy. The darling mispronunciations of childhood!—dear me, there's no music that can touch it; and how one grieves when it wastes away and dissolves into correctness, knowing it will never visit his bereaved ear again. Well, how good it was to be able to carry that gracious memory away with me!

I approached England the next morning, with the wide highway of salt water all to myself. There were ships in the harbor, at Dover, but they were naked as to sails, and there was no sign of life about them. It was Sunday; yet at Canterbury the streets were empty; strangest of all, there was not even a priest in sight, and no stroke of a bell fell upon my ear. The mournfulness of death was everywhere. I couldn't understand it. At last, in the further edge of that town I saw a small funeral procession—just a family and a few friends following a coffin—no priest; a funeral without bell, book or candle; there was a church there, close at hand, but they passed it by, weeping, and did not enter it; I glanced up at the belfry, and there hung the bell, shrouded in black, and its tongue tied back. Now I knew! Now I understood the stupendous calamity that had overtaken England. Invasion? Invasion is a triviality to it. It was the INTERDICT![3]

I asked no questions; I didn't need to ask any. The Church had struck; the thing for me to do was to get into a disguise, and go warily. One of my servants gave me a suit of his clothes, and when we were safe beyond the town I put them on, and from that time I traveled alone; I could not risk the embarrassment of company.

A miserable journey. A desolate silence everywhere. Even in London itself. Traffic had ceased; men did not talk or laugh, or go in groups, or even in couples; they moved aimlessly about, each man by himself, with his head down, and woe and terror at his heart. The Tower[4] showed recent war-scars. Verily, much had been happening.

Of course I meant to take the train for Camelot. Train! Why, the station was as vacant as a cavern. I moved on. The journey to Camelot was a repetition of what I had already seen. The Monday and the Tuesday differed in no way from the Sunday. I arrived, far in the night. From being the best electric-lighted town in the kingdom and the most like a recumbent sun of anything you ever saw, it had become simply a blot—a blot upon darkness—that is to say, it was darker and solider than the rest of the darkness, and so you could see it a little better; it made me feel as if maybe it was symbolical—a sort of sign that the Church was going to *keep* the upper hand, now, and snuff out all my beautiful civilization just like that. I found no life stirring in the sombre streets. I groped my way with a heavy heart. The vast castle loomed black upon the hill-top, not a spark visible about it. The

---

3. Exclusion from certain church offices, sacraments, or privileges; here applied to an entire country.

4. An anachronism, as the Tower of London was not begun until the eleventh century.

Beard depicts a church figure about to snuff out the candle of nineteenth-century enlightenment; a similar eclipse motif appears in several of his drawings. In a drawing a few pages after this one, a bat representing the Church appears to be attempting to blow out the torch of the Statue of Liberty (which was dedicated three years before the publication of the novel).

drawbridge was down, the great gate stood wide, I entered without challenge, my own heels making the only sound I heard—and it was sepulchral enough, in those huge vacant courts.

## Chapter XLII

### WAR!

I found Clarence, alone in his quarters, drowned in melancholy; and in place of the electric light, he had re-instituted the ancient rag-lamp, and sat there in a grisly twilight with all curtains drawn tight. He sprang up and rushed for me eagerly, saying:

"Oh, it's worth a billion milrays to look upon a live person again!"

He knew me as easily as if I hadn't been disguised at all. Which frightened me; one may easily believe that.

"Quick, now, tell me the meaning of this fearful disaster," I said. "How did it come about?"

"Well, if there hadn't been any queen Guenever, it wouldn't have come so early; but it would have come, anyway. It would have come on your own account, by and by; by luck, it happened to come on the queen's."

"*And* Sir Launcelot's?"

"Just so."

"Give me the details."

"I reckon you will grant that during some years there has been only one pair of eyes in these kingdoms that has not been looking steadily askance at the queen and Sir Launcelot—"

"Yes, King Arthur's."

—"and only one heart that was without suspicion—"

"Yes—the king's; a heart that isn't capable of thinking evil of a friend."

"Well, the king might have gone on, still happy and unsuspecting, to the end of his days, but for one of your modern improvements—the stock-board. When you left, three miles of the London, Canterbury and Dover were ready for the rails, and also ready and ripe for manipulation in the stock market. It was wildcat,[5] and everybody knew it. The stock was for sale at a give-away. What does Sir Launcelot do, but—"

"Yes, I know; he quietly picked up nearly all of it, for a song; then he bought about twice as much more, deliverable upon call; and he was about to call when I left."

"Very well, he did call. The boys couldn't deliver. Oh, he had them—and he just settled his grip and squeezed them. They were

---

5. Financially irresponsible; produced outside the bounds of standard or legitimate business practices.

laughing in their sleeves over their smartness in selling stock to him at 15 and 16 and along there, that wasn't worth 10. Well, when they had laughed long enough on that side of their mouths, they rested-up that side by shifting the laugh to the other side. That was when they compromised with the Invincible at 283!"

"Good land!"

"He skinned them alive, and they deserved it—anyway, the whole kingdom rejoiced. Well, among the flayed were Sir Agravaine and Sir Mordred, nephews to the king. End of the first act. Act second, scene first, an apartment in Carlisle castle,[6] where the court had gone for a few days' hunting. Persons present, the whole tribe of the king's nephews. Mordred and Agravaine propose to call the guileless Arthur's attention to Guenever and Sir Launcelot. Sir Gawaine, Sir Gareth, and Sir Gaheris will have nothing to do with it. A dispute ensues, with loud talk; in the midst of it, enter the king. Mordred and Agravaine spring their devastating tale upon him. *Tableau*.[7] A trap is laid for Launcelot, by the king's command, and Sir Launcelot walks into it. He made it sufficiently uncomfortable for the ambushed witnesses—to-wit, Mordred, Agravaine, and twelve knights of lesser rank, for he killed every one of them but Mordred; but of course that couldn't straighten matters between Launcelot and the king, and didn't."

"Oh, dear, only one thing could result—I see that. War, and the knights of the realm divided into a king's party and a Sir Launcelot's party."

"Yes—that was the way of it. The king sent the queen to the stake, proposing to purify her with fire. Launcelot and his knights rescued her, and in doing it slew certain good old friends of yours and mine—in fact, some of the best we ever had; to-wit, Sir Belias le Orgulous, Sir Segwarides, Sir Griflet le Fils de Dieu, Sir Brandiles, Sir Aglovale—"[8]

"Oh, you tear out my heartstrings."

"—wait I'm not done yet—Sir Tor, Sir Gauter, Sir Gillimer—"

"The very best man in my subordinate nine. What a handy right-fielder he was!"

—"Sir Reynold's three brothers, Sir Damus, Sir Priamus, Sir Kay the Stranger—"

"My peerless short-stop! I've seen him catch a daisy-cutter in his teeth. Come, I can't stand this!"

---

6. The town is located in the extreme north-west of England, not far south of the Scottish border; the castle was built on a bluff north of the city in 1092 and enlarged later.

7. A stationary, silent grouping of actors in a theatrical production when the action is suddenly arrested. Clarence is describing recent events as if he were summarizing a play.

8. The list is from Malory, XX.viii, except that the epithet for Sir Griflet, "le Fils de Dieu" (the Son of God) does not appear. Elsewhere in Malory, however, he is called "le Fise de Dieu."

—"Sir Driant, Sir Lambegus, Sir Herminde, Sir Pertilope, Sir Perimones, and—whom do you think?"

"Rush! Go on."

"Sir Gaheris, and Sir Gareth—both!"

"Oh, incredible! Their love for Launcelot was indestructible."

"Well, it was an accident. They were simply on-lookers; they were unarmed, and were merely there to witness the queen's punishment. Sir Launcelot smote down whoever came in the way of his blind fury, and he killed these without noticing who they were. Here is an instantaneous photograph one of our boys got of the battle; it's for sale on every news stand. There—the figures nearest the queen are Sir Launcelot with his sword up, and Sir Gareth gasping his latest breath. You can catch the agony in the queen's face through the curling smoke. It's a rattling battle-picture."

"Indeed it is. We must take good care of it; its historical value is incalculable. Go on."

"Well, the rest of the tale is just war, pure and simple. Launcelot retreated to his town and castle of Joyous Gard, and gathered there a great following of knights. The king, with a great host, went there, and there was desperate fighting during several days, and as a result, all the plain around was paved with corpses and cast iron. Then the Church patched up a peace between Arthur and Launcelot and the queen and everybody—everybody but Sir Gawaine. He was bitter about the slaying of his brothers, Gareth and Gaheris, and would not be appeased. He notified Launcelot to get him thence, and make swift preparation, and look to be soon attacked. So Launcelot sailed to his Duchy of Guienne, with his following, and Gawaine soon followed, with an army, and he beguiled Arthur to go with him. Arthur left the kingdom in Sir Mordred's hands until you should return—"

"Ah—a king's customary wisdom!"

"Yes. Sir Mordred set himself at once to work to make his kingship permanent. He was going to marry Guenever, as a first move; but she fled and shut herself up in the Tower of London. Mordred attacked; the Bishop of Canterbury dropped down on him with the Interdict. The king returned; Mordred fought him at Dover, at Canterbury, and again at Barham Down. Then there was talk of peace and a composition. Terms, Mordred to have Cornwall and Kent during Arthur's life, and the whole kingdom afterward."

"Well, upon my word! My dream of a republic to *be* a dream, and so remain."

"Yes. The two armies lay near Salisbury.[9] Gawaine—Gawaine's head is at Dover Castle, he fell in the fight there—Gawaine appeared to Arthur in a dream, at least his ghost did, and warned him to refrain

9. Southwest of London, near Stonehenge.

from conflict for a month, let the delay cost what it might. But battle was precipitated by an accident. Arthur had given order that if a sword was raised during the consultation over the proposed treaty with Mordred, sound the trumpet and fall on! for he had no confidence in Mordred. Mordred had given a similar order to *his* people. Well, by and by an adder bit a knight's heel; the knight forgot all about the order, and made a slash at the adder with his sword. Inside of half a minute those two prodigious hosts came together with a crash![1] They butchered away all day. Then the king—however, we have started something fresh since you left—our paper has."

"No? What is that?"

"War correspondence!"

"Why, that's good."

"Yes, the paper was booming right along, for the Interdict made no impression, got no grip, while the war lasted. I had war correspondents with both armies. I will finish that battle by reading you what one of the boys says:

Then the king looked about him, and then was he ware of all his host and of all his good knights were left no more on live but two knights, that was Sir Lucan de Butlere, and his brother Sir Bedivere: and they were full sore wounded. Jesu mercy, said the king, where are all my noble knights becomen? Alas that ever I should see this doleful day. For now, said Arthur, I am come to mine end. But would to God that I wist where were that traitor Sir Mordred, that hath caused all this mischief. Then was King Arthur ware where Sir Mordred leaned upon his sword among a great heap of dead men. Now give me my spear, said Arthur unto Sir Lucan, for yonder I have espied the traitor that all this woe hath wrought. Sir, let him be, said Sir Lucan, for he is unhappy; and if ye pass this unhappy day, ye shall be right well revenged upon him. Good lord, remember ye of your night's dream, and what the spirit of Sir Gawaine told you this night, yet God of his great goodness hath preserved you hitherto. Therefore, for God's sake, my lord, leave off by this. For blessed be God ye have won the field: for here we be three on live, and with Sir Mordred is none on live. And if ye leave off now, this wicked day of destiny is past. Tide me death, betide me life, saith the king, now I see him yonder alone, he shall never escape mine hands, for at a better avail shall I never have him. God speed you well, said Sir Bedivere. Then the king gat his spear in both his hands, and ran toward Sir Mordred, crying, Traitor, now is thy death day come. And when Sir Mordred heard Sir Arthur, he ran until him with his sword drawn in his hand. And then King Arthur smote Sir Mordred under the shield, with a foin of his spear throughout the body more than a fathom. And when Sir Mordred felt that he had his death's wound, he thrust himself, with the might

1. Details of how the battle began are from Malory, XXI.iv, as is the pretended war correspondent's report.

that he had, up to the but of King Arthur's spear. And right so he smote his father Arthur with his sword holden in both his hands, on the side of the head, that the sword pierced the helmet and the brain-pan, and therewithal Sir Mordred fell stark dead to the earth. And the noble Arthur fell in a swoon to the earth, and there he swooned oft-times."

"That is a good piece of war correspondence, Clarence; you are a first-rate newspaper man. Well—is the king all right? Did he get well?"

"Poor soul, no. He is dead."

I was utterly stunned; it had not seemed to me that any wound could be mortal to him.

"And the queen, Clarence?"

"She is a nun, in Almesbury."[2]

"What changes! and in such a short while. It is inconceivable. What next, I wonder?"

"I can tell you what next."

"Well?"

"Stake our lives and stand by them!"

"What do you mean by that?"

"The Church is master, now. The Interdict included you with Mordred; it is not to be removed while you remain alive. The clans are gathering. The Church has gathered all the knights that are left alive, and as soon as you are discovered we shall have business on our hands."

"Stuff! With our deadly scientific war-material; with our hosts of trained—"

"Save your breath—we haven't sixty faithful left!"

"What are you saying? Our schools, our colleges, our vast workshops, our—"

"When those knights come, those establishments will empty themselves and go over to the enemy. Did you think you had educated the superstition out of those people?"

"I certainly did think it."

"Well, then, you may unthink it. They stood every strain easily—until the Interdict. Since then, they merely put on a bold outside—at heart they are quaking. Make up your mind to it—when the armies come, the mask will fall."

"It's hard news. We are lost. They will turn our own science against us."

"No they won't."

"Why?"

"Because I and a handful of the faithful have blocked that game. I'll

2. Now Amesbury, about seven miles from Salisbury.

tell you what I've done, and what moved me to it. Smart as you are, the Church was smarter. It was the Church that sent you cruising— through her servants the doctors."

"Clarence!"

"It is the truth. I know it. Every officer of your ship was the Church's picked servant, and so was every man of the crew."

"Oh, come!"

"It is just as I tell you. I did not find out these things at once, but I found them out finally. Did you send me verbal information, by the commander of the ship, to the effect that upon his return to you, with supplies, you were going to leave Cadiz—"

"Cadiz! I haven't been at Cadiz at all!"

—"going to leave Cadiz and cruise in distant seas indefinitely, for the health of your family? Did you send me that word?"

"Of course not. I would have written, wouldn't I?"

"Naturally. I was troubled and suspicious. When the commander sailed again I managed to ship a spy with him. I have never heard of vessel or spy since. I gave myself two weeks to hear from you in. Then I resolved to send a ship to Cadiz. There was a reason why I didn't."

"What was that?"

"Our navy had suddenly and mysteriously disappeared! Also as suddenly and as mysteriously, the railway and telegraph and telephone service ceased, the men all deserted, poles were cut down, the Church laid a ban upon the electric light! I had to be up and doing—and straight off. Your life was safe—nobody in these kingdoms but Merlin would venture to touch such a magician as you without ten thousand men at his back—I had nothing to think of but how to put preparations in the best trim against your coming. I felt safe myself—nobody would be anxious to touch a pet of yours. So this is what I did. From our various works I selected all the men—boys I mean—whose faithfulness under whatsoever pressure I could swear to, and I called them together secretly and gave them their instructions. There are fifty-two of them; none younger than fourteen, and none above seventeen years old."

"Why did you select boys?"

"Because all the others were born in an atmosphere of superstition and reared in it. It is in their blood and bones. We imagined we had educated it out of them; they thought so, too; the Interdict woke them up like a thunderclap! It revealed them to themselves, and it revealed them to me, too. With boys it was different. Such as have been under our training from seven to ten years have had no acquaintance with the Church's terrors, and it was among these that I found my fifty-two. As a next move, I paid a private visit to that old cave of Merlin's—not the small one—the big one—"

"Yes, the one where we secretly established our first great electric plant when I was projecting a miracle."

"Just so. And as that miracle hadn't become necessary then, I thought it might be a good idea to utilize the plant now. I've provisioned the cave for a siege—"

"A good idea, a first rate idea."

"I think so. I placed four of my boys there, as a guard—inside, and out of sight. Nobody was to be hurt—while outside; but any attempt to enter—well, we said just let anybody try it! Then I went out into the hills and uncovered and cut the secret wires which connected your bedroom with the wires that go to the dynamite deposits under all our vast factories, mills, workshops, magazines, etc., and about midnight I and my boys turned out and connected that wire with the cave, and nobody but you and I suspects where the other end of it goes to. We laid it under ground, of course, and it was all finished in a couple of hours or so. We shan't have to leave our fortress, now, when we want to blow up our civilization."

"It was the right move—and the natural one; a military necessity, in the changed condition of things. Well, what changes *have* come! We expected to be besieged in the palace some time or other, but—however, go on."

"Next, we built a wire fence."

"Wire fence?"

"Yes. You dropped the hint of it yourself, two or three years ago."

"Oh, I remember—the time the Church tried her strength against us the first time, and presently thought it wise to wait for a hopefuler season. Well, how have you arranged the fence?"

"I start twelve immensely strong wires—naked, not insulated— from a big dynamo in the cave—dynamo with no brushes except a positive and a negative one—"

"Yes, that's right."

"The wires go out from the cave and fence-in a circle of level ground a hundred yards in diameter; they make twelve independent fences, ten feet apart—that is to say, twelve circles within circles—and their ends come into the cave again."

"Right; go on."

"The fences are fastened to heavy oaken posts only three feet apart, and these posts are sunk five feet in the ground."

"That is good and strong."

"Yes. The wires have no ground-connection outside of the cave. They go out from the positive brush of the dynamo; there is a ground-connection through the negative brush; the other ends of the wire return to the cave, and each is grounded independently."

"No-no, that won't do!"

"Why?"

"It's too expensive—uses up force for nothing. You don't want any ground-connection except the one through the negative brush. The other end of every wire must be brought back into the cave and fastened independently, and *without* any ground-connection. Now, then, observe the economy of it. A cavalry charge hurls itself against the fence; you are using no power, you are spending no money, for there is only one ground-connection till those horses come against the wire; the moment they touch it they form a connection with the negative brush *through the ground*, and drop dead. Don't you see?— you are using no energy until it is needed; your lightning is there, and ready, like the load in a gun; but it isn't costing you a cent till you touch it off. Oh, yes, the single ground-connection—"

"Of course! I don't know how I overlooked that. It's not only cheaper, but it's more effectual than the other way, for if wires break or get tangled, no harm is done."

"No, especially if we have a tell-tale in the cave and disconnect the broken wire. Well, go on. The gatlings?"[3]

"Yes—that's arranged. In the centre of the inner circle, on a spacious platform six feet high, I've grouped a battery of thirteen gatling guns, and provided plenty of ammunition."

"That's it. They command every approach, and when the Church's knights arrive, there's going to be music. The brow of the precipice over the cave—"

"I've got a wire fence there, and a gatling. They won't drop any rocks down on us."

"Well, and the glass-cylinder dynamite torpedoes?"

"That's attended to. It's the prettiest garden that was ever planted. It's a belt forty feet wide, and goes around the outer fence—distance between it and the fence one hundred yards—kind of neutral ground, that space is. There isn't a single square yard of that whole belt but is equipped with a torpedo. We laid them on the surface of the ground, and sprinkled a layer of sand over them. It's an innocent looking garden, but you let a man start in to hoe it once, and you'll see."

"You tested the torpedoes?"

"Well, I was going to, but—"

"But what? Why, it's an immense oversight not to apply a—"

"Test? Yes, I know; but they're all right; I laid a few in the public road beyond our lines and they've been tested."

"Oh, that alters the case. Who did it?"

"A Church committee."

"How kind!"

"Yes. They came to command us to make submission. You see they didn't really come to test the torpedoes; that was merely an incident."

"Did the committee make a report?"

3. Rapid-firing, multi-barrel gun invented by Richard Jordan Gatling (1818–1903). Clemens fired a Gatling gun in the Colt Arms Factory at Hartford during his visit there in 1868.

"Yes, they made one. You could have heard it a mile."

"Unanimous?"

"That was the nature of it. After that I put up some signs, for the protection of future committees, and we have had no intruders since."

"Clarence, you've done a world of work, and done it perfectly."

"We had plenty of time for it; there wasn't any occasion for hurry."

We sat silent awhile, thinking. Then my mind was made up, and I said:

"Yes, everything is ready; everything is shipshape, no detail is wanting. I know what to do, now."

"So do I: sit down and wait."

"No, *sir!* rise up and *strike!*"

"Do you mean it?"

"Yes, indeed! The *de*fensive isn't in my line, and the *of*fensive is. That is, when I hold a fair hand—two-thirds as good a hand as the enemy. Oh, yes, we'll rise up and strike; that's our game."

"A hundred to one, you are right. When does the performance begin?"

"*Now!* We'll proclaim the Republic."

"Well, that *will* precipitate things, sure enough!"

"It will make them buzz, I tell you! England will be a hornet's nest before noon to-morrow, if the Church's hand hasn't lost its cunning—and we know it hasn't. Now you write and I'll dictate—thus:

## PROCLAMATION[4]

BE IT KNOWN UNTO ALL. Whereas the king having died and left no heir, it becomes my duty to continue the executive authority vested in me, until a government shall have been created and set in motion. The monarchy has lapsed, it no longer exists. By consequence, all political power has reverted to its original source, the people of the nation. With the monarchy, its several adjuncts died also; wherefore there is no longer a nobility, no longer a privileged class, no longer an Established Church: all men are become exactly equal, they are upon one common level, and religion is free. A *Republic is hereby proclaimed*, as being the natural estate of a nation when other authority has ceased. It is the duty of the British people to meet together immediately, and by their votes elect representatives and deliver into their hands the government.

I signed it "The Boss," and dated it from Merlin's Cave. Clarence said:

"Why, that tells where we are, and invites them to call right away."

---

4. Clemens was particularly pleased with what he saw as the similarity between Morgan's proclamation and that issued in Brazil when its emperor was overthrown at about the time the novel was published. A copy of the novel marked by Clemens, now in the Mark Twain Papers, indicates that in his readings he omitted the clause "when other authority has ceased."

"That is the idea. We *strike*—by the Proclamation—then it's their innings. Now have the thing set up and printed and posted, right off; that is, give the order; then, if you've got a couple of bicycles handy at the foot of the hill, ho for Merlin's Cave!"

"I shall be ready in ten minutes. What a cyclone there is going to be to-morrow when this piece of paper gets to work! . . . . . It's a pleasant old palace, this is; I wonder if we shall ever again—but never mind about that."

## Chapter XLIII

### THE BATTLE OF THE SAND-BELT

In Merlin's Cave—Clarence and I and fifty-two fresh, bright, well educated, clean-minded young British boys. At dawn I sent an order to the factories and to all our great works to stop operations and remove all life to a safe distance, as everything was going to be blown up by secret mines, *"and no telling at what moment—therefore, vacate at once."* These people knew me, and had confidence in my word. They would clear out without waiting to part their hair, and I could take my own time about dating the explosion. You couldn't hire one of them to go back during the century, if the explosion was still impending.

We had a week of waiting. It was not dull for me, because I was writing all the time. During the first three days, I finished turning my old diary into this narrative form; it only required a chapter or so to bring it down to date. The rest of the week I took up in writing letters to my wife. It was always my habit to write to Sandy every day, whenever we were separate, and now I kept up the habit for love of it, and of her, though I couldn't do anything with the letters, of course, after I had written them. But it put in the time, you see, and was almost like talking; it was almost as if I was saying, "Sandy, if you and Hello-Central were here in the cave, instead of only your photographs, what good times we could have!" And then, you know, I could imagine the baby goo-gooing something out in reply, with its fists in its mouth and itself stretched across its mother's lap on its back, and she a-laughing and admiring and worshiping, and now and then tickling under the baby's chin to set it cackling, and then maybe throwing in a word of answer to me herself—and so on and so on—well, don't you know, I could sit there in the cave with my pen, and keep it up, that way, by the hour with them. Why, it was almost like having us all together again.

I had spies out, every night, of course, to get news. Every report made things look more and more impressive. The hosts were gathering, gathering; down all the roads and paths of England the knights were riding, and priests rode with them, to hearten these original Crusaders, this being the Church's war. All the nobilities, big and little, were on their way, and all the gentry. This was all as was expected. We should thin out this sort of folk to such a degree that the people would have nothing to do but just step to the front with their republic and——

Ah, what a donkey I was! Toward the end of the week I began to get this large and disenchanting fact through my head: that the mass of the nation had swung their caps and shouted for the republic for about one day, and there an end! The Church, the nobles, and the gentry then turned one grand, all-disapproving frown upon them and shriveled them into sheep! From that moment the sheep had begun to gather to the fold—that is to say, the camps—and offer their valueless lives and their valuable wool to the "righteous cause." Why, even the very men who had lately been slaves were in the "righteous cause," and glorifying it, praying for it, sentimentally slabbering over it, just like all the other commoners. Imagine such human muck as this; conceive of this folly!

Yes, it was now "Death to the Republic!" everywhere—not a dissenting voice. All England was marching against us! Truly this was more than I had bargained for.

I watched my fifty-two boys narrowly; watched their faces, their walk, their unconscious attitudes: for all these are a language—a language given us purposely that it may betray us in times of emergency, when we have secrets which we want to keep. I knew that that thought would keep saying itself over and over again in their minds and hearts, *All England is marching against us!* and evermore strenuously imploring attention with each repetition, ever more sharply realizing itself to their imaginations, until even in their sleep they would find no rest from it, but hear the vague and flitting creatures of their dreams say, *All England*—ALL ENGLAND!—*is marching against you!* I knew all this would happen; I knew that ultimately the pressure would become so great that it would compel utterance; therefore, I must be ready with an answer at that time—an answer well chosen and tranquilizing.

I was right. The time came. They *had* to speak. Poor lads, it was pitiful to see, they were so pale, so worn, so troubled. At first their spokesman could hardly find voice or words; but he presently got both. This is what he said—and he put it in the neat modern English taught him in my schools:

"We have tried to forget what we are—English boys! We have tried to put reason before sentiment, duty before love; our minds approve, but our hearts reproach us. While apparently it was only the nobility, only the gentry, only the twenty-five or thirty thousand knights left alive out of the late wars, we were of one mind, and undisturbed by any troubling doubt; each and every one of these fifty-two lads who stand here before you, said, 'They have chosen—it is their affair.' But think!—the matter is altered—*all England is marching against us!*

Oh, sir, consider!—reflect!—these people are our people, they are bone of our bone, flesh of our flesh,[5] we love them—do not ask us to destroy our nation!"

Well, it shows the value of looking ahead, and being ready for a thing when it happens. If I hadn't foreseen this thing and been fixed, that boy would have had me!—I couldn't have said a word. But I *was* fixed. I said:

"My boys, your hearts are in the right place, you have thought the worthy thought, you have done the worthy thing. You are English boys, you will remain English boys, and you will keep that name unsmirched. Give yourselves no further concern, let your minds be at peace. Consider this: while all England *is* marching against us, who is in the van? Who, by the commonest rules of war, will march in the front? Answer me."

"The mounted host of mailed knights."

"True. They are 30,000 strong. Acres deep, they will march. Now, observe: none but *they* will ever strike the sand-belt! Then there will be an episode! Immediately after, the civilian multitude in the rear will retire, to meet business engagements elsewhere. None but nobles and gentry are knights, and *none but these* will remain to dance to our music after that episode. It is absolutely true that we shall have to fight nobody but these thirty thousand knights. Now speak, and it shall be as you decide. Shall we avoid the battle, retire from the field."

"NO ! ! !"

The shout was unanimous and hearty.

"Are you—are you—well, afraid of these thirty thousand knights?"

That joke brought out a good laugh, the boys' troubles vanished away, and they went gaily to their posts. Ah, they were a darling fifty-two! As pretty as girls, too.

I was ready for the enemy, now. Let the approaching big day come along—it would find us on deck.

The big day arrived on time. At dawn the sentry on watch in the corral came into the cave and reported a moving black mass under the horizon, and a faint sound which he thought to be military music. Breakfast was just ready; we sat down and ate it.

This over, I made the boys a little speech, and then sent out a detail to man the battery, with Clarence in command of it.

The sun rose presently and sent its unobstructed splendors over the land, and we saw a prodigious host moving slowly toward us, with the steady drift and aligned front of a wave of the sea. Nearer and nearer it came, and more and more sublimely imposing became its aspect; yes, all England was there, apparently. Soon we could see the innumerable banners fluttering, and then the sun struck the sea of armor and set it all aflash. Yes, it was a fine sight; I hadn't ever seen anything to beat it.

5. Variation of Adam's statement about Eve, Genesis 2:23.

At last we could make out details. All the front ranks, no telling how many acres deep, were horsemen—plumed knights in armor. Suddenly we heard the blare of trumpets; the slow walk burst into a gallop, and then—well, it was wonderful to see! Down swept that vast horseshoe wave—it approached the sand-belt—my breath stood still; nearer, nearer—the strip of green turf beyond the yellow belt grew narrow—narrower still—became a mere ribbon in front of the horses—then disappeared under their hoofs. Great Scott! Why, the whole front of that host shot into the sky with a thunder-crash, and became a whirling tempest of rags and fragments;[6] and along the ground lay a thick wall of smoke that hid what was left of the multitude from our sight.

Time for the second step in the plan of campaign! I touched a button, and shook the bones of England loose from her spine!

In that explosion all our noble civilization-factories went up in the air and disappeared from the earth. It was a pity, but it was necessary. We could not afford to let the enemy turn our own weapons against us.

Now ensued one of the dullest quarter-hours I had ever endured. We waited in a silent solitude enclosed by our circles of wire, and by a circle of heavy smoke outside of these. We couldn't see over the wall of smoke, and we couldn't see through it. But at last it began to shred away lazily, and by the end of another quarter-hour the land was clear and our curiosity was enabled to satisfy itself. No living creature was in sight! We now perceived that additions had been made to our defences. The dynamite had dug a ditch more than a hundred feet wide, all around us, and cast up an embankment some twenty-five feet high on both borders of it. As to destruction of life, it was amazing. Moreover, it was beyond estimate. Of course we could not *count* the dead, because they did not exist as individuals, but merely as homogeneous protoplasm, with alloys of iron and buttons.

No life was in sight, but necessarily there must have been some wounded in the rear ranks, who were carried off the field under cover of the wall of smoke; there would be sickness among the others—there always is, after an episode like that. But there would be no reinforcements; this was the last stand of the chivalry of England; it was all that was left of the order, after the recent annihilating wars. So I felt quite safe in believing that the utmost force that could for the future be brought against us would be but small; that is, of knights. I therefore issued a congratulatory proclamation to my army in these words:

SOLDIERS, CHAMPIONS OF HUMAN LIBERTY AND EQUALITY: Your General congratulates you! In the pride of his strength and the vanity of his renown, an arrogant enemy came against you. You were ready. The conflict was brief; on your side, glorious. This

---

6. In a copy of the novel which he marked for reading, Clemens added "that blotted out the sun," thus invoking the eclipse image once again.

mighty victory having been achieved utterly without loss, stands without example in history. So long as the planets shall continue to move in their orbits, the BATTLE OF THE SAND-BELT will not perish out of the memories of men.

THE BOSS

I read it well, and the applause I got was very gratifying to me. I then wound up with these remarks:

"The war with the English nation, as a nation, is at an end. The nation has retired from the field and the war. Before it can be persuaded to return, war will have ceased. This campaign is the only one that is going to be fought. It will be brief—the briefest in history. Also the most destructive to life, considered from the standpoint of proportion of casualties to numbers engaged. We are done with the nation; henceforth we deal only with the knights. English knights can be killed, but they cannot be conquered. We know what is before us. While one of these men remains alive, our task is not finished, the war is not ended. We will kill them all." [Loud and long continued applause.]

I picketed the great embankments thrown up around our lines by the dynamite explosion—merely a lookout of a couple of boys to announce the enemy when he should appear again.

Next, I sent an engineer and forty men to a point just beyond our lines on the south, to turn a mountain brook that was there, and bring it within our lines and under our command, arranging it in such a way that I could make instant use of it in an emergency. The forty men were divided into two shifts of twenty each, and were to relieve each other every two hours. In ten hours the work was accomplished.

It was nightfall, now, and I withdrew my pickets. The one who had had the northern outlook reported a camp in sight, but visible with the glass only. He also reported that a few knights had been feeling their way toward us, and had driven some cattle across our lines, but that the knights themselves had not come very near. That was what I had been expecting. They were feeling us, you see; they wanted to know if we were going to play that red terror on them again. They would grow bolder in the night, perhaps. I belived I knew what project they would attempt, because it was plainly the thing I would attempt myself if I were in their places and as ignorant as they were. I mentioned it to Clarence.

"I think you are right," said he; "it is the obvious thing for them to try."

"Well, then," I said, "if they do it they are doomed."

"Certainly."

"They won't have the slightest show in the world."

"Of course they won't."

"It's dreadful, Clarence. It seems an awful pity."

The thing disturbed me so, that I couldn't get any peace of mind for thinking of it and worrying over it. So, at last, to quiet my conscience, I framed this message to the knights:

> TO THE HONORABLE THE COMMANDER OF THE INSURGENT CHIVALRY OF ENGLAND: You fight in vain. We know your strength—if one may call it by that name. We know that at the utmost you cannot bring against us above five and twenty thousand knights. Therefore, you have no chance—none whatever. Reflect: we are well equipped, well fortified, we number 54. Fifty-four what? Men? No, *minds*—the capablest in the world; a force against which mere animal might may no more hope to prevail than may the idle waves of the sea hope to prevail against the granite barriers of England. Be advised. We offer you your lives; for the sake of your families, do not reject the gift. We offer you this chance, and it is the last: throw down your arms; surrender unconditionally to the Republic, and all will be forgiven.
>
> (Signed).    THE BOSS

I read it to Clarence, and said I proposed to send it by a flag of truce. He laughed the sarcastic laugh he was born with, and said:

"Somehow it seems impossible for you to ever fully realize what these nobilities are. Now let us save a little time and trouble. Consider me the commander of the knights yonder. Now then, you are the flag of truce; approach and deliver me your message, and I will give you your answer."

I humored the idea. I came forward under an imaginary guard of the enemy's soldiers, produced my paper, and read it through. For answer, Clarence struck the paper out of my hand, pursed up a scornful lip and said with lofty disdain—

"Dismember me this animal, and return him in a basket to the base-born knave who sent him; other answer have I none!"[7]

How empty is theory in presence of fact! And this was just fact, and nothing else. It was the thing that would have happened, there was no getting around that. I tore up the paper and granted my mistimed sentimentalities a permanent rest.

Then, to business. I tested the electric signals from the gatling platform to the cave, and made sure that they were all right; I tested and re-tested those which commanded the fences—these were signals whereby I could break and renew the electric current in each fence independently of the others, at will. I placed the brook-connection under the guard and authority of three of my best boys, who would alternate in two-hour watches all night and promptly obey my signal, if I should have occasion to give it—three revolver-shots in quick

---

7. Here the English edition reads: "Disembowel me this animal, and convey his kidneys to the base-born knave, his master; other answer have I none!" Clemens reluctantly changed the wording on the proof sheets for the American edition, but the English remained unaltered.

succession. Sentry-duty was discarded for the night, and the corral left empty of life; I ordered that quiet be maintained in the cave, and the electric lights turned down to a glimmer.

As soon as it was good and dark, I shut off the current from all of the fences, and then groped my way out to the embankment bordering our side of the great dynamite ditch. I crept to the top of it and lay there on the slant of the muck to watch. But it was too dark to see anything. As for sounds, there were none. The stillness was death-like. True, there were the usual night-sounds of the country—the whir of night-birds, the buzzing of insects, the barking of distant dogs, the mellow lowing of far-off kine—but these didn't seem to break the stillness, they only intensified it, and added a grewsome melancholy to it into the bargain.

I presently gave up looking, the night shut down so black, but I kept my ears strained to catch the least suspicious sound, for I judged I had only to wait and I shouldn't be disappointed. However, I had to wait a long time. At last I caught what you may call indistinct glimpses of sound—dulled metallic sound. I pricked up my ears, then, and held my breath, for this was the sort of thing I had been waiting for. This sound thickened, and approached—from toward the north. Presently I heard it at my own level—the ridge-top of the opposite embankment, a hundred feet or more away. Then I seemed to see a row of black dots appear along that ridge—human heads? I couldn't tell; it mightn't be anything at all; you can't depend on your eyes when your imagination is out of focus. However, the question was soon settled. I heard that metallic noise descending into the great ditch. It augmented fast, it spread all along, and it unmistakably furnished me this fact: an armed host was taking up its quarters in the ditch. Yes, these people were arranging a little surprise party for us. We could expect entertainment about dawn, possibly earlier.

I groped my way back to the corral, now; I had seen enough. I went to the platform and signalled to turn the current onto the two inner fences. Then I went into the cave, and found everything satisfactory there—nobody awake but the working-watch. I woke Clarence and told him the great ditch was filling up with men, and that I believed all the knights were coming for us in a body. It was my notion that as soon as dawn approached we could expect the ditch's ambuscaded thousands to swarm up over the embankment and make an assault, and be followed immediately by the rest of their army.

Clarence said:

"They will be wanting to send a scout or two in the dark to make preliminary observations. Why not take the lightning off the outer fences, and give them a chance?"

"I've already done it, Clarence. Did you ever know me to be inhospitable?"

"No, you are a good heart. I want to go and—"

"Be a reception committee? I will go, too."

We crossed the corral and lay down together between the two inside fences. Even the dim light of the cave had disordered our eyesight somewhat, but the focus straightway began to regulate itself and soon it was adjusted for present circumstances. We had had to feel our way before, but we could make out to see the fence posts now. We started a whispered conversation, but suddenly Clarence broke off and said:

"What is that?"

"What is what?"

"That thing yonder?"

"What thing—where?"

"There beyond you a little piece—a dark something—a dull shape of some kind—against the second fence."

I gazed and he gazed. I said:

"Could it be a man, Clarence?"

"No, I think not. If you notice, it looks a lit—why it *is* a man!—leaning on the fence."

"I certainly believe it is; let's us go and see."

We crept along on our hands and knees until we were pretty close, and then looked up. Yes, it was a man—a dim great figure in armor, standing erect, with both hands on the upper wire—and of course there was a smell of burning flesh. Poor fellow, dead as a door-nail, and never knew what hurt him. He stood there like a statue—no motion about him, except that his plumes swished about a little in the night wind. We rose up and looked in through the bars of his visor, but couldn't make out whether we knew him or not—features too dim and shadowed.

We heard muffled sounds approaching, and we sank down to the ground where we were. We made out another knight vaguely; he was coming very stealthily, and feeling his way. He was near enough, now, for us to see him put out a hand, find an upper wire, then bend and step under it and over the lower one. Now he arrived at the first knight—and started slightly when he discovered him. He stood a moment—no doubt wondering why the other one didn't move on; then he said, in a low voice, "Why dreamest thou here, good Sir Mar—" then he laid his hand on the corpse's shoulder—and just uttered a little soft moan and sunk down dead. Killed by a dead man, you see—killed by a dead friend, in fact. There was something awful about it.

These early birds came scattering along after each other, about one every five minutes in our vicinity, during half an hour. They brought no armor of offence but their swords; as a rule they carried the sword ready in the hand, and put it forward and found the wires with it. We would now and then see a blue spark when the knight that caused it was so far away as to be invisible to us; but we knew what had happened, all the same, poor fellow; he had touched a charged wire with his sword and been elected. We had brief intervals of grim stillness, interrupted with piteous regularity by the clash made by the falling of an iron-clad; and this sort of thing was going on, right along, and was very creepy, there in the dark and lonesomeness.

We concluded to make a tour between the inner fences. We elected to walk upright, for convenience sake; we argued that if discerned, we should be taken for friends rather than enemies, and in any case we should be out of reach of swords, and these gentry did not seem to have any spears along. Well, it was a curious trip. Everywhere dead men were lying outside the second fence—not plainly visible, but still visible; and we counted fifteen of those pathetic statues—dead knights standing with their hands on the upper wire.

One thing seemed to be sufficiently demonstrated: our current was so tremendous that it killed before the victim could cry out. Pretty soon we detected a muffled and heavy sound, and next moment we guessed what it was. It was a surprise in force coming! I whispered Clarence to go and wake the army, and notify it to wait in silence in the cave for further orders. He was soon back, and we stood by the inner fence and watched the silent lightning do its awful work upon that swarming host. One could make out but little of detail; but he could note that a black mass was piling itself up beyond the second fence. That swelling bulk was dead men! Our camp was enclosed with a solid wall of the dead—a bulwark, a breastwork, of corpses, you may say. One terrible thing about this thing was the absence of human voices; there were no cheers, no war cries: being intent upon a surprise, these men moved as noiselessly as they could; and always when the front rank was near enough to their goal to make it proper for them to begin to get a shout ready, of course they struck the fatal line and went down without testifying.

I sent a current through the third fence, now; and almost immediately through the fourth and fifth, so quickly were the gaps filled up. I believed the time was come, now, for my climax; I believed that that whole army was in our trap. Anyway, it was high time to find out. So I touched a button and set fifty electric suns aflame on the top of our precipice.

Land, what a sight! We were enclosed in three walls of dead men! All the other fences were pretty nearly filled with the living, who were stealthily working their way forward through the wires. The sudden glare paralyzed this host, petrified them, you may say, with astonishment; there was just one instant for me to utilize their immobility in, and I didn't lose the chance. You see, in another instant they would have recovered their faculties, then they'd have burst into a cheer and made a rush, and my wires would have gone down before it; but that lost instant lost them their opportunity forever; while even that slight fragment of time was still unspent, I shot the current through all the fences and struck the whole host dead in their tracks! *There* was a groan you could *hear!* It voiced the death-pang of eleven thousand men. It swelled out on the night with awful pathos.

A glance showed that the rest of the enemy—perhaps ten thousand strong—were between us and the encircling ditch, and pressing forward to the assault. Consequently we had them *all!* and had them past help. Time for the last act of the tragedy. I fired the three appointed revolver shots—which meant:

"Turn on the water!"

There was a sudden rush and roar, and in a minute the mountain brook was raging through the big ditch and creating a river a hundred feet wide and twenty-five deep.

"Stand to your guns, men! Open fire!"

The thirteen gatlings began to vomit death into the fated ten thousand. They halted, they stood their ground a moment against that withering deluge of fire, then they broke, faced about and swept toward the ditch like chaff before a gale. A full fourth part of their force never reached the top of the lofty embankment; the three-fourths reached it and plunged over—to death by drowning.

Within ten short minutes after we had opened fire, armed resistance was totally annihilated, the campaign was ended, we fifty-four were masters of England! Twenty-five thousand men lay dead around us.

But how treacherous is fortune! In a little while—say an hour—happened a thing, by my own fault, which—but I have no heart to write that. Let the record end here.

## *Chapter XLIV*

### A POSTSCRIPT BY CLARENCE

I, Clarence, must write it for him. He proposed that we two go out and see if any help could be afforded the wounded. I was strenuous against the project. I said that if there were many, we could do but little for them; and it would not be wise for us to trust ourselves among them, anyway. But he could seldom be turned from a purpose once formed; so we shut off the electric current from the fences, took an escort along, climbed over the enclosing ramparts of dead knights, and moved out upon the field. The first wounded man who appealed for help, was sitting with his back against a dead comrade. When the Boss bent over him and spoke to him, the man recognized him and stabbed him. That knight was Sir Meliagraunce,[8] as I found out by tearing off his helmet. He will not ask for help any more.

---

8. According to Malory, XIX.ix, Sir Meliagraunce had been killed by Launcelot some time before.

We carried the Boss to the cave and gave his wound, which was not very serious, the best care we could. In this service we had the help of Merlin, though we did not know it. He was disguised as a woman, and appeared to be a simple old peasant goodwife. In this disguise, with brown-stained face and smooth shaven, he had appeared a few days after the Boss was hurt, and offered to cook for us, saying her people had gone off to join certain new camps which the enemy were forming, and that she was starving. The Boss had been getting along very well, and had amused himself with finishing up his record.

We were glad to have this woman, for we were short handed. We were in a trap, you see—a trap of our own making. If we stayed where we were, our dead would kill us; if we moved out of our defences, we should no longer be invincible. We had conquered; in turn we were conquered. The Boss recognized this; we all recognized it. If we could go to one of those new camps and patch up some kind of terms with the enemy—yes, but the Boss could not go, and neither could I, for I was among the first that were made sick by the poisonous air bred by those dead thousands. Others were taken down, and still others. To-morrow—

*To-morrow.* It is here. And with it the end. About midnight I awoke, and saw that hag making curious passes in the air about the Boss's head and face, and wondered what it meant. Everybody but the dynamo-watch lay steeped in sleep; there was no sound. The woman ceased from her mysterious foolery, and started tip-toeing toward the door. I called out—

"Stop! What have you been doing?"

She halted, and said with an accent of malicious satisfaction:

"Ye were conquerors; ye are conquered! These others are perishing—you also. Ye shall all die in this place—every one—except *him*. He sleepeth, now—and shall sleep thirteen centuries. I am Merlin!"

Then such a delirium of silly laughter overtook him that he reeled about like a drunken man, and presently fetched up against one of our wires. His mouth is spread open yet; apparently he is still laughing. I suppose the face will retain that petrified laugh until the corpse turns to dust.

The Boss has never stirred—sleeps like a stone. If he does not wake to-day we shall understand what kind of a sleep it is, and his body will then be borne to a place in one of the remote recesses of the cave where none will ever find it to desecrate it. As for the rest of us—well, it is agreed that if any one of us ever escapes alive from this place, he will write the fact here, and loyally hide this Manuscript with the Boss, our dear good chief, whose property it is, be he alive or dead.

### END OF THE MANUSCRIPT

Final P. S. by M. T.

The dawn was come when I laid the Manuscript aside. The rain had almost ceased, the world was gray and sad, the exhausted storm was sighing and sobbing itself to rest. I went to the stranger's room, and listened at his door, which was slightly ajar. I could hear his voice, and so I knocked. There was no answer, but I still heard the voice. I peeped in. The man lay on his back, in bed, talking brokenly but with spirit, and punctuating with his arms, which he thrashed about, restlessly, as sick people do in delirium. I slipped in softly and bent over him. His mutterings and ejaculations went on. I spoke—merely a word, to call his attention. His glassy eyes and his ashy face were alight in an instant with pleasure, gratitude, gladness, welcome:

"O, Sandy, you are come at last—how I have longed for you! Sit by me—do not leave me—never leave me again, Sandy, never again Where is your hand?—give it me, dear, let me hold it—there—now all is well, all is peace, and I am happy again—*we* are happy again, isn't it so, Sandy? You are so dim, so vague, you are but a mist, a cloud, but you are *here,* and that is blessedness sufficient; and I have your hand; don't take it away—it is for only a little while, I shall not require it long. . . . . Was that the child? . . . . Hello-Central! . . . She doesn't answer. Asleep, perhaps? Bring her when she wakes, and let me touch her hands, her face, her hair, and tell her good-bye. . . . . . Sandy! . . . . . Yes, you are there. I lost myself a moment, and I thought you were gone. . . . Have I been sick long? It must be so; it seems months to me. And such dreams! such strange and awful dreams, Sandy! Dreams that were as real as reality—delirium, of course, but *so* real! Why, I thought the king was dead, I thought you were in Gaul and couldn't get home, I thought there was a revolution; in the fantastic frenzy of these dreams, I thought that Clarence and I and a handful of my cadets fought and exterminated the whole chivalry of England! But even that was not the strangest. I seemed to be a creature out of a remote unborn age, centuries hence, and even *that* was as real as the rest! Yes, I seemed to have flown back out of that age into this of ours, and then forward to it again, and was set down, a stranger and forlorn in that strange England, with an abyss of thirteen centuries yawning between me and you! between me and my home and my friends! between me and all that is dear to me, all that could make life worth the living! It was awful—awfuler than you can ever imagine, Sandy. Ah, watch by me, Sandy—stay by me every moment—*don't* let me go out of my mind again; death is nothing, let it come, but not with those dreams, not with the torture of those hideous dreams—I cannot endure *that* again. . . . . . . . Sandy? . . . . . ."

He lay muttering incoherently some little time; then for a time he lay silent, and apparently sinking away toward death. Presently his fingers began to pick busily at the coverlet,[9] and by that sign I knew that his end was at hand. With the first suggestion of the death-rattle in his throat he started up slightly, and seemed to listen; then he said:

"A bugle? . . . . . It is the king! The drawbridge, there! Man the battlements!—turn out the—"

He was getting up his last "effect;" but he never finished it.

### THE END[1]

---

9. Traditionally thought to be a sign of impending death, as with Falstaff, as reported in *Henry V*, II.iii.

1. In the first edition these words appear beneath Dan Beard's drawing of Morgan, Sandy, and Hello-Central apparently united in heaven, while in the foreground Death has killed Time and smashed his hourglass. A separate sheet at the end of the manuscript shows that at one point Clemens intended to supply an appendix which would support "the assertion that there were no real gentlemen & ladies before our century" by printing extracts from various historical and literary works, "where printable." Among the authors to be included were Fielding, Richardson, Goldsmith, Rousseau, and Zola. (*A Connecticut Yankee in King Arthur's Court*, ed. Bernard L. Stein [Berkeley: University of California Press, 1979], p. 515.)

# Backgrounds and Sources

# King Arthur†

The romantic figure of King Arthur has probably some historical basis, and there is reason to think that, as Nennius states, he was a chieftain or general *(dux bellorum)* in the 5th or 6th cent. The 'Annales Cambriae' place the battle of Mount Badon, 'in which Arthur carried the cross of our Lord Jesus Christ on his shoulders', in 518, and the 'battle of Camlan, in which Arthur and Medraut fell', in 539. The contemporary chronicler Gildas makes no mention of Arthur (though he refers to the battle of Badon), nor do some of the principal Welsh bards of the 6th and 7th cents. But there is mention of him in certain ancient poems contained in the 'Black Book of Carmarthen' and more especially in the ancient Welsh romance 'Kilhwch and Olwen,' where he figures with Kay, Bedivere, and Gawain (Gwalchmei). But this Arthur is a king of fairyland, and the author of the tale is building, in Matthew Arnold's words, with the 'materials of an older architecture, greater, cunninger, and more majestical'. In fact, Arthur and several other characters in the Arthurian legend can be traced to figures in the ancient Celtic pantheon (Rhys, 'Studies in the Arthurian Legend', 1901), but their working up and fashioning was, in the wide sense of the word, English (Saintsbury, 'The Flourishing of Romance' in P. E. L.). Rhys suggests that there were originally two Arthurs, the British god and the human general, whose characters have become blended in legend.

Arthur first takes definite form as a romantic hero in the 'Historia Regum Britanniae' of Geoffrey of Monmouth, a work in which the author's imagination played a very large part. In this narrative Arthur is the son of Uther Pendragon (Welsh = chief leader in war) and Ygaerne (Igraine), wife of Gorlois of Cornwall, whom Uther wins by the help of Merlin's magic. The elves bestow on him long life, riches, and virtures. At the age of 15 he becomes king of Britain and wars against Scots, Picts, and Saxons. With his sword 'Caliburn' (Excalibur) he slays Childric, defeats the heathen, and conquers Scotland, Ireland, Iceland, and the Orkneys. He marries Guanhamara (Wenhaver, Guinevere), a lady of noble Roman family. He conquers many lands on the Continent. His court is at Caerleon on Usk. He is summoned to pay tribute to the Emperor Lucius of Rome, resists, and declares war. Guanhamara and the kingdom are left in Modred, his nephew's, charge. On his way to Rome he slays the giant of St. Michael's Mount. Walwain (Gawain), his ambassador, defies the emperor and bears himself bravely in the ensuing combat. Arthur is about to enter Rome when he receives warning that Modred has seized

† From *The Oxford Companion to English Literature*, ed. Sir Paul Harvey, 4th ed. (Oxford: Clarendon Press, 1967), pp. 42–43.

261

Guanhamara and the kingdom. He returns with Walwain, who is slain on landing. Modred retreats to Cornwall, and in a final battle on the Camel, is slain with all his knights. Arthur is mortally wounded, and is borne to the island of Avalon for the healing of his wounds. Guanhamara takes the veil.

This story was developed by the Norman writer Wace, who added many details. The 'Round Table' is first mentioned by him, a device to settle the disputes as to precedence among Arthur's knights. The wounded king is expected to return from Avalon and resume his kingdom. Wace's work served as the basis of the 'Brut' of Layamon, the first English record of the 'noble deeds of England', which adds many romantic details, and a fairy element, to the story. Elves are present at Arthur's birth, his sword and spear are of magic origin. After the final battle at Camelford, Arthur is borne off to Argante in Avalon, in a magic boat.

The Arthurian story was also developed in the French *Matière de Bretagne,* by such writers as Marie de France and Chrétien de Troyes, and later by Robert de Baron. Arthur became the centre of a mass of legends in various tongues. A number of these, dealing with various personages, Merlin, Launcelot, Tristram, etc., were gradually associated with him. He is the central figure only in the narratives of his earlier years and of his final battles and death. In the other tales his court is merely the rallying-point for the various adventurous knights. He ceases to be the model of purity and valour, and yields in importance to Gawain and Launcelot.

The story of Arthur, as summarized above, is the foundation of Malory's 'Morte Darthur,' but the greater part of this work is occupied with the exploits of the Knights of the Round Table, the quest of the Holy Grail, the loves of Launcelot and Guinevere and of Tristram and Iseult. *     *     *


# WASHINGTON IRVING

## [The Total Eclipse]†

*     *     *

In this extremity, a fortunate idea presented itself to Columbus. From his knowledge of astronomy, he ascertained that within three days there would be a total eclipse of the moon in the early part of the night. He sent, therefore, an Indian of Hispaniola, who served as his

† From Washington Irving, *The Life and Voyages of Christopher Columbus* (New York: G. P. Putnam, 1868), II, 457–58 (Book 16, chapter 3). Hank Morgan credits his eclipse stratagem to "Columbus or Cortez, or one of those people." The event took place during Columbus' fourth voyage, in 1504.

interpreter, to summon the principal caciques to a grand conference, appointing for it the day of the eclipse. When all were assembled, he told them by his interpreter, that he and his followers were worshipers of a Deity who dwelt in the skies, who favored such as did well, but punished all transgressors. That, as they must all have noticed, he had protected Diego Mendez and his companions in their voyage, because they were in obedience to the orders of their commander, but had visited Porras and his companions with all kinds of afflictions in consequence of their rebellion. This great Deity, he added, was incensed against the Indians who refused to furnish his faithful worshipers with provisions, and intended to chastise them with famine and pestilence. Lest they should disbelieve this warning, a signal would be given that night. They would behold the moon change its color, and gradually lose its light; a token of the fearful punishment which awaited them.

Many of the Indians were alarmed at the prediction, others treated it with derision—all, however, awaited with solicitude the coming of the night. When they beheld a dark shadow stealing over the moon, they began to tremble; with the progress of the eclipse their fears increased, and when they saw a mysterious darkness covering the whole face of nature, there were no bounds to their terror. Seizing upon whatever provisions were at hand, they hurried to the ships, threw themselves at the feet of Columbus, and implored him to intercede with his God to withhold the threatened calamities, assuring him they would henceforth bring him whatever he required. Columbus shut himself up in his cabin, as if to commune with the Deity, and remained there during the increase of the eclipse; the forests and shores all the while resounding with the howlings and supplications of the savages. When the eclipse was about to diminish, he came forth and informed the natives that his God had deigned to pardon them, on condition of their fulfilling their promises; in sign of which he would withdraw the darkness from the moon.

When the Indians saw that planet restored to its brightness, and rolling in all its beauty through the firmament, they overwhelmed the admiral with thanks for his intercession, and repaired to their homes, joyful at having escaped such great disasters. Regarding Columbus with awe and reverence, as a man in the peculiar favor and confidence of the Deity, since he knew upon earth what was passing in the heavens, they hastened to propitiate him with gifts; supplies again arrived daily at the harbor, and from that time forward there was no want of provisions.

# W. E. H. LECKY

## [The Ascetic Saints]†

\* \* \*

There is, perhaps, no phase in the moral history of mankind, of a deeper or more painful interest than this ascetic epidemic. A hideous, sordid, and emaciated maniac, without knowledge, without patriotism, without natural affection, passing his life in a long routine of useless and atrocious self-torture, and quailing before the ghastly phantoms of his delirious brain, had become the ideal of the nations which had known the writings of Plato and Cicero and the lives of Socrates or Cato. For about two centuries, the hideous maceration of the body was regarded as the highest proof of excellence. St. Jerome declares, with a thrill of admiration, how he had seen a monk, who for thirty years had lived exclusively on a small portion of barley bread and of muddy water; another, who lived in a hole and never ate more than five figs for his daily repast; a third, who cut his hair only on Easter Sunday, who never washed his clothes, who never changed his tunic till it fell to pieces, who starved himself till his eyes grew dim, and his skin 'like a pumice stone,' and whose merits, shown by these austerities, Homer himself would be unable to recount. For six months, it is said, St. Macarius of Alexandria slept in a marsh, and exposed his body naked to the stings of venomous flies. He was accustomed to carry about with him eighty pounds of iron. His disciple, St. Eusebius, carried one hundred and fifty pounds of iron, and lived for three years in a dried-up well. St. Sabinus would only eat corn that had become rotten by remaining for a month in water. St. Besarion spent forty days and nights in the middle of thorn-bushes, and for forty years never lay down when he slept, which last penance was also during fifteen years practised by St. Pachomius. Some saints, like St. Marcian, restricted themselves to one meal a day, so small that they continually suffered the pangs of hunger. Of one of them it is related that his daily food was six ounces of bread and a few herbs; that he was never seen to recline on a mat or bed, or even to place his limbs easily for sleep; but that sometimes, from excess of weariness, his eyes would close at his meals, and the food would drop from his mouth. Other saints, however, ate only every second day; while many, if we could believe the monkish historian, abstained for whole weeks from all nourishment. St. Macarius of Alexandria is said during an entire week to have never lain down, or eaten anything but a few uncooked herbs

†From W. E. H. Lecky, *History of European Mortals from Augustus to Charlemagne* (New York: Appleton, 1872), II, 114–119, 386–88. The account Hank Morgan gives in Chapter XXII is based on the first passage. The second, Lecky's footnotes on the king's touch, is used as a basis for Chapter XXVI.

on Sunday. Of another famous saint, named John, it is asserted that for three whole years he stood in prayer, leaning upon a rock; that during all that time he never sat or lay down, and that his only nourishment was the Sacrament, which was brought him on Sundays. Some of the hermits lived in deserted dens of wild beasts, others in dried-up wells, while others found a congenial resting-place among the tombs. Some disdained all clothes, and crawled abroad like the wild beasts, covered only by their matted hair. In Mesopotamia, and part of Syria, there existed a sect known by the name of 'Grazers,' who never lived under a roof, who ate neither flesh nor bread, but who spent their time for ever on the mountain side, and ate grass like cattle. The cleanliness of the body was regarded as a pollution of the soul, and the saints who were most admired had become one hideous mass of clotted filth. St. Athanasius relates with enthusiasm how St. Antony, the patriarch of monachism, had never, in extreme old age, been guilty of washing his feet. The less constant St. Pœman fell into this habit for the first time when a very old man, and, with a glimmering of common sense, defended himself against the astonished monks by saying that he had 'learnt to kill not his body, but his passions.' St. Abraham the hermit, however, who lived for fifty years after his conversion, rigidly refused from that date to wash either his face or his feet. He was, it is said, a person of singular beauty, and his biographer somewhat strangely remarks, that 'his face reflected the purity of his soul.' St. Ammon had never seen himself naked. A famous virgin named Silvia, though she was sixty years old, and though bodily sickness was a consequence of her habits, resolutely refused, on religious principles, to wash any part of her body except her fingers. St. Euphraxia joined a convent of one hundred and thirty nuns, who never washed their feet, and who shuddered at the mention of a bath. An anchorite once imagined that he was mocked by an illusion of the devil, as he saw gliding before him through the desert a naked creature black with filth and years of exposure, and with white hair floating to the wind. It was a once beautiful woman, St. Mary of Egypt, who had thus, during forty-seven years, been expiating her sins. The occasional decadence of the monks into habits of decency was a subject of much reproach. 'Our fathers,' said the abbot Alexander, looking mournfully back to the past, 'never washed their faces, but we frequent the public baths.' It was related of one monastery in the desert, that the monks suffered greatly from want of water to drink; but at the prayer of the abbot Theodosius, a copious stream was produced. But soon some monks, tempted by the abundant supply, diverged from their old austerity, and persuaded the abbot to avail himself of the stream for the construction of the bath. The bath was made. Once, and once only, did the monks enjoy their ablutions, when the stream ceased to flow. Prayers, tears, and fastings were in vain. A whole year passed. At last the abbot destroyed the bath, which was the object of the Divine displeasure, and the waters flowed afresh. But of all the evidences of the loathsome excesses to which this spirit was carried, the life of St. Simeon Stylites is probably the most remarkable. It would be difficult to conceive a more horrible or disgusting picture than is given of the penances by which that saint commenced his ascetic career. He had bound a rope around him so that it became imbedded in his flesh, which putrefied around it. 'A horrible stench, intolerable to the bystanders, exhaled from his body, and worms dropped from him whenever he moved, and they filled his bed.' Sometimes he left the monastery and slept in a dry well, inhabited, it is said, by dæmons. He built successively three pillars, the last being sixty feet high, and scarcely two cubits in circumference, and on this pillar, during thirty years, he remained exposed to every change of climate, ceaselessly and rapidly bending his body in prayer almost to the level of his feet. A spectator attempted to number these rapid motions, but desisted from weariness when he had counted 1,244. For a whole year, we are told, St. Simeon stood upon one leg, the other being covered with hideous ulcers, while his biographer was commissioned to stand by his side, to pick up the worms that fell from his body, and to replace them in the sores, the saint saying to the worm, 'Eat what God has given you.' From every quarter pilgrims of every degree thronged to do him homage. A crowd of prelates followed him to the grave. A brilliant star is said to have shone miraculously over his pillar; the general voice of mankind pronounced him to be the highest model of Christian saint, and several other anchorites imitated or emulated his penances.

\* \* \*

# W. E. H. LECKY

## [The King's Touch]†

'The days on which the miracle [of the king's touch] was to be wrought were fixed at sittings of the Privy Council, and were solemnly notified by the clergy to all the parish churches of the realm. When the appointed time came, several divines in full canonicals stood round the canopy of state. The surgeon of the royal household introduced the sick. A passage of Mark xvi. was read. When the words "They shall lay their hands on the sick and they shall recover," had been pronounced, there was a pause, and one of the sick was brought to the

† From W. E. H. Lecky, *History of European Morals from Augustus to Charlemagne* (New York: Appleton, 1872), I, 386–88. This mate- rial is presented in two footnotes. The account given in Chapter XXVI of the novel derives from this source.

king. His Majesty stroked the ulcers. . . . Then came the Epistle, &c.
The Service may still be found in the Prayer Books of the reign of
Anne. Indeed, it was not until some time after the accession of George
I. that the University of Oxford ceased to reprint the Office of healing,
together with the Liturgy. Theologians of eminent learning, ability,
and virtue gave the sanction of their authority to this mummery, and,
what is stranger still, medical men of high note believed, or affected to
believe, it. . . . Charles II., in the course of his reign, touched near
100,000 persons. . . . In 1682 he performed the rite 8,500 times. In
1684 the throng was such that six or seven of the sick were trampled to
death. James, in one of his progresses, touched 800 persons in the
choir of the cathedral of Chester.'—Macaulay's *History of England*,
c.xiv.

One of the surgeons of Charles II., named John Brown, whose
official duty it was to superintend the ceremony, and who assures us
that he has witnessed many thousands touched, has written an ex-
tremely curious account of it, called *Charisma Basilicon* (London,
1684). This miraculous power existed exclusively in the English and
French royal families, being derived, in the first, from Edward the
Confessor, in the second, from St. Lewis. A surgeon attested the
reality of the disease before the miracle was performed. The king hung
a riband with a gold coin round the neck of the person touched; but
Brown thinks the gold, though possessing great virtue, was not essential to the cure. He had known cases where the cured person had sold,
or ceased to wear, the medal, and his disease returned. The gift was
unimpaired by the Reformation, and an obdurate Catholic was converted on finding that Elizabeth, after the Pope's excommunication,
could cure his scrofula. Francis I. cured many persons when prisoner
in Spain. Charles I., when a prisoner, cured a man by his simple
benediction, the Puritans not permitting him to touch him. His blood
had the same efficacy; and Charles II., when an exile in the Nether-
lands, still retained it. There were, however, some 'Atheists, Sad-
ducees, and ill-conditioned Pharisees' who even then disbelieved it;
and Brown gives the letter of one who went, a complete sceptic, to
satisfy his friends, and came away cured and converted. It was popularly, but Brown says erroneously, believed that the touch was peculiarly efficacious on Good Friday. An official register was kept for every
month, in the reign of Charles II., of the persons touched, but two
years and a half appear to be wanting. The smallest number touched
in one year was 2,983 (in 1669); the total, in the whole reign 92,107.
Brown gives numbers of specific cases with great detail. Shakespeare
has noticed the power (*Macbeth*, Act iv. Scene 3). Dr. Johnson,
when a boy, was touched by Queen Anne; but at that time few
persons, except Jacobites, believed the miracle.

# W. E. H. LECKY

## [Financing the Mansion House]†

\* \* \*

A very scandalous form of persecution, in which, however, religious motives had no part, was practised in the last years of George II. and the early years of George III. by no less a body than the Corporation of the City of London. In 1748 that Corporation made a bye-law imposing a fine of 400*l*. and 20 marks on any person who, being nominated by the Lord Mayor for the office of Sheriff, refused to stand the election of the Common Hall, and 600*l*. on anyone who, being elected, refused to serve. The proceeds of these fines were to be employed in building the New Mansion House, which had just been begun. But the office of Sheriff was one of those in which no one could serve who had not previously taken the Sacrament according to the Anglican rite, and it was, therefore, one of those from which Dissenters were excluded. It would appear almost incredible, if the facts were not amply attested, that under these circumstances the City of London systematically elected wealthy Dissenters to the office in order that they should be objected to and fined, and that in this manner it extorted no less than 15,000*l*. The electors appointed these Dissenters with a clear knowledge that they would not serve, and with the sole purpose of extorting money. One of those whom they selected was blind; another was bedridden. Sometimes the victims appealed against the sentence, but the case was brought in the first instance before a City court, which always gave verdicts for the Corporation, and the cost of appeals against the whole weight of the City influence was so great that few men were rich enough or determined enough to encounter it.\* \* \*

† From W. E. H. Lecky, A *History of England in the Eighteenth Century* (New York: Apple-ton, 1882). III, 538. Hank Morgan presents this information in Chapter XXV of the novel.

# Composition and Publication

# The Author and the Novel

## SAMUEL L. CLEMENS

### The "Tournament" in A.D. 1870†

Lately there appeared an item to this effect, and the same went the customary universal round of the press:

> A telegraph station has just been established upon the traditional site of the Garden of Eden.

As a companion to that, nothing fits so aptly and so perfectly as this:

> Brooklyn has revived the knightly tournament of the Middle Ages.

It is hard to tell which is the most startling, the idea of that highest achievement of human genius and intelligence, the telegraph, prating away about the practical concerns of the world's daily life in the heart and home of ancient indolence, ignorance, and savagery, or the idea of that happiest expression of the brag, vanity, and mock-heroics of our ancestors, the "tournament," coming out of its grave to flaunt its tinsel trumpery and perform its "chivalrous" absurdities in the high noon of the nineteenth century, and under the patronage of a great, broad-awake city and an advanced civilization.

A "tournament" in Lynchburg[1] is a thing easily within the comprehension of the average mind; but no commonly gifted person can conceive of such a spectacle in Brooklyn without straining his powers. Brooklyn is part and parcel of the city of New York, and there is hardly romance enough in the entire metropolis to re-supply a Virginia "knight" with "chivalry," in case he happened to run out of it. Let the reader, calmly and dispassionately, picture to himself "lists"—in Brooklyn; heralds, pursuivants, pages, garter king-at-arms—in Brooklyn; the marshalling of the fantastic hosts of "chivalry" in slashed doublets, velvet trunks, ruffles, and plumes—in Brooklyn; mounted on omnibus and livery-stable patriarchs, promoted, and referred to in cold blood as "steeds," "destriers," and "chargers," and divested of their friendly, humble names—these meek old "Jims" and "Robs" and "Charleys," and renamed "Mohammed," "Bucephalus," and "Saladin"—in Brooklyn; mounted thus, and armed with swords and shields and wooden lances, and cased in pasteboard hauberks, mor-

---

† From *The Galaxy* (July 1870) pp. 135–36.   1. Virginia.

ions, greaves, and gauntlets, and addressed as "Sir" Smith,[2] and "Sir" Jones, and bearing such titled grandeurs as "The Disinherited Knight," the "Knight of Shenandoah," the "Knight of the Blue Ridge," the "Knight of Maryland," and the "Knight of the Secret Sorrow"—in Brooklyn; and at the toot of the horn charging fiercely upon a helpless ring hung on a post, and prodding at it intrepidly with their wooden sticks, and by and by skewering it and cavorting back to the judges' stand covered with glory—this in Brooklyn; and each noble success like this duly and promptly announced by an applauding toot from the herald's horn, and "the band playing three bars of an old circus tune"—all in Brooklyn, in broad daylight. And let the reader remember, and also add to his picture, as follows, to wit: when the show was all over, the party who had shed the most blood and overturned and hacked to pieces the most knights, or at least had prodded the most muffin-rings, was accorded the ancient privilege of naming and crowning the Queen of Love and Beauty—which naming had in reality been done *for* him by the "cut-and-dried" process, and long in advance, by a committee of ladies, but the crowning he did in person, though suffering from loss of blood, and then was taken to the county hospital on a shutter to have his wounds dressed—these curious things all occurring in Brooklyn, and no longer ago than one or two yesterdays. It seems impossible, and yet it is true.

This was doubtless the first appearance of the "tournament" up here among the rolling-mills and factories, and will probably be the last. It will be well to let it retire permanently to the rural districts of Virginia, where, it is said, the fine mailed and plumed, noble-natured, maiden-rescuing, wrong-redressing, adventure-seeking knight of romance is accepted and believed in by the peasantry with pleasing simplicity, while they reject with scorn the plain, unpolished verdict whereby history exposes him as a braggart, a ruffian, a fantastic vagabond, and an ignoramus.

All romance aside, what shape would our admiration of the heroes of Ashby de la Zouch[3] be likely to take, in this practical age, if those worthies were to rise up and come here and perform again the chivalrous deeds of that famous passage of arms? Nothing but a New York jury and the insanity plea could save them from hanging, from the amiable Bois-Guilbert and the pleasant Front-de-Boeuf[4] clear down to the nameless ruffians that entered the riot with unpictured shields and did their first murder and acquired their first claim to respect that day. The doings of the so-called "chivalry" of the Middle Ages were absurd enough, even when they were brutally and bloodily in earnest, and when their surroundings of castles and donjons, savage

<hr>

2. The original name for the hero of *A Connecticut Yankee* was Sir Robert Smith.
3. Scene of the great tournament in Sir Walter

Scott's *Ivanhoe* (1819).
4. Both are characters in *Ivanhoe*.

landscapes and half-savage peoples, were in keeping; but those doings gravely reproduced with tinsel decorations and mock pageantry, by bucolic gentlemen with broomstick lances, and with muffin-rings to represent the foe, and all in the midst of the refinement and dignity of a carefully-developed modern civilization, is absurdity gone crazy.

Now, for next exhibition, let us have a fine representation of one of those chivalrous wholesale butcheries and burnings of Jewish women and children, which the crusading heroes of romance used to indulge in in their European homes, just before starting to the Holy Land, to seize and take to their protection the Sepulchre and defend it from "pollution."

# SAMUEL L. CLEMENS

## The Great Revolution in Pitcairn†

Let me refresh the reader's memory a little. Nearly a hundred years ago the crew of the British ship *Bounty* mutinied, set the captain and his officers adrift upon the open sea, took possession of the ship, and sailed southward. They procured wives for themselves among the natives of Tahiti, then proceeded to a lonely little rock in mid-Pacific, called Pitcairn's Island, wrecked the vessel, stripped her of everything that might be useful to a new colony, and established themselves on shore.

Pitcairn's is so far removed from the track of commerce that it was many years before another vessel touched there. It had always been considered an uninhabited island; so when a ship did at last drop its anchor there, in 1808, the captain was greatly surprised to find the place peopled. Although the mutineers had fought among themselves, and gradually killed each other off until only two or three of the original stock remained, these tragedies had not occurred before a number of children had been born; so in 1808 the island had a population of twenty-seven persons. John Adams, the chief mutineer, still survived, and was to live many years yet, as governor and patriarch of the flock. From being mutineer and homicide, he had turned Christian and teacher, and his nation of twenty-seven persons was now the purest and devoutest in Christendom. Adams had long ago hoisted the British flag and constituted his island an appanage of the British crown.

To-day the population numbers ninety persons—sixteen men, nine-

---

† From the *Atlantic Monthly*, 43 (1879), 295–302. Obvious similarities exist between this piece and *A Connecticut Yankee*. In both an American comes into a British society and attempts to change it radically. Although he is at first successful, his revolution is ultimately overthrown.

teen women, twenty-five boys, and thirty girls—all descendants of the mutineers, all bearing the family names of those mutineers, and all speaking English, and English only. The island stands high up out of the sea, and has precipitous walls. It is about three-quarters of a mile long, and in places is as much as half a mile wide. Such arable land as it affords is held by the several familes, according to a division made many years ago. There is some live stock—goats, pigs, chickens, and cats; but no dogs, and no large animals. There is one church-building—used also as a capitol, a schoolhouse, and a public library. The title of the governor has been, for a generation or two, "Magistrate and Chief Ruler, in subordination to her Majesty the Queen of Great Britain." It was his province to *make* the laws, as well as execute them. His office was elective; everybody over seventeen years old had a vote—no matter about the sex.

The sole occupations of the people were farming and fishing; their sole recreation, religious services. There has never been a shop in the island, nor any money. The habits and dress of the people have always been primitive, and their laws simple to puerility. They have lived in a deep Sabbath tranquility, far from the world and its ambitions and vexations, and neither knowing nor caring what was going on in the mighty empires that lie beyond their limitless ocean solitudes. Once in three or four years a ship touched there, moved them with aged news of bloody battles, devastating epidemics, fallen thrones, and ruined dynasties, then traded them some soap and flannel for some yams and breadfruit, and sailed away, leaving them to retire into their peaceful dreams and pious dissipations once more.

On the 8th of last September, Admiral de Horsey, commander-in-chief of the British fleet in the Pacific, visited Pitcairn's Island, and speaks as follows in his official report to the admiralty:

> They have beans, carrots, turnips, cabbages, and a little maize; pineapples, fig trees, custard-apples, and oranges; lemons, and cocoanuts. Clothing is obtained alone from passing ships, in barter for refreshments. There are no springs on the island, but as it rains generally once a month they have plenty of water, although at times in former years they have suffered from drought. No alcoholic liquors, except for medicinal purposes, are used, and a drunkard is unknown. . . .
>
> The necessary articles required by the islanders are best shown by those we furnished in barter for refreshments: namely, flannel, serge, drill, half-boots, combs, tobacco, and soap. They also stand much in need of maps and slates for their school, and tools of any kind are most acceptable. I caused them to be supplied from the public stores with a Union Jack for display on the arrival of ships, and a pit-saw, of which they were greatly in need. This, I trust, will meet the approval of their lordships. If the munificient people of England were only aware of the wants of this most deserving little

colony, they would not long go unsupplied. . . .

Divine service is held every Sunday at 10.30 A.M. and at 3 P.M., in the house built and used by John Adams for that purpose until he died in 1829. It is conducted strictly in accordance with the liturgy of the Church of England, by Mr. Simon Young, their selected pastor, who is much respected. A Bible class is held every Wednesday, when all who conveniently can attend. There is also a general meeting for prayer on the first Friday in every month. Family prayers are said in every house the first thing in the morning and the last thing in the evening, and no food is partaken of without asking God's blessing before and afterward. Of these islanders' religious attributes no one can speak without deep respect. A people whose greatest pleasure and privilege is to commune in prayer with their God, and to join in hymns of praise, and who are, moreover, cheerful, diligent, and probably freer from vice than any other community, need no priest among them.

Now I come to a sentence in the admiral's report which he dropped carelessly from his pen, no doubt, and never gave the matter a second thought. He little imagined what a freight of tragic prophecy it bore! This is the sentence:

One stranger, an American, has settled on the island—*a doubtful acquisition*.

A doubtful acquisition, indeed! Captain Ormsby, in the American ship *Hornet*, touched at Pitcairn's nearly four months after the admiral's visit, and from the facts which he gathered there we now know all about that American. Let us put these facts together in historical form. The American's name was Butterworth Stavely. As soon as he had become well acquainted with all the people—and this took but a few days, of course—he began to ingratiate himself with them by all the arts he could command. He became exceedingly popular, and much looked up to; for one of the first things he did was to forsake his worldly way of life, and throw all his energies into religion. He was always reading his Bible, or praying, or singing hymns, or asking blessings. In prayer, no one had such "liberty" as he, no one could pray so long or so well.

At last, when he considered the time to be ripe, he began secretly to sow the seeds of discontent among the people. It was his deliberate purpose, from the beginning, to subvert the government, but of course he kept that to himself for a time. He used different arts with different individuals. He awakened dissatisfaction in one quarter by calling attention to the shortness of the Sunday services; he argued that there should be three three-hour services on Sunday instead of only two. Many had secretly held this opinion before; they now privately banded themselves into a party to work for it. He showed certain of the women that they were not allowed sufficient voice in the prayer-meetings; thus another party was formed. No weapon was beneath his notice; he even descended to the children, and awoke discontent in their breasts because—*as he* discovered for them—they had not enough Sunday-school. This created a third party.

Now, as the chief of these parties, he found himself the strongest power in the community. So he proceeded to his next move—a no less important one than the impeachment of the chief magistrate, James Russell Nickoy; a man of character and ability, and possessed of great wealth, he being the owner of a house with a parlor to it, three acres and a half of yam-land, and the only boat in Pitcairn's, a whaleboat; and, most unfortunately, a pretext for his impeachment offered itself at just the right time.

One of the earliest and most precious laws of the island was the law against trespass. It was held in great reverence, and was regarded as the palladium of the people's liberties. About thirty years ago an important case came before the courts under this law, in this wise; a chicken belonging to Elizabeth Young (aged, at that time, fifty-eight, a daughter of John Mills, one of the mutineers of the *Bounty*) trespassed upon the grounds of Thursday October Christian (aged twenty-nine, a grandson of Fletcher Christian, one of the mutineers). Christian killed the chicken. According to the law, Christian could keep the chicken; or, if he preferred, he could restore its remains to the owner and receive damages in "produce" to an amount equivalent to the waste and injury wrought by the trespasser. The court records set forth that "the said Christian aforesaid did deliver the aforesaid remains to the said Elizabeth Young, and did demand one bushel of yams in satisfaction of the damage done." But Elizabeth Young considered the demand exorbitant; the parties could not agree; therefore Christian brought suit in the courts. He lost his case in the justice's court; at least, he was awarded only a half-peck of yams, which he considered insufficient, and in the nature of a defeat. He appealed. The case lingered several years in an ascending grade of courts, and always resulted in decrees sustaining the original verdict; and finally the thing got into the supreme court, and there it stuck for twenty years. But last summer, even the supreme court managed to arrive at a decision at last. Once more the original verdict was sustained. Christian then said he was satisfied; but Stavely was present, and whispered to him and to his lawyer, suggesting, "as a mere form," that the original law be exhibited, in order to make sure that it still existed. It seemed an odd idea, but an ingenious one. So the demand was made. A messenger was sent to the magistrate's house; he presently returned with the tidings that it had disappeared from among the state archives.

The court now pronounced its late decision void, since it had been made under a law which had no actual existence.

Great excitement ensued immediately. The news swept abroad over

the whole island that the palladium of the public liberties was lost—
maybe treasonably destroyed. Within thirty minutes almost the entire
nation were in the court-room—that is to say, the church. The
impeachment of the chief magistrate followed, upon Stavely's motion. The accused met his misfortune with the dignity which became
his great office. He did not plead, or even argue; he offered the simple
defense that he had not meddled with the missing law; that he had kept
the state archives in the same candle-box that had been used as their
depository from the beginning; and that he was innocent of the
removal or destruction of the lost document.

But nothing could save him; he was found guilty of misprision of
treason, and degraded from his office, and all his property was confiscated.

The lamest part of the whole shameful matter was the *reason*
suggested by his enemies for his destruction of the law, to wit: that he
did it to favor Christian, because Christian was his cousin! Whereas
Stavely was the only individual in the entire nation who was *not* his
cousin. The reader must remember that all these people are the
descendants of half a dozen men; that the first children intermarried
together and bore grandchildren to the mutineers; that these grand-
children intermarried; after them, great and great-great-grandchildren
intermarried; so that to-day everybody is blood kin to everybody.
Moreover, the relationships are wonderfully, even astoundingly,
mixed up and complicated. A stranger, for instance, says to an is-
lander:

"You speak of that young woman as your cousin; a while ago you
called her your aunt."

"Well, she *is* my aunt, and my cousin, too. And also my stepsister,
my niece, my fourth cousin, my thirty-third cousin, my forty-second
cousin, my great-aunt, my grandmother, my widowed sister-in-
law—and next week she will be my wife."

So the charge of nepotism against the chief magistrate was weak.
But no matter; weak or strong, it suited Stavely. Stavely was immediately elected to the vacant magistracy, and oozing reform from
every pore, he went vigorously to work. In no long time religious
services raged everywhere and unceasingly. By command, the second prayer of the Sunday morning service, which had customarily
endured some thirty-five or forty minutes, and had pleaded for the
world, first by continent and then by national and tribal detail, was
extended to an hour and half, and made to include supplications in
behalf of the possible peoples in the several planets. Everybody was
pleased with this; everybody said, "Now *this* is something *like*." By
command, the usual three-hour sermons were doubled in length. The
nation came in a body to testify their gratitude to the new magistrate.
The old law forbidding cooking on the Sabbath was extended to the

prohibition of eating, also. By command, Sunday-school was privileged to spread over into the week. The joy of all classes was complete. In one short month the new magistrate had become the people's idol!

The time was ripe for this man's next move. He began, cautiously at first, to poison the public mind aginst England. He took the chief citizens aside, one by one, and conversed with them on this topic. Presently he grew bolder, and spoke out. He said the nation owed it to itself, to its honor, to its great traditions, to rise in its might and throw off "the galling English yoke."

But the simple islanders answered:

"We had not noticed that it galled. How does it gall? England sends a ship once in three or four years to give us soap and clothing, and things which we sorely need and gratefully receive; but she never troubles us; she lets us go on our own way."

"She lets you go your own way! So slaves have felt and spoken in all the ages! This speech shows how fallen you are, how base, how brutalized you have become, under this grinding tyranny! What! has all manly pride forsaken you? Is liberty nothing? Are you content to be a mere appendage to a foreign and hateful sovereignty, when you might rise up and take your rightful place in the august family of nations, great, free, enlightened, independent, the minion of no sceptered master, but the arbiter of your own destiny, and a voice and a power in decreeing the destinies of your sister-sovereignties of the world?"

Speeches like this produced an effect by and by. Citizens began to feel the English yoke; they did not know exactly how or whereabouts they felt it, but they were perfectly certain they did feel it. They got to grumbling a good deal, and chafing under their chains, and longing for relief and release. They presently fell to hating the English flag, that sign and symbol of their nation's degradation; they ceased to glance up at it as they passed the capital, but averted their eyes and grated their teeth; and one morning, when it was found trampled into the mud at the foot of the staff, they left it there, and no man put his hand to it to hoist it again. A certain thing which was sure to happen sooner or later happened now. Some of the chief citizens went to the magistrate by night, and said:

"We can endure this hated tyranny no longer. How can we cast it off?"

"By a *coup d'état.*"

"How?"

"A *coup d'état.* It is like this: everything is got ready, and at the appointed moment I, as the official head of the nation, publicly and solemnly proclaim its independence, and absolve it from allegiance to any and all other powers whatsoever."

"That sounds simple and easy. We can do that right away. Then what will be the next thing to do?"

"Seize all the defenses and public properties of all kinds, establish martial law, put the army and navy on a war footing, and proclaim the empire!"

This fine program dazzled these innocents. They said:

"This is grand—this is splendid; but will not England resist?"

"Let her. This rock is a Gibraltar."

"True. But about the empire? Do we *need* an empire and an emperor?"

"What you *need*, my friends, is unification. Look at Germany; look at Italy. They are unified. Unification is the thing. It makes living dear. That constitutes progress. We must have a standing army and a navy. Taxes follow, as a matter of course. All these things summed up make grandeur. With unification and grandeur, what more can you want? Very well—only the empire can confer these boons."

So on the 8th day of December Pitcairn's Island was proclaimed a free and independent nation; and on the same day the solemn coronation of Butterworth I., Emperor of Pitcairn's Island, took place, amid great rejoicings and festivities. The entire nation, with the exception of fourteen persons, mainly little children, marched past the throne in single file, with banners and music, the procession being upward of ninety feet long; and some said it was as much as three-quarters of a minute passing a given point. Nothing like it had ever been seen in the history of the island before. Public enthusiasm was measureless.

Now straightway imperial reforms began. Orders of nobility were instituted. A minister of the navy was appointed, and the whale-boat put in commission. A minister of war was created, and ordered to proceed at once with the formation of a standing army. A first lord of the treasury was named, and commanded to get up a taxation scheme, and also open negotiations for treaties, offensive, defensive, and commercial, with foreign powers. Some generals and admirals were appointed; also some chamberlains, some equerries in waiting, and some lords of the bedchamber.

At this point all the material was used up. The Grand Duke of Galilee, minister of war, complained that all the sixteen grown men in the empire had been given great offices, and consequently would not consent to serve in the ranks; wherefore his standing army was at a standstill. The Marquis of Ararat, minister of the navy, made a similar complaint. He said he was willing to steer the whale-boat himself, but he *must* have somebody to man her.

The emperor did the best he could in the circumstances: he took all the boys above the age of ten years away from their mothers, and pressed them into the army, thus constructing a corps of seventeen privates, officered by one lieutenant-general and two major-generals.

This pleased the minister of war, but procured the enmity of all the mothers in the land; for they said their precious ones must now find bloody graves in the fields of war, and he would be answerable for it. Some of the more heartbroken and unappeasable among them lay constantly in wait for the emperor and threw yams at him, unmindful of the body-guard.

On account of the extreme scarcity of material, it was found necessary to require the Duke of Bethany, postmaster-general, to pull stroke-oar in the navy, and thus sit in the rear of a noble of lower degree, namely, Viscount Canaan, lord justice of the common pleas. This turned the Duke of Bethany into a tolerably open malcontent and a secret conspirator—a thing which the emperor foresaw, but could not help.

Things went from bad to worse. The emperor raised Nancy Peters to the peerage on one day, and married her the next, notwithstanding, for reasons of state, the cabinet had strenuously advised him to marry Emmeline, eldest daughter of the Archbishop of Bethlehem. This caused trouble in a powerful quarter—the church. The new empress secured the support and friendship of two-thirds of the thirty-six grown women in the nation by absorbing them into her court as maids of honor; but this made deadly enemies of the remaining twelve. The families of the maids of honor soon began to rebel, because there was nobody at home to keep house. The twelve snubbed women refused to enter the imperial kitchen as servants; so the empress had to require the Countess of Jericho and other great court dames to fetch water, sweep the palace, and perform other menial and equally distasteful services. This made bad blood in that department.

Everybody fell to complaining that the taxes levied for the support of the army, the navy, and the rest of the imperial establishment were intolerably burdensome, and were reducing the nation to beggary. The emperor's reply—"Look at Germany; look at Italy. Are you better than they? and haven't you unification?"—did not satisfy them. They said, "People can't *eat* unification, and we are starving. Agriculture has ceased. Everybody is in the army, everybody is in the navy, everybody is in the public service, standing around in a uniform, with nothing whatever to do, nothing to eat, and nobody to till the fields—"

"Look at Germany; look at Italy. It is the same there. Such is unification, and there's no other way to get it—no other way to keep it after you've got it," said the poor emperor always.

But the grumblers only replied, "We can't *stand* the taxes—we can't *stand* them."

Now right on top of this the cabinet reported a national debt amounting to upward of forty-five dollars—half a dollar to every individual in the nation. And they proposed to fund something. They had heard that this was always done in such emergencies. They proposed duties on exports; also on imports. And they wanted to issue bonds; also paper money, redeemable in yams and cabbages in fifty years. They said the pay of the army and of the navy and of the whole government machine was far in arrears, and unless something was done, and done immediately, national bankruptcy must ensue, and possibly insurrection and revolution. The emperor at once resolved upon a high-handed measure, and one of a nature never before heard of in Pitcairn's Island. He went in state to the church on Sunday morning, with the army at his back, and commanded the minister of the treasury to take up a collection.

That was the feather than broke the camel's back. First one citizen, and then another, rose and refused to submit to this unheard-of outrage—and each refusal was followed by the immediate confiscation of the malcontent's property. This vigor soon stopped the refusals, and the collection proceeded amid a sullen and ominous silence. As the emperor withdrew with the troops, he said, "I will teach you who is master here." Several persons shouted, "Down with unification!" They were at once arrested and torn from the arms of their weeping friends by the soldiery.

But in the mean time, as any prophet might have foreseen, a Social Democrat had been developed. As the emperor stepped into the gilded imperial wheelbarrow at the church door, the social democrat stabbed at him fifteen or sixteen times with a harpoon, but fortunately with such a peculiarly social democratic unprecision of aim as to do no damage.

That very night the convulsion came. The nation rose as one man—though forty-nine of the revolutionists were of the other sex. The infantry threw down their pitchforks; the artillery cast aside their cocoanuts; the navy revolted; the emperor was seized, and bound hand and foot in his palace. He was very much depressed. He said:

"I freed you from a grinding tyranny; I lifted you up out of your degradation, and made you a nation among nations; I gave you a strong, compact, centralized government; and, more than all, I gave you the blessing of blessings—unification. I have done all this, and my reward is hatred, insult, and these bonds. Take me; do with me as you will. I here resign my crown and all my dignities, and gladly do I release myself from their too heavy burden. For your sake I took them up; for your sake I lay them down. The imperial jewel is no more; now bruise and defile as ye will the useless setting."

By a unanimous voice the people condemned the ex-emperor and the social democrat to perpetual banishment from church services, or to perpetual labor as galley-slaves in the whale-boat—whichever they might prefer. The next day the nation assembled again, and rehoisted the British flag, reinstated the British tyranny, reduced the nobility to the condition of commoners again, and then straightway turned their diligent attention to the weeding of the ruined and neglected yam patches, and the rehabilitation of the old useful industries and the old healing and solacing pieties. The ex-emperor restored the lost trespass law, and explained that he had stolen it—not to injure any one, but to further his political projects. Therefore the nation gave the late chief magistrate his office again, and also his alienated property.

Upon reflection, the ex-emperor and the social democrat chose perpetual banishment from religious services in preference to perpetual labor as galley-slaves "*with* perpetual religious services," as they phrased it; wherefore the people believed that the poor fellows' troubles had unseated their reason, and so they judged it best to confine them for the present. Which they did.

Such is the history of Pitcairn's "doubtful acquisition."

# SAMUEL L. CLEMENS

## Legend of the "Spectacular Ruin"†

\*    \*    \*

The captain of the raft, who was as full of history as he could stick, said that in the Middle Ages a most prodigious fire-breathing dragon used to live in that region, and made more trouble than a tax-collector. He was as long as a railway-train, and had the customary impenetrable green scales all over him. His breath bred pestilence and conflagration, and his appetite bred famine. He ate men and cattle impartially, and was exceedingly unpopular. The German emperor of that day made the usual offer: he would grant to the destroyer of the dragon, any one solitary thing he might ask for; for he had a surplusage of daughters, and it was customary for dragon-killers to take a daughter for pay.

So the most renowned knights came from the four corners of the earth and retired down the dragon's throat one after the other. A panic arose and spread. Heroes grew cautious. The procession ceased. The dragon became more destructive than ever. The people lost all hope of succor, and fled to the mountains for refuge.

At last Sir Wissenschaft,[1] a poor and obscure knight, out of a far country, arrived to do battle with the monster. A pitiable object he was, with his armor hanging in rags about him, and his strange-shaped knapsack strapped upon his back. Everybody turned up their noses at him, and some openly jeered him. But he was calm. He simply inquired if the emperor's offer was still in force. The emperor said it was—but charitably advised him to go and hunt hares and not en-

† From *A Tramp Abroad* (1880), Chapter 17.    1. The name means "science."

danger so precious a life as his in an attempt which had brought death to so many of the world's most illustrious heroes.

But this tramp only asked—"Were any of these heroes men of science?" This raised a laugh, of course, for science was despised in those days. But the tramp was not in the least ruffled. He said he might be a little in advance of his age, but no matter—science would come to be honored, some time or other. He said he would march against the dragon in the morning. Out of compassion, then, a decent spear was offered him, but he declined, and said, "spears were useless to men of science." They allowed him to sup in the servants' hall, and gave him a bed in the stables.

When he started forth in the morning, thousands were gathered to see. The emperor said:

"Do not be rash, take a spear, and leave off your knapsack."

But the tramp said:

"It is not a knapsack," and moved straight on.

The dragon was waiting and ready. He was breathing forth vast volumes of sulphurous smoke and lurid blasts of flame. The ragged knight stole warily to a good position, then he unslung his cylindrical knapsack—which was simply the common fire-extinguisher known to modern times—and the first chance he got he turned on his hose and shot the dragon square in the center of his cavernous mouth. Out went the fires in an instant, and the dragon curled up and died.

This man had brought brains to his aid. He had reared dragons from the egg, in his laboratory, he had watched over them like a mother, and patiently studied them and experimented upon them while they grew. Thus he had found out that fire was the life principle of a dragon; put out the dragon's fires and it could make steam no longer, and must die. He could not put out a fire with a spear, therefore he invented the extinguisher. The dragon being dead, the emperor fell on the hero's neck and said:

"Deliverer, name your request," at the same time beckoning out behind with his heel for a detachment of his daughters to form and advance. But the tramp gave them no observance. He simply said:

"My request is, that upon me be conferred the monopoly of the manufacture and sale of spectacles in Germany."

The emperor sprang aside and exclaimed:

"This transcends all the impudence I ever heard! A modest demand, by my halidome! Why didn't you ask for the imperial revenues at once, and be done with it?"

But the monarch had given his word, and he kept it. To everybody's surprise, the unselfish monopolist immediately reduced the price of spectacles to such a degree that a great and crushing burden was removed from the nation. The emperor, to commemorate this generous act, and to testify his appreciation of it, issued a decree commanding everybody to buy this benefactor's spectacles and wear them, whether they needed them or not.

So originated the wide-spread custom of wearing spectacles in Germany; and as a custom once established in these old lands is imperishable, this one remains universal in the empire to this day. Such is the legend of the monopolist's once stately and sumptuous castle, now called the "Spectacular Ruin."

\* \* \*

# SAMUEL L. CLEMENS

## The New Dynasty†

Power, when lodged in the hands of man, means oppression— *insures* oppression: it means oppression *always:* not always consciously, deliberately, purposely; not always severely, or heavily, or cruelly, or sweepingly; but *oppression*, anyway, and *always*, in one shape or another. One may say it cannot even lift its hand in kindness but it hurts somebody by the same act whereby it delivers a benevolence to his neighbor. Power cannot be so righteously placed that it will neglect to exercise its great specialty, Oppression. Give it to the King of Dahomey, and he will try his new repeating rifle on the passers-by in the courtyard; and as they fall, one after another, it hardly occurs to him or to his courtiers that he is committing an impropriety; give it to the high priest of the Christian Church in Russia, the Emperor, and with a wave of his hand he will brush a multitude of young men, nursing mothers, gray headed patriarchs, gentle young girls, like so many unconsidered flies, into the unimaginable hells of his Siberia, and go blandly to his breakfast, unconscious that he had committed a barbarity; give it to Constantine, or Edward IV, or Peter the Great, or Richard III, or a hundred other monarchs that might be mentioned, and they slaughter members of their own family, and need no opiates to help them sleep afterward; give it to Richard II, and he will win the grateful tears of a multitude of slaves by setting them free—to gain a vital point—and then laugh in their faces and tear up their emancipation papers, and promise them a bitterer and crueler slavery than ever they imagined before, the moment his point has been gained; give it to the noblesse of the Middle Ages, and they will claim and seize wandering freedmen as their serfs; and with a totally unconscious irony will put upon THEM the burden of proving that they

† Reprinted in Paul J. Carter, Jr., "Mark Twain and the American Labor Movement," *New England Quarterly*, 30 (1957), 383–88. Clemens' article was read to the Monday Evening Club, Hartford, Connecticut, March 22, 1886. Many of the attitudes expressed in *A Connecticut Yankee* are anticipated here.

are freedmen and not serfs; give it to the Church, and she will burn, flay, slay, torture, massacre, ruthlessly—and neither she nor her friends will doubt that she is doing the best she can for man and God; give it suddenly to the ignorant masses of the French monarchy, maddened by a thousand years of unspeakable tyranny, and they will drench the whole land with blood and make massacre a pastime; give power to whomsoever you please, and it will oppress; even the horse-car company will work its men eighteen hours, in Arctic cold or Equatorial heat, and pay them with starvation: and in expanded or in otherwise modified form, let the horse-car company stand for a thousand other corporations and companies and industries which might be named. Yes, you may follow it straight down, step by step, from the Emperor to the horse-car company, and wherever power resides it is used to oppress.

Now so far as we know or may guess, this has been going on for a million years. Who are the oppressors? The few: the king, the capitalist, and a handful of other overseers and superintendents. Who the oppressed? The many: The nations of the earth; the valuable personages; the workers; they that MAKE the bread that the soft-handed and the idle eat. Why is it right that there is not a fairer division of the spoil all around? BECAUSE LAWS AND CONSTITUTIONS HAVE ORDERED OTHERWISE. Then it follows that if the laws and constitutions should change around and say there SHALL be a more nearly equal division, THAT would have to be recognized as right. That is to confess, then, that in POLITICAL SOCIETIES, IT IS THE PREROGATIVE OF MIGHT TO DETERMINE WHAT IS RIGHT; that is the prerogative of Might to create Right—and uncreate it, at will. It is to confess that if the banded voters among a laboring kinship of 45,000,000 of persons shall speak out to the other 12,000,000 or 15,000,000 of a nation and command that an existing system of rights and laws be reversed, that existing system has in that moment, in an absolutely clear and clean and legal way, become an obsolete and vanishing thing—has utterly ceased to exist, and no creature in all the 15,000,000 is in the least degree privileged to find fault with the act.

We will grant, if you please, that for uncounted ages, the king and the scattering few have oppressed the nations—and have held in their hands the power to say what is right and what is not. Now was that power real, or was it a fiction? Until to-day it was real; but FROM to-day, in THIS country, I take heart of grace to believe, it is forevermore dust and ashes. For a greater than any king has arisen upon this the only soil in this world that is truly sacred to liberty; and you that have eyes to see and ears to hear may catch the sheen of his banners and the tramp of his marching hosts; and men may cavil, and sneer, and make wordy argument—but please God he will mount his throne: and he will stretch out his sceptre, and there will be bread for the hungry, clothing for the naked, and hope in eyes unused to hoping; and the sham nobilities will pass away, and the rightful lord will come to his own.

There was a time for sneering. In all the ages of the world and in all its lands, the huge inert mass of humbler mankind,—compacted crush of poor dull dumb animals,—equipped from its centre to its circumference with unimaginable might, and never suspecting it, has made bread in bitter toil and sweat, all its days for the feeble few to eat, and has impotently raged and wept by turns over its despised households of sore-hearted women and smileless children—and that was a time for sneering. And once in a generation, in all ages and all lands, a little block of this inert mass has stirred, and risen with noise, and said it could no longer endure its oppressions, its degradation, its misery—and then after a few days it has sunk back, vanquished, mute again, and laughed at—and that also was a time for sneers. And in these later decades, single mechanical trades have banded themselves together, and risen hopefully and demanded a better chance in this world's fight; and when it was the bricklayers, the other trades looked on with indifferent eye—it was not their fight; and when this or that or the other trade revolted, the ten millions in the other trades went uninterested about their own affairs—it was not their quarrel;—and that also was a time to sneer—and men did sneer. But when ALL the bricklayers, and all the bookbinders, and all the cooks, and all the barbers, and all the machinists, and all the miners, and blacksmiths, and printers, and hod-carriers, and stevedores, and housepainters, and brakemen, and engineers, and conductors, and factory hands, and horse-car drivers, and all the shop-girls, and all the sewing-women, and all the telegraph operators: in a word, all the myriad of toilers in whom is slumbering the reality of that thing which you call Power, not its age-worn sham and substanceless spectre,—when these rise, call the vast spectacle by any deluding name that will please your ear, but the fact remains, a NATION has risen! And by certain signs you may recognize it. When James Russell Lowell makes his courteous appeal for the little company of American authors before a Committee of the United States Senate—who listen as their predecessors have for sixty years listened to authors' appeals, with something of indifference due a matter of small weight intruded by a faction inconsequent and few—and sits down and his place is taken by a foreman of a printing office, clad in unpretending gray, who says "I am not here as a printer; I am not here as a brick-layer, or a mason, or a carpenter, or as any other peculiar or particular handicrafts man; but I stand here to represent ALL the trades, ALL the industries, all brethren of ANY calling that labor with their hands for their daily bread and the bread of their wives, and their little children, from Maine to the Gulf, and from the Atlantic to the Pacific; and when I speak, out of my mouth issues the voice of five millions of men!"—when THAT thunderpeal falls, it is time for the Senatorial lethargy to show sign of life, to show interest, respect—yes, reverence, supple and eager recognition of the master, and to know what might be the King's messenger's commands. And the Senators realize that indeed such time has come.

The authors had with slender hopefulness indicated what they would like the Congress to do; in the other case, without any insolence of speech or bearing, but reposeful with the clear consciousness of unassailable authority, the five-million-voiced printer DICTATED to the Congress—not anything which it MUST do, but certain things which it must NOT do. And that command will be heeded.

This was the first time in this world, perhaps, that ever a nation did actually and in its own person, not by proxy, speak. And by grace of fortune I was there to hear and see. It seemed to me that all the gauds and shows and spectacles of history somehow lost their splendor in this presence; their tinsel and lacquer and feathers seemed confessed and poor, contrasted with this real blood and flesh of majesty and greatness. And I thought then, and still think, that our country, so wastefully rich in things for her people to be proud of, had here added a thing which transcended all that went before. Here was the nation in person speaking; and its servants, *real*—not masters *called* servants by canting trick of speech—listening. The like could not be seen in any other country, or in any other age.

They whom that printer represented are in truth the nation: and they are still speaking. Have you read their Manifesto of demands? It has a curiously worn and old and threadbare sound. And it IS old. It is older than the Scriptures. It is as old as Tyranny—old as Poverty—old as Despair. It is the oldest thing in this world—being as old as the human voice. In one form or another it has wearied the ears of the fortunate and the powerful in all the years of all the ages. And always it seemed the fretful cry of children—the fretful cry of a stranger's children, not one's own—and was not listened to; and did not need to be listened to, since as a matter of course they were crying for the moon, crying for the impossible. So one thought, without listening—without examining. But when *all* the children in a little world cry, one is roused out of his indifference by the mere magnitude of the fact—and he realizes that perhaps something IS the matter; and he opens his ears. And what does he hear? Just what he has heard countless times before, as a mere dead formula of words; but now that his attention is awake, he perceives that these words have meaning. And so he—that is, you—do at last listen, do at last con the details of this rag of immemorial antiquity, this Manifesto of Wrongs and Demands, with alert senses. And straightway the thing that springs to your surprised lips when you are confronted by one or two of the things in that list, is the ejaculation, "Is it possible that so plain and manifest a piece of justice as this, is actually lacking to these men, and must be asked for?—has been lacking to them for ages, and the world's fortunate ones did not know it; or, knowing it could be indifferent to it, could endure the shame of it, the inhumanity of it?" And the thought follows in your mind, "Why this is as strange as that a famishing child should want its common right, the breast, and the mother-heart not divine it; or, divining it, turn away indifferent."

Read their Manifesto; read it in a judicial spirit, and ponder it. It impeaches certain of us of high treason against the rightful sovereign of this world; the indictment is found by a competent jury, and in no long time we must stand before the bar of the Republic and answer it. And you will assuredly find counts in it which not any logic of ours can controvert.

Many a time, when I have seen a man abusing a horse, I have wished I knew that horse's language, so that I could whisper in his ear, "Fool, you are master here, if you but knew it. Launch out with your heels!" The working millions, in all the ages, have been horses—were horses; all they needed was a capable leader to organize their strength and tell them how to use it, and they would in that moment be master. They have FOUND that leader somewhere, to-day, and they ARE master—the only time in this world that ever the true king wore the purple; the only time in this world that "By the grace of God, King" was ever uttered when it was not a lie.

And we need not fear this king. All the kings that have ruled the world heretofore were born the protectors and sympathizing friends and supporters of cliques and classes and clans of gilded idlers, selfish pap-hunters, restless schemers, troublers of the State in the interest of their private advantage. But this king is born the enemy of them that scheme and talk and do not work. He will be our permanent shield and defence against the Socialist, the Communist, the Anarchist, the tramp, and the selfish agitator for "reforms" that will beget bread and notoriety for him at cleaner men's expense; he will be our refuge and defence against these, and against all like forms of political disease, pollution, and death.

How will he use his power? *To oppress*—at first. For he is not better than the masters that went before; nor pretends to be. The only difference is, he will oppress the few; they oppressed the many; he will oppress the thousands, they oppressed the millions; but he will imprison nobody, he will massacre, burn, flay, torture, exile nobody, nor work any subject eighteen hours a day, nor starve his family. He will see to it that there is fair play, fair working hours, fair wages: and further than that, when his might has become securely massed and his authority recognized, he will not go, let us hope, and determine also to believe. He will be strenuous, firm, sometimes hard—he *must* be—for a while, till all his craftsmen be gathered into his citadel and his throne established. Until then let us be patient.

It is not long to wait; his day is close at hand: his clans are gathering, they are on their way; his bugles are sounding the call, they are answering; every week that comes and goes, sees ten thousand new crusaders swing into line and add their pulsing footfalls to the thunder-tread of his mighty battalions.

He is the most stupendous product of the highest civilization the world has ever seen—and the worthiest and the best; and in no age but this, no land but this, and no lower civilization than this, could he ever have been brought forth. The average of his genuine, practical, valuable knowledge—and knowledge is the truest right divine to power—is an education contrasted with which the education possessed by the kings and nobles who ruled him for a hundred centuries is the untaught twaddle of a nursery, and beneath contempt. The *sum* of his education, as represented in the ten thousand utterly new and delicate and exact handicrafts, and divisions and subdivisions of handicrafts, exercised by his infinite brain and multitudinous members, is a sum of knowledge compared to which the sum of human knowledge in any and all ages of the world previous to the birth-year of the eldest person here present in this room, was as a lake compared to the ocean, the foothills compared to the Alps; a sum of knowledge which makes the knowledge of the elder ages seem but ignorance and darkness; even suggests the figure of a landscape lying dim and blurred under the stars, and the same landscape revealed in its infinitude of bloom, color, variety, detail, under the noontide sun. Without his education, he had continued what he was, a slave; with it, he is what he is, a sovereign. His was a weary journey, and long: the constellations have drifted far from the anchorages which they knew in the skies when it began; but at last he is here. He is here,—and he will remain. He is the greatest birth of the greatest age the nations of this world have known. You cannot sneer at him—that time has gone by. He has before him the most righteous work that was ever given into the hand of man to do: and he will do it. Yes, he is here; and the question is not—as it has been heretofore during a thousand ages—What shall we do with him? For the first time in history we are relieved of the necessity of managing his affair for him. He is not a broken dam this time—he is the Flood!

## SAMUEL L. CLEMENS

## To Mrs. Jervis Langdon†

[York, England, July, 1873]

\* \* \* the stately city walls, the castellated gates, the ivy-grown, foliage-sheltered, most noble and picturesque ruin of St. Mary's

---

† From *Mark Twain's Letters*, ed. Albert Bigelow Paine (New York: Harper, 1917), I, 208. Mrs. Langdon was Clemens' mother-in-law. This and the following letter indicate that, as Alan Gribben (see Bibliography) has shown, Clemens knew the Arthurian material before he obtained a copy of Malory's *Morte d'Arthur* in December 1884.

Abby, suggesting *their* date, say five hundred years ago, in the heart of Crusading times and the glory of English chivalry and romance; * * * the hint here and there of King Arthur and his knights and their bloody fights with Saxon oppressors round about this old city more than thirteen hundred years gone by:* * *

## SAMUEL L. CLEMENS

### To Mrs. Cincinnatus A. Taft†

[Aug. 14, 1883]

* * *

* * * Do not tell us he [Cincinnatus Taft] shall not be himself again; nor that he must withdraw and clothe another in the semblance of his art and skill and send him in his place—for what is Sir Kay in Sir Launcelot's armor, but only Sir Kay, after all, and not Sir Launcelot?

* * *

## GEORGE WASHINGTON CABLE

### [Buying a Copy of *Morte d'Arthur*]‡

* * *

One night we were in Rochester together. It was Saturday night, and for a wonder we were without an engagement that night, so we started out for a walk; we had gone a few steps when we found a bookstore, and at the same moment it was beginning to rain. I said: "Let us go in here." He said: "I remember I have not provided myself with anything to read all day to-morrow." I said: "We will get it here. I will look down that table, and you look down this." Presently I went over to him and said I had not found anything that I thought would interest him, and asked him if he had found anything. He said no, he had not; but there was a book he did not remember any previous acquaintance with. He asked me what that book was.

"Why," I said, "that is Sir Thomas Malory's *Morte d'Arthur*." And he said: "Shall we take it?" I said: "Yes; and you will never lay it down

† From *Susy and Mark Twain*, ed. Edith Colgate Salisbury (New York: Harper & Row, 1965), p. 170. The date is given by Salisbury as August 17, but August 14 appears to be correct. The passage clearly anticipates the appearance of Sir Kay and Sir Launcelot in the early chapters of the novel.

‡ Quoted in Arlin Turner, *Mark Twain and George W. Cable* (Lansing: Michigan State University Press, 1960), pp. 135–36. Cable's remarks were originally made at a memorial service in New York City, November 30, 1910.

until you have read it from cover to cover." It was easy to make the prophecy, and, of course, it was fulfilled. He had read in it a day or two, when I saw come upon his cheekbones those vivid pink spots which every one who knew him intimately and closely knew meant that his mind was working with all its energies. I said to myself: "Ah, I think Sir Thomas Malory's *Morte d'Arthur* is going to bear fruit in the brain of Mark Twain." A year or two afterward, when he came to see me in my Northampton home, I asked him what he was engaged in, and he said he was writing a story of *A Yankee at the Court of King Arthur*. I said: "If that be so, then I claim for myself the godfathership of that book." He said: "Yes; you are its godfather." I can claim no higher honor than to have the honor to claim that here and now, to-night, and to rejoice with you that we are able to offer a tribute to our affection to the memory of Mark Twain.

# SAMUEL L. CLEMENS

## From *Mark Twain's Notebooks and Journals*†

\*   \*   \*

Dream of being a knight errant in armor in the middle ages.

Have the notions & habits of thought of the present day mixed with the necessities of that. No pockets in the armor. No way to manage certain requirements of nature. Can't scratch. Cold in the head—can't blow—can't get at handkerchief, can't use iron sleeve. Iron gets red hot in the sun—leaks in the rain, gets white with frost & freezes me solid in winter. Suffer from lice & fleas. Make disagreeable clatter when I enter church. Can't dress or undress myself. Always getting struck by lightning. Fall down, can't get up. See Morte DArthur.

\*   \*   \*

Fall of '84[1]—while Cable & I were giving readings. Cable got a Morte d'Arthur & gave it me to read. I began to make notes in my head for a book. Nov. 11 '86 I read the first chapter (all that was then written), at Governor's Island & closed the reading with an outline of the probable contents of the future book. Wrote the book (The Yankee at Arthur's Court in '87 & '88, & published it in December '89. (Shall, anyway.)

Nov. 19 '89. SL C

\*   \*   \*

† From *Mark Twain's Notebooks & Journals*, III (1883–1891), ed. Robert Pack Browning, Michael B. Frank, and Lin Salamo (Berkeley. University of California Press, 1979), 78–79, 86, 216–17, 413, 415, 420.
1. This paragraph is written vertically across the preceding one.

Have a battle between a modern army, with gatling guns—(automatic) 600 shots a minute, <with one pulling of the trigger,> torpedos, balloons, 100-ton cannon, iron-clad fleet &c & Prince de Joinville's Middle Age Crusaders.[2]

\* \* \*

Wouldn't fight the knight with a lance, "but I will just try him a whirl with a hay-fork—& I bet I'll show him that I warn't brought up on a Conneticut [sic] farm for nothing."

(Bring out as a holiday book.
Title, "The Lost Land."

First part written on ancient yellow parchment, (palimpsest) the last chapter on fresh new paper, laid, hand-made, with watermark, British arms & "1885." In palimpsest one catches remnants of monkish legends. Get them from Wm of Huntingdon.

He mourns his lost land—has come to England & revisited it, but it is all changed & become old, so old!—& it was so fresh & new, so virgin before. Winchester does not resemble Camelot, & the Round Table (has at least seen a life-size picture of the one there in James I's time (See State Trials) is not a true one.[3] Has lost all interest in life—is found dead next morning—suicide.

He is also grieving to see his sweetheart, so suddenly lost to him. Maledisant? But not Isolde. Elaine? No, she is dead. He saw her arrive.[4]

\* \* \*

Country placed under an interdict.

Why not let him arrive just as the dumb boatman arrives with Elaine's body?

\* \* \*

An excommunicated person—carry him through what he had to stand. We assist him—& here begin my troubles & long fight with the church, & my eventual defeat.

\* \* \*

I make a *peaceful* revolution & introduce advanced civilization. The Church overthrows it with a 6 year interdict.

\* \* \*

2. Jean de Joinville (c. 1224–1317) wrote an important history of the Seventh Crusade.

3. In the Great Hall at Winchester (sometimes indentified as the site of Camelot) hangs a round table thought to date from the thirteenth century. It of course has no real association with King Arthur.

4. Elaine la Blank, the fair maid of Astolat, was so in love with Launcelot that when he refused either to marry her or to become her lover she died. At her request her body was borne by boat (guided only by a mute boatman) to Arthur's court. Both Malory and Tennyson describe the incident.

The first thing I want to teach is *disloyalty* till they get used to disusing that word *loyalty* as representing virtue. This will beget independence—which is loyalty to one's best self & principles, & this is often disloyalty to the general idols & fetishes.

\* \* \*

Competition of bards. Break, break, break; the Fair Maid of Astolat; some exploit of Lancelot. (to curry favor with the Queen) from Idyls. Sensation. Hint that I was "prepared." I demand an instant competition. The bard breaks down, showing that his barbarous previous effort had been memorized. I whirl in some more Tennyson, with a touch of Shak & Browning & take the cake. King says, "Strike the lyre"—I lay him out.

## FROM THE NEW YORK *SUN* AND THE NEW YORK *HERALD*

## [The 1886 Reading at Governor's Island]†

Last night's monthly meeting of the Military Service Institution on Governor's Island was made entertaining by Mark Twain, who read a paper, the announcement of which caused the thronging of the old museum hall. Gen. W. T. Sherman and Gen. Schofield were present. Gen. James B. Fry presided.

Mr. Clemens said that that which he was about to read was part of a still uncompleted book, of which he would give the first chapter by way of explanation, and follow it with selected fragments, "or outline the rest of it in bulk, so to speak; do as the dying cowboy admonished his spiritual adviser to do, 'just leave out the details, and heave in the bottom facts.' "

Mr. Clemens's story is the autobiography of Sir Robert Smith of Camelot, one of King Arthur's knights, formerly a manufacturer of Hartford, Conn. Robert Smith says of himself:

"I am a Yankee of the Yankees, a practical man, nearly barren of sentiment or poetry. . . ." [Quotation continues, more or less as in the novel; the Yankee is captured by Sir Kay.]

---

† On November 11, 1886, at Governor's Island, in New York harbor, Clemens read to the Military Service Institute from what was to become "A Word of Explanation" and at least the first three chapters of *A Connecticut Yankee.* He also briefly outlined further events which were to occur in the novel. His title was "The War Experiences of a Connecticut Yankee at King Arthur's Court" and the Yankee was named Robert (or Bob) Smith. The text given here is a composite of "Yankee Smith of Camelot," New York *Sun,* November 12, 1886, p. 1, and "Mark Twain's Yankee Knight," New York *Herald,* November 12, 1886, p. 10. (A third account, "Mark Twain's New Lecture/A Yankee's Adventures at the Court of King Arthur," appeared in the New York *World,* November 12, 1886, p. 2.)

And so the two wander on together, and amid scenes of human life that afford the author many opportunities for quaint philosophic contrasts and dry humor, until they come to Camelot, to the court of King Arthur. Fanciful and curious are the reflections of the transposed Yankee about that place—which he at first thinks must be the asylum—in its country of soft, reposeful summer landscape, as lovely as a dream and lonesome as Sunday; where the air was full of the smell of flowers and the buzzing of insects and the twittering of birds, and there were no people or wagons or life or anything going on.

Very vividly he portrays the scene at Camelot, where King Arthur, with his knights, sits at a round table as big as a circus ring, and 300 dogs fight for bones around them, while the musicians are in one gallery high aloft and the ladies in another. But before he gets in there he seeks information from a plain-looking man, in the outer court, saying to him," 'Now my friend, do me a kindness. . . .' [Quotation continues, as in Chapter Two of the novel.] I shall never see my friends again—never see my friends any more: they won't be born for as much as a thousand years."

The speaker had often been interrupted by laughter, but at the originality and fun of that conceit his auditors laughed until they cried, and kept on laughing with renewed outbursts over and over again. How the cute Yankee determined to get at the bottom facts about the year by watching for a total eclipse of the sun that he remembered the almanac of 1884 had spoken of as having occurred in 528, will have to be learned from the book when it appears.

"I made up my mind to two things. . . . [Quotation continues, as in Chapter Two.] 'Clarence, if your name should happen to be Clarence, what's the name of that duck, that galoot [in the novel the word is "apparition"], who brought me here?' "

The galoot turned out to be Sir Kay, the Seneschal. In the natural course of the story came the charming description of the interior of King Arthur's castle, leading up to a royally funny account of the competitive lying of the gallant knights about their feats at arms. The transposed Smith looked upon the knights as a sort of "white Indians," admired their bigness and their simplicity, and eventually concluded:

"There didn't seem to be brains enough in the entire nursery to bait a fishhook. . . ." [Quotation continues, as in Chapter Three of the novel.]

Everybody goes to sleep when Merlin reels off that same old story about Excalibur. Guinevere makes eyes at Launcelot in a way that would have got him shot in Arkansas. King Arthur orders the Yankee to go to some unknown place not down in any map, capture a castle, kill the colossal saucer-eyed ogre who owned it, and release sixty royal princesses. Of course he went, but he reflected:

"Well, of all the damn contracts this is the boss. Why, I offered to sublet it to Sir Launcelot at ninety days and no margin. But no, he'd got a better thing to do—a whole menagerie of giants and a Vassar College full of jugged princesses. Lots of princesses this year, and all of 'em in trouble. Go and lick the ogre and set loose his summer boarders, hey? Not if I can compromise with him. Never saw such a bull-headed lot as these Round Table knights. They never think of doing anything by strategy. All they know is to fight. They haven't any brains. I asked Sir Galahad to lend me a map, so as I could locate the ogre's castle. He thought it was something to eat. These Round Table duffers are nothing but grown up children."

Sir Bob Smith dons his armor—his "boiler iron straight jacket"— and sallies forth. The sun warmed it up like any other stove, and presently he felt that if he couldn't get out he'd drown in his own sweat, and as he jolted along on his horse it sounded like a heavy tray of dishes falling down cellar. "It may not be delicate to say it," said Sir Bob, "but the Lord has so made us that when we perspire we want to scratch, and the more we can't scratch, the more we want to." He suffers untold torture because he wants to scratch his back, his head, his leg, his arm, his foot, and he can't move in his iron suit. He'd give a million—or his note for it—if he could only scratch. A thunder storm comes up and he is scared because he thinks that he is nothing but a perambulating lightning rod. The rain comes in through the joints of his boiler iron, and he wants to trade his lance for an umbrella.

He finally comes to the conclusion that a hardware suit is N.G. and that without it he can dodge around and tucker out any duffer in armor, lasso him and yank him in. So he arms himself with a lasso. He doesn't tackle the ogre, but goes back and tells a majestic lie about it like the rest of the Knights, and the King thinks it's all right and that he has sent to their homes the released princesses, C.O.D. He easily discounts the simple Knights of the Round Table in lying about his achievements, showing what an educated nineteenth century man can do in the lofty realms of that art, and becomes a favorite of the King and finally the boss of the kingdom.

He took a contract from King Arthur to kill off, at one of the great tournaments, fifteen kings and many acres of hostile armored knights. When, lance in rest they charge by squadrons upon him, he behind the protection of a barbed wire fence charged with electricity mowed them down with Gatling guns that he had made for the occasion. He found that the "education of the nineteenth century is plenty good enough capital to go into business in the sixth century with," and the next year he was running the kingdom all by himself on a moderate royalty of forty per cent.

He spoiled the ogre business; cleared out the fuss and flummery of romance and put King Arthur's kingdom on a strictly business basis. Inside of three and a half years the improvement was complete.

Cast-iron clothes had gone out of fashion. Sir Launcelot was running a kind of Louisiana lottery. The search for the Holy Grail had been given up for a hunt for the Northwest Passage. King Arthur's 140 illustrious Knights had turned themselves into a stock Board, and a seat at the Round Table was worth $30,000.

# SAMUEL L. CLEMENS

## Letters about *A Connecticut Yankee*

### To Mary Mason Fairbanks†

Hartford Nov. 16/86.

Dear Mother Fairbanks:

The story isn't a satire peculiarly, it is more especially a *contrast*. It merely exhibits under high lights, the daily life of the [imaginary Arthurian] time & that of to-day; & necessarily the bringing them into this immediate juxtaposition emphasizes the salients of both. Only two or three chapters of the book have been written, thus far. I expect to write three chapters a year for thirty years; then the book will be done. I am writing it for posterity only; my posterity: my great grand-children. It is to be my holiday amusement for six days every summer the rest of my life. Of course I do not expect to publish it; nor indeed any other book—though I fully expect to write one other book besides this one; two others, in fact, if one's autobiography may be called a book—in fact mine will be nearer a library.

Of course in my story I shall leave unsmirched & unbelittled the great & beautiful *characters* drawn by the master hand of old Malory (if he drew them—at any rate he gave them to *us*)—I am only after the *life* of that day, that is all: to picture it; to try to get into it; to see how it feels & seems. I shall hope that under my hand Sir Galahad will still remain the divinest spectre that one glimpses among the mists & twilights of Dreamland across the wastes of the centuries; & Arthur keep his sweetness & his purity, and Launcelot abide & continue "the kindest man that ever strake the sword," yet "the sternest knight to his mortal foe that ever put spear in the rest;"[1] & I should grieve indeed if the final disruption of the Round Table, & the extinction of its old tender & gracious friendships, & that last battle—the Battle of the

---

† From *Mark Twain to Mrs. Fairbanks*, ed. Dixon Wecter (San Marino, Calif.: Huntington Library, 1949), pp. 257–58.
1. Clemens is quoting the speech of Sir Ector de Maris over the body of Launcelot in Malory, XXI. xiii. In his eulogy of General Grant re-ported in the *Hartford Courant*, July 24, 1885, Clemens quotes at length from this passage, praising its "noble and simple eloquence" and declaring it unequalled until Lincoln's Gettysburg Address.

Broken Hearts, it might be called—should lose their pathos & their tears through my handling.

\* \* \*

### To Charles L. Webster†

Elmira
3 August 1887

\* \* \*

\* \* \* If the canvassing book can with *certainty* be gotten ready and distributed by the 12th or 15th of September, let me know, for I want relief of mind; the fun, which was abounding in the Yankee at Arthur's Court up to three days ago, has slumped into funereal seriousness, and this will not do—it will not answer at all. The very title of the book requires fun, and it must be furnished. But it can't be done, I see, while this cloud hangs over the workshop.

\* \* \*

### To Theodore Crane‡

*Friday, October 5, 1888.*
\* \* \* I began here Monday morning, and have done eighty pages since. I was so tired last night that I thought I would lie abed and rest to-day; but I couldn't resist. I mean to try to knock off to-morrow, but it's doubtful if I do. I want to finish the day the machine finishes, and a week ago the closest calculations for that indicated Oct. 22—but experience teaches me that the calculations will miss fire as usual.

\* \* \*

### From Edmund Clarence Stedman*

To S. L. Clemens.

July 7, 1889.
Yes, I read your "Connecticut Yankee at King Arthur's Court," last week—i.e., as soon as the package came to me—and didn't need any stimulus, either. Fact is, I went through it in two evenings with great wonderment and satisfaction—as completely out of my present world

† From *Mark Twain's Letters to His Publishers,* ed. Hamlin Hill (Berkeley: University of California Press, 1967), pp. 221–22.

‡ From Albert Bigelow Paine, *Mark Twain: A Biography* (New York: Harper, 1912), pp. 874–75. Crane was the husband of Livy Clemens' adopted sister. The "machine" is the Paige typesetter, on which Clemens had spent a great deal of money.

* From *Life and Letters of Edmund Clarence Stedman* (New York: Moffat, Yard, 1910), II, 370–72. Clemens had sent a now-lost typescript of the novel to Stedman; consequently, the page numbers he cites are not those of the first edition or of the existing manuscript.

and its toils and troubles, as I was when I first read the "Arabian Nights." *Then* I was a boy of ten years, a Connecticut Yankee in the Court of Haroun al Raschid. There were two deaths in Old Judge Stedman's, my great-uncle's, house,—at Norwich, where I was "raised,"—and they had to filch and hide the "Arabian Nights" to make me wash up and go to the funerals.

After living out of the real world with you, for two nights, I had to go to the Chinese Theatre on the third, where I found equally unusual entertainment, and so let myself down easily to every-day life.

My belief is, on the whole, that you have written a great book, in some respects your most original, most imaginative,—certainly the most effective and sustained. It isn't so learned and pedantic as "Pantagruel" and it doesn't need to be—but why it should not be preserved, somewhat as Rabelais' work has been, even in this age of endless bookmaking by "Type-Setters and Distributors," is more than I can see. Whether the ordinary critical reader will take in its *real* claims to *importance*, is a serious question. But here and there somebody will, and that somebody, soon or late, will open the senses of the dullards.

To some extent, this manuscript is an extension of the text called "The Prince and the Pauper"—and perhaps 'twould not have been written, or not written as well, but for that pioneer. . . . The little book was checkers: this is chess.

*Some* blasted fool will surely jump up and say that Cervantes polished off Chivalry centuries ago, etc. After a time he'll discover, perhaps, that you are going at the *still existing* radical principles or fallacies which made "chivalry" possible once, and servility and flunkeyism and tyranny possible now.

However, I am most impressed by the magnificently riotous and rollicking imagination and humor and often poetry, of the whole work. You have let your whole nature loose in it at the prime of your powers. Of course, when *you* let yourself loose, 'tis somewhat like a stallion just out of the paddock, but 'tis remarkable how finished, and in what good taste, your whole work—considering the theme and its possibilities—is. There is scarcely anything which I wished to change—in so long a book one finds a few matters *out of tone*, and to these I now refer you—fearlessly, in spite of your just anathemas scored against the typewriter. If you don't like it you may lump it!

I have handed, then, to Mr. Hall, the following notes, *all* I cared to make (after very close and hostile reading):

I. Sir Thomas Malory—*not Mallory.*

Page 34 (line 7) "*at myself*"(?)

Pages 34, 119, 120—"*soil a sewer*"—"*sewer*," "*try soap on a sewer*," etc. The illustration is poor and commonplace, the word offensive, the image not happily chosen. Unworthy of the writer. Too superlative—hence *ineffective*.

P. 127, etc., I presume you have thoroughly foreseen and are ready to meet, the holy horror of the Church in general, and the "Protestant Episcopal Church" in particular, at this and other matters here and there. You yourself bear down on the *dull persistency* with which both the oppressors and the oppressed stick to their systems. No matter how elevated your aim, how inoffensive your general meaning, the Church will say: Our title, like a lady's name, shouldn't be made free with, etc. There will be various rows and rumpuses, but these, as I understand it, you calculate upon,—and will not lose your head, or try to explain, or *get mad over public stupidity?*

P. 139, "damned and welcome for all I care" a trifle out of tone for a Brother Jonathan.

P. 183, The peculiar early-manner—of Mark Twain-ish exaggeration, first half of this page is *out of keeping*, and mars the *vraisemblance.*

. . . . . . . . . . .

P. 222, You have *queried* this page, but there is nothing on it which I object to in the least.

Pp. 383–84, It seems to me that a good deal of this *technical* humor (as I should call it) is rather a failure, and might be rewritten to advantage. The 4,000,000-lbs.-of-meat calculation is a lapse towards your very early manner. 'Tis important to be *in keeping*, near the climax and end of the book.

Nothing can be finer than the chapter where the Yankee Knight at Arms, in his new suit of mail, starts forth with the Damosel. Poetry and prose, by turns, and perfect as a whole. The entire story is managed with great skill, so as to seem quite possible, even probable, throughout. Personally, I have no doubt of its absolute truth as a narrative.

I suppose the *sale* of this unusual book will depend somewhat on the "working capacity" of your firm. But it will make a great noise, at all events, if sent to every prominent critical journal and newspaper here and in Great Britain.

### To William Dean Howells†

Elmira, N.Y., Aug. 5/89.

Dear Howells:

Mrs. Clemens will not listen to reason, or argument; or supplication: I've *got* to get you to read the book. I have stood the pelting for all

† From *Mark Twain–Howells Letters*, ed. Henry Nash Smith and William M. Gibson (Cambridge: Harvard University Press, 1960), I, 608–609, 610–11, 613, 621, 624–25. As early as January 18, 1886, Howells had written Clemens: "That notion of yours about the Hartford man waking up in King Arthur's time is capital. There is a great chance in it" (I, 550).

these months; but I am only human, & I am tuckered out. I have stood between you & this sorrow with a steadfastness which there is none but me to admire; but I admire it. I wouldn't have done it for another man; & I can never do it again, even for you, for I am permanently debilitated.

But you will not have to take it at a bite. I will spread it thin, & leave resting-spells all along. The proofs, thoroughly corrected, & then revised & re-corrected, shall go to you as revises, from time to time, from the office in New York.

If Mrs. Clemens could have sat down & read the book herself, I could have got you off, maybe, but she has not had an hour's use of her eyes for reading since she had the pink-eye six months ago. So she is afraid I have left coarsenesses which ought to be rooted out, & blasts of opinion which are so strongly worded as to repel instead of persuade. I hardly think so. I dug out many darlings of these sorts, & throttled them, with grief; then Steadman [sic] went through the book & marked for the grave all that *he* could find, & I sacrificed them, every one. So you see your work has been lightened for you the best I could. Now then, God be with you!

Yours Ever

Mark.

Elmira, Aug. 24/89.

Dear Howells:

If you should be moved to speak of my book in The Study, I shall be glad & proud—& the sooner it gets in, the better for the book; though I don't suppose you *can* get it in earlier than the November number— why, no, you can't get it in till a month later than that. Well, anyway I don't think I'll send out any other press copy—except perhaps to Stedman. I'm not writing for those parties who miscal themselves critics, & I don't care to have them paw the book at all. It's my swan-song, my retirement from literature permanently, & I wish to pass to the cemetery unclodded.

I judge that the proofs have begun to reach you about this time, as I had some (though not revises), this morning. I'm sure I'm going to be charmed with Beard's pictures. Observe his nice take-off of Middle-Age art—dinner-table scene.[1]

Ys sincerely

Mark

Hartford, Sept. 22/89.

Dear Howells:

It is immensely good of you to grind through that stuff for me; but it gives peace to Mrs. Clemens's soul, & I am as grateful to you as a body can be.

1. Clemens is referring to Beard's illustration captioned "The Round Table," which appeared between Chapters I and II.

I am glad you approve of what I say about the French Revolution. Few people will. It is odd that even to this day Americans still observe that immortal benefaction through English & other monarchical eyes, & have no shred of an opinion about it that they didn't get at second hand. Next to the 4th of July & its results, it was the noblest & the holiest thing & the most precious that ever happened in this earth. And its gracious work is not done yet—nor anywhere in the remote neighborhood of it.

Don't trouble to send me all the proofs; send me the pages with your corrections on them, & waste-basket the rest.

We issue the book Dec. 10; consequently a notice that appears Dec. 20 will be just in good time.

I am waiting to see your Study set a fashion in criticism. When that happens—as please God it must—consider that if you lived three centuries you couldn't do a more valuable work for this country, or a humaner. As a rule a critic's dissent merely enrages, & so does no good; but by the new art which you use, your dissent must be as welcome as your approval, & as valuable. I do not know what the secret of it is, unless it is your attitude—man courteously reasoning with man & brother, in place of the worn & wearisome critical attitude of all this long time—superior being lecturing a boy.

Well, my book is written—let it go. But if it were only to write over again there wouldn't be so many things left out. They burn in me; & they keep multiplying & multiplying; but now they can't ever be said. And besides, they would require a library—& a pen warmed-up in hell.

Ys Ever

Mark.

[Hartford] Nov. 22/89.

Dear Howells:

These are immense days! Republics & rumors of republics, from everywhere in the earth. There'll be plenty to sneer & depreciate & disenthuse—on the other hand, whoso can lift a word of the other sort, in the name of God let him pipe up! I want to print some extracts from the Yankee that have in them this new (sweet) breath of republics. It is not that I wish to advertise my book, but that I want the book to speak now when there's a listening audience, alert & curious to hear—& try to make that audience hear with profit.

*   *   *

Hartford, Dec. 23/89.

Dear Howells:

The magazine came last night, & the Study notice[2] is just great. The satisfaction it affords me could not be more prodigious if the book

<hr/>

2. Howells' review of A *Connecticut Yankee* was published in his "Editor's Study" section of *Harper's Magazine* for January 1890. It is reprinted in this volume.

deserved every word of it; & maybe it does; I hope it does, though of course I can't realize it & believe it. But I am your grateful servant, anyway & always.

\* \* \*

## To Sylvester Baxter†

[Nov. 20, 1889]

Dear Mr. Baxter,—Another throne has gone down, and I swim in oceans of satisfaction. I wish I might live fifty years longer; I believe I should see the thrones of Europe selling at auction for old iron. I believe I should really see the end of what is surely the grotesquest of all the swindles ever invented by man—monarchy. It is enough to make a graven image laugh, to see apparently rational people, away down here in this wholesome and merciless slaughter-day for shams, still mouthing empty reverence for those moss-backed frauds and scoundrelisms, hereditary kingship and so-called "nobility." It is enough to make the monarchs and nobles themselves laugh—and in private they do; there can be no question about that. I think there is only one funnier thing, and that is the spectacle of these bastard Americans—these Hamersleys and Huntingtons and such—offering cash, encumbered by themselves, for rotten carcases and stolen titles. When our great brethren the disenslaved Brazilians frame their Declaration of Independence, I hope they will insert this missing link; "We hold these truths to be self-evident: that all monarchs are usurpers, and descendants of usurpers; for the reason that no throne was ever set up in this world by the will, freely exercised, of the only body possessing the legitimate right to set it up—the numerical mass of the nation."

You already have the advance sheets of my forthcoming book in your hands. If you will turn to about the five hundredth page, you will find a state paper of my Connecticut Yankee in which he announces the dissolution of King Arthur's monarchy and proclaims the English Republic. Compare it with the state paper which announces the downfall of the Brazilian monarchy and proclaims the Republic of the United States of Brazil, and stand by to defend the Yankee from plagiarism. There is merely a resemblance of ideas, nothing more. The Yankee's proclamation was already in print a week ago. This is merely one of those odd coincidences which are always turning up. Come, protect the Yank from that cheapest and easiest of all charges—plagiarism. Otherwise, you see, he will have to protect himself by charging approximate and indefinite plagiarism upon the official servants of our majestic twin down yonder, and then there

† From *Mark Twain's Letters*, ed. Albert Bigelow Paine (New York: Harper, 1917), I, 519–21. Baxter reviewed *A Connecticut Yankee* very favorably in the *Boston Herald* on December 15. His review is reprinted in this volume.

might be war, or some similar annoyance.

Have you noticed the rumor that the Portuguese throne is unsteady, and that the Portuguese slaves are getting restive? Also, that the head slave-driver of Europe, Alexander III, has so reduced his usual monthly order for chains that the Russian foundries are running on only half time now? Also that other rumor that English nobility aquired an added stench the other day—and had to ship it to India and the continent because there wasn't any more room for it at home? Things are working. By and by there is going to be an emigration, may be. Of course we shall make no preparation; we never do. In a few years from now we shall have nothing but played-out kings and dukes on the police, and driving the horse-cars, and whitewashing fences, and in fact overcrowding all the avenues of unskilled labor; and then we shall wish, when it is too late, that we had taken common and reasonable precautions and drowned them at Castle Garden.

### To Clara Clemens†

[July 20, 1890]

* * * It's a secret that isn't to be breathed outside of the family—the new play, the Yankee in Arthur's Court, has bored the very soul out of me. Four level hours I listened, today, in misery. Taylor has made a rattling, stirring, & spectacular, & perhaps taking play, & has shown dramatic talent & training; *but* his handling of archaic English is as ignorant & dreadful as poor Mrs. Richardson's[1]; & he has captured but one side of the Yankee's character—his rude animal side, his circus side; the good heart & the high intent are left out of him; he is a mere boisterous clown, & oozes slang from every pore. I told Taylor he had degraded a natural gentleman to a low-down blackguard. He thinks he can modify him & refine him—but I doubt it. However, the awful ordeal is over & Taylor is gone. He is a very old friend of mine, & a good fellow; so I was careful to say nothing harsh about his work; but if he had been a stranger I should have said things that would have hurt. This is the very last play that I ever mean to have anything to do with.

\* \* \*

### To Clara Clemens Gabrilowitsch‡

Hamilton [Bermuda], March 10 [1910]

\* \* \*

† From *The Love Letters of Mark Twain*, ed. Dixon Wecter (New York: Harper, 1949), pp. 257–58.
1. Abby Sage Richardson's dramatization of *The Prince and the Pauper* was a distinct failure.

‡ Reprinted in Clara Clemens [Gabrilowitsch], *My Father, Mark Twain* (New York: Harper, 1931), p. 289. Clemens must have meant twenty rather than thirty years, since only twenty-one years had passed since the novel's publication.

Yesterday I read "A Connecticut Yankee at [sic] King Arthur's Court" for the first time in more than 30 years. I am prodigiously pleased with it—a most gratifying surprise.

# SAMUEL L. CLEMENS

## From *The Autobiography of Mark Twain*†

\* \* \*

A *Connecticut Yankee in King Arthur's Court* was an attempt to imagine, and after a fashion set forth, the hard conditions of life for the laboring and defenseless poor in bygone times in England, and incidentally contrast these conditions with those under which the civil and ecclesiastical pets of privilege and high fortune lived in those times. I think I was purposing to contrast that English life, not just the English life of Arthur's day but the English life of the whole of the Middle Ages, with the life of modern Christendom and modern civilization—to the advantage of the latter, of course. That advantage is still claimable and does creditably and handsomely exist everywhere in Christendom—if we leave out Russia and the royal palace of Belgium.

The royal palace of Belgium is still what it has been for fourteen years, the den of a wild beast, King Leopold II, who for money's sake mutilates, murders and starves half a million of friendless and helpless poor natives in the Congo State every year, and does it by the silent consent of all the Christian powers except England, none of them lifting a hand or a voice to stop these atrocities, although thirteen of them are by solemn treaty pledged to the protecting and uplifting of those wretched natives. In fourteen years Leopold has deliberately destroyed more lives than have suffered death on all the battlefields of this planet for the past thousand years. In this vast statement I am well within the mark, several millions of lives within the mark. It is curious that the most advanced and most enlightened century of all the centuries the sun has looked upon should have the ghastly distinction of having produced this moldy and piety-mouthing hypocrite, this bloody monster whose mate is not findable in human history anywhere, and whose personality will surely shame hell itself when he arrives there—which will be soon, let us hope and trust.

The conditions under which the poor lived in the Middle Ages were hard enough, but those conditions were heaven itself as compared with those which have obtained in the Congo State for these past

† From *The Autobiography of Mark Twain*, ed. Charles Neider (New York: Harper, 1959), pp. 271–72. The passage was written or dictated December 5, 1906.

fourteen years. I have mentioned Russia. Cruel and pitiful as was life throughout Christendom in the Middle Ages, it was not as cruel, not as pitiful, as is life in Russia today. In Russia for three centuries the vast population has been ground under the heels, and for the sole and sordid advantage of a procession of crowned assassins and robbers who have all deserved the gallows. Russia's hundred and thirty millions of miserable subjects are much worse off today than were the poor of the Middle Ages whom we so pity. We are accustomed now to speak of Russia as medieval and as standing still in the Middle Ages, but that is flattery. Russia is way back of the Middle Ages; the Middle Ages are a long way in front of her and she is not likely to catch up with them so long as the Czardom continues to exist.

# SAMUEL L. CLEMENS

## [A Rejected Preface]†

My object has been to group together some of the most odious laws which have had vogue in the Christian countries within the past eight or ten centuries, and illustrate them by the incidents of a story.

There was never a time when America applied the death-penalty to more than fourteen crimes. But England, within the memory of men still living, had in her list of crimes 223 which were punishable by death! And yet from the beginning of our existence down to a time within the memory of babes England has distressed herself piteously over the ungentleness of our Connecticut Blue Laws. Those Blue Laws should have been spared English criticism for two reasons:

1. They were so insipidly mild, by contrast with the bloody and atrocious laws of England of the same period, as to seem characterless and colorless when one brings them into that awful presence.

2. *The Blue Laws never had any existence.* They were the fancy-work of an English clergyman; they were never a part of any statute-book. And yet they could have been made to serve a useful and merciful purpose; if they had been injected into the English law the dilution would have given to the whole a less lurid aspect; or, to figure the effect in another way, they would have been coca mixed into vitriol.

I have drawn no laws and no illustrations from the twin civilizations of hell and Russia. To have entered into that atmosphere would have defeated my purpose, which was to show a great and genuine progress

---

† From Albert Bigelow Paine, *Mark Twain: A Biography* (New York: Harper, 1912), pp. 1656–57. This and two other draft prefaces were written by Clemens in 1888–89 but were not included in the novel. All three appear in Bernard Stein's edition (Berkeley: University of California Press, 1979), pp. 516–18.

in Christendom in these few later generations toward mercifulness—a wide and general relaxing of the grip of the law. Russia had to be left out because exile to Siberia remains, and in that single punishment is gathered together and concentrated all the bitter inventions of all the black ages for the infliction of suffering upon human beings. Exile for life from one's hearthstone and one's idols—this is rack, thumb-screw, the water-drop, fagot and stake, tearing asunder by horses, flaying alive—all these in one; and not compact into hours, but drawn out into years, each year a century, and the whole a mortal immortality of torture and despair. While exile to Siberia remains one will be obliged to admit that there is one country in Christendom where the punishments of all the ages are still preserved and still inflicted, that there is one country in Christendom where no advance has been made toward modifying the medieval penalties for offenses against society and the State.

# The Dan Beard Illustrations

## DANIEL CARTER BEARD

### [Making the Illustrations for A Connecticut Yankee]†

\* \* \*

Mr Fred Hall, Mark Twain's partner in the publishing business, came to my studio in the old Judge Building and told me that Mark Twain wanted to meet the man who had made the illustrations for a Chinese story in the *Cosmopolitan*[1] and he wanted that man to illustrate his new book, *A Connecticut Yankee in King Arthur's Court*. The manuscript was sent to me to read. I read it through three times with great enjoyment. Then I met Mr Clemens by appointment in his little office on Fourteenth Street, not far from the corner of Fifth Avenue.

Fourteenth Street was then the abode of artists, writers and illustrators, whose studios seemed to be the pioneer fringe which pushed ahead of the business houses as they moved uptown. There was no elevator in this building. When I climbed to Mark Twain's office, if I was a little short of breath, it was not from the exercise so much as the awe I felt in the presence of a man who stood so high in my esteem. I stood before this shaggy-headed man, first on one foot and then on the other, not knowing how to open the conversation. He did not rise but turned his head slowly toward me, drawling, "Sit down. "In regard to the illustrations you are to make," he said, "I only want to say this. If a man comes to me and wants me to write a story, I will write one for him; but if he comes to me and wants me to write a story and then tells me what to write, I say, 'Damn you, go hire a typewriter,' " meaning a stenographer. In saying this, he did not blow the smoke from his mouth, but it seemed to roll out slowly like round, bulbous clouds, in perfect rhythm with his words, with which the smoke was so intimately connected that I remember it as if what he said were vocalized cumulus clouds of tobacco smoke. If the building had been burning down it would not have hurried him a bit. He would have leisurely arose and, while complaining of the interruption, just as leisurely have found his way downstairs.

† From Dan Beard's autobiography, *Hardly a Man Is Now Alive* (New York: Doubleday, Doran, 1939), pp. 336–38.

1. "Wu Chih Tien, The Celestial Empress," in the March 1889 *Cosmopolitan*.

In making the illustrations for his book I referred to a collection of photographs of people of note. When I wanted a face or a figure to fit a character in the story I looked over this collection of photographs and made free use of them, not as caricatures or portraits of the people themselves, but for the dress, pose, or their whole figure and features as best fitted the character I was to depict. The captain of our boat club, holding a halberd in his hand, posed for one of the initial letters as a sentry dressed with a sealskin. For the Yankee himself I used George Morrison, a real Connecticut Yankee who was experimenting in a photoengraving establishment adjoining my studio. The charming actress Annie Russell appears in the pages as Sandy, the heroine. Sarah Bernhardt is there as a page. In fact no one held too lofty a position to escape my notice if I thought he or she possessed the face or figure suited to the character I wished to draw.[2] I had more fun making the drawings for that book than any other book I ever illustrated.

I made about four hundred illustrations[3] in seventy working days. The first illustration was that of a knight with lance set charging on the Yankee, who was climbing a tree. This pleased Mr Clemens very greatly. In the corner of the illustration there is a helmet as a sort of decoration with the visor partly open, of which Mark said, "The smile on that helmet is a source of perennial joy to me." When I finished the book he wrote:

DEAR MR BEARD—
   Hold me under everlasting obligations. There are a hundred artists who could have illustrated any other of my books, but only one who could illustrate this one. It was a lucky day I went netting for lightning bugs and caught a meteor. Live forever.[4]

Sad to say, the illustrations which so pleased Mark Twain and delighted people all over the world grievously offended some big advertisers. The offending illustrations were removed from further editions. Not only did the book feel the force of the displeasure of this group, but it is significant that after its publication Mark Twain was ruined financially and my work was boycotted for many years by all the prominent magazines, with the exception of *Life* and *Cosmopolitan*. I, too, went practically broke, but Mark Twain died a wealthy man and I lived to find my work in great demand.

\*     \*     \*

2. Among other notables appearing in the illustrations: Alfred, Lord Tennyson (as Merlin); the Price of Wales, later Edward VII; his son the Duke of Clarence; Kaiser Wilhelm of Germany; and the financier Jay Gould (as the slave driver).

3. Apparently an exaggerated figure. There were 220 illustrations in the first edition.
4. The text of this letter, dated November 11, 1889, varies in some respects from Beard's version.

## DANIEL CARTER BEARD

### [The Character of the Yankee]†

"Now," he [Clemens] said, "Mr. Beard, you know the character of the Yankee. He is a common, uneducated man. He's a good telegraph operator; he can make a Colt's revolver or Remington gun—but he's a perfect ignoramus. He's a good foreman for a manufacturer, can survey land and run a locomotive; in other words he has neither the refinement nor the weakness of a college education. In conclusion I want to say that I have endeavored to put in all the coarseness and vulgarity into the Yankee in King Arthur's Court that is necessary and rely upon you for all the refinement and delicacy of humor your facile pen can depict."

## SAMUEL L. CLEMENS

### To Dan Beard‡

Elmira, N.Y., Aug. 28, '89

My Dear Mr. Beard:

I have examined the pictures a good many times, and my pleasure in them is as strong and fresh as ever. I do not know of any quality they lack. Grace, dignity, poetry, spirit, imagination, these enrich them and make them charming and beautiful; and wherever humor appears it is high and fine, easy, unforced, kept under mastery, and is delicious.

You have expressed the King as I wanted him expressed; both face and figure are noble and gracious, and set forth the man's character with a satisfying eloquence. And he is clothed as he should be clothed—it was a proper subject for the dainty workmanship of the pencil. You have made a darling of a Guenevere, and the architectural setting adds effect to her soft young grace and beauty. I like the Yankee every time. You have got him down fine where he is naked in the dungeon, supporting the initial letter.

I enjoy the humor of the sky-towering monster (the fineness of the work, too) and of the interview between the Yankee and the page in the dungeon, and the Yankee's opening adventure with Sir Kay—enjoy it exceedingly; and there is something about the smile of that helmet in

† Quoted in "Mark Twain, the Man, as Dan Beard Knew," *San Francisco Examiner*, April 25, 1910, p. 16.

‡ From Cyril Clemens, "Unpublished Letters to Dan Beard," *Mark Twain Quarterly*, 7, ii (1945), 22.

the left foreground of the latter which is a perpetual delight to me. I could go into much further detail without saying all my say and expressing all my pleasure—but what I mainly wanted to put on paper was the fact that I appreciate the pictures and hold myself your obliged servant.

Yours Sincerely,

S. L. Clemens.

## SAMUEL L. CLEMENS

### To a Reader†

Dec. 20, 1889

Dear Sir:

I should not be able to tell you anything about the picture, as I did not make it or suggest it. You will have to apply to its author, Mr. Dan Beard, "Judge" Building, New York. He illustrated the book throughout without requiring or needing anybody's suggestions; and to my mind the illustrations are better than the book—which is a good deal for me to say, I reckon. I merely approved of the pictures—and very heartily, too, the slave-driver along with the rest.

S. L. Clemens.

## HENRY NASH SMITH

### [Beard's Illustrations]‡

\* \* \*

\* \* \* The supposed bearing of the book on contemporary society is emphasized and extended in Beard's illustrations, which, as some reviewers noticed, constituted a drastic reading-in of radical doctrines only faintly suggested, or not suggested at all, in Mark Twain's text. Most of Beard's drawings are deft, witty commentaries on the story, but far too many of them are crude cartoons that make their point only by means of elaborate labels. In this fashion Beard ascribes to Mark Twain a number of slogans and battle cries of current left-wing groups such as the Single-Taxers and the Anti-Monopolists

---

† From Cyril Clemens, "Unpublished Letters to Dan Beard," *Mark Twain Quarterly*, 7, ii (1945), 22. The recipient of the letter apparently was L. E. Parkhurst. The model for the slave driver was Jay Gould.

‡ From *Mark Twain's Fable of Progress: Political and Economic Ideas in "A Connecticut Yankee"* (New Brunswick, N.J.: Rutgers University Press, 1964), pp. 79–81.

with whom he had had no previous association. One of Beard's more extreme flights of fancy shows two allegorical female figures representing Justice in the sixth and nineteenth centuries, each peeking out from behind the bandage covering her eyes, and each holding a balance in which a hammer marked "Labor" is outweighed—in the sixth century by a crown or coronet labeled "Title," in the nineteenth century by a moneybag labeled "$1000000."

There are numerous other illustrations of this sort, the total effect of which was well described by an anonymous critic in Henry George's New York *Standard:*

> Though but little is said in the book about specific social or political reforms, it is impossible to read these extracts [quoted in the review] without seeing that the great American humorist has been moved by the spirit of democracy. Human equality, natural rights, unjust laws, class snobbery, the power of the rich and the dependence and oppression of the poor, are subjects of frequent allusion in the text; and whatever of definiteness the text may lack in pointing out the fundamental cause and radical cure for wrongs, is admirably supplied by Dan Beard in the illustrations.

A particularly dubious inference from the story—almost certainly misrepresenting the views of Mark Twain, who was never disposed to question private rights in property—is set forth in one of the illustrations reproduced by the *Standard.* Over the caption "The Coming Eclipse," the drawing shows a sun labeled "Divine Right of Kings VI Cen" about to be obscured by a sphere labeled "The Earth Belongs to the People XIX Cen," while a huddled throng kneel or lift up their hands in salutation. The passage near which the drawing is placed does contain a denunciation of the divine right of kings by the Yankee, but there is nothing in the text to support Beard's single-tax doctrine about ownership of natural resources.

A more defensible use of illustrations to go beyond the letter of the text is Beard's amusing depiction of living Englishmen in the guise of unsympathetic characters in the story. He gives to Merlin the venerable features of Tennyson, and to a "chuckleheaded" nobleman the countenance of the Prince of Wales. But the distinction between legitimate and illegitimate interpretation of the book in Beard's drawings was of no moment to Mark Twain, who complicated the task of future critics by unqualified praise of the illustrations as a whole. One can only conclude that by the time he had finished the book he was perfectly willing to accept the opinions of his associates about its meaning. Howells also asserted that Beard had accurately captured the spirit of the text. In the general humanitarian and Populist enthusiasm, fine shades of doctrine were of little interest to either the writer or his readers.

\*　　\*　　\*

# The English Edition

DENNIS WELLAND

## [Clemens, Chatto, and the English Edition]†

\* \* \*

\* \* \* on 6 May 1889, Chatto, writing to Webster & Co. on a totally different subject, concluded with a request for 'any further particulars of Mr Clemens' proposed new book "Mr. Smith of Camelot"', which we hope may be published this season'. Fred Hall referred the enquiry to Clemens and one of them must have written encouragingly to England, for Chatto, remitting the royalties on 3 July observed:

> There are many enquiries for the "Yankee at the Court of King Arthur" which I suppose is the same as "Mr Smith of Camelot" with a stronger title. I am glad to learn that it is approaching completion, and I hope you will soon be able to let us have some proofs in order that we may get to work in the preparation of the English edition.

Mark Twain's reply to this straightforward and goodnatured request is one of the most remarkable and least explicable letters in his entire correspondence with Andrew Chatto. Since its publication by Paine in 1917 it has given rise to more misconceptions about their relationship and about the book itself than any other single factor, and the problem is complicated still further by discrepancies between the text of the letter as Paine prints it and the text received by Chatto. I reproduce here the wording of Clemens's autograph original which still survives in the Chatto & Windus files:

Hartford, July 16/89

Dear Mr. Chatto,
 Your statement and drafts came yesterday for £364, for which I thank you and endorse your opinion that its a very good return for an off year.[1]
 I have revised the "Yankee" twice; Stedman has critically read it and pointed out to me some needed emendations; Mrs Clemens has read it and made me strike out many passages and soften others; I

---

† From Dennis Welland, *Mark Twain in England* (London: Chatto & Windus, 1978), pp. 134–39. Welland here refutes the often-repeated assertion that the English publisher insisted that Clemens modify the novel to make it more acceptable to his readers.

1. Welland points out earlier (p. 133) that "an off year" was a phrase Clemens typically used in acknowledging receipt of royalties from Chatto. It was a joke between the two rather than an indication that the year was actually a poor one.

have read chapters of it in public several times where Englishmen were present, and have profited by their suggestions. Next week I shall make a *final* revision. After that, if it still isn't blemishless I can't help it, and ain't going to try.

Now mind you, I have taken all this pains because I wanted to say a Yankee mechanic's say against monarchy and its several natural props, and yet make a book which you would be willing to print exactly as it comes to you, without altering a word.

*We* are spoken of (by *Englishmen*!) as a thin-skinned people. It is you that are thin-skinned. An Englishman may write with the most brutal frankness about any man or any institution among us, and we re-publish him without dreaming of altering a line or a word. But England cannot stand that kind of a book, written about herself. It is England that is thin-skinned. It causeth me to smile, when I recal [sic] the modifications of my language which have been made in my English Editions to fit it for the sensitive English palate.

Now as I say, I have taken laborious pains to so trim this book of offence that you'll not lack the nerve to print it just as it stands. I'm going to get the proofs to you just as early as I can. I want you to read it carefully. If you can publish it without altering a single word or omitting one, go ahead. Otherwise, please hand it to J. R. Osgood in time for him to have it published at my expense. This is important, for the reason that the book was not written for America, it was written for England. So many Englishmen have done their sincerest best to teach us something for our betterment, that it seems to me high time that some of us should substantially recognize the good intent by trying to pry up the English nation to a little higher level of manhood in turn.

Sincerely yours,<br>S. L. Clemens

In the Mark Twain Papers at Berkeley an unsigned typescript on Charles L. Webster & Co. notepaper is substantially identical to this except in very minor details ($364 instead of £364, in the first paragraph, for instance), so the responsibility for the editing of the published version is indisputably Paine's.

Paine produces a much more formal letter which opens uncharacteristically, dispenses with preliminaries, and achieves an immediate and defensive aggressiveness:

> Gentlemen,—Concerning the Yankee, I have already revised the story twice; and it has been read critically by W. D. Howells and Edmund Clarence Stedman, and my wife has caused me to strike out several passages which have been brought to her attention, and to soften others. Furthermore, I have read chapters of the book in public. . . .

Paine does not date the letter and implies that it was written after the book's American publication, which is plainly wrong. We have Howells's own statement, in a letter to Clemens, that he did not begin reading the book until 18 September, so Paine's introduction of a reference to him here is also wrong. Paine does not print the two sentences at the end of this paragraph ('Next week . . . ain't going to try'); this, like his omission of the opening paragraph, his spelling out of the contractions 'you'll' and 'I'm' in the final paragraph, and his ending 'Very truly yours', increases the cold formality of the letter. In the final sentence of the fourth paragraph both typescript and Paine have 'read'; 'recal', spelt thus, occurs elsewhere in Clemens's correspondence too, but the difference is not crucial. In the same sentence Paine prints 'them' for 'it', thus suggesting that it is the English editions that have been adapted where Clemens only claims that the language has been altered; in the typescript 'it' is in type and 'them' substituted in pencil, but in the original at Chatto & Windus Clemens certainly wrote 'it'.

Obviously some of Paine's changes are more significant than others; the reasons why he made them at all can only be conjectured— perhaps to strengthen the letter by giving it a more unified tone—and are less important than the implications of the letter itself, for despite the discrepancies between the two versions, it is still substantially the same letter and still very strange. Introducing it, Paine comments:

> The *Yankee* did not find a very hearty welcome in England. English readers did not fancy any burlesque of their Arthurian tales, or American strictures on their institutions. Mark Twain's publishers had feared this, and asked that the story be especially edited for the English edition. Clemens, however, would not listen to any suggestion of the sort.

It is a legitimate inference from either text of the letter, but it is obviously not supported by the facts.

The date and the opening reference to the receipt of the royalties confirm that Chatto's letter of 3 July (already quoted) was the latest in the series: in that and in all his other references to the book the publisher had expressed nothing but enthusiasm for it—certainly no fears or reservations. Two ideas are now introduced for the first time which one would have expected Clemens to have raised with Chatto before this: first, that the English editions of earlier books had been doctored to suit 'the sensitive English palate'; second, that *A Connecticut Yankee* 'was not written for America, it was written for England'. The first is demonstrably untrue, the second is at best suspect. The over-riding necessity to secure copyright by 'simultaning' had, as has been shewn, always imposed on the British publisher a production-schedule so tight and so hand-to-mouth that any serious editing would have been impracticable, even if it had been contemplated—and we find no evidence that it had. Textual variations between the English and the American editions of *Tom Sawyer* were, as we have seen, fortuitous, and the language of the English text was in many instances more colloquial than the American. There had been no attempt at 'modifications' to 'that unchristian dialect' in *Huckleberry Finn*, although Clemens seems subsequently almost to have wished that there had. His quarrel with Hotten had been over the attribution of specific pieces to him, not over any modifications to language; Routledge had allowed him to authorise the texts used, and any changes introduced into the English *Innocents Abroad* were made by Mark Twain, not required by Routledge. The whole accusation is as strikingly at variance with the correspondence and the relationship between Clemens and Chatto since 1876 as is the remarkable suggestion that Chatto might 'lack the nerve to print it just as it stands'. Nothing in their previous correspondence prepares us for this or justifies the truculence of Clemens's attitude here. The reiterated insistence on the sacredness of the author's text (it occurs five times in this letter) had never before been raised in that correspondence nor had it needed to be.

Paine's editing obscures some very curious shifts of tone within the letter itself (in the version that reached Chatto) that are clearly significant but are difficult to explain. The amiability of the opening paragraph with its use of the 'off-year' joke could hardly have led the publisher to expect what followed. The emphasis on revisions meticulously carried out at the suggestion of Stedman, Olivia, and the anonymous Englishmen does not wholly accord with the self-confident brashness of the 'Yankee mechanic's' vernacular 'I can't help it, and ain't going to try'. Even if one hears in that not brashness so much as weariness with the whole process of revision, there is still an inconsistency of tone. The vernacular also contrasts with a rhetoric somewhat out of place in a letter, so that one would hardly have blamed Chatto had he reproached Clemens, as Queen Victoria reproached Gladstone, for 'addressing us as though we were a public meeting'. Alternatively, he might have suggested that, like the Player Queen, Mark Twain seemed to 'protest too much'.

In fact he did neither. He did not reply until 8 August, by which time a date of publication had been proposed, and his only comment was dignified and restrained: 'I am very pleased to learn that the Yankee at the Court of King Arthur is to be published on December 10th next. I do not think there is any possibility of your writing anything I should not be pleased to publish'. To have been no more perturbed than this by Clemens's outburst, or at least to resist the temptation to retaliate, argues, on Chatto's part, a shrewd knowledge of and liking for his correspondent rather than indifference or pusillanimity. In one respect, however, Clemens may have been less than delighted by Chatto's quiet reassurance, for he had in the interim caused Webster & Co. to write, on 5 August, an even more specific letter to London.

We enclose a form of Preface for the English Edition of Mr Clemens' new book. This will differ materially from the Preface of the Am. Edition. We will send you two sets of sheets and would like if possible, to have you make arrangements with Baron Tauchnitz. There will probably be some portions of the book which you may not care to publish, although we think such passages are very rare. Mr Clemens suggests that at the end of Chapter XXVI what he says in regard to 'royal grants' you may wish to leave out: we will mark this portion in the proofs we send you. In reading over the proofs, please advise us of such portions as you wish to leave out and we will communicate with Mr Clemens regarding same.

We understand of course, that the book is a satire on English Royalty and Nobility, but as we have said it is a pleasant one, and one with the exception of an occasional passage, that no one should take offence at. All these changes should be made before the plates are cast as it would be quite difficult to do so afterwards. . . .

From this it is even clearer than from Clemens's letter that no proofs had been despatched to Chatto, so that he could not possibly have 'asked that the story be especially edited for the English edition'. This letter tends to minimise the iconoclastic nature of the book that Clemens had emphasized; the chapter reference should be to XXV rather than XXVI; the instructions as to when the changes should be made are hardly necessary; and the preface, instead of being enclosed, had to be sent on the next day. An explanation of why a different form of Preface was considered necessary would have been interesting but is not forthcoming. The Preface to the English edition consists of only one unsigned paragraph; the American edition follows this with a second, discussing the Divine Right of Kings, and the name MARK TWAIN. However, in the Berg Collection of the New York Public Library there is a proof of the one-paragraph text with 'Proof of Chatto's Preface' written on it. It is date-stamped 18 August 1889, and at the bottom are the words 'All right. SLC' in Clemens's holograph. Apparently he is approving the version sent to England two weeks earlier. The most likely reason for dropping the second paragraph might be that its facetiousness, especially in the closing sentences, could encourage the English reader, for whom the book purported to be specially written, to underestimate its seriousness of purpose even before beginning on it.

Chatto did not demur at the Preface, nor did he propose any cuts, but totally ignored both the general and the specific suggestions Webster & Co. had made. Thus, far from the English publishers being apprehensive about the book, the only suggestions for toning it down came from the author himself and, at his instigation, from his American publisher. It is as though Mark Twain positively *wanted* cuts to be made and would have been happier still had Chatto declined to publish the book at all. Behind the hectoring tone of his letter, so

unusual in his correspondence with Chatto, behind its factual inaccuracies and the injustice of its allegations, there lies, I believe, a very
troubled mind. Whatever praise Stedman or others had bestowed or
might bestow on the book, Mark Twain himself knew only too well
with how much difficulty he had written it; 'if it still isn't blemishless I
can't help it, and ain't going to try' tacitly admits as much. He must
also have known that, as Henry Nash Smith and others have demonstrated, the inner logic of his story had taken command and
defeated the optimistic faith in democracy it was supposed to have
celebrated. He must have realised that it was a scathing condemnation, not of 'monarchy and its several natural props', not of British
institutions and 'English manhood', but of human nature and the
faith in human nature on which Western democracy is ultimately
based. To insist that it is the English alone who are under attack is to
divert attention (Mark Twain's as much as anyone else's) from the
condemnation of American civilisation that the book also involves. If
the British could be induced to take umbrage at it, the diversionary
tactic would be even more effective, the author's criticism would be
vindicated, and he would be recognised as a man with a serious
message. The paranoiac insistence on the sacrosanctity of the text, not
one word of which is to be changed, is similarly evidence of a belief in
the importance of what he has revealed; the pretence that only the
non-democratic and thin-skinned English would wish to tamper with
its disguises conveniently the full import of the revelation.

Melville, having completed *Moby-Dick*, told Hawthorne 'I have
written a wicked book, and feel spotless as the lamb'. Mark Twain
believed that he too had written a wicked book but, always a victim of
that conscience against which he inveighed in *Huckleberry Finn* and
in this book itself, could not bring himself to feel spotless. The letter to
Chatto is a desperate attempt to transfer that guilt to other shoulders
and, in so doing, to change its nature. What Poe would have recognised as the imp of the perverse in Mark Twain would have liked
nothing better than the outright banning of the book in England: the
tone in which he could then have said 'I told you so!' would have
sounded conveniently like Anglophobia rather than the deeper and
more genuine misanthropy that he was still trying to deny even to
himself. Aghast at the subversive implications of his fable, he feels that
if it is attacked (especially by the British) he is proved right but his
misanthropy will be increased; if it is not attacked, then he has failed
in his attempt to attract serious attention, and his despair at his
imperceptive fellow human beings is intensified.

\* \* \*

# Criticism

# Early Views

## SYLVESTER BAXTER

## [Nothing More Delicious]†

Of all the extraordinary conceits that have germinated in his fruitful imagination, nothing more delicious has ever occurred to Mark Twain than that of running riot among the legendary times of our ancestral race by placing 'A Connecticut Yankee in King Arthur's Court.' These quoted words form the title of the latest successor to *Innocents Abroad*. Here is a rare field for the unbridled play of fancy, and right bravely has the author used his opportunity. There is a most audacious rollicking around among the dusty bric-a-brac of chivalry—which is not handled at all gently—and a merry tossing about of poetic finery in a way that ruthlessly exposes in their literal ugliness the illusively mantled facts. Of course there is most abundant fun, and Mark Twain's rich humor never coursed more freely than here, where just provocation is never absent. But there is much more than this; the sources of the claims of aristocratic privileges and royal prerogatives that yet linger in the world are so exposed to the full glare of the sun of 19th century common sense, are shown in so ridiculous an aspect, that the work can hardly fail to do yeoman service in destroying the still existing remnants of respect for such pretentions. Through the book there is a steady flowing undercurrent of earnest purpose, and the pages are eloquent with a true American love of freedom, a sympathy with the rights of the common people, and an indignant hatred of oppression of the poor, the lowly and the weak, by the rich, the powerful and the proud. While much false glamour is dispelled by resolving it into absurdity under the touchstone of truth, the book is marked by real beauty, by a poetry of style worthy of its rich material, with much sympathetic tenderness, as well as frankness of speech. The quaint early English speech is handled with the same artistic skill that characterized the author's facile handling of the stately Elizabethan in that lovely idyll of childhood, *The Prince and the Pauper*, and the constant admixture of a concisely expressive American vernacular thereto makes a contrast of lingual coloring that is unspeakably delightful.

We may fancy that the same matter-of-fact Englishman who seriously reasoned that certain statements in *Innocents Abroad* were

† From the Boston *Sunday Herald*, December 15, 1889, p. 17.

preposterously absurd, and could not be based upon fact, might again step forward to break a lance against this book by showing, from historical and philological data, that such a language could not possibly have been spoken in the sixth century, since the English tongue did not exist, and that the use of Norman French names before the conquest is anachronistic in the highest degree! But this is an excursion back into the England of the chronicles, and not of strict chronology, and that eminent ethnologist, Tylor, would undoubtedly perceive with delight the accuracy of scientific perception in the treatment of human nature which marks the book. For, in order to characterize with truth a past period we must make ourselves familiar with some existing state of society that is analogous therewith. Only under such conditions can a faithful historical romance be written, for otherwise the writer cannot fail to modernize his work, and falsify its life with 19th century sentiments that could not have been known in a previous age. By resorting to the principle that 'distribution in time' is paralleled by 'distribution in space,' we may solve many a problem. So there is a certain aspect of sober truth in this most fanciful tale, and, just as the Connecticut Yankee went back into the days of King Arthur's court, so might he go out into the world today, into Central Asia or Africa, or even into certain spots in this United States of ours, find himself amidst social conditions very similar to those of 1300 years ago, and even work his astonishing 19th century miracles with like result. For it is a fact that, when Frank Hamilton Cushing astounded the Zuni Indians with an acoustic telephone constructed of two tomato cans and a string, they deemed him a magician, and tried him for witchcraft. And, for parallels of the inhumanities which, as we here read of them, seem to have been left far behind us in the track of the centuries, we have but to look with George Kennan into the dungeons of Siberia, [1] and, in our own country, read the records of the investigations into the horrors of the almshouses, jails and lunatic hospitals here in this enlightened commonwealth of Massachusetts so late as the time of Horace Mann, or look to the record of the nameless barbarities of negro slavery alive in the memories of men still young. How the conscience and the sympathies of the world have quickened with the advent of the railway, the steamship and the telegraph! We have, after all, but just passed out across the threshold of the dark ages, and, in view of the few steps we have taken, we can hardly doubt that we are yet to make an infinitely mightier progress into the light of a genuine civilization, putting far behind us the veneered barbarism of the present, that still retains the old standards of conduct and intercourse for our guidance in all 'practical' affairs.

As an instance of the scientific fidelity of this book in its picture of

1. George Kennan's articles on Russia, published in *The Century Illustrated Monthly* *Magazine* in 1887–88, are often cited as one of the sources used in the writing of the novel.

mediaeval society, we may take this from the description of the company at King Arthur's Round Table, around which there was an average of about two dogs to one man, watching for bones:[2]

\* \* \*

The following also illustrates an exact perception of the essentially savage traits of such a people: 'Finally it occurred to me all of a sudden that these animals didn't reason; that they never put this and that together; that all their talk showed that they didn't know a discrepancy when they saw it.' Again, when Sir Sagramour le Desirous caught a chance remark of the Yankee applied to some one else and thought it meant for him, and so challenged him to the memorable encounter that took place several years after, and was fought with lariat versus lance, the 'Sir Boss,' as he was called said: 'Whenever one of those people got a thing into his head, there was no getting it out again. I knew that, so I saved my breath, and offered no explanations.' The foregoing characterizations might apply equally well to a tribe of Dakota Indians, to their hardly more civilized foes, the cowboys of the plains, to the mountaineers of Tennessee and Georgia, or even to the savages in our great city slums.

By some strange means, perhaps more marvellous than those by which Edward Bellamy transferred the hero of *Looking Backward* forward to the year 2000, the Yankee is carried back 1300 years in time, and in the record of his adventures affords us another and very instructive sort of *Looking Backward*.

\* \* \*

The advance in the art of popular bookmaking in the past two decades is illustrated by the contrast between *Innocents Abroad* and this volume. In illustration, the progress is particularly notable. Even a child of today would turn in contempt from the crude woodcuts of the former to the beautiful pen-and-ink drawings by Dan Beard that adorn the new work. These drawings are graceful, picturesque and thoroughly characteristic of the spirit of the book. Many of them embody instructive allegories, as, for instance, in a cut of Justice, with her scales, one containing the heavy hammer of 'Labor' and the other baubles of 'Aristocracy,' but the latter made to outweigh the former by means of the string of 'Self-interest,' artfully attached to the toe of 'Law,' who stands by; another, in a similar vein, shows the Justice of the 19th century and Justice of the sixth century standing opposite each other, and simultaneously remarking, 'Sister, your blind is disarranged,' for, with the same manner of string attached to the toe of each, 'Money' is made to outweight 'Labor' by the former, just as titles are made heavier in the balance of the latter. One little cut shows

2. Baxter here quotes the last two paragraphs of Chapter II.

'Decorations of Sixth Century Aristocracy' as 'Rewards for all Babes Born Under Specified Conditions,' such as 'Slave Driver,' 'Robber of Unarmed Savages,' 'Robber of Orphans,' 'Absorber of Taxes,' 'Murderer of Rivals,' etc., the whole supported by 'Honi soit qui mal y pense!' Another illustrates the remark of the king concerning a peasant: 'Brother! to dirt like this?' by depicting the three phases of oppression of man by man, first by violence under the sword of royal power, then by the book of 'law,' making man subject to the slave driver's lash, and last, the subjection of the workingman to the millions of the monopolist. A strong and spirited picture of an arrogant slave driver shows in its face the unmistakable portrait of a celebrated American billionaire and stock gambler.[3]

We are so accustomed to regard England of today as 'essentially a republic, with a monarchical head,' that it seems strange that the utterances of this book, so thoroughly in accordance with accepted American ideas, should find any difficulty in obtaining publicity in England, yet so strong is the prejudice there still that its English publisher has cut out some of the best passages, including a portion of the preface, with some persiflage about 'the divine right of kings.'[4]

# WILLIAM DEAN HOWELLS

## [His Wonder-Story][†]

\* \* \* [It][1] describes without caricature, in a democratic commonwealth, and on the verge of the twentieth century, an ideal of life entirely stupid, useless, and satisfied, and quite that which Mark Twain has been portraying in his wonder-story of *A Connecticut Yankee at the Court of King Arthur*. Mr. Hamerton's French noble of the year 1890 is the same man essentially as any of that group of knights of the Round Table, who struck Mr. Clemens's delightful hero as white Indians. In his circle, achievement, ability, virtue, would find itself at the same disadvantage, without birth, as in that of Sir Launcelot. When you contemplate him in Mr. Hamerton's clear, passionless page, you feel that after all the Terror was perhaps too brief, and you find yourself sympathizing with all Mr. Clemens's

---

3. Jay Gould.
4. As is shown in Welland's essay (reprinted above) the only omission made in the English edition was the second paragraph of the preface, and even that change seems not to have originated with the English publisher, Andrew Chatto.
† From *Harper's Magazine*, 80 (January 1890), 319–21. Howells was, of course, one of Clemens' closest friends and had read proof before the novel was published. He had already declared to Clemens that the book was "charming, original, wonderful," "good in fancy, and sound to the core in morals," "every kind of a delightful book," and "glorious—simply noble" (*Mark Twain–Howells Letters*, II, 612, 614, 617).
1. A chapter of Philip Gilbert Hamerton's *French and English: A Comparison*, which Howells was also reviewing.

robust approval of the Revolution.

Mr. Clemens, we call him, rather than Mark Twain, because we feel that in this book our arch-humorist imparts more of his personal quality than in anything else he has done. Here he is to the full the humorist, as we know him; but he is very much more, and his strong, indignant, often infuriate hate of injustice, and his love of equality, burn hot through the manifold adventures and experiences of the tale. What he thought about prescriptive right and wrong, we had partly learned in *The Prince and the Pauper*, and in *Huckleberry Finn*, but it is this last book which gives his whole mind. The elastic scheme of the romance allows it to play freely back and forward between the sixth century and the nineteenth century; and often while it is working the reader up to a blasting contempt of monarchy and aristocracy in King Arthur's time, the dates are magically shifted under him, and he is confronted with exactly the same principles in Queen Victoria's time. The delicious satire, the marvellous wit, the wild, free, fantastic humor are the colors of the tapestry, while the texture is a humanity that lives in every fibre. At every moment the scene amuses, but it is all the time an object-lesson in democracy. It makes us glad of our republic and our epoch; but it does not flatter us into a fond content with them; there are passages in which we see that the noble of Arthur's day, who battened on the blood and sweat of his bondmen, is one in essence with the capitalist of Mr. Harrison's[2] day who grows rich on the labor of his underpaid wagemen. Our incomparable humorist, whose sarcasm is so pitiless to the greedy and superstitious clerics of Britain, is in fact of the same spirit and intention as those bishops who, true to their office, wrote the other day from New York to all their churches in the land:

> It is a fallacy in social economics, as well as in Christian thinking, to look upon the labor of men and women and children as a commercial commodity, to be bought and sold as an inanimate and irresponsible thing. . . . The heart and soul of a man cannot be bought or hired in any market, and to act as if they were not needed in the doing of the world's vast work is as unchristian as it is unwise.

Mr. Clemens's glimpses of monastic life in Arthur's realm are true enough; and if they are not the whole truth of the matter, one may easily get it in some such book as Mr. Brace's *Gesta Christi*,[3] where the full light of history is thrown upon the transformation of the world, if not the church, under the influence of Christianity. In the mean time, if any one feels that the justice done the churchmen of King

2. Benjamin Harrison, president of the United States, 1889–93.

3. Charles L. Brace's *Gesta Christi, or, A History of Humane Progress under Christianity* was published in London in 1880. Howells had written Clemens (II, 614) that it was "a pity you don't let us see how when ever Christ himself could get a chance, all possible good was done" and recommended that he read Brace's book.

Arthur's time is too much of one kind, let him turn to that heart-belonging scene where the brave monk stands with the mother and her babe on the scaffold, and execrates the hideous law which puts her to death for stealing enough to keep her from starving. It is one of many passages in the story where our civilization of to-day sees itself mirrored in the cruel barbarism of the past, the same in principle, and only softened in custom. With shocks of consciousness, one recognizes in such episodes that the laws are still made for the few against the many, and that the preservation of things, not men, is still the ideal of legislation. But we do not wish to leave the reader with the notion that Mr. Clemens's work is otherwise than obliquely serious. Upon the face of it you have a story no more openly didactic than *Don Quixote*, which we found ourselves more than once thinking of, as we read, though always with the sense of the kindlier and truer heart of our time. Never once, we believe, has Mark Twain been funny at the cost of the weak, the unfriended, the helpless; and this is rather more than you can say of Cid Hamet ben Engeli.[4] But the two writers are of the same humorous largeness; and when the Connecticut man rides out at dawn, in a suit of Arthurian armor, and gradually heats up under the mounting sun in what he calls that stove; and a fly gets between the bars of his visor; and he cannot reach his handkerchief in his helmet to wipe the sweat from his streaming face; and at last when he cannot bear it any longer, and dismounts at the side of a brook, and makes the distressed damsel who has been riding behind him take off his helmet, and fill it with water, and pour gallon after gallon down the collar of his wrought-iron cutaway, you have a situation of as huge a grotesqueness as any that Cervantes conceived.

The distressed damsel is the Lady Corisande,[5] he calls her Sandy, and he is troubled in mind at riding about the country with her in that way; for he is not only very doubtful that there is nothing in the castle where she says there are certain princesses imprisoned and persecuted by certain giants, but he feels that it is not quite nice: he is engaged to a young lady in East Hartford, and he finds Sandy a fearful bore at first, though in the end he loves and marries her, finding that he hopelessly antedates the East Hartford young lady by thirteen centuries. How he gets into King Arthur's realm, the author concerns himself as little as any of us do with the mechanism of our dreams. In fact the whole story has the lawless operation of a dream; none of its prodigies are accounted for: they take themselves for granted, and neither explain nor justify themselves. Here he is, that Connecticut man, foreman of one of the shops in Colt's pistol factory, and full to the throat of the invention and the self-satisfaction of the nineteenth century, at the court of the mythic Arthur. He is promptly recognized as a being of

4. Pretended author of Don Quixote's adventures in Cervantes' novel (1605, 1615).     5. Actually, "Alisande."

extraordinary powers, and becomes the king's right-hand man, with the title of The Boss; but as he has apparently no lineage or blazon, he has no social standing, and the meanest noble has precedence of him, just as would happen in England to-day. The reader may faintly fancy the consequences flowing from this situation, which he will find so vividly fancied for him in the book; but they are simply irreportable. The scheme confesses allegiance to nothing; the incidents, the facts follow as they will. The Boss cannot rest from introducing the apparatus of our time, and he tries to impart its spirit, with a thousand most astonishing effects. He starts a daily paper in Camelot; he torpedoes a holy well; he blows up a party of insolent knights with a dynamite bomb; when he and the king disguise themselves as peasants, in order to learn the real life of the people, and are taken and sold for slaves, and then sent to the gallows for the murder of their master, Launcelot arrives to their rescue with five hundred knights on bicycles. It all ends with the Boss's proclamation of the Republic after Arthur's death, and his destruction of the whole chivalry of England by electricity.

We can give no proper notion of the measureless play of an imagination which has a gigantic jollity in its feats, together with the tenderest sympathy. There are incidents in this wonder-book which wring the heart for what has been of cruelty and wrong in the past, and leave it burning with shame and hate for the conditions which are of like effect in the present. It is one of its magical properties that the fantastic fable of Arthur's far-off time is also too often the sad truth of ours; and the magician who makes us feel in it that we have just begun to know his power, teaches equality and fraternity in every phrase of his phantasmagory.

He leaves, to be sure, little of the romance of the olden time, but no one is more alive to the simple, mostly tragic poetry of it; and we do not remember any book which imparts so clear a sense of what was truly heroic in it. With all his scorn of kingcraft, and all his ireful contempt of caste, no one yet has been fairer to the nobility of character which they cost so much too much to develop. The mainly ridiculous Arthur of Mr. Clemens has his moments of being as fine and high as the Arthur of Lord Tennyson; and the keener light which shows his knights and ladies in their childlike simplicity and their innocent coarseness throws all their best qualities into relief. This book is in its last effect the most matter-of-fact narrative, for it is always true to human nature, the only truth possible, the only truth essential, to fiction. The humor of the conception and of the performance is simply immense; but more than ever Mr. Clemens's humor seems the sunny break of his intense conviction. We must all recognize him here as first of those who laugh, not merely because his fun is unrivalled, but because there is a force of right feeling and clear thinking in it that never got into fun before, except in *The Bigelow* [sic] *Papers.* [6] Throughout, the text in all its circumstance and meaning is supplemented by the illustrations of an artist who has entered into the wrath and the pathos as well as the fun of the thing, and made them his own.

This kind of humor, the American kind, the kind employed in the service of democracy, of humanity, began with us a long time ago; in fact Franklin may be said to have torn it with the lightning from the skies. Some time, some such critic as Mr. T. S. Perry (if we ever have another such) will study its evolution in the century of our literature and civilization; but no one need deny himself meanwhile the pleasure we feel in Mr. Clemens's book as its highest development.

# FROM THE LONDON *DAILY TELEGRAPH*

## [King Arthur or Jay Gould?]†

At this holiday season, in books and newspapers, on stage and in drawing-room, the poet and the painter, the author, the actor, and the dramatist compete with one another to bring before young and old scenes and suggestions of beauty, heroism, purity, and truth. One writer is an exception. MARK TWAIN sets himself to show the seamy side of the legendary Round Table of King ARTHUR'S time. He depicts all the vices of feudalism—the licentiousness of the nobles, their arrogance and insolence to the middle classes, their neglect of the poor, their hours of gluttony and idleness, varied by raids and brawls and riotous disorders. He describes how a Yankee visiting the Court uses modern inventions, defeats the best warriors, and redresses the wrongs of the poor. It is quite possible that a serious purpose underlies what otherwise seems a vulgar travesty. We have every regard for MARK TWAIN—a writer who has enriched English literature by admirable descriptions of boy life, and who in *The Prince and the Pauper* has given a vivid picture of mediæval times. A book, however, that tries to deface our moral and literary currency by bruising and soiling the image of King ARTHUR, as left to us by legend and consecrated by poetry, is a very unworthy production of the great humourist's pen. No doubt there is one element of wit—incongruity—in bringing a Yankee from Connecticut face to face with feudal knights; but sharp contrast between vulgar facts and antique ideas is not the only thing necessary for humour. If it were, then a travelling Cockney putting a flaming tie round the neck of the 'Apollo Belvidere,' or sticking a clay pipe

6. By James Russell Lowell, originally pub-
lished 1846–48.                    † An anonymous review, January 13, 1890.

between the lips of the 'Venus de Medici,' would be a matter-of-fact MARK TWAIN, and as much entitled to respect. Burlesque and travesty are satire brought down to the meanest capacity, and they have their proper province when pretentious falsehoods put on the masks of solemnity and truth. Stilted tragedies, artificial melodramas, unnatural acting, are properly held up to ridicule on the stage or in parodies. The mannerisms of a popular writer like CARYLE, BROWNING, or even TENNYSON, may, through caricature, be good-humouredly exposed; but an attack on the ideals associated with King ARTHUR is a coarse pandering to that passion for irreverence which is at the basis of a great deal of Yankee wit. To make a jest of facts, phrases, or words— Scriptural, heroic, or legendary—that are held in awe or reverence by other men is the open purpose of every wilting on a Western print, who endeavours to follow in the footsteps of ARTEMUS WARD, BRET HARTE, and MARK TWAIN. They may finally be successful enough to destroy their own trade. They now live by shocking decent people who still retain love for the Bible, HOMER, SHAKESPEARE, SCOTT, and TENNYSON; but when they have thoroughly trained a rising generation to respect nothing their irreverence will fall flat.

The stories of King ARTHUR that have come down to us represent in legendary form not any historical fact, but an ideal of kingship and knighthood which had birth in the hearts and aspirations of mediæval men. This was their ideal of what a King amongst his warriors ought to be, and the beautiful image has fired the thoughts and purified the imagination of millions of men and women for many generations. Will this shrine in human souls be destroyed because a Yankee scribe chooses to fling pellets of mud upon the high altar? The instincts of the past and the genius of TENNYSON have consecrated for ever 'the goodliest fellowship of famous knights Whereof this world holds record.' The Round Table is dissolved, but we can still 'delight our souls with talk of knightly deeds,' as they at Camelot in the storied past. We can still apply the image of the ideal knight as a criterion of modern worth. King ARTHUR swore each of his followers to 'reverence his conscience as his King, To ride abroad redressing human wrongs, To speak no slander, no, nor listen to it, To honour his own word as if his GOD's, To lead sweet lives in purest chastity. To love one maiden only, cleave to her, And worship her by years of noble deeds.' Such an oath presented to a modern Yankee would seem to convey in almost every phrase a covert insult to American institutions. In a land where commercial fraud and industrial adulteration are fine arts we had better omit appeals to 'conscience.' The United States are not likely to 'ride abroad redressing human wrong'—as they never gave a dollar or a man to help Greece, Poland, Hungary, or Italy in their struggles to be free. 'To speak no slander, no, nor listen to it,' would utterly uproot America's free press—based to a great extent on scandalous personalities. Loving one maiden only and cleaving to her must seem too 'high-toned' in the States, where there are many facilities for ready divorce. So far MARK TWAIN is right as a Western iconoclast to pelt with sarcasm ideals which are not included in the Constitution or customs of the United States. Yet, in spite of all that America has done or can do to deface images of self-sacrifice and beauty, there are chosen souls in her own borders who have fulfilled the heroic ideals of the olden time. The Abolitionists of New England encountered great perils when they first set out to redress the great human wrong of negro slavery, and they fought as noble a contest against organised iniquity as any knight of ARTHUR'S Court. They faced political obloquy, mob violence, loss of limb, sometimes of life, and the falling away of friends and relatives, because they had inherited the old instinct of knights, to lead lives of duty to their fellow-men. They were jeered and derided by the MARK TWAINS of the day, but their foresight was proved at the end of the war, when the world recognised the two-fold result, 'a nation saved, a race delivered.' What, too, would have been the fate of the Republic if no ideal image of their country shone before the souls of the men who died to save the Union? Coward souls at the North said, 'It will cost much money and many lives to re-conquer the South: let them go; let the Republic break up; what is a country to us?' but a chivalry that came down from British ancestors animated the men who followed GRANT, and they kept to their high purpose until the field was won. Where was MARK TWAIN then? Why did he not satirise the patriotism that would not let a Republic be mutilated? Why did he not sneer at Yankee reverence for a paper Constitution not a hundred years old? Why did he not sing the glories of trade as better than any preservation of the Union or liberation of negro slaves?

Even if we look at the real feudalism idealised in the legends of King ARTHUR, it was not all evil. No doubt there were licentious nobles at all times, and there were great landlords who were occasionally cruel to the peasants in their fields. The change to modern times, however, is not all a gain. A great lord of old held his possessions by 'suit and service'; he was bound to follow his King to the wars. Now he owns his broad lands free of duty, and may live a life of shameful luxury when he likes. The peasant of the olden times was not always in distress. The country was thinly peopled; he had as much land as he wanted; the woods were full of wild game, the streams of fish; except on occasions of rare famine he was fed well. Such a thing as an eviction was unknown, and for one good reason—the lord was not only bound to serve the King, but to bring men for his army; consequently he had an interest in raising on his estates a body of faithful followers. The modern landlord drives his peasants into the towns, where, uncared for by him, they degenerate and die in slums. We must remember, too, that the vices of the past were characteristic of rough times; they were the sins of brutality, not of fraud. A bad knight of the feudal age wronged a maid or widow, and refused redress; but what are the offences of a commercial age? In America and in England, to a lesser extent, financial swindling is elaborately organised. The wicked man of modern times does not couch his lance against the weak or lowly; he sends out a prospectus. In twelve months the widow and the orphan are breadless; the promoter and the financier have added another twenty thousand to their stores. Were King ARTHUR to descend in New York to-morrow he would make for Wall-street, where he would find a host of men whose word is as good, and as bad, as their bond—railway schemers who plunder the shareholders of a continent, and are ever intent by every device of falsehood and of plot to deceive each other and to defraud the public. Talk of the inequality of man! King ARTHUR and the meanest menial in his halls were nearer to each other in conditions of life than the tramp in the slums of New York and the ASTORS, VANDERBILTS, and JAY GOULDS who have piled up millions extracted from the pockets of less successful men. The Republic is a 'land of liberty,' yet its commerce, its railways, and its manufactures are in the hands of a few cliques of almost irresponsible capitalists, who control tariffs, markets, and politics in order that they may be enriched, to the disadvantage of the masses. Which, then, is to be most admired—the supremacy of a knight or the success of a financier? Under which King will the Americans serve—the ideal or the real? Will they own allegiance to King ARTHUR or JAY GOULD?

## WILLIAM T. STEAD

### Mark Twain's New Book: A Satirical Attack on English Institutions†

In selecting as the Novel of the Month Mark Twain's new story, *A Yankee at the Court of King Arthur*, I am aware that I expose myself to many remonstrances. There is a certain profanation in the subject, and withal a certain dulness in its treatment. It is not a novel; it is a ponderous political pamphlet, and so forth and so forth. Nevertheless, to those who endeavour to understand what the mass of men who speak English are thinking, as opposed to those who merely care about what they think they ought to be thinking, this book of Mark Twain's is one of the most significant of our time. It is notable for its faults quite as much as for its virtues, and for the irreverent audacity of its original conception as much as for the cumbrous and strenuous moralising

† From the London *Review of Reviews*, February 1890, pp. 144–56.

which makes it at times more like one of Jonathan Edwards' sermons[1] than a mere buoyant and farcical bubbling up of American humour.

Mark Twain is one of the few American authors whose writings are popular throughout the English-speaking world. Our superfine literary men of culture who pooh-pooh the rough rude vigour of the American humorist represent a small clique. Mark Twain gets 'directlier at the heart' of the masses than any of the blue-china set of nimminy-pimminy criticasters. In his own country, if we may judge from the remarks[2] in the January *Harper*, *A Yankee at the Court of King Arthur* has been received with an enthusiasm which it has hitherto failed to evoke on this side of the Atlantic. We read there that

> the delicious satire, the marvellous wit, the wild, free, fantastic humour, are the colours of the tapestry, while the texture is a humanity that lives in every fibre. We can give no proper notion of the measureless play of an imagination which has a gigantic jollity in its feats, together with the tenderest sympathy. The humour of the conception and of the performance is simply immense; but more than ever Mr. Clemens's humour seems the sunny break of his intense conviction.

What a contrast this to the frigid condemnation of the *Speaker*: 'In his last book Mr. Clemens failed to make us laugh by any method, even the worst. He is not only dull when he is offensive, but perhaps even more dull when he is didactic.' Yet I make free to say that the vote of the mass of English people would be on the side of the American and against the English critic. For what our critical class has failed to appreciate is that the Education Act has turned out and is turning out millions of readers who are much more like the Americans in their tastes, their ideas, and their sympathies than they are to the English of the cultured, pampered, and privileged classes. The average English-speaking man is the product of the common school in America, of the public elementary school in Britain and Australia. His literary taste is not classical but popular. He prefers Longfellow to Browning, and as a humorist he enjoys Mark Twain more than all the dainty wits whose delicately flavoured quips and cranks delight the boudoir and the drawing-room. This may be most deplorable from the point of view of the supercilious æsthetes, but the fact in all its brutality cannot be too frankly recognised.

Another circumstance which gives significance to the book is the fact that it is the latest among the volumes whereby Americans are revolutionising the old country. The two books which have given the greatest impetus to the social-democratic movement in recent years have both come to us from America. Henry George's land nationali-

---

1. The most famous sermon by the American Puritan preacher was "Sinners in the Hands of an Angry God," delivered at Enfield, Connecticut, in 1741.
2. By William Dean Howells.

sation theories were scouted by the superfine, but they have gained a firm hold of the public mind. His book[3] has circulated everywhere, and is still circulating. Of another kind, but operating in the same direction, is Edward Bellamy's *Looking Backwards* [*sic*], which has supplied our people with a clearly written-out apocalypse of the new heaven and the new earth that are to come after the acceptance of the Evangel of Socialism. Mark Twain's book is a third contribution in the same direction. His Yankee is a fierce and furious propagandist of anti-monarchical and aristocratic ideas. Under the veil of sarcasms levelled at King Arthur we see a genial mockery of the British monarchy of to-day, with its Royal grants and all its semi-feudal paraphernalia. Nor is it only at British abuses Mark Twain levels his burly jests. He thwacks the protectionist American as readily as the aristocratic Briton. There is something infinitely significant in the very form of his satire. If there is nothing sacred to a sapper, neither can there be anything sacred to a descendant of the men of the *Mayflower*, who has all the fervour of Mr. Zeal-for-the-Lord-Busy[4] and the confident, complacent assurance of Sam Slick,[5] who dismissed unceremoniously the authority of Plato or Aristotle with the observation that we need not heed what they said as there were no railways in their times. Here is the New England Democrat and Puritan as passionately sympathetic with the common man as the nobles and knights whom he scourges were sympathetic with men of their order, determined to avenge the injustice of centuries and by holding the mirror up to face to punish the chivalric age by showing how it treated the common man. It is not longer enough to judge systems of to-day by the effect which they have upon Hodge the ploughman and Bottom the weaver,[6] the war must be carried into the enemy's camp, the verdict of history must be reversed, and all our ideals of the past transformed in the light of this new and imperious interrogation.—The labouring man, what did that age or that institution make of him?

Tennyson sang the idyls of the King, and as long as the world lasts Sir Thomas Malory's marvellous old Romance will fill the hearts and imaginations of men with some far-off reflection of the splendours and the glories of that child-like age. But truly he sang 'the old order changeth, giving place to the new,' of which can we have a more notable and even brutal illustration than the apparition of this vulgar Yankee realist, with his telephones and his dynamite, his insufferable slang and his infinite self-conceit, in the midst of King Arthur's Court,

3. *Progress and Poverty* (1879), Henry George's major work, proposed a tax on land as a remedy for social ills. Certain of Dan Beard's illustrations for *A Connecticut Yankee* support George's ideas.
4. Zeal-of-the land Busy is a religious charlatan in Ben Jonson's *Bartholomew Fair* (1614).

5. The central character of Thomas Chandler Haliburton's *The Clockmaker* (1837) and other sketches.
6. Hodge is a typical name for an English country fellow; Bottom was the leader of the Athenian rustics in Shakespeare's *A Midsummer Night's Dream*.

applying to all the knighthood of the Round Table the measure of his yard-stick,—the welfare of the common man? It is the supreme assertion of the law of numbers, of the application of the patent arithmetical proposition that ten is more than one, to the problems of politics and of history.

Tennyson himself, in the 'Last Tournament,' supplied a vivid picture, which may well serve as a frontispiece of Mark Twain's vision:—

> Into the hall swaggered, his visage ribbed
> From ear to ear with dog whip-weals, his nose
> Bridge-broken, one eye out and one hand off,
> And one with shattered fingers dangling, lame;
> A churl, to whom indignantly the king,
> 'My churl, for whom Christ died; what evil beast
> Hath drawn his claws athwart thy face? or fiend,
> Man, was it who marr'd heaven's image in thee thus?'[7]

The churl for whom Christ died is the centre of Mark Twain's story, which is a long and a passionate attempt to suggest that the evil beast who marred the visage of the poor wretch was the three-headed chimera of Monarchy, Aristocracy, and Church. There is much strange misreading of history caused by the extent to which Mark Twain has allowed the abuses of institutions to obscure their use.

# FROM THE BOSTON *LITERARY WORLD*

## [This Melancholy Product of the American Mind][†]

Mark Twain's latest book, which his publishers have brought out in a handsome volume, seems to us the poorest of all his productions thus far. The conceit of taking a Yankee of this generation of telephones and the electric light back to King Arthur's Court may please some minds, if presented in a story of moderate length, but there can be few who will really enjoy it when long-drawn out to the extent of nearly six hundred pages. Whatever value Mr. Clemens might have incidentally imparted to his burlesque by giving something like a correct picture of the customs of the time in which the mythical King flourished is entirely absent. He has crowded into his picture a great number of episodes illustrating 'ungentle laws and customs' which are historical, indeed; but he says:

It is not pretended that these laws and customs existed in England

---

7. Lines 57–64 of "The Last Tournament" (1871) one of the sections of Tennyson's *Idylls of the King*.

† An anonymous review from the Boston *Literary World*, 21 (February 15, 1890), 52–53.

in the sixth century; no, it is only pretended that, inasmuch as they existed in the English and other civilizations of far later times, it is safe to consider that it is no libel upon the sixth century to suppose them to have been in practice in that day also. One is quite justified in inferring that wherever one of these laws or customs was lacking in that remote time, its place was competently filled by a worse one.

Mr. Clemens' method of writing history would justify him in picturing the Connecticut of the seventeenth century as afflicted with loose divorce customs and great corruption at the polls—or something worse—simply because these are vices of the nineteenth century! To crowd into a representation of one age the social evils of all its successors known to us, and to omit those special redeeming features of the time which made life tolerable, is a very irrational proceeding.

The serious aim under Mark Twain's travesty is the glorification of American Protestant democracy. The effort fails through the extreme partiality of the procedure. Even a Mark Twain, the persistent teacher of irreverence for great men and great events, should have some little respect left for fair play. Mr. Clemens' previous books have been bad enough in their strong encouragement of one of the worst tendencies in a democratic State, the inclination to sheer flippancy and unmanly irreverence in the face of the natural sanctities of private life and the grand heroisms of human history. But this volume goes much further in its endeavor to belittle a century surrounded with romantic light by men of later times, who thus fell back upon poetry as a slight relief to the hard prose of their actual lot. A buffoon, like the hero of this tale, playing his contemptible tricks where Sir Thomas Malory has trod with a noble teaching of knightly courtesy, and uttering his witless jokes where Tennyson has drawn so many a high moral of true gentleness, is a sorry spectacle. It is not calculated to make a reflecting person proud of a shallow and self-complacent generation which can enjoy such so-called humor.

The one consolation to be derived from this melancholy product of the American mind in the ninth decade of the nineteenth century is that, equally in its serious and in its jesting parts, it must bring about a healthy reaction in some of its admiring readers because it overshoots the mark; because its history is perverse, in its one-sided accumulation of evils; and because its humor will be wearisome in the extreme when its falsity is seen.

When Mr. Clemens relates his Life on the Mississippi with characteristic American exaggeration, we cannot fail to laugh and become friends. But when he prostitutes his humorous gift to the base uses of historical injustice, democratic bigotry, Protestant intolerance, and nineteenth-century vainglory, we must express the very sincere animosity we feel at such a performance. If anything could be less of a credit to our literature than the matter of this book, it certainly is the illustrations which disfigure it. A Protestant of the Protestants himself, the writer of this review cannot refrain from thus freeing his soul in the cause of literary decency when the Roman Catholic Church, that is to say the Christian Church in one of the noblest periods of its history, is thus grossly assailed by the writer and the illustrator of this tiresome travesty.

## ANDREW LANG

### [He Has Not the Knowledge]†

* * * I have abstained from reading his work on an American at the Court of King Arthur, because here Mark Twain is not, and cannot be, at the proper point of view. He has not the knowledge which would enable him to be a sound critic of the ideal of the Middle Ages. An Arthurian Knight in New York or in Washington would find as much to blame, and justly, as a Yankee at Camelot. *   *   *

## RUDYARD KIPLING

### [The Yankee Animal]‡

*     *     *

LATER.—Oh shame! Oh shock! O fie! I have been reading the new book which you also will have read by this time—the book about the yankee animal in the court yard. It's *   *   * but I don't believe he ever wrote it; or, if he did, I am certain that if you held it up to a looking glass or picked out every third word or spelled it backward you would find that it hid some crystal clean tale as desirable as Huck Finn.

## CHARLES WHIBLEY

### [A Bull in The China-Shop of Ideas]*

*     *     *

* * * Mark Twain the humourist is a bull in the china-shop of ideas. He attempts to destroy what he could never build up, and assumes that his experiment is eminently meritorious. When, as in A

---

† "The Art of Mark Twain," *Illustrated London News*, February 14, 1891, p. 222. This statement appears in a long article written in response to Clemens' request that Lang defend him against the British critics.
‡ From "Rudyard Kipling on Mark Twain,"

New York *Herald*, August 17, 1890, p. 5. The comment comes at the end of a long, appreciative article about Kipling's visit to Clemens at Elmira, N.Y.
* From "Musings Without Method," *Blackwood's Magazine*, 182 (1907), 279–286.

*Yankee at the Court of King Arthur,* he gave full rein to his fancy, he achieved such a masterpiece of vulgarity as the world has never seen. His book gives you the same sort of impression which you might receive from a beautiful picture over which a poisonous slug had crawled. The hint of magnificence is there, pitilessly deformed and defaced. That Mark Twain is in perfect sympathy with his creature is perfectly evident. He frankly prefers Hartford, Conn., to Camelot. He believes that in all respects his native land is superior to the wisest and noblest society that the eye of Arthur saw or any other eye has seen. He is sure that refinement and 'gentility' were unknown before his own time. The Knights of the Round Table, he declares, used words which would have made a Comanche blush. 'Indelicacy is too mild a term to convey the idea.' In our own nineteenth century, he informs us, 'the earliest samples of the real lady and real gentleman discoverable in English history—or in European history, for that matter—may be said to have made their appearance.' That is what it is to be a humourist. But even if we permit the humour we must still question the historical accuracy of the statement, and regret that Mark Twain ever thought it necessary to comment upon the ancients, against whom he cherishes a fierce antipathy.

His verbal humour, if less reckless than his history, is far more dismally deplorable. Here is his comment upon Merlin: 'He is always blethering around in my way, everywhere I go; he makes me tired. He don't amount to shucks as a magician.' Who can resist this amazing humour? And again, who, save a churl, would refuse the tribute of a laugh to the following exquisite criticism of the same wonder-worker? 'Merlin's stock was flat,' writes Mark Twain, 'the King wanted to stop his wages: he even wanted to banish him; but I interfered. I said he would be useful to work the weather, and attend to small matters like that, and I would give him a lift now and then when his poor little parlour-magic soured on him.' Isn't there a snigger in every word of it? And before this brilliancy must we not confess that humour, like delicacy and all the other virtues, made its first appearance in the nineteenth century and in America?

\* \* \*

## ALBERT BIGELOW PAINE

### [His Literary Worst and Best]†

\* \* \*

\* \* \* *A Connecticut Yankee in King Arthur's Court* is nothing less than a brief for human rights and human privileges. That is what it

† From Albert Bigelow Paine, *Mark Twain: A Biography* (New York: Harper, 1912), pp. 890–91. Paine was Mark Twain's official biographer.

is, and it is a pity that it should be more than that. It is a pity that he should have been beset by his old demon of the burlesque, and that no one should have had the wisdom or the strength to bring it under control.

There is nothing more charming in any of Mark Twain's work than his introductory chapter, nothing more delightful than the armoring of the Yankee and the outset and the wandering with Alisande. There is nothing more powerful or inspiring than his splendid panoramic picture of the King learning mercy through his own degradation, his daily intercourse with a band of manacled slaves; nothing more fiercely moving than that fearful incident of the woman burned to warm those freezing chattels, or than the great gallows scene, where the priest speaks for the young mother about to pay the death penalty for having stolen a halfpenny's worth, that her baby might have bread. Such things as these must save the book from oblivion; but alas! its greater appeal is marred almost to ruin by coarse and extravagant burlesque, which destroys illusion and antagonizes the reader often at the very moment when the tale should fill him with a holy fire of a righteous wrath against wrong. As an example of Mark Twain at his literary worst and best the *Yankee* ranks supreme. It is unnecessary to quote examples; one cannot pick up the volume and read ten pages of it, or five pages, without finding them. In the midst of some exalted passage, some towering sublimity, you are brought suddenly to earth with a phrase which wholly destroys the illusion and the diviner purpose. Howells must have observed these things, or was he so dazzled by the splendor of its intent, its righteous charge upon the ranks of oppression, that he regarded its offenses against art as unimportant. This is hard to explain, for the very thing that would sustain such a great message and make it permanent would be the care, the restraint, the artistic worthiness of its construction. One must believe in a story like that to be convinced of its logic. To lose faith in it—in its narrative—is absolutely fatal to its purpose. The *Yankee in King Arthur's Court* not only offended the English nation, but much of it offended the better taste of Mark Twain's own countrymen, and in time it must have offended even Mark Twain himself. Reading it, one can visualize the author as a careering charger, with a bit in his teeth, trampling the poetry and the tradition of the romantic days, the very things which he himself in his happier moods cared for most. Howells likened him to Cervantes, laughing Spain's chivalry away. The comparison was hardly justified. It was proper enough to laugh chivalry out of court when it was a reality; but Mark Twain, who loved Sir Thomas Malory to the end of his days, the beauty and poetry of his chronicles; who had written *The Prince and the Pauper*, and would one day write that divine tale of the Maid of Orleans; who was himself no more nor less than a knight always ready to redress wrong, would seem to have been the last person to wish to laugh it out of romance.

And yet, when all is said, one may still agree with Howells in ranking the *Yankee* among Mark Twain's highest achievements in the way of "a greatly imagined and symmetrically developed tale." It is of that class, beyond doubt. Howells goes further:

> Of all the fanciful schemes in fiction it pleases me most, and I give myself with absolute delight to its notion of a keen East Hartford Yankee finding himself, by a retroactionary spell, at the court of King Arthur of Britain, and becoming part of the sixth century with all the customs and ideas of the nineteenth in him and about him. The field for humanizing satire which this scheme opens is illimitable.

Colossal it certainly is, as Howells and Stedman agreed: colossal in its grotesqueness as in its sublimity. Howells, summarizing Mark Twain's gifts (1901), has written:

> He is apt to burlesque the lighter colloquiality, and it is only in the more serious and most tragical junctures that his people utter themselves with veracious simplicity and dignity. That great, burly fancy of his is always tempting him to the exaggeration which is the condition of so much of his personal humor, but which when it invades the drama spoils the illusion. The illusion renews itself in the great moments, but I wish it could be kept intact in the small, and I blame him that he does not rule his fancy better.

All of which applies precisely to the writing of the *Yankee in King Arthur's Court*. Intended as a fierce heart-cry against human injustice—man's inhumanity to man—as such it will live and find readers; but, more than any other of Mark Twain's pretentious works, it needs editing—trimming by a fond but relentless hand.

# Recent Criticism

## JOHN B. HOBEN

## [So Much Divine Comedy]†

\*    \*    \*

It is true that Mark Twain's last major work, like even the best of his books, contains some passages "which were only good enough for the corner of a newspaper." The opening scene, padded with the Malory excerpt "How Sir Launcelot Slew Two Giants," drags. Attention is not engaged until the stranger begins his curious story. The narrative mood shifts from the comic to the pathetic in Chapter XXVII, and the ensuing incidents of the smallpox hut ending with the witch-hanging are amateurishly conceived and written. Nevertheless, the story triumphs over its structural defects as surely as does *Don Quixote* or *Gulliver's Travels*, both of which embody incidents contrary to the spirit of the whole. The success is partly due to the fact that the reader accepts much under "the lawless operation of a dream" which would otherwise disturb him—as Howells observed in his *Harper's* review.

"A Yankee mechanic's say against monarchy and its several natural props" miraculously escapes the nationalistic bias and fury so apparent in the notebook entries and in many of the Arnold tracts. Too much has been made of the indignant blasts in *A Connecticut Yankee* and not enough emphasis placed on its dominant tone of genial mockery.

Clemens, of course, prefers the nineteenth century to the sixth; but he is not blind to the imperfections of the American eighties. Trade-union haters and high-wage protectionists are ridiculed in Chapter XXXIII. Under The Boss's reforms the Round Table is converted into the Stock Exchange, with Sir Launcelot president of the board. The advertising of Peterson's prophylactic toothbrush is a hilarious gibe at American business methods. Then, as the final master touch, the outcome of the Yankee's ruthless republican revolution is left undetermined. The endeavor to prove one civilization superior to another is as fruitless as the quest for the Holy Grail.

Some critics interpret the finale as revealing Mark Twain with one foot over the precipice of despair, as a symptom of his forthcoming fulminations against the "damned human race." There is a measure

† From John B. Hoben, "Mark Twain's *Connecticut Yankee*: A Genetic Study," *American Literature*, 18 (1946), 217–18. Footnotes have been omitted.

of truth in the view because pessimism always lurked as a pressure within his paradoxical nature ready to rush to the surface. But is not the climactic mood, in fact, the dominant tone of the *Yankee*, the very essence of Mark Twain's humor at its best? It may assume the shape of fantasy, travesty, or extravaganza, but inwardly it is the human spirit reducing the mysteries of life to livable proportions.

So the unpromising germ cell of a burlesque on knight-errantry, conceived in the fall of 1884, finally comes to life as a robust Yankee mechanic who ironically attempts to lift the British out of their slough of medievalism. And Matthew Arnold's indictment of American Philistinism and cultural mediocrity provided an inner drive to the narrative which was languishing in 1886. Some aspects, however, of the origin of *A Connecticut Yankee* defy complete analysis.

How is it that Mark Twain succeeds in writing his most purposeful satire in the midst of a period when he is dissipating so much energy on his publishing firm, the Paige typesetter, and other enterprises? Usually his works lack even one clearly etched purpose. In the *Yankee* he handles the various levels of social, political, religious, and literary satire in a commendable manner. No adequate answer can be given. Perhaps Howells put his finger on the enigma when he said, "We feel that in this book our arch-humorist imparts more of his personal quality than in anything else he has done."

The greatest miracle is that the pen "warmed-up in hell" shed so much divine comedy. For wherever the *Yankee's* defiance has made an enemy, its good-natured, rough-hewn advocacy of the rights of man has won a thousand friends.

## HOWARD G. BAETZHOLD

### [The Composition of A *Connecticut Yankee*]†

No rumblings of animosity toward England accompanied the first stage of the novel that became *A Connecticut Yankee*. Clemens' initial inspiration for the book resulted primarily from his fascination with the archaic diction and the chivalric derring-do that he found in Malory. Some of the passages in *Le Morte Darthur* remained his favorites for life. The tale of Arthur's passing he considered "one of the most beautiful things ever written in English," and Sir Ector's lament for Launcelot no less than "perfect." But the knightly adventures appealed likewise to his sense of the ridiculous. During the remainder of the reading tour, he and Cable often badgered their friends and each other in Malory's "quaint language," with Clemens gleefully dubbing

† From *Mark Twain and John Bull: The British Connection* (Bloomington: Indiana University Press, 1970), pp. 102, 104–15, 118–20, 123–24, 127–30. Footnotes are by Baetzhold.

Ozias Pond, brother of their tour manager, "Sir Sagramore le Desirous."[1]

The first notebook "germ" for the Connecticut Yankee's adventures in King Arthur's England emerged from a similar mood of raillery and burlesque sometime that December of 1884: "Dream of being a knight errant in armor in the Middle Ages. Have the notions and habits of thought of the present day mixed with the necessities of that. No pockets in the armor. [No way to manage certain requirements of nature.] Can't scratch. Cold in the head—can't blow—can't get a handkerchief, can't use iron sleeve. Iron gets redhot in the sun—leaks in the rain, gets white with frost and freezes me solid in winter. Makes disagreeable clatter when I enter church. Can't dress or undress myself. Always getting struck by lightning. Fall down and can't get up. [See Morte Darthur.]"

Though Clemens later said that he immediately began to make mental notes for the book, he did not get the story itself under way until late in the fall of 1885—almost a year later. Among the notebook entries at that time, one set down a format and a possible conclusion. The Yankee's story was to be preserved as a journal written on ancient yellowed parchment—a palimpsest with "remnants of monkish legends" showing through. The final chapter, however, was to be on new paper, embossed with the British coat-of-arms and the current year's date, 1885. At the end, perhaps as a sort of parallel to the pathos of King Arthur's death in Malory's eloquent account, Clemens envisioned the Yankee back in modern England, distressed by the changes he saw there. Mourning his "lost land," so "fresh & new, so virgin before," and now "old, so old!" he was to lose all interest in life and be "found dead next morning—suicide."[2]

By early February, the writing was well begun, though business pressures constantly threatened to tear the author away from his work. When they finally did so, near the end of February or beginning of March, he had managed to finish "A Word of Explanation" and the first three chapters (as they appear in the published book). But then the time-traveler from Hartford languished in Arthur's castle for almost a year and a half.[3]

1. *MTB*, III, 1320; Nbk 19, p. 25; SLC to OLC, 2/4/85, *LLMT*, p. 230.

2. Nbk 20, p. 33, quoted in my "The Course of Composition of *CY*," *AL*, XXXIII (May, 1961), 197. The nostalgic tone and reference to a lost love suggest that Clemens might have been remembering his legend of Dilsberg Castle, invented for *TA*, Ch. XIX (*MT&EB*, p. 135). The notion of the Yankee's eventual conflict with the Church was apparently stirring in his mind, for shortly after the "suicide" entry he noted: "Country placed under an interdict" (Nbk 20, p. 34). Here he was possibly recalling the Pope's threat in Malory (Bk. XX, Ch. xiii) to use the Interdict against Arthur. The summer before, he had listed a description of England under the Interdict invoked against King John as one of the "Picturesque Incidents in History and Tradition" that he hoped to compile into a book (Nbk 19, p. 32).

3. SLC to CLW, 12/16/85, 2/13/86, *MTBus*, pp. 343, 355; WDH to SLC, 1/16/86, *MTHL*, II, 550. SLC to Charles C. Buel, an assistant editor of the *Century*, mentions on 2/26/86 that a chapter or two of the book he is working on will be good material for the magazine when he finishes (Berg).

Clemens did rouse him briefly on November 11, 1886, for an appearance at the Military Service Institution on Governors Island in New York Bay. There, to an enthusiastic audience of high-ranking military officials and their guests, the author read "all that was then written" and then presented an "outline" of his hero's subsequent adventures.[4] Detailed reports of the performance in the next day's New York *Sun* and *Herald*, and a squib in the *Tribune*, show that the part he read followed the final version of the book through Chapter Three, describing the inventive superintendent of the Colt Arms Factory, his awakening in Arthur's England and capture by Sir Kay; the festivities in Camelot, highlighted by the lies of the boastful knights; and finally, Merlin's putting the company to sleep by telling his "old story for the thousandth time." The remainder of the story as outlined was, however, far different from the final version.

Probably echoing Clemens' own statement of his purpose, the *Tribune* noted that the tale was "intended to bring into sharp contrast the days of the 'idyls of the king' with the present system of life." A few days later the author himself wrote Mrs. Fairbanks that the new book was not going to be "a satire peculiarly" but "more especially a *contrast*" [his italics] between "the daily life of the time & that of today." Taken together, the first three chapters and the "outline" suggest that this contrast would play upon the humorous clashes between the bumptious and somewhat vulgar modernity of the Yankee and the romantic world of chivalry as conceived by Malory, Scott, and Tennyson.[5] * * *

From the Yankee's awakening in Arthurian England through the end of Chapter Three, the published novel shows this burlesque contrast of ancient and modern dominating the action.[6] The few signs of medieval cruelty that do appear, seem to be there primarily as local color rather than as an attack on the feudal system itself. The Yankee's bruised and battered fellow-prisoners are not representatives of the downtrodden peasantry, but are knights—"big boobies," whose stoicism deserved neither admiration nor pity since it resulted from mere "animal training" rather than essential bravery. * * *

In these three chapters, too, more than in the rest of the book, the favorable side of Clemens' initial reaction to Malory is apparent. The

4. *MTN*, p. 171. For a fuller discussion of the Governors Island reading, see my " 'The Autobiography of Sir Robert Smith of Camelot': MT's Original Plan for *A Connecticut Yankee*," *AL*, XXXII (Jan., 1961), 456–461.

5. *MTF*, p. 257, 11/16/86; *MTFP*, p. 48.

6. The tone of the original "dream" idea is very much in evidence as the Yankee awakes to be greeted by Sir Kay in words appropriated from Balin's challenge to Lanceor (Malory, II, v)— "Fair Sir, will ye just? [*sic*]"—and replies, "Will

I which?" His lack of surprise at seeing a knight, his comments on the circus, and his mistaking the towers of Camelot for Bridgeport suggest also that Clemens was drawing some of the Yankee's characteristics from his interest in the great sensation-salesman, P. T. Barnum [Hamlin Hill, "Barnum, Bridgeport, and *The Connecticut Yankee*," *AQ*, XVI (Winter, 1964), 615–616]. Clemens and Barnum corresponded during the 1870's (MTP).

castle at Camelot, as the Yankee describes it, is itself "full of loud contrasts." Above the snarls and growls of dogs fighting for scraps flung from the banquet tables sounds the "gracious and courtly" speech of knights and ladies. Though childish and gullible, the knights exhibit a "manliness" and a certain "lofty sweetness." More specifically, the Yankee notes "the majesty and greatness" of Launcelot's glance and bearing and "the noble benignity and purity" which characterize Arthur and Galahad. The disrespectful rat in Chapter Three who climbs on the sleeping King's head during Merlin's story and dribbles crumbs in his face "with naïve and impudent irreverence" was not added to the manuscript until much later.

Clemens was not merely soft-soaping Mrs. Fairbanks, then, when he assured her that he intended to leave "unsmirched & unbelittled the great & beautiful *characters* drawn by the master hand of old Malory," and at the same time reiterated his pleasure in certain passages in *Le Morte Darthur*.[7]

As for the actual tales from Malory quoted or referred to in these early chapters, their primary purpose was to emphasize the readiness of this "childlike and innocent" lot of people to accept as gospel any account of chivalric exploits, no matter how extravagant. The fact that Merlin's story puts the audience to sleep reflects not on the tale itself, but on the fact that the garrulous magician has told it so many times. For here Merlin is not presented as a sinister force but as a bumbling egotist, whom the clever Yankee will have little trouble outwitting.

The "outline" of the subsequent episodes with which Clemens entertained his Governors Island audience shows that the Yankee (here called Sir Robert Smith) would have continued to exploit his native shrewdness and knowledge of tools and machinery to win wealth and power for himself. Finding that he could not dodge Arthur's commission to rescue sixty captive princesses from a neighboring ogre, he would decide first to "compromise" with the ogre rather than resort to direct combat, and finally, to ignore the mission entirely and merely "tell a majestic lie about" it "like the rest of the knights." His illustration of what "an educated man of the nineteenth century can do in the lofty realms of that art," in turn, would make his rapid rise to power all but certain.

Within a year, Sir Bob was to be running the entire kingdom "at a moderate royalty of forty percent." Within three and a half, he would have cleared away all the "fuss and flummery of romance," and put the kingdom on a "strictly business basis." Launcelot would be con-

---

7. *MTF*, p. 258, 11/16/86. He hoped that Sir Galahad would still remain "the divinest spectre that one glimpses among the mists & twilights of Dreamland," that Arthur would "keep his sweetness & his purity," and that Launcelot would "abide & continue 'the kindest man that ever strake the sword,' yet 'the sternest knight to his mortal foe that ever put spear in the rest.'" He would be reluctant, too, to destroy the tears and pathos inherent in the dissolution of the Round Table and in the last great battle, which he termed "the Battle of the Broken Hearts."

ducting "a kind of Louisiana lottery," the quest for the Holy Grail would give way to a search for the Northwest Passage, and the 140 knights of Arthur's Court would form a Stock Board, with seats at the Round Table selling for $30,000. [8]

Sir Bob's skill at prevarication, his "moderate" forty per cent royalty, and his other manipulations indicate that certain contemporary practices were to be fair game for Clemens' burlesque along with the "fuss and flummery of romance," though the latter would, of course, provide the primary target.

Among the "germs" for other episodes that were later expanded, Clemens mentioned the possibility of Sir Bob's using a lasso to defeat his cumbersome competitors and later employing an electrically charged barbed-wire fence and battery of Gatling guns to halt "squadrons" of hostile knights. But in the early version, the guns and electricity were pressed into service not to destroy the whole chivalry of England, but merely to win a victory over King Arthur's enemies in one of the great tournaments.

Clemens apparently did not tell his audience of his plan for the Yankee's eventual suicide in modern England. Either he had already abandoned the idea or preferred not to reveal the entire plot. He was probably not greatly concerned with the ending at this time, for in the letter already mentioned, he told Mrs. Fairbanks that he intended to find his "holiday entertainment" for thirty years in writing just three chapters of the novel each summer.

When he picked up the story the next summer, however, he did not stop at three chapters but wrote more than *sixteen*—Chapters Four through Twenty and part of Twenty-one (except for Chapter Ten, "The Beginnings of Civilization," which he inserted in 1888). Therefore, by mid-September, despite several delays resulting from business worries, he had seen the Yankee through his rise to Bossdom, introduced the demoiselle Alisande la Carteloise (Sandy) into the furtherelaborated quest for the captive princesses (now forty-five rather than sixty), and had brought the wanderers through the horrors of Morgan le Fay's castle to the portals of the Valley of Holiness. [9]

But sometime between the Governors Island reading and the summer of 1887, Clemens' concept of the story of the Yankee's role seems to have changed drastically. Instead of merely profit for himself and for the king's treasury, the Yankee's primary goal became no less than total reform of political and social evils in Arthur's kingdom. Instead of dodging the encounter with the ogre, he would carry the quest through to its vivid conclusion that the princesses (and by implication,

8. My summary is from the Hartford *Courant*, 11/13/86 (reprinted from the New York *Sun*, 11/12/86) and the New York *Herald*, 11/12/86. Louisiana established a state lottery in 1886, which operated until it was outlawed in 1895.

9. For documentation of the chronology of work on the remainder of the novel, see my "The Course of Composition of *A Connecticut Yankee*," *AL*, XXXIII (May, 1961), 195–214.

all royalty and nobility) were hogs. And instead of using his Gatling gun and electrified fence simply against Arthur's enemies, he would ultimately add the devastating power of dynamite and turn his weapons against the whole chivalry of England and the "superstitions" for which it stood.

The reasons for the shift in purpose doubtless were complicated ones. In some respects, of course, the change made the novel a much more logical next step from *Life on the Mississippi* and *Huckleberry Finn* than the original contrast would have been. Its examination of the influences of chivalry and of the effects of slavery of various sorts embody some of the most serious concerns of the earlier books. But new emphases are also apparent. In the discussions of the advantages of free-trade over protection, for instance, the author would embody his admiration for the policies of Grover Cleveland. More important, during these years Clemens developed a new sympathy for equalitarian democracy.

The breakdown of his earlier mistrust stemmed partly from his interest in the activities of the Knights of Labor in 1886. Intrigued by the group's potentialities for improving conditions for the masses, he had treated the Monday Evening Club meeting of March 22, 1886, to a flowery eulogy that hailed the workers as "The New Dynasty." Admitting that power inevitably resulted in oppression, he argued that because this dynasty would be concerned with the nation's good rather than with the selfish interests of a small clique, it need not be feared. Rather, it would form a permanent defense "against the Socialist, the Communist, the anarchist, the tramp, and the selfish agitator for 'reforms,' " and "against all like forms of political disease, pollution and death."[1] Many of the attitudes and comments of that speech Clemens would transfer almost verbatim to the *Yankee* a year and a half later.

But given the difference between the "outline" at Governors Island and the new themes that emerged the following summer, something else must have contributed to this change. Whatever other elements helped produce the critical mass, Clemens' growing antagonism toward England was a major catalyst to the explosion.

In examining the events of these months and the immediately succeeding years, it is important to note that Clemens' quarrel with England did not result in a broadside blast at *all* English attitudes. Rather, he directed his fire only at those that seemed obstacles to progress and the preservation of human dignity. In becoming a Mugwump he had moved closer to the views of the British Liberal Party, for

1. DV 80, MTP, published in Paul J. Carter, "MT and the American Labor Movement," *NEQ*, XXX (Sept., 1957), 383–388; reprinted in *Twainian* (Sept.–Oct., 1960), 2, 4. In February, 1887, also, Clemens spoke again to the Monday Evening Club on "Machine Culture," praising the inventive skill of the American workman. (Parts of this address perhaps survive in *The American Claimant*, Ch. X, in one of the speeches at the Mechanics Club).

as Louis J. Budd has said, the Mugwumps "were well-defined politically as the American branch of middle-class Liberalism."[2]

Clemens had kept in fairly close touch with developments in England ever since his visits during the 1870's. Besides reading newspapers and periodicals, he corresponded with British friends like Frank Finlay, a long-time member of the Liberal Reform Club. At various times during the middle and late 1880's, reports from abroad evoked direct reactions in his notebooks. In 1885, for instance, he speculated briefly at one point on the future of the Liberal Party and the possibility that Lord Rosebery might become the next Prime Minister. In July, 1888, he would applaud the progress of the Local Government Bill, a Liberal measure hotly debated for several years in both Parliament and the press. Copying a July 1 news report from London that the Liberals were welcoming the bill's passage through committee as "almost a revolution, which transfers control of county affairs from the privileged few to the people," he added his own cheer: "There—the handwriting on the wall! There's a day coming!"[3]

As Budd has correctly observed, many of the "improvements" that the Yankee came to propose for Arthurian England were those which Britain's Liberals—and especially the party's Radical wing—were currently advocating. In an unpublished essay of 1888 or 1889, also, Clemens' listing of major steps in England's "slow climb from chattel slavery" all but summarized the principles for which the Liberals had been fighting over the years. Yet it was a new sense that the evils of monarchy and aristocracy had continued into the present, even in the England he had loved so well during the 1870s, that accounts for most of the themes in *A Connecticut Yankee* not envisioned in the earlier "outline."

The outlook for Liberal legislation in 1886 and 1887 was less than bright. In the spring of 1885, the fall of Gladstone's ministry had aroused great interest in the United States, and many had watched with deep concern the general election that followed. American public opinion very largely reflected that of the New York *Herald* and other newspapers. For them Gladstone was the champion of progress, staunchly opposing the obstructionist tactics of the British aristocracy and landed gentry. Many were dismayed, therefore, when even those whom the Liberals' Reform Act of 1885 had recently enfranchised, flocked in large numbers to vote the Conservative ticket.

Though Clemens' reactions to the sweeping Conservative victory had apparently not jelled sufficiently by November, 1886, to find their way into his "outline," other irritants soon stirred him up. Reports that autumn of Welsh riots against enforced tithing led to a notebook blast at this "frightful tax" which so harassed the poor. From those reports,

2. *MTSP*, p. 110.

3. Nbk 18, p. 23; 23 I, p. 11, quoted in *MTSP*, p. 122; see also pp. 120–121.

too, he gleaned an incident about a poor woman's reaction to the tithe-collector priest, which he would incorporate into the *Yankee* the following summer. Very likely he also read about the use of government troops to disperse the crowds who had gathered in Trafalgar Square to protest against unemployment, and about the Scottish crofters' demonstrations against their landlords for setting aside grazing lands as private deer-parks.[4] If not, England was still specifically on his mind during these months, for another notebook entry proposed that he write up a comparison of "the Englishman 100 years ago" and "the Englishman of To-Day."[5]

Other rumblings sounded early in 1887, when Matthew Arnold's opinion of General Grant's *Memoirs* came to his attention. Though the review (which first appeared in the January and February issues of *Murray's* magazine) was more complimentary than critical, Clemens did not let its few objections go unchallenged. He was no doubt ruffled a good deal by Arnold's repetition of his objections to American boasting, especially now that the criticism was implicitly aimed at Grant.

With both the defense of a friend and possible book sales at stake, Clemens welcomed the opportunity for counterattack provided by an invitation to address a reunion of the Army and Navy Club of Connecticut on April 27, the anniversary of Grant's birthday. Concentrating on Arnold's criticisms of certain grammatical constructions, he drew for logistical support on H. H. Breen's *Modern English Literature: Its Blemishes and Defects* in order to "prove" that the general's grammatical faults were no more numerous nor serious than those of many universally acknowledged literary masters. Finally, after firing at certain stylistic flaws in the review itself, he flung Arnold's charges of American chauvinism back in his face with a flowery tribute to the grandeur of the *Memoirs* and their soldier-author, "who, all untaught by the silken phrase-makers, linked words together with an art surpassing the art of the schoolmen."[6]

A more important stimulus to the *Yankee's* change of direction, however—perhaps the primary one—was a book sent by an English acquaintance, which arrived in May, 1887, barely a month before Clemens resumed work on the novel. This bit of potential dynamite, *The People's History of the English Aristocracy*, was the work of another British correspondent, a London printer and Radical prop-

4. *MTN*, pp. 190–191. For mention of Trafalgar Square demonstrations and crofters' riots, see R. H. Gretton's *A Modern History of the British People*, 1880–1910 (Boston, 1913), I, 195. Gretton cites the files of the London *Times* as his chief source of "dates and facts" and *Punch* as his authority for some of "the popular interests of the moment." His book, therefore, is an excellent source for matters of current interest in England during the years covered by his study.

5. Notebook 21, TS, pp. 32–33, Mark Twain Papers.

6. *MTS(P)*, p. 137. See also John Y. Simon, ed., *General Grant by Matthew Arnold with a Rejoinder by MT* (Carbondale, Ill., 1966).

agandist named George Standring, who edited his own magazine, *The Republican* (later called *The Radical*), and also wrote for several other Liberal and free-thought journals.

\*    \*    \*

If *The People's History* did not actually inspire Clemens to give new directions to *A Connecticut Yankee*, it at least crystallized his decision to do so. In its vivid expression of the most vehement strains of current Liberal and Radical sentiments, it treated many of the same themes which came to dominate the *Yankee*. Standring's major premise was that England's only hope lay in replacing the monarchy with a republic. He charged particularly that the vast wealth of the aristocracy allowed it to control not only the House of Lords, but also the mercantile interests, the professions, the military services, and even "that one bulwark which the nation is supposed to possess against tyranny—the House of Commons." Among the causes of this deplorable situation, he isolated two principal evils: the feudal laws of primogeniture and entail, and, almost more important, the British devotion to the "fetish of nobility," which kept the commoner in a state of slavery more hopeless than if his chains were real ones.[7]

As evidence that the nobility was completely unworthy of respect, much less of loyalty and devotion, Strandring presented the "case histories" of most of England's noble families, tracing them from their beginnings to the present day. Emphasizing those that had originated in the guilty amours of kings and courtesans, he marshalled an amazing catalogue of "crimes," both serious and petty. And to hammer home his point, he almost invariably capped each recital with a sarcastic jibe like that following an account of the misdeeds of Thomas Howard, Third Duke of Norfolk: "Yet this is the stock to which our nobility point with pride when they prate over their long descent."

Clemens' wide reading in English history had made him familiar with much of Standring's "evidence."[8] But nowhere in one place and in such detail had he found the intimate stories of so many of England's noble houses. He was so enthusiastic about *The People's History*, in fact, that soon after its arrival in May, he proposed to publish it with some of his longtime favorites in a high-priced edition, to be called "Royalty and Nobility Exposed." St. Simon's *Memoires* and "the English printer's little book" would come first, with Taine's *Ancient Regime* and Carlyle's *French Revolution* following almost immediately, and then, sometime later, "The White Slave—Mining Life in Wales—Margravine of Bayreuth."[9]

7. *The People's History of the English Aristocracy*, 2d. ed. (London, 1891), Chapter I, passim. Direct quotations in this and following paragraph: Introduction (unnumbered), and pp. 1, 6, 16, 165.
8. By this time, too, he had probably read such books as Andrew Carnegie's popular *Trium-phant Democracy* (1886), which also urged the establishment of a republic in Britain. Clemens' gift copy from Carnegie, however, was from the 1888 edition. (*A1911*, p. 14).
9. Notebook 21, TS, p. 49, Mark Twain Papers.

Though that project (and also several later plans for introducing *The People's History* to American readers) failed to materialize,[1] there is no doubt that Standring's book served as an important agent in focusing Clemens' attention on aristocratic abuses in England. Furthermore, its very position in the proposed edition, preceding even such old friends as Taine and Carlyle, not only testifies to Clemens' high regard for the volume, but shows him placing England squarely alongside France as a perpetrator of the ancient evils. No longer was he affirming (as he had in 1879) that the British lacked the essential savagery which had allowed the French to continue the "atrocious privileges" of the nobility down through the ages. Here was firsthand evidence from a native-born Englishman that British slavery to a totally corrupt ideal was far from dead.

If Standring's vituperations had not totally convinced Clemens that the "fetish of nobility" was still potent in England, the reports that June of Queen Victoria's Jubilee would certainly have completed the job. Seldom had adulation reached such a peak as in the crowds who lined the streets on June 20 to cheer the parade to Westminster Abbey. According to contemporary newspaper accounts, no fewer than three kings (of Denmark, Belgium, and Greece) marched in the colorful procession, along with "the Crown Princes of every throne in Christendom, and of some outside Christendom."[2] The particular cortege which followed Victoria's carriage—her three sons, five sons-in-law, and nine grandsons and grandsons-in-law—provided an eloquent reminder that Victoria's numerous progeny had linked Britain with most of the other thrones of Europe. Whether it was the descriptions of the Jubilee, or merely the sneers of Standring and other Liberals which impressed him, Clemens himself was to allude to Victoria's fertility in his novel, not once but twice.[3]

Less than two months later, struck by how radically one's attitudes could change without one's being conscious of the alterations, Clem-

---

1. In May, 1887, Clemens reminded himself to "Hand the nobility book to a publisher" (Nbk 21, p. 47) and in September thought of including a copy of *The People's History* as a bonus for purchasers of *A Connecticut Yankee* (Nbk 22 I, p. 5). Early in 1889 he saw Standring's views as "An Englishman on England" forming an eloquent contrast to those of "Englishmen on America" like Matthew Arnold and Sir Lepel Griffin (whom Arnold had cited in his criticisms of the U.S.). At the same time, presumably to make Standring's comments widely available, he proposed to publish companion volumes of Arnold, Griffin, and Standring in paper covers at twenty-five cents each (Nbk 23 II, pp. 54–55). That fall he even got so far as drafting a title page for an "Authorized American Edition" of *The People's History* to be called *English Royalty and Nobility* (A1911, p. 11). But again some-

thing interfered, and the project was shelved again, permanently, even though as late as November 24 Clemens was urging Fred Hall to "pile on the printers" so that copies could be on the booksellers' counters and in the hands of reviewers when CY issued on December 10 (SLC to Hall, 11/24/89, *MTLP*, p. 257).

2. Gretton, *Modern History of the British People*, I, 211.

3. In Ch. XL, Clarence facetiously argues that after Arthur's demise a royal family of cats should be established, whose obvious virtues would inspire other nations of Europe to request "catlings from our own royal house" for their rulers. In an attack on royal grants, added to Ch. XXV in the proof stage, the Yankee cites the excessive costs arising from the fact that these "royalties . . . were a long-lived race and very fruitful."

ens described to Howells the progress of his own ideas regarding monarchy and aristocracy since his first reading of Carlyle's *French Revolution* in 1871, at which time he had sided with the moderate Girondins. "Every time I have read it since, I have read it differently—being influenced & changed little by little, by life & environment (& Taine & St. Simon): & now I lay the book down once more, & recognize that I am a Sansculotte—And not a pale characterless Sansculotte, but a Marat. Carlyle teaches no such gospel: so the change is in *me*—in my vision of the evidences." Obviously Clemens had come by this time to regard the French Revolution, despite its excesses, in much the same terms as he later described it (again to Howells)—as "the noblest & the holiest" event in history next to the Fourth of July and its aftermath. Yet he was also convinced that its "gracious work" was not yet finished—"not anywhere in the remote neighborhood of it."[4]

In the novel itself, signs of the storm that was about to break appeared almost immediately in Chapter Four. Following Sir Dinadan's hoary jokes and Sir Kay's lies about capturing the Yankee, a sharper tone begins to emerge as the narrator turns his attention to Arthurian morals. Where earlier he had spoken of "gracious and courtly speech," he now describes the knights' and ladies' "language that would make a Comanche blush." More significantly, he adds that reading *Tom Jones*, *Roderick Random*, "and other books of that kind" had convinced him that bawdy conversation "and the morals and conduct which such talk implies" were common among English ladies and gentlemen "clear into our own nineteenth century. . . ."

Some critics have denied that these remarks indicate a shift in the novel's tone, or at least that they can be attributed to any new antagonism toward England. Clemens had, to be sure, said much the same thing about the coarseness of *Tom Jones* in 1879. But in terms of *A Connecticut Yankee* itself, the comments on language and morals are more sharply critical of the Arthurians than those in the preceding chapters. The connection of the crudity and immorality with later centuries, including the nineteenth, also implies a considerable extension of the scope of the novel's satire. Furthermore, the immediate inspiration for the Yankee's remarks very likely came from Standring's *People's History*. Around the time he wrote the passage, Clemens made a list of some fourteen sources that could be included in an appendix, to support his charges that laxity in language and morals had lingered far beyond the medieval era.[5] Of those included, he had

---

4. SLC to WDH, 8/22/87; 9/22/89, *MTHL*, II, 595, 613.
5. Reminding himself to "make an appendix in support of the assertion that there were no real gentlemen and ladies before our century," he cited besides "Standring's book," Madame

Campan's memoirs of Marie Antoinette, Taine's *Ancient Regime*, St. Simon's *Memoires*, Cellini's *Autobiography*, memoirs of Madame du Barry and the Margravine of Beyreuth, Rousseau's *Confessions*, the writings of Lord Herbert of Cherbury and Emile Zola, "Field-

probably read Standring's book most recently and could hardly have failed to note such vivid examples of aristocratic elegance as the Duchess of Marlborough, whose "volleys of oaths and streams of foul language would have done credit to a Billingsgate fish-fag," or the subsequent remark of a law-clerk that though he did not know her, he "was sure she was a lady of quality, *as she swore so dreadfully*" [Standring's italics].

The *People's History* also contributed at least supporting evidence for the later extension of these observations on morals in the Yankee's comment (Chapter Fourteen), that the "squaws" of these Arthurian "Comanches" were always ready "to desert to the buck with the biggest string of scalps at his belt." Was he thinking of various ladies in *Le Morte Darthur*—like the damsel (in Book Ten, Chapter Eighty-three) who became the property of Sir Epinogris, Sir Helior, and Sir Safere, in rapid succession? (But most of Malory's females are passive and submissive.) Standring's anthology of aristocratic misdeeds, on the other hand, not only cites the "flood of filth and garbage" from English divorce courts as representing "the daily life of the Modern English Aristocracy," but also records how Lady Shrewsbury, disguised as a page, attended the duel between her husband and George Villiers, second Duke of Buckingham, and *"when her husband lay cold and dead on the ground . . . rode off with his murderer"* [again Standring's italics].[6] The possible play on the first syllable of *Buck*-ingham's name in Clemens' Indian metaphor is also intriguing.

The immediately following episodes, too, give important indications of Clemens' current antagonisms (which will appear in another context), but he managed to remain pretty well detached from his protagonist through the destruction of Merlin's Tower in Chapter Seven. With the Yankee's first direct diatribe against English reverence for rank and pedigree in Chapter Eight, however, the mask slips considerably. Invoking the same sort of scorn which Standring had so often heaped upon British bondage to the "fetish of nobility"—and in much the same language—the author makes the Yankee sneer at the "inherited ideas" that made ostensibly free Englishmen into slaves, proud to grovel before king, Church, and noble, and grateful even for the snubs which invariably greet their devotion. "*Any* kind of royalty, howsoever modified, *any* kind of aristocracy, howsoever pruned, is rightly an insult," Hank Morgan says. Thereafter, the humorist makes the connection with the present even more obvious with the Yankee's ironic observation that in Arthur's Britain, "just as in the remote England of my birth-time, the sheep-witted earl who could claim long

ing's chief novels, and Richardson's and Miss Burney's, and even *Vicar of Wakefield.*" From these he would select "instances where printable" and explain "that others (note their places)

are not" (Separate ms. sheet included with *Yankee* ms., Berg).

6. Standring, p. 61; Introduction; p. 42.

descent from a king's leman . . . was a better man than I was."

\* \* \*

Work on the novel lagged in late August or early September, though the author still hoped to complete the book that fall. But once back in Hartford, he soon gave up. "This kind of rush is why parties write no books," he complained to Mrs. Fairbanks on November 25, after listing some of his recent business and social activities.[7]

During that fall and winter his animosity toward England continued to make itself evident, and several incidents furnished specific impetus for later chapters of *A Connecticut Yankee.* In November, suspiciously close on the heels of a visit from Charles Dickens (the novelist's son) and his daughter, Clemens growled that a "cessation of hospitalities to traveling English" had occurred "because English manners could not be endured." Shortly thereafter, another notebook entry suggested that "English Breeding as Exhibited in the United States" was "a prodigious theme," well-calculated to make "all England blush." Obviously, there was little left, by this time, of the tolerance shown to critical English visitors in *Life on the Mississippi.* The following spring Clemens reacted even more vigorously to Matthew Arnold's "Civilization in the United States" which appeared in the April issue of *Nineteenth Century.* Touched off by a request for a rebuttal from *Forum* editor Lorettus D. Metcalf, the outburst was nonetheless sincere. Early in April a single notebook sentence proclaiming that "Matthew Arnold's civilization" was *"superficial polish"* began a barrage whose reverberations would echo through scores of notebook and manuscript pages during the next two years.[8]

Whether the outraged American immediately plunged into the furious fragmentary replies that remain among the unpublished manuscripts in the Mark Twain Papers (one of which specifically mentions an editor's request) is not certain. By June 13, however, he had projected a future book entitled "English Criticism on America, Letters to an English Friend," and a week later was filling his notebook with ammunition that could serve equally well for that book or for the attack on Arnold.

Though Clemens never did complete his article for the *Forum*, his various fulminations found their way into several drafts of some half-dozen essays, mostly unfinished, but altogether totalling more than a hundred manuscript pages. Repeatedly he lambasted Arnold's

---

7. *MTF*, p. 262. As late as September, Clemens had made tentative plans to issue the novel the following spring, predicated upon finishing it by Nov. 15 (Nbk 22 I, p. 2).
8. Nbk 22 II, pp. 37, 64; five items after the latter reference, recalling a dream in which Americans greeted the Archangel Michael "with a hearty and friendly 'Hello Mike!' " he ironically admitted: "No, there *is* no reverence with us." (All quoted in my "Course of Composition of CY," p. 206, as is quotation from Nbk 22 II, p. 69 in the following paragraph). For Metcalf's request see *MTHL*, II, 600–601.

definition of "civilization," and above all the Englishman's insistence that "a spirit of reverence" was the quintessential element of any truly civilized society. He was particularly irked, also, by Arnold's charge that the deplorable lack of reverence among Americans stemmed not only from an irresponsible press, but from their unfortunate "addiction to the 'funny man'."

Yale University provided the platform for his only public reference to Arnold that summer. In accepting their honorary Master of Arts degree, he answered the slur on American humorists, and at the same time all but defined the purpose which had come to dominate *A Connecticut Yankee* in 1887. The degree, he said, represented a tribute to all humorists, a tribute made all the more "forcible and timely" by "the late Matthew Arnold's sharp rebuke to the guild of American 'funny men' in his latest literary delicacy." It would remind the world of the humorist's real purpose: "the deriding of shams, the exposure of pretentious falsities, the laughing of stupid superstitions out of existence . . . ," a purpose which made him "the natural enemy of royalties, nobilities, privileges, and all kindred swindles, and the natural friend of human rights and human liberties."[9]

This is the mood in which Clemens took up Hank Morgan's story again soon after the ceremony in New Haven. Though the battle lines had long been drawn, Arnold's essay obviously had made him more determined than ever to laugh those "stupid superstitions" out of existence.

More specifically, the long notebook diatribes which began late in June by charging that the "absence of an irreverent press" had permitted Europe to exist for a thousand years "merely for the advantage of half a dozen seventh-rate families called Monarchs, and some hundreds of riffraff sarcastically called Nobles,"[1] help to determine the point at which Clemens resumed Hank Morgan's adventures. Just at the paragraph in Chapter Twenty-one where Sandy assembles the "princesses" in the castle dining room (and both paper and handwriting change in the manuscript), Hank echoes his creator's renewed antagonism toward English subservience to rank and caste. Observing the ironic picture of Sandy waiting personally upon the hogs, he comments that her attitude manifested "in every way the deep reverence which the natives of her island, ancient and modern, have always felt for rank, let its outward casket and the mental and moral contents be what they may."

\* \* \*

9. Hartford *Courant*, 6/22/88, p. 5, col. 1. Arnold had died on April 15, hence the reference to the "late" Matthew Arnold.

1. *MTN*, p. 195. Many of these notes were preparations for a speech to be delivered the following Sept. 20 (in response to the toast, "The American Press") at an Encampment of the Army of the Cumberland in Chicago (Nbk 22 II, p. 67; 23 I, pp. 1, 2).

The Valley episodes reflect other issues currently receiving much attention in England, as does Chapter Ten, "The Beginnings of Civilization." Clemens wrote Chapter Ten sometime late in the summer of 1888, when he apparently realized he had not adequately prepared for various details like the appearance of the telephone and newspaper in the Holy Valley.[2] There he established a four-year period between the tournament of Chapter Nine and the beginning of the quest with Sandy, and summarized the Yankee's accomplishments. Besides a network of telephone and telegraph lines and the newspaper (with Clarence as editor), the Yankee creates technical schools, a "teacher-factory," and military and naval academies, revises the revenue system, and establishes a "complete variety" of protestant sects. In addition he underlines the Church's commanding role by stressing the need to keep all these projects (except the newspaper and revenue systems) secret for fear of ecclesiastical opposition.

Traditionally, the Yankee's plans for improving England have been seen in terms of American technological and industrial development. Yet along with ideas derived from Lecky's works (to be considered presently), recent discussions in English newspapers and journals very likely contributed to the picture. Clemens was no doubt aware, for instance, that the matter of public education, especially technical education, was a vital issue in England during 1887 and 1888. In 1887 various members of Parliament had introduced into the House of Commons a bill for publicly supported technical education, only to see it by-passed in favor of other legislation. In another area, certain British Liberals had for some time advocated a reduction in Church control of English schools. A Royal Commission was appointed to study the matter. But when this essentially Conservative group reported, it recommended only a few changes, primarily in teacher training and the methods of paying salaries. Moreover, besides voting 15-5 in favor of maintaining the voluntary (private) school system rather than increasing public support of education, it suggested that religious instruction be increased rather than decreased.[3]

The efforts of journalists to draw public attention to the need for reform increased. During 1888 the *Nineteenth Century* alone devoted some twenty articles to educational problems. Of these, ten dealt specifically with the need for increased technical education. In the February number, Thomas Henry Huxley declared his disappointment that the Technical Instruction Bill had been dropped, and another writer called the lack of action on that bill one of the most important Parliamentary failures of the preceding year. But, though many in England would have sided with the opinion of the anarchist

2. Other details: the supplies requisitioned from Clarence for the "restoration" of the fountain, and the appearance of the "West Pointer" at the competitive examination.
3. See Gretton, I, 210, 220, 228, 243.

Prince, Peter Kropotkin, who declared in June that technological training was the boon that would usher in a "reign of plenty," there were those who demurred. In July, for instance, a British nobleman, Lord Armstrong, argued that the workingman would benefit far more from additional instruction "of a religious and moral nature" than from technical education. And despite all the arguments in favor of improving technical training in British schools, those who agreed with Lord Armstrong temporarily prevailed, for the Education Act did not come before the Parliament again until 1889 (after *A Connecticut Yankee* had been completed). That the Yankee established public schools, the "teacher-factory," and other training schools for technical skills therefore probably reflects more than merely a tribute to American know-how.

Some of the Yankee's specific technological achievements can also be read as satiric thrusts at England's backwardness. Though Edison had invented the incandescent lamp in 1879 and New York had completed the world's first central power plant for electric lighting two years later, it was not until 1888 (again the very year in which Clemens wrote most of his novel) that house-to-house lighting became practicable in London. Before that, each electrical installation had required its own separate power plant, and even in 1888 the two companies formed that year confined their activities chiefly to areas where theaters, clubs, and hotels assured sufficient consumption to make the operation profitable.

\* \* \*

Almost all of these elements—technological backwardness, aristocratic opposition to education, abuses in the military system, reverence for hereditary rank, and the close association of Church and State in matters of aristocratic prerogatives—Clemens molded especially skillfully into the Chapter Twenty-five episode in which the Yankee's West Pointer and two young nobles compete for a lieutenancy in the newly established army. Though the humorist's longtime aversion to corrupt practices in the American civil service system may also have added its bit, England was the primary target.

Along with W. E. H. Lecky's pointed comment (in *The History of England in the Eighteenth Century*) that in most areas of competition, aristocratic lineage invariably overshadowed intellectual eminence,[4] any number of Standring's acid remarks could have served as the immediate inspiration for this episode. But Clemens probably also remembered W. S. Gilbert's vivid spoof of Parliamentary obtuseness in *Iolanthe* (1882). The fact that he had already adapted the "jackdaws strut in peacock feathers" line from *Pinafore* for Hank Morgan's earlier

4. *Eighteenth Century*, I, 227. Clemens was reading this work in 1888. See notes to Ch. VII, *post*.

blast at aristocratic pretensions doubles the temptation to see in the Arthurian contest echoes of Strephon's "shocking proposal" (in Act II) to "throw the Peerage open to Competitive Examination," and Lord Tolloller's rejoinder that "with a House of Peers with no grandfathers worth mentioning, the country must go to the dogs."

Clemens' barbs fly thick from the very beginning of the episode. Some Americans might miss the shaft in Hank's identification of the chief examiner as "the officer known to later centuries as Norroy King-at-Arms." But English readers would immediately recognize the allusion to the Herald's College, the authority since 1483 in all matters of noble genealogy.[5] The Church's concern with hereditary rank is also assailed, both in the Yankee's remark that of course the examiners were all priests, and in the vivid passage where Hank is rebuked for questioning the requirement that candidates for commissions prove that they are descended from at least four generations of nobility, When the chief examiner tells him that his query "impugns the wisdom of our Holy Mother Church herself," since a similar rule applies to the canonization of saints, Hank hammers home the basic likeness between the aristocratic and ecclesiastical "superstitions" with the only overtly satiric comment in the episode: "In the one case a man lies dead-alive four generations—mummified in ignorance and sloth—and that qualifies him to command live people . . . and in the other case, a man lies bedded with death and worms four generations, and that qualifies him for office in the celestial camp."

The humorist's principal source for his attack on the "four-generation" rule for Army officerships was Carlyle's *French Revolution* which cites the requirement as the brain-child "in comparatively late years" of a French Minister of War, who sought to reduce the excessive number of requests for commissions. Carlyle explains, too, that this solution to the immediate problem had had a more serious effect. By establishing a barrier between the old and the new nobility, as well as by increasing still further the gulf between commoner and noble, it created a harsher contrast between classes in France.[6] This concept Clemens put to excellent use, first in King Arthur's explanation that the rule prevented peers "of more lofty lineage" from scorning military service because of the presence of those "of too recent blood," and later in the Examining Board's final choice between the candidates.

As the examination begins, the Board eliminates the Yankee's West Pointer immediately, refusing at first even to question him when they

---

5. They would also doubtless identify the two other members of the Board as the two other ruling members of the College: Garter King of Arms and Clarenceux King of Arms.

6. *FrRev*, II, 2, ii. Taine also briefly mentions the rule (*Ancient Regime*, p. 64), and Clemens, in a note for an appendix, cites both Taine and Carlyle as supporting sources (Nbk 24, p. 15).

discover that his father was a weaver. But then it relents enough to let Hank Morgan conduct the examination into the cadet's other qualifications for officership. The youth's obvious skill and his fund of technical knowledge of course count for nothing compared with the "real" qualifications of the two nobles. Though the first, Sir Pertipole, is thoroughly stupid and the second is his "twin, for ignorance and incapacity," both possess the requisite four generations of nobility.

In the Board's final choice of Sir Pertipole's rival, Clemens adapted Carlyle's distinction between the "old" and "new" nobility so as to create a double irony. Sir Pertipole's great-grandfather had been elevated to "the sacred dignity of the British nobility" as first Baron of Barley Mash, for having built a brewery. But though the author here subtly supports the contemporary objections to the "beerage" in England, this fact is not what disqualifies Sir Pertipole. Presumably he means to imply that the "beer peerages" are just as legitimate as any others. What does win the place for the other young noble is the character of the wife of his line's founder. Sir Pertipole's ancestress had been a chaste and gracious gentlewoman. But when his rival reveals that *his* great-great grandmother had been "a king's leman" who climbed "to that splendid eminence by her own unholpen merit from the sewer where she was born," the examiner proclaims this lineage to be "the true nobility . . . the right and perfect intermixture . . . the blood all Britain loves and reverences."

In thus defining the "old" nobility, the humorist once again underlined the pet aversion he shared with George Standring—the unwarranted pride of most British aristocrats in their noble heritage and the irrational slavery of British commoners to the "fetish of nobility." In reconsidering the passage later, he may have thought, in fact, that the final phrase of the examiner's accolade resembled some of Standring's sarcasms too closely, or at least considered it too direct a statement, for he ultimately deleted it from the manuscript.

Clemens' biting satire of the young nobles in this episode is likewise identical in spirit with Standring's snorting indignation over such anomalies as one of Nell Gwyn's sons being commissioned Colonel of a cavalry regiment at age fifteen, even though (as Standring adds) "like many royal and aristocratic officers of today, he did nothing besides drawing his pay."[7] Such observations doubtless lay behind the Yankee's subsequent scheme to establish the King's Own Regiment, exclusively for nobles, and with absolute independence in time of war. With the nobles flocking to such an infinitely attractive company, the

7. *People's History*, p. 29. He doubtless also noticed Standring's reference (p. 145) to the bastard son of the Duke of Clarence—"this offspring of a prostitute actress"—who, at fourteen, was not only a Cornet in the Tenth Regiment of Light Dragoons, of which the Prince of Wales was Colonel, but was "*senior to four other Cornets*" [Standring's italics].

rest of the army could then be officered by "nobodies" like the West Pointer, "selected on the basis of mere efficiency." In the conclusion of this "Competitive Examination" chapter Clemens took a final fling at the aristocratic code, scoring the inequities in the awards of pensions and allowances, esecially as these came to members of the Royal Family. Here again he parallels Standring.[8]

There is a fascinating possibility that the timely arrival on bicycles of Launcelot and his five hundred knights (in Chapter Thirty-eight) carries a contemporary implication. In 1888 some of England's local Volunteer companies, whose role in their country's defense system received much discussion, were introducing cycling into their maneuvers. But, as one historian has said with almost classic restraint, "the high bicycle did not lend itself well to such uses."[9] Did the thought of soldiers in full military gear pedalling furiously down the highway so overwhelm Clemens that he could not resist enhancing the absurdity by having his cumbersome armored knights mount similar steeds?

Once the Valley episodes were finished, progress on the novel during September and October was more rapid. The book was going so well, in fact, that on October 5 Clemens hopefully named October 22 as the date when both the novel and the Paige typesetter might be finished. Again his calculations proved over-optimistic. But by some time in March[1] the holocaust of the Sand-Belt had burned itself out, and the author had brought the Yankee back to die in modern England, not by suicide as in his original plan, but still, in a way, yearning for his "lost land."

8. *People's History*, pp. 149, 161–163, and passim. See also *MTN*, p. 207. Clemens may also have known some of Standring's shorter pamphlets like *Court Flunkeys: Their Work and Wages* (London: Freethought Publishing Co., n.d.) and "Does Royalty Pay?" *The Atheistic Platform*, X (1884), 174–160). The "pensions" passage was a late addition to CY, for sometime during the proof stage of the novel Clemens reminded himself to "Insert royal grant" (Nbk 24, p. 13) immediately following the discussion of how Hank planned to increase military efficiency by establishing the King's Own Regiment. This, too, is where he pointed directly at Victoria, blaming the vast expense of the royal grants on the fact that the rulers of the "Pendragon stock" were so "long-lived" and "fruitful."

In view of all these contemporary implications, one wonders if the great English stock booms of 1886–88 did not influence the Yankee's stock-manipulations as much as Clemens' knowledge of financial activities in the U.S. Some of the arguments advanced in England during the mid-80's by the proponents of bimetallism, also, seem reflected in Hank's substitution of new nickels for the old and worn goldpieces traditionally given to participants in the Royal Touch ceremony. Even more likely, the emphasis on the savings which resulted from Hank's financial reforms may have resulted from the publicity accorded the success of G. J. Goschen, Chancellor of the Exchequer, in converting the greater part of Britain's funded debt to a lower rate of interest in 1888. See Gretton, I, passim.

9. Gretton, I, 239.

1. SLC to Theodore Crane, 10/5/88, *MTL*, II, 500. A letter from Webster & Co. dated 4/16/89 (MTP) reports the completion of two typewritten copies of the ms.

## JAMES D. WILLIAMS

### Revision and Intention in Mark Twain's
### A *Connecticut Yankee*†

In 1889, Mark Twain got free advertising for his forthcoming "keen and powerful satire of English Nobility and Royalty" by free-swinging attacks on England and all things un-American. On December 10, for example, in an interview in the New York *Times,* he derided English publishers who refused to print his "utter contempt for their pitiful Lords and Dukes" and then—with notable inconsistency—went on to deplore the dissemination of foreign literature in America. Americans, he asserted, could afford "to look down and spit upon miserable titled nonentities." He was carried away by indignation as he bemoaned the existence of "perfectly respectable women" in America who were willing "to sell themselves to anything bearing the name of Duke." And finally, if we may trust the interviewer, he stated flatly that his purpose in A *Connecticut Yankee* was to "get at" the Englishman by satirizing "the shams, laws, and customs of today under pretense of dealing with the England of the sixth century."

These remarks were in line with the advertising policy Mark Twain and his publisher Fred Hall had agreed on—"whatever makes fun of royalty and nobility . . . will suit the American public well"[1]—and might have been largely a bid for sales. But Mark Twain's letters and notebook entries prove that his Anglophobia was not merely for public consumption. It is now generally agreed that during the late 1880's he went through a phase of extreme hostility to England—especially to English aristocracy—accompanied by high confidence in the beneficence of American democracy, capitalism, and technology. But the precise effect of these shifting opinions on A *Connecticut Yankee* is less easy to determine, although it is clear that Mark Twain's conception of the novel was anything but stable during composition. The statement of intention quoted above, for example, might be contrasted with his 1886 assertion that he was "only after the life of that day, that is all; to picture it; to try to get into it; to see how it feels and seems."[2] Authorial comments such as these have given rise to the current belief that the *Yankee* began as a simple "contrast" but for various reasons—primarily Mark Twain's resentment of English criticisms of America—became a satire after the third chapter had been com-

† From *American Literature,* 36 (1964–65), 288–97. Footnotes are by Williams.
1. Hall to Clemens, Oct. 16, 1889 (Mark Twain Papers; subsequently referred to as MTP).
2. *Mark Twain to Mrs. Fairbanks,* ed. Dixon Wecter (San Marino, Calif., 1949), p. 257.

pleted.[3] This view is both critically misleading and unsupported by what we know of the actual planning and revising of A *Connecticut Yankee*.

I

To begin with, we can establish no point in time, or in the text, as marking a clear change in general intention. Even with the novel nearly half finished, Mark Twain insisted that "fun" was its primary purpose[4] and planned to accompany it with a free copy of Malory.[5] And yet he had long believed that the society of the "Middle Ages" was not simply quaint but radically evil and falsely glamorized. History provided him with intense moral issues as well as opportunities for comic irreverence, and as an artist who delighted in broad strokes he was deeply involved with the past. He had once considered giving a contemporary setting to *The Prince and the Pauper*, but found that it did not seem "real."[6] His favorite "answer" to English critics of America was to refer them to their national past.[7] Even his unwritten but cherished appendix to A *Connecticut Yankee* was simply an attack on the manners and morals of the eighteenth century.[8] It could not have supported his contention that the novel satirized by indirection the "shams, laws and customs of today." Moreover, he made his claim only briefly and at a time when his animosity towards England was being freely vented in notebook entries, letters, and interviews, which apparently afforded him the same sort of relief as did his "unmailed letters."

In A *Connecticut Yankee*, Mark Twain presented a series of pathetic and outrageous scenes of brutal oppression in forms largely non-existent in the England and America of the 1880's. Even his ridicule of such perennial follies as credulity, snobbery, and superstition was cast in terms generally flattering to his readers.[9] He assumed that British criticism of the *Yankee* proceeded from wounded sensibilities, but for most English readers the satire was surely a slap on the wrist rather than a body blow. It was specifically the unavoidable contem-

3. John Hoben reached this conclusion in "Mark Twain's 'Connecticut Yankee,' a Genetic Study," *American Literature*, XVIII, 197–218 (Nov., 1946). Hoben overestimated the influence of Matthew Arnold on the *Yankee*. (The one certain reference to Arnold in the novel—a humorous disquisition on "shall" and "will" —was cut prior to publication.) Howard G. Baetzhold corrects some of Hoben's conclusions, but agrees with him that Mark Twain's intentions changed at this point in composition ("The Course of Composition of A *Connecticut Yankee*: A Reinterpretation," *American Literature*, XXXIII, 195–214, May, 1961).

4. Clemens to Webster and Hall, Aug. 15, 1887 (Berg Collection).

5. Notebook 22, p. 5 (MTP).

6. Albert B. Paine, *Mark Twain: A Biography* (New York, 1912), II, 597.

7. Examples may be found in *Mark Twain's Notebook, Speeches*, ed. A. B. Paine (New York, 1935). p. 150, and in Paine 91a (MTP).

8. MS II, final page. (All references to the manuscript of A *Connecticut Yankee* are to the holograph in the Berg Collection of the New York Public Library.)

9. *Atlantic Monthly*, LXV, 286 (Feb., 1890), concluded that the *Yankee* gave the feudal system some hard knocks, "but as the feudal system is dead there is no great harm done and the moral purpose shines"; the Boston *Literary World*, Feb. 15, 1890, pp. 52–53, asserted the *Yankee* was designed for "a shallow, self-complacent generation."

porary English parallels to Mark Twain's Arthurdom that inspired English critics to describe the satire in the *Yankee* as "stale," "second-hand," and "very trite."[1]

It is difficult, therefore, to accept a recent writer's assertion that "most critics now agree that *A Connecticut Yankee* was written to point up the injustices both of Victoria's England and of Mark Twain's America."[2] If such agreement exists, it is based on the understanding that what is apparently peripheral in the novel reflects the author's central intention. To classify the *Yankee* as an "inverted satire" is both to misread it and to damn it. In the context of Mark Twain's inveterate antimedievalism, we cannot infer a single initial intention from the series of burlesque "contrasts" which he rarely used but continued to plan almost until the *Yankee* was completed.[3] Ambiguities in tone were present from the beginning, when he outlined a heavily nostalgic love story similar to the Dillsberg legend in *A Tramp Abroad* or planned the destruction of a medieval army by a few men with modern weapons[4]— an "effect" adumbrating the cruelly adolescent "dream of glory" element in the *Yankee*. Perhaps the most significant departure from initial intentions was the decision to submit King Arthur to his own cruel laws, a procedure borrowed from *The Prince and the Pauper*.[5] It should be noted that with the novel half finished, and at a time when he was stuffing his notebooks with scathing attacks on contemporary England, Mark Twain deliberately turned to the sort of historical cruelties which could only blunt and muffle satiric concern with the present.

The current theory that Mark Twain's attitude toward King Arthur and his knights became more severely critical beginning with the fourth chapter mistakes tangential remarks for a major shift in tone. Hank Morgan sees Arthurdom from the beginning in terms of the ante bellum South of *Life on the Mississippi*. The picturesque and legendary Camelot becomes on closer inspection a wretched Arkansas village plus a castle. Hogs wallow in the mud amid hordes of unwashed children. Freemen humbly salute Sir Kay, who contemptuously ignores them. Chained slaves are in evidence. The knights are presented as credulous liars, insensitive to suffering, brainless, ver-

1. See the *Speaker*, I, 49 (Jan. 11, 1890); *Athenaeum*, XCV, 211 (Feb. 15, 1890); and London *Literary World*, XLI, 43–45 (Jan. 17, 1890).

2. Gladys Bellamy, *Mark Twain as a Literary Artist* (Norman, Okla., 1950), p. 312. Bernard De Voto once labeled as "a cheap sneer" and an "asininity" the view that *A Connecticut Yankee* is primarily concerned with feudalism (*Mark Twain's America*, Boston, 1932, p. 212 n.). He was defending Edmund C. Stedman's comment that the *Yankee* attacked the "*still existing* radical principles or fallacies" which had once

made chivalry possible (July 7, 1889, MTP). A similar claim could be made for many effective satires, whatever the object and however dated the specific instances.

3. Many of them can be found in Notebook 20, p. 34; Notebook 23 (I), pp. 20–21; and Paine 91 (MTP).

4. Notebook 18, p. 17 (MTP).

5. When the idea occurred to him, he abandoned a comic presentation of the Boss's sickness and Marinel's ghastly cures (MS I, 484–II, 6).

bose, and dirty. Like the village loafers in *Huckleberry Finn*, they delight in dog fights. Hank Morgan's conclusion that he is in an asylum recalls "The Tournament in A.D. 1870,"[6] in which Mark Twain labeled the knight "a braggart, a ruffian, a fantastic vagabond and an ignoramus." The fact that the knights are described as unconsciously indelicate in the fourth chapter of the *Yankee* is no sign that Mark Twain's attitude toward them had changed. He had already dubbed them "White Indians," and verbal and sexual indecency had long been part of his catalogue of the evils of an aristocratic past.[7] The first important intrusion of a satiric tone inappropriate to the narrator did not occur until Chapter VIII, a tirade on reverence, nobility, and the Catholic Church. Thereafter, the narrative mask was frequently discarded, and humor often entirely subordinated to moral indignation and pathos. The chapters on Morgan le Fay's dungeons, for example, were written under the influence of a rereading of Carlyle, and Mark Twain himself was troubled by their "funeral seriousness."[8] But his zaniest burlesque continued to crop up in the midst of his angriest, most pathetic, and melodramatic scenes.

II

Mark Twain claimed he had carefully eliminated passages in the *Yankee* that were potentially offensive to the English, thus suggesting that the original text had a sharper satiric thrust. But the available evidence does not support his assertion that he and Stedman had dug out many "darlings" so that the publisher Chatto would accept the novel.[9] On the contrary, several passages added to the manuscript during revision were among the novel's most direct attacks on royalty and the Church;[1] and one of the latest additions—a passage on the Royal Grant—was a clear sally against a still existing abuse.[2] The manuscript leads one to believe that most cuts in the text were made more with general propriety than national sensibilities in mind. The *Yankee* was advertised as "thoroughly clean, wholesome, humorous, instructive, and patriotic,"[3] but Mark Twain's notebook suggestions

6. He concluded in the earlier (1870) work that if knights were to reappear in the modern world "nothing but a New York jury and the insanity plea" could save them from hanging.

7. In 1879 he had decided the English were "a very fine and pure and elevated people," but that prior to the nineteenth century they had been "small improvement upon the Shoshone Indians" (*Mark Twain's Notebook*, p. 150).

8. On August 22, 1887, he wrote to Howells that he had just read *The French Revolution* again (*Mark Twain-Howells Letters*, ed. Henry N. Smith and William Gibson, Cambridge, Mass., 1961, II, 595). A week earlier he had written to Webster and Hall that he had completed 350 pages of manuscript. The seigneur in Morgan le Fay's dungeon who had walled up a

township well was borrowed from *The French Revolution*, I, vi, 3.

9. *Mark Twain-Howells Letters*, II, 609.

1. The comments on the Catholic Church in Chapter VIII, and those on the "two Reigns of Terror" in Chapter XIII, were afterthoughts of uncertain date.

2. These three paragraphs at the end of Chapter XXV are not in the manuscript. They may have been inspired by George Standring's attack on Victoria's use of the royal grant in "Does Royalty Pay?" in *The Atheistic Platform*, ed. Annie Besant and Charles Bradlaugh (London, 1884), pp. 154–156.

3. Publisher's announcement at the rear of the prospectus for *A Connecticut Yankee*.

for direct satire of contemporary England often had decidedly vulgar or sexual overtones. Particularly if one considers discarded plans for the novel as well as eliminated passages, it appears that Mark Twain's chief aims in revision were to tone down some of the wildest burlesque, to eliminate the "vulgar," and to modify attacks on the Church that might also have offended Protestants.

Some discarded burlesque inspirations for the *Yankee* were not unlike incidents in the published novel. Among them was the plan to have the Boss place bets on a hermit during a competition in austerities.[4] Another involved a contest among bards, which the Boss would win by reciting Tennyson and Shakespeare.[5] But a number of the jokes that occurred to Mark Twain during composition undermined whatever unity of character and tone he had managed to establish. For example, the story that the Boss repeats fifteen times at the monastery—until his English audience "disintegrates"—was initially about a "celebrated jumping frog of Calaveras County."[6] And Sandy's version of the same tale originally broke all hearts in the adjacent nunnery. The nuns' tears washed away a wing of the asylum, drowned sixty orphans, and gave Merlin the chance to claim he had started up the fountain. Another briefly considered burlesque impulse was in direct conflict with the romantic nostalgia of the love story. The Boss would sadly forego marriage with the talkative Sandy because of an "obstacle" which would not be overcome until a bout of scarlet fever had left her hilariously deaf and dumb.[7]

Most of the discarded ideas for the *Yankee* stemmed from a fairly mechanical proliferation of burlesque "contrasts" which Mark Twain continued to jot down as late as 1888. At various times he planned to include knights charging a locomotive, getting their picture taken, insuring their armor, "dating" the Lady of Shallott by phone, and engaging in a number of other activities of the "grailing by rail" variety.[8] With fourteen chapters completed, he planned the Boss's introduction of steam engines, fire companies, aluminum, vaccination, and lightning rods,[9] but the whole business of technological innovation failed to catch his deeper interest, and it was probably not until the novel was near completion that he added some summarizing passages on this subject.[1]

The "germ" of the *Yankee* developed into a good example of unrestrained burlesque calmed down in revision. In the earlier version, Sandy threw rocks at Hank's helmet while she called balls and strikes, and only after braining the horse did she manage to jar the helmet loose with the shaft of a lance.[2] An equally unrestrained but

4. MS I, 235.
5. MS I, 152; cf. Notebook 23 (I), p. 21 (MTP).
6. MS I, 436.
7. DeVoto 21, oversize (MTP).
8. See Paine 91; Notebook 20, p. 34; and

Notebook 23 (I), pp. 13–17, 19–20 (MTP).
9. MS I, 235.
1. All of Chapter X (MS I, 166 A–J) was a later insertion. See Baetzhold, p. 212 n.
2. MS I, 199–202.

funnier account[3] of the Boss's wildly successful farming and real estate speculation in "hermit dirt" was omitted—perhaps as vulgar. Other major elisions were the "Letter from the Recording Angel"[4]—a satire of American business worked into the novel with obvious strain—and the Boss's lengthy and absurd calculations of casualties during the battle of the Sand Belt, which Stedman objected to as "technical humor" and which made a shambles of any significance the final catastrophe was intended to have.

A number of "vulgar" passages were cut from A *Connecticut Yankee*, including some *doubles entendres* inspired by the tails of Sandy's "princesses," a comparison of hermits and sewers, and several references to nakedness. (Chief among the latter was a passage on the effect of putting undershirts on nude statues, an idea Mark Twain had already presented—using fig leaves—in A *Tramp Abroad*.) Two comments on the sexual immorality of medieval clergy were toned down. All that remains of them are the merry songs of Morgan le Fay's chaplain and the mere presence of a foundling home in the Valley of Holiness. Finally, he eliminated two long passages on the Boss's plan to erect monuments to royal mistresses as the true "divine right" rulers of England.[5] These passages, on which the second paragraph of the *Yankee* preface seems to comment, might have been regarded as particularly offensive to the English, even though Swift, for example, had less humorously made the same point in the previous century; but mistresses, royal or otherwise, were not really appropriate in a thoroughly clean and wholesome book from which such words as "bastard," "prostitute," "rump," "buttocks," "damn," "nipple," "stark naked," "disemboweled," and "devil" had been carefully stricken.

Charles Webster, as the publisher of the Pope's biography, could assure Mark Twain that Catholics did not buy books anyway;[6] but there were a number of passages in the *Yankee* that even Protestants might have found offensive, and while Mark Twain wished to instruct, he had no desire to offend.[7] Nevertheless, he may have agreed with Webster on Catholic reading habits, since on the one hand he inserted in the manuscript the direct and extreme attack on the Catholic Church in Chapter VIII, but on the other omitted the lengthy comparison of Sandy's veneration of pigs with the (Presbyterian) doctrine of infant damnation.[8] The desire to avoid offense may not have been the only reason for cutting the latter passage, in which the

3. MS I, 481–482.
4. MS I, 370–396 (deleted pages in MTP).
5. MS II, 221–226 and 235–237; the idea may go back ten years to his amusement over the Albert Memorial as a monument to mediocrity. See "Diary Notes in England," p. 107 (MTP).
6. Webster to Clemens, July 30, 1889 (MTP).
7. Offensive religious implications were left out of all promotional material (Hall to Clemens, Oct. 16, 1889, and Webster to Clemens, April 18, 1889; MTP). In a reading given at West Point he used the phrases "state church" and "go-as-you please church" rather than "Catholic" and "Protestant" (Paine 10, MTP).
8. MS I, 362–363.

Boss suddenly and untypically despises his own feeling of superiority to Sandy. He recalls an American trick of placing a tall mirror at one end of a dimly lit room, so that a stranger assumes it is a door which someone is approaching from the other side. After vainly trying to dodge by his own reflection, the stranger calls it a fool, idiot, and ass before realizing that he is addressing himself. Similarly, the Boss concludes, Sandy slobbering over hogs is simply the mirror image of his recent American Presbyterian self. The lesson that we should at least pretend to honor each other's superstitions is perfectly apt and typical of Mark Twain, but it tends to undercut both the theme of moral progress and the character of the narrator, who was originally conceived as an "innocent" mask for satire of religiosity.

Some other eliminated comments on religion also involved inconsistencies in characterization. Thus it was clearly inappropriate for Sandy to deride burnt offerings and votive candles to the Virgin.[9] The Boss himself was at first envisioned as a "Brother Jonathan," complete with pious ejaculations *à la* George Cable,[1] but either his foolish piety or his increasingly direct comments on religion had to be sacrificed. (At one point, for example, Mark Twain planned to have the Boss convert the hermit Marinel to Presbyterianism as a punishment for his dreadful cures.[2] Marinel would be delighted, since a Presbyterian hermit is a sort of ultimate in the revolting.) Finally, almost all indirect satire of religiosity was cut, and the Boss's Presbyterianism ceased to be a subject to ridicule. The fading of Hank Morgan as an "innocent" point of view for religious satire was paralleled by his increasing historical and literary sophistication. Mark Twain continued to use him as an "ignoramus" for indirect satire on such subjects as chromos, but verbal revisions show that he often gave his narrator a deliberately literate or even literary style, and late additions like the passage on the joys of intellectual work[3] suggest how little concern he finally had for his original conception of a shrewd and pious buffoon.

Many of the undeveloped or discarded ideas for satire of England in the *Yankee* did not occur to Mark Twain until 1888 or later and were frequently of dubious propriety. The subject of Anglo-American marriages, for example, provoked his unrestrained contempt. He thought of having market reports on rich girls from a republic and a bench show of mongrel children,[4] in his notebook he went so far as to suggest that the English dukes "bought" by American heiresses were for the most part syphilitic.[5] A less virulent idea from 1887—the Boss's still undetected substitution of chimpanzees for the royal family[6]—appeared in the novel in the moderated form of Clarence's proposal for a family of royal cats.

9. MS I, 410–411.
1. MS I, 56, 115.
2. DV24; see also Notebook 23 (I), pp. 15, 18 (MTP).
3. MS II, 87v.
4. Notebook 24, p. 29 (MTP).
5. Notebook 23 (I), p. 21 (MTP).
6. Notebook 21 (I), p. 21 (MTP).

Discarded but unobjectionable ideas for satire of contemporary England involved such relatively minor "abuses" as the use of lithographed sermons, the sale of advowsons, and the privateness of English public parks.[7] But such topics must have struck him as rather tame, and as late as the summer of 1889 he was hoping to add to the *Yankee* a chapter in which women would be stripped and whipped, though the only possible contemporary reference was to Russia.[8] Clearly, Mark Twain's appetite for scenes of extreme brutality and pathos contributed to the frustration of his belated attempts to satirize "the shams, laws, and customs" of contemporary England.

### III

The notebook entries, the manuscript, and the published novel do not support the thesis that *A Connecticut Yankee* began simply as a humorous contrast and then—because of a conscious change in intention—became at a specific point an "inverted satire." Throughout the period of composition, Mark Twain's ability to resist the "damned human race" theme was uncertain, but specific outbursts against contemporary England were for the most part too late, or too tame, or too indelicate for inclusion in the novel. The *Yankee* works out in action ideas on chivalry, slavery, and progress which had been dominant in Mark Twain's thinking for twenty years. His Anglophobia, on the other hand, had shallow roots and was poor in associations. (Even in 1883, after all, he had seen England as the greatest of all nations.[9]) Consequently, and despite his claims to the contrary, he seems to have had more trouble *including* satire of England in his novel than in toning it down or eliminating it. His 1889 references to the *Yankee* as an attack on England were certainly not detached estimates of his intentions during composition nor of his actual accomplishment. And however great may be our interest in the conflicting historical and social philosophies underlying the *Yankee*, the novel survives neither as a theory of history nor as an "inverted satire," but rather as a giddy, shrewd, and violent realization of that ordinary fantasy in which a hostile world is reduced to impotence before the unchanged yet conquering dreamer.

# JAMES D. WILLIAMS

## The Use of History in Mark Twain's
## *A Connecticut Yankee*†

Despite Mark Twain's prefatory disclaimer of any pretense to historical accuracy, a number of early reviewers of *A Connecticut Yankee*

---

7. Notebook 23 (I), pp. 17–21 (MTP).
8. Notebook 23 (II), p. 60 (MTP): cf. Mark Twain's letter to the editor of *Free Russia* (*Mark Twain's Letters*, New York, 1917, II, 537–539).

9. Paine 91a (MTP).
† From *PMLA*, 80 (1965), 102–10. Footnotes are by Williams.

saw it as fundamentally historical and consequently "a very irrational proceeding."[1] William Thomas Stead, who read the *Yankee* with sympathetic insight and thought it a highly significant novel, conceded that it contained "much strange misreading of history."[2] And Andrew Lang, in a spirited defense of Mark Twain against his English detractors, admitted that he had not read the *Yankee* because its author did not have "the knowledge which would enable him to be a sound critic of the Middle Ages."[3]

The historical accuracy of backgrounds and incidents in *A Connecticut Yankee* can hardly be a major issue in itself. However, the novel does embody a philosophy of history, as recent critics have emphasized.[4] Consequently, the following examination of Mark Twain's use of history does not aim at a detailed description of sources, but rather at the presentation of sufficient evidence to warrant a few general conclusions.

Mark Twain's attempts at historical accuracy in *A Connecticut Yankee* were sporadic and strictly limited by the demands of farce, outrage, or the theme of progress. He drew his material largely from modern historians and largely from post-Renaissance history. Since for the most part he was collecting examples of misery and injustice, the modernity of his material implied increasingly narrow chronological limits for his theme of social and moral progress. Indeed, by 1889, with the roads back so often leading to an image of mother-and-babe-at-the-stake, he had worked himself into the position that "there is today but one civilization in the world, and it is not yet thirty years old."[5] The intensity of his moral reaction to historical evil and his desire to "realize" that evil contributed to Mark Twain's vision of an outrageously corrupt (yet esthetically satisfying) "past" which undermined his meliorism by threatening to subsume the present and even the future of a damned human race.

Mark Twain's historical ambitions in the *Yankee* clearly underwent changes during the course of composition. He claimed in early 1886 that he had been "saturating" himself with "the atmosphere of the day and the subject,"[6] and on 16 November 1886 he wrote to Mrs. Fairbanks that he was "after the life of that day, that is all; to picture it; to try to get into it; to see how it feels and seems."[7] There is plentiful evidence—including *The Prince and the Pauper*—for doubting that

1. *The Literary World* (Boston), XXI (15 Feb. 1890), 52–53.
2. *The Review of Reviews* (Feb. 1890), p. 144.
3. *Illustrated News of the World* (14 Feb. 1891). Mark Twain had requested Lang to defend him as an entertainer of the "Belly and the Members" (*Letters*, ed. A. B. Paine, New York, 1917, pp. 525–528). Lang had written an appreciation of Malory's prose style for the H. Oskar Sommer edition of *Le Morte D'Arthur* the year before, and he may have found a parody of Malory particularly unwelcome.

4. Roger B. Salomon, *Twain and the Image of History* (Yale Studies in English, No. 150; New Haven, 1961), p. 102; Henry Nash Smith, *Mark Twain* (Cambridge, Mass., 1962), p. 138.
5. *Speeches*, ed. A. B. Paine (New York, 1923), p. 151.
6. Samuel Charles Webster, *Mark Twain, Business Man* (Boston, 1946), p. 355.
7. *Mark Twain to Mrs. Fairbanks*, ed. Dixon Wecter (San Marino, Calif., 1949), p. 257.

he was ever so free of a thesis as the last remarks imply. At a reading given in Baltimore some two years later, he asked his audience to compare the "mighty miracles" of science in the nineteenth century with the "trivial miracles" and "humbug magicians" of the Middle Ages, to "conceive of the blank and sterile ignorance of that day and contrast it with the vast and many-sided knowledge of this."[8] And in the original preface to the *Yankee*, he explicitly abandoned historical actualities for a "higher" truth: "My object has been to group together some of the most odious laws which have had vogue in the Christian countries within the past eight or ten centuries, and illustrate them by the incidents of a story."[9]

Oddly enough, however, he was not fully aware of the extent to which such a procedure involved him in historical inaccuracies, since twenty years later he could still speak of having attempted to imagine and set forth "not just the English life of Arthur's day but . . . the whole of the Middle Ages."[1] The various assumptions which allowed him to believe he had done so are of continuing interest to us. We can perhaps get a clearer view of what they were and of how they affected the tone and structure of *A Connecticut Yankee* by examining a few of the historical readings on which Mark Twain drew in writing his novel.

I

Aside from *Le Morte D'Arthur* itself, and perhaps a handful of chronicles in the Bohn library,[2] Mark Twain relied on secondary sources for his knowledge of medieval life. Much of the historical material in the *Yankee* was used initially in *The Prince and the Pauper*,[3] and comparatively little of it was of medieval provenance. Notebook references during the period of composition suggest the moral and historical bias in his preparation. He was increasingly interested in finding instances of "the abyss of depravity into which it is possible for human nature to sink." Such abysses, according to his favorite historian William Lecky, furnished "striking proofs of the reality of the moral progress we have attained."[4] The same bias resulted in Mark Twain's 1885 plans for a "Picturesque History,"[5] a collection of human stupidities and cruelties drawn from the Middle

8. DeVoto 21 (oversize), in the Mark Twain Papers, subsequently referred to as MTP; © 1965 by the Mark Twain Company.

9. A. B. Paine, *Mark Twain, A Biography* (New York, 1912), p. 1656.

1. *Mark Twain in Eruption*, ed. Bernard De-Voto (New York, 1940), p. 211.

2. Mark Twain referred to "scant chronicles" in his Baltimore reading of 1888. His secretary in later life, Isabel Lyon, stated in 1933 that he had read "deeply" in the Early English Chronicles collected in the Bohn library, and that he wrote *A Connecticut Yankee* under their in-

spiration. The "chronicles" available in the Bohn library in 1882 were: *Bede's Ecclesiastical History of England, The Anglo-Saxon Chronicles, The Chronicles of the White Rose of York, Chronicles of the Crusades*, Joinville's *Memoirs of Saint Louis*, and Froissart's *Chronicles*.

3. See Walter Blair, *Mark Twain and Huck Finn* Berkeley, Calif., 1960), pp. 135–145, 179–186, 310–313.

4. *A History of European Morals* (New York, 1911), I, 110.

5. Notebook 19, pp. 31–32 (MTP).

Ages and the Renaissance, which never progressed beyond the papal interdict during the reign of King John. Both the "Picturesque History" and the *Yankee* were undertaken in what was still a conscious agreement with Lecky's conclusions about moral progress.

Although Mark Twain's chance reading of Malory in 1884 was the occasion for the inception of *A Connecticut Yankee*, neither *Le Morte D'Arthur* nor Tennyson's *Idylls*, which he also planned to use,[6] contributed a great deal to the published novel. Of course about a dozen pages in *A Connecticut Yankee* are quoted from Malory, and Mark Twain depended on him for archaic phrases as well as for proper names. But the novel was formed in far more significant ways by the influence of William Edward Hartpole Lecky's *History of European Morals* and *History of England in the Eighteenth Century*.

Several of Mark Twain's borrowings from Lecky are already common knowledge. Among them are the story of the holy fountain, most of the material on the hermit saints in the Valley of Holiness,[7] and the Boss's illustrative anecdote of the building of the Mansion House.[8] But Mark Twain's debt to what he termed the "noble" and "beautiful" *History of European Morals* has yet to be fully explored.

We might first consider Lecky's attitude toward the writing of history: "Wrapt in the pale winding-sheet of general terms, the greatest tragedies of history evoke no vivid images in our minds, and it is only by a great effort of genius that an historian can galvanize them into life."[9] In a letter to Howells, Mark Twain had once written that his purpose in *The Prince and the Pauper* was "to afford a realizing sense of the exceeding severity of the laws of that day."[1] In a similar vein, Hank Morgan discusses the difference between "mere knowledge" and "realization" at the beginning of Chapter vi, echoing Lecky's belief that "an act of realization is a necessary antecedent and condition of compassion" and that "any influence that augments the range and power of this realizing faculty is favourable to the amiable virtues."

Lecky's influence on *A Connecticut Yankee* was both positive and negative. In his own copy of *A History of European Morals*, for example, Mark Twain scored a passage on the credulity and intolerance of the Middle Ages, described by Lecky as "lower than any other period in the history of mankind" in all the intellectual virtues.[2] And in the *Yankee*, of course, Mark Twain insisted on and frequently illustrated the brainlessness and credulity of Arthur's subjects. On the

6. Notebook 23 (I), p. 21 (MTP).

7. *European Morals*, II, 107–111.

8. *A History of England in the Eighteenth Century* (New York, 1888), III, 538; see Notebook 23 (I), p. 19 (MTP).

9. *European Morals*, I, 133.

1. *Mark Twain-Howells Letters*, ed. Henry Nash Smith and William M. Gibson (Cambridge, Mass., 1960), I, 291.

2. For this and all subsequent references to Mark Twain's marginal notations in Lecky, see *The Twainian*, XIV (May 1955–December 1956). Chester L. Davis, who edited the notations for *The Twainian*, believes Mark Twain made them in 1906. Walter Blair, on the contrary, believes that some, and perhaps all, were written much earlier; see *Mark Twain and Huck Finn*, p. 401, n. 6.

other hand, when the historian admitted that Christianity tended to emphasize the passive rather than the active virtures, Mark Twain commented that the Church did not raise up the slave, but "degraded all conditions of men to the slave's level." This charge became the burden of Hank Morgan's tirade against the Catholic Church in Chapter viii. Again, in disagreement with Lecky's praise of the Church for its opposition to suicide, Mark Twain noted: "It gives me a very real pang to read of a prevented suicide, and a very real feeling of gratitude to read of a successful one." In Chapter xiii the Boss adopts the same attitude: "If the freeman, grown desperate with his tortures, found his life unendurable under such conditions, and sacrificed it and fled to death for mercy and refuge, the gentle Church condemned him to eternal fire, the gentle law buried him at midnight at the crossroads with a stake through his back, and his master the baron or the bishop confiscated all his property and turned his widow and his orphans out of doors."[3]

There are a number of historical details in the *Yankee* which were probably drawn from the *History of European Morals*. The King's touching of the scrofulous in Chapter xxvi seems to have been based on Lecky's description of that ceremony, which was in turn based on Macaulay.[4] The Roman law which condemns King Arthur and the Boss to death in Chapter xxxvii was described by Lecky as follows: "An atrocious law, intended to secure the safety of the citizens, provided that if a master were murdered, all the slaves in his house, who were not in chains or absolutely helpless through illness, should be put to death" (I, 302).

Finally, there are many fairly tenuous parallels. For example, Lecky's "poor lunatic" who in 1359 declared himself the brother of the archangel Michael and a daily commuter between heaven and hell (II, 87) is similar to Sandy's "maniac"—the Recording Angel—whose story was originally a part of the *Yankee*. And Lecky's account of how Apuleius was attacked for praising tooth powder (II, 148) brings to mind the Boss's huckstering of "Noyoudont."

Turning to Lecky's *History of England in the Eighteenth Century*, we find the story of a young woman whose husband had been impressed.[5] She was gradually reduced to starvation, whereupon she resorted to shoplifting, was caught, and with her child in her arms was led to execution (III, 583). Lecky told another story of an eighteenth century trial:

> a girl of twenty-two was hanged for receiving a stolen piece of check from an accomplice who had stolen it. Such crimes were at this

3. He could also have found scorn for the Christian condemnation of suicide in Charles Ball's *Autobiography* (See below).
4. *European Morals*, I, 363–364 n.
5. The press gang was a subject Mark Twain

planned to include in the *Yankee*. The Boss would break the system by "mistakenly" impressing nobles. See Notebook 23 (I), p. 19 (MTP).

time scarcely ever capitally punished, but the poor girl had unfortunately drunk too freely before the trial, and was insolent in the dock. The prosecutor, a simple, honest man, who had no idea that such a punishment would be inflicted was driven almost distracted by remorse and did not long survive the shock. (VI, 251)

Mark Twain probably drew on both these accounts in composing the scene of emotional outrage in Chapter xxxv of the *Yankee*. He eliminated any elements—such as the drinking—which might limit the reader's sympathy with the young woman and dwelt unashamedly on the pathetic aspects of the story.[6]

In addition the *Yankee* contains a good number of minor elements which were probably found in *England in the Eighteenth Century*. Among them may be references to the laws of Elizabeth and James I which allowed magistrates to fix wages and regulate occupations, or to the fact that pilloried men were often pelted to death,[7] or that women were burned in England as late as 1790. In connection with the latter subject, Lecky told the story of an old "witch" who was tortured and killed while her two daughters pleaded in vain for mercy (II, 89–90). This historical incident is paralleled by the burning of the Baptist women in *The Prince and the Pauper* and is approximately repeated (using a beautiful young mother) in the *Yankee*, with the added melodramatic twist that the slave-driver views the burning as a mere expedient for warming his valuable slaves back to life.

Lecky also helped to form Mark Twain's conviction that there had been no ladies and gentlemen anywhere prior to the nineteenth century. He described at length the "universal coarseness" of eighteenth-century manners, a coarseness Mark Twain planned to illustrate by including liberal extracts from eighteenth-century novels in an appendix to the *Yankee*. In sum, even though much of the material available in Lecky's works could have been found elsewhere—in Hume, for example, or in John Lingard's twenty-volume *History of England*[8]—the few definite examples of borrowing from Lecky support the conclusion that much of the common historical information in the novel was derived from the same source.

## II

Reinforcing Lecky's influence on the *Yankee* was a work Mark Twain had used extensively in writing *The Prince and the Pauper*. This was *The True-Blue Laws of Connecticut and New Haven*, edited by J. Hammond Trumbull and published at Hartford in 1876. Trumbull

---

6. The incident in *The Prince and the Pauper* of the stolen pig—whose owner is horrified to learn of the possible punishment for the culprit—is probably based on the same passage in Lecky.

7. Lecky, VI, 233, and I, 549; see also Notebook 23 (I), p. 24 (MTP). Both references are included in the Boss's conversation with Dow-

ley in Ch. xxxiii. In *The Prince and the Pauper* (Ch. xxviii), the pilloried Hendon comes close to injury at the hands of the crowd.

8. Miss Isabel Lyon, in a 1933 Letter (Berg Collection, New York Public Library), stated that Lingard was Mark Twain's constant reference during the writing of *A Connecticut Yankee*.

was a member of the Monday Evening Club, so Mark Twain had no doubt heard him speak on the general subject of punitive law. In an 1889 notebook entry, he indicated that he planned to use extracts from Trumbull in an appendix to support the historicity of incidents in the *Yankee*. [9] One such incident was surely the London scene of "a man being boiled to death in oil for counterfeiting pennies," which was apparently based on Trumbull's account of poisoners boiled to death under Henry VIII and counterfeiters who in Hamburg were slowly boiled in oil as late as 1616. [1] Trumbull's list of crimes punished by death in sixteenth- and seventeenth-century England included stealing a woolen cloth—for which the young mother in Chapter xxxv of the *Yankee* is hanged—and killing a deer—for which the young husband in Morgan Le Fay's dungeon is being racked to death. The whole spirit of A *Connecticut Yankee* reflects Trumbull's own theme-defining quotation from Phillimore's *History of England During the Reign of George III:* "It is difficult to find, in the history of the most despotic countries in the darkest ages, proofs of more stupid and revolting injustice . . . The reader of the state trials . . . might almost imagine that he is reading the narrative of Gregory of Tours, or the history of some tribe in the infancy of civilization" (p. 14). The last phrase in this quotation is paralleled by the Boss's reference to knights as "White Indians" and Mark Twain's own comparison of the English of earlier centuries to Shoshone Indians. [2]

### III

Originally, one of the hardest-worked devices in the *Yankee* for attacking "divine-right" monarchy was the topic of royal mistresses and the power they had often had over kings and nations. In the manuscript of *A Connecticut Yankee* there are two lengthy passages on the Boss's plan to erect monuments to such royal mistresses. [3] These passages were probably cut for the sake of general propriety, so that in the published novel we have only the brief and humorous reference to the subject in the "Preface." Mark Twain's ideas on royal mistresses—no doubt garnered from many sources—were derived in part from his reading of Henri Forneron's *The Court of Charles II, 1639–1734.* This is the story of "a French harlot's progress at Whitehall." Forneron presented a picture of a sexually depraved aristocracy, claiming that in seventeenth-century England all reforming power and self-discipline had been transferred to America and that the corrupt court had become the tool of Louis XIV through Louise de Kerouaille's power over Charles II. Mark Twain's notebooks indicate Forneron as the probable source—though perhaps only a corroboration—of his definition of a nobleman as the product of a

9. Notebook 24, p. 15 (MTP).
1. *The True-Blue Laws*, p. 13.
2. *Mark Twain's Notebook*, ed. A. B. Paine

(New York, 1935), p. 150.
3. Manuscript, II, 221–226 and 235–237 (Berg Collection).

king crossed with a prostitute, an idea which appears in the *Yankee* during the competitive examinations for army commissions.[4] After discussing the ennobling of Lady Castlemaine's children, Forneron wrote that in a few years England would be happy to see "a House of Peers extracted out of the blood Royal."[5] At another point he claimed that "the blood of Charles II runs in the veins of many peers of the realm of Great Britain" (p. 293). Finally, Mark Twain's conviction that "England pensions the rich whore with millions, the poor private with a shilling a month"[6] might be compared with the following passage from Forneron: "the British parliament, which thinks £1200 a year enough to relieve the distressed families of authors, artists, scientists, and other benefactors of their country, continues to pay the Duke of Richmond £19,000 a year in virtue of the secret services rendered to Louis XIV by his ancestress Louise de Keroualle" (p. 307).

Forneron is only one of a whole group of historians whose specific influence on Mark Twain can be determined only after lengthy research, since historical material by its very nature renders borrowing difficult to trace. Before passing to the influence on *A Connecticut Yankee* of a few relatively obscure writers, we can at least suggest some relations between the *Yankee* and the works of Saint Simon, Taine, and Carlyle. In Saint Simon's *Memoirs*, which he would have liked to publish,[7] Mark Twain found a vivid picture of a corrupt court, an insane preoccupation with rank and precedence, and a people being starved and squeezed dry by taxation. He once told Howells that Saint Simon had transformed him into a *sans-culotte*,[8] and his reading of the *Memoirs* is probably reflected both in the Boss's condemnation of "ten centuries of wrong and shame and misery" in Chapter xiii and in his assertion that there were two Reigns of Terror, the one minor and momentary and the other "not to be mated in hell." Saint Simon would also seem to be in the background of the passages on the opening of Morgan Le Fay's dungeon. When the Regent restored liberty to a number of political prisoners in the Bastille, one old man was discovered who had been there thirty-five years without knowing why he was arrested and without ever having been examined.[9] Morgan Le Fay's "inherited" prisoner is a similar case.

Mark Twain admired Taine's *The Ancient Regime* and in his projected appendix to the *Yankee* he planned to use excerpts from Taine relating to unjust imprisonments and the requirement that army officers be able to establish descent from three generations of nobility.[1] There was also a good deal of material in *The Ancient*

4. Notebook 22 (II), p. 40; see also Notebook 23 (I), p. 3 (MTP).
5. *The Court of Charles II* (London, 1886), p. 62.
6. Notebook 24, p. 3 (MTP); © 1965 by The Mark Twain Company.
7. Notebook 21, p. 49 (MTP).
8. *Mark Twain–Howells Letters*, p. 595.
9. *Memoirs* (trans. Bayle St. John, London, 1888), III, 56.
1. Notebook 24, p. 14 (MTP).

*Regime* on the Church's extraction of tithes from an impoverished people and on wild game as "the tyrant of the peasant." Taine's accounts of how the peasant's crops were often ruined by animals he was afraid to injure, and of how he was punished if the lord's fruit trees were damaged,[2] probably underlie passages listing the injustices inflicted on peasants in Chapter xiii and xxix of *A Connecticut Yankee*. Mark Twain may have read Taine's *Notes on England* as well. If so, its attack on English servility towards rank must have pleased him. Taine observed at one point that few artists and writers were admitted into the drawing rooms of nobility in England. When they were admitted, they appeared not as equals but as "lions and curiosities."[3] This complaint seems echoed by the Boss's conviction that Arthur's nobles admired him as an "elephant" but despised him because he lacked a title.

Mark Twain's comments in *A Connecticut Yankee* on "naked kings and mechanics" suggest that he had read *Sartor Resartus*. (A copy of it in his library bore the date 1888 on the flyleaf.)[4] But his favorite work by Carlyle was *The French Revolution*, which he read at least once during the composition of the *Yankee* and which he described to Mrs. Fairbanks as "one of the greatest creations that ever flowed from a pen."[5] The seigneur who walled up the only fountain of a township was almost definitely borrowed from *The French Revolution*.[6] He is a prisoner in Morgan Le Fay's dungeon, and instead of releasing him with the others, the Boss permits him to be hanged. In addition, the Boss's comment in Chapter xiii on the impoverished freemen—"they were the nation, the actual nation"—seems to echo Carlyle's summary of the Deliberations of D'Orleans: "The Third Estate is the Nation" (I, iv, 1). One can guess that Carlyle had an important and manifold influence on the composition of the *Yankee*, but specific borrowing from him was very limited.

## IV

In a group of "Tributes to Mark Twain" published in *The North American Review* in 1910, Andrew Carnegie wrote that Mark Twain had once confided, "much to my surprise, that the idea of 'A Yankee at the Court of King Arthur' came from reading my first literary outburst; written at high noon, when the sun casts no shadow, *Triumphant Democracy*; also he called my attention to the heading of a

---

2. *The Ancient Regime* (trans. John Durand, New York, 1885), I, ii and iii.

3. *Notes on England* (trans. W. F. Rae, New York, 1885), p. 242.

4. Anderson Auction Company Catalogue, 7 and 8 Feb. 1911.

5. *Mark Twain to Mrs. Fairbanks*, p. 207. He planned to use excerpts in the appendix to the *Yankee*; see Notebook 24, p. 14 (MTP).

6. *The French Revolution* (New York, 1956), I, vi, 3. The borrowing seems quite certain because Twain had just finished reading *The French Revolution* when he wrote this scene. Cf. *Mark Twain-Howells Letters*, p. 595, and the chronology of composition in Harold G. Baetzhold's "The Course of Composition of A Connecticut Yankee: A Reinterpretation," AL, XXXIII (May 1961), 195–214.

chapter in 'Pudd'nhead Wilson,' of which I was the author."[7] That the "idea" for A *Connecticut Yankee* came from *Triumphant Democracy* need not be considered, but Mark Twain may well have borrowed a few suggestions from Carnegie, whom he described in 1892 as "great enough to make his power felt as a thinker and a literary man."[8] On one level, at least—the level of uncontainable happy pride over the American invention of sleeping and parlor cars—the two men had much in common. And Mark Twain owned a copy of *Triumphant Democracy*, presented to him by Carnegie and inscribed with the "regards of his fellow Republican."

One suspects a good deal of wry self-knowledge in Mark Twain's observation that Carnegie only spoke his mind when there was no danger in it. "He thinks he is a scorner of kings and emperors and dukes, whereas he is like the rest of the human race: a slight attention from one of these can make him drunk for a week and keep his happy tongue wagging for seven years."[9] At any rate, *Triumphant Democracy* was as hotly antiaristocractic as the *Yankee*. At the same time, it was far more consistently optimistic, since it quite lacked the novel's humorous, irritable, and bitter recognition of human perversity. In short, the two books are a good index of the definite but limited similarities between the two men, and there are apparent verbal echoes of *Triumphant Democracy* both in the *Yankee* and in Mark Twain's notebooks.

Carnegie, for example, saluted "the coming national hymn which is to live and vibrate round the world when royal families are extinct as dodos. God speed the day! A royal family is an insult to every other family in the land."[1] An 1888 notebook entry by Mark Twain reads: "Royalty and nobility in *our* day. Those dodos and pterodactyls!"[2] And Carnegie's belief that a royal family was an insult to other families was shared by the Boss, who in Chapter xiii asks the freemen if they agree that "a certain hundred families should be raised to dizzy summits of rank, and clothed on with offensive transmissible glories and privileges to the exclusion of the rest of the nation's families."

Carnegie also despised the "dudes" who affected English fashions. In the manuscript of the *Yankee* Mark Twain expressed a scorn for the "dudes" and "Dudesses" who "aped English high society dress, and grossness of manner, mispronunciation, and appetite for the compliment of a snub from a noble."[3] Finally, Carnegie's congratulations to America for its daily transformation of "victims of feudal tyranny" into

7. *The North American Review*, CXCI (1910), pp. 827 ff. In *The Ordeal of Mark Twain* (New York, 1920), p. 142, Van Wyck Brooks accepted *Triumphant Democracy* as the inspiration of A *Connecticut Yankee*.
8. *Mark Twain's Letters*, ed. A. B. Paine (New York, 1917), p. 578.

9. *Mark Twain in Eruption* (New York, 1940), p. 42.
1. *Triumphant Democracy* (New York, 1886), p. 9.
2. Notebook 23 (I), p. 11 (MTP).
3. Manuscript, I, 147B (Berg Collection).

"republican Americans" implied historical and psychological assumptions that Mark Twain was in the process of abandoning, but which briefly made the Boss's "man factory" possible. The mixture of contempt and admiration which Mark Twain felt for Carnegie reflected his own ambivalence toward the ideas which the millionaire could still embrace and proclaim without a trace of hesitation.

### V

In the summer of 1889 Mark Twain noted the fact that against the four Englishmen on America—Sir Lepel Griffin, Matthew Arnold, Dickens, and Mrs. Trollope—stood a lone "Englishman on England."[4] This lone Englishman was George Standring, whose "exposure" of England Mark Twain wished to "carry down" and publish for twenty-five cents.[5] Standring was an English printer, a socialist, and an editor of *The Republican*. His *People's History of the English Aristocracy* (London, 1887) was a compact illustration of the thesis that throughout historic times the English aristocracy had been "a disgrace to their country and to humanity." Standring was capable of an infectious moral rage in his attacks on primogeniture, on "loyalty," on wild-game laws, and on the power of royal concubines. He taunted the English nobility for its insolent assumption of superiority despite its descent from harlots, for its inveterate opposition to every popular freedom, and for its absurd monopoly of military rank. He brought his history up to the mid-nineteenth century and in an introductory note mentioned "the flood of filth and garbage" from the divorce courts as "portraying *the daily life of the modern English Aristocracy*." He concluded the volume with a call for the establishment of an English republic.

In a letter in the Mark Twain Papers, dated 7 May 1887, Standring mentioned that he was sending a copy of his *People's History* to Mark Twain. This book's influence both on the *Yankee* and on Mark Twain's attitudes towards England merits additional study. But Standring wrote other "exposures" which Mark Twain may have read. One of his penny pamphlets summarizes his views of Victoria's usefulness to the nation. "Does Royalty Pay?" appeared in a group of fortnightly publications under the general title of *The Atheistic Platform* (London, 1884), edited by Annie Besant and Charles Bradlaugh. (Bradlaugh, whose biography Standring wrote, was charged by Matthew Arnold in "Numbers" with wishing to banish the New Testament from the schools.) Standring's pamphlet was a direct attack on the English constitutional monarchy of the 1880's, which Mark Twain only a few years earlier had believed far superior to democracy.[6] According to Standring, monarchy was simply "a costly sham." Like Mark Twain—who briefly planned to include a nearby "cuckoo

4. Notebook 23 (II), p. 54 (MTP).
5. Clemens to Hall, 24 November 1889 (Berg Collection).
6. See *Mark Twain to Mrs. Fairbanks*, p. 208.

kingdom" in the *Yankee*[7]—Standring emphasized the foreign extraction of English monarchs and specifically attacked the royal grant. (Mark Twain reminded himself to work something on royal grants into the *Yankee*.[8] The three paragraphs on this topic at the end of Chapter XXV are not in the holograph manuscript.) Standring's suggestion that a rubber stamp might economically be substituted for the monarch was similar to Clarence's suggestion in the *Yankee* that a family of royal cats be established.

Two of the clearest instances of direct influence on *A Connecticut Yankee* involve Edward Jarvis and Charles Ball. During the summer of 1888, Mark Twain jotted down in his notebook the reminder to "Take that Atlantic and make showing of how much a day's wages would buy."[9] Additional notes made a year later identify this reference as an article by Edward Jarvis, "The Increase of Human Life,"[1] from which Twain planned to excerpt passages in substantiation of the Boss's statistics in the conversation on prices and wages in Chapter xxxiii of the *Yankee*.

Jarvis attacked the romantic view of the past and praised human progress in recent centuries. He put particular stress on inventions and the listings in patent offices as sure indicators of that progress. (The Boss considers a patent office the first necessity of a civilization. Mark Twain intended to develop this theme in the *Yankee*, but never got around to it.)[2] Jarvis believed that modern comforts were essential to "the fullness of life attained only in the highest civilizations" (p. 581). However, he presented statistics on wages and prices drawn largely from the sixteenth century and later. In using such material as the basis for the Boss's discussion of sixth-century economics, Mark Twain characteristically assumed that living standards steadily worsened as one went back in time. In estimating wages, he applied Jarvis' method of computing how many days a worker needed to earn a particular piece of goods. Thus Jarvis wrote that a mechanic in the late sixteenth century could earn a "stuff gown" for his wife in seven and one-half days (p. 712). The Boss mentions that it took a farm woman forty-two days in the sixth century to earn that same stuff gown. He then goes on to predict that wages would be six times higher in seven hundred years, twenty times higher in 950 years, and two hundred times higher in 1290 years (i.e., in 1890). Prices, in the meantime, would have risen only four times. These figures correspond approximately to Jarvis' estimates of the rate of increase in real wages from the sixteenth to the nineteenth century (p. 711). Even more than Jarvis, the Boss implies that "real wages" are an absolute standard for measuring the relative quality of human life in various times and places.

7. Notebook 23 (II), p. 60 (MTP).
8. Notebook 24, p. 13 (MTP).
9. Notebook 23 (I), p. 14 (MTP).

1. *The Atlantic Monthly*, XXIC (Oct., Nov., Dec. 1869), 495–502, 581–598, 711–718.
2. Manuscript, I, 153 (Berg Collection).

The list of trades in Chapter xxxiii of A *Connecticut Yankee*—carpenter, dauber, mason, painter, blacksmith, wheelwright—was probably taken directly from the third part of Jarvis' article, as were many of the consumer goods used to illustrate prices. (This reliance on Jarvis led to the inclusion of a seventeenth-century turkey for the sixth-century feast at Marco's. But the illustrator, Dan Beard, objected to the turkey as an anachronism, and a goose was substituted.)[3] While some of the economic points made by the Boss were clearly based on Mark Twain's own experience of inflated money, the bulk of the data for the entire chapter on "Sixth-Century Political Economy" was supplied by Jarvis.

In commenting on this chapter, Bernard DeVoto claimed that Mark Twain never misapplied the proportionate values of the sixth and nineteenth centuries.[4] Proportionate values over the centuries involve very complex reckonings, but DeVoto's statement at any rate gives an exaggerated impression of Mark Twain's thoroughness in method. Hermit shirts, for example, were sold for a dollar and a half, which was the price of fifty cows or a blooded race horse. According to the price list for the dinner at Marco's then, fifty cows were no more valuable than thirty suckling pigs, and a slave (the Boss, at least) was worth all of six hundred head of cattle. But Mark Twain could have found in his copy of Lingard's *History* that a slave in early England was worth only four oxen.[5] Like the Boss, Mark Twain was aiming at "effects" and felt no obligation to be scrupulously accurate or consistent in his rendering of historical detail.

Mark Twain's awareness of a number of other aspects of medieval life was either derived from, or reinforced by, Jarvis' article. Smallpox, for example, as the great killer miraculously stamped out by vaccination, was discussed by Jarvis (p. 502) and appeared in the *Yankee*, although Mark Twain never got around to including in the novel the compulsory vaccination program which he had planned.[6] Another example of probable borrowing of historical details is suggested by the description of early Renaissance housing which Jarvis quoted from Erasmus: "The floors of the houses generally were made of nothing but loam, and are strewed with rushes, which being constantly put on fresh, without a removal of the old, remain lying there, in some cases, for twenty years, with fishbones, broken victuals, and other filth, impregnated with the excretions of dogs, children, and men" (p. 585). Mark Twain seems to have turned this information into the joke about stratified family histories which concludes the episodes of Sandy's pigs. Finally, he may also have borrowed a number of comments on such things as the scarcity of glass and carpets.

3. Fred Hall to Clemens, 16 October 1889 (MTP).

4. *Mark Twain's America* (Cambridge, Mass.,

1932), p. 273.

5. *History of England* (London, 1883), I, 417.

6. Notebook 23 (II), p. 60 (MTP).

In sum, Jarvis supplied Mark Twain with a number of historical details and a method for calculating real wages on which a major incident in the novel was based. Jarvis, with his unrestrained praise of man's moral and material progress, and his assertion that the latter was a necessary precondition of the former, was a strong voice in the choir of writers and historians who were assuring a restless Mark Twain of the salvation inherent in republican technology.

## VI

A major object of attack in *A Connecticut Yankee* was slavery, and it was clearly the American brand which provided most of the material for Mark Twain's presentation. In the summer of 1889 he planned to use excerpts from "Charles Ball" in an appendix to substantiate the historicity of the slave scenes in Chapters xxi and xxxiv.[7] But he abandoned this plan, perhaps because he had decided that the *Yankee* was to be presented as a satiric retort to contemporary English critics of America.

Charles Ball's *Slavery in the United States*[8] purported to be the personal reminiscences of an illiterate Negro slave. It contained several accounts of slaves horribly tortured or burned alive by mobs, and emphasized the belief (shared by the Boss) that one of the most vicious aspects of slavery was its brutalization of the slave owners.[9] Ball—like the Boss in Chapter xiii—defended those slaves who chose suicide, ironically describing the opposition of proprietors to such an escape and the Church's refusal of Christian burial to slaves who killed themselves (p. 70). Unlike Lecky, Ball did not think Christianity had done much for the slave, since the main virtue it preached was obedience to masters (p. 15), a view of the Church with which Mark Twain was in complete accord.[1]

The group of slaves met by Sandy and the Boss have much in common with the chained slaves being driven south in Ball's book (p. 48). The women in Ball's group are tied with ropes, but the men, like those in the *Yankee*, wear iron collars with padlocks, a 100-foot chain passing through the hasp of each padlock.[2] The men are also handcuffed in pairs by one-foot chains. Like Mark Twain's slaves, they receive only scraps of food and sleep bundled together on naked floors.

Mark Twain borrowed several incidents from Ball. There is one young mother in the *Yankee* whose child is taken from her while she is forced to lie on the ground and expose her body for a lashing. Later she

7. Notebook 24, p. 13 (MTP).

8. It was published in New York in 1837 as part of the Cabinet of Freedom Series. An 1859 edition bears the title *Charles Ball's Autobiography, or Fifty Years in Chains*.

9. *Slavery in the United States*, pp. v, viii. Like Mark Twain's Morgan Le Fay, a Southern slave owner, according to Ball, was free to murder a slave as long as he paid for him.

1. See his marginal comment on *European Morals, II, 72*, in *The Twainian*, XIV (May–June 1955).

2. Ball, p. 37. Some of Mark Twain's description of the slave gang was probably drawn from George Kennan's current articles on Russia. See Howard Baetzhold, "The Course of Composition of *A Connecticut Yankee*: A Reinterpretation," pp. 207–211.

is freed from her chains at the shop of a wayside smith. An argument follows between the trader and the buyer over who should pay the smith,[3] and finally the woman is wrenched from her husband's arms and dragged off shrieking. This scene was probably derived from two scenes in Ball. The first involves a female slave—Lydia—who also is forced to lie on the ground and expose herself for whipping while she holds her child in her arms. (Lydia—like the woman slaves in the *Yankee*—prays for the death of her child.)[4] The second recounts Ball's own separation from his mother, who runs after him weeping until whipped back into line by the trader (p. 17). In phrasing similar to Hank Morgan's as he watches a slave family broken up and listens to screams receding in the distance, Ball says that "the terrors of the scene return with painful vividness" after fifty years. Finally, in Ball's book a slave auction takes place on July fourth while in the background an orator praises American freedoms and the concept that all men are created equal (pp. 125–126). Mark Twain used this incident in the *Yankee*, omitting the date, of course, and shifting the praise to "our glorious British liberties" while the Boss and the King are being sold off.

## VII

The instances gathered here of the probable or definite influence of various historians on *A Connecticut Yankee* suggest several conclusions. The historical reading behind the novel was wide but eclectic, and there is no evidence that Mark Twain attempted any thorough or scholarly historical preparation. Despite his early statements of intention, he made no serious effort to present accurately the "life of the day." His failure to do so was not proof that he simply did not have "the knowledge which would enable him to be a sound critic of the Middle Ages." It was rather that he did not have the temperament or the desire. His fairly impressive historical knowledge was entirely at the service of humor on the one hand, and a philosophy of history on the other. The result is that the "historical" world of *A Connecticut Yankee* lacks almost all the redeeming features which generally make harsh lives bearable.

It is also evident, however, that even as Mark Twain forced history to serve his own views, those views were in the process of being changed. The fact that his historical material was drawn for the most part from relatively modern times suggests at least one basis for his deepening distrust of the meliorism preached by the historians on whom he most relied. Civilization, he was beginning to feel, had barely begun. Furthermore, history was becoming for him almost exclusively a source of material for moral indignation rather than for anachronistic farce. In *A Connecticut Yankee* he increasingly—if by

---

3. Ball, p. 72, describes a similar incident.     4. Ibid., pp. 151, 159.

no means consistently—looked for historical examples of cruelty and injustice as the cores for successive narrative episodes. The shift within the *Yankee* itself from farce towards bitter humor and indignation parallels that larger pattern of changing emphasis which characterizes Mark Twain's work in its totality.

# KENNETH S. LYNN

## The Volcano†

\*   \*   \*

### II

An early memorandum on *A Connecticut Yankee in King Arthur's Court* reads as follows: "He mourns his lost land—has come to England & revisited it, but it is all changed & become old, so old!—& it was so fresh & new, so virgin before. . . . Has lost all interest in life—is found dead next morning—suicide." Twain's terrible sense of loss that resulted from his 1882 trip to the river is easily recognizable in these fatalistic lines, thus prompting the question: Does the Yankee's journey to Arthurian England symbolize the doomed effort of a Twain hero to get back to the Happy Valley? If it does, then there is something radically wrong with the popular theory that *A Connecticut Yankee* is a happy book which triumphantly celebrates American democracy as a Heaven-on-earth.

According to this theory, the novel expresses Twain's growing sympathy with the political and economic aspirations of the masses; his faith in a machine civilization and his pride in America's industrial accomplishment; his hatred for the ignorance and superstition of the Middle Ages and the Catholic Church; and his patriotic desire to twist the British lion's tail, a desire lately inflamed by Matthew Arnold's criticism of General Grant's memoirs and of certain vulgar aspects of American life. Even a sensible critic like Kenneth R. Andrews, ordinarily attuned to the ambivalences of Mark Twain's mind, says of *A Connecticut Yankee* that the novel asserts Twain's approval of the society of his time "unmistakably and enthusiastically." Individual sentences in the novel seem to lend this interpretation weight, but they do so only if their context, both within the book and within the over-all context of Twain's writings, is ignored. Like his Yankee hero, Twain was a passionately loyal American, but by the late '80s his revolt against the Republican party had blossomed into a wholesale contempt for America's business civilization. The nation's institutions, he

† From Kenneth S. Lynn, *Mark Twain and Southwestern Humor* (Boston: Little, Brown, 1959), pp. 249–58.

said, had fallen into rags which were totally unable "to protect the body from winter, disease, and death." For all the quotations about the glories of industrial democracy, et cetera, that can be gleaned from the book, Twain's early memorandum on the despairing suicide of the novel's hero testifies to the somberness of the imagination which created *A Connecticut Yankee.*

In many ways, the novel is the most "Southwestern" book Twain ever wrote, and the first evidence of this is that it begins with a frame. Starting with an encounter between "Mark Twain" and "a curious stranger" in Warwick Castle, the novel leads us by degrees deep into a dream. As the story proper begins, we feel that sense of being in a strange and topsy-turvy world where things are familiar, and yet not, which is one of the most distinctive qualities of the dream-state. Thinking that he recognizes contemporary Bridgeport, the dreaming narrator is told that the town is King Arthur's Camelot. On closer inspection, however, the place turns out to look very much like Bricksville, Arkansas, in the days when Huck Finn was a boy: "The streets were mere crooked alleys, unpaved; troops of dogs and nude children played in the sun . . . ; hogs roamed and rooted contentedly about, and one of them lay in a reeking wallow in the middle of the main thoroughfare." The crazy impression that the stranger's journey into the medieval past has also transported him simultaneously to the pre-Civil War Southwest is reinforced in a multitude of ways—by the Crockett-like tall tales which the knights of the Round Table are forever spinning; by the "Southern" emphasis of Arthur's courtiers on personal honor and the immaculate virtue of fair ladies; and by the fact that a large segment of the population is held in involuntary servitude. The very characteristics of the Valley society which in Twain's view Mrs. Trollope had every right to denounce—"slavery, rowdyism, 'chivalrous' assassinations, sham Godliness"—precisely define the Arthurian world into which the stranger from Connecticut wanders.

He is a strange man, this stranger. Although a Yankee mechanic from Hartford, Hank Morgan speaks with disconcerting familiarity of Arkansas journalism, steamboating, and sunsets on the Mississippi, while his narrative style makes him sound like a grown-up Huck Finn. Except that Hank is Huck with a vengeance. The gentle boy who was so ashamed of the human race that he seceded from society has grown into an aggressive adult who wishes not to escape from a fallen Eden, but rather to uplift it, who dreams—inside his own dream—of turning Bricksville-like Camelot into a St. Petersburg with modern conveniences. And yet despite his Utopianism, he has a relentless and unforgiving contempt for the human race. In Hank's curious view, the people whom he proposes to help are animals who aren't worth the trouble: "Finally it occurred to me that these animals didn't reason," he says. "Why, they were nothing but rabbits," he says. "The people had inherited the idea that all men without title . . . were creatures of no more consideration than so many animals, bugs, insects, whereas I had inherited the notion that human daws who can consent to masquerade in the peacock-shams of inherited dignities and unearned titles, are of no good but to be laughed at." From that last quotation it is possible, of course, to extract an endorsement of democracy, and critics have done so, but the imagery in which the endorsement is cast reflects a view of humanity as degraded beyond the power of any political system to redeem it. Hank Morgan, unlike the narrators of the Southwestern tradition, makes no moral distinctions between the Gentleman and the Clown, but in democratically consigning everyone, regardless of social rank, to the category of human daws the Yankee can hardly be described as the triumphant voice of American egalitarianism.

Anesthetized by his contempt, Hank Morgan is able to laugh uproariously at the spectacle of human suffering. In *A Connecticut Yankee,* the detached and callous joking that was one of the distinguishing marks of the Southwestern tradition abruptly re-emerges. To be sure, much of the humor in the novel follows the usual Twain formula of drawing attention to the minor discomforts of the innocent abroad—Hank Morgan trying to scratch an itch while wearing a suit of armor, for example. But some of the jokes are shockingly cruel. "There are times," the Yankee says, "when one would like to hang the whole human race and finish the farce," a vengeful wisecrack indeed, and one which serves as the prelude to a number of exceedingly sadistic pranks. By profession a maker of guns, revolvers, and cannon—which he significantly calls "labor-saving machinery"— Hank Morgan is a Sut Lovingood with all the latest weapons at his disposal, a backwoods prankster with technological know-how.

Nevertheless, this strange man from Hartford has entered history in order to redeem it. He desires to give the people a "new deal" (a phrase which Franklin Roosevelt did *not* get from *A Connecticut Yankee*), and the drama of the novel consists in his attempt to create a new and better society, a Heavenly City of machines, in backward Camelot. If the Happy Valley no longer existed in the past, perhaps it could be recreated in the future, bigger and better than ever.

Discovering that King Arthur is an "extinct volcano," the Yankee mechanic comes to power by displaying an assortment of nineteenth-century tricks, most of them volcanic in nature. "I made about three passes in the air, and then there was an awful crash and that old tower leaped into the sky in chunks, along with a vast volcanic fountain of fire that turned night to noonday. . . . It rained mortar and masonry the rest of the week." With the resources of a kingdom now under his command, he secretly creates the modern world, and the way in which he describes his creation is of the utmost significance: "It was fenced away from the public view, but there it was, a gigantic and unassailable fact—and to be heard from yet, if I lived and had luck. There it was, as sure a fact and as substantial a fact as any serene volcano, standing innocent with its smokeless summit in the blue sky and giving no sign of the rising hell in its bowels." Standing for the creative flux of a new and better life, Hank Morgan's volcano image also implies a hellish instrument of destruction, to be used against all contemptible creatures who forcibly resist Utopia. As it did in the United States in the 1850s, the volcano in Arthurian England prophesies a civil war between the old order and the new.

For with the introduction of democratic institutions and technological marvels, England is divided in two: the Yankee versus the chivalric knights, "hard unsentimental commonse-sense and reason" versus a feudalistic romanticism. When the war comes, it is horrible. Volcanic explosions now cause more than mortar to rain down: "It resembled a steamboat explosion on the Mississippi; and during the next fifteen minutes we stood under a steady drizzle of microscopic fragments of knights and hardware and horseflesh." Finally, the struggle ends—with the Yankee victorious. "Slavery was dead and gone," he says exultantly, and "the march of civilization was begun. How did I feel? Ah, you never could imagine it." Schools, mines, and factories come out into the open; the telegraph, the telephone, the phonograph, the typewriter, and the sewing machine are introduced; the Round Table is now employed for "business purposes." Progress, energy, and prosperity have become a reality.

If Twain had concluded his novel with this rosy, postwar picture, *A Connecticut Yankee* would take its place beside Edward Bellamy's *Looking Backward* and Howells' *A Traveler from Altruria* as one of those bright prophecies of a brave new world a-coming which flooded the American literary market in the closing decades of the nineteenth century. For in a troubled era, many Americans turned to Utopian fictions for reassurance, and Twain might well have tailored his novel to the popular taste of the moment, as he had done some years earlier in *The Prince and the Pauper*. But Twain conceived of *A Connecticut Yankee* as his farewell to literature, and he wrote it according to the requirements of his personal vision of history, without regard for the market place. "What saves history from triviality," Salvador de Madariaga has said, "is that in its core it is a tragedy"; what saves *A Connecticut Yankee* from being a trivial book is its awareness of that fact. The novel therefore belongs in American literature not with the shallow prophecies of Bellamy and Howells, but alongside *The Education of Henry Adams*.

### III

That Twain should have heard, as Adams did, the sound of doom in the humming of the dynamos is at first glance a surprising fact, especially when one considers the personal history of Mark Twain during the decade in which he conceived and wrote A *Connecticut Yankee*. It was in the '80s that Twain's lifelong enthusiasm for machines reached its apogee.

From the day that Mark Twain first grasped the wheel of a steamboat and felt the power that machines could deliver into a man's hands, he had been an inveterate inventor of gadgets. He also invested money numerous times in the brain children of other men. An engraving process called the Kaolotype, a steam-railway brake, a hinged pants button, a self-pasting scrapbook, a patent steam generator, a steam pulley, a new method of marine telegraphy, a new kind of watch, a new kind of mechanical organ, all these things and many, many more claimed the attention, the money, and the dreams of Mark Twain. Then, in the '80s, he became more deeply involved than ever before, both financially and emotionally, in a grandiose scheme of mechanical perfection.

In the year 1880, Twain purchased two thousand dollars' worth of stock in the Paige typesetting machine, then being brought to completion in the Colt arms factory in Hartford. Soon he put his name down for another three thousand dollars' worth. Five years later, the machine was still not workable, but by this time Twain's faith in it had grown into an obsession. James W. Paige, the inventor of the typesetter, he believed to be "a poet; a most great and genuine poet, whose sublime creations are written in steel." When Paige offered him a half-interest in the machine in exchange for thirty thousand dollars, Twain eagerly accepted. In 1886, the year in which Twain began to work on A *Connecticut Yankee*, Paige came to him for another four thousand dollars. Twain supplied it; and at the rate of three to four thousand dollars every month thereafter, poured his fortune into the "most wonderful typesetting machine ever invented." Offered a half interest in the Mergenthaler linotype in exchange for his interest in the Paige patents, Twain loftily refused. Once the Paige machine was on the market it would bring in annual rentals, Twain calculated, of fifty-five million dollars.

Meantime, Twain was rapidly running out of money. (At Christmastime, 1887, for example, he was able to send his sister only fifteen dollars because, as he wrote to her, he was "a little crowded this year by the type-setter.") The completion of the machine thus became a race against the exhaustion of Twain's funds. All through 1888, while Twain worked steadily and hard on A *Connecticut Yankee*, Paige and the master mechanics he had assembled around him in Pratt and Whitney's shops (the scene of the operations had been shifted from the Colt factory some time before) seemed tantalizingly close to finishing the machine. Finally, in January of 1889, the long task was completed. "The machine is finished!" Twain wrote to a London publisher. "This is by far the most marvelous invention ever contrived by man. And it is not a thing of rags and patches; it is made of massive steel, and will last a century." To Orion he exclaimed, "It's a cunning devil, is that machine! . . . All the other inventions of the human brain sink pretty nearly into commonplace, contrasted with this awful mechanical miracle. Telephones, telegraphs, locomotives, cotton gins, sewing machines, Babbage calculators, Jacquard looms, perfecting presses, Arkwright's frames—all mere toys, simplicities! The Paige Compositor marches alone and far in the lead of human inventions." "In two or three weeks," he added as an afterthought, "we shall work the stiffness out of her joints and have her performing as smoothly and softly as human muscles, and then we shall speak out the big secret and let the whole world come and gaze." In two or three weeks, however, the machine was breaking types, and Paige tore it apart again to see what the trouble was. Once more, Twain had to reach into his pocket every month for another three thousand dollars; with his other hand he wrote the concluding chapters of *A Connecticut Yankee*.

In the fall of 1889, after he had finished reading page proofs on the novel, Twain attempted to sell one hundred thousand dollars in Paige stock to Senator John P. Jones, in order to raise additional funds for the insatiable machine. Neither Jones, nor any other capitalist, was interested. With all of his financial resources committed, and unable to raise any outside aid, Twain was now irrevocably headed down the road that would take him away from his comfortable life in Hartford, bankrupt both him and the publishing firm he controlled, and bring him at last to that bitter December day in Paris in 1894 when he learned that the Paige machine had definitively failed. "It hit me like a thunder-clap," he wrote to his Standard Oil friend H. H. Rogers. "It knocked every rag of sense out of my head, and I went flying here and there and yonder, not knowing what I was doing, and only one clearly defined thought standing up visible and substantial out of the crazy storm-drift—that my dream of ten years was in desperate peril and . . . [that] I must be there and see it die." "Don't say I'm wild," he added some hours later. "For really I'm sane again this morning."

This final, agonizing episode in the history of Mark Twain and the typesetter took place well after his completion of *A Connecticut Yankee*. Up to the point of finishing the book and well beyond it, Twain continued to believe in James W. Paige and his wonderful machine, and Hank Morgan's excited plans for improving the world through technological ingenuity undoubtedly reflect that belief. Indeed, it may very well be that Paige partially inspired the character of Hank Morgan, who in his nineteenth-century identity, after all, was a superintendent of mechanics in a Connecticut arms factory. (Trooping back and forth, in 1885, between Paige's workshop in Hartford and his Nook Farm desk, did not Twain begin to wonder what the world would be like if it were run by a poet whose sublime creations were written in steel? And was it not then that he decided to write a novel on the subject?) As he moved, however, toward the conclusion of *A Connecticut Yankee*, Paige and his typesetter may have begun to have a somewhat less exhilarating effect on Twain's creative imagination. "A cunning devil," was now his name for the machine; having drained him of so much of his wealth, having tantalized and frustrated him a thousand times, it is a wonder he did not call the thing a Frankenstein's monster. The early memorandum that Twain wrote on *A Connecticut Yankee* suggests that right from the beginning he conceived of Hank Morgan's story as a tragedy: like Veblen, Twain believed that the modern technologist could create the world anew, but doubted that society would permit him to do so. In the final chapters of the novel, however, the tragedy becomes something more than simply the downfall of a genius who could not sell his up-to-date ideas to an animalistic people. It becomes the story of a man who is the victim of his own inventions. The steamboat catastrophe with which the cub pilot's education had concluded flowers horribly in *A Connecticut Yankee* into a machine-created cataclysm in which no one is spared, including Hank Morgan, as if Twain now sensed that the Paige typesetter was uncontrollable—that it not only could not be stopped from breaking types, but that it would end by smashing his very life to bits. Translating a foreboding sense of personal disaster into a public one, Twain envisioned the world-wide explosions of the mechanically marvelous twentieth century.

When the war of the future comes, and the "sheep" swarm down upon them from all sides, Hank Morgan and his sidekick Clarence fight back with all the latest weapons, including Gatling guns, dynamite, and electrified fences. The story of their last stand is quintessentially Twainian: their only allies in the struggle against a depraved society are boys—"a darling fifty-two" of them; their place of refuge (how could it be otherwise?) is a cave. Fifty-two Tom Sawyers in a cave, commanded by a "curious stranger," mowing down the enemy, electrocuting him, drowning him, blowing him sky-high in volcanic explosions, until the stench from twenty-five thousand corposes seeps into the cave and the boys (no longer as lucky as Tom Sawyer) all die of asphyxiation, while the Yankee—transposed once more to the nineteenth century—cries out one last time for the Paradise he has lost, and then falls back dead: this, in Mark Twain's history, is the way the world ends.

*　　*　　*

## JAMES M. COX

### A *Connecticut Yankee in King Arthur's Court*: The Machinery of Self-Preservation†

A *Connecticut Yankee in King Arthur's Court* holds much the same position in Mark Twain's work that *Pierre* occupies in Melville's. Before both books stand single masterpieces; after them come books of genuine merit, books even greater than they themselves are, but books more quietly desperate, as if the creative force behind them had suffered a crippling blow and had trimmed itself to the storm of time. And both books reach resolutions involving self-destruction. Melville's hero is a writer so caught in the ambivalences of love and creativity that suicide becomes his last refuge. Twain's Hank Morgan, a robust superintendent of a machine shop who has been plunged into a sixth-century feudal world, discovers himself in the role of a superman inventor who can remake the world. And he does remake it—only to blow up his technological marvels and defeat himself. Despite a certain audacity of conception, however, both works disintegrate into extravagant failures; indeed, their desperate resolutions suggest a desperation behind the fiction, as if the writer were involved in destroying a part of himself, thereby breaking an identification with a threatening aspect of his psychic life. In these works reality and fiction coalesce in such a way that the writer is drawn more and more into his creation until he can end it all only by fighting his way out.

Such a struggle is particularly evident in A *Connecticut Yankee*. Indeed, there is probably no better description of the quality of the book that Twain's famous reply to Howells' praise of the novel: "Well, my book is written—let it go. But if it were only to write over again there wouldn't be so many things left out. They burn in me; and they keep multiplying and multiplying; but now they can't ever be said. And besides, they would require a library—and a pen warmed up in hell." Two main assumptions animate Twain's hyperbole: (1) that the book is an incomplete expression of repressed attitudes; (2) that the remaining attitudes are self-generatively threatening the writer's personality. Both these assumptions point to the final incompleteness of A *Connecticut Yankee*; indeed, Twain's remark to Howells is in its way a remarkably accurate summary of the novel. It is not my purpose to go beyond that summary but to determine what is being summarized. For Twain's remark will not define the novel, but the novel will define—or better, *realize*—the remark. By beginning with the novel, I

† From *Yale Review*, 50 (1960), 89–102. Professor Cox revised the last two paragraphs for inclusion of the essay in *Mark Twain: A Collection of Critical Essays*, ed. Henry Nash Smith (Englewood Cliffs, N.J.: Prentice-Hall, 1963). The revised paragraphs appear in this Norton Critical Edition.

hope to go on to show the forces which burned in Twain, the terms he attempted to make with them in *A Connecticut Yankee,* and the terms his genius finally made with him.

The form of *A Connecticut Yankee* is what we may call an inverted Utopian fantasy, and a graphic way to see that inversion is to compare Twain's novel with Edward Bellamy's *Looking Backward,* which appeared in 1887 and was a best seller by the time the *Yankee* was ready for publication. Bellamy's fantasy involves a dream in which Julian West is precipitated into the future, where, faced with the material and ideological evolution evident in the year 2000 A.D., he sees his own nineteenth century in a perspective at once meager and startling. Through all this experience, West is the observer, the listener, the interrogator who assimilates the persuasive criticism which the imaginary age affords.

Twain, however, instead of going into an imaginary land outside history where the terms of criticism could operate abstractly and logically, plunged into history, and his novel became a going backward in order to look forward. Hank Morgan, the superintendent of a Colt Arms machine shop, thus emerges into the sixth-century Arthurian world and is able to see this feudal pastoral from the presumable advantage of democratic industrialism. But unlike Julian West, Morgan is not the amazed, yet credulous listener. Unable to resist the lure of potential power residing in his technological advantage, he "invents" labor-saving devices, instigates reforms, and organizes the people until he is finally able to proclaim a republic in England. For a brief moment his regime prevails, but the Church, never quite defeated, plays upon the superstition of the populace, declares an interdict, and revolts against the Yankee's authority. He in turn blows up his world along with the assaulting forces of the past, until, surrounded by electrocuted knights he is condemned to a thirteen-century sleep by Merlin. Morgan is the chief actor of his chronicle; just as his nineteenth-century machine shop colloquial vernacular collides with the Maloryese which Twain ascribes to the Arthurian subjects, his political philosophy comes to grips with the aristocratic assumptions of the King's realm.

In saying that *A Connecticut Yankee* is an extravagant failure, I do not mean to imply that the book lacks amusing incidents, for there are happy moments when Twain exploits the incongruities inherent in his conception of a Yankee mechanic clattering through the world of chivalry. Thus, Hank's burlesque of knighthood retains a certain pungency. His mounting the knights on bicycles or forcing them to wear placards advertising such items as Persimmons Soap or Peters Prophylactic Toothbrushes are memorable examples of Twain's rowdy humor; and Morgan's harnessing the incidental power of a praying ascetic in order to operate a shirt factory shows a recklessness of taste which still has power to shock a safe gentility. Taken as a whole, however, the book is a grim reading experience, for as Morgan assumes power in the Arthurian world the fantasy begins to rout the criticism and progression degenerates into mere sequence. The waste of energy which results is perhaps most manifest in the startling disproportion between Hank Morgan's emotion and his reason. His consuming indignation so outstrips his critical intelligence that his ideas are reduced to clamorous fulminations and noisy prejudices causing him to become an object of curiosity instead of an agent of ideas.

Nor is curiosity an inappropriate response, since one of Morgan's most characterizing compulsions is his urge to draw attention to himself. His indignation, his prejudices, his achievements, his incessant boasting, and finally his style—which is overstatement from the moment he greets us until he finally collapses under Merlin's spell—are all manifestations of his desire to show off. Wherever he appears, the Yankee must shine, and more than food or woman or even life itself he loves the effect. He himself in a rare moment of insight observes that the crying defect of his character is his desire to perform picturesquely. Thus he plans his actions with an eye for their stage value, usually specializing in technicolor explosions and other noisy demonstrations which electrify his audiences. Even the sad-faced Mark Twain ruefully observes of the Yankee's dying call to arms, "He was getting up his last 'effect'; but he never finished it."

Constantly advertising his ideas, his mechanical aptitude, and his stagey jokes, Morgan becomes a grotesque caricature of the enlightenment he advocates. He prances and struts through every conceivable burlesque, flaunting himself before the stunned Arthurian world into which he bursts until he becomes the real buffoon of his own performance. More mechanical than any of the gadgets in which he specializes, he grinds laboriously through his "acts," his only means of attracting attention being to run faster and faster, to do bigger and bigger things, until the mechanism of his character flies apart. And fly apart it finally does. There is an ironic appropriateness in the ending of the novel when Morgan, trapped in his cave by the stench from the rotting bodies of his victims and condemned to a thirteen-century sleep by Merlin, emerges deranged before us—adrift in space, unmoored from time.

Mark Twain was aware of the Yankee's limitations, going so far as to confide to Dan Beard, who was to illustrate the book, "The Yankee of mine . . . is a perfect ignoramus; he is boss of a machine shop, he can build a locomotive or a Colt's revolver, he can put up and run a telegraph line, but he's an ignoramus nevertheless." And he insisted in a letter to Mrs. Fairbanks that he did not intend the book as a satire but as a *contrast* between two radically different ages. In view of

Morgan's career and Twain's own statements, it is small wonder that certain critics have maintained that Twain was satirizing not the sixth century but the nineteenth. Thus Parrington insisted that Twain was "trimming his sails to the chill winds blowing from the outer spaces of a mechanistic cosmos," and Miss Gladys Carmine Bellamy has more recently observed that the book is a "fictional working out of the idea that a too-quick civilization breeds disaster."

Plausible though such arguments are in the light of the Yankee's ultimate failure, the tone of the novel often goes in precisely the opposite direction; for although the Yankee finally destroys himself, Twain's major investment in the novel is in the Yankee's attitudes. After all, most of those attitudes were the same ones Mark Twain swore by at one time or another during his public life, and the usual response to the novel has been that Twain was lampooning monarchy and chivalry. Furthermore, there is abundant evidence that Twain intended just such criticism. As early as 1866, Twain was attacking feudalism in the Sandwich Islands; and his belief in the superiority of democracy to monarchy goes back to the very beginning of his career; his hatred of an established church stretches equally far back—and further forward. Thus, ten years after the Yankee's diatribes against the ancient authority of the church, Twain still retained enough of his old animus against organized religion to mount a sustained, logical attack against Mary Baker Eddy, whose Christian Science he feared would become the official religion of the Republic. Finally, Matthew Arnold's strictures upon American culture particularly exasperated Twain, and there is clear evidence that some of the Yankee's attitudes are a direct response to Arnold's criticisms.

But in turning his narrative over to Morgan, Twain sacrificed whatever satiric intent he may have had in mind, for instead of converting the indignation which stands behind satire into the ironic observation, apparent indifference, and mock innocence which constitute it, Twain paraded his indignation in front of the world to be criticized. Moreover, the person of the Yankee stood between the idea and its dramatization, short-circuiting logic in such a welter of emotion that he became the problem with which Twain had to deal.

The nature of Twain's struggle is implicit in the slender frame around the story. Chronically incapable of erecting the complex plots which he thought characterized the novel, Twain often resorted to stock devices for getting into his narratives. But, as Walter Blair has pointed out, in his hands those devices become significant form charged with his own motives. In this frame, Twain employed the author-meets-narrator stratagem, managing to gain an excuse for telling his tale at the same time he introduced his hero. Following a guided tour through Warwick Castle, itself a representative of the stock past of the tourist's imagination, Twain encountered a stranger "who wove such a spell about me that I seemed to move among the shadows and dust and mold of a gray antiquity, holding speech with a relic of it." The very rhetoric which Twain ascribes to himself is filled with the clichés of travelogue nostalgia. Throughout this brief introduction, Twain portrays himself as a dewy-eyed tourist bent on caressing images of the past. In this moment of sentimental retrospection while the guide attempts to explain the presence of a bullet hole in an ancient piece of armor, the stranger appears, like a fabulous genie come from a bottle, and into Twain's ear alone proclaims himself the author of the bullet hole. The "electric surprise of this remark" momentarily shatters the tourist Mark Twain's retrospective dream, and by the time he recovers, the stranger has disappeared. That evening, however, sitting by the fire at the Warwick Arms "steeped in a dream of the olden time," Twain is again abruptly confronted by the stranger, who, knocking upon the door to interrupt the dream, takes final charge of the narrative.

What the artist Mark Twain makes apparent in this brief frame is that Morgan is a projection, or, more accurately, an anti-mask of the tourist Mark Twain's stock nostalgia. For just as Morgan has put a bullet hole through the antique armor, so does he puncture the sentimental dream of the past. Moreover, he comes unbidden to menace at the same time he accompanies the dreamer on the journey back into time. Speaking with a casual and confident authority, he even announces that he is the antithesis of sentimentality: "I am a Yankee of Yankees—and practical; yes, and nearly barren of sentiment, I suppose—or poetry, in other words." His narrative is appropriately preserved on a palimpsest, since the Yankee's personal history is the record of an effort to overwrite the past.

The Yankee's role, as it is defined in the frame, is one of burlesquing "Mark Twain's" tourist version of the past. The one emotion which is anathema to Morgan is reverence, and wherever he encounters the posture—whether in sentimental nostalgia or in a feudal aristocracy—his reaction is one of aggressive ridicule. This unqualified irreverence was by no means new in Twain's work. It was a necessary adjunct to a writer whose own creative impulse was essentially nostalgic. When we look upon Twain's work we realize that the past—his personal past—was his own armor. His great work is staged within his and America's remembered Southern geography of boyhood which the indignation and mechanization of the Civil War had reduced to the status of an island in the remote past. Although Twain shared the indignation enough to transplant himself morally and literally into the Hartford neighborhood of Harriet Beecher Stowe, his creative imagination discovered itself in the primal world before the War. Sentimental as his longing for the past could be—he speaks in his *Autobiography* of "the pathetic past, the beautiful past, the dear and lamented past"—it nevertheless inspired at the same time it drove him back upon his memory. The rich cargo he brought back from these "voyages into the uncharted sea of recollection," as he once called them, redeemed the meagerness of his wish to go.

One of Twain's chief protections against this intense longing for the past was his capacity for burlesque. Burlesque was the reality principle which could both mock and check the nostalgic impulse, and as early as *The Innocents Abroad* Twain had mastered the technique of shifting from platform nostalgia to burlesque. One of his favorite stances in all of his writing is along that borderland where pathos dissolves into broad ridicule, and it is often difficult to tell whether Twain is trapped in clichés or simply exploiting them. This complexity of vision characterizes much of *The Innocents Abroad* and even manifests itself in the very pun in the title of *A Tramp Abroad*. Indeed, Twain's success in writing travel books comes largely from his pervasive concern with attitudes toward history.

But Hank Morgan is more than merely an agent of ridicule; he goes beyond burlesque to threaten the whole existence of the past—any past. The image of Camelot into which he erupts is a "soft, reposeful summer landscape, as lovely as a dream and as lonesome as Sunday. The air was full of the smell of flowers and the buzzing of insects, and the twittering of birds, and there were no people, no wagons, there was no stir of life, nothing going on." Here is one of those ambivalent descriptions so recurrent in Twain's work. It is almost sentimental, almost, indeed, a cliché, and yet it could be Jackson's Island or Holiday's Hill, or the vision from a raft on the Mississippi. It is that summer idyl around which Twain perpetually revolved and in which his memory forever renewed itself.

Even Morgan feels the spell of its beauty, but his indignation at the slavery he discovers within its borders arouses him to destroy the sanctuary. He is finally a Connecticut *Yankee*, and slavery in Arthur's kingdom outrages him as much as slavery in Missouri. It is the archetypal evil justifying his determination to overthrow the past. What enables him to accomplish his task is his ability as an inventor and a businessman. What we have, in effect, is a Tom Sawyer fantasy being played out by an adult who, in an increasingly menacing way, means business. At the end of the fantasy, Morgan is electrocuting knights so rapidly and so thoroughly that there is no way of identifying the dead. They are merely an alloy of brass and buttons. Just as Twain drives the Yankee as clown through act after act of burlesque, he also drives the republican gadgeteer through a long line of inventions to destruction. And yet just as burlesque had been a valuable component of Twain's earlier humor, the prefigurations of Hank Morgan businessman are among his most celebrated character creations.

There is, for example, Twain himself in *Roughing It*, the restless and passionate victim of gold fever; there is Colonel Sellers, the extravagant speculator whose thoughts, fairly humming with infinite inventions and projects, are invested in a golden tomorrow at the same time they are busy preparing for it; there is Samuel Clemens in *Old Times on the Mississippi*, the adventurer on steamboats, his adventure itself a kind of Arabian Night's tale of youthful ambition realized; and finally there is Tom Sawyer, that shrewd boyhood businessman always so caught in a vision of his future glory that he cannot resist showing himself off at every opportunity. These dreaming characters often fail in their prophecies, but their presence in Twain's world is prophetic, just as their power for Twain, and for us, is compelling. They are, all of them, great characters, and without them Twain's literary achievement would have been vastly less significant than it was. Proof of their almost independent being within Twain's mind is the fact that Colonel Sellers and Tom Sawyer have assumed a mythic life outside the fiction in which they appeared. Twain himself must have sensed the alarming potential of such characters when he refused to carry Tom Sawyer into manhood on the grounds that he would "just lie like all other one-horse men in literature and the reader would conceive a hearty contempt for him." By keeping Tom trapped in the idyl of the past—or as DeVoto aptly phrased it, "the phantasy of boyhood"—Twain could transform the dream work which produced Tom into dream play.

Although Twain usually managed to control these characters *in* literature, he could not confine the creative forces behind them to literature alone. By the time he wrote *Huckleberry Finn*, they were not only operating inside the novel in the person of Tom Sawyer, who, interestingly enough, threatened to turn the novel upside down with his burlesque; they were encroaching from the outside as well, having led Twain from investments in a steam generator, a steam pulley, a new method of marine telegraphy, a watch company, an insurance house, a new process of engraving (the kaolatype) into two huge projects: the Webster Publishing Company, in which Twain was chief investor and senior partner; and the Paige typesetting machine. Even while Twain was feverishly working on *Huckleberry Finn*, he revealed the tension of his divided life in a bluntly urgent letter to Charles L. Webster: "I cannot answer letters; I can ill spare the time to read them; my time is brief. I cannot be interrupted by vinyard business or any *other* . . . You are my businessman; & business I myself will *not* *transact*. . . . I won't talk business—I will perish first. I hate the very idea of business in all its forms." The speculative urges, which had once been both source and subject of his literary capital, had become a threat to his life as a writer, and he was forced to feed his literary productions into his business holdings: *Huckleberry Finn* was the first book published by the Webster Publishing Company.

Twain's publishing interests did not, however, demand nearly so much of his attention, energy, and capital as the Paige typesetting machine. From 1881, when he first became interested in it, until 1894, when the bankruptcy to which it brought him forced him to abandon it, the machine devoured $300,000 of his money. At the height of his obsession, in 1888, the same year in which he wrote most of *A Connecticut Yankee,* he was spending three thousand dollars per month on the invention. Even these figures fail to reflect the awe with which he regarded the machine. To his brother Orion he described the reverent silence which gripped those who watched it in operation for the first time. "All the witnesses," he wrote, "made written record of the immense historical birth—the first justification of a line of movable type by machinery—and also set down the hour and the minute."

He spoke of it as a cunning devil at one time; at another, he contended that it was next to man in intricacy at the same time it surpassed him in perfection; at still another, he wrote that he loved to sit by the machine by the hour and merely contemplate it. Never was Twain more enamored of an object, unless it was Olivia Langdon; if she was the goddess he revered, it was the demon who possessed him and on whom he wasted his fortune and almost sacrificed his sanity. In his obsessed vision, the machine was both an intricate world and a mechanical brain whose infinitely interrelated parts he could half comprehend. It became for him, as Tom Burnham has wisely suggested, the concrete embodiment, the diagram, from which his mechanistic philosophy and psychology took their inspiration. More than that, the machine was uniquely wedded to the printed word; it was, after all, a kind of automatic writer capable of working tirelessly with speed and precision.

This then was the mechanical miracle whose advent Twain anxiously awaited, as he proceeded with his work on the *Yankee.* On October 5, 1888, he was able to write to Theodore Crane, his wife's brother-in-law:

> I am here in Twichell's house at work with the noise of the children and an army of carpenters to help. Of course they don't help, but neither do they hinder. It's like a boiler factory for racket . . . but I never am conscious of the racket at all, and I move my feet into position of relief without knowing when I do it . . . I was so tired last night that I thought I would lie abed and rest, today; but I couldn't resist . . . I want to finish the day the machine finishes, and a week ago the closest calculations for that indicated October 22—but experience teaches me that their calculations will miss fire as usual.

The letter might well stand as a foreword to *A Connecticut Yankee.* The process of composition as Twain describes it—a dully driven effort which goes on almost outside himself—is perfectly explained by his wish to finish the book on the day the machine was to be completed. Twain was saying, in effect, that he was a machine-driven writer; more important, he revealed that the novel had come to have a strange identification with the machine. There is, however, the hint of fatal doubt about the Paige contraption. To accommodate one's writing to its schedule was to be involved in a frustrating regimen of uncertainty. We know that the machine was not perfected on October 22; neither was the novel completed on that date. Not until the summer of 1889, after seasons of supreme hope punctuated by periods of depression or anxious alarm about the mechanical marvel, did Twain succeed in bringing the novel to its conclusion.

That Twain could bring the book to an end at all and break the vicious identification between it and the machine signifies a victory for the writer. For Hank Morgan is to a large extent the concrete embodiment of Twain's obsession with Paige's invention. At least, available evidence argues the plausibility of such a conclusion. Intruding into Twain's reverie, he assumes the power in the book that he held in the Hartford world outside the novel. In the cosmos of the novel, however, Twain is the Yankee's master; although the Yankee is Boss of the machine world he imposes upon the face of the Arthurian landscape, Twain operates the machinery of the novel and compels the Yankee to jump through act after act with ever increasing velocity until all his improvisations are exhausted. In bringing Morgan to death Twain was symbolically killing the machine madness which possessed him. If the devices Twain employs in the narrative do not always succeed as art—even if they are mere parts of the machinery of this mechanical novel—the novel nevertheless remains an act of personal salvation, its machinery the machinery of self-preservation.

For instead of being the "Divine Amateur" which he has been called, Twain was finally a professional writer; writing was his last protection. Just as he relied upon his art to protect himself from the financial embarrassments into which his amateur business ventures were leading him, so did he turn to it as we have seen, to reestablish psychic control over those unleashed creative forces which were wreaking havoc in his private life. In endeavoring to regain control of those forces, Twain was preparing himself against the inevitable fall which awaited him in time. When, in 1894, Henry Rogers, the Standard Oil tycoon whose experience and advice had come to Twain's rescue during his financial failure, wrote that the typesetter had to be relinquished as a total loss, Twain replied from Europe:

> I seemed to be entirely expecting your letter, and also prepared and resigned; but Lord, it shows how little we know ourselves and how easily we can deceive ourselves. It hit me like a thunder-clap. It knocked every rag of sense out of my head, and I went flying here and there and yonder not knowing what I was doing, and only one

clearly defined thought standing up visible and substantial out of the crazy storm-drift—that my dream of ten years was in desperate peril and out of the 60,000 or 70,000 projects for its rescue that came flocking through my skull not one would hold still long enough for me to examine it and size it up.

The entire action of Twain's book, published five years earlier, was more than a mere prophecy of the disaster toward which the machine obsession was tending; it was an acting out beforehand of the experience itself and hence a preparation for the end it prophesied. Indeed, the last scene of the novel in which "Mark Twain" hears the Yankee's confused and futile attempt to keep hold of a reality which is dissolving into dream is a rehearsal of Twain's own dilemma as the crisis of his fortunes approached. Writing to Mrs. Theodore Crane in 1893, Twain could only say:

> I dreamed I was born and grew up and was a pilot on the Mississippi and a miner and a journalist in Nevada and a pilgrim in the Quaker City, and had a wife and children and went to live in a villa at Florence—and this dream goes on and on and sometimes seems so real that I almost believe it is real. I wonder if it is? But there is no way to tell, for if one applies tests they would be part of the dream, too, and so would simply aid the deceit. I wish I knew whether it is a dream or real.

The book could not prevent the disasters; it could only prepare for them, but in its way it represented a victory of the writer over the businessman. In viewing that victory one is almost led to believe that Merlin, who has been crossed, belittled, and ridiculed by the Yankee throughout the book, is—as he was for so many writers during the nineteenth century—the prototype of the artist who emerges from humiliation and shame to exercise his magic power at the last.

Such an interpretation would grossly oversimplify the matter, however, for neither is Twain's victory so dramatic nor the division between writer and businessman so precipitous. As he himself revealed in his letters to Howells, the book failed to express completely the attitudes which burned in him. They were left to burn themselves out in his experience. And I have already suggested that Twain's interest in business was a result of his creative imagination overflowing into his life. To deplore his commercial ventures is to forget that both publishing companies and typesetters are not wholly unrelated to literary creation. After all, the fact that *Huckleberry Finn* was the first product of Twain's publishing house is as gratifying as the knowledge that Thoreau was at one time a manufacturer of pencils.

The figure of the Yankee reveals how closely knit the activities of writing and business were in Twain's mind. The Yankee was not simply a businessman, but an *inventor*, and his power, which was as benign inside the creative imagination as it was malign outside it, was indissolubly linked with Twain's artistic life. To kill the Yankee even symbolically was a serious undertaking, representing a crippling of the inventive imagination, as if Twain were driven to maim himself in order to protect himself. It is not surprising that Twain considered this radical redefinition of himself as a logical end of his writing life. He went so far as to notify Howells that his career was over and that he wished "to pass to the cemetery unclodded." Of course, Twain's career was not over. He wrote again and again because there were financial necessities which required it and because there were personal disasters to come of even greater magnitude than those he was facing.

And A *Connecticut Yankee* is a rehearsal for that writing as much as it was a preparation for the experience which was to come. I do not have the space to examine in detail the last phase of Twain's career, but I do want to stress a single, salient aspect in which the Yankee anticipated the work to come. A look at the important fiction which Twain wrote after 1889 reveals that a particular figure tends to dominate them—a stranger, who ultimately becomes the Mysterious Stranger. Just as the burlesquer and the incipient businessman had appeared early in Twain's work, so had this stranger. In "The Celebrated Jumping Frog" he had come into the decayed mining camp of Angels and, in order to win a bet from Jim Smiley, had poured enough shot into the jumping frog Dan'l Webster to paralyze him. But even in this story, the stranger is simply required by the terms of the story. His character is never defined and he remains no more than a shadowy personage necessary to the plot.

A *Connecticut Yankee* marks his full emergence into the foreground of Twain's comic world, for Hank Morgan is the stranger who intrudes into "Mark Twain's" reverie and into the charmed Arthurian paradise. As Twain describes him in the frame, he is strangely detached in countenance and manner, possessed of an all-knowing air as if he were present at the creation of the universe. The role this stranger comes to assume in Twain's fiction—his *act* we might say—is one of disturbing the peace. Into quiet, complacent communities he comes disrupting the society by unmasking and turning it upon itself. Thus Pudd'nhead Wilson, another Yankee stranger, enters Dawson's Landing, drolly observes the community, taking its fingerprints until he alone can disclose the crime which lies hidden at the heart of the society. And the man that corrupted Hadleyburg is a stranger who, somehow wronged by the community in the veiled past, takes elaborate revenge on it by means of a diabolically conceived joke which reveals the moral sham of the society. The stranger is last incarnated in the role of Philip Traum, the Mysterious Stranger, who pronounces the universe a dream.

The stranger's different avatars do not obscure certain distinguishing aspects of his character. He is first of all gaining a curious revenge on the world, a revenge usually taking the form of a practical joke.

Second, he has a penchant for philosophy, his thought generally following a pattern of cracker barrel mechanistic determinism. Thus the Yankee, Pudd'nhead, and Philip Traum all insist that man is a machine who must obey the laws of his "make," that he cannot fully create anything. Third, the stranger invents the plots which expose the community. In this last sense, the stranger's plots become the form of Twain's work after *A Connecticut Yankee.* Both *Huckleberry Finn* and *A Connecticut Yankee* are primarily episodic novels, but the plot device which provides the frame of the *Yankee* becomes the essential form of the later work. The whole plot of *Pudd'nhead Wilson,* for example, pivots on mistaken identity devices.

We cannot certainly define the stranger's full significance in Twain's work, but *A Connecticut Yankee* shows that he is in large part the mechanics of Twain's comedy—the showman who, prior to the Yankee's appearance, was contained behind the dead-pan mask of innocence or within the world of boyhood play. In the figure of the Yankee he emerges into the world of manhood to speak for himself and run the show. Though Mark Twain killed the Yankee he could never quite contain the stranger again.

Thus, in much the same way that its motive turns within it from creation toward destruction, the book stands as a turning point in Twain's career. The work is not a destructive act however; rather it is an incomplete creative gesture, leaving an opening—a ligature—between the form and creative personality of the artist. As such a gesture, *A Connecticut Yankee* is what we may call Mark Twain's treaty with his Genius, for Hank Morgan in the last analysis is the unmasked demon—the practical joker and compulsive showman—so much a part of Mark Twain's humor. Seen in such a way the book is a great comedian's nightmare vision of himself, grotesquely exposing the secret manipulator behind the mechanism of the comic performance. The terms of the treaty may not be as favorable as we would wish, but they were the best that Twain could make with the fatalities of his art. Revealing as it does the inexorable logic of a creative life, the book stands as a channel marker which Mark Twain left behind him in his precarious voyage downstream.

# LOUIS J. BUDD

## Uncle Sam†

* * * Arnold's last essay warned that "if one were searching for the best means to efface and kill in a whole nation the discipline of respect, the feeling for what is elevated, one could not do better than

† From *Mark Twain, Social Philosopher* pp. 134–44. Footnotes are by Budd. (Bloomington: Indiana University Press, 1962).

take the American newspapers." Fifteen years earlier Twain had sounded the same warning more sweepingly, but in this new context he wrote "The American Press," which arraigned British editors for lulling the masses with solemn clichés. Just as anxious as Carnegie to set a better example, Hank insisted on starting up a newspaper as soon as possible. Though his *Weekly Hosannah and Literary Volcano* also burlesqued our own backwoods press so vividly that Arnold seemed not so wrong after all, Twain was primarily saying that even this smeary tabloid was an improvement for England.

Perhaps with a margin of flattery, because he was about to ask Carnegie to invest in his sagging enterprises, Twain wrote in 1890 that *Triumphant Democracy* was a "favorite" of his and went on, "I am reading it again, now & firing up for a lecture which I want to deliver on the other side one of these years."[1] But Carnegie had only stiffened the trans-Atlantic storm; its sources were innumerable. For instance Twain most probably knew about the very popular *King Solomon's Mines* (1885)—which got further publicity from an argument over whether an eclipse that its heroes exploited the way Hank did was astronomically on time. In any event Hank contrasts neatly with Rider Haggard's Englishmen: they use science and modern gadgets against an African tribe to get at a diamond mine; he wants to spread the light of progress. This role as a Prometheus, it should be noted, likewise contrasts with and soon dwarfs the passages of objective fiction that hint at his brash "circus side."

A titan in practicality also, Hank brought along the technical skill that is, Twain implied, a special talent of his country. In his doings the telephone, Edison's lightbulb, and the Colt revolver get more play than the steam engine or spinning jenny. At the time most of his pet devices were impressively new; New York had just put in electrocution as more humane than hanging, and the barbed wire on which the knights died had just proved its worth out on the cattleraising plains. The ending—which desperately solved the problem of leaving the chain of history unbroken after all—did not mean technology is a menace, however.

Pumped by high pressure advertising, a flood of the latest American gadgets had been ready to irrigate a parched Britain; Hank's proposal to establish a "Republic on the American Plan" was baited with the lure of solid comfort. He did not stop with patentable, workaday devices. His skill with a lariat reminded Londoners how they had enjoyed their first look at Buffalo Bill's Wild West show; the knights he taught to clank awkwardly around a baseball diamond were proving that Americans had come up with a better game than gentlemanly cricket. When

1. Letter dated March 17—in New York Pub. Lib. Copyright by the Mark Twain Company, 1962. Carnegie claimed that Twain told him the idea for the *Yankee* came from reading his book—"Tributes to Mark Twain,"*North Amer. Rev.*, CXCI (June, 1910), 827.

the All-Stars got back from spreading the news through a world tour in 1888, Twain was there to salute baseball as the "very symbol . . . of the drive and push and rush and struggle of the raging, tearing, booming nineteenth century!"[2] Hank's message was pointed up with a vibrant idiom that also fitted such an era. His sixth-century friends, who talked in murky circles, soon envied his forceful vernacular, and when Sandy imitated it she was gaily thumbing her nose at complaints that American influences were corrupting Victorian speech. If Hank found any feature of old England really worth saving, he never let on. Like Carnegie, he had given clear warning—heave the inefficient past overboard or miss the wave of the future on which Americans were steaming ahead.

The parallels with Carnegie included what was left unsaid to England and what was ignored at home. *Triumphant Democracy* had shown the partisans of laissez faire that they could appeal to natural rights as profitably as anybody. Unsuspecting that his name would soon stand out in labor troubles more starkly than Carnegie's, George Pullman acclaimed it as a model of soothing and faultless logic; but beneath the skyscraping rhetoric lay shallow footings. Carnegie assumed that the ballot-box held all the equality needed, that only a formally entrenched class got unfair advantages and so progess—as Twain put it—came "at the expense of royalties, priesthoods & aristocracies."[3] Carnegie also assumed that democracy should be judged by the pile of steel and steel appliances produced. By this standard it was criminal to doubt the rightness of a society whose industrial graphs had risen so far from the day when there were no railroads and factories or, as Hank found, not even matches or mirrors.

Though the Whig party in the United States sorely missed having a titled class to inveigh against, Daniel Webster had covered up its conservatism by hurrahing for the anti-royalists in Europe. Without his trained shrewdness Carnegie and Twain came close to the same effect. Instead of challenging abuses that were straining the seams of American laissez faire, Hank's best fighting speeches faced across the Atlantic, just like Twain's hardest sally at the doctrine of a negative state:

> The English laws don't allow a man to shoot himself, but you see these people don't want to make a law to prevent a man's committing half-suicide & being other-half murdered by overwork—& his family left destitute. No legislation to strengthen the hands of the despised strugglers. Why doesn't the Church (which is part of the aristocracy) leave tithes and other robberies to "voluntary action"?[4]

2. Walter F. Frear, *Mark Twain and Hawaii*, 501. John M. Ward, *Baseball* (Philadelphia, 1888), 9–33, spent much time denying that the game was derived from cricket.

3. MTP, Paine 102B.
4. Reprinted in Foner, 165, from Nbk for Feb., 1890.

Enraged, he was invoking the specter that would soon haunt laissez faire—the use of the state to protect victims of unguided supply and demand or to equalize the power balance. Yet he never spoke out for the campaigns to get an eight-hour day here, and his appeals to lowerclass militancy were shaped to the ears of the Old World "commoner" rather than the captives of New York City sweatshops.

This does not mean that Twain was insincere or connived at a diversion: he believed he was fighting evil's crack regiment. In the heat of desperate battle he could rush beyond the old Lockean contract and argue, "That government is not best which best secures mere life and property—there is a more valuable thing—manhood," and he could propose to judge any system strictly by how it serves the "whole people."[5] Though many a conservative was finally ready to shout agreement with such ideas if they were kept abstract, Twain could even sweep on to ringing statements about writing not for the upper crust but for the "mighty mass of the uncultivated who are underneath," for the "Belly and the Members" of the social organism. Until his assistant convinced him that they would lose money, he thought seriously of putting *A Connecticut Yankee* and possibly *Huckleberry Finn* and *The Prince and the Pauper* into twenty-five cent editions as a major shift from his long policy of holding the price of his books distinctly high.

Yet Twain's sympathy for the underdog never went seriously beyond orthodox limits, which were relaxing under not only a spreading demand for fair play but also a sense that unions—as Twain's "The New Dynasty" said—might be "our permanent shield and defence" against the leftist "agitator for 'reforms' that will beget bread and notoriety for him at cleaner men's expense." If Twain was discussing politics with his best suit on, he could get painfully close to putting himself in the very cleanest group, and if their expense was concerned he could be all business. When the Paige machine looked like a sure bet to take over every big printing plant, he bridled at protests that it would throw human typesetters out of work and coldly insisted that technology has been "Labor's savior, benefactor; but Labor doesn't know it, & would ignorantly crucify it." The most distrubing fact is that he could just as easily waver toward man in general or even relapse into believing the "majority of all peoples are fools." Like Voltaire in hating superstition he often despised the masses for holding on to it. In his novels most of the mob that the self-reliant thinker tries to enlighten are dull and unwilling pupils, easily scared into quitting school; friendly and plebeian Hank sometimes changes suddenly into a superman outwitting a species that is basically despicable.

Twain's attitudes toward the common man finally make sense only within the pattern of Liberalism, which—even when it was not dubious about the average voter's wisdom—kept a wall between political

5. *Notebook*, 210; *Letters*, 525–28; Smith-Gibson, 610.

and economic democracy. As he was writing A *Connecticut Yankee* he carefully denied that he meant more than giving every man the same "legal right & privilege." More positively, he praised the United States as an arena "where inequalities are infinite—not limited, as in monarchies; where the inequalities are measured by degrees & shades of degrees of difference in capacity, not by accidental differences in birth; where 'superior' & 'inferior' are terms which state facts, not lies."[6] As to what happens if some men turn out too superior at amassing money, he was unclear. From the vantage point of a mild socialism Howells later concluded his friend "had not thought out any scheme for righting the economic wrongs we abound in."

If pressed, Twain would have answered that technology will take care of most wrongs. Though Hank used raw coercion now and then, Twain felt guilty about it, blaming religious knots that were too deep for applied science to smooth away.[7] Hank's legislative program was very simple, and he almost never mentioned it after bragging that the "very first official thing I did, in my administration—and it was on the very first day of it, too—was to start a patent office; for I knew that a country without a patent office and good patent laws was just a crab." In 1888 Twain visited Thomas Edison at his laboratory with the zestful respect for applied science that let Hank beat Merlin hands down. Clowning over the quirks of a burglar alarm or storming impatiently at a sick telephone did not keep Twain from believing that the inventor was the supreme wizard, the catalyst, the dynamo, the solar engine that turned loose rays into profits if it was not wrecked by priests and kings or unions or the stock-market wolves who cause disturbing panics in Wall Street and grab too big a share. Unhumble Carnegie went so far as to say that the industrialist also gets too much more than the practical genius who spins wealth out of his brains. Hank was a grease stained cousin of Carnegie's ideal man who, with a hardheaded sense learned in the factory, handles his money as a trust fund piled up by applied science.

The inventive genius seemed to need some ink stained disciples too, especially for clearing away the mental cobwebs and false idols. In time there were enough volunteer iconoclasts to sound like an organized movement, with Twain considering himself a head executioner at "this wholesome and merciless slaughter-day" for the outmoded.[8] Yet the fetish of a negative state rode safely above the slaughter, and rooting out the old obstacles to laissez faire carried over

6. MTP, Paine 102B (on the same kind of paper as the last part of "Yankee" MS) and DV 128 (6)—clearly to be ascribed by internal evidence to the late 1880's. (copyright by the Mark Twain Company, 1962) *My Twain*, 80–81.
7. *Notebook*, 199; MTP, DV 24—a passage omitted from the *Yankee*, Walter F. Taylor, *The Economic Novel in America* (Chapel Hill, 1942), 146, has an excellent analysis of Twain's

attitude toward the machine. "Yankee" MS, I, 153, includes: "I shall have considerable to say about my patent office by & by, in its proper place."
8. *Letters*, 520; Percy Douglas, "Iconoclasm Necessary to Progress," *North Amer. Rev.*, CXLVIII (June, 1889), 768–69; Thomas P. Neill, *The Rise and Decline of Liberalism* (Milwaukee, 1953), 36–37.

into opposing any plan for setting up a safety code. Confidently, Twain was willing to have the present and future ride on the same few principles with which he judged the past:

> Let us say, then, in broad terms, that any system which had in it any one of these things—to wit, human slavery, despotic government, inequality, numerous and brutal punishments for crime, superstition almost universal, and dirt and poverty almost universal—is not a real civilization, and any system which has none of them is.[9]

As a guide for federal policy after 1890, this left the main circuit open to a new kind of baron who soon made the public clamor for trust-busting.

For that matter Twain had livewire ambitions on his own. Paying taxes during the 1880's on property assessed at over a hundred thousand dollars, he needed a big income, and he got into the stock market with both feet. Among his bad buys was a holding company organized to plant Yankee capital in Europe. Thinking big in an expansive age he even wrote to Leland Stanford and General Grant about chartering a railroad from Constantinople to the Persian Gulf. Doubtless he had visions of this line carrying progress along with the payload, just as he was stubborn in backing the typesetter because it would benefit mankind as well as his bank account. As a publisher, however, he was too busy shoring up his list prices to worry about improving the world: "Macy has Grant books for sale cheap. We must assault him, next." Because he—too hopefully—scented a big killing he promoted an official biography of Pope Leo XIII and looked for other manuscripts that were good gambles "in these piping times of pious pow-wow."[1]

As always Wall Street and business proved sadly unpredictable. It was a comfort to have one major front covered with a nerveless, homegrown Liberal like Grover Cleveland in the White House. Cleveland stood unbendingly for cash and carry government and against any kind of "paternalism," even federal seed-grain for Texas counties baked by drought. His narrow defeat in 1888 stunned Twain almost beyond profanity. However, for longer than any other period in his life, Twain felt public affairs were moving well enough and dabbled in them with pleasure. To say that *A Connecticut Yankee* falls into nostalgia for a pre-industrial Eden is to play up a minor thread instead of the bold, obvious pattern. When he gave a public reading from the first batch of manuscript, he ended up with liplicking about how much power and money a modern man could swing if he were dumped into the benighted past.[2]

Beneath Twain's unique verve and the bizarre plot *A Connecticut*

9. "On Foreign Critics," *Speeches*, 150–51.
1. Letter to Charles Webster on June 20,

1887—Berg Coll.; Webster, 347.
2. New York *Sun*, Nov. 12, 1886.

*Yankee* was inseparably entwined with its times. In 1886 an ex-congressman and friend from Washoe days sent Twain a clipping of his latest Fourth of July oration, which declared we had improved on our British heritage so evidently as to set an example for the mother country; Twain passed it on to his circle after jotting, "It is fine. . . . Preserve it." A *Connecticut Yankee* said almost nothing new as it leaped back thirteen centuries to look forward; the very gimmick of bringing the past and present face to face was common property. In another variation, Charles Heber Clark's *The Fortunate Island* (1882) imagined a floating bit of England that had drifted away in Arthur's time. Revering tradition and wallowing in a devil-ridden ignorance complete with hermits, its natives are mystified by a ship-wrecked American whose suitcase full of scientific devices puts the official conjurer out of business. Given to plundering raids by habit, the nobility are tamed by the castaway, who deflates a panoplied bully with his revolver. Twain insisted he had not borrowed from this thin fantasy. It is easy to believe him after finding the same basic ideas in many other sources including the later fiction of Bret Harte[3]—whom he despised too much by then to borrow anything from.

Indeed A *Connecticut Yankee* fitted current ideas so well that it was virtually a manifesto summing up the Gilded Age just before times changed with a vengeance. It assumed progress as a booming fact; and, ironically adapting the classic Whig historians by using England as the zero mark, gloated over the rise of science and political freedom. Set against the ludicrously feudal past, the United States needed no defense beyond loud cheers emphasizing mostly its wealth and technical skills. Because it had come so far and was pounding ahead so fast, the American system was obviously sound in spite of minor flaws. In the grand perspective its flaws did not justify criticism from the inside by the leftist or even the Populist, and it towered over the Old World as the model for industrial republics of the future.

A popular manifesto must slide over the tangles caused by man's imperfect nature or the tensions of unregulated progress. The chance that the masses and industrialism may clash was just dimly suggested; Twain still did not doubt that social harmony will be sweetest if everybody is encouraged to make as much money as possible in almost any way. The chance that the elements of human nature may clash was made much clearer—without his intending it to be. Hank exults in his appeal to reason; yet he expects his struggles and declares that the finest quality of Arthur's knights was their spirit of "emulation." Seemingly, man is both rational and fiercely competitive. But self interest, it turned out, can be short sighted and work for the wrong side along with heredity and conditioning. At such moments, when

3. Margaret Duckett, "The 'Crusade' of a Nineteenth-Century Liberal," *Tenn. Stud, In Lit.*, IV (1959), 109–20.

Twain's dark view of character blocked his optimistic theory of history. Hank raged he would like to "hang the whole human race and finish the farce." How could he be sure about the future if people were so intractable? And if they were not, society was supposed to roar on improving—into what? The smashing logic of *A Connecticut Yankee* worked best at hindsight. By 1890 most Americans, while committed to worshipping progress, were wary of predicting any serious change in social and economic patterns. Ironically, the changes in the next ten years would take the bounce out of Twain's confidence.

Of course *A Connecticut Yankee* also holds the stamp of Twain's personal emphases and interests. In some places his old fondness for burlesque is uppermost, in others his old ambition to recreate the past from an insider's viewpoint. Always driven to chart man's basic makeup, in 1883–84 he started a novel that—besides tracing feudalism in Hawaii—would show the lifelong grip of whatever religious system the child is taught. The crucial fact is that, once again, topical interests won out. This novel soon limped to a halt and the guiding ideas took third or fourth billing in *A Connecticut Yankee*, which was finished with enthusiasm to spare. Even as literary burlesque it had immediate point as an answer to Tennyson, who jarred Liberals everywhere by accepting a baronetcy in 1884 and next publishing an indictment of modern progress in "Locksley Hall Sixty Years After."

Twain began *A Connecticut Yankee* by 1886, kept it moving along fairly well, and made final revisions during the summer of 1889. If he had a shaky spread of motives at first, he aimed more and more at the current situation in England as he went on.[4] In the prospectus his firm gave its salesmen, the heaviest weight fell on the trans-Atlantic message:

> The book answers the Godly slurs that have been cast at us for generations by the titled gentry of England. . . . Without knowing it the Yankee is constantly answering modern English criticism of America, and pointing out the weakness and injustice of government by a privileged class. . . . It will be to English Nobility and Royalty what Don Quixote was to Ancient Chivalry.

Unquestionably, Twain edited this prospectus if he did not write it. While the comparison with Cervantes needs excuse as the usual exuberance of publishers' claims, he lavished much effort on *A Connecticut Yankee* with much success. Its teeming imagination, its parade of vivid characters, and its often sensitive pacing deserve more praise than they have had. Its sweep is finally uneven, as every reader knows, but the troughs feel so low partly because the crests swell so

---

4. Besides Howells', American reviews that especially saw the anti-British point were in the Boston *Herald*, Dec. 15, 1889, p. 17; "Literary Gossip," *American Standard* (San Francisco), May 17, 1890; *National* (Quincy, Calif.), July 5, 1890.

high. Though Twain must have piloted a steamboat better than his books, the mistakes in *A Connecticut Yankee* can too easily be exaggerated. A critic should make sure he questions its art rather than its attitudes and at least understands them before he brushes the book off as confused if not chaotic.

Like a majority of Americans at the time, Twain fits reasonably well within the school known to the nineteenth century as Liberalism, though it will not pass as liberal today, especially after the realignments of the 1930's. At most, *A Connecticut Yankee* sometimes took positions staked out by British Radicals like Labouchere, who busily defended the gulf between himself and Marx or the utopian socialist or any kind of defector from private enterprise. Yet humanity and a sense of fair play led Twain so far that some labor groups in the United States decided his book was on their side.[5] When he snatched up the banners under which the middleclass was forcing the nobility to disgorge, he was eloquently sincere; his flaming calls to revolt against self-appointed masters are great statements of that right, and his genius at phrasemaking left memorable appeals for self-respecting manliness and political equality. Their immediate purpose has gone down the stream of time but they will be useful for years to come.

# HENRY NASH SMITH

## The Ideas in a Dream†

### I

The diverse strains of thought and feeling that converge in the character of Mark Twain's Yankee are all aspects of American self-consciousness in the later nineteenth century, but we can distinguish two clusters of images embodied in this protagonist that derive from radically different sources and are never fully synthesized. In some of his roles the Yankee is a figure out of the past. He is an avatar of the American Adam dwelling in the Garden of the World, whose vague but resplendent features can be discerned in Cooper's Natty Bumppo, the yeoman farmer dear to agrarian tradition, Frederick Jackson Turner's frontiersman, and the idealized "self" of Whitman's *Leaves of Grass*.[1] Because the Yankee is a transatlantic innocent confronting an ancient and corrupt Europe, he also resembles the narrator of *The Innocents Abroad*. In fact, he belongs to the long line of vernacular

5. Foner, 176; letter to Twain from George H. Warner, dated Nov. 17, 1891—Berg Coll.
† From *Mark Twain's Fable of Progress: Political and Economic Ideas in "A Connecticut Yankee"* (New Brunswick, N.J.: Rutgers University Press, 1964), pp. 67–70, 82–89, 104–8. Footnotes are by Smith.
1. A half-dozen recent studies bearing on the figure of the American Adam are discussed by Frederic I. Carpenter in "The American Myth': Paradise (to Be) Regained," *PMLA*, LXXIV (December, 1959), 599–606.

protagonists in Mark Twain's books which includes the tenderfoot in *Roughing It*, the cub pilot in *Life on the Mississippi* and, of course, Huck Finn. The Yankee's colloquial language, his lowly rural origins, his uncultivated practical common sense, and his magnificent indifference toward the pretensions of titled aristocrats all attest to this side of his ancestry. Yet he also embodies significant traits that are foreign to Mark Twain's earlier vernacular characters. One of these novelties is his command of industrial technology. Another is his highly developed political awareness. He is a constitutional and legal theorist and is well versed in the outstanding events of modern history. He knows what he is trying to do in a way that sets him apart from his predecessors.

Although the Yankee is a philistine with reference to the arts, his consciousness of his historical mission makes him an intellectual. Unlike Huck Finn, who is not at ease with concepts, the Yankee is passionately devoted to general ideas such as progress, civilization, justice, equality before the law, universal suffrage, representative government, free trade, and separation of church and state. His principles are American in the sense that they were cherished by virtually all Americans in the nineteenth century, but they are too abstract for folklore and too serious to be useful in comedy, oral or otherwise. In characterizing Hank Morgan, Mark Twain attempted to engraft upon an almost entirely nonintellectual tradition of folk humor an ideology of enlightenment and republicanism.

In the broadest sense, we may say that Mark Twain was trying to depict a protagonist who represented the American common man functioning within an exemplary industrial and political order which he himself created. To put the matter in yet more general terms, Mark Twain was asking himself whether the American Adam, who began as representative of a preindustrial order, could make the transition to urban industrialism and enter upon a new phase of his existence by becoming a capitalist hero. Many of the confusions in the character and actions of Hank Morgan—particularly the extent to which he both is and is not an entrepreneur and businessman—take on clarity and meaning if we examine them in the light of this over-all intention. I shall therefore examine first the vernacular elements in Mark Twain's Yankee and then the functions dictated by his ideology.

II

The vernacular humor of Hank Morgan is his most obvious trait. The device of burlesquing Malory creates almost endless comic opportunities in the handling of romantic conventions of chivalry as if they governed everyday life in Arthurian Britain. To the newcomer from the nineteenth century the inhabitants naturally seem at first simply lunatics. Later he thinks of them as "big boobies" or "white Indians" or tame animals. He analogizes their yarns about forests and enchantments drear with tall tales of the American West, ridicules Malory's endless paratactic sentences as a medium of conversation, takes a common-sense reductionist view of the Grail quest, and notes the impropriety of having high-born damsels accompany knights-errant on long overland journeys without a chaperon. At its best, the burlesque is so brilliant that it disarms criticism, as in the excursion to the enchanted pigsty.

As the story develops, however, the burlesque leads into a bitter vein of satire growing out of the fact that the narrator is an American in conflict with Englishmen. Mark Twain becomes preoccupied with American resentments against nineteenth-century Britain. The years during which he was working on *A Connecticut Yankee* were a period when his patrotism (or rather, his jingoistic nationalism) reached a peak of intensity.[2] The book and its protagonist were thus markedly influenced by an outraged national pride.* * *

* * *

## IV

The transition from a comic to a melodramatic mode evident in the passages that wrung Howell's heart indicates that Mark Twain had begun to draw upon a store of ideas and attitudes quite different from the motives he had taken over from native-backwoods humor. He had implied as much when he told Mrs. Fairbanks he was writing a contrast of civilizations. The contrast, of course, was between poverty-stricken, ignorant, tyrannical feudalism and the enlightened industrial capitalism of the nineteenth century. Mark Twain, in common with virtually all his contemporaries, held to a theory of history that placed these two civilizations along a dimension stretching from a backward abyss of barbarism toward a Utopian future of happiness and justice for all mankind. The code name for the histori-cal process thus displayed was progress, and in nineteenth-century America it had the status of a secular theology.[3]

The current notion of progress had a considerable basis in Mark Twain's own experience. For he had himself passed from the tranquil preindustrial world of Hannibal in the 1840's to Hartford in the highly industrialized Connecticut Valley, where during most of the 1880's he had been preoccupied with what he considered the most amazing of modern inventions, the Paige typesetter. The sixth-century Britain of Hank Morgan's adventures shows many points of similarity to the slaveholding Missouri of Mark Twain's childhood. The prewar South, for example, is described in *Life on the Mississippi* as having been debilitated by a chivalry-disease contracted from reading Walter

2. Louis J. Budd assembles evidence concern-ing Mark Twain's Anglophobia in *Mark Twain: Social Philosopher*, Bloomington, Indiana, 1962, pp. 118–144.

3. Salomon, *Twain and the Image of History*, ch. I ("History and the American Writer"), ch. II ("Twain and the Whig Hypothesis").

Scott's medieval romances,[4] and in *Pudd'nhead Wilson* Mark Twain
would implant a hollow but fanatically cherished ideal of chivalry in
Dawson's Landing, one of his many versions of Hannibal.[5] The
institution of slavery introduced unhistorically into Arthurian Britain
is documented with incidents drawn from the supposedly authentic
*Autobiography* of Charles Ball, an American Negro slave. Hank
Morgan explicitly compares the peasants of Abblasoure Manor with
the misguided poor whites who served in the ranks of the Confederate
Army to defend an aristocratic order that kept them degraded and
impoverished. Most significant of all, perhaps, the landscape of Britain is described by means of words and images identical with those
Mark Twain would apply in his *Autobiography* to the Quarles Farm
near Hannibal that he had known as a boy.[6]

Thus Mark Twain's own observation had deeply impressed upon
him the pattern of rapid transition from a backward agrarian society
with corrupt institutions and ideals to an industrial society enjoying all
the benefits of machine technology and enlightened republican government. The contrast between medieval and modern civilizations
was, accordingly, the obvious conceptual framework for the Yankee's
adventures in Arthurian Britain.

The most obvious exemplification of progress in the story is the
Yankee's technological achievements—his creation of a complex of
factories, railways, and telegraph and telephone lines. This aspect of
the contrast between civilizations is an allegory of the industrial
revolution; its emphasis is primarily economic. But the contrast also
has a political aspect in the depiction of outrageous laws by means of
which the nobles of Arthur's realm oppress the people. In this respect
the story is an allegory of the French Revolution, which the Yankee
mentions with enthusiasm.

Hank Morgan was meant to be a representative American both in
his practical knowledge of machines and in his devotion to republican
institutions. But at different times Mark Twain emphasized first one
aspect and then the other. His introductory remarks for readings from
the unfinished manuscript before a Baltimore audience in January
1888 stressed the Yankee's technology:

> Conceive of the blank & sterile ignorance of that day, & contrast
> it with the vast & many-sided knowledge of this. Consider the trivial
> miracles & wonders wrought by the humbug magicians & enchant-
> ers of that old day, & contrast them with the mighty miracles
> wrought by science in our day of steam & electricity. Take a
> practical man, thoroughly equipped with the scientific [magic]

4. Budd, *Mark Twain: Social Philosopher*, pp. 89–90.

5. Henry N. Smith, *Mark Twain: The De- velopment of a Writer*, Cambridge, Mass.,

1962, pp. 174–175.

6. Henry N. Smith, *Mark Twain: The De- velopment of a Writer*, pp. 156–157.

enchantments of our day & set him down alongside of Merlin the head magician of Arthur's time, & what sort of a show would Merlin stand?[7]

Here, evidently, "civilization" is equated with knowledge, and knowledge with technology. Chapter X of the novel, describing the creation of the Yankee's hidden industrial system, is entitled "Beginnings of Civilization." To mention only one other passage, when Clarence reports his preparations for a last stand in Merlin's cave, he explicitly refers to "all our vast factories, mills, workshops, magazines, etc." as "our civilization."

After the book was published Mark Twain continued on various occasions to interpret "civilization" in similar fashion. Thus in an unpublished reply to Paul Bourget's criticism of the United States (probably written in 1894) he sets out to list the components of modern civilization, most of which he claims as American contributions. The first five items are political and legal: "Political Liberty," "Religious Liberty," "Reduction of Capital Penalties," "Man's Equality before the Law," and "Woman's rights." But No. 6 is "Application of Anaesthesia in Surgery." And with No. 7 ("The First Approximately Rational Patent Law") and No. 8 ("Development of Patents") he begins a list of mechanical inventions that reaches almost one hundred items before the writer begins to tire of the game.[8]

Despite Mark Twain's stated beliefs, however, the theme of technological advance is only meagerly dealt with in *A Connecticut Yankee*. Man-factories are mentioned, but the only products of the Yankee's system of technical education that appear on stage are the fifty-two shadowy boy technicians in the cave at the end, none of them given an identity or even a name, and none represented as performing any concrete action. Despite Mark Twain's occasional efforts to give fictional substance to the Yankee's mechanical prowess, he actually performs no constructive feat except the restoration of the holy well; and it will be recalled that the technology in this episode does not go into repairing the well, but into the fraudulent display of fireworks with which he awes the populace.

One of the reasons why the Yankee provides so little actual demonstration of his technological skill is his curious passivity during most of the narrative. After emphasizing at the outset the protagonist's ability to build or invent all kinds of machinery, Mark Twain seems strangely reluctant to make use of this power in the story. By far the longest and most vivid sequences are those in which the Yankee is not a mover and shaker but a spectator or victim of feudal oppression. The

---

7. DV 21, in Mark Twain Papers. The word "magic" has been canceled.
8. "Have We Appropriated France's Civilization?" DV 317, in Mark Twain Papers. Mr.

Salomon comments on the definition of civilization implied here (*Twain and the Image of History*, pp. 31–32).

narrative viewpoint in these chapters resembles that in the middle section of *Huckleberry Finn,* where the Duke and the King dominate Huck by the threat of turning Jim in as a runaway slave. Huck is powerless to resist and can merely record the brutality and degradation he witnesses in the towns along the shore of the Mississippi. Through almost five hundred pages of *A Connecticut Yankee* Hank Morgan is restrained for one reason or another from full exercise of the powers theoretically conferred on him at the outset when he is made "perpetual minister and executive" to the King, "the second personage in the Kingdom, as far as political power and authority were concerned." During his first seven years in office he postpones overt action because he must build his factories and workshops before he can openly defy the Church and the nobles. He is constrained by opinion at the court to set out on his travels with Sandy, during which he ceases to function as an executive. The device of sending the Yankee traveling about the kingdom in disguise with the King is yet another way of depriving him temporarily of administrative responsibility; and having him sold into slavery renders him completely helpless. Thus through the greater part of the book the Yankee is unable to enact the role of entrepreneur that Mark Twain putatively assigns to him. His program for industrializing Britain appears only in such trivial items as the knights made to serve as traveling salesmen or the bicylces on which Launcelot and the Knights ride from Camelot to London.

Furthermore, even when the stage is set for exhibitions of modern technology, the effect falls short of expectation. Again and again—in the Yankee's exploitation of the eclipse, in the destruction of Merlin's tower, in the restoration of the well—a minimum of science or technology is overlaid by elaborate and essentially fraudulent display. Hank Morgan is at least half as much a pretender as Merlin is; the spectacle surrounding his miracles has hardly more empirical basis than do Merlin's charms and spells, the "fol-de-rol" of which he is so scornful. The reader eventually begins to wonder whether Mark Twain may not have been unduly influenced by the current habit of speaking about science and technology as mysterious and magical. When the Yankee refers to his "miracles," he is perhaps only half joking. His statement to Merlin, "I am going to call down fire and blow up your tower," claims a quasi-mythical status that Mark Twain seems inclined to grant him; for the spark that ignites the charges of gunpowder is precisely the moment chosen by the Yankee for his theatrical demonstration.

To regard the engineer's work as supernatural is of course to view it with the awe of an outsider, an uncomprehending layman. The fact is that despite Clemens' interest in gadgets and machines—particularly the Paige typesetter—he did not really understand what the experts were doing; indeed, no one without technical training could have understood it. The technological feats that Mark Twain ascribes to his protagonist had not entered deeply enough into his experience to be fully grasped by his imagination. Wordsworth had predicted that the poet would "be ready to follow the steps of the Man of Science . . . carrying sensation into the midst of objects of the science itself," but only when "these things shall be familiar to us, . . . manifestly and palpably material to us as enjoying and suffering beings."[9] Melville had learned whaling by shipping before the mast, and he could therefore work this relatively primitive technology into the fabric of his fiction. But no American writer in the 1880's knew enough about even the simplest power-driven machines to subdue them to the uses of literature. For that matter, has anyone yet been able to write the fictional interpretation of modern technology that Mark Twain tried to produce?

Magic, of course, can be black as well as white; and along with the implication that the Yankee's machines will work miracles for the good of mankind, the reader notices strong hints that they are potentially a menace. Since this evidence has been discussed by several critics, all that need be said here is that the twenty-five thousand rotting corpses left before the cave when the electrically charged fences and Gatling guns have done their work are but the culimination of a series of half-buried suggestions all through the narrative. In an often quoted passage in Chapter X, for example, the Yankee compares his hidden factories to a "serene volcano, standing innocent with its smokeless summit in the blue sky and giving no sign of the rising hell in its bowels."

\* \* \*

## VIII

Mark Twain could not work out adequately his contrast of medieval and modern civilizations because the protagonist who represented the modern world in the story was an inadequate vehicle for depicting the industrial capitalism. In more metaphorical terms, the American Adam representing an older agrarian or pre-agrarian order could not be made into a Prometheus creating and administering an economic system comparable in complexity to the actual economic system of post-Civil War America.

Adam and Prometheus—American Adam and American Prometheus—are cultural symbols, and to state Mark Twain's dilemma in these terms is to imply that the failure of his undertaking in *A Connecticut Yankee* was due to forces affecting all perceptive men of his generation—including for example Henry Adams, who found that the modern world resisted his effort to interpret it by means of scientific concepts, and Frederick Jackson Turner, whose archetypal fron-

9. In the Preface to the second edition of *Lyrical Ballads* (1800).

tiersman was even less able than Hank Morgan to function in an urban industrial society because he knew nothing about machine technology.[1] Warner and Howells, of course, were condemned to failure from the beginning because they had no categories of interpretation except a set of outmoded moral principles.

Yet if Hank Morgan's story can be read as a parable dealing with the same historical subject as *The Education of Henry Adams*, his defeat is also due to a conflict within Mark Twain's mind between a conscious endorsement of progress and a latent revulsion against the non-human imperatives of the machine and all it stood for in the way of discipline and organization.[2] Again, Mark Twain was not alone in experiencing such emotions; much evidence has been gathered to demonstrate the existence of a "covert culture" in this country from the early nineteenth century onwards which associated machines with images of destruction and menace.[3] But his latent hostility to machines and technological progress was unusually strong. Even though he disclaimed exact fidelity to history, his choice of medieval Britain as the setting for his fable meant that he could not hope to represent the Yankee's undertaking as permanently successful. Mark Twain may not have realized fully at the outset what the implications of this decision were, but they must have been present in his mind in some fashion. Let me mention again the evidences in the story itself that he felt a nostalgia for a half-remembered, half-imagined preindustrial world: the images associated with his uncle's farm near Hannibal that crop up so vividly in his descriptions of landscapes in Arthurian Britain; the hints that the Yankee's industrial system is a potential menace; the consistently destructive effects of technology in the story; and above all the strange ending of the framework narrative, in which the dying Yankee proclaims himself to be "a stranger and forlorn" in the modern world, "with an abyss of thirteen centuries yawning . . . between me and all that is dear to me, all that could make life worth the living!"

These words are addressed in delirium to his beloved Sandy; his yearning for his Lost World is expressed in conventional terms, but it is nevertheless erotic. Since the Lost World is also identified with memories of childhood, one might conjecture that Mark Twain's latent hostility to industrialism is related to the psychological conflict between Eros and civilization that Herbert Marcuse has explored.[4] But the prelogical fantasies of this sort are buried too deeply to be more

1. Henry N. Smith, *Virgin Land: The American West as Symbol and Myth*, Cambridge, Mass., 1950, pp. 257–260.

2. Mark Twain's impatience of restraint was deeper than the contrast of civilizations. In the original dream it was the armor, the symbol not of modern technology but of medieval civilization (especially tyranny?), that was so uncomfortable for the dreamer.

3. Bernard Bowron, Leo Marx, and Arnold Rose, "Literature and Covert Culture," *American Quarerly*, IX (Winter, 1957), 382–383.

4. *Eros and Civilization: A Philosophical Inquirty into Freud*, Boston, 1955.

than glimpsed. The overt narrative presents a conflict expressed in terms more congruous with Hank Morgan's announced effort to bring enlightenment and progress to medieval Britain. He identifies the force that has defeated him as "superstition," the structure of habit imposed on all men by the conditions of their lives in society. Another name for this ineradicable evil is "training," the conditioning that implants reverence for established authority in every man's mind from childhood. The brute fact is that men love their chains and turn against the saviors who would force freedom on them. In the final sequence of the novel, the human fear of rationality seems categorical and primal: it is a secularized version of Original Sin, and no means of redemption is in sight.

Mark Twain's proclamation of this doctrine through a protagonist with whom he is now fully identified reveals an absolute despair. It is true that his comments on the book after it was finished show he was not fully conscious of its meaning. Nevertheless, at some point in the composition of this fable he had passed the great divide in his career as a writer. What had happened to him was too complex to be made out at this distance in time, but one aspect of it is clear. When he found it impossible to show how the values represented by his vernacular protagonist could survive in an industrial society, he lost his faith in the value system of that society. Henceforth he worked as a writer in a kind of spiritual vacuum. His imagination was virtually paralyzed. He was never again able to reach the level of his achievement in *Adventures of Huckleberry Finn*. Frustrated in his attempt to come to terms with the industrial revolution, he gave up the modern world for lost, and during the rest of his career devoted most of his energy to composing variations on the theme expressed in his slogan of "the damned human race." That indomitable writer's imagination of his spent itself for two decades in a series of demonstrations that, as the dying Yankee believed, the world is too absurd to be anything but a dream.

## DAVID KETTERER

### Epoch-Eclipse and Apocalypse: Special "Effects" in A *Connecticut Yankee*†

Hank Morgan's use of a solar eclipse to impress upon King Arthur and his court that a magician superior to Merlin stands before them is, undoubtedly, the most impressive episode in A *Connecticut Yankee in*

† From *PMLA*, 88 (1973), 1104–14. Footnotes are by Ketterer, who has slightly revised the article for publication here.

King Arthur's Court, Mark Twain's time-travel version of the international novel. Arthur is at least as affected as the reader and, as a consequence, Hank is transformed from being a prisoner into being the Boss. But perhaps the reader does not appreciate that on a symbolic level, this blotting out and temporary displacement of one heavenly body by another parallels the "transposition of epochs—and bodies [human and stellar]" which is the donnée of the novel—the displacement of nineteenth-century America by sixth-century Britain and, subsequently, the displacement, first tentative then total, of sixth-century Britain by nineteenth-century America. By equating this "epoch-eclipse" with the apparent extinction of the sun, Mark Twain is implying that the posited world transformation is an event of apocalyptic proportions. In the Revelation of John the Divine, as in traditional symbology, fire is the instrument of apocalypse and, thus, Mark Twain's use of the sun is this context is most appropriate.[1]

Because this revelation is a continuing process the book is repeatedly given to fiery reminders of the epoch-eclipse; indeed, the work is remarkable for the number of explosions that occur and for images that draw on the sun's various qualities: its fieriness, its circularity, its color, and its role as a source of light.[2] I hope to demonstrate that all these instances depend upon "The Eclipse" chapter for their essential meaning.

If all the rather intricate connections that I shall argue for are not immediately obvious to the reader, still less are they apparent to Hank, even though as the narrator he is the source of all the information. Hank, a narrowly pragmatic exhibitionist and something of a boor, is incredibly obtuse, unaware and quite incapable of questioning his own attitudes. These limitations manifest themselves in a hackneyed and exaggerated speech which admirably serves the purposes of comedy and burlesque at the expense both of Arthur's England and of himself as a representative nineteenth-century "Yankee." But what Hank's style does not allow for, as James M. Cox has made very clear, is enough "analytic intelligence or wit to discharge his growing indignation" when the novel moves from an essentially burlesque to an essentially satiric stance.[3] In other words, because Hank cannot func-

---

1. Cf. the symbolic vision of an eclipsed and dying sun in H. G. Wells's *The Time Machine* and the ambiguous use of an eclipse in the film *Pharaoh*, ambiguous because there is no verification as to whether it is temporary or terminal. See also Revelation viii.12 where a variety of eclipses occur: "And the fourth angel sounded, and the third part of the sun was smitten, and the third part of the moon, and the third part of the stars; so as the third part of them was darkened, and the day shone not for a third part of it, and the night likewise."

2. It is possible, of course, that the obsession with fire in *A Connecticut Yankee* and in the Mysterious Stranger manuscripts is not without a biographical foundation. According to Dixon Wecter in his *Sam Clemens of Hannibal* (Boston: Houghton, 1952), pp. 253–56. Mark Twain's recurrent concern with death by fire is to be associated with a guilt feeling about his brother Henry who died in a steamboat explosion and about the drunk who burned up in jail because Mark Twain had given him matches.

3. See James M. Cox, *Mark Twain: The Fate of Humor* (Princeton, N. J.: Princeton Univ. Press, 1966), p. 205, Ch. ix, "Yankee Slang," et passim.

tion satisfactorily as a satiric norm and because, outside of the frame, there is no "Mark Twain" narrator, the novel lacks an acceptable perspective on reality. The reader has only the very limited perspective implied by Hank's style, a perspective that would certainly not generate and would seemingly deny the possiblity of any subtle imagistic design. Thus my analysis of imagistic patterning infers a sophisticated consciousness that is otherwise explicitly absent from the novel. I will attempt to explain why Mark Twain excluded from his satire a normative and intelligent consciousness that might have provided a convincing source for imagistic significance in favor of a philistine who is a most unconvincing source.

II

Lest the reader miss the sun's function as an apocalyptic image, Mark Twain is careful to associate the eclipse with that biblical prefiguration of the Apocalypse, the Flood: "when the silver rim of the sun pushed itself out, a moment or two later, the assemblage broke loose with a vast shout and came pouring down like a deluge to smother me with blessings and gratitude." It is assumed that Hank's incantation, timed with the astronomical process, is the causal factor. So it is that Hank escapes death at the stake by fire or, in symbolic terms, survives the apocalypse and successfully enters the new world. Previously, after being hit on the head in the nineteenth century, the old "world went out in darkness," like a light. Now we learn that "the eclipse had scared the British world almost to death: that while it lasted the whole country . . . was in a pitiable state of panic, and the churches, hermitages, and monkeries overflowed with praying and weeping poor creatures who thought the end of the world had come." As Hank notices "my eclipse beginning," he exclaims, "I was a new man." During the eclipse he put on the new man as he "struggled with these awkward sixth-century clothes" which befit his new status.

To exhibit further his power, and thus to consolidate his position, Hank arranges the first of many explosions. His "magic" causes Merlin's tower, an apocalyptic symbol in its own right, to blow up: "I made about three passes in the air, and then there was an awful crash and that old tower leaped into the sky in chunks, along with a vast volcanic fountain of fire that turned night to noonday [previously, noonday had been turned into night since the eclipse occurred at approximately twelve noon], and showed a thousand acres of human beings groveling on the ground in a general collapse of consternation." It is my contention that the symbolic relationship between the eclipse and this explosion, pointed up here by the specific time reversal, applies to the remaining explosive fires in the book.[4]

---

4. Henry Nash Smith notes an additional connection between the two events in that the thunderstorm Hank requires "to ignite his charges" "appears as fortuitously as the eclipse." See *Mark Twain's Fable of Progress: Political and Economic Ideas in* A Connecticut Yankee (New Brunswick, N.J.: Rutgers Univ. Press, 1964), p. 53; see also p. 86.

No sooner has Hank adjusted to the displacement of the nineteenth century by the sixth than he attempts to reverse the process. It is his particular aim to replace the monarchy and the aristocracy with a democracy and thus the only title he is willing to accept is that of "THE BOSS," which was granted by the entire nation.[5] Just as the moon threw the sun into shadow during the eclipse, so democracy will eclipse monarchy. "I was no shadow of a king; I was the substance; the king himself was the shadow," affirms Hank. And in a voice reminiscent of Huckleberry Finn's, Hank continues, "It is enough to make a body ashamed of his race to think of the sort of froth that has always occupied its thrones without shadow of right or reason." Is it a mistake to deduce from the shadow image the light necessary to produce shadow and from there to recall the sun once more? Dan Beard's illustrations, which accompanied the original text, frequently make overt what Mark Twain only implied: in a drawing of the solar eclipse the sun is symbolic of the "Divine Right of Kings VI ceny" while the moon, which bears the legend "The Earth belongs to the People XIX ceny," casts the "shadow of right and reason."

Surreptitiously, Hank manages to install most nineteenth-century technical improvements, notably electric light and, thereby, the emergent nineteenth century is associated with explosive fire: "There it was, as sure a fact, and as substantial a fact as any serene volcano, standing innocent with its smokeless summit in the blue sky [the sun is shining!] and giving no sign of the rising hell in its bowels." Meanwhile, in his despair at turning Sandy, his traveling companion, into a pragmatic nineteenth-century American woman, Hank can conceive the transformation only by blowing her up: "It may be that this girl had a fact in her somewhere, but I don't believe you could have . . . got it with the earlier forms of blasting, even; it was a case for dynamite." The attention paid to Hank's pipe, which causes Sandy to faint and the freeman to flee ("They thought I was one of those fire-belching dragons"), is not accidental. Its forceful effect may be more accurately attributed to its function as a symbol of the apocalyptic change associated with Hank. Surely, the episode in which Hank routs "half a dozen armed men and their squires" is a little too fantastic in anything other than symbolic terms. "You should have seen the wave go to pieces and scatter!" and all at the sight of "a column of white smoke through the bars of my helmet." As Roger B. Salomon has noted, Hank is a Prometheus bringing to the Middle Ages the fire of the nineteenth century.[6] Just as Prometheus is assisted by Hercules, so

5. According to Juliette A. Trainor in her note, "Symbolism in *A Connecticut Yankee in King Arthur's Court*," *MLN*, 66 (June 1951), 382–85, Hank's strongest antagonists, the church and the monarchy, are represented by the two giants killed by Lancelot in the Malory account which the narrator is reading prior to Hank's entrance.

6. See Ch. vi, "The Fall of Prometheus," in *Twain and the Image of History* (New Haven, Conn.: Yale Univ. Press, 1961).

Hank's displacement depends upon being hit on the head by "a fellow we used to call Hercules." Note also that Hank's father, like Vulcan, "was a blacksmith."

Hank announces in his Tom Sawyer voice, "You can't throw too much style into a miracle," and takes pains to include the apocalyptic element in his restoration of the dry fountain in the Valley of Holiness. "Then I touched off the hogshead of rockets, and a vast fountain of dazzling lances of fire [here fire and flood are identified] vomited itself toward the zenith with a hissing rush, and burst in mid-sky into a storm of flashing jewels!" The eclipse occurred at midday on 21 June, the time at which the sun is at its zenith in the western hemisphere, its point of greatest strength, and, in traditional symbology, a point of exit from the world of time and space.[7] The cry of exultation that follows the eclipse might be an appropriate response to the sight of the jeweled New Jerusalem descending from the sky's zenith, although mention of "flashing jewels" may not itself warrant such an extention. This event is written up in the newspaper Hank has founded, the *Weekly Hosannah and Literary Volcano*, with the phrase, "INFERNAL FIRE AND SMOKE AND THUNDER!" in large print. The column, "Local Smoke and Cinders," is presented as being representative of the rest of the paper. If Marshall McLuhan is right about the impact of the Gutenberg revolution, and, at a later point, Gutenberg, along with Watt, Arkwright, Whitney, Morse, Stephenson, and Bell are credited, "after God," as "the creators of this world," Hank could find no surer means than a newspaper to displace a sixth-century reality by a nineteenth-century reality. It is then meaningful and in no way accidental that the newspaper by its titles and headline is associated with apocalyptic heat. No wonder that Hank, reading this first edition, feels, "Yes, this was heaven."

### III

Hank and Arthur's journey through the kingdom is made with the intention of opening Arthur's eyes to that reality of sixth-century England which Hank has become aware of in the earlier part of the book. There are two disconnected worlds or realms of experience in

---

7. Hank is quite specific in his information "that the only total eclipse of the sun in the first half of the sixth century occurred on the 21st of June, A.D. 528, O.S. [presumably Old System hence the Julian Calendar], and began at 3 minutes after 12 noon." Because Mark Twain has symbolic reasons for the particular day and time, historical accuracy is not to be expected. However, given that Theodor Ritter Von Oppolzer's *Canon of Eclipses* (Vienna, 1887), which remains the standard work on the subject, was, coincidentally, published during the 5 years from Dec. 1884 to May 1889 when Mark Twain was working intermittently on A *Connecticut Yankee*, it might be expected that he would have checked for a year in the early 6th century in which a total eclipse of the sun was visible from Britain. But not so, apparently. In A.D. 528, O.S. the 4 eclipses that occurred, on 6 Feb., 6 March, 1 Aug., and 30 Aug., were all partial. An eclipse of the sun that was total and the nearest such to Mark Twain's year did occur, according to the *Canon of Eclipses* on 1 Sept. in A.D. 538, O.S. Nevertheless, whether or not Mark Twain checked this matter still cannot be verified because, as the later portion of my argument indicates, it is most appropriate that the eclipse cannot be anchored to "reality."

sixth-century England, since the romantic experience of Arthur, his knights, and the aristocracy is quite distinct from the actual living conditions of the majority of the population. The nineteenth-century experience is similarly dual—there is the technological utopia which Hank believes in, his own form of romanticism, and the dehumanized Armageddon which is much closer to a possible future reality. There are, then, essentially four worlds in *A Connecticut Yankee*: two negative visions of the sixth century and the nineteenth century and two corresponding positive visions. Mark Twain's purpose is to have Arthur undergo an apocalypse of mind in recognizing the negative reality of his time and, subsequently, to have Hank undergo a similar apocalyptic revelation concerning the negative reality of his epoch. The effect of this movement is, of course, to imply an essential lack of differentiation between the sixth century and the nineteenth century.

While traveling incognito with the king, Hank engineers another miracle—another explosion—to dispose of some troublesome knights, providing an objective correlative for Arthur's dawning realization about the sham of chivalry. By noting that the conflagration "resembled a steamboat explosion on the Mississippi," Hank associates it with a new and different world and, consequently, with the notion of apocalyptic transformation. A fifth instance of fire (and of the "decrees of God," according to the priests), the manor-house fire and the death of the lord of the manor, is intended as symbolic of the end of an old feudal world. For accompaniment, "there was an ear-splitting explosion of thunder, and the bottom of heaven fell out; the rain poured down in a deluge"—the mixture of fire and flood as before.

Admittedly somewhat indirectly, the relationship between fire and revelation or apocalypse is indicated during Marco's fantastic feast. Marco, we are told, "was in Paradise" as "the madam piled up the surprises with a rush that *fired* [emphasis mine] the general astonishment up to a hundred and fifty in the shade." When the count is tallied, surprise is registered by the general exclamation, "God be with us in the day of disaster," implying the end of the world. It is my conviction that such details are not fortuitous.

Hank's efforts to update the sixth-century economy allow Mark Twain to draw symbolically on a further characteristic of the sun—its circularity. Dan Beard diagrams the revolution as a coinlike sun emerging over the horizon. Around its edges are the words "free trade." The new "currency" which Hank introduces, plus the notion of "a trade union, to *coin* [emphasis mine] a new phrase," must be seen for the puns contained if these measures are to impart their total meaning; likewise the description of the "gun-purse" which uses different-sized shot for money and which Hank offers as an explanation for the phrase, "Paying the shot." In other words, the new money and the new world of mind that it signifies entails destruction. To be effective, revolutionary ideas must be circulated—hence the rather weird information regarding the gun-purse that "you could carry it in your mouth" wherefrom, of course, might issue that "Paying the shot" line which "would still be passing men's lips, away down in the nineteenth century."

It is Arthur's experience as a slave—as a part of the slave band that Hank had witnessed earlier—that, more than anything else, encourages the emergence of his new awareness and heroic stature. Once again the revelation and reversal of fortune is accompanied by fire as the slaveholders smoke Arthur and Hank out of the tree in which they were hiding: "They raised their pile of dry brush and damp weeds higher and higher, and when they saw the thick cloud begin to roll up and smother the tree, they broke out in a storm of joy-clamors." One might recall here Hank's earlier experience when "the fagots were carefully and tediously piled about my ankles, my knees, my thighs, my body," just prior to the eclipse. I would, incidentally, not insist upon the addition of the symbolic dimension to all the incidents and images involving fire, were it not for two factors: one, the apparently deliberate referral back to the eclipse which most of these fiery verbal details encourage and, two, the coincidence of these combustible elements with moments of major transformation and revelation.

In a subsequent episode, Hank and Arthur, still slaves, witness the burning of a witch: "They fastened her to a post; they brought wood and piled it about her; they applied the torch, while she shrieked and pleaded and strained her two younger daughters to her breast; and our brute, with a heart solely for business, lashed us into position about the stake and warmed us into life and commercial value by the same fire which took away the innocent life of that poor harmless mother." Again, we recall the possibility of Hank's similar fate at the stake but the incident is particularly important to the process of revelation that Arthur is undergoing. In addition, this incident illustrates exceptionally well the dual nature of an apocalypse: it is both destructive and creative. Shortly afterwards, Hank and Arthur witness a similar atrocity—the hanging of a young girl after a priest has pulled her baby from her arms. The priest pledges to look after the child: "You should have seen her face then! Gratitude? Lord, what do you want with words to express that? *Words are only painted fire; a look is the fire itself* [my emphasis]. She gave that look, and carried it away to the treasury of heaven, where all things that are divine belong." Here fire is specifically equated with divine will and thereby with apocalyptic revelation. Fire figures yet again in the next episode which features "a man being boiled to death in oil for counterfeiting pennies," perhaps for inability to adapt to Hank's new currency?

## IV

Hank and Arthur are finally rescued, Arthur with his neck in a noose, when five hundred knights, seemingly having harnessed the power and aggression of the sun itself, come cycling to his aid in response to Hank's telephone call: "Lord, how the plumes streamed, how the sun flamed and flashed from the endless procession of webby wheels!" Hank describes this spectacle as "the grandest sight that ever was seen." Yet at a later point, when a similarly sun-coated army ("the sun struck the sea of armor and set it all aflash") aligns itself *against* Hank, the impression is even more formidable: "I hadn't ever seen anything to beat it." In between these two moments Hank suffers a major reversal. The remaining action consists of an escalated series of violent encounters between Hank, or the nineteenth century, and Arthur's knights, or the sixth century. The association of the knights with the sun is not accidental. This climactic Armageddon is a kind of literal equivalent to the solar eclipse. But whereas the solar eclipse, seemingly, signaled the displacement of the sixth century by the nineteenth for the people of Arthur's England and the displacement of the nineteenth century by the sixth for Hank, the concluding Armageddon signifies, for the world of King Arthur, a final if costly victory of the sixth-century reality over that of the nineteenth century and, for Hank personally, a displacement of the sixth century by the nineteenth century. In a sense, then, both sides win and both sides lose.

The tournament between Hank and Sir Sagramour is, in reality, "a duel not of muscle but of mind," a "mysterious and awful battle of the gods," because the real conflict is between two magicians, Hank and Merlin. It is described in terms of a conflict between the elements of fire and air. Sir Sagramour, and after him other knights, engage Hank in combat to the repeated blasts of apocalyptic bugles. All fall prey to the "snaky spirals" of Hank's lasso which is linked with a whirlwind. Thus, when Hank "whirled" out of Sir Sagramour's path the action occasions a "whirlwind of applause" while, afterwards, Lancelot falls "with the rush of a whirlwind." Sir Lancelot is described as "the very sun of their shining system" while one of his predecessors charges "like a house afire." Sir Lancelot's fall is greeted with a "thundercrash of applause." After Merlin steals his lasso, Hank is compelled to use his revolver to halt the five hundred knights who then bear down upon him. Hank's subsequent challenge to take on, with fifty assistants, "*the massed chivalry of the whole earth and destroy it*" is not taken up initially. However, the double syntactic ambiguity of the italicized section of the challenge (the words "massed chivalry" may be a description of the "whole earth," the "it" may refer back to the "whole earth") allows for the implication that he will destroy the whole world and makes the cosmic and apocalyptic nature of the upcoming conflict readily apparent.

Following the civil war between the king's army and Sir Lancelot's over Guinevere which began when Lancelot thwarted the king's intention to "purify her with fire" (we might well recall once more

Hank's own experience at the stake) and the civil war between Arthur's group and Sir Mordred's for possession of the kingdom, during which Arthur is killed, both Hank and Mordred find themselves bereft of power by force of the Church Interdict. However, Clarence, Hank's chief helper, having done "a world of work" has prepared Merlin's cave for a siege, whereupon Hank declares his republic. (Actually the cave is as much Plato's as Merlin's, given Twain's concern with the nature of reality, a concern I take up in section v, below.) At the battle of the sand-belt, Hank, Clarence, and fifty-two boys, one for each week of the solar year, prepare to take on the Church army. The detailed description of Hank's fortification is meaningful. Twelve electrified wire fences circle concentrically the cave while the mined sand-belt lies around the outer fence. The planetary, somewhat Copernican setup of this design, confused possibly with the twelve signs of the zodiac "*belt*" to create a mix of sixth-century and nineteenth-century cosmologies, suggests to me that the sand-belt, presumably yellow in color, be symbolically identified as the path of the sun. If this is the case, Hank's choice of analogy in the congratulatory proclamation to his army is deliberate: "So long as the planets shall continue to move in their orbits, the BATTLE OF THE SAND-BELT will not perish out of the memories of men." It would seem that Twain intends some equation between the battle and cosmological phenomena, an eclipse of the sun, for example.

The ensuing holocaust has all the requisite apocalyptic features. The knights first advance to "the blare of trumpets" only to be "shot into the sky with a thunder-crash, and become a whirling tempest of rags and fragments." The "smell of burning flesh" is noticeable at first and then the carnage itself becomes visible when Hank "touched a button and set fifty electric suns aflame on the top of our precipice." The solar eclipse turned day into night, now Hank turns night into day. (To our ears, incidentally, the reference to "fifty electric suns" gains in intensity with its ominous implications of megatonnage.) When the eclipse was total the multitude "groaned with horror." Now, as a host of knights are electrocuted, "There was a groan you could *hear!*" The "deluge" of congratulations which Hank received for returning the sun now becomes a "withering deluge of fire" directed at the remaining knights. The deluge here is both literal and metaphorical, composed of both fire and water since Hank opens the sluice gates in order to fill the now surrounding ditch, caused by the explosion of the torpedoes, and thus drown many of the knights like Pharaoh's army. My point here is that these ordered repetitions are purposeful.

Hank's victory is pyrrhic only. Merlin, who, for his first accomplishment in the novel, had sent all of Arthur's court to sleep during his droning rehearsal of Arthur's adventures with the Lady of the Lake, now works his most effective enchantment. Disguised as a woman, he puts the wounded Boss to sleep for thirteen centuries—a magical accomplishment more truly impressive than any of Hank's. But Merlin's victory, too, is short-lived. A moment later, in the midst of a delirious cackle, he electrocutes himself. Subsequently, the remainder of Hank's followers gradually die for reasons which Clarence explains: "We were in a trap you see—a trap of our own making. If we stayed where we were, our dead would kill us; if we moved out of our defences, we should no longer be invisible. We had conquered; in turn we were conquered." In the event "any one of us ever escapes alive from this place, he will write the fact here, and loyally hide this Manuscript with the Boss." There is no such addenda—presumably no one survivied. Clarence is right and the "end of the manuscript" is *the* end. Following the end, we obtain the truly apocalyptic revelation, a revelation indirectly hinted at throughout, namely that the sixth century does not displace the nineteenth century in any real sense nor does the nineteenth century displace the sixth century because there is no essential difference between them.

V

The eclipse of the sun is a false apocalyptic image, *at least in the sense I have so far implied*. And the same goes for the related fiery, circular, luminous yellow elements which I have been cataloging. They are all "effects" insofar as they relate to the usurpation of one historical world of mind by another. Nevertheless these elements, outside of Hank's usage of them, do have a "factual" and symbolic reality as apocalyptic imagery insofar as they herald the revelation that any apocalyptic transformation, from an Eden in the past to a utopia in the future, is all myth. We are gradually made aware that the most startling fact about the sixth century in relation to the nineteenth is the lack of significant differentiation. It is no accident that Hank's story is inscribed on a palimpsest and that underlying his writing are "Latin words and sentences: fragments from old monkish legends." The common parchment is more important than the apparent differences imbedded in successive historical records. And it is this essential lack of differentiation that prepares the reader for the genuine apocalyptic revelation with which the book concludes.

Careful attention to the imagery associated with the sun is in itself revealing. Shortly after his spectacular demonstration, Hank draws attention to the current belief that "he could have blown out the sun like a candle." There is some irony in this statement as the sun-candle world of mind comes to be associated with nineteenth-century America and not sixth-century Britain. This process gets under way with Hank's decision to wait for an opportune moment before *flooding* sixth-century England with nineteenth-century electric light: "I was turning on my light one-candle-power at a time, and meant to continue to do so." Nevertheless, he was ready, like God, to "flood the midnight world with light any moment." Somewhat weirdly, except within the context of this process, Hank, in full armor, speaks of himself as being "snug as a candle in a candle-mould." And, at the end of the novel, when Hank appears to be losing ground to the church, Dan Beard provides an illustration of a monk snuffing the candle of the nineteenth century, an illustration presumably based on this description of Camelot:

> From being the best electric-lighted town in the kingdom and the most like a recumbent sun of anything you ever saw, it was becoming simply a blot—a blot upon darkness—that is to say, it was darker and solider than the rest of the darkness, and so you could see it a little better; it made me feel as if maybe it was symbolical—a sort of sign that the Church was going to *keep* the upper hand, now, and *snuff out* [my emphasis] all my beautiful civilization just like that.

Once again, snuffing out the candle and the eclipse of the sun are clearly related although the import is completely reversed. But this confusion seems to imply that, if the two transformations can be imaged in the same terms, perhaps the similarities between the two epochs are more important than the differences.

Similarities between sixth-century Britain and nineteenth-century America assert themselves from the very beginning. Conscious of the sorry state of his fellow prisoners who are dragged before King Arthur's court, Hank identifies them as "white Indians" on the following basis: "*they* have served other people so in their day; it being their own turn, now, they were not expecting any better treatment than this; so their philosophical bearing . . . is mere animal training." The game of "Cowboys and Indians" is then seen appropriately as equivalent to knight-errantry. Accordingly, Hank refers to the continuation of Sandy's interminable account of chivalric adventure as "the trail of the cowboys."

The major common denominator is slavery. In large measure Mark Twain's source for the Old World of the sixth century is the pre-Civil War South. Perhaps the slave master in this account of what befalls a fatigued slave inspired Beard's later portrait of "The Slave Driver" as Jay Gould:[8]

8. Tony Tanner makes this point in "The Lost America—The Despair of Henry Adams and Mark Twain." He also notes that the Round Table "comes to have an uncanny resemblance to the stock exchange and the final civil war is precipitated by a shady deal reminiscent of the railroad frauds of the Seventies." See Tanner's 1961 article, "The Lost America—The Despair of Henry Adams and Mark Twain," as reprinted in *Mark Twain: A Collection of Crit-* *ical Essays*, ed. Henry Nash Smith (Englewood Cliffs, N.J.: Prentice-Hall, 1963), p. 162. And Smith in *Mark Twain: The Development of a Writer* (Cambridge, Mass.: Harvard Univ. Press, 1962) demonstrates that the words and images used to describe the British landscape are identical to those used later by Mark Twain to describe, in his *Autobiography*, Quarles Farm near Hannibal, pp. 174–75.

She dropped on her knees and put up her hands and began to beg and cry and implore, in a passion of terror, but the master gave no attention. He snatched the child from her, and then made the men-slaves who were chained before and behind her throw her on the ground and hold her there and expose her body; and then he laid on with his lash like a madman till her back was flayed, she shrieking and struggling the while, piteously. One of the men who was holding her turned away his face, and for this humanity he was reviled and flogged.

The slave "who had turned away his face" turns out to be her husband and Hank, a few sentences later, also "turned away" as the girl is forced to abandon her husband and child in order to be taken away by her purchaser. It would seem, then, that the same impulses, sadistic and humanitarian, are common to sixth-century and nineteenth-century man. At a later point in the novel, when Arthur and Hank are themselves slaves, an additional parallel becomes apparent. Unable to prove that he is a freeman, the king is sold as a slave and Hank notes, "this same infernal law had existed in our own South in my own time."

Furthermore, the way in which the common people support the baron reminds Hank "of a time thirteen centuries away, when the 'poor whites' of our South who were always despised and frequently insulted, by the slave-lords around them, and who owed their base condition simply to the presence of slavery in their midst, were yet pusillanimously ready to side with slave-lords in all political moves for the upholding and perpetuating of slavery and did also finally shoulder their muskets and pour out their lives in an effort to prevent the destruction of that very institution which degraded them." "Why, it was like reading about France and the French, before the ever-memorable and blessed Revolution," Hank exclaims when he learns that for three days in a week freemen work on their bishop's road for no pay. Economic thinking is as muddled in King Arthur's time as in Hank's day, due to the failure to realize that the important thing is not how much you earn but how much you can purchase with it. Hank "recalls" that, "in the time of our great civil war in the nineteenth century," a worker in the North earned fewer dollars than his counterpart in the South but he was twice as rich as the Southerner because of the much higher purchasing power of his dollar.

Mark Twain was fond of blaming Sir Walter Scott for causing the Civil War by romanticizing aristocratic behavior. It becomes apparent, in *A Connecticut Yankee*, that Scott's predecessor in this activity is Malory, who presented a similarly romantic version of chivalry. Mark Twain derides Malory by parody in Merlin's opening story, the style of which is later taken up by Sandy's rambling narrative. Lest we forget this equation between Malory and Scott, Mark Twain is at pains, on a number of occasions, to introduce Scott in the context of King Arthur's court. Shocked by the indecency of the aristocratic tongue in the sixth century, Hank recognizes he is the victim of brainwashing: "Suppose Sir Walter, instead of putting the conversations into the mouths of his characters, had allowed the characters to speak for themselves. We should have had talk from Rachel and Ivanhoe and the soft Lady Rowena which would emabarrass a tramp in our day." And it is not accidental that the phrase "great Scott" is one of Hank's favorite expletives in the face of the incredible naïveté of a Sandy or a Dowley.

From this comparison between Malory and Scott it is but a short step to the recognition that men are all the same under the skin. Hank refers with approval to a prisoner's critical assertion that, "if you were to strip the nation naked and send a stranger through the crowd, he couldn't tell the king from a quack doctor, nor a duke from a hotel clerk." The later portion of the narrative with the king and the Boss traveling incognito effectively bears out this point. Nor is there any fundamental distinction between good and evil.[9] The essential similarity between the sinister Morgan Le Fay and our hero, Hank Morgan, pointed to by their common name, becomes increasingly obvious as the book goes on. As Edmund Reiss suggests, Hank's surprise at Morgan Le Fay's beauty is a means of indicating the ambiguity of good and evil but "what appalls the Yankee in the character of Morgan Le Fay are the same insensitivities Mark Twain objects to in the Yankee's character."[1] Unlike her husband, "an extinct volcano . . . his fire was out," but like fiery Hank, Morgan Le Fay is "a Vesuvius. As a favour, she might consent to warm a flock of sparrows for you, but then she might take that very opportunity to turn herself loose and bury a city." A further distinction is eroded when we learn of Hank's factory where he plans "to turn groping and grubbing automata into *men*" which raises, in the modern reader's mind, the equal likelihood of turning men into automata.

What superficial distinctions do exist are all a consequence of training and "inherited ideas":

> For instance, those people had inherited the idea that all men without title and a long pedigree, whether they had great natural gifts and acquirements or hadn't, were creatures of no more consideration than so many animals, bugs, insects; whereas I had inher-

9. As Robert Regan argues in his *Unpromising Heroes: Mark Twain and His Characters* (Berkeley: Univ. of California Press, 1966), pp. 168–84, many of Hank's problems arise because, for much of the novel, he does insist on a moral distinction. In Regan's terms, he makes the mistake of distinguishing morally between two father figures, Arthur and Merlin, who are actually identical. However, in the context of my argument that *A Connecticut Yankee* proposes an essential lack of distinction between people, Regan's structural complaint that, toward the end of the book, interest shifts from Hank to Arthur, loses much of its force.

1. See Edmund Reiss's "Afterword" to the Signet Edition of *A Connecticut Yankee* (New York: New American Library, 1963), p. 325.

ited the idea that human daws who can consent to masquerade in the peacock-shams of inherited dignity and unearned titles, are of no good but to be laughed at.

At a later point, Hank spells the matter out in greater detail:

> Training—training is everything; training is all there is *to* a person. We speak of nature; it is folly; there is no such thing as nature; what we call by that misleading name is merely heredity and training. We have no thought of our own, no opinions of our own; they are transmitted to us, trained into us. All that is original in us, and therefore fairly creditable or discreditable to us, can be covered up and hidden by the point of a cambric needle, all the rest being atoms contributed by and inherited from, a procession of ancestors that stretches back a billion years to the Adam-clam or grasshopper or monkey from whom our race has been so tediously and ostentatiously and unprofitably developed.

Since man is essentially, then, without free will, he might fittingly be considered allegorically as a slave, which is how Dan Beard presents him, chained by two iron balls of debt.[2] Men are imprisoned by a system and a continual "Catch 22" situation. For example, the legal entanglement surrounding *le droit du seigneur* reminds Hank of the "way in which the aldermen of London ['Yankees in disguise'] raised the money that built the Mansion House." Dissenters, not being eligible to run or serve as sheriffs, were nominated or elected so that they might then contribute the £400 fine for refusing to be a candidate for office or the £600 fine for refusing to serve after being elected! £15,000 in fines was thereby raised.

Clearly, since our recognition of material reality depends upon our ability to make meaningful distinctions, the discovery that meaningful distinctions do not exist would tend to throw that state of reality into question. It is, then, a relatively small step from demonstrating an essential homogeneity to asserting that there is no reality or that reality is a dream—the truly apocalyptic revelation of the postscript.

### VI

There is, however, one further logical intermediary step: the business of eradicating any distinction between reality and appearance or reality and unreality. It is all shown to be a matter of phenomenology. Toward the end of the book, Hank's entire conception of reality comes to depend upon the health of his child. Thus this description of her recovery:

> Then our reward came: the centre of the universe turned the corner and began to mend. Grateful? It isn't the term. There *isn't* any term

2. There is an additional leveling tendency to relate everybody in terms of the child metaphor. See Albert E. Stone, *The Innocent Eye: Child-hood in Mark Twain's Imagination* (New Haven, Conn.: Yale Univ. Press, 1961), pp. 167–73.

for it. You know that, yourself, if you've watched your child through the Valley of the Shadow and seen it come back to life and sweep night out of the earth [like the sun] with one all illuminating smile that you could cover with your hand.

In context, this image of the creation is most appropriate and in no way inflated. Elsewhere it is implied that the attainment of the apocalyptic world of heaven is possible through intellectual activity: "The poorest paid architect, engineer, general, author, sculptor, painter, lecturer, advocate, legislator, actor, preacher, singer, is constructively in heaven when he is at work!" Is this not an apocalypse of mind?

Now is the appropriate time to recall Hank's status in the novel as narrator because the perceptual idiopathic bias which his child's recovery highlights is endemic. To the degree that all events are filtered through the hardheaded burlesque "Yankee" consciousness of Hank the entire account is "unreal." Hank's idiosyncracies translate themselves into a style that is ultimately as "unreal" as the Malory romance he ridicules. For example, although one might speak descriptively of Hank's "ordeal" at the stake, the use of quotation marks should be taken as ironic because Hank is simply insufficiently serious and insufficiently aware to experience the incident as more than a spectacular show, albeit somewhat uncomfortable.[3] Similarly Hank's practical and rather callous application of the energy expended by the bowing hermit on his pillar to run a sewing machine, reflects on his total incomprehension of the realities of religious ardor.

The image of the saintly hermit standing against the "background of sky," producing energy at the rate of "1244 revolutions in 24 minutes and 46 seconds" to make shirts which "sold like smoke" shares certain qualities with the sun and now I can perhaps seek to justify further my imagistic use of the sun as a viable approach to the novel. My point is that Mark Twain's narrative strategy blurs the distinction between an event or incident object considered externally and the subjective image whereby events and objects are understood. Given that Mark Twain's aim is an impression of the unreality of reality, a clue to the novel's "reality principle" may logically be found in imagery, by definition unreal, particularly since the entire narrative, as a statement of Hank's consciousness, may be conceived as having the same ontological status as imagery. There is then good reason for the disjunction which I raise in my introduction. Mark Twain chooses to dissociate his intricate imagistic patterns from a poetic consciousness capable of comprehending them and instead locates them in the mundane, "effective" rhetoric of a practical man because such a stance turns out to be an extreme but representative form of unreality. Ultimately the form of Hank's narrative *is* the

---

3. I am grateful to James M. Cox for this portion of my argument.

primary reality of the novel and it is there that the ambiguous imagistic import of the eclipse is appropriately if paradoxically "grounded." Indeed, the "truth" of the novel has much to do with what appears to exist but which is independent of factual justification.

Mark Twain's point about the idiopathic nature of perception is more strongly made by dramatizing the weird conceptions of sixth-century humanity—of Sandy in particular. Where Hank sees pigs in a sty she sees enchanted princesses in an enchanted castle. Sandy ponders:

> And how strange is this marvel, and how awful—that to the one perception it is enchanted and dight in a base and shameful aspect; yet to the perception of the other it is not enchanted, hath suffered no change, but stands firm and stately still, girt with its moat and waving its banners in the blue air from its towers.

Although men differ only in their training, the differences that do exist are sufficiently powerful to mold external reality! It is indeed tempting, incidentally, to extend the connotations of the sand-belt to the name Sandy!

A little later, Hank elaborates on this episode with the swine to explain the basic problem he experiences in understanding the sixth century. The statement involves what might be described as a philosophical apocalypse:

> Everybody around her believed in enchantments; nobody had any doubts; to doubt that a castle could be turned into a sty, and its occupants into hogs, would have been the same as my doubting, among Connecticut people, the actuality of the telephone and its wonders,—and in both cases would be absolute proof of a diseased mind, an unsettled reason. Yes, Sandy was sane; that must be admitted.

Accordingly, Hank reasoned that he must keep quiet about his intuition that "the world was not flat" nor was it supported by pillars and protected by a canopy from a universe of water, unless he wished to be taken for a madman.

To confuse swine with members of the aristocracy and then a few pages on to refer to the band of slaves, who perambulate through the novel, as "bundled together like swine" is not just a matter of being uncomplimentary to the nobility nor is it just a means of pointing to an essential lack of distinction between animals, nobles, and slaves. It is more especially, a further and final confusion of reality and unreality. The slave chain, as I have argued, is an image of humanity. Hank and the king do not suddenly become slaves toward the end of the novel to be "sold at auction, like swine"; this is but a concrete manifestation of their continual situation. But this conception of human reality, linked to Sandy's unique perception of swine, is equally a picture of human unreality. The swine image comes to stand for both the aristocracy and the slaves but primarily for the force of illusion.

The apocalyptic discovery with which the book is concerned is the understanding that no apocalyptic transformation has occurred. The true apocalyptic revelation is not that the sixth-century world is so different but that it is identical and identically unreal. In this context, the concluding doubt in Hank's mind as to which is the dream, the sixth century or the nineteenth century, makes perfect sense. Apparently back in the nineteenth century, Hank, delirious, believes he is speaking to Sandy in the sixth century:

> I seemed to be a creature out of a remote unborn age, centuries hence, and even *that* was as real as the rest! Yes, I seemed to have flown back out of that age into this of ours, and then forward to it again, and was set down, a stranger and forlorn in that strange England, with an abyss of thirteen centuries yawning [pun intended?] between me and you.

He begs Sandy to shield him from "these hideous dreams." This revelation is in alignment with, but does not depend for justification upon, those other moments in the book when the reality of a dream world is particularly pressing. Can we be sure that everything is not merely the narrator's dream? After all, Hank's second entrance occurs after midnight and after the narrator has read a stretch of Malory with the intention that it put him to sleep.[4] In fact, as Mark Twain's notebook entry tells us, his original idea for the story derived from a dream following his reading Malory, "a dream of being a knight errant in armor in the middle ages."[5] And perhaps it is not irrelevant to note that Dan Beard pictures the stranger's story as emanating from a combined pipe-smoke-dragon created by the narrator and Hank. At any rate, Camelot is "as lovely as a dream" and Hank "moved along as one in a dream." Toward the end of the book, Hank's dreams are of the nineteenth century: "In my dreams, along at first, I still wandered thirteen centuries away, and my unsatisfied spirit went calling and harking all up and down the unreplying vacancies of a vanished world."

The apocalyptic solution implied in *A Connecticut Yankee* and, subsequently, stated directly in one of the Mysterious Stranger manuscripts and in the symbolic writings of Twain's later years is that all

---

4. As James M. Cox aptly comments, "*A Connecticut Yankee in King Arthur's Court:* The Machinery of Self-Preservation," "just as Morgan has put a bullet hole through the antique armor which the narrator is nostalgically examining in Warwick Castle, he punctures the sentimental dream of the past" when he interrupts the narrator's reverie to proclaim his responsibility. See Cox's 1960 article, as reprinted in *Mark Twain: A Collection of Critical Essays,* p. 121. Cox, then, sees the narrator as an antimask of Hank. However, if, as I have suggested, Mark Twain is arguing that distinctions between people are illusory anyway, the point is pretty much a quibble.

5. Notebook #18, 24 October, 1883—4 April 1885, TS, p. 11, Mark Twain Papers, Univ. of California, Berkeley.

reality is a dream.[6] Apparently the inhabitants of sixth-century Britain were absolutely correct in their intuition that the eclipse of the sun betokens the end of the world. As an image, the eclipse and the related details chronicled earlier connote not the transformation of realities but the end of reality, the final apocalypse. The images of apocalypse that figure in Hank's final pronouncements suggest the impact of such an extreme philosophical position: "A bugle. . . . It is the king! . . . Turn out the—" Are we not justified in hypothesizing the adjective "apocalyptic" before bugle, in identifying "the king" as God rather than Arthur, and, in completing the phrase, as "turn out the—" light, recall, a final time, the episode detailing the extinction of the sun which now darkens both the sixth century and the nineteenth century? The frame narrator interprets this as Hank, "getting up his last 'effect' " but the quotation marks around "effect" are fortunate. In a reality that turns out to be a dream, a special effect must be granted its measure of actuality.

## EVERETT CARTER

## The Meaning of A *Connecticut Yankee*†

Interpretations of Mark Twain's fiction about knight errantry, A *Connecticut Yankee in King Arthur's Court*, have changed with successive generations of American commentators. Like the Spanish readers of *Don Quixote*, American readers of A *Connecticut Yankee* have divided into "hard" critics who have seen the book as an attack on sentimentalism about the past, and, increasing in number, those "soft" critics who have read it as either ambivalent or an an attack on technology and the American faith in material progress.[1] The terms

6. *Mark Twain's Mysterious Stranger Manuscripts*, ed. W. M. Gibson (Berkeley: Univ. of California Press, 1967), pp. 404–405; and see *Mark Twain's Which Was the Dream? and Other Symbolic Writings of the Later Years*, ed. John S. Tuckey (Berkeley: Univ. of California Press, 1967). As H. Bruce Franklin indicates in his *Future Perfect: American Science Fiction of the Nineteenth Century* (New York: Oxford Univ. Press, 1966), pp. 375–78, there is the further connection that, in A *Connecticut Yankee* and that late symbolic unfinished work, *The Great Dark*, Mark Twain has broken into the genre of science fiction.

† From *American Literature*, 50 (1978), 418–40. Footnotes are by Carter.

1. Among the "hard" critics are Louis Budd, *Mark Twain, Social Philosopher* (Bloomington, Ind., 1962), Howard Baetzhold, *Mark Twain*

*and John Bull* (Bloomington, Ind., 1970) and most social historians who have alluded to the work as a summary of nineteenth-century faith in technology; see, for example, Carl N. Degler, *The Age of Economic Revolution, 1876–1900* (Glenview, Ill., 1967), p. 198. Among the "soft" critics have been: Alan Guttman, "Mark Twain's Connecticut Yankee: Affirmation of the Vernacular Tradition?" *New England Quarterly*, XXXIII (June, 1960), 232–237; Henry Nash Smith, *Mark Twain: The Development of a Writer* (Cambridge, Mass., 1962), and *Mark Twain's Fable of Progress* (New Brunswick, N.J., 1964); James M. Cox, "A *Connecticut Yankee in King Arthur's Court*: The Machinery of Self-Preservation," *Yale Review*, L (Autumn, 1960), 89–102; and Kenneth Lynn, *Mark Twain and Southwestern Humor* (Boston, 1959).

"hard" and "soft" are those of a scholar commenting upon the division between schools of commentaries on *Don Quixote*, the "hard" critics of Cervantes' masterpiece insisting upon its defense of reality, the "soft" critics interpreting the work as a defense of the dauntless power of the imagination to remake reality nearer to the dream.[2]

The new "soft" reading of *Don Quixote* has been essential to interpretations of Spanish culture; Unamuno, the first of the "soft" critics of our century, suggested that Don Quixote, rejecting the miserable real for the hopeless dream, is the symbol of what is good, holy, and tragic in the Spanish soul. The fact that one modern American commentator[3] has suggested that the Yankee's enemy, Merlin, plays a similar role in Mark Twain's romance is an index of how far criticism has come from the nineteenth-century assumptions that *A Connecticut Yankee* was a satire on English chivalry. Like the controversy over *Don Quixote*, the controversy about the Yankee has been couched in terms that leave no doubt that for twentieth-century readers there is something eponymous about Hank Morgan. Hank is not only a Connecticut Yankee; he is *The* Yankee, and his fate, like the fate of Cervantes' hero and of the book in which he appears, is more than a falling out among scholars; it has something to do with a country's feeling about itself and its role in the Western world. In 1889, most readers, the illustrator Dan Beard among them, thought they were reading a book about a Yankee's praiseworthy attempt to make a better world. In the second half of the twentieth century, some critics, among them our most influential, have seen it as a premonition of what they assume is an American danger to the world: a story that ends in massive destruction of a large number of the inhabitants of an underdeveloped country is obviously suggestive to the modern mind.

My purpose here is to try to find out what is the probable meaning of *A Connecticut Yankee*. In doing so, I accept both the terminology and the method of E. D. Hirsch's *Validity in Interpretation*. Hirsch urges the distinction between "meaning" and "significance," with "meaning" restricted to the meaning that the author meant.[4] I address myself to this meaning alone. About significance I shall not comment. No one is going to convince the modern readers who see the book as a reinforcement of their dread of American technological progress that it is anything other. I shall not try. I shall simply try to answer the question: "What, in all probability, and on the basis of all the internal and external evidence, did Mark Twain mean by the total fiction *A Connecticut Yankee in King Arthur's Court?*"

2. Oscar Mandel, "The Function of the Norm in *Don Quixote,* "*Modern Philology*, LV (Feb., 1959), 154–163.

3. Cox, "A Connecticut Yankee in King Arthur's Court, The Machinery of Self-Preservation," p. 100.

4. E. D. Hirsch, Jr., *Validity in Interpretation* (New Haven, Conn., 1967).

In evaluating the external evidence which bears upon the novel's meaning, the first problem to resolve is the probable attitude of Mark Twain towards his narrator, Hank Morgan. Did Mark Twain identify with and sympathize with Hank? Or did he create a narrator whom the reader must criticize, whose attitudes the reader is directed to reject? The answer to this question need not suppose constant authorial identification with the narrator: Mark Twain, after all, had been completely one with Huck Finn's "sound heart" and yet he had satirized minor aspects of Huck's attitude. All that need be asked is "did the writer generally identify with and approve of his narrator and the general course of his narrator's behavior?"

The external evidence that Mark Twain disbelieved in Hank's values consists of a statement to Dan Beard that the Yankee is "an ignoramus."[5] The context of this expression is a description of the protagonist in so favorable a light that Beard made his portraits of the Yankee uniformly sympathetic, although obviously Beard's Yankee is far from refined. Mark Twain, himself a philistine, would not have regarded this as a serious shortcoming. However, he made Hank even more philistine than himself, and Hank's blindness to the beauties of medieval painting and tapestry provides one of the relatively rare instances of Twain's satirizing his protagonist.

Against this lone piece of dubious evidence outside the work itself which might indicate the author's adverse attitude towards the narrator, there are arrayed several indications that Mark Twain sympathized deeply with his Connecticut Yankee. The notebook entries that announce the first glimmerings of the idea for the book, and Twain's working notes for the development of the plot identify the author with the protagonist, suggest he is like Mark Twain's hero, Ulysses S. Grant, and use the first person in outlining the story: "I gave a knight a pass to go holy-grailing. . . . I did everything I could to bring knight-errantry into contempt." After saying that "the whole tribe" will be away on the quest, Twain asks: "Is here my chance to push a R R along, while they are out of my way?"[6] After writing the first thirty-two chapters, he paused to think about the conclusion of his book, and he wrote himself a memorandum: "I make a *peaceful* revolution and introduce advanced civilization."[7]

Even more directly, Mark Twain is on record as approving of his

5. Quoted in A. B. Paine, *Mark Twain: A Biography* (New York, 1912), p. 887.
6. The Mark Twain Papers, Box 41 #4, Bancroft Library, University of California, Berkeley. The working notes will be published as one of the appendices to the forthcoming MLA-CEAA edition of *A Connecticut Yankee in King Arthur's Court*, ed. Bernard L. Stein, with an Introduction by Henry Nash Smith, Berkeley, [1979]. Permission to quote unpublished excerpts from the papers has been kindly granted by the trustees of the Mark Twain Estate, Frederick Anderson, curator.
7. The Mark Twain Papers. This material will be published in *Mark Twain's Notebooks and Journals* (cited hereafter as *NB&J*), Volume III, 1883–1891, ed. Robert Pack Browning, Michael B. Frank, and Lin Salamo (Berkeley [1978]), p. 415.

protagonist. The circumstances which led to his expression of approval were these: Howard Taylor had asked for and had received permission to rework the novel for the stage. When Twain read the dramatization he was disappointed, and he focused his criticism on Taylor's failure to do justice to the Yankee. "The new play," Twain wrote his wife, ". . . has captured but one side of the Yankee's character—his rude animal side, his circus side; the good heart & the high intent are left out of him. . . . I told Taylor he had degraded a natural gentleman to a low-down blackguard."[8]

The external evidence seems weighted in Hank's favor; the internal evidence which bears upon Mark Twain's attitude towards his narrator concerns the Yankee's philistinism and his seemingly inhuman attitude towards the chivalry he is trying to destroy. His philistinism is announced at the beginning: Hank describes himself as "nearly barren of sentiment . . . or poetry. . . ." He stands amid medieval glories of sculpture, painting, and tapestry and complains that there is no "insurance-chromo, or at least a three-color-God-Bless-Our Home over the door." But this lack of a refined aesthetic sense is a minor flaw (and probably not a flaw, at all, in the eyes of Mark Twain). More serious are the several instances where Hank sounds close to megalomania in his desire to reform the medieval world. When he declares, near the end, referring to the massed knights, "We will kill them all," he seems like the Hitler to whom one "soft" commentary has come close to comparing him. "There is a time," Hank says, "when one would like to hang the whole human race. . . ." He describes with apparent relish the "steady drizzle of microscopic fragments of knights and hardware and horse-flesh" that result from his use of dynamite. He considers using "a person of no especial value" to place a bomb down a well. He hooks up a repetitively bowing hermit to a machine and, after he wears him out, he unloads him on Sir Bors de Gans. Finally he approves (although he had not himself prepared) the electrified fences that wipe out England's chivalry.

These constitute an almost complete list of the charges against Hank. If we add to them his willingness to cheat in business, to hang some musicians who play off-key, and to murder a boring would-be humorist, we have the complete indictment. But there is evidence to support a contention that the author did not consider these actions as fundamentally immoral or as more than occasionally and humanly foolish. In the instance of Hank's apparently callous actions, Twain either agreed with their necessity or, in less important cases, took it for granted that his audience would understand the comic-epic tone which permits us to laugh unreservedly at the obliteration of Tom in a Tom and Jerry cartoon, without agonizing about the realities of pain.

8. *The Love Letters of Mark Twain*, ed. Dixon Wecter (New York, 1949), pp. 257–258.

For example, when Hank asks Clarence if some committee members had made their report (they had just walked over a landmine), Clarence answers that it was "unanimous." Until the final pages, when Twain's rage against aristocratic privilege got out of hand, Twain was working confidently in the comic world of frontier humor where overstatement about death and destruction was a standard mode of evoking laughter. Many of the seemingly inhuman reactions of Hank take this form, a form linked to the author's own perhaps tasteless but nevertheless comic hyperbole.

Others of Hank's actions are meant to be taken seriously, and in these instances there is a weight of evidence to indicate Twain's sympathies with his protagonist. When planning the activities of the narrator, he not only used the "I," but in the writing sometimes forgot that he was using a specious rather than an actual first-person. Hank's enormous pride when the first newspaper comes out, and as he watches the favorable reaction of a reader, is not the feeling of a Connecticut factory foreman, but rather that of a Missouri journalist: "Yes, this was heaven; I was tasting it once, if I might never taste it more." When Hank expresses his views of England and Russia, they are views that Mark Twain held and which were according to the two most thorough accounts of the genesis of *A Connecticut Yankee*, the major impulses for the revival of his interest in the narrative in 1887–1888;[9] Hank's words are usually paraphrases of Twain's letters and notebook entries during those years. He could look into the future, says Hank, and see England "erect statues and monuments to her unspeakable Georges and other royal and noble clothes-horses, and leave unhonored the creators of this world—after God— Gutenberg, Watt, Arkwright, Whitney, Morse, Stephenson, Bell." Said Mark Twain in a speech in Baltimore in January, 1889, "Conceive of the blank and sterile ignorance of that day, and contrast it with the vast and many-sided knowledge of this. Consider the trivial miracles and wonders wrought by the humbug magicians and enchanters of that old day, and contrast them with the mighty miracles wrought by science in our day of steam and electricity."[1]

From the opening of the tale to its end, Mark Twain treated his alter-ego sympathetically, weighting plot and characterization heavily in his favor. When, at the beginning, Clarence unwittingly dooms him to seeming certain death by his well-meaning acceleration of the date of execution, Hank is considerate of the boy's feelings even at the moment that would tempt most men to relieve their own feelings in recrimination: "I had not the heart to tell him," says Hank, "his

9. Howard G. Baetzhold, "The Course of Composition of A *Connecticut Yankee*," *American Literature*, XXXIII (Jan., 1961), 456–461 and John B. Hoben, "Mark Twain's A *Connecticut Yankee*: A Genetic Study," *American Literature*, XVIII (Nov., 1946), 197–218.
1. The Mark Twain Papers, Box 41, DV #21.

good-hearted foolishness had ruined me." When Hank comes upon a dying woman in a peasant's hut, he comforts her, and stays with her even when he knows she is dying of small-pox. "Let me come in and help you—you are sick and in trouble," are his words. His aim in urging the king to travel incognito and his motivation for allowing himself to be kept in the chain-gang, is to open the king's eyes to the horrors of slavery. When they are opened, and the king says he will abolish the evil institution, Hank says he is "ready and willing to get free, now," for his mission has been accomplished. A thoroughly middle-class husband and father, Hank is properly concerned for the good name and well-being of his wife and child. He marries Sandy because he is "a New Englander and in my opinion this sort of partnership [their unwedded companionship] would compromise her." Their marriage results in "the dearest and perfectest comradeship that ever was." The illness of their child compels his absence at the crucial moment of his new country's history: the child is sick; the good father unhesitatingly takes her to the sea-shore. Dan Beard, the illustrator of the first edition, underscored the firm position of the Yankee at the heart of middle-class values with his full-page illustration of a benign and solicitous Yankee, standing next to a beautiful and adoring Sandy, both holding the recumbent "Hello Central," while on the wall behind them is the inevitable framed embroidery of "God Bless Our Home."[2]

Most important of all, Twain sympathetically gave Hank a fatal, but entirely praiseworthy weakness: a reluctance to use violence when the opinion of the sansculotte Mark Twain of 1888 was that bloodshed is the only means of accomplishing major social change. It is "the immutable law," says Hank, echoing sentiments Mark Twain had confided to Howells, "that all revolutions that will succeed must *begin* in blood, whatever may answer afterward. . . . What this folk needed, then, was a Reign of Terror and a guillotine, and I was the wrong man for them." In the end, it is Hank's humanitarianism (viewed by Clarence as his "mistimed sentimentalities") that causes his final tragic sleep. Clarence reports that Hank proposed to go out to help the wounded knights; Clarence strenuously opposes the project; Hank insists, and it is on this errand of mercy that he is treacherously stabbed by one of the knights. Clarence, in what are almost the final words of the epilogue, calls Hank "our dear good chief."

Hank, the eponymous Yankee, then, is a good and trustworthy narrator whose weaknesses are occasionally satirized but who usually carries the burden of authorial attitudes. This fact about the narrator is

2. Mark Twain was delighted with his illustrator: "What luck it was to find you!" he wrote Beard. "There are hundreds of artists who could illustrate any other book of mine, but there was only one who could illustrate this one." *Mark Twain's Letters*, ed. A. B. Paine (New York, 1917), II, 511.

central to the answer of the next and the most important question: the meaning of A Connecticut Yankee with regard to the progress of mankind through the application of reason to the physical and social world, an application that has resulted in the technological society. When Hank engages in his duel with Merlin and with knight errantry, the duel is not simply a conflict between two men, but between two ways of life, between two cultures with their attendant deities, "a mysterious and awful battle of the gods": the god of science on the one hand, the god of superstition on the other. "I was a champion . . . ," Hank says, "but not the champion of the frivolous black arts, I was the champion of hard unsentimental common-sense and reason."

There are three pieces of external evidence that might support a proposition that A Connecticut Yankee is not a book in praise of commonsense and reason, but is rather an attack on these and a defense of a lost world of the imagination. One is a notebook entry written very early in the gestation of the work when Twain predicted that his Yankee would mourn "his lost land" and would be "found a suicide."[3] A second piece of external evidence is the fact that Twain was outraged, in August or September, 1887, by the Langdon family's sharp business practices, a concern which led him to write a section, unused in the final version, satiric of nineteenth-century commercialism. The third piece of external evidence is the most famous: Twain's letter to Howells, after the dean of American letters had read and praised the book: Twain replied that there were many things left unsaid, that if he were to say them it would take "a pen warmed-up in hell."[4]

All three pieces of evidence are ambiguous, but all three more logically support a view that the meaning of the work is a defense of the American nineteenth century than the reverse. The early notebook reference to Hank's longing for a sixth-century, a "new" and "virgin" England can be read as a reference to the century and the country as Hank had reformed them, a land and a time that held the memories of his wife and child, a time and a land that, in the same entry, he contrasts with the degradation not of nineteenth-century America, but of nineteenth-century England. Concerning his anger at Andrew Langdon's sharp business practices: Twain's awareness of the curse of financial greed had long been a motive of his satire; since The Gilded Age, sixteen years before, he had deplored this disease in a system that he otherwise considered far superior to those of other lands and times. To satirize those ancient evils which persisted into the present was consistent with his reformist purposes; it was this meliorist urge that Dan Beard pointed up by using the face of Jay Gould on the body of the medieval slave-driver, and that William Dean Howells and Clar-

3. NB&J. III. 216.
4. Mark Twain–Howells Letters, ed. Henry Nash Smith and William M. Gibson (Cambridge, Mass., 1960), II, 613.

ence Stedman noticed in their reviews. What is more significant than the fact that Twain continued to criticize the shortcomings of his contemporary society is the fact that, in the final version of *A Connecticut Yankee*, he decided to omit a specific satire of this example of a contemporary evil.

The third, and more often quoted bit of external evidence, consists of that cry to Howells that he would need a "pen warmed-up in hell" to say the unsaid things of *A Connecticut Yankee*. There is little reason to believe that the unsaid things would have been attacks on common-sense, republicanism, and technology. There is every reason to believe that the unsaid things were further scathing attacks on monarchy, foreign despotisms, and aristocratic pretensions. Exactly two months after his cry for a hell-warmed pen, he crowed to Howells that "These are immense days. . . . There'll be plenty to sneer & depreciate & disenthuse—on the other hand, who can lift a word of the other sort, in the name of God let him pipe up! I want to print some extracts from the Yankee that have in them the new (sweet) breath of republics."[5] The same week he wrote the hell-warmed pen letter, he wrote to Sylvester Baxter to gloat over the fall of the Brazilian monarchy, and to link the last chapters of *A Connecticut Yankee* with that happy demise.[6] Within three months he wrote to his English publisher: "I wanted to say a Yankee mechanic's say against monarchy and its several natural props."[7] From 1885 to 1889 his notebooks and letters are full of rage against English arrogance, Russian tyranny, commercial speculation and greed, and those prolongations of medieval prejudices into the nineteenth century which made the South and the slavery system the subject of nostalgic sentimentalizing. These had been the evils against which Twain had been fulminating for years; he had never expressed the need for a weapon with which to attack technological progress and liberal democracy, while he had often raged against royalty, aristocracy, and hereditary privilege. To take the angry satirist's cry for a pen warmed in hell as a cry for a tool with which to attack republican progress would be an improbable introduction of a new and unexpected attitude; to take the phrase as a reference to his hatred of those past and foreign institutions about which he had frequently expressed himself would be a more probable inference.

The letter to his English publisher constitutes one of six direct, unambiguous statements of authorial purpose, six declarations of intent which provide a substantial body of support for a reading of *A Connecticut Yankee* as a defense of democracy, technology, and progress. Every time Mark Twain expressed himself about what he meant in writing the book, he tried to say bluntly that he was defend-

5. *Mark Twain–Howells Letters*, II, 621.    7. *Mark Twain's Letters*, II, 524–525.
6. *Mark Twain's Letters*, II, 520.

ing the American nineteenth century and attacking a brutish and inhumane past. The letter to the English publisher not only made the identification between author and narrator: "I wanted to say a Yankee mechanic's say . . . ," but it went on to declare: ". . . the book was not written for America; it was written for England. So many Englishmen have done their sincerest to teach us something for our betterment that it seems to me high time that some of us should substantially recognize the good intent by trying to pry up the English nation to a little higher level of manhood in turn."[8] Twain's changing the name of the Yankee from the neutral "Robert Smith" to a familiar form of the name of the pirate who harried English trade routes is, in this context, no reflection on the character of Hank Morgan, but is rather the humorist's signal of the direction of his satire. Twain's angry response to English criticism of America, and his defense of his country, was one of his preoccupations in the years he was writing *A Connecticut Yankee*; he has left notes for a talk attacking English and defending American society: ". . . If you scrape off our American crust of shabby politicians," the unfinished draft reads, "you will find a nation underneath of as sterling a character, & with as high purposes at heart. . . ."[9] The draft did not complete the terms of the comparison, but the meaning is unambiguous. Equally unequivocal is the introduction to several excerpts from *A Connecticut Yankee* which appeared in the *Century Magazine* in November, 1889. There Twain described the work as "a bitter struggle for supremacy . . . , Merlin using the absurd necromancy of the time and the Yankee beating it easily and brilliantly with the more splendid necromancy of the nineteenth century—that is, the marvels of modern science." After a few chapters, Twain wrote a summary of the plot: "Meantime the Yankee is very busy; for he has privately set himself the task of introducing the great and beneficent civilization of the nineteenth century, and of peacefully replacing the twin despotisms of royalty and aristocratic privilege with a 'Republic on the American plan.' . . ."[1] In 1906, he dictated his memories about the book; they were that he had been ". . . purposing to contrast that English life . . . with the life of modern Christendom and modern civilization—to the advantage of the latter, of course."[2]

In addition to these declarations of purpose in letter, introduction, and memoir, Twain wrote three prefaces that announce the intended meaning of the work. One, published as an appendix in A. B. Paine's biography, accounts for the fact that he chose England, and not Russia (or Belgium) as the object of his satire. "I have drawn," he wrote, "no

8. *Ibid.*
9. The Mark Twain Papers, Box 41 #5.
1. "*A Connecticut Yankee in King Arthur's Court* by Mark Twain," *Century Magazine,*

XXXIX (Nov., 1889), 74, 77.
2. Autobiographical Dictation of December 5, 1906, The Mark Twain Papers.

laws and no illustrations from the twin civilizations of Hell and Russia. To have ventured into that atmosphere would have defeated my purpose: which was to show a great & genuine progress in Christendom in these few later generations, toward mercifulness—a wide and general relaxing of the grip of the law."[3] This was one of his tries at an introduction; another emphasized that his attack was not only upon the false worship of the English past, but upon the sentimentalizing of history in general: "The strange laws," this unpublished preface went, "which one encounters here and there in this book, are not known to have existed in King Arthur's time, of course, but it is fair to presume that they did exist, since they still existed in Christian lands in far later times—times customarily called, with unconscious sarcasm, 'civilized and enlightened.' The episodes by which these laws are illustrated in this book are not invention, but are drawn from history; not always from English history, but mainly from that source. Human liberty—for white people—may fairly be said to be one hundred years old this year; what stood for it in any previous century of the world's history cannot be rationally allowed to count."[4] This seems clear enough, but even more to the point was another unpublished preface that was directed at the reader who might make the mistake of preferring the past to the present: "One purpose of the book," Mark Twain wrote, "is to entertain the reader—if it may have the happy luck to do that. Another is, to remind him that what is called Christian Civilization is so young and new that it had not yet entered the world when our century was born. . . . If any are inclined to rail at our present civilization, why there is no hindering him; but he ought to sometimes contrast it with what went before, & take comfort—and hope, too."[5]

In the face of this evidence of authorial purpose, few commentators have implied that Mark Twain intended to write an attack on progress and technology. Instead, modern revision of the work's meaning has either ignored the question of authorial intent (after all, academic critics had been warned off by the dread of committing "the intentional fallacy") or has argued that authorial intent was subverted by the act of creation: behind the new commentaries has hovered the critical ideology which insists upon the independence of the work of art: "trust the tale, not the teller." The tale, for the "soft" critics, tells us that the Yankee is at least a well-meaning fool or at most an authoritarian villain whose obsession with technology brings about the destruction of civilization. This interpretation was proposed in 1950, by Gladys Bellamy who summarized the work as meaning that a "too-quick civilization brings disaster,"[6] thus placing blame for the ending on

3. The Mark Twain Papers, Box 41 #10.
4. The Mark Twain Papers, Box 47 #7.
5. The Mark Twain Papers, Box 41 # 2. The three prefaces will appear as Appendix ˈ ɔ in the

MLA-CEAA edition.
6. Bellamy, *Mark Twain as Literary Artist*, p. 314.

Hank. The new reading received its most influential formulation in 1962 when Henry Nash Smith described the working of Mark Twain's unruly genius: "He had planned a fable illustrating how the advance of technology fosters the moral improvement of mankind," Smith wrote. "But when he put his belief to the test by attempting to realize it in fiction, the oracle of his imagination, his intuition, the unconsciously formulated conclusions based on his observation and reading, his childhood heritage of Calvinism, at any rate some force other than his conscious intention convinced him that his belief in progress and human perfectibility was groundless." The support for this view came, as it must, from a close reading of the romance with special attention to the ending: "The raw aggression expressed in Mark Twain's description of the slaughter of the knights reveals a massive disillusionment and frustration."[7] James Cox had earlier agreed that a subconscious obsession took over the meaning of the work, and argued that the Yankee became an "anti-mask," a burlesque caricature of the Enlightenment, a symbol of the "machine madness" which possessed Mark Twain, and that he had to kill by killing its embodiment in Hank Morgan. While admitting that Twain's disenchantment with the machine did not come until five years after finishing A Connecticut Yankee, Cox argued that the successive postponements of the completion of Paige's typesetter caused the book to become "more than a mere prophecy of the disaster toward which the machine obsession was tending; it was an acting out beforehand of the experience itself." Cox's analysis goes on to suggest that in viewing the final triumph of Merlin, one is "almost" led to believe that the necromancer is "the prototype of the artist who emerges from humiliation and shame to exercise his magic powers at the last."[8]

While occasionally concerned with internal evidence drawn from other portions of the book, these revisions of A Connecticut Yankee's meaning have usually concentrated on the conclusion: the catastrophic scenes of the slaughter of the knights, the destruction of the technological civilization, the triumph of Merlin, the thirteen-century-long sleep of the Yankee, and his sad death while calling out for his lost life in the sixth century. Any interpretation of the meaning of the romance must address itself to the construction of the plot of A Connecticut Yankee with particular attention to its development towards this ending: towards the electrocution of the knights, the dynamiting of the factories, and the defeat of the Yankee. What were the causes of the Yankee's failure? Who and what was responsible for the downfall of his civilization?

To support a contention that this ending constitutes a subconsious inversion of the author's conscious intention, several necessary condi-

7. Smith, Mark Twain, pp. 169–170.
8. Cox, "A Connecticut Yankee in King Ar-
thur's Court: The Machinery of Self-Preservation," p. 100.

tions would have to be proven. One is that there was a sudden shift, an undermining of the author's meaning as the work progressed, a reversal of previous mood and tone. The second is that the ending was unusually, even unbearably painful for the author: certainly a subconsious fear that exploded previous convictions and that subverted conscious desires would be something to which he would be loathe to return. A third is that the sadness of the ending, the change from comedy to tragedy, was a statement about human institutions and not about man's cosmic fate, a statement about society and not about metaphysics. An ending that described common-sense, reason, and technology as destructive forces inside of history would be truly a subversion of authorial intent; a plot whose denouement showed an awareness of the immutable human condition, condemned to eventual earthly separation from home and love, would be a shift in mood, but not a change in social commitment: within the larger, inescapable terms of human existence, this ending might say, men can still make choices that will make society better or worse; the crucial point is whether the Yankee offered a better choice than that which was offered in the past.

First the question: was the ending an unforeseen reversal of previous plans for the novel? It seems not to have been. From the beginning, as we have seen, Mark Twain planned an ending in which the Yankee would "mourn his lost land." In Chapter 8, "The Boss," a chapter written in the summer of 1887[9] a full eighteen months before he wrote the ending, Mark Twain put in Hank's mouth the following prediction about the conclusion of his adventure: "Yes, in power I was equal to the king. At the same time there was another power that was a trifle stronger than both of us put together. That was the Church. I do not wish to disguise that fact. I couldn't if I wanted to. But never mind about that, now; it will show up in its proper place, later on." Then, in September, 1888, still nine months before he wrote the conclusion, Twain made the entry in his notebook where he both identified himself with the protagonist, and then summarized the ending: "I make a *peaceful* revolution and introduce advanced civilization. The Church overthrows it with a 6 year interdict."[1]

The frustration of England's premature progress, the failure of the Yankee to reform the medieval world was the ending Mark Twain had decided upon possibly as early as 1885, probably as early as 1887, and certainly by the autumn of 1888. It was no sudden change, no turning of a creator's subconsious against his conscious wishes. Furthermore the very form of the ending—the carnage of the knights, electrocuted by charged barbed wire and mowed down by machine guns—had been one of the earliest incidents Mark Twain had devised; he had

9. Baetzhold, "The Course of Composition of *A Connecticut Yankee*," p. 199.

1. The Mark Twain Papers. This material will be published in *NB&J*. III, 216.

written of precisely this kind of battle in 1886, when no more than three chapters had been completed. Some of these "adventures of Sir Robert Smith of Camelot" were read before the Military Service Institute of Governor's Island on November 11, 1886. According to a reporter's version, Sir Robert Smith "took a contract from King Arthur to kill off, at one of the great tournaments, fifteen kings and many acres of hostile armored knights. When, lance in rest, they charge by squadrons upon him, he, behind the protection of a barbed wire fence charged with electricity, mowed them down with Gatling guns that he had made for the occasion."[2] After finishing the book in 1889, Twain gave another reading of it before a military audience, this time the cadets of West Point. He included the scene of the Battle of the Sand-Belt, and in his reading notes—a paste-up of pages from the first edition—he identified the 52 loyal "boys" with the audience before him, substituting the word "cadet" for "boy" when the latter first appeared, and ended his reading with a description of the military victory: ". . . the campaign was ended, we fifty-four were masters of England! Twenty-five thousand men lay dead around us." Then he crossed out the remaining paragraphs that dealt with Hank's wounding and his defeat.[3]

The carnage at the end, then, is no aberration but a conventional mode of frontier hyperbole in which Mark Twain frequently indulged, which he had planned for three years to be part of his novel, and which he read with obvious relish before audiences properly appreciative of the progress of military weaponry; one may deplore its childish ferocity or its possibly misplaced admiration, but one can scarcely use it to prove a sudden reversal of authorial intent, or a pathological change in customary style. Above all, since Mark Twain conceived the scene early and returned with relish to it late, he was obviously untraumatized by its possible implications for his belief in the blessings of technology.

The ending, then, was both planned by and was untraumatic for its author; it was something Mark Twain had decided upon early, and with unusual care for an author who was self-admittedly a poor constructor of plots. But there is certainly a difference in tone between the ending of A *Connecticut Yankee* and almost everything Mark Twain had written before; all of his previous works had concluded "happily": *The Gilded Age* with Washington Hawkins coming to his senses; *The Prince and the Pauper* with the regaining of the Prince's position and with the improved fortunes of the pauper; *Tom Sawyer* with the finding of Injun Joe and the winning of the reward; *Huckleberry Finn* with the freedom of Jim from slavery and of Huck

---

2. Howard G. Baetzhold, "The Autobiography of Sir Robert Smith of Camelot: Mark Twain's Original Plan for A *Connecticut Yankee*," *American Literature.* XXXII (Jan., 1961), 459.
3. The Mark Twain Papers, Box 41 #1.

from his father's tyranny; *Life on the Mississippi* with paeans to Northern progress. The sense of weariness and sadness at the end of *A Connecticut Yankee* is a changed tone. Very early in its writing, Mark Twain knew that the Yankee would have to lose and began to prepare his readers for his hero's downfall. The crucial question is: to what causes did the book assign the Yankee's failure? Were they causes inherent in the Yankee's beliefs or moral structure? Did Hank cause the terrible ending of *A Connecticut Yankee?* Or did Mark Twain take care to assign the reasons for the disaster to other elements of history? And what did this assignation of guilt tell us about forces in history that should be encouraged, and those discouraged, in order to achieve a better society?

Mark Twain made Hank but a minor, and morally guiltless, cause of the final catastrophe: he was too humane in his efforts to reform an evil society. With Hank absent, drawn from his post by the needs of a sick child, forces that the romance identifies as evil and reactionary, and that Hank (still according to the authorial voice) had been too soft-hearted to make impotent, these forces nullify his reforms. In self-defense and in defense of a small besieged band of royal followers, victims of an unprovoked aggression by armored soliders who outnumber them 500–1, soldiers who would torture and kill them and then reinstitute serfdom and slavery, Hank uses advanced technology to destroy the enemy. There is no evidence that Twain thought Hank's self-defense reprehensible. The major causes of the disaster, as Twain described them, are, first, the growing corruption of the Round Table, specifically the adultery of Launcelot and Guenever, and second, and most important, the opening that this corruption made for the exercise of the decisive cause: the power of an absolute church.

The corruption of the Round Table was fixed as a moving force in the denouement from the beginning of the conception of *A Connecticut Yankee*. Immediately after he outlined the burlesque of knight-errantry for the Military Institute of Governor's Island in 1886, Twain reassured Mrs. A. W. Fairbanks that he would not besmirch the work she loved, the *Morte Darthur*, and its "beautiful" characters.[4] He did not keep his promise with regard to the whole of Malory's romance; it comes in for pretty rough treatment in Chapter XV; but as a counterpoint to the broad burlesque of knight errantry and of its chronicler, Mark Twain introduced and intermittently sustained the serious traditional subplot concerning the gallant and praiseworthy members of the chivalric orders: Galahad, Launcelot, and, above all, the king himself. The king is more than a king, says Hank, he is "a man." Galahad, the Yankee tells us, has a "noble benignity and purity." Launcelot has "majesty and greatness," and it is he who comes riding

4. *Mark Twain to Mrs. Fairbanks*, ed. Dixon Wecter (San Marino, Calif., 1949), p. 258.

to Hank's rescue—on a bicycle. The part of the *Morte Darthur* that Mark Twain seized upon was the tragic and fatal adultery that resulted in the waste of Malory's admirable characters; in *A Connecticut Yankee* it was this crime against nineteenth-century middle-class morality that leads directly to the death of that portion of the chivalry of England that was praiseworthy, leaving only the dregs of aristocracy to be destroyed by Hank and Clarence and their fifty-two loyal cadets.

The adultery is suggested as early as the third chapter, upon Hank's first view of the Knights of the Round Table. He sees the queen fling the kind of "furtive glances at Sir Launcelot that would have got him shot in Arkansas, to a dead certainty." A few moments later, the court explodes in a riot of indecency, using language that "would make a Comanche blush." Hank is stripped, and stands before the knights and ladies "naked as a pair of tongs." Queen Guenever, says Hank, "was as naïvely interested as the rest." Dan Beard obligingly emphasized the meaning of this scene by drawing a small picture of Guenever, looking anything but naïve, as she presumably appraises the object before her. In Chapter XXVI, written during the summer of 1886, Hank describes the mournful look of King Arthur, when Hank suggests that he tell Guenever that he is going away. "Thou forgettest," says the king, "that Launcelot is here; and where Launcelot is, she noteth not the going forth of the king, nor what day he returneth." Hank then observes: "Yes, Guenever was beautiful, it is true, but take her all around she was pretty slack." When Hank returns from his trip of mercy to find his partially reformed country in ruins, Clarence tells him of the Civil War that resulted when Arthur found out about Guenever's and Launcelot's adultery; it is a tale of the destruction of all of the worthy knights, of the death of Arthur, and of the queen's retirement to a nunnery. Moral slackness had destroyed what was good in knight errantry.

Sexual immorality, however, was but a contributory cause of the disaster; it had been but the weakening of the body politic, making it susceptible to the final fatal disease. The disease, announced by Mark Twain in both notebook and text, was the power of the absolute church. It was a power exercised when both the adultery of court life and the morally opposite fidelity of Hank to wife and family made it possible for the Church to exercise its latent strength. While Hank is away, caring for his child, the Church, stronger than both Hank and the king, makes its move; the Church, Hank says sadly when he returns from France, was going to "*keep* the upper hand, now, and snuff out all my beautiful civilization. . . ." Again, Dan Beard obliged by visualizing these lines in a full-page illustration of a smirking monk placing a bishop's miter over a bright candle labeled "19th Century," and entitling the drawing: "Snuffing Out the Candle."

The failure of the Yankee, then, is accounted for: minor blame is assigned to Hank for the venial sin of sentimentality, major blame to the mortal sins of Launcelot and Guenever and, most important, of the reactionary church. In only one place in the narrative is there the suggestion that progress through technology itself is the wrong course of humanity. This is the paragraph where Hank, describing his hidden factories, uses the analogy of a volcano, and compares them to the lava's "rising hell": "Unsuspected by this dark land," Hank says, "I had the civilization of the nineteenth century booming under its very nose! . . . There it was . . . as substantial a fact as any serene volcano, standing innocent with its smokeless summit in the blue sky and giving no sign of the rising hell in its bowels."

Comparing technology to a hell, the metaphor seems on the face of it to be loaded with negative feelings about the beneficence of applied science. Perhaps. One might also observe that "hell" did not always have negative connotations for an author who would rather be consigned to the Puritan hell than the Puritan heaven, who asked for his pen to be warmed in the infernal regions, and who might quite typically have described what was going to happen to aristocracy and church as, from their standpoint, a diabolical eruption. Furthermore the possibly negative import of the metaphor is contradicted by the surrounding allusions where technology is associated with light, and backward England with darkness.

The metaphor of the volcano is the one piece of internal evidence that might support the view that the cause of the disaster was technology itself; everywhere else there is the suggestion that Hank's prescription for the cure of social ills—the prescription of the faith in progress through reason, common sense, and applied science—is sound. What is perhaps true, although the internal evidence is far from clear, is that the general metaphysical framework in which this belief was embedded began to show signs of stress by the time Mark Twain was finishing *A Connecticut Yankee*. This framework had been built of a certain view of human nature—that it is essentially good—, and a corresponding view of universal law—that it too is moral and tends to work by assuring the betterment of human institutions over the course of history. Both optimisms are questioned by the conclusion of Mark Twain's fiction.

The disappointment Hank suffers when he returns to find not only the chivalry of England massed against him, but the people of England as well, revives his (and Mark Twain's) latent ambivalance towards the common man and towards the doctrine of his natural goodness. Where at the beginning of his adventures in medieval England, Hank used the word "muck" literally, to describe the streets of Camelot, Hank uses the term at the end of the novel to describe the people themselves: "Imagine such human muck as this; conceive of this folly!" This constitutes the "massive disillusionment" to which revisionist criticism of *A Connecticut Yankee* refers. It is incontestable that the Yankee is disappointed, and that his faith in humanity has been shaken. However, it had never been a faith without an admixture of both doubt and realism; earlier in the work, Hank had faced the problem posed for his hope of progress by the complex nature of man, and had come out of the experience with a renewed, if chastened, conviction that in the main there is enough good in human nature to justify a hope for society's improvement. The situation was this: travelling incognito, Hank and the king had come upon a frightful example of the operations of the archaic customs of England, laws that had resulted in mass cruelties and executions. Hank found that the peasants support the lords. "The painful thing," he observed, ". . . was the alacrity with which this oppressed community had turned their cruel hands against their own class. . . . It was depressing to a man with a dream of a republic in his head." Then, as it often did, the distance between narrator and author collapsed, and Mark Twain began to talk of his own experiences, experiences in the American South outside the range of a descendant of New England blacksmiths and horsedoctors: "It reminded me of a time thirteen centuries away, when the 'poor whites' of our South . . . were . . . pusillanimously ready to side with slave-lords . . . for the upholding and perpetuating of slavery." There was a redeeming factor, however, a small one, but enough to modify Hank's pessimism: "secretly the 'poor white' did detest the slave-lord and feel his own shame." This was enough "for it showed that a man is at bottom a man . . ." That this is straightforward and not ironic is made clear a moment later when Hank describes the bravery of one of the peasants and declares: "There it was, you see. A man *is* a man, at bottom. Whole ages of abuse and oppression cannot crush the manhood clear out of him." Yes, he continues, "there is plenty good enough material for a republic in the most degraded people that ever existed. . . ." Then, as mask and author once more abruptly coalesce, he adds: "—even the Russians." At this point, the most extended discussion of the problem of the moral nature of man in *A Connecticut Yankee*, Hank concluded: "there was no occasion to give up my dream yet a while." The abandonment of the dream would be forced not by the nature of man, but by the nature of radically corrupt human institutions.

The second part of the metaphysical structure that supported the American belief in progress was an attitude toward the power behind history, be it God, Nature, or Universal Law: the sense that the movement of events was both purposeful and, in the long run, moral. There is some support for the proposition that Mark Twain's shaky allegiance to his faith was undergoing stress, and that the stress is reflected in the ending of *A Connecticut Yankee*. When the Yankee is described in Twain's notebook as "mourning his lost land," when in the frame of the narrative he smiles "one of those pathetic, obsolete smiles of his," when, in his dreams, he still wanders "thirteen centuries away," his unsatisfied spirit ". . . calling and harking all up and down the unreplying vacancies of a vanished world," we seem to have taken a long step toward the final pessimisms of *The Mysterious Stranger*. If, in his longing for his vanished world, Hank is longing for Camelot as Camelot, and if he feels himself a stranger in the nineteenth century as the nineteenth century, then, indeed, A *Connecticut Yankee*, as fiction, subverted its author's announced intention.

That this is not true can be proven by an examination of the portrait of medieval England as we find it in A *Connecticut Yankee*. The sixth century landscapes are idyllic, but its villages are vile and the life of its people is a hell for all but noble and aristocrat. It is a pastoral land whose dream-like beauty is, for Hank, "as lonesome as Sunday." In the course of his incognito wanderings, Hank comes upon a telegraph station of his underground army of progress. "In this atmosphere of telephones and lightning communication . . . ," Hank says, "I was breathing the breath of life again after long suffocation. I realized then, what a creepy, dull, inanimate horror this land had been to me all these years."

The apparently idyllic land contained a culture that made a horror out of natural goodness. Even the most favored of the aristocrats were prevented from enjoying it. The most eloquent description of pre-technological England, a description full of sentimental cliches like "sylvan solitudes," comes at the beginning of the chapter called "Slow Torture," a chapter devoted to the intolerable life inside a coat of armor. A second flowery passage describing "blessed God's untainted dew-freshened, woodland-scented, air" comes after the description of Morgan le Fay's tortured victims, and is followed by Hank's description of the suffocation of mind and body in "the moral and physical stenches of that intolerable old buzzard-roost."

This pretechnological England, naturally beautiful, humanly terrible, was transformed by Hank without, apparently, harming the landscape. Like "another Robinson Crusoe," he invented, contrived, created, and made a good society. "Consider the three years sped," he said proudly. "Now look around on England. A happy and prosperous country, and strangely altered. Schools everywhere, and several colleges. . . . Slavery was dead and gone; all men were equal before the law; taxation had been equalized. The telegraph, the telephone, the phonograph, the type-writer, the sewing machine, and all the thousand willing and handy servants of steam and electricity were working their way into favor. . ." The list of accomplishments goes on, and ends with: "I was getting ready to send out an expedition to discover America."

There is reason to believe, then, that Hank's longing is not for a pretechnological Eden, but for an England that the Yankee, like Robinson Crusoe, had made bearable by the exercise of his ingenuity. However, more powerful motives than nostalgia operated at the end of *A Connecticut Yankee* to give the comedy its serious turn. One was Mark Twain's consideration of a cyclical, repetitive theory of the movements of history. While the immediate cause of the downfall of Hank's society was the immorality of the Queen, Clarence suggests, without contradiction, that the end would have come "by and by," and would be caused by Hank himself. Merlin's taunt: "Ye were conquerors, ye are conquered," has the ring of the mockery of the goddess of Fortune, the deity of an inevitable turning back upon itself of all human enterprise.

The second tragic motive, and a more important one, was Mark Twain's growing awareness, at the age of fifty, of the inevitable private failures of men, whatever the fate of their societies. Men must die; men must be separated from their earthly loves. Except for those fortunate, or self-deluding, enough to have a traditional religious faith, men must face the fact that time is man's enemy, cutting him away from his worldly affections. Hank's final delirium is entirely about these private sadnesses; he raves about Sandy and about their child, not about politics or technology. The bathetic ending of *A Connecticut Yankee* has nothing to do with the relative merits of republics or monarchies, progress or tradition. This is the human condition, says the novel's ending; but given the unalterable limits of this condition, man can still ask the question: what should man then do? And the answer *A Connecticut Yankee* gives, just as Mark Twain's tract *What Is Man?*, written years later, would give, is that within the severe restrictions and limitations of man's condition, he can try to act for human, for worldly improvement.

The available evidence, then, external and internal, suggests that the meaning of *A Connecticut Yankee* is, as the author repeatedly said it was, that the American nineteenth century, devoted to political and religious liberalism and to technology, was better than the traditional past. The efforts of modern men to continue a progress towards a fulfillment of material goals is shown to be a worthy mission of man. Mark Twain's fictional excursion into history was, as he insisted it was, for the purpose of saying to the reader: you've been poor following European models; you've become rich following American models; rich is better. Twentieth-century interpreters who find an opposed significance in the work must ask themselves whether that significance is an "appropriate" extension of authorial meaning.

# Selected Bibliography

The bibliography which follows does not include items which have been excerpted in the body of the book, since full bibliographical information has already been given. The most complete bibliography is Thomas Asa Tenney, *Mark Twain: A Reference Guide* (Boston: G. K. Hall, 1977), which is being supplemented annually in *American Literary Realism*, beginning with 10 (1977), 327–412. Another checklist is Maurice Beebe and John Feaster, "Criticism of Mark Twain: A Selected Checklist," *Modern Fiction Studies*, 14 (1968), 93–139.

## GENERAL STUDIES

Andrews, Kenneth R. *Nook Farm: Mark Twain's Hartford Circle*. Cambridge: Harvard University Press, 1950.

Baldanza, Frank. *Mark Twain: An Introduction and Interpretation*. New York: Barnes & Noble, 1961.

Bellamy, Gladys Carmen. *Mark Twain as a Literary Artist*. Norman: University of Oklahoma Press, 1950.

Blair, Walter. *Horse Sense in American Humor*. Chicago: University of Chicago Press, 1942.

Blues, Thomas. *Mark Twain and the Community*. Lexington: University of Kentucky Press, 1970.

Brooks, Van Wyck. *The Ordeal of Mark Twain*. Rev. ed. New York: E. P. Dutton, 1933.

Covici, Pascal, Jr. *Mark Twain's Humor: The Image of a World*. Dallas: Southern Methodist University Press, 1962.

Cox, James M. *Mark Twain: The Fate of Humor*. Princeton: Princeton University Press, 1966.

De Voto, Bernard. *Mark Twain's America*. Boston: Little, Brown, 1932.

Ferguson, DeLancey. *Mark Twain: Man and Legend*. Indianapolis: Bobbs-Merrill, 1943.

Foner, Philip S. *Mark Twain, Social Critic*. New York: International Publishers, 1958.

Franklin, H. Bruce. "Mark Twain and Science Fiction." In *Future Perfect: American Science Fiction of the Nineteenth Century*. New York: Oxford University Press, 1966.

Geismar, Maxwell. *Mark Twain: An American Prophet*. Boston: Houghton Mifflin, 1970.

Gerber, John C. "The Relation Between Point of View and Style in the Works of Mark Twain." In *Style in Prose Fiction: English Institute Essays, 1958*. New York: Columbia University Press, 1959.

Gibson, William M. *The Art of Mark Twain*. New York: Oxford University Press, 1976.

Gribben, Alan. *Mark Twain's Library: A Reconstruction*. Boston: G. K. Hall, 1980.

Gross, Seymour L. "Mark Twain and Catholicism." *Critic*, 17 (1959), 9, 12, 88–91.

Kaplan, Justin. *Mr. Clemens and Mark Twain*. New York: Simon and Schuster, 1966.

Long, E. Hudson. *Mark Twain Handbook*. New York: Hendricks House, 1958.

Moore, Olin Harris. "Mark Twain and Don Quixote." *PMLA*, 37 (1922), 324–46.

Regan, Robert. *Unpromising Heroes: Mark Twain and His Characters*. Berkeley: University of California Press, 1966.

Rubin, Louis D., Jr. "Mark Twain and the Post-War Scene." In *The Writer in the South: Studies in a Literary Community*. Athens: University of Georgia Press, 1972.

Salomon, Roger B. *Twain and the Image of History*. New Haven: Yale University Press, 1961.

Sloane, David E. E. *Mark Twain as a Literary Comedian*. Baton Rouge: Louisiana State University Press, 1979.

Smith, Henry Nash. *Mark Twain: The Development of a Writer*. Cambridge: Harvard University Press, 1962.

Spengemann, William C. *Mark Twain and the Backwoods Angel: The Matter of Innocence in the Works of Samuel L. Clemens.* Kent, Ohio: Kent State University Press, 1966.

Stone, Albert E. *The Innocent Eye: Childhood in Mark Twain's Imagination.* New Haven: Yale University Press, 1961.

Taylor, Walter F. "Mark Twain and the Machine Age." *South Atlantic Quarterly,* 37 (1938), 384–96.

Wagenknecht, Edward. *Mark Twain: The Man and His Work.* 3rd ed. Norman: University of Oklahoma Press, 1967.

Wiggins, Robert A. *Mark Twain, Jackleg Novelist.* Seattle: University of Washington Press, 1964.


## A CONNECTICUT YANKEE


Allen, Gerald. "Mark Twain's Yankee." *New England Quarterly,* 39 (1966), 435–46.

Andersen, Kenneth, "The Ending of Mark Twain's *A Connecticut Yankee in King Arthur's Court.*" *Mark Twain Journal,* 14, iv, (1969), 21.

———. "Mark Twain, W. D. Howells, and Henry James: Three Agnostics in Search of Salvation." *Mark Twain Journal,* 15, i, (1970), 13–16.

Aspiz, Harold. "Lecky's Influence on Mark Twain." *Science & Society,* 26 (1962), 15–25.

Baetzhold, Howard G. " 'The Autobiography of Sir Robert Smith of Camelot': Mark Twain's Original Plan for *A Connecticut Yankee.*" *American Literature,* 32 (1961), 456–61.

———. "The Course of Composition of *A Connecticut Yankee:* A Reinterpretation." *American Literature,* 33 (1961), 195–214.

———. "An Emendation in *A Connecticut Yankee.*" *CEAA Newsletter,* 1 (1968), 10.

Berthold, Dennis. "The Conflict of Dialects in *A Connecticut Yankee.*" *Ball State University Forum,* 18, iii, (1977), 51–58.

Bertolotti, D. S., Jr. "Mark Twain Revisits the Tailor." *Mark Twain Journal,* 13, iv, (1967), 18–9.

Burnam, Tom. "Mark Twain and the Paige Typesetter: A Background for Despair." *Western Humanities Review,* 6 (1951–52), 29–36.

Butcher, Philip. " 'The Godfathership' of *A Connecticut Yankee.*" *CLA Journal,* 12 (1969), 189–98.

Canby, Henry Seidel. "Hero of the Great Know-How: Mark Twain's Machine-Age Yankee." *Saturday Review of Literature,* 20 October 1951, pp. 7–8, 40–41.

Clemens, Cyril. "Dan Beard and the Connecticut Yankee." *Hobbies,* 79, viii (1974), 134, 136.

David, Beverly R. "The Unexpurgated *A Connecticut Yankee:* Mark Twain and His Illustrator, Daniel Carter Beard." *Prospects,* 1 (1975), 99–117.

Dinan, John S. "Hank Morgan: Artist Run Amuck." *Massachusetts Studies in English,* 3 (1972), 72–77.

Douglas, Ann. "Art and Advertising in *A Connecticut Yankee:* The 'Robber Baron' Revisited." *Canadian Review of American Studies,* 6 (1975), 182–95.

Duram, James G. "Mark Twain and the Middle Ages." *Wichita State University Bulletin,* University studies #88, 47 (1971), 3–16.

Edwards, Peter G. "The Political Economy of Mark Twain's 'Connecticut Yankee.' " *Mark Twain Quarterly,* 8, iv, (1950) 2, 18.

Ensor, Allison R. "Mark Twain's Yankee and the Prophet of Baal." *American Literary Realism,* 14 (1981), 38–42.

Fetterley, Judith. "Yankee Showman and Reformer: The Character of Mark Twain's Hank Morgan." *Texas Studies in Literature and Language,* 14 (1973), 667-79.

Foster, Edward F. "*A Connecticut Yankee* Anticipated: Max Adeler's *Fortunate Island.*" *Ball State University Forum,* 9, iv, (1968), 73–76.

Girgus, Sam B. "Conscience in Connecticut: *Civilization and Its Discontents* in Twain's Camelot." *New England Quarterly,* 51 (1978), 547–60.

Gribben, Alan. " 'The Master Hand of Old Malory': Mark Twain's Acquaintance with *Le Morte D'Arthur.*" *English Language Notes,* 16 (1978), 32–40.

Griffith, Clark. "Merlin's Grin: From 'Tom' to 'Huck' in *A Connecticut Yankee.*" *New England Quarterly,* 48 (1975), 28–46.

Guttman, Alan. "Mark Twain's Connecticut Yankee: Affirmation of the Vernacular Tradition?" *New England Quarterly*, 33 (1960), 232–37.

Hall, Robert A., Jr. "Cultural Sybolism in Mark Twain's *Connecticut Yankee*." *Annali dell Istituto Universitario Orientale, Napoli, Sezione Germanica*, 2 (1959), 127–40.

Hansen, Chadwick. "The Once and Future Boss: Mark Twain's Yankee." *Nineteenth-Century Fiction*, 28 (1973), 62–73.

Hill, Hamlin. "Barnum, Bridgeport, and *The Connecticut Yankee*." *American Quarterly*, 16 (1964), 615–16.

Henderson, Harry B., III. "Twain: The Varieties of History and *A Connecticut Yankee*." In *Versions of the Past: The Historical Imagination in American Fiction*. New York: Oxford University Press, 1974.

Holmes, Charles S. "*A Connecticut Yankee in King Arthur's Court*: Mark Twain's Fable of Uncertainty." *South Atlantic Quarterly*, 61 (1962), 462–72.

Hough, Robert L. "Twain's Double-Dating in 'A Connecticut Yankee.'" *Notes & Queries*, n.s., 15 (1968), 424–25.

Jones, Joseph. "Mark Twain's *Connecticut Yankee* and Australian Nationalism." *American Literature*, 40 (1968), 227–31.

Kahler, William V. "Mark Twain: Adult Hero of Daniel Carter Beard." *Mark Twain Journal*, 18, iii, (1976), 1–4.

Kegel, Paul. "Henry Adams and Mark Twain: Two Views of Medievalism." *Mark Twain Journal*, 15, iii, (1970), 11–21.

Klass, Philip. "An Innocent in Time: Mark Twain in King Arthur's Court." *Extrapolation*, 16 (1974), 17–32.

Lorch, Fred W. "Hawaiian Feudalism and Mark Twain's *A Connecticut Yankee in King Arthur's Court*." *American Literature*, 30 (1958), 50–66.

Maynard, Reid. "Mark Twain's Ambivalent Yankee." *Mark Twain Journal*, 14, iii, (1969), 1–5.

McKee, John DeWitt. "*A Connecticut Yankee* as a Revolutionary Document." *Mark Twain Journal*, 11, ii, (1960), 18–20, 24.

———. "Three Uses of the Arming Scene." *Mark Twain Journal*, 12, iv, (1965), 18–19, 21.

Roades, Sister Mary Teresa. "*Don Quixote* and *A Connecticut Yankee in King Arthur's Court*." *Mark Twain Quarterly*, 2, iv, (1938), 8–9.

Roemer, Kenneth M. "The Yankee(s) in Noahville." *American Literature*, 45 (1973), 434–37.

Rogers, Rodney O. "Twain, Taine, and Lecky: The Genesis of a Passage in *A Connecticut Yankee*." *Modern Language Quarterly*, 34 (1973), 436–47.

Rust, Richard D. "Americanisms in *A Connecticut Yankee*." *South Atlantic Bulletin*, 33, iii, (1968), 11–13.

Schroth, Evelyn. "Mark Twain's Literary Dialect in *A Connecticut Yankee*." *Mark Twain Journal*, 19, ii, (1978), 26–29.

Spofford, William K. "Mark Twain's Connecticut Yankee: An Ignoramus Nevertheless." *Mark Twain Journal*, 15, ii, (1970), 15–18.

Stessen, Lawrence. "The Businessman in Fiction." *Literary Review* [Fairleigh Dickinson University], 12 (1969), 281–89.

Towers, Tom H. "Mark Twain's *Connecticut Yankee*: The Trouble in Camelot." In *Challenges in American Culture*. Ed. by Ray B. Browne et al. Bowling Green, Ohio: Bowling Green University Popular Press, 1970.

Trainor, Juliette A. "Symbolism in *A Connecticut Yankee in King Arthur's Court*." *Modern Language Notes*, 66 (1951), 382–85.

Turnbull, Deborah Burger. "Hank Morgan as American Individualist." *Mark Twain Journal*, 20, ii (1980), 19–21.

Tuveson, Ernest Lee. "A Connecticut Yankee in the Mystical Babylon." In *Redeemer Nation: The Idea of America's Millennial Role*. Chicago: University of Chicago Press, 1968.

Wilson, James D. "Hank Morgan, Philip Traum, and Milton's Satan." *Mark Twain Journal*, 16, iv (1973), 20–21.

Wilson, Robert H. "Malory in the *Connecticut Yankee*." [University of Texas] *Studies in English*, 27 (1948), 185–206.

Wysong, Jack P. "Samuel Clemens' Attitude Toward the Negro as Demonstrated in *Pudd'nhead Wilson* and *A Connecticut Yankee in King Arthur's Court*." *Xavier University Studies*, 7, ii, (1968), 41–57.